THE ECONOMICS OF LOCATION

AUGUST LÖSCH

The Economics of Location

TRANSLATED FROM THE SECOND REVISED EDITION
BY WILLIAM H. WOGLOM WITH THE ASSISTANCE OF
WOLFGANG F. STOLPER

NEW HAVEN: YALE UNIVERSITY PRESS

©, 1954, by Yale University Press.
Printed in the United States of America by
J. H. Furst Company, Baltimore, Maryland
and reprinted by The Murray Printing Company,
Forge Village, Massachusetts.
First published, November, 1954
Second printing, April, 1959
All rights reserved. This book may not be
reproduced, in whole or in part, in any form
(except by reviewers for the public press),
without written permission from the publishers.
Library of Congress catalog card number 52-9268

Translator's Note

THE TRANSLATOR gratefully acknowledges the indispensable help of two distinguished economists.

Dr. Edgar M. Hoover, while on the staff of the President's Council of Economic Advisers, read the entire translation in manuscript and furnished a great many valuable suggestions.

Wolfgang F. Stolper, professor of economics at the University of Michigan, also read the manuscript through. A fellow student of Lösch under Schumpeter, in Bonn, Germany, and a close lifelong friend thereafter, he was able to interpret some expressions peculiar to the author that otherwise might have remained obscure.

The translator has profited throughout, too, by the advice and assistance of the staff of the Yale University Press.

W. H. W.

Teaneck, New Jersey, May, 1952

Grateful acknowledgment is made to the Social Science Research Council for a grant which facilitated the translation.

August Lösch in Memoriam

WRITTEN amid privations and war, *The Economics of Location* bears witness to a combination of rare strength of character, intellect, and warmth of personality in its author which is not frequently found in scientific works in any language.

August Lösch was born in 1906. He died shortly after the end of hostilities on May 30, 1945, at least partially as the result of that very strength of character which forbade him to make any compromises with the National Socialist regime. He never even considered taking a government or academic position in which he would have had to swear a personal oath of allegiance to Hitler. The willingness to accept a professorship *after the war*, which he expressed in the foreword to the second edition of his book, speaks for his courage as well as for his solitude. It is for this reason that though we have omitted this note from the American edition we have not felt free to change any of the many passages in which his love for his homeland of Swabia is fervently expressed. For what has been hypocrisy in many others who turn their love of country to account, in Lösch is a reminder that there are men who can combine passion with intellect, love of home with a cosmopolitan view.

Even a glance at *The Economics of Location* is enough to convince the reader that its author was an extraordinary personality. All of Lösch's work is original in a double sense of the term. He asked significant new questions and he added significantly to the answers given by others to older questions. Like most truly original persons, Lösch appreciated the contributions of others. *The Economics of Location* contains an immense number of references to other works. But two things stand out: Lösch never hesitated to quote anyone whether or not he belonged to the " wrong " nation or " race "—which was by no means easy at the time he was writing this book. And he never quoted merely to criticize. This book, a substantial piece of work, not only gives credit where credit is due; it shows an appreciation of the achievement of others without accepting anything, including the author's own contribution, as final truth. Yet no man had more passion for truth, more feeling for the fact that truth must come before originality.

Lösch's first publication concerned the transfer problem and grew out of a seminar paper. His first major piece of work was a booklet about the economic consequences of a declining population, perhaps the best discussion of the problem in terms of classical (in the sense of pre-Keynesian) theory that exists. The subject was set as a prize question and Lösch won the contest. Because he believed in personal freedom, including the taking of risks, he chose to publish the booklet himself, using the prize money for the purpose. That book and his next major work, on *Population Cycles and Business Cycles*, dealt with the economics of population. Both show all the characteristics of a modern economist who attempts to fuse theory and facts in one indissoluble whole. The books are concisely written; no superfluous introductions ease the reader into the subject matter. Nor does Lösch spare the reader concise reasoning or a multitude of facts.

It may not be without interest to give the main results of Lösch's population study in some detail, since the relation of population growth and business cycles has aroused new interest through the Keynes-Hansen-Terborgh discussion, through the stagnation thesis and criticisms of it, and again through the fact that the forties and early fifties have been a period of prosperity which has also witnessed the largest absolute increase of population in the history of the United States.

The question whether population cycles cause business cycles requires different answers, according to Lösch, in the precapitalist and the capitalist eras. During the capitalist era population movements are neither necessary nor sufficient to explain the fluctuations of the economy. Nevertheless Lösch establishes the fact that in Germany industrial production as a rule increased quickly following a population increase. Indeed, during the periods 1861–1913 and 1923–33 he finds only two exceptions to this relationship. Since the economic development of growing nations takes to a large extent the form of increased housing and capital equipment for the increased numbers of people, as well as of increased amounts of consumers' goods, it is not unexpected that the rhythm of population movements and of business cycles should largely coincide. Furthermore, the growth of the economy to accommodate a growing population entails smaller risks than the adaptation to changes brought about by technological progress and the creation of new markets. Thus, in Lösch's own words, although " population growth does not create business cycles, it shapes their course."

This kind of discussion is quite familiar today. But Lösch antedates the Keynesian discussion. If his contribution is formulated in terms of any one particular frame of reference, it is in terms of Spiethoff's or perhaps Schumpeter's rather than Keynes' theoretical language. His contribution is distinguished by solid statistical verification and arguments largely missing in the Anglo-American discussion.

The Economics of Location, like his book on population cycles, exhibits the characteristics of a man blessed at the same time with originality and a sense of tradition and history. Lösch knew and used the traditional theories of location from von Thünen on. Yet he succeeded in bringing new insights even to so well-developed a theory as that of the famous Thünen rings. His criticism of Alfred Weber's location theory is essentially that voiced by Schumpeter.[1] Weber's solution is in terms of partial equilibrium theory and as such is a brilliant piece of work. But the partial equilibrium approach means that among the other things which have to be assumed as given are demand, the location of raw materials, and the location of markets. What remains to be accomplished, therefore, once a satisfactory solution of the partial equilibrium problem has been found, is the development of a general equilibrium approach.

This is precisely one of Lösch's major contributions. He had Ohlin's and Palander's work to build on, and gratefully acknowledged both—in spite of the fact that he was already working out his own ideas when they published their contributions. It is nevertheless fair to say that Lösch was the first to present a full general equilibrium system describing in abstract the interrelationship of all locations. To be sure, he did not go beyond counting equations and unknowns. But this in itself is a major achievement which, in its precision, had eluded his intellectual forebears. Again his achievement sets the stage for the next step in the development of the general theory of location: the development of the dynamics of locations. Lest we lose patience and courage it may be well to remember that it was over sixty years before dynamics was added to the Walrasian system.

Lösch himself has pointed out that his system of equations shares the weakness of any general theory which is too all-inclusive to be applicable. This was one of the reasons why he developed his theory of economic regions. However, the theoretical framework itself is useful for a number of problems for which it must, of course, be narrowed down and made specific. It is surely no accident that one of the most useful pieces of theoretical and empirical research,

---

1. In *Schmollers Jahrbuch*, XXXIV (1910), 1356 ff.

The Economics of Location

Leontief's input-output analysis, which has opened up entirely new vistas, is based on the most general Walrasian system. And the application of input-output analysis to regional data, attempted by Isard, for the same reason will have to come to terms with the general theory of location which, in a sense, is simply the application of the Walrasian system to an economy in which distance is also a variable. Finally, anyone who works with regional economies of the real world knows that interregional relationships assume greater importance the smaller the region considered. Any theory which enables the scholar to keep these mutual relationships in mind therefore fulfills an important function in empirical research.

Lösch's discussion of the nature of economic regions is probably his most original contribution. To be sure, here too he has in Ohlin a magnificent predecessor. Yet there are enough differences to mark Lösch's work as something entirely new. The novelty could be characterized in different ways. Lösch does not assume his region or define it, for example, by means of factor mobility; nor does he assume the existence of markets, sources of raw materials, or even transport lines. Instead he develops the structure of a region, that is, the interrelationship of all relevant variables, with a minimum of assumptions which, with true genius, are deliberately chosen to be as generalized as possible. The very lack of realism reminds one of the theory of comparative cost which also substituted for the trivial realism that grapes could not be grown in Scotland the brilliant proof that an inefficient producer could not be undersold in all goods.

To put it differently, Lösch does not ask for the definition of a region by means of which to analyze it, nor does he search for particular characteristics. His region is not defined by factor mobility—for factor mobility is also permissible between regions— nor by " homogeneity," nor by " self-sufficiency," though the last and possibly also the first of these characteristics can, *after* his discussion of the nature of a region, be read into it. Instead his question concerns the interrelationship of individual production and consumption units, the eventual location of markets and producing centers, of transport lines, of distribution of population and cities, all to be simultaneously and mutually determined. What matters is the complicated structure, the *Gestalt*, not the average characteristics of an area. The relevance of these ideas to the problems of underdeveloped countries is obvious, and their application in specific cases may turn out to be extremely useful.

The statistician and empirical scholar may well point out that

x

statistics cannot possibly be assembled for all points of the United States but must of necessity be combined for smaller or larger areas. This is true enough, though perhaps less true than it seems at first, since the aggregations themselves are based on the detailed individual data originally collected. And even to the extent to which it is true, it is less damaging than at first appears. The bulk of Lösch's book consists of applications of his ideas to data, chiefly to American data. This alone indicates their fruitfulness for empirical research. But again, anyone working with regional data knows that little can be done with the data of a single region in isolation without considering interrelationships with other areas. The income of a region depends, of course, on its productivity, but just as clearly on the prices of its exports and imports. As soon as this is pointed out, the structure—industrial, agricultural, population, capital, etc.—again becomes of paramount importance. In a similar manner interregional wage differentials cannot be understood without an awareness of the structure both of a region and its relationships with the outside world.

The Economics of Location is not easy reading. This is partly due to the evident pressure under which it was written. In a few places it may be because important passages from the first edition which were omitted from the second German edition to save space have been reinserted in the American edition in the appropriate places. But basically it is due to the very newness of the ideas: not enough time has as yet elapsed since the publication of the book to lead to simplification, a streamlining as it were, of the formulations. Lösch's work opens up new vistas and new avenues of research. No greater compliment could be paid to it than its being taken up where Lösch left off and carried on to new formulations and achievements. The highest praise of this book will be if in the future it can be said that the work it has stimulated has made it obsolete.

WOLFGANG F. STOLPER

Ann Arbor, Michigan
1953

Preface to First Edition

JUST AS THE THEORY of economic development considers time, so this book will include space in its approach to economics, not only in the case of individual problems, as has been done before, but throughout the entire field. It proposes to view all economic activities geographically. In principle all economic theory can be reformulated thus from a spatial aspect. But every exploration of new territory will concentrate first on the investigation of what is most interesting. I have been less interested in outlining a theory that is complete than one that is capable of further development; and I believe, for example, that, on the basis of the theoretical foundation given, dynamics could easily be introduced into the spatial picture. If the fundamental idea of the work is sound, omissions and errors in details should not weigh too heavily. It is of little importance, too, that some of my partial results have already become known in the meantime, since I have written this book not for its details but because of its broad view.

Obviously it was necessary first to integrate the scattered results of previous research and—what is particularly important in this special field—bring them into harmony with general economic theory. But over and above that, this investigation develops a systematic location theory, a new theory of foreign trade, and perhaps the first general analysis of the nature of economic regions. These, Parts II and III, are the kernel of the whole book.

The relation of the present investigations to my previous ones is this: Those dealt with the relations between *peoples* and the economy whereas this treats of the relations between *space* and the economy. Or, seen from the standpoint of population, the subject there was its development in time and here, on the contrary, its distribution in space.

I conceived the plan of the present work ten years ago, as a young student. At that time I could not foresee the practical interest that these questions would arouse today, or that the underlying principle of the book, its recognition of local stability in the widest sense, for which I then thought I had to do battle, would have prevailed so completely in the meantime. Throughout this whole period I have never discussed the basic features of my idea. But just because I was so sure of my course, at first instinctively and then more and more consciously, I could absorb in detail so much of the information and suggestions that streamed in upon me without losing myself in a welter of theories or facts. It is therefore impossible to give a complete list of all those who assisted in my investigation with advice, criticism, or information, or by cooperating in so many ways. For their constant readiness to help I thank first of all my teachers, Arthur Spiethoff, in Bonn; Walter Eucken, in Freiburg; and Joseph Schumpeter, at Harvard University. My obligation is especially great to the Rockefeller Foundation, which generously made possible my two trips of investigation through all North America, and the publication of their results. I sincerely thank, also, the Paul Stelzmann Fund, in Freiburg, for helping me through a critical situation. To Professor Wassily Leontief I am indebted for valuable suggestions, and mention in gratitude at least the following others: Professors Taussig, Chamberlin, and v. Haberler of Harvard, headquarters for my American investigations; the members of the Cowles Commission and Professors Roos and Hotelling, with whom I spent a never-to-be-forgotten summer in Colorado Springs; Professors Evans in Berkeley; Garver in Minneapolis; Hoover in Ann Arbor; Riefler, then in Princeton, and Whittlesey; Spengler in Durham; Dr. Christaller in Freiburg; and numerous other economists and geographers at the universities already mentioned as well as at those in Chicago, Baton Rouge, Iowa City, and Chapel Hill. I received the warmest cooperation from the Internal Trade Branch of the Dominion Bureau of Statistics, in Ottawa, and the Retail Price Division of the Bureau of Labor Statistics, in Washington, whose director, Mrs. S. Stewart, took special interest in the question of regional price differences. Dr. Constantine E. McGuire, of Washington, opened up many possibilities to me in the friendliest manner. Minister Barton, in Ottawa, and Vice-President Powell, treasurer Stewart, and other officers of the Federal Reserve Banks in Minneapolis and St. Louis; Messrs. McGregor, of the Dominion Tariff Board (Ottawa), Young, of the Bureau of Mines (Washington), Charles L. Horn and J. Bell of Minneapolis, A. Edwards, F. W. Olin, and Col. Jackson of St. Louis, not to mention many other officials, librarians, and economists, freely gave me information. In Germany I availed myself of the excellent opportunities for work at the Institut für Weltwirtschaft in Kiel. I shall still have an opportunity to thank a few persons in the text, but there remain many more whose help I value even though I cannot call them by name here. Last but not least I thank my mother and my fiancée, who facilitated the accomplishment of this wearisome task at great personal sacrifice.

There are mathematical calculations in this book, because it is reprehensible not to trust reason and rest content with vague words and hazy sentiments. But there are also speculation and philosophizing where the frontiers of the calculable are crossed, and especially where the meaning of the whole is to be interpreted. As for mathematics, I have neither sought nor shunned it, but have simply employed it where it was superior to other methods. He who has a better command of it may be willing to forgive me for the ponderous presentation; he who is less well schooled in mathematics may skip the dry proof if only he accepts the results. On the other hand, nothing was further from my mind than to be satisfied with a cold mathematical consideration. This would resemble a mere brick shell that is not yet ready for occupation; a skeleton without flesh or blood. But it meant giving up a number of original intentions, even those that I most cherished. Here, indeed, I believe it is impossible to do without a solid foundation. One can erect a large or a small house on a foundation, adding more or taking away to create comfort; but building materials without a foundation remain a formless mass. This is sufficiently proved by the many well-meant endeavors to achieve a living science immediately, and without rigid thinking. In such a neglected field as location theory it required many years of hard work before even a tenable intellectual structure could be erected. Yet I hope that even in its objective restraint it testifies to a sense of reality and to a belief.

I was fortunate in being able to develop and test my views through the more readily understandable conditions in America. Though a foreigner slips more easily into error, my presentation on the whole may show even the American reader the economy of his country from a new viewpoint, and thus serve in some small degree to express my thanks for the help and hospitality experienced there in a hundred different ways.

It was not easy for me largely to forego the attractive task of applying what had thus been tested to our more complicated German conditions and analyzing the pertinent facts. But apart from all foreign studies and the wide applicability of the resulting ideas, my youthful experiences in a little Swabian town constitute the real background of this book. I am convinced that we rarely learn to know any conditions as intimately as those among which we grew up. We can judge with certainty only a small understandable and familiar world like this, and we transfer the findings to large problems afterward. My Swabian homeland constitutes such a world in miniature, if any economic landscape at all can be said to do so. To have my original experiences there confirm my final theories gives me a real sense of security, and so I dedicate this book to the land of my birth, the land that I love.

AUGUST LÖSCH

Heidenheim (Württemberg)
Autumn, 1939

Preface to the Second Edition

THE FAVORABLE RECEPTION accorded this book, long since out of print, beyond the circle of German economists and even abroad,[1] in other sciences, and especially among practical economists, encouraged my resolve to publish a new edition, although for a long time conditions prevented me from making many of the changes that I should have liked to make. Nevertheless I have at least worked out more clearly my location theory, which in the first edition was merely a preliminary study; added some new material on geographic price differences; supplied what was most necessary to the regional planning made timely by the war; and presented the transfer problem in better form, so far as monetary problems relate to it.[2] In addition, those who are familiar with the first edition will discover new observations, statistics, and illustrations here and there. Occasionally the presentation could be simplified, but nothing decisive would be achieved: the indescribable difficulties under which the book was first written so compressed and reduced what is valid, beyond mere impressions, that only he who studies it thoroughly will be able fully to exhaust its contents.

However, a few hints may be of service to those who hurry through it. Entrepreneurs may be especially interested in pages 396–420; bankers in 461–476 and 505 ff., monetary experts in 276–

---

1. The plans for translation were upset by the Second World War. In America the book is evidently being circulated on microfilm, being unobtainable in any other form. (Only a handful of copies for review reached the United States before the war shut off the supply.—Translator.)

2. My book on money will contain more on this subject. (Because of the premature death of the author this book has never appeared—However, a lengthy article, " Theorie der Währung," appeared posthumously in the Weltwirtschaftliches Archiv, Vol. LXII (1949), 35–88.—W. F. S.)

304 and 317–324; price control officials 263, 333, and 452–507; geographers and statisticians in 365–507; sociologists in 66–91 and 223–262; and transportation specialists in pages 127, 170–191 and 440–444. Students may skip Part I, and at first the mathematics as well. Those interested in town and regional planning will consider especially pages 329–357 and 440–444, Part IV in general and, finally, the basic material in Parts I and II, which is not alway easy. Here they will find what economics has to offer today about the spatial aspects of the economy.

In addition, of course, the utilization of many ideas for practical planning needs to be further developed. The commission to prepare this work I owe to the friendly interest of the Secretary of State Dr. Muhs, Director of the Reichsstelle für Raumordnung. In this connection I recall with pleasure my conversations with his collaborators, Ministerialdirigent Dr. Teubert, First Baurat Köster, Dr. Puttkammer, and Diplomvolkswirt Wiesener. But above all I am indebted for much to my compatriot, Oberregierungsrat Dr. Isenberg, a pioneer in regional research. Then, too, the contribution of those who helped to make the book technically possible is not to be underestimated today. As for the rest, the thanks expressed in the first edition as well as its dedication still apply.

When the first edition was written I lacked the money, and now I lack the time, to carry my plans to completion. Most of my powers were then consumed, instead of in actual work, in merely making this possible. For generous though the help intended for science may often be, little of it reaches the garret rooms where truth is sought. But in the meantime I was able to test the new views on many theoretical or pressing practical problems. Whether these concerned wide areas (*Grossraum*) and the drawing of boundaries, the establishment of towns and new settlements, or such apparently remote subjects as currency, foreign trade, the formation of prices, and market forms, they have proved fruitful throughout. A new economics is coming into existence. But not enough time remains to make it secure in peace on all sides, and since I do not wish to offer what may be attractive at the moment but would not stand a rigid test I have given up the publication of most of my results, even though I could use some of them in my memoranda. It is not easy to stand before this rich harvest with hands tied if one has within his grasp a new method for practicing and analyzing economics.

AUGUST LÖSCH

Kiel
Autumn, 1943

Contents

Translator's Note	v
August Lösch in Memoriam, by Wolfgang Stolper	vii
Preface to the First Edition	xiii
Preface to the Second Edition	xvi
List of Figures	xxiii
List of Tables	xxvii

I. Location   1
   A. Systematic Presentation of the Location Problem   3
      1. The Meaning of the Location Problem   4
      2. Specific Locations   5
         a. Effects of Locations upon One Another   5
         b. The Relative Position of Locations   9
      3. Areal Boundaries   13
         a. Boundaries between Simple Areas   13
         b. Boundaries between Areal Systems   13
   B. Selected Problems of Location   15
      4. Industrial Location Theory   16
         a. The General Principle   16
         b. Practical Execution   17
      5. The Theory of Agricultural Location   36
         a. Partial (One-sided) Orientation   36
         b. Comprehensive Solution   60
         c. Agricultural and Industrial Location Theory: A Comparison   63
      6. Site and Reasons for Town Settlement   68
         a. Reasons for Town Settlement   68
         b. The Site of Town Formation   80
      7. Site and Cause of Belt Formation   85
         a. Belts of Locations Producing Identical Goods   85
         b. Belts of Different Locations   90
      8. The Problem of General Location Patterns   92

		a. The Equilibrium of Locations	94
		b. The Separation of Locations	98
		c. Conclusion	99
II.	Economic Regions		101
	A.	Economic Regions under Simple Conditions	105
		9. The Market Area	105
		10. The Network of Markets	109
		a. Continuous Distribution of Population	109
		b. Discontinuous Distribution of Population	114
		c. Regional Networks	122
		11. The System of Networks	124
		a. The General Pattern	124
		b. Special Cases	130
		12. The Network of Systems	135
		a. The Relation of Landscapes to One Another	135
		b. The Boundary Region	136
		c. Results	137
	B.	Economic Regions under Difficult Conditions	138
		13. Some New Factors	139
		a. Economic Differences	139
		b. Natural Differences	178
		c. Human Differences	191
		d. Political Differences	196
		14. Further Restriction of Market Areas	211
		15. Economic Regions in Reality	215
		a. Spatial Arrangement	215
		b. On a Chaotic Interpretation	219
III.	Trade		223
	A	Description of Equilibrium	223
		16. Six Cardinal Problems of the Division of Labor and Their Interrelations	223
		17. The Six Cardinal Problems of the Division of Labor Discussed Individually	226
		a. The Occupation of a Person	226
		b. The Personnel of an Industry	**236**

	c. The Locality of a Person	240
	d. The Occupants of a Locality	245
	e. The Industry in a Locality	248
	f. The Locality of an Industry	255
	g. Conclusion	262
18.	Price Gradients	263
B. Disturbance of the Equilibrium		264
19.	Self-Regulation	265
	a. Transfer of Products During Short-run Disturbances (The Transfer Problem)	265
	b. Redistribution of the Factors of Production with Long-run Disturbances (The Combination Problem)	305
	c. What Remains of the Classical Theory?	312
20.	Regulation from Without	315
	a. Regulation of the Transfer of Products (The Transfer Problem)	316
	b. Regulation of the Distribution of Factors of Production (The Combination Problem)	324
	c. The Practical Value of Economic Theory	357
IV. Examples		361
A. Location		365
21.	Locations of Production	365
	a. Uniform Distribution	365
	b. Uneven Distribution	376
	c. National Boundaries as Factors in Location	382
22.	The Location of Towns	389
B. Economic Areas		395
23.	Simple Market Areas	395
	a. The Significance of Distance for the Individual Enterprise	396
	b. Description of Market Areas	402
	c. The Economic Importance of Distance	427
24.	Regional Systems	431
	a. Number, Spacing, and Size of Towns	431

	b. Spatial Arrangement of Towns	438
	c. The Function of Towns	439
	d. Town Plans	440
25.	Frontier Regions	445
C. Trade		452
26.	Price Levels in Space	452
	a. Prices of Factors of Production	452
	b. Product Prices	476
	c. Cost of Living	490
27.	Price Changes in Space	496
	a. Spatial Differences in the Movement of Commodity Prices	496
	b. Spatial Differences in the Movement of Interest	505
Epilogue. On Space		508

Subject Index	509
Name Index	517

List of Figures

1. The concentration of locations	11
2. The construction of isodapanes	19
3. Consumption and production as functions of distance	37
4. Effect of increased freight on the demand for a cheap and for an expensive product	45
5. Rent per acre as a function of distance	49
6. Intersection of two profitability planes	50
7. Thünen case	53
8. Inversion of the Thünen rings	53
9. Contradiction between figures 8a and 8e	55
10. Comparison of rent per hectare of Thünen case and in its inversion	55
11. Potato market	56
12. Corn market	56
13. Rent per hectare during transition	56
14. Illustration of case 18 of the complete system	58
15. Mixed cropping and rings	58
16. Size of the producing unit in a) industry and b) agriculture	64
17. Supply of the same market by several entrepreneurs	70
18. Suitability of different soils for different products	86
19. Location of crops as a function of soil quality and distance	88
20–22. Derivation of the demand cone and the market area from the demand curve for the product as function of distance and the cost curves	106
23. Development of market areas from the large circle to the final small hexagon	110
24–26. The three smallest market areas	117
27. The ten smallest economic areas	118
28. Theoretical pattern of an economic landscape	125
29. Theoretical pattern of an economic landscape, but without nets	125
30. Indianapolis and environs	125

31. Toledo and environs	125
32. The transport lines in the ideal economic landscape	127
33. Location of regional centers in the complete system	128
34. Regions with equal structure, $k = 3$	128
35. Regions with equal structure, $k = 4$	132
36. Regions with equal structure, $k = 7$	132
37. Part of a square economic landscape	134
38–39. Location of landscapes in respect to one another	135
40. Comparison of individual demand with respect to the c. i. f. and f. o. b. price	140
41. Various types of total demand curves	145
42. Factory price and distance	149
43. Three individual demand curves with respect to f. o. b. price as function of distance, corresponding total revenue curves, and corresponding transport cones	151
44. Geometric solution of limits of price differentiation	154
45. Comparison of price discrimination, uniform f. o. b. price, and uniform c. i. f. price	161
46. Price cones of agricultural products around towns	167
47. Similarity of price differentiation for goods and spatial freight differentiation through zonal tariffs	172
48. Effect of new large-scale economies on size of market area	176
49. Comparison of market area in thickly settled and thinly settled regions, with equal cost curves	181
50. The law of refraction	184
50. Schematic representation of efficient route from Hawaii to New Orleans via Panama Canal and possible Nicaragua cut	186
52. Effect of gate cities on market and supply areas	190
53. Economic and political borders	204
54. Schematic representation of the six basic questions of the division of labor	224
55. Population density of northeastern Europe, 1930	258
56. Effects of a price inflation on market areas	268
57. The spread of price changes	271
58. World-wide price waves	304
59. Possible effect of customs union on demand and price	341
60. Reduction of market areas by a tariff	341

List of Figures xxv

61. Member banks of the Federal Reserve Bank of Chicago in Iowa, January 1, 1926 — 366
62. Bank locations in the nine northwest counties of Iowa, 1926 — 366
63. Principal European fairs, 1921 — 367
64. Agricultural population per square mile in North America (United States, 1930; Canada, 1931) — 375
65. Rotation of crops as a function of distance from a village — 382
66. Distribution of towns in Iowa, 1930 — 389
67. Distribution of towns in England, 1910 — 389
68. Increase in distance between towns west of Chicago — 390
69. Parceling of fields on a farm in the Administrative District of Herrenberg — 400
70. Size of wholesale market areas by goods, 1929 — 404
71. Encirclement of a small town by a large town — 411
72. Market area of a house in Kansas City for fine woolen clothing and overalls and work clothes — 413
73. Market areas of five hardware trade centers — 415
74. Method of determining retail market areas — 418
75. Sales area for building lumber and cement, Cedar County, Iowa — 418
76. Supply and market areas for Muscatine, Iowa — 419
77. Hierarchy of supply areas for tung oil — 420
78–79. The great world wheat markets, 1928–29 — 421
80. England as a corner market at the center of world trade routes, 1936 — 425
81. Distance and foreign trade — 429
82. Shape and street network of a small town — 442
83. The French hinterland of Geneva — 445
84. Influence of the drawing of the boundary upon the market area of Bischofswerder, East Prussia — 446
85. The network of railways on the American-Canadian border — 447
86. The financial sphere of influence of El Paso, 1914 — 448
87. Price of land in Nordhorn, 1926–29 — 453
88. Value of agricultural units around Stuttgart and Heilbronn, 1935 — 454
89. Gradation of wages in the German Empire, 1941 — 457

90. The Stuttgart commuting area	457
91. Monthly wage, without board, of agricultural workers, United States, 1933	458
92. Price in dollars for resoling and heeling a pair of shoes, United States, 1936	459
93. Price in cents for laundering a man's shirt, United States, 1936	459
94. Increase in the rate of interest with distance from New York, 1919–25	462
95. Increase in the rate of interest with distance from Houston, Texas, 1936	465
96. Spatial pattern of wheat prices in the United States, 1910–14	478
97. Producer prices for potatoes, United States, 1906–15	480
98. Retail prices of potatoes, United States, 1936	480
99. Isotimes for soap, United States and Canada, 1936	488
100. Westward movement of the depression in Iowa, 1929–31	497
101. Comparison of house rents in the United States and Canada, 1929–37	500
102. The ratio of price levels in the North and South in the United States and its dependence upon tariff policy, 1820–1935	502

List of Tables

1. Classification of locations	34
2. Complete system of spatial order in agriculture for two crops	39
3. Symbols of spatial arrangement	95
4. System of equations I	97
5. Demand as a function of regional shape	111
6. The ten smallest possible market areas	119
7. Calculation of n	119
8. Regions with homogeneous structure	131
9. International trade	227
10. Interpersonal trade	228
11. Comparative efficiencies (comparative advantages) of the countries	229
12. Order of comparative advantages	231
13–14. Example of determination of the price of land	255
15. Transfer and construction of currency	282
16. Transfer with different reserve ratios	283
17. System of methods for regional planning	347
18. Significance of regional production in the United States, 1929	368
19. Surplus, self-sufficient and deficit regions	369
20. Employment per 1,000 inhabitants, East Prussia, Württemberg, Ruhr, Reich	373
21. Frequency distribution of towns in Iowa, 1930, by size and distance	391
22. Distances separating towns in various parts of the United States	392
23. Distances separating English towns, 1910	394
24. Selling cost and distance	398
25. Relation of sales radius to cost in certain wholesale trades	399
26. Size of market areas for wholesale trade in the United States according to goods, 1929	405
27. Size of wholesale market areas by cities, 1929	407
28. Distance and size of demand in wholesale trade, by counties	409

29. Distance and size of demand in retail trade for similar places in three counties in Iowa — 410
30. Distance and size of demand — 412
31. Source of wheat imports, by importing country and exporting country, 1928–29 — 423
32. Germany's share in the foreign trade of European countries, 1928 — 430
33. Structure of region, with $k = 3$ — 431
34. Regional systems in Iowa, theory and reality — 435
35. Increase in interest rate on bank loans with distance in Texas, 1936 — 465
36. Increase in interest rate on bank deposits with distance, Texas, 1936 — 466
37. Orange prices and distance — 481
38. Local differences in nonagricultural retail prices in the United States and Canada, 1936 — 487
39. Comparison of price movements on the American-Canadian border, 1915–37 — 499
40. National price increase after devaluation in Canada and the United States — 500

UNNUMBERED TABLES

One-to-one correspondence between international and interpersonal trade — 235

Relation of physical yield of various crops to the proportion of total production of the United States by New England, Middle Atlantic, and East North Central States — 376n.

Selling cost dependent on distance as percentage of total cost, United States — 397

Freight per ton-mile relative to factory price, Germany — 397n.

Theoretical and actual number of places in Christaller system — 432

Expenses of national banks as percentage of deposits, 1935 — 470

Spread of interest rates between New York and twenty-seven financial centers in the South and West, 1923–35 — 505

PART ONE. LOCATION

OUR EXISTENCE in time is determined for us, but we are largely free to select our location. This is influenced, though not dictated, by our place of origin. Finding the right location is essential to successful life, but it is essential also to a successful enterprise, to the establishment of a lasting settlement—in short, to group survival. In addition, a suitable location must be a location for the right events. On closer examination, these originally simple problems constantly divide and subdivide anew. Thus presentation, unlike investigation, must begin by introducing some order into this rapidly confusing abundance of problems.

A. Systematic Presentation of the Location Problem [1]

NO MAN-MADE SYSTEM can avoid the arbitrary. None is conclusive for we do not know the final cause of things. We know only a mutual relationship, not a simple series of causes from beginning to end, from above to below. It is basically immaterial where our presentation begins, since we cannot linger over the parts without considering the whole. If a system is regarded as an order of preference, the emphasis lies heavily on the word *order*. We *order* our facts according to viewpoints that are important to us. Hence the same thing appears again and again but is seen differently, whereas in a proper sequence, in an ideal system, it would have a unique place. Just as the first three parts of this book imply no clear-cut separation, so classification within this as within all other sections is only a matter of convenience. This is already shown by the fact that not until the third part does the argument expand into a comprehensive view of economics in space and the division of labor in general. Here we limit ourselves to the narrower problem that forms the subject of traditional location theory, namely, where a particular economic activity is to be found. In judging the manifold contributions to this theme it is helpful to fix their place in the theory. Moreover, only thus can we recognize the basic problems.

---

1. This concise review presupposes in its details some familiarity with the subject. Hence the beginner should merely glance at first over pp. 5–14.

Chapter 1. The Meaning of the Location Problem

THE QUESTION of actual location must be distinguished from that of the rational location. The two need not coincide. Interest in the first is divided between identifying and explaining a site, and may concern itself either with an individual case and thus be essentially historical in character, or with a behavior that is typical at least for an epoch. From this follow rules for the considerations by which entrepreneurs let themselves be guided in choosing an actual location. It is often important to know this. But it would be dangerous to conclude that what is must also be rational since otherwise it could not exist, and that any theoretical determination of the correct location would therefore be superfluous. Such a capitulation to reality is as useful as the advice of those who on principle contradict no one: a contemptible attitude that is satisfied to accept one's era instead of serving it. Of what value is a science that does not observe Schiller's valiant watchword: " Live with thy century, but be not its creature; give to thy contemporaries, but give what they need, not what they laud "?[1] No! The real duty of the economist is not to explain our sorry reality, but to improve it. The question of the best location is far more dignified than determination of the actual one.

---

1. Ueber die ästhetische Erziehung des Menschen, 9. Brief.

Chapter 2. Specific Locations

a. EFFECT OF LOCATIONS UPON ONE ANOTHER

THE PRINCIPLES for a rational choice of location vary according to whether we view them (as entrepreneurs) from the standpoint of the individual, or (as regional planners) from the standpoint of the whole. According to the point of view we perceive only one factor determining location, or two.

§1. THEORY OF LOCATION FOR AN INDIVIDUAL FIRM

α. *Choice of Location for the Economic Unit*

The problem is: Given all locations but one, to determine this.[1] The individual solves this problem according to his best advantage. (This is the first general tendency.) As a rule, he must find the most favorable center of a production, sales, or supply area. The first two cases concern the location of a producer, the third that of a consumer.

1. *Location for a Producer.* The situation of available means of production, of competition, and of consumption must be known as geographical data, but the significance of these factors is variable in the extreme. For the location of a farm it is highly important that its production be areal, whereas its market may be thought of as punctiform. For a typical nonfarm enterprise the situation is reversed, and the theory of agricultural location differs therefore from that of industrial location. The latter has been discussed especially by Weber though in very simple terms, to be sure; the former, by J. H. von Thünen.[2]

2. *Location of a Consumer.* His location depends upon the location of the producers and of neighboring centers of consump-

---

1. The pricing problem of an individual enterprise is no different. As in any one individual case price can be explained by costs, so any one location can be explained by others. The general theory of pricing must not, of course, follow this circular reasoning, and neither must the general theory of location. In either case only a system of simultaneous equations can properly demonstrate the interdependence.
2. J. H. von Thünen, *Der Isolierte Staat in Beziehung auf Landwirtschaft und Nationalökonomie* (Hamburg, 1826), §11 and elsewhere.

tion. This case was especially important in the Middle Ages: An inland town would develop only where the neighboring towns left it an adequate source of agricultural supplies. The situation is fundamentally similar today for cotton mills, flour mills, slaughter houses, and so on. Some discussion of this subject is to be found in the literature on economic history (Sombart), though as far as I am aware its theory has not been so thoroughly worked out as that of the first case.

β. *Repercussions of Individual Choices of Location*

In adopting the viewpoint of the individual economic unit we appear to have freed ourselves from the general interdependence of locations, and thus to be able to give a more exact solution than that contained in the general equations of location to be discussed below. But certain repercussions immediately appear, which radiate from the desired location back to those that determine it. As long as we consider only the first and nearest of the determining locations (as in what follows) we still deal with a problem of partial equilibrium. But as soon as we endeavor to take account of all interactions we are faced with general interdependence (as in §2).

1. *Influence on Competitors.* When the new enterprise has chosen its location competitors may re-examine theirs. This difficult problem was first suggested by H. Hotelling,[3] but treated on such simplified assumptions that his conclusion (a tendency to agglomeration) cannot be generalized. Under uniform conditions in a free market the individual has no latitude in the choice of his location. The problem can thus have practical importance only either during the transition to equilibrium or, in equilibrium itself, only in those industries where human or natural differences play a role or where a single enterprise produces a large part of total output. After production has been divided among individual firms, a residue may remain in this case that is too small to permit the existence of an additional firm, yet large enough to allow those already established to operate well to the right of Chamberlin's point.[4] These enterprises then have some latitude of choice, and may fight among themselves for the most advantageous location.

2. *Influence on Customers and Suppliers.* We can distinguish effects on the form and the substance of their activities.

(aa) *Effects on Form.* First, the form of consumption as a

---

3. Harold Hotelling, "Stability in Competition," *Economic Journal*, 1929, pp. 41-57.
4. See below, p. 109, note 1.

function of distance. Given the location of its production, the consumption of a particular product may assume different forms, depending on the distance from the site of its manufacture. For example, it might prove advantageous to ship a large machine already assembled to a near-by purchaser. The additional cost of shipping a bulky machine rather than its parts will be more than offset, up to a certain distance from the factory, by savings in the cost of mounting. Beyond this critical distance, on the other hand, the machine will be shipped knocked down.[5]

Second, the form of production as a function of distance. Given the place of consumption of a product, the particular form in which it is produced may vary with the distance from that place. By form of production may be meant intensiveness, that is, the method of cultivation (Thünen); or the stage to which factory production is carried out locally. If local finishing is more expensive than centralized finishing, perhaps because the advantages of large-scale production cannot be utilized so fully, but freight per unit of consumption is less when a product is shipped in finished rather than crude condition, then it may pay at a certain distance from the consumer to ship frozen meat, say, instead of livestock for slaughter. In these cases the final product always remains the same. From this we must distinguish the cases in which different end products such as fresh milk, cream, or butter are prepared from the same original products, depending on the distance from the consumer. We then deal no longer with different competing forms, but with different products—the subject of the next section.

(bb) *Influences on the Substance of Economic Activity*. First, the object of consumption as a function of distance. Suppose competing goods are produced in the same place. Where each will be consumed may depend on the distance from their origin.[6] Consider, for example, rich and poor ores, both mined at the same spot, the former below, the later at the surface. Since the cheap ore is therefore cheaper per consumption unit, though more expensive to ship, it has an advantage in the neighborhod of the mine, while the rich ore is purchased only by more distant iron works.

Second, the object of production as a function of distance. We come to the other half of Thünen's famous statement of the problem, the first half of which concerned the form of production as a function of distance from the market. Suppose the locations for the

5. See below, p. 37.
6. See W. Launhardt, *Mathematische Begründung der Volkswirtschaftslehre* (Leipzig, 1885), p. 164.

consumption of various products to coincide in a town. These products compete for land for their cultivation. Thünen has shown that under certain conditions their cultivation is arranged in rings around the market. We shall return to this problem later.[7]

§2. THE GENERAL THEORY OF LOCATION

α. *General Equations of Location*

If we wish to be precise and to consider the influence of the selection of a particular location on all other locations—in the example of Thünen just mentioned, for instance, the repercussions of the location of our town not only on the particular farms that supply it, but on all agriculture and on all other towns—then we enter upon the general theory of location. The repercussions, strictly speaking, are transformed into mutual relations, and it ceases to be meaningful to pick out one location and examine its relation to its neighbors in isolation. We are faced with the interdependence of all locations. Equilibrium of the location system can therefore no longer be charted, but can be represented only by a system of equations that are insoluble in practice. The conditions that they express, rather than the equations themselves, are of great interest indeed. For they contain the conditions for the functioning of the whole system and are therefore more important than all that the special location theory has to offer in the way of realistic details. With the general equations we encounter the other basic force that determined location: the tendency to equalization of the advantages of the individual economic units and (in a market into which entry is possible) the maximization of the number of competitors.[8]

β. *The Simplifying Theory of Economic Regions*

Between the theory of individual locations and that of location patterns stands the theory of economic regions. It shares with the former the advantage of geometric representation, with the latter a breadth of subject. It shows the universal interdependence of

---

7. An industrial parallel appears when different goods are made from the same raw material with different weight losses. See O. Engländer, *Theorie des Güterverkehrs und der Frachtsätze* (Jena, 1924), pp. 129 f.

8. As the latter eliminates profits (though absence of profits, on the other hand, does not assure maximization of the number of independent economic existences) one may speak roughly of a tendency toward equalization and elimination of profits; i.e., of an equalization of incomes among independents and between them and dependents. Later we shall assume free entry to markets as a more desirable situation, and thus treat both tendencies together.

locations with such simplifications that it can be charted. It neglects in particular natural inequalities and in some though not all respects urban demand. It considers the relations between all producers and consumers of the same goods, and between the producers of different goods at least in so far as they are significant for the establishment of major cities and main transport arteries. If the suppressed factors are introduced it is quite probable that the picture would be somewhat changed, but it is unlikely that it will be wholly invalidated. Because of their importance, a separate part of this book will be devoted to economic regions.

b. THE RELATIVE POSITION OF LOCATIONS

§1. THE BASIC TYPES

We shall now discuss the results of a rational choice of location. Definite and characteristic combinations emerge between the places where a commodity is produced and those where it is consumed, depending on their numbers and locations. In the market as a whole there may well be a hundred such, which usually will split up into smaller groups of which the majority find it advantageous to deal principally with one another, or exclusively so if the products of the individual manufacturers are homogeneous. Every group is a submarket. Those submarkets that have immediate contact with each other, as well as those markets that are not split up into further subdivisions, may be reduced to a few basic types: It occurs only rarely that a single producing center deals with a single consuming center. Yet nonagricultural location theory has preferred to base itself on this limiting case. As a rule, several producers are grouped about one consumer, or several consumers about one producer. We speak accordingly of *regions of supply* or *of demand*, and include both under the term *market areas*.

These two basic types of positional relations are the core of every determination of a location, areas of demand playing a larger role in the nonagricultural theory and areas of supply in the agricultural. The latter has been discussed principally by Thünen, the former by Launhardt, and the borderline cases by Weber. It makes little difference whether the number of locations distributed throughout the market area is large, as in agriculture, or small, as it often is with nonagricultural enterprises. According to circumstances we deal with complete or with incomplete market areas, but fundamentally the situation is the same. Nor is it altered if a center of production included many independent enterprises in the same line of business, each of which supplies the entire area. In respect to their common area of demand they may be treated as one firm, and their supply curves may correspondingly be added.[9] From this it follows that the nature of the area is determined not by the number of buyers or sellers, but by the number and position of their locations.[10,11] The locations of the producers and consumers of the same product, as well as of different products, may be situated anywhere or may be agglomerated. These agglomerations are important enough to be treated as a special problem.

§2. Agglomeration of Locations

α. Punctiform Agglomeration

The questions why the best locations for many producers (or consumers) sometimes coincide, why production in some places is so unusually great, and why and where towns grow, are one and the same. The answer must distinguish between agglomeration of locations for the production of similar commodities and that for the production of different commodities. As to the former category, we set aside the case where a particular place has only a single large firm that has merely attracted a few local enterprises to the spot. At present we shall discuss how several similar and *independent* enterprises can exist in the same place as the result of purely rational considerations; that is, if either mergers or migration of some firms could occur without friction. In large cities, finally, the concentration of similar and different enterprises may occur together. The relation of all these agglomerations to one another is subject to special laws, which will be discussed in Part II.

β. Areal Agglomerations

With punctiform agglomerations the individual locations, or at least their centers, coincide. Areal agglomerations are distinguished by the fact that the locations of their centers lie close together

---

9. Otherwise some product differentiation would have to exist.

10. If numbers alone were relevant—i. e., if locations were evenly distributed—areas of supply would result if in the economy as a whole the number of production centers exceeded that of consumption centers, and vice versa for areas of demand.

11. The nature of the area is in turn an essential factor determining the market form, together with the number and importance of buyers and sellers, their market behavior, and their complementarity. It was a mistake to think that the market form—i. e., the method and results of price formation—could be known merely from the number of buyers and sellers without their locational pattern. In general, the traditional market forms acquire an essentially different content as soon as they are seen geographically. But there is neither time nor space to develop this here.

Specific Locations

without, however, coinciding. This has the important consequence that in the latter case the market areas of the various locations remain separate though close together, whereas in the former they coincide precisely near the concentration of locations but in turn may be of wide extent. An example of an areal agglomeration of locations is the network of the supply areas of cotton gins in the United States, which are distributed with fair regularity throughout the cotton belt and are also restricted to it. An example of punctiform agglomeration of locations is the factories producing men's collars, practically all of which are situated in Troy, New York, but

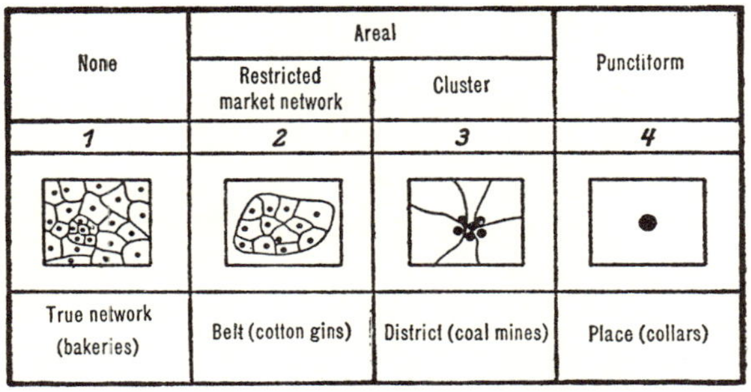

None	Areal		Punctiform
	Restricted market network	Cluster	
1	*2*	*3*	*4*
True network (bakeries)	Belt (cotton gins)	District (coal mines)	Place (collars)

Fig. 1. The Concentration of Locations

whose market includes the whole of the United States. There is, however, a third, intermediate, form. Most of the American coal mines are not concentrated at one site, though they are restricted to a relatively small territory. Nevertheless they do not supply arbitrarily those areas that lack coal. The importance of overlapping coal shipments is somewhat overestimated. They depend partly on quality differences.[12] In the main they are the result of irrational freight rates. On the whole it may be said, therefore, that each section of the coal-producing area has its own special outlets.[13]

12. Thus the steel works in the Chicago area get their coal from the Pittsburgh region because the coal from the much nearer Illinois fields is not suitable for coking.
13. Even with small districts this makes good sense: it prevents crosshauls within a district that is already overburdened with traffic. When this district is of even relatively small extent a sensible organization of the markets becomes difficult. Imagine a circular coal deposit, and assume the demand to be so small that only the mines at the periphery are kept busy. Then each mine will supply a sharply defined sector of the surrounding territory. With increasing demand it will pay to work the mines in the next inner ring. Strictly speaking, therefore, rather than the entire coal field only an outer ring is worked, whose width varies with demand. The nearer the mines are to the periphery the larger is the rent they yield. The situation would be simplest if coal, like cotton, say, were collected at a few cents at the edge of the circle and then

Hence in areal agglomeration of locations for the same industry we must distinguish the *belt*, where the market networks are compressed close together; and the *district*, where the markets are separated, while only their centers are compressed. Figure 1 pictures the differences of the last two agglomerations from complete dispersal on the one hand to punctiform concentration on the other.

Hitherto we have been discussing only the case of a single industry. But there is an areal as well as a punctiform agglomeration of locations for different activities: the so-called industrial areas. In their structure they resemble partly belts and partly districts.

---

redistributed from these. Producers' and consumers' rents would vary then only with their distances from these collecting centers. Their supply and sales areas would be easily determined. In reality the situation is somewhat more complex, but it is not worth while to go into the details here.

Chapter 3. Areal Boundaries

a. BOUNDARIES BETWEEN SIMPLE AREAS

Besides the locations themselves, the lines that separate them in areal distribution are of interest, and, in punctiform distribution, the areas of influence. We must therefore distinguish between (1) *boundaries between different kinds of goods* (i. e., areas that produce or consume different kinds of goods), and (2) *boundaries between different kinds of markets* (i. e., areas that sell the same product in different markets, or buy from them). Thünen's rings are an example of the first; separation of the sales areas for two competing enterprises in different locations is an example of the second. We may also call the latter the boundaries of competing locations, the former the boundaries of competing goods.

The boundaries separating areas of competing locations delimit the supply and demand areas of identical goods. The boundaries separating areas of competing goods delimit the areas of production or consumption of different goods, or at least of different forms of goods.

The latter are already given with the position of all locations, but the former must be calculated from the locations. With homogeneous goods the boundaries are sharp if buyers and sellers are scattered and numerous, and if the center of each area is treated as though the other centers did not exist. Otherwise the markets overlap and the boundaries become indistinct.

b. BOUNDARIES BETWEEN AREAL SYSTEMS

There are systems in which the areas for different goods are separate (as in the Thünen case) or overlap (as in economic provinces). Depending on the system, we get only boundary lines (1) or boundary zones (2). Boundary lines between both kinds of areal system have two things in common: Both include boundaries between simple areas, and, with intrinsic similarity of both towns and provinces, both separate market areas for the same marginal good. The same Thünen ring lies on either side of the border, referring, however, to different towns; and with economic provinces we find on either side of the boundary market areas of the same good that correspond to each other and have the largest necessary extension. But if the towns or provinces are of different size, the goods on the two sides of the boundary are also different. Any kind of Thünen rings meet, and may change as one walks along the boundary. Similarly, when the economic provinces are unequal, the marginal goods are different.

The distinction between boundary lines and boundary zones is this: The former constitute a sharp boundary between two towns or major cities in so far as these rival each other. The latter exist only between major cities, and indicate the boundary area in which "loophole" markets are found, that is, markets belonging wholly to neither of the two districts even though both are by nature wholly similar. They arise from the fact that where markets meet district boundaries empty corners appear that in themselves are too small to afford room for another independent enterprise, and that can be made large enough only by combination with similar corners in the adjoining province. We shall see later that these boundary zones extend from the edge of the district about two thirds of the way toward its principal city, but that they become less important as they approach it. Boundary zones are not distinguished by any particular price situation. Boundary lines and simple boundaries introduced under (a), on the contrary, are lines of equal profit to the producer or of equal prices to the consumer.

B. Selected Problems of Location[1]

IT IS neither possible nor really necessary to answer here every problem on location that has systematically been raised in the preceding section. They are not all of equal importance, and the nature of the solution of the individual cases would not differ greatly. It will suffice, therefore, to demonstrate a few typical methods of treating the problem. Once the procedure is thoroughly grasped there will be no difficulty in applying it to other and more complex situations.

The following pages will discuss two groups of questions concerning the choice of location seen from the standpoint of the individual economic unit (industrial and agricultural location theory), two problems on the agglomerations of locations (formation of towns and belts), and two divisions of the general theory of location (of which only the locational equations will be introduced in this part; the fundamental discussion on economic regions will be presented separately).

---

1. In a few places throughout the following discussion certain findings on economic regions have been anticipated, whose proof cannot be given until Part II.

Chapter 4. Industrial Location Theory

a. THE GENERAL PRINCIPLE

The location of an industrial enterprise is selected by the entrepreneur. His choice rests upon subjective considerations. He will, of course, bear objective facts in mind, but these alone cannot dictate location. Thus it is conceivable that under exactly the same external conditions two entrepreneurs may choose entirely different locations. The available range [1] for their decision depends upon the size of their possible entrepreneurial profits.[2] They will share only the formal aim, which is to choose their location so that the utility shall be as great as possible. Whether they have hit upon the right one can be determined only later, of course, for even after mature consideration they will chose " with their fingers crossed." [3]

1. Imitating entrepreneurs easily forget that this range is more restricted for them than for the abler pioneers. A location that may yield the latter some profit, though not the greatest possible, may result in losses to the former. Therefore they should not simply take the locations of leading enterprises as a guide, or without further thought attach themselves to an already existent agglomeration of their industry.

2. Here enter all those eccentricities that skeptics like to advance as examples of the irrationality and antitheoretical nature of actual events. For instance, a producer may frequently locate his plant so that he can pursue his favorite hobby on the side. The preference of English businessmen and their wives for life in the south of England has been said to play an important role in the southward migration of British industry. (PEP, *Political and Economic Planning: Report on the Location of Industry* [London, 1939], p. 46.) But as long as such a capricious choice costs no more than the entrepreneurial profit, it is still consistent with theory.

3. There are two reasons for this: the practical difficulty of determining exactly under given conditions how good a site really is, and the fundamental impossibility of foreseeing how these conditions will change. Dynamically there is no best location, because we cannot know the future. What follows is therefore meant to apply to static conditions. That the measurement of utility itself is dubious will be discussed later.

The degree of uncertainty connected with a location varies, of course. The scale runs from the security of old farms, manorial estates, or mercantile establishments inherited for generations that have seen their owners through all vicissitudes; through virtually permanent positions that their occupants hold for life (rural pastorates); through the multitude of industrial enterprises that under prudent management may last for a few generations, or may move away or collapse at any moment; down to itinerant folk of all sorts—musicians and poets, scientists and preachers, inventors, mercenaries, reformers and seekers after the Holy Grail, for all of whom the existing order holds no place, who can only choose between being ascetics or prostitutes and

The chosen location may turn out to be only subjectively a failure, or even objectively so. An entrepreneur fails subjectively when the personal success expected from the chosen location is not realized, objectively, when he goes into bankruptcy because his choice, seen also from the standpoint of the economy as a whole, proved to be wrong.[4]

b. PRACTICAL EXECUTION

In order to fix exactly the point of greatest utility we should have to bear in mind more considerations than would be scientifically possible, let alone practically convenient. An approximate formula for the choice of a location, however, depends on how many of the factors that influence a careful decision are eliminated. Obviously all irregular influences must be removed, since comprehensible rules can be established only for the effects of the regular. If we disregard all locally conditioned priceless utilities, the entrepreneur will choose the location of greatest real profit. If we discover no spatial regularity in the price level of the things he consumes, which will certainly be true for corporations, it will be best to eliminate such a cost-of-living pattern also. The goal will then become the location of the greatest nominal profit.

§1. ONE-SIDED ORIENTATION

α. *Cost Orientation*

Nominal profit is the difference between money cost and money receipts. As receipts depend on many irregular factors, industrial location theory has generally disregarded them. Thus Weber considered demand to be wholly inelastic. This assumes among other things that an areal boundary that separates neighboring competitors is fixed once and for all. The factory would then be situated at the point of lowest c. i. f. costs (cost, insurance, freight).

---

whose proper location is the highway, where they are torn between home and the world. The fate of List is repeated every day. [Friedrich List (1789–1846), a German economist, vigorously championed protective tariffs for infant industries, customs unions, and government development of railroads and merchant marine. Because of his views he was forced into exile for several years and upon returning to Germany was sentenced to imprisonment, but pardoned when he promised to emigrate. In 1825 he entered the United States and later became a citizen. Because of illness and financial difficulties he finally took his own life.—W. H. W.]

4. Bankruptcy does not necessarily mean the elimination of the unfit, but mainly the preservation of an order that derives its dignity through its distinction from chaos and not really through having accomplished something just or meaningful (except perhaps the maximum of free will, though not, as was formerly believed, the maximum utility). See below, p. 92, note 2.

1. TRANSPORT ORIENTATION

The cost of production depends upon local price differences and the amounts of factors of production and other things required. If these inequalities are finally abolished by the *ceteris paribus* assumption, only transport costs remain to be minimized. These alone almost always show spatial regularity, and their contribution toward determining location has therefore become the principal item in the ruling theory.

(aa) *The Point of Minimum Transport Cost.* Location theory up to now recognizes three methods for determining the point of minimum transport cost, that is, the place where total freight costs per unit are lowest.

1. *Construction of the Point of Minimum Transport Cost in the Locational Triangle by the Proposition of Exterior Angles.* This solution was first discovered by W. Launhardt,[5] and rediscovered a generation later by Alfred Weber.[6] In recent years T. Palander [7] has contributed an extensive discussion of this solution. The method is only touched upon here, because it is of neither great theoretical nor great practical importance. It applies only when the number of necessary sources of materials and places of consumption together amount to 3, and freight costs are proportional to weight and distance.

2. *The Mechanical Model.* Perforations are made in a stiff map at the sites of material sources and markets. Threads bearing determinate weights are passed through these holes and tied together in one knot. The position of rest for the knot is the desired location of production. The problem of finding the point of lowest freight costs is identical with that of finding the position of equilibrium in a system of forces. The mathematical proof is given by Palander.[8] The weights on the threads are proportional to the quantities to be moved. Let A, B, and C be raw material sites, of which 3, 2, and 0.5 tons respectively are needed to produce 1 ton of finished product; and let D, E, and F be markets consuming 80, 15, and 5 per cent of

---

5. His first easily accessible paper is "Die Bestimmung des zweckmässigsten Standorts einer gewerblichen Anlage," *Zeitschrift des Vereins Deutscher Ingenieure,* 1882, pp. 106–115.

6. Alfred Weber, *Ueber den Standort der Industrien,* Pt. I (Tübingen, 1909). Translated and edited by C. J. Friedrich as *Alfred Weber's Theory of the Location of Industries* (Chicago, 1928).

7. Tord Palander, *Beiträge zur Standortstheorie* (Uppsala, 1935), pp. 139–145.

8. *Op. cit.,* p. 141.

the total output respectively. Then the weights for the points A to F must be related as $3 : 2 : 0.5 : 0.8 : 0.15 : 0.05$. (For the history and bibliography of this method see footnotes 5–7.) The field of applicability of this method is wider, however; it can be used for any desired number of production and market sites, though again only when freight rates are proportional to distance.

3. *Isodapanes.*[9] Alfred Weber's isodapanes are lines of equal total freight per unit of product; that is, lines connecting points for which a definite combination of hauls is equally expensive. The combination consists of the shipment of raw materials and intermediate products to, and shipments of the finished product from,

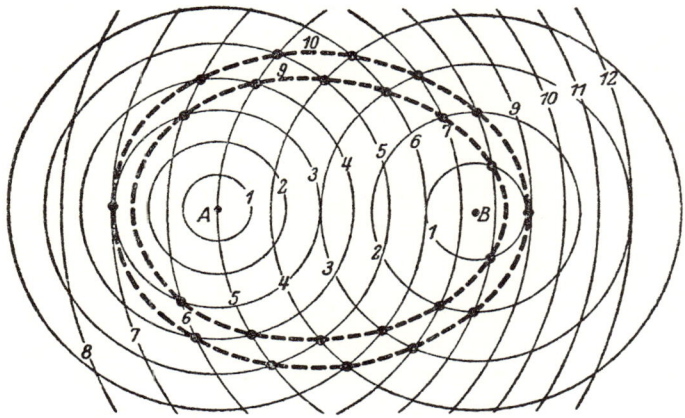

Fig. 2. The Construction of Isodapanes

the factory. Isodapanes must be distinguished from *isovectures*: lines representing equal unit freight rates for simple transport to and from a certain place. For a homogeneous transport surface, isovectures are concentric circles that follow one another at equal intervals for similar freight differences. They are proportional to distance as one proceeds outward from the center, and follow one another generally at increasing intervals for a graduated tariff. If the transport area is traversed by especially cheap lines of transportation (railroads, canals), combined transports result (e. g., by rail and truck) [10] and the isovectures are distorted. Isovectures serve for the construction of isodapanes. They are drawn for the transport of that

---

9. Palander (*op. cit.*, p. 305) has reviewed the various " iso " lines.
10. Brilliantly discussed by Palander, *op. cit.*, pp. 337–360.

quantity of goods which is required for the production and sale of a unit of finished product. Thus, in the foregoing example, the isovecture for 3 tons is drawn around A, that for 2 tons around B, and so on. The nearest isovecture around A is the line up to which 3 tons of the particular raw material can be shipped for the total expenditure of 1 monetary unit (isovecture 1); the next line connects the places to which the shipment of 3 tons from A will cost 2 monetary units (isovecture 2), and so on. It is simplest always to derive one family of isodapanes from two families of isovectures, as shown in Figure 2. On the assumption of a freight rate proportional to distance, the isovectures 1–12 are drawn around A, and 1–8 around B; the isodapanes constructed from the two sets of isovectures are drawn in as the broken lines 9 and 10. Isodapane 10, for example, connects all points to which the freight of 3 tons of raw materials from A and of 2 tons from B will cost together 10 monetary units. On it there lie, for instance, the points of intersection of isovecture 4 around A and of isovecture 6 around B, and also the points of intersection of both isovectures 5. Next a group of higher order isodapanes is constructed in exactly the same way until finally, in the highest group, all movements of goods between the production site looked for and the six points A to F are included. Of these highest order isodapanes only the innermost bearing the lowest cardinal number is of real interest in the present context, because it surrounds the minimum total cost of transportation; i. e., the most advantageous location for production. Isodapanes have the advantage over the mechanical model that, like it, they can be used for any desired number of locations, but, in addition, they can be used for any number of transportation lines and transport tariffs.

4. *The Principle of Substitution.* According to this principle the sum of freight increases equals the sum of freight decreases for infinitesimal deviations from the desired location.[11] While it merely characterizes the minimum point, it indicates at the same time the possibility of calculating it from the equations for the surface representing total freight.

(bb) *Limiting Position of the Point of Minimum Transport Cost.* Ever since the time of Weber, special interest has been devoted to those special situations where production has been drawn to a favored point. In addition to transshipment points and nodal points, we also designate as favored points the sites where the factors of

---

11. A. Predöhl, "Das Standortproblem in der Wirtschaftstheorie," *Weltwirtschaftliches Archiv*, XXI (1925), 294–321. The principle is stated on p. 306.

production,[12] consumers, or competitors are to be found.[13] Under what conditions does the point of lowest total freight costs coincide with one of these favored sites?

Four cases may be imagined with a tariff proportional to distance. The first is *weight ratios*. If the weight on one of the threads in the mechanical model (p. 18) is greater than the sum of the remaining weights, the position of rest for the system of forces will coincide with the point of insertion for the large weight. In the Lorraine iron industry, for example, the weight ratios before World War I were: 3 tons of ore + 1 ton of coke = 1 ton of pig iron. Thus the weight of the ore was greater than the sum of the two other weights. The attraction of the Lorraine minette basin would have been even greater had not the freight rate for coke from the Ruhr to Lorraine exceeded that for the shipment of ore from Lorraine to the Ruhr.[14] The poorer the ores that have to be smelted, the greater the attraction of their deposits. Hence the iron industry moves today more and more toward the ore. A typical example of weight-conditioned attraction toward the consumer is offered by the brewing industry. The weight of the water added is greater than the weight lost by hops, malt, and fuel.

The relative positions of the various locations are the second reason for the coincidence of the point of minimum transport cost with one of the favored points. What has just been described occurs

---

12. If these are present but only in insufficient number one can speak of a favored point or site only with reservations.

13. There may be some doubt whether a central location between neighboring competitors belongs here. Such a location may be highly important as a guess in respect to a possible general neighborhood but it is difficult to define in theory, since it is not a stable point; indeed, under realistic assumptions such a point can be defined only through maximization of profits. Such an intermediate location is probable if, first, in transport orientation the freight rate on raw material is low compared with that on the finished product (in the German railway tariff the highest rate for manufactured goods by the carload is almost five times, the less-than-carload rate almost thirty times, as high as for coal!), so that production would be carried out exactly at the center of consumption; if, second, in orientation by total costs instead or besides, location of raw material and labor are about evenly distributed; if, third, in orientation by return the buyers are scattered (at the desired point the sales cone would have to be intersected least by the neighboring ones); or if, fourth, in orientation by profits everything coincides: high freight on manufactured goods, and wide dispersion of raw material sites, labor, and the markets. This case leads to production for a well-rounded exclusive territory. Eggers and Umlauf have called this " area-bound " production. Part II will be devoted to this topic.

14. H. Schumacher, " Die Wanderung der Grossindustrie in Deutschland und in den Vereinigten Staaten," *Schmollers Jahrbuch*, 1910, pp. 451–482. Buchman *et al.*, *Die Standorte der Eisen- und Stahlindustrien der Welt* (Berlin, 1927).

not only when one of the weights exceeds the sum of the others, but also when it exceeds their resultants. The resultant for any given weight depends on the relative positions of the points of insertion of the weights.[15]

Third, *established lines of communication* have the result that the costs of transportation are always smallest at one of the perforations (location of raw material or of consumption) or nodes, as can be readily seen on the mechanical model. Only at such favored places can the opposing forces affect each other by altering the angle of attack, whereas between these points they remain constant. Hence the nodes have the advantage that from them a larger number of places can be directly reached than from other points, which might perhaps be preferred if a transport *area* existed.

The first three causes for the limiting special locations consisted in a reduction of transport cost. The fourth cause lies in a saving of transshipment cost. This factor, among others, accounts for the location of industries at transport junctions, including seaports. Even where transports do not pass a transshipment point, the cost of reloading would nevertheless be saved if the production site were moved directly to the source of a factor of production instead of simply near it. This shift will occur as long as the increase in line-haul costs is less than the saving in terminal costs.

We now replace the simple tariff proportional to distance by *differential tariffs*. First, according to the type of goods: The freight rate for the finished good is often higher. This works out exactly as though the ordinary rate prevailed but the finished product were heavier than it actually is (Weber's "ideal" weight). It alters nothing in our analysis except that location at the site of consumption becomes more probable. Not so, secondly, when rates are graduated according to length of haul. Graduated tariffs favor shipment over long distances and hence favor as locations the starting points and terminals of transportation systems (location of raw materials or of consumption) rather than intermediate or transshipment points.[16]

---

15. For the simple case of the location triangle I refer as an example to Palander's figure 8 (*op. cit.*, p. 144). If a consumption site K lies in one of the cross-hatched areas, we have a normal case: the site of production lies within the location figure. If K lies in the dotted area, goods are produced at the point of consumption. If it lies in the area of broken lines, goods are produced at the source of raw material. Many scattered areas of consumption easily give the raw material site the preponderance of influence in the location of production.

16. The contrast with a straight mileage tariff is well brought out by Palander's figures (*op. cit.*, p. 318). The legends must, however, be transposed.

The recent development of automobile transportation counteracts some of the factors discussed that influence the limiting special location. It undermines the preferred position of railway stations in general and that of favored special points in particular. The advantages of transshipment points are less frequently felt because transshipment is less frequent when motor trucks are employed. Location near consumption—whether it is concentrated in large cities or distributed over open country—becomes less advantageous because with competition truck rates are regulated more by immediate cost than by "what the traffic will bear." Thus it is hardly possible to burden finished goods with higher rates. Markets and locations of raw materials, finally lose their power to attract when, as in the case of the motor truck, mileage tariffs supplant graduated freight rates.[17]

To this extent the truck has a decentralizing effect on the location of industry. It breaks up agglomerations that depend only on differentiated freight tariffs but, under conditions still to be discussed, it encourages agglomerations that depend upon lower production costs by eliminating scattered rural locations.

2. ORIENTATION ACCORDING TO PRODUCTION COSTS

Production costs by themselves may sometimes determine location exclusively, but if so, always in marginal situations. The generally indefinite *technical* orientation by production must be separated from this case. Only where one or a combination of several factors of production are exhaustible, immobile, and unique, does production necessarily occur at this location if at all. In the main, these will be instances of resources whose occurrence in the necessary minimum quantities is especially rare, of some special climate, or of gifted men who refuse to migrate.

3. ORIENTATION ACCORDING TO TOTAL COSTS

(aa) *Location of Lowest C.I.F. Costs.* As a rule the costs of production cannot be separated from the freight cost on raw material, and often it is not desired to separate them from the freight cost on the finished product. In such cases they affect location only in combination with the latter, e. g., when several scattered raw materials have to be combined, or when several sources of supply are available. In our examples on page 18 let there be two sources for the first, mobile raw material, for which the cost at A_1 is 10 marks per ton

---

17. Thus the automobile is superior to the railroad for short hauls, for express freights, and for goods on which freight rates are high.

whereas in remote A_2 it is only 5 marks. By ordering from A_2, 15 marks on every ton of finished product can be saved. But let the total freight per ton of finished product for the combination $A_1, B \cdots F$ at the point of minimum transport cost be 20 marks less than at the minimum point for the combination $A_2, B \cdots F$. The more expensive but nearer source, A_1, would therefore be preferred. Hence freight costs decide the choice among sources, and production costs [18] the choice among points of lowest freight rates. In short, the most favorable location depends upon both, and therefore upon total costs.[19]

(bb) *Special Location of the Point of Lowest Total Cost.* Here many things must be distinguished. First, total costs may attract an enterprise to a favored point even though neither production costs nor cost of distance is a minimum there, provided that the sum of

---

18. Spatial differences in production costs rest upon the fact, as Ohlin has frequently emphasized, that the factor endowment of different regions varies, and that these factors are combined in varying proportions and thus affect production in different degrees. However, spatial price differences are not simply the result of local differences in scarcity. Because of the mobility of the factors of production and of their products, the relative scarcities themselves are a result of the particular spatial price system. It is necessary to emphasize interdependence at this point, instead of merely citing physical factors (climate, natural resources, human characteristics) as causes of local differences in production costs. But it will not do to reduce spatial price differences entirely to variations in freight cost, and thus orientation according to total costs to transport orientation, since the price differences may be smaller than the freight costs. The difficulty could be surmounted, to be sure, by pushing the significance of space too far, and developing the whole theory of production as a theory of transportation. Obviously every step in production could always be reduced in the last analysis to spatial movement.

19. Again the substitution principle characterizes the minimum point: For small changes in location, the sum of cost increases must equal the sum of cost decreases. If costs were known as a function of latitude and longitude, their minimum point could be determined on principle algebraically instead of by Weber's geometrical solution. Predöhl (*loc. cit.*) introduced the marginal principle into the theory of industrial location. The substitution equilibrium is harder to define here, however, than in price theory. Predöhl to the contrary (*op. cit.*, p. 314, but in agreement with other passages), it does not matter that equally priced *amounts* of means of production, whose price varies locally, may be substituted for one another without change in physical *return* (which here includes transportation to the buyer). It is not the change in physical cost (which may be restricted to transportation or be wholly absent) that is relevant, but in *money cost*; and not in two factors, but in two combinations of *all* factors (which may differ in amount and/or value). The entire combination varies even with *small* changes in location (in contradistinction to substitution at the same place) and its total costs must remain constant. With larger displacements, say to a place of cheap labor, total costs may nevertheless decrease. As soon as there are several points of minimum cost the marginal principle fails to indicate the best (discontinuous substitution).

the two costs is a minimum. Second, in cases that remain indeterminate in respect to production orientation, total costs permit a decision as to where, if anywhere, the special location is reached. It may, for example, happen that a factor of production is immobile but not irreplaceable, or that it is found in several places. The conditions of production decide only that in the case of replaceable factors some special location may be, and in the case of more frequently found factors certainly will be, chosen. Only total cost can decide among the various possibilities. Again Weber's isodapanes are employed.[20] But instead of giving each of the highest isodapanes the cardinal number that corresponds to the total freight for each unit of product when it is produced on a particular isodapane, we may set down the difference between this figure and the freight costs at the minimum point. This new number indicates by how many monetary units the total freight costs per unit of product increase, when production is moved away from the optimum transport point onto the corresponding isodapane.

If, for example, local wage differences are to be considered, we can indicate in the same way by how much the labor cost per unit is greater or less than at the point of lowest freight costs.[21] Instead of at the place of lowest freight cost, the plant will then be set up where the saving in wages less the additional freight costs is greatest.

Third, where production is technically restricted to a unique location, and where location by partial cost leads to a special location, this special location will be necessarily confirmed by the effect of total cost. The special location may perhaps be confirmed by the effect of total cost when the plant has been transport oriented.

Fourth, if costs of transport alone lead to an unequivocal[22] special location, this location can be shifted to another favored point as

20. A. Weber, *op. cit.*, pp. 100–103; English ed., pp. 102–104.
21. Occasionally the spatial picture of wages will be so regular that isotims of labor can also be drawn; that is, lines connecting points of equal wages. Moreover, as "iso-lines" or "contour lines" can be interpolated within certain limits, L. von Bortkiewicz was probably not correct on this point in his otherwise wholly pertinent criticism of Weber. Bortkiewicz prefers empirical calculation even when nothing but freight and labor costs are taken into account, because isodapanes themselves are simply made up of similar individual empirical calculation and only afterwards compared with individual labor markets, which is a more complex procedure than the finding of freight cost in general for these sites alone. (" Eine geometrische Fundierung der Lehre vom Standort der Industrien," *Archiv für Sozialwissenschaft*, XXX [1910], 759 ff. The criticism is found on page 770.)
22. A special location according to transport orientation is almost always unequivocal. Even with several minimum points, one will generally be the cheapest because there are several sources of supply to choose from.

soon as the prices of factors are taken into consideration that either are found in different places or, though mobile, do not give rise to freight cost.[23] Whenever production costs by themselves lead to an unequivocal special location that is determined not exclusively on technical but perhaps only on economic grounds,[24] the simultaneous consideration of transportation costs may likewise lead to removal to another favored point.

Finally, orientation by total costs may even eliminate the special location in such cases instead of merely changing it.

β. *Orientation by Gross Receipts*

1. LOCATION OF THE MOST FAVORABLE MARKET

A plant can be established at a place where revenue is greatest rather than where outgo is smallest.[25] Still more one-sided than the choice of the place of largest sales would be establishment according to one of their components, quantity and price. Orientation by quantity would look more toward the number of buyers, orientation by price toward their purchasing power. The former, therefore, would favor populous districts; the latter, prosperous ones; both prefer a location away from competition.

2. SPECIAL LOCATION OF THE POINT OF GREATEST GROSS RECEIPTS

Regard for gross receipts alone forces production to the location of the consumer, if the market is technically tied to the buyer (the corresponding phenomenon on the expenditure side is production tied to an immobile factor of production), and if purchasers cannot or will not change their location (the corresponding phenomenon is irreplaceable production factors.[26]). If such areas of consumption

---

23. Local taxes, capital, and labor, for example. Capital is almost never immobile, and labor at most in respect to definite kinds and definite amounts. But the cost of changing their locations cannot, except for commuters, be treated as are other transportation costs. It is incurred only once and connected with the locality in question.

24. When all production elements are present in one or several places and thus no transportation is technically necessary for purposes of production, the only or cheapest source will be chosen in orientation by production, whereas in orientation by total costs the combination of factors from different places, or a location nearer the market, may be still more advantageous.

25. "... in the absence of decisive natural factors ... industries tend to be located within easy reach of the market." *Royal Commission on the Distribution of the Industrial Population (Barlow Commission) Report* (London, 1940) (Cmd. 6153), p. 48.

26. As a rule the location of consumers depends in turn, at least in principle, on the local prices of the production technically tied to them.

exist everywhere (the corresponding phenomenon with natural factors is ubiquitous occurrence), the fact of a special location means nothing; if several possible locations exist, the special location is technically indeterminate; that is, it is a necessary but not sufficient condition for the choice of a location. Then receipts are the governing factor. The special location is technically unequivocal only when all buyers, or at least a sufficient number, live in one place.

§2. THE CORRECT PROCEDURE

α. *Orientation by Profit*

In so far as they dominate in practice, all the points of view so far discussed may perhaps explain an actual location, but except in special cases no single one shows the right location. This depends neither upon expenses nor upon gross receipts alone, to say nothing of any individual cost or receipt component. Their significance may well be considered singly at the beginning of the analysis, but the final and sole determining factor is their balance: the net profit. In a free economy, the correct location of the individual enterprise lies where the net profit is greatest.[27]

Of course, even the procedures discussed above represented attempts to find this optimum point. For when receipts, say, are given, the location of the greatest profit coincides with that for the lowest c. i. f. costs. But a consideration of the variability of gross revenue should make use beyond a one-sided orientation by costs; we should not, with Weber, regard gross revenue as constant by assuming a given demand and price. Actually, demand varies with price[28] in part directly, in part via the size of the market area; and it varies also with the site of production chosen. The connection between price, demand, and location is such that for each possible factory price, for example, the greatest total demand will be realized with a different location of the plant, because with every change in price the market area assumes another form (even if, as will usually happen, neighboring competitors do not change their locations too), and because the demand of individual markets changes in different proportions. Even in the simple case of a linear demand curve, an increase in price would restrict the demand from distant points by a

---

27. This does not exclude deviations for extra-economic reasons, in so far as profits permit.

28. In other words, sales rise as prices fall: (1) at the expense of competitors and (2) at the expense of other products. Not only does the demand curve shift to the right, but actual demand moves downward on the new curve as well.

larger percentage than that from nearer ones. The factory location that would result in the greatest total demand would thus be more strongly affected by the location of neighboring markets when prices are high than when they are low. That is, the optimum location would shift with each change in price. As soon as this variability in demand is taken into account [29] all of Weber's constructions on the supply side collapse again.[30] For it becomes meaningless to wish to find the point of lowest cost. The minimum transport point and isodapanes cease to exist. The minimum point vanishes because, as soon as the boundaries of the market area are changeable, the average freight costs would be smallest if nothing were sold beyond the location of the factory—indeed, if the factory itself were finally to disappear! Isodapanes, on the other hand, can be constructed only when a shift in location does not itself bring about a shift in demand.

It is hardly necessary to go further into this matter. Weber's solution for the problem of location proves to be incorrect as soon as not only cost but also sales possibilities are considered. His fundamental error consists in seeking the place of lowest cost.[31]

29. A. Robinson has recently criticized this omission by Weber. Review of S. R. Dennison, *The Location of Industry and the Depressed Areas* (Oxford, 1939), in *Economic Journal*, L (1940), 267.

30. This does not exclude the possibility that isodapanes may aid in the determination of locations not only of production, but also of consumption, and of raw materials, whenever two of the three categories of location are given. (See Palander, *op. cit.*, pp. 159 ff.) In the first case, local wage differences may be taken into account, as described above; in the other two cases, differences in f. o. b. cost of materials. (*Ibid.*, pp. 162–165.)

In the intermediate case, the problem may be to include simultaneously both kinds of local differences in manufacturing costs in the calculations. This, too, can be done in principle. All isodapanes (i. e., lines of equal freight cost) merely become isotims (i. e., lines of equal price, or, in this case, of equal total unit cost). With their help we can determine the area for which any particular combination of production sites and raw material sources (at least with constant cost) will be superior to every other combination. The lines separating such areas are indifference lines, or "isostants," i. e., lines of minimum cost points. However, one must not overlook the fact that such a construction presupposes a knowledge of production locations, and is therefore not suited to their discovery. Nor does it permit consideration of the influence of changing demand upon costs any more than does the construction of isodapanes.

31. This applies also to all modern location theories (those of Predöhl, Palander, and Ritschl among others) in so far as they are based on Weber. See my review of Palander's *Beiträge zur Standorttheorie* in *Schmollers Jahrbuch*, 1938, and my reply to Ritschl, " Um eine neue Standorttheorie: Eine Auseinandersetzung mit Ritschl," *Weltwirtschaftliches Archiv*, LIV (1941), 1*–11*.

This by no means excludes the incorporation into a new location theory of parts of his theory which, though destroyed as a whole, nevertheless is a great achievement.

This is as absurd as to consider the point of largest sales as the proper location. Every such one-sided orientation is wrong. Only search for the place of greatest profit is right,

But where is this to be found? A geometrical solution becomes impossible as soon as price and quantity are added to the two spatial variables, for it can be applied to three variables at most. Yet algebraic treatment leads to equations of an insoluble degree. This complexity stems from the facts that, as already explained, there is more than one geographical point where the total demand of a surrounding district is at a maximum, and that from these points outward total demand does not decrease according to a simple function.[32] We are thus reduced to determine separately for every one of a number of virtual factory locations the total attainable demand, and for similar reasons the best volume of production as a function of factory price (market and cost analysis). The greatest profit attainable at each of these points can be determined from the cost and demand curves, and from this the place of greatest money profit, the optimum location, can be found. Now the procedure is no longer theoretical, however, but simply empirical testing, since the result holds only for the locations actually examined and cannot be interpolated. As all points in an area can never be analyzed in this manner, we cannot exclude the possibility that among the locations not examined there may be one that would yield a higher return than the most advantageous of those investigated. There is no scientific and unequivocal solution for the location of the individual firm, but only a practical one: the test of trial and error. Hence Weber's and all the other attempts at a systematic and valid location theory for the individual firm were doomed to failure.

For example, Weber's method could be employed in deciding between dispersed settlement of farmers and village settlement. For in this case demand is actually given as a first approximation as far as the location, amount, and market price and the number of products are concerned (but see p. 60, note 41). Thus economically it remains only to locate the farms in such a way that the total costs of transportation to the farmer as producer, vendor, and consumer are minimized.

Advocates of the classical theory of international trade which regards countries as points and the market area as given can explain the international division of labor also by means of the minimum transport point (see W. H. Dean, *The Theory of the Geographic Location of Economic Activities* [Ann Arbor, 1938], pp. 24 ff., from the dissertation), or at least introduce the conditions of transportation into the theory of comparative cost.

32. Nor does a substitution equilibrium prevail here any longer. Even with small departures from the best location the cost may change, if their change is as great as that of the proceeds.

Yet science does offer something to the practical investigator of locations. First, it teaches him to avoid the errors of one-sided orientation, wherein generally an investigator may arrive at wrong conclusions more often than right ones. Second—and this is really the most important—the theory and statistics of areas with or without insufficient locations (that is, our theory seen from the practical side of the individual firm) indicates not at what spot, but in what neighborhood, a new location must be sought. For the actual choice we can at least provide a list of favored points that should by all means be appraised in addition to the approximate center of gravity of the market area, even though it might be advisable to avoid them since their market areas are often more than saturated. But there might be so many of these points that it would be worth while to know which ones deserved further examination. Here, too, theoretical considerations help, together with the findings of statistics and the results of practical experience.[33]

33. To that end it is necessary to determine on the cost side which point of supply of production factors offers the greatest saving as a location. Thus for each individual cost items we must know: (a) their shares in the total costs (chief cost factors of an industry); (b) the extent of their geographical differences (cheapest sources for the main cost factors as compared with the most expensive). The former can be only approximately calculated since the share itself varies from place to place. In the latter, geographical price differences include the costs of transportation. For most cost factors the price will be lowest at one of their points of supply. Local taxes, of course, have no point of supply; workers may be willing to accept lower wages in an attractive place to which they must first migrate. Goods may be cheaper away from the place where they are produced because of dumping or of smaller trade margins. The saving in costs is presumably greatest where those factors are cheapest (a) whose share in total costs and (b) whose geographical price differences are especially large; with factors where only (a) or (b), or neither, has a high value considerable savings are less probable. Whether this first presumption was justified can be determined for any given place only after the cost of factors that are not particularly cheap is taken into account. However, to calculate total production costs one must include demand, whose extent often determines the height of the costs and always decides whether they can be borne. Thus one ends up with an unavoidable calculation of the chances of profit in a particular locality. As a location where the most important cost factor was especially cheap may nevertheless prove a failure in the end the suggestion of such a location can be only a hint, worth following up, but nothing more. Similarly, and with results of equal value, places may be selected from the standpoint of demand and appraised where the product presumably might bring a particularly high price or command a particularly large market. But, above all, points more or less in the center of their expected sales areas should be considered, and even before that the favored points in their vicinity.

These reflections are applicable to entire industries. If systematic lists are prepared of the characteristics of various industries (technical restrictions, cost structure, market conditions); of various sites (supplies, prices, location); and of locations already appraised, the locations and possibilities of dislocation that are especially probable or

Finally, the effect of single location factors, and the co-operation of at least the most important ones, can be shown in a series of typical though greatly simplified cases. This would aid directly in the discussion of practical location questions, or at least provide a model.[34] The irregularity of even such standardized situations makes a systematic presentation of their solution impossible, just as the irregularity of conditions in any actual case usually prevents a scientific solution. Even Lehmann-Lenoir, who applied Weber's theory, proceeded only by trial and error.[35]

The situation is somewhat simpler when a factory is to be moved rather than newly established. At any rate cost analysis offers the lesser difficulty. But how is one to discover in advance what demand may be expected at the various eligible locations?' Here the much-criticized " basing-point system " may be an important help. It consists in charging the customer freight from a point different from the point of production. By considering one eligible location after another as a basing point, the effect on demand will be almost [36] as though the industry had been experimentally established at these various places, while the risk of actual investment is not incurred.[37]

β. *Special Location of the Point of Greatest Profit*

In comparison with one-sided orientation, an orientation by profits could produce new special locations at favored points where neither outlay is lowest nor proceeds are highest, but where their difference is greatest. There is, however, no industry in which this would necessarily be the case.

With complete orientation, production necessarily takes place at a favored point only when it requires an irreplaceable or immobile

---

improbable can be determined for different industries. Conversely, it can be stated for individual locations whether they are likely to attract industries, and which ones. Thus far, however, we lack systematic cost analyses for the different industries, and especially geographic price analyses of the individual cost factors.

34. Our conclusions on the economic importance of distance for the individual firm, for example, on the geographic gradation of prices, and many others are of direct practical interest.

35. F. Lehmann-Lenoir, *Les verreries suisses. Etude comparative de leur répartition territoriale effective et de celle résultant de la " Reine Theorie des Standorts " d'Alfred Weber* (Soleur, 1940), pp. 217 ff.

36. In some respects, for example where the advantages of actual contact are concerned, it makes a difference whether the industry is actually moved or not.

37. Producers with branches can establish new enterprises more easily than those with but one plant, since the former can draw more reliable geographic comparisons from actual experience than if they had to rely on estimates alone.

production factor or consumer, or a still rarer combination of such factors or consumers (technically conditioned special location) whether at one place (definite special location) or several (indefinite special location). In the latter instance the location will be determined by the simultaneous consideration of all the other location factors, including proceeds, in contradistinction to one-sided orientation by total costs. Definite technically conditioned special locations will necessarily be confirmed by profit calculations; others, which depended on one-sided orientation, may be so confirmed. Should production be carried on at a special location when only proceeds (a purely economic restriction) or transportation costs are considered, it can always be shifted or eliminated by inequality in production costs, and usually [38] by the changeability of demand (as son as the market area is no longer sharply defined.)

In retrospect, it is clear that special locations are probably more numerous with one-sided than with complete orientation. In reality, they are therefore more significant than they would be in a rational world. Only a few obvious and easily surveyed factors are generally taken into account in choosing a location, and often enough all but a single one are eliminated as trifling because a real comparison would be far too difficult. Thus it happens that special locations are more common in reality than they should rationally be.

§3. Orientation and Especially Favorable Locations

Up to now *orientation* has had several meanings in the literature of location. It may mean the motives for or the outcome of a choice of location. In the former case it denotes the factors that are taken into account either (1) exclusively or (2) as especially important. We have employed the term only in the sense of (1): transport orientation, orientation by production costs, total costs, proceeds, and possibly by profits.[39]

In the second case one (3) describes or at the same time (4) gives

---

38. If a special location depends on established lines of communication, demand conditions alone cannot as a rule eliminate it; if it depends on weight ratios, demand conditions can eliminate it only if the finished product predominates (provided that the tariff is not graduated and that all costs imposed by distance except freight are insignificant). This predominance may be lost when the finished product is shipped to several places, so that only the resultant of these divided forces is operative. If, on the other hand, a raw material predominates, nothing can alter this, no matter how the consumers are distributed.

39. As well as (extra-economically) by the technical conditions of production.

Industrial Location Theory

reasons for the result of the choice. The first of these simply names an actual situation at the source of a location factor after that factor, but it remains an open question whether this factor is also responsible for the choice (we shall call this " situation " at the source of supply for raw material, etc.). The second implies that the factor at whose location production is situated has obviously caused the choice. This explanation is meaningful only in the case of technical restriction. It is sufficient for one,[40] and a necessary (though only partial explanation) for several sources of the same kind (it is better to speak of definite or indefinite " technical restriction " to sources for raw material, etc.—d_1 in Table 1).[41] But it may mean only that the actual site is rational though not technically due to the factor located in the same place. (We call this either " economic " or " extra-economic " restriction to a point of consumption, etc.—d_2 and d_3 in Table 1.)[42]

40. Apart from the fact that whether or not production will pay at all depends also on every other factor influencing profit. (See Predöhl, *op. cit.*, p. 294.)

41. As such technical restrictions are imposed mainly though not entirely by nature, the influence of nature on the choice of a location may be briefly sketched. The natural causes for local differences in the economic scarcity of means of production may be divided into (1) their natural abundance, first as to the number and second as to the extent of their sources; and (2) their technical suitability for shipment (mobile or immobile).

According to the number of the sources of supply, production is: (1) With immobile means of production unconditionally dependent on source *technically* and *economically* (one source); conditionally dependent (several sources); or free to choose a source (ubiquity through occurrence). (2) All mobile means of production allow technical independence of their source, no matter what the number of their sources (ubiquity through transportation).

Thus a location's technical independence of its sources predominates except where immobile factors of production are found at only one or a few sites. Technical ubiquity need not be economic, however, and vice versa. A locally varying *economic* scarcity of factors of production can only limit still further the possibilities of a production location that are already narrowed by technical scarcity. It cannot extend them.

In addition to influencing the choice of a location through sources and the technique of transportation, nature influences it through the technique of production, which, however, depends not solely upon nature but also upon price relationships. Nevertheless, nature does affect in this way the kind and relative amounts to be shipped. (The extent of the weight loss is only one factor among others.)

42. It is clear how protean the all-too-popular concept of orientation is. When it is said, for example, that an industry is " oriented to raw material," does the phrase mean: (a) That in choosing a location attention need be paid to raw materials alone? But to which of several? To the cost of its production or of its transportation? To its quality or its quantity? Or (b) that the raw material merely plays the most important role among several location factors? Or (c) simply that the production in question usually occurs at a source of raw material, whatever the reason? Or (d) do we refer to an industry that for technical reasons can be carried on only at this source? If there

"Especially favorable location," the situation of production at a favored site, is for any particular type of orientation: (*aa*) *definite*, when only one, or (*bb*) *indefinite*, when a whole group of favored sites could provide the desired location. In (*bb*) it is certain only

Table 1

			Motives for Choice of Location					Explanation of special location
			(a) Partial (one-sided)	(b) All factors considered	Extra-economic			
			Orientation					
	Ordinary location		1	4	7			
Result of choice of location	(c) Special location	(bb) Indefinite	—	—	8	Technically conditioned	Necessary	
			—	—	9			
		(aa) Definite	2	5	—	Technically and economically	(cc) (d₁)	
			—	—	10	Technically and extra-economically	Fortuitous (dd)	
			3	6	—	Economically (d₂)		
			—	—	11	Extra-economically (d₃)		

The letters refer to the categories set up in the text.

that there is a special location; in (*aa*) the situation of this special location is determined. This is (*cc*) necessary when based upon a technical restriction; (*dd*) fortuitous when the restriction is only economic or even extra-economic. A fortuitous special location is

are several raw materials, is "orientation to raw material" an adequate explanation for any actual location? Or, finally, should a raw material source happen to prove the most suitable location when several or all factors are considered, is "orientation to raw material" only subsidiary to transport orientation, orientation by production, or complete orientation? It would obviously be better to describe the situation in plain words.

always definite (e. g., transport orientation); a necessary one may be indefinite (as with orientation by technical restrictions on production).[43] A rational special location is always definite, but a definite one is not always rational.

Table 1 shows the relation between orientation and special location in their various meanings. One-sided orientation need not lead to a special location (Space 1), and special location does not necessarily presuppose one-sided orientation (Spaces 5, 6, 8–11).[44] "Technical restriction" means in the nature of things a special location, but this remains uncertain (Space 8) unless costs (Space 2), profits (Space 5) or extra-economic considerations (Space 10) are also taken into acount—with the exception of an unavoidable technical restriction at one single source of supply (Space 9). In this case only will even one-sided orientation necessarily provide a rational special location, because by way of exception it is synonymous with orientation by profits. As a rule, however, no single factor can indicate a location. All influence it, many favor it, but none determines it. Many reasons lie behind its choice.[45,46]

43. Transport orientation is merely an economic restriction; orientation by production may be also a technical restriction.

44. For example, it does not follow from location in a market area that easy sales determined the choice of this location in whole or even in part. In many other cases, on the contrary, the location of consumers has a great influence on the choice of location, though it is concealed because the resultant of the various forces favors another location, which appears to be independent of consumption.

45. The location of any particular coal mine, for instance, cannot be fully explained by the presence of coal. Only the whole relationship between production and demand that results in profits will make clear why coal is mined at just this spot and at no others. Which of the possible mines will actually be worked depends among other things on its technical productivity and the local prices of the factors of production on the one hand (cost curve), and transport relations to the market (demand curve) on the other. Thus, whereas over half of the American coal deposits are said to lie in the Rocky Mountains (Sten de Geer, "The American Manufacturing Belt," *Geografiska Annaler,* 1927, pp. 233–359), unlike the coal fields in the Appalachians, they have not attracted many industries nor are they worked to any great extent because of of their unfavorable location. Although coal is widely distributed, coal mining is rather concentrated. Hence " orientation by raw material," or more exactly " restriction by raw material," is not an adequate explanation here, where this factor is only one of those taken into account. By itself, therefore, it is a false explanation for the special location.

46. The relation of special location to orientation, even in the meanings that we do not employ, is this: Special location is the possible but not inevitable *result of* orientation in the sense of (*a*) or (*b*); on the contrary, it is the necessary *condition for* orientation in the sense of (*c*) or (*d*).

Chapter 5. The Theory of Agricultural Location

As far as industry is concerned, we have discussed thus far only the location of an additional enterprise. That is, we have considered the location problem from the standpoint of the individual firm. Later we shall describe in detail how industry as a whole is located. With agriculture, this more general statement of the problem—namely, where a particular product is grown—is of greater interest from the very first. At the same time a second important problem is solved: what is to be produced in a particular place or by what particular enterprise.

a. PARTIAL (ONE-SIDED) ORIENTATION

These problems, too, can be simplified by ignoring some of the factors that should properly be considered. Of the various problems, the importance of location has been most thoroughly examined (by Thünen). Later we shall discuss changes in the quality of the soil, and in demand. When we finally consider the remaining factors, especially joint demand and supply, local wage differences,[1] and local variations in prices to the enterprise, we shall move to an orientation that takes all factors into account. But here, too, as with industrial location, we shall have to forego a geometrical solution.

§1. SYSTEM BASED ON THÜNEN'S THEORY

α. Preliminary Remarks

Thünen regarded industrial locations as given, and deduced agricultural locations from them. Basically he discussed a special case of reactions to the choice of the location of an individual enterprise (Fig. 3).

Let O be the site of an enterprise that sells its product in two forms, one of which is cheaper to produce per unit of consumption while the other is cheaper to ship. Let OA be the factory price for a machine and AB the cost of knocking it down for shipment

---

[1] G. Pavlovsky, Zur Frage der räumlichen Ordnung der Landwirtschaft, *Internationale Landwirtschaftliche Rundschau*, I, 33 (1942), 337–373.

and reassembling it at the purchaser's. Transport cones are drawn from A and B that give the c. i. f. prices for various distances. The cone above A is more acute because it costs more to ship a bulky or delicate machine in assembled form. Nevertheless, up to the distance OD the delivered price is lower for the assembled machine, and only beyond D will it be shipped knocked down.[2]

Still another situation is elucidated by Figure 3. Suppose that different competing products rather than different forms of the same product are produced at O. Let the first of these two products be cheaper to produce per unit of consumption but more expensive

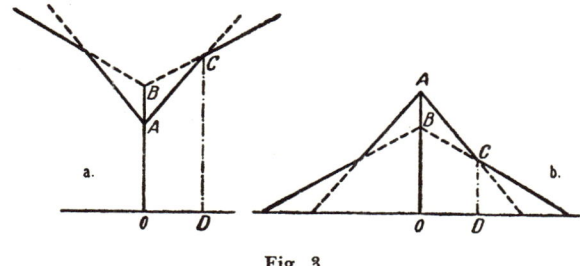

Fig. 3.

to ship (low-grade surface-mined ore); let the other be more expensive to produce but in return cheaper to ship (rich ore mined underground). The market area for the poor ore will therefore extend from the mine to the distance OD, and only then will the ring be reached within which it is cheaper to smelt the rich ore.[3]

Figure $3b$ illustrates similar cases, except that O is now no longer the center of production, but of consumption, and the rings around O are now conversely rings of different productions. Suppose that a certain product raised in the neighborhood of O is purchased there in crude or finished condition. Assume that processing on the spot is more expensive because it must be carried out on a small scale, but that it will save freight charges because it decreases weight. For example, let OA be the price paid for potatoes by starch factories

---

2. Another example is cotton, which for shipment over long distances requires the additional process of compression in large presses. Similarly, with lignite the calorific value and manufacturing costs are greater per unit of weight for briquettes, so that these are sold in a distant market.

3. If OA is the low price of electric current from a large power station erected in a coal district, and AB the loading costs of coal (i. e., costs independent of distance) plus the additional cost of small power stations, and if the costs that depend on distance are lower for coal than for electricity, current will be transmitted in the vicinity and coal shipped to distant points. See C. Pirath, *Die Grundlagen der Verkehrswirtschaft* (Berlin, 1934), pp. 201 ff.

at O, and AB the amount by which the cost of local reduction to starch exceeds that at a center. The vertices of the cones drawn from A or B then represent the grower's price for potatoes as a function of distance. For all farmers in the region OD it will clearly be more advantageous to ship potatoes to the town to be worked up at a center, whereas those at a greater distance will do better to ship starch.

The same figure, 3b, throws light on still another situation, which is of special interest in the present connection. Let O be the market for different products rather than for different forms of the same product. One, potatoes, yields economic rent OA per hectare when raised in the immediate vicinity of O, whereas corn yields only rent OB there. The picture changes with increasing distance from O, because a greater weight of potatoes than of corn can be harvested from a hectare. The freight charges for sending these yields to O will therefore be higher for potatoes. With increasing distance the freight absorbs the rent from potatoes more quickly than that from corn, and from the distance OD outward only corn rather than potatoes will be raised. Thus cultivation of the various crops is spread out in rings around the market.

β. *Possible Cases*

The famous Thünen rings represent special cases. The reasons for and the limitations of this solution will be clearer when its place in a complete system is seen. For this purpose the following symbols have been chosen:

Independent Variables

A: Outlay per hectare, in marks
E: Yield per hectare, in centners
p: Market price per centner
k: Distance from market, in kilometers
f: Freight per centner per kilometer

Derived Variables

$a = \dfrac{A}{E}$: Outlay per centner, in marks
$\pi = p - kf$: Local price per centner
$r = \pi - a$: Local profit per centner
$R = rE = E(p - kf) - A$: Rent per hectare
$m = p - a$: Highest profit per centner
   (= highest freight possible without loss to producer)

Agricultural Location

Table 2. COMPLETE SYSTEM OF SPATIAL ORDER IN AGRICULTURE FOR TWO CROPS

Case No.	Relative Size of Variables			Variables Fulfill Condition No. (m)						Crop Produced					
				Always		Sometimes		Never		Monoculture		Polyculture			
										Unconditioned	Conditioned	Unconditioned	Conditional		
													Cultivated together	Rings	
	E_1 to E_2	A_1 to A_2	p_1 to p_2	1	2	1	2	1	2	I	II	I or II	I and II side by side	I inside	II inside
1		>	>	.	.	×	×	.	.	.	.	0	.	0	.
2		>	=	.	.	×	×	.	.	.	.	0	.	0	.
3		>	<	.	.	×	×	.	.	.	.	0	.	0	.
4		=	>	×	.	.	.	.	×	0	.	.	.	.	.
5	>	=	=	×	.	.	.	.	×	0	.	.	.	.	.
6		=	<	.	.	×	×	.	.	.	.	0	.	0	.
7		<	>	×	.	.	.	.	×	0	.	.	.	.	.
8		<	=	×	.	.	.	.	×	0	.	.	.	.	.
9		<	<	.	.	×	×	.	.	.	.	0	.	0	.
10		>	>	.	.	×	×	.	.	.	.	0	.	0	.
11		>	=	.	×	.	.	×	.	.	0	.	.	.	.
12		>	<	.	×	.	.	×	.	.	0	.	.	.	.
13		=	>	×	.	.	.	.	×	0	.	.	.	.	.
14	=	=	=	.	.	.	.	×	×	.	.	.	0	.	.
15		=	<	.	×	.	.	×	.	.	0	.	.	.	.
16		<	>	×	.	.	.	.	×	0	.	.	.	.	.
17		<	=	×	.	.	.	.	×	0	.	.	.	.	.
18		<	<	.	.	×	×	.	.	.	.	0	.	0	.
19		>	>	.	.	×	×	.	.	.	.	0	.	.	0
20	>	>	=	.	×	.	.	×	.	.	0	.	.	.	.
21		>	<	.	×	.	.	×	.	.	0	.	.	.	.
22		=	>	.	.	×	×	.	.	.	.	0	.	.	0
23	<	=	=	.	×	.	.	×	.	.	0	.	.	.	.
24		=	<	.	×	.	.	×	.	.	0	.	.	.	.
25		<	>	.	.	×	×	.	.	.	.	0	.	.	0
26		<	=	.	.	×	×	.	.	.	.	0	.	.	0
27		<	<	.	.	×	×	.	.	.	.	0	.	.	0

(m) See text for definition of conditions, p. 40.

Table 2 contains all possible variations of the relative magnitudes of the first three independent variables for two crops, I and II.

γ. Spatial Order

We seek those cases where both crops are raised. Only then does the problem of their spatial order arise. Both crops will be grown when one yields a greater rent per hectare at the center of the area and the other at its periphery. The condition under which I will yield a greater rent at the center than II is $R_1 > R_2$. This yields:

$$\text{First Condition: } 1 < \frac{E_1 \cdot p_1 - A_1}{E_2 \cdot p_2 - A_2} \qquad (1)\,^4$$

The condition under which II will yield a greater rent at the periphery is: $R_1 < R_2$. This gives

$$\text{Second Condition: } \frac{E_1 \cdot p_1 - A_1}{E_2 \cdot p_2 - A_2} < \frac{E_1}{E_2} \qquad (2)\,^5$$

4. This is derived as follows:
$$R_1 > R_2.$$
substituting
$$E_1 \cdot (p_1 - kf) - A_1 > E_2 \cdot (p_2 - kf) - A_2.$$
Since at the center of production $k = 0$, this becomes
$$E_1 \cdot p_1 - A_1 > E_2 \cdot p_2 - A_2.$$
By dividing this becomes
$$\frac{E_1 \cdot p_1 - A_1}{E_2 \cdot p_2 - A_2} > 1.$$

5. This is derived as follows:
$$R_1 < R_2.$$
By substitution we get
$$E_1 \cdot (p_1 - kf) - A_1 < E_2 \cdot (p_2 - kf) - A_2.$$
But at the periphery
$$kf = p_2 - a_2.$$
Therefore
$$E_1 \cdot (p_1 - p_2 + a_2) - A_1 < E_2 (p_2 - p_2 + a_2) - A_2$$
$$E_1 p_1 - E_1 p_2 + E_1 a_2 - A_1 < E_2 p_2 - E_2 p_2 + E_2 a_2 - A_2.$$
Simplifying and substituting $a_2 = \dfrac{A_2}{E_2}$, we get:
$$E_1 p_1 - E_1 p_2 + \frac{E_1 A_2}{E_2} - A_1 < E_2 p_2 - E_2 p_2 + \frac{E_2 A_2}{E_2} - A_2$$
$$E_1 p_1 - E_1 p_2 + \frac{E_1 A_2}{E_2} - A_1 < 0$$
$$E_1 p_1 - A_1 < E_1 p_2 - \frac{E_1 A_2}{E_2} = \frac{E_1 E_2 p_2 - E_1 A_2}{E_2} = \frac{E_1}{E_2}(E_2 p_2 - A_2).$$
Dividing by $(E_2 p_2 - A_2)$ we get
$$\frac{E_1 p_1 - A_1}{E_2 p_2 - A_2} < \frac{E_1}{E_2} \qquad \text{Q. E. D.}$$

Agricultural Location

Both conditions combined:

$$1 < \frac{E_1 p_1 - A_1}{E_2 p_2 - A_2} < \frac{E_1}{E_2} \qquad (3)$$

First we establish for what variations of A, E, and p conditions (1) and (2) are fulfilled. Table 2 shows that of 27 cases condition (1) alone is always fulfilled in 7, and that condition (2) alone is always fulfilled in 7 further cases. In the first 7 the cultivation of crop II will nowhere be advantageous; in the other 7 only crop II will be grown.

In 12 additional cases our assumption on the relative magnitudes of A, E, and p is not sufficient to decide between the different crops. They leave it open whether only one or both together will be planted. The latter will occur either when both conditions are fulfilled or when neither is. This depends on the exact numerical value of A, E, and p. If both conditions are fulfilled or if neither one is, cases 10 and 18 differ from the remaining 10. Since in both cases $E_1/E_2 = 1$, both conditions can never be met. On the other hand, it has the same effect that for $(p_1 - p_2) = (a_1 - a_2)$ both conditions are unfulfilled at the same time.[6] The cultivation of both crops simultaneously is then possible as in the other 10 cases. They can even be grown side by side in adjoining sectors within the same ring instead of in successive rings only, as in the other 10 cases.

For the remaining 10 cases certain relative values for A, E, and p exist for which both conditions are fulfilled. *The choice of a crop is then a function of distance.* In all cases where $E_1 > E_2$ crop I will necessarily be grown in the inner ring. In all cases where $E_1 < E_2$ it will just as necessarily be grown in the outer ring. If $E_1 = E_2$, only one of the crops in question can be grown eco-

---

6. To prove that when $(p_1 - p_2) = (a_1 - a_2)$ neither condition (1) nor condition (2) can be fulfilled:

$$(p_1 - p_2) = (a_1 - a_2) = \frac{A_1}{E_1} - \frac{A_2}{E_2}.$$

If $E_1 = E_2$, as assumed in cases 10 to 18, it follows that

$$p_1 - p_2 = \frac{A_1 - A_2}{E_1} = \frac{A_1 - A_2}{E_2}$$

$E_1(p_1 - p_2) = A_1 - A_2$; therefore $E_1 p_1 - A_1 = E_2 p_2 - A_2$.
Dividing by the right side:

$$\frac{E_1 p_1 - A_1}{E_2 p_2 - A_2} = 1$$

But condition (1) requires that this expression be greater than unity; condition (2) requires that it be smaller than unity.—W. F. S.

nomically as a rule, with the following three exceptions: in cases 10 and 18, already mentioned, it is possible under certain conditions, and in case 14, the median case of the whole system, it is always possible, to plant both crops side by side. We shall now examine more closely those 10 of the 27 cases in which rings may be formed.

8. *Reason for the Formation of Rings*

1. *More Exact Reasons.* For the choice of a crop to depend upon distance, conditions (1) and (2) must be simultaneously fulfilled. When crop I should be grown in the inner ring, equation (3) shows that the following must be true: [7]

$$E_2(p_2 - a_2) < E_1(p_1 - a_1) < E_1(p_2 - a_2)$$

or

$$E_2 m_2 < E_1 m_1 < E_1 m_2 \quad \text{or} \quad E_1 m_1 > E_2 m_2$$

Since $m_1 < m_2$, it follows that $E_1 > E_2$.

Thus crop I brings in the greater total profit $(E_1 m_1)$, but the smaller profit per unit (m_1). From this it follows that the physical yield E_1 per unit of area is greater.[8] The first inequality makes it certain that crop I is superior at the market; the second, that it is superior only there. If both inequalities are fulfilled—that is, if rings are established at all—the product with the greater return by weight will be cultivated in the inner ring.[9] The exact reason why the superiority of crop I is lost with distance from the market is that freight charges absorb its unit profit more quickly,[10] until a

7. Derived as follows:

$$1 < \frac{E_1 p_1 - A_1}{E_2 p_2 - A_2} < \frac{E_1}{E_2}; \qquad (3)$$

since $a = A/E$, $A = aE$; substituting in (3),

$$1 < \frac{E_1 p_1 - a_1 E_1}{E_2 p_2 - a_2 E_2} < \frac{E_1}{E_2}$$

$$1 < \frac{E_1(p_1 - a_1)}{E_2(p_2 - a_2)} < \frac{E_1}{E_2}.$$

Multiplying through and simplifying:

$$E_2(p_2 - a_2) < E_1(p_1 - a_1) < E_1(p_2 - a_2) \qquad \text{Q. E. D.}$$

8. Geometrically this means (in the same order) that in Figure 7a *I* cuts the *M*-axis farther from, the distance axis nearer to, the origin, and hence is steeper than II. The point of intersection with the *km*-axis marks the greatest possible distance for shipment (m/f), which for crop I is smaller.

9. This is neither an additional nor a sufficient condition for ring formation, but a necessary one (though it is already contained in the two others). It cannot, therefore, replace either of these.

10. A more detailed analysis would have to take into account that the price of the

point is arrived at where this is no longer outweighed by the greater yield per hectare: the boundary line between the two crops has been reached.[11]

same physical input also varies with distance and with the possible freight. Near a town, labor especially becomes more expensive and agricultural machines cheaper.

Let us sketch at least briefly the manner in which nominal agricultural wages depend on distance from the market. Suppose that the amounts in the laborer's budget are independent of price; that agricultural and industrial commodities can be combined into a general commodity of which the amounts l and i are supposed to be consumed per year. Let f be the freight per unit of quantity and distance, and p_l or p_i the unit price in the town; suppose finally that the real wage is the same everywhere ($R = l + i =$ a constant).

How does the nominal wage (Na) vary with the distance (a)? The nominal wage equals quantity times the price of agricultural and industrial goods:

$$Na = l(p_l - af) + i(p_i + af) = lp_l + ip_i + af(i - l).$$

Of these, lp_l and ip_i are constants, whereas $af(i - l)$ depends on distance. Whether the nominal wage will decrease or increase with distance from the town will therefore depend upon whether a greater weight of agricultural or of industrial goods is consumed.

Even today agricultural goods are likely to preponderate. The urban annual consumption per capita is roughly 500 kg. of food and 400 kg. of coal. The rural laborer receives by way of the town perhaps 60 kg. of industrial goods and 80 kg. of food (in the country potatoes, milk, flour, and meat make up three fourths of all foodstuffs). He uses less coal than the town dweller because he burns wood, and besides coal does not always reach the country from a town. Thus one can count on only about 140 kg. of urban products as against 420 kg. of rural products. Much depends upon fuel.

A second reason why agricultural wages decrease with distance from a town is that house rents are lower because the ground itself is cheaper (as a result of the small agricultural rent and lower density of population) and because natural building materials, being nearer, are less expensive. A third reason is the greater surplus population, which often increases with distance from the town, together with the incomplete mobility of this surplus. Fourth, the agricultural laborer saves transport cost and local taxes, since local services can safely be lower. In the fifth place, he has more incidental and intangible income (land for gardening, the possibility of breeding small animals, and a more natural way of life). Sixth, he buys some things from farmers at lower cost. Finally, agricultural wages, lowered for the reasons just cited, are reciprocally depressed still further to a certain degree (by lower trade margins, for example). On the other hand, the migration of the abler inhabitants to towns, where they can specialize according to their particular gifts, does not explain a real difference in efficiency wages as between town and country, though it does explain such a differential among country dwellers in favor of the skilled trades.

11. The matter can be expressed this way also: The total freight is proportional to the physical yield, but total gross profit (money receipts less cost of production) for crop I is less than proportional to the physical yield, since $m_1 < m_2$. In other words: The gross profit on crop I is greater than that on crop II by a smaller percentage than its physical yield, which influences the cost of transportation. Hence for the same distance the latter makes up a greater percentage of the gross profit for crop I, and this difference in percentages increases with distance. The originally greater net profit for I, therefore, shrinks more quickly with increasing freight costs, and finally drops below that for crop II.

2. Determination of the Transition. At the limit $R_1 = R_2$, or $E_1(p_1 - kf) - A_1 = E_2(p_2 - kf) - A_2$. Hence

$$k = \frac{E_2 p_2 - E_1 p_1 + A_1 - A_2}{f(E_2 - E_1)};$$

or

$$k = \frac{1}{f}\left(\frac{E_1 m_1 - E_2 m_2}{E_1 - E_2}\right)^{12}$$

The distance k of the transition from the center is directly proportional to the difference in gross profits before deduction of freight charges, and inversely proportional to the freight rate and the difference in physical yield. If the equation is written as

$$kf = (E_1 m_1 - E_2 m_2) / (E_1 - E_2)$$

the left side corresponds to the marginal cost (in freight) and the right to the marginal receipts (over and above production costs) per centner. Thus every production spreads out until at the edge of its ring the rising marginal cost curve intersects the marginal revenue curve.

This differs from the usual discussion of marginal adjustments of an individual firm only in that in the latter case marginal cost refers to production, whereas here it refers to transport cost. The two problems of the amount and the location of production are thereby solved simultaneously. If rings I and II represent areas of intensive and extensive cultivation of the same commodity, between which no transition is possible, the difference from the usual discussion of marginal adjustments consists only in the fact that here, with increasing distance, the marginal cost for a great part of the product (namely, that by which I is more intensive than II) *suddenly* rises above marginal revenue. This leads to an abrupt transition to extensive cultivation.

12. This is reached as follows:

$$k = \frac{E_2 p_2 - E_1 p_1 + A_1 - A_2}{f(E_2 - E_1)}$$

as $a = A/E$, $A = aE$; therefore

$$k = \frac{E_2 p_2 - E_1 p_1 + a_1 E_1 - a_2 E_2}{f(E_2 - E_1)}$$

$$= \frac{1}{f} \cdot \frac{E_2(p_2 - a_2) - E_1(p_1 - a_1)}{E_2 - E_1};$$

substituting $m = (p - a)$, and multiplying numerator and denominator by (-1), we get

$$k = \frac{1}{f} \cdot \left(\frac{E_1 m_1 - E_2 m_2}{E_1 - E_2}\right). \quad \text{Q. E. D.} \quad\quad -\text{W. F. S.}$$

3. *Popular Reasons.* The sequence of spatial order is often explained plausibly and on a common-sense basis, even by Thünen,[13] by saying that the " lighter " or the " dearer " good is produced farther out, because with it freight is less important.[14] If this vague formulation means the commodity that costs more per pound, that is, of which fewer pounds can be bought for one mark, the statement is false. In case 1 of Table 2, for example, the cheaper

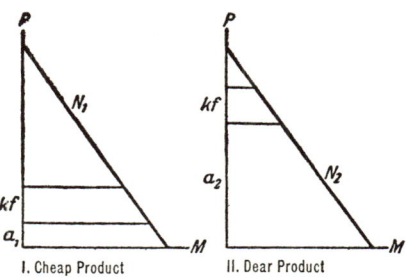

Fig. 4. Effect of increased freight on the demand for a cheap and for an expensive product

commodity is cultivated on the outside.[15] It is sometimes said, also, that the more extensively grown crop comes from outside. This is true if only the smaller physical yield per hectare [16] is meant, independent of outlay. This condition is in fact necessary but not

13. H. v. Thünen, *Der Isolirte Staat in Beziehung auf Landwirtschaft und Nationalökonomie* (Wäntig edition, Jena, 1921), p. 12.

14. The assertion that the more expensive commodity can " bear more freight " is manifestly incorrect in this general form. If N in Figure 4 is the demand curve and a the cost of production, the same freight, kf, reduces the demand for the more expensive commodity (II) to almost nothing, whereas it hardly affects that for the cheaper one (I). Naturally, with a differently shaped demand curve the situation *may* be reversed. See O. Engländer, " Emil Sax' Verkehrsmittel und die Lehre vom Verkehr," *Schmollers Jahrbuch*, 1924, pp. 265–305. " The transportability of goods does not depend on their value " (*ibid.*, p. 276).

15. Example: Corn is grown near the River Plate and wheat farther away, not because the latter is dearer but because its yield per hectare with an appropriately intensive cultivation is smaller (contrary to the otherwise excellent discussion by A. Rühl, *Das Standortproblem in der Landwirtschaftsgeographie* [Berlin, 1929], p. 120).

The specific gravity of goods is of as little import as their value; only the yield by weight of each unit of area is decisive. On a par with it are higher freight rates, easy spoilage, or transportation of food or manure through and beyond the town (transportation in an opposite direction).

16. Or, which amounts to the same thing, reduction by drying, cleaning, butchering, and so on. In wartime, when transportation is difficult, this concentration is carried

sufficient, since it is still possible that the extensive or intensive crop will be cultivated everywhere. But if "extensive" means " smaller outlay per unit of area or of weight," this statement, too, is false. For example, in case 9 both are greater for the product cultivated in the outer ring.

ε. *An Example of Thünen Rings*

The popular example of ring formation in the sale of milk may serve as an illustration of the subject now under discussion.[17] When we arrange the possible products in the order milk (I), cream (II), and butter (III), it is immediately known that the yield per acre, E, falls in that order, whereas the outlay per acre, A, and market price, p, rise. This is case 9 in Table 2, and it will be

very far in areas that are distant from their markets, so that a relatively small shipping space can transport the same useful load.

Weight is decreased by: (1) Eliminating everything superfluous or less important; e. g., shipping powdered instead of fluid milk; fruit juices instead of fruit; with rising freight rates frozen meat rather than iced, then meat with bones removed, later canned, finally dried, until at last perhaps only hides are shipped. (2) Further processing (bacon instead of corn; dried eggs instead of barley; butter fat instead of oil crops). Volume can be decreased by compression also.

This diminution in the bulk of the same commodity in areas far removed from their markets is, as Engländer rightly said (*Theorie des Güterverkehrs und der Frachtsätze* [Jena, 1924], p. 118), only a special case of decrease of the yield in weight per unit of area away from the market, except that the one case concerns different kinds of commodities and the other concerns different forms of the same commodity. Furthermore, greater durability or ease of handling is equivalent to a smaller yield per hectare in lowering the freight. A. Petersen (*Die fundamentale Standortlehre Thünens, wie sie bisher als Intensitätslehre missverstanden wurde und was sie wirklich besagt* [Jena, 1936], p. 16) correctly deduces from this that certain refining enterprises (such as distilleries, dairies, sugar refineries, plants for the manufacture of starch and the preserving and canning of food, and grain mills) may have a wholly rational location in East Prussia, though they are far from their markets. He errs, however, in believing that the compatibility of such intensity at a distance from the market with the Thünen theory had been overlooked until then. Adam Smith had already shown that the two-fold freight charge causing low agricultural and high industrial prices is conducive to industrial development in remote areas. The industries employ the heavy products of the soil cheaply on the spot and in return ship a smaller weight in low-quality goods to markets nearby, and a smaller weight in high quality goods to more distant markets. (*An Inquiry into the Nature and the Causes of the Wealth of Nations* [London, 1811], Book 3, end of Chapter 3, where also there are interesting observations on the dynamics of location.) A large increase in population strengthens, whereas the scarcity of capital associated therewith checks, this tendency toward industrialization. Example: Balkan States (see A. Lösch, *Was ist vom Geburtenrückgang zu halten?* [Heidenheim, 1932]).

17. Here we may proceed as though milk, cream, and butter were completely separate products.

realized from the preceding analysis that it does not necessarily lead to the formation of rings. It is, on the contrary, possible that one or two of the products are not provided at all. We know, further, that if rings are formed the sequence of the products cannot be changed. If with a certain distance from the market it is more profitable to make butter than to supply milk,[18] but if at the same time it is always less advantageous than to separate cream,[19] butter making can evidently not be spatially inserted between milk and cream but must cease entirely. The inner product must necessarily show the greater physical yield per acre.

Example: [20]

		E Yield per hectare (kg.)	A Outlay per hectare (pfennigs)	p Market price (pfennigs)
I	Milk	25	250	20
II	Cream	2.5	300	160
III	Butter	1	350	380

Freight per kg. and km.: 0.10 pfennig

$$a = A/E$$

hence

$$a_1 = 10; \quad a_2 = 120; \quad a_3 = 350$$

$$m = p - a$$

hence

$$m_1 = 10; \quad m_2 = 40; \quad m_3 = 30$$

Conditions for ring establishment [21] between

I and II: $E_2 m_2 < E_1 m_1 < E_1 m_2$; $\quad 100 < 250 < 1000$: Fulfilled
I and III: $E_3 m_3 < E_1 m_1 < E_1 m_3$; $\quad 30 < 250 < 750$: Fulfilled
II and III: $E_3 m_3 < E_2 m_2 < E_2 m_3$; $\quad 30 < 100 > 75$: Not met *

* II is always more advantageous than III.

---

18. The producer of milk who is near his market has a good location, not merely because of the difficulties of shipment but mainly because of the high yield per acre (in Germany the marketable surplus of milk in weight is greater than that of grains). This yield by weight in sheep breeding is hardly 1 per cent, so that it pays only on very poor soil.

19. This is necessarily the case when $m_2 > m_3$, even though butter is the " lighter " and " dearer " commodity.

20. See also E. M. Hoover, *Location Theory and the Shoe and Leather Industries* (Cambridge, Mass., 1937), pp. 30–33.

21. See above, pp. 40 f., where this inequality has been developed.—W. H. W.

Boundary line between I and III at kilometers

$$k = \frac{1}{f}\left(\frac{E_1 m_1 - E_3 m_3}{E_1 - E_3}\right) = \frac{1}{0.1}\ \frac{250-30}{24} = 92$$

But at 92 km. the rent from II is already greater than that from III.[22] Thus butter making is never started. To make it possible, m_3 must rise above m_2. This will happen as soon as the butter shortage raises its price to at least 400 pfennigs. Then $m_3 = 50$, whereas m_2 is only 40. Now butter will be produced rather than cream at distance $k = \frac{1}{0.1}\left(\frac{100-50}{1.5}\right) = 333$ km. With a sufficiently pressing demand such a price change can provide relief in those cases where the production of a commodity seems impossible. For example, in case 4 of Table 2 only commodity I can be produced, not commodity II. If the price of commodity II were to rise as a result, and if the urgency of the demand should drive its price above that of commodity I, the situation obtaining for case 4 would change to that for case 6, where the simultaneous production of both commodities is possible.

ζ. *Interregional Trade*

Of course this relative change in prices does not always occur. It may be defeated by the shape of the demand curve, or by outside influences. If imports, for instance, prevent the price of butter from rising, the production of domestic butter will be impossible. The single broken line in Figure 5 shows the rent from butter when the price is depressed in this way; it falls to zero (with distance) before intersecting the more rapidly decreasing rent on cream. On the other hand, as is easily seen, a slight decrease in price caused by imports is enough to push the rent on cream below the line of dots and dashes and, unless butter is also imported, to exclude the domestic production of cream thereby. The butter ring then borders directly on the milk ring.

A threat to the cream and milk rings by competition from another economic region is much more improbable, of course, than exclusion of the butter ring. Then the paradox arises that as soon as foreign competition, through a lowering of costs, say, is able to send in not only butter but also cream, and perhaps even milk, the situation of the domestic butter industry improves again. The area of domestic production is reduced as a whole, to be sure, but if the rent from cream should be lowered too it may very well fall

---

22. $R_2 > R_3$; $E_2(p_2 - 92f) - A_2 > E_3(p_3 - 92f) - A_3$
   $77 > 21$.

Agricultural Location

again somewhere below the previously reduced rent on butter (as —·—·— in *B'* under — — —). Assume that somewhere abroad there is an " island " where production costs are only half as much and, when freight is neglected and with the prices prevailing at *O*, permit a gross profit two and a half times as great as that in the domestic area of supply. Then suitable rings can be established around *O* whose radii, of course, will be two and a half times as long. Now imagine the " island " of cheap production costs to be moved slowly from far away toward the market; at first it will not be able to compete despite its own low costs, because of high freight rates.

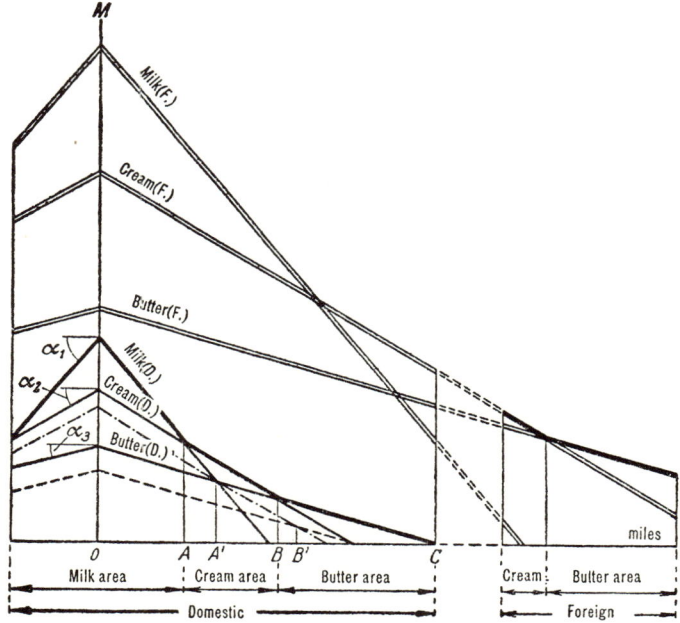

Fig. 5. Rent per acre as a function of distance
tg α: freight per mile on the physical yield per acre

Moved farther inward toward the market, this area reaches first the butter ring, and in order to compete in cream and fresh milk too it must approach very close to the market. That is to say, *the goods enter interregional trade in the sequence in which they were prepared far away for the market.*[23] If this sequence is different in the importing and the exporting country, that of the latter will prevail under similar freight rates.

23. For example, the quantities of Canadian exports to the United States increase in the following order: fresh milk, cream, butter, and cheese.

η. The Spatial Order of Production Systems

What we have found for various lines of production can be employed also for various degrees of intensity of cultivation of the same commodity, in the nine cases where $p_1 = p_2$.[24,25] There is a boundary line, of course, only when no gradual transition between intensive and extensive cultivation exists. This holds, also, when I and II each represent a whole assortment of commodities; that is, if they represent a production system, if only these commodities are actually cultivated in both systems, even though in different proportions and with different intensity.[25] As soon as there are transitions between these proportions and these degrees of intensity, however,

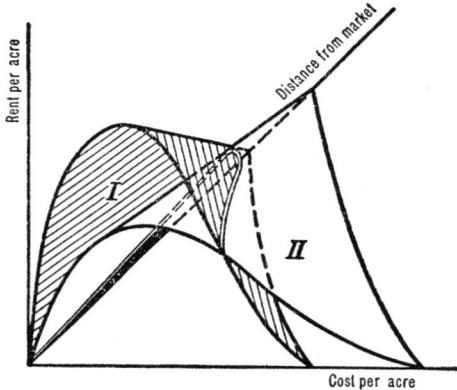

Fig. 6. Intersection of two profitability planes

the spatial boundary lines between the systems disappear. But if I and II stand for different branches of agriculture (i. e., different commodities), there is a clear demarcation even when both have variable degrees of intensity (Fig. 6). Since every commodity can be cultivated as a rule with any desired variations in intensity,

---

24. Here we can equate the inner ring to intensive, and the outer rings to extensive, cultivation (in any one of the meanings previously mentioned), since case 2 and case 26 are the only ones among those permitting the formation of rings in which $p_1 = p_2$. In both cases the outlay and the yield per hectare are greater in the inner ring, and a moment's thought will show that rings can be formed only (in place of the alternatives that only commodity I or commodity II is cultivated) if, for case 2, $E_1/E_2 < A_1/A_2$; that is, if intensity is maintained with diminishing returns (if the returns decrease greatly, of course, only II may be cultivated). In any case $a_1 > a_2$; thus the second criterion of intensity given on p. 40 is fulfilled too.

25. An example: Thünen found rotation of crops (K) in the vicinity of a market more advantageous than the three-fallow system (D). Thus his numerical example

Thünen rings are subject to the further restriction that in general they appear *only with different commodities*.

θ. Several Centers of Consumption

When production is not grouped about one center of consumption as has been assumed up to now, but about several, these select their own sources of supply from the environment of the foremost producer if they are near enough (see Fig. 45). The rings under discussion form around each new center, but in a region of many towns there is no room for the outer ones; they are displaced toward its margin. The number of displaced rings increases with the density of towns. For the inner rings the individual town is the marketing center, for the outer ones the agglomeration of towns. Thus with the growth of northwestern Europe more and more branches of agriculture with a low yield per acre, such as sheep breeding, grain growing, and the production of some feeds, of butter and of cheese, moved overseas and to eastern Europe.[26] This development, first described in detail by H. Engelbrecht,[27] has been discussed recently by H. Backe.[28]

---

must fulfill our three conditions (p. 40.). In fact (Thünen: *op. cit.*, p. 121, §14a), with K compared to D the physical yield of rye is greater everywhere $(1,710 > 1,000)$, the profit per hectare greater within (for instance in the market where the grower's price is $1\frac{1}{2}$ taler: $1,818 > 1,119$); the profit per bushel, on the contrary, is smaller even in the market $(1,818/1,710 < 1,119/1,000)$. Since according to Thünen (*ibid.*, p. 36) the yield of rye would be proportional to the total yield (which we rather doubt), this example would generally hold also for a comparison of both production systems as a whole.

Historical significance: Thünen proved, in opposition to Thaer, that adoption of the English rotation of crops is advantageous only up to a certain distance from the market; just as List showed, in opposition to the classical writers, that free trade is profitable only from a certain stage of development onward. In other words, as List proved the temporally limited validity of the English theories of the time, so Thünen proved their spatial limitation.

26. Exceptions are explained by the fact that besides location, which has been the sole basis of our theoretical deductions, other factors play a part in reality: duties and subsidies, natural fertility (English sheep breeding on poor soil), freight rates (coastal regions like England enjoy cheap sea freights), the necessities of joint production, extra-economically conditioned curbs on adaptation to new situations, and so on.

27. See G. Pavlovsky, "Zur Frage der räumlichen Ordnung der Landwirtschaft," *Internationale Landwirtschaftliche Rundschau*, I, 33 (1942), 345 ff.

28. H. Backe, *Um die Nahrungsfreiheit Europas* (Leipzig, 1942), pp. 35–61.

§2. Inversion of Thünen Rings

α. *Technique of Presentation*

We shall now examine the formation of rings according to Thünen's theory by means of an example that can be subsumed under case 6 of Table 2. Twice the weight of potatoes (I) as of corn (II) is harvested from one acre with the same outlay. In order for rings to be established, the further conditions (see p. 92) $m_1 < m_2$ and $E_1/E_2 > m_2/m_1$ must be met. Since $E_1 = 2E_2$, the conditions can be rewritten $m_1 < m_2 < 2m_1$; or, since $a_2 = 2a_1$ also $p_1 - a_1 < p_2 - 2a_1 < 2(p_1 - a_1)$. This is true when $a_1 < p_2/2$ and $p_2 - a_1 > p_1 > p_2/2$. We start out from a price limit $p_1 = 6$ and $p_2 = 12$ per hundredweight. This is the lower limit for potatoes, for if the price sank below half that for corn no more potatoes would be raised. At these prices there should be a demand for exactly twice as many hundredweight of potatoes as of corn, so that the area devoted to both will be the same.

In order to simplify Figures 7b and 7d, the demand curves have the same slope, which involves a greater elasticity of the demand for potatoes. The example is further clarified if the market is regarded as a line rather than a point (like a river valley with many towns). Then the rings become zones, and the demand is proportional to their breadth. We also assume here—and this will turn out to be significant—that the commodity with the higher yield per hectare (potatoes) will be cultivated in the zone nearest the market. This will be true, as we have seen, if rings are formed at all. Again, the production of each commodity considered alone is supposed to be in equilibrium; that is to say, neither potatoes nor corn yields a rent at their respective margins of cultivation.

As for the technique of presentation, it should be noted that the scale employed for the quantity of corn is twice that for the quantity of potatoes, and that it is to be reckoned from the actual boundary between I and II, whereas the town line is always the zero point for the quantity of potatoes. Thus, in contradistinction to the supply curve, the demand curve N_2 must undergo a parallel shift by the same amount and in the same direction with every shift of the zero point. In this way the supply curve K (production cost plus freight) and the aerial view of the agricultural area can be directly compared. The production costs plus freight for every point in the area can be read off from a point directly above or below it on the corresponding supply curve.

Agricultural Location

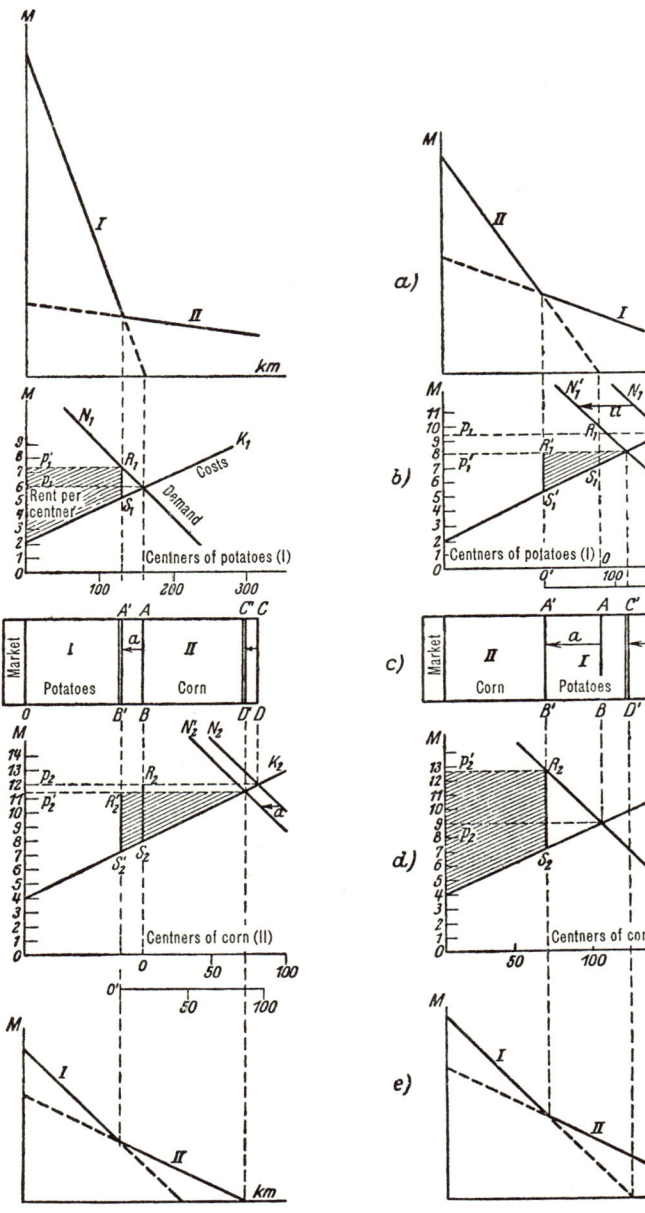

Fig. 7. Thünen case   Fig. 8. Inversion of the Thünen rings

It is now immediately clear that no equilibrium exists. At the boundary line AB in Figure 7c (which gives a bird's-eye view) the rent on potatoes is 0, on corn R_2S_2, per hundredweight. The cultivation of corn is therefore extended at the expense of potatoes, and p_2 falls to p_2'; on the other hand, p_1 rises and all the conditions for ring formation are now fulfilled ($a_1 = 2$; $p_1' = 7.5$; $p_2' = 11.5$; substitution in $a_1 < p_2/2$ gives $2 < 3.75$; substitution in $p_2 - a_1 > p_1 > p_2/2$ gives $9.5 > 7.5 > 5.75$). The rent changes with prices, falling for II and rising for I. When the profit on a hundredweight of potatoes is equal to half that on the same amount of corn $(R_1S_1 = R_2'S_2'/2)$ final equilibrium will have been reached. The cultivation of potatoes is then diminished by the area $A'B'BA$, total cultivation by the smaller area $C'D'DC$. So far everything agrees with Thünen's theory, and an already familiar case has been so extensively discussed only to demonstrate the technique of presentation.

β. Inversion of Rings

We shall now change one single assumption. We shall suppose that potatoes are being imported from America and that the fields lying near the town are not available for potato raising, their use being determined by long tradition. The new crop is therefore assigned to more distant fields, where an unsuccessful experiment will not cause any serious loss of profit. If we start once more from the same situation: equilibrium for each individual crop without regard to alternative possibilities, potatoes are now superior at the boundary line AB (Fig. 8c), where corn and potatoes meet. Their cultivation will therefore be extended at the expense of corn by the area a until the rent of corn per hundredweight at the boundary line $A'B'$ is again twice that of potatoes; the return per hectare will consequently be the same for both crops. When this point has been reached, equilibrium apepars at first to prevail, *although the Thünen rings have been inverted!*

This is a curious situation. Figure 8a shows [29] that a shift of the boundary toward the left would make the cultivation of corn at the new boundary more advantageous, and that a shift toward the right would favor the cultivation of potatoes. To this extent the boundary $A'B'$ in Figue 8c is actually the only possible equilibrium position—so far as equilibrium really is decided at the

---

29. Figures 7a and 8a show the rent per hectare at the boundary as a function of the position of the boundary.

boundary. But according to Figure 8e, on the contrary,[30] the boundary line thus found marks also the boundary between potatoes and corn; only it appears (this boundary being assumed as given) that at least for the moment it will be more advantageous to plant the *other* crop at every point away from the boundary. To the left of the dividing line the cultivation of potatoes, not corn, will yield the greater rent per hectare; the reverse is true to the right of the line.

γ. *The Critical Assumption*

The contradiction between Figures 8a and 8e (summarized in Fig. 9) can be resolved.[31] Suppose it has already been decided

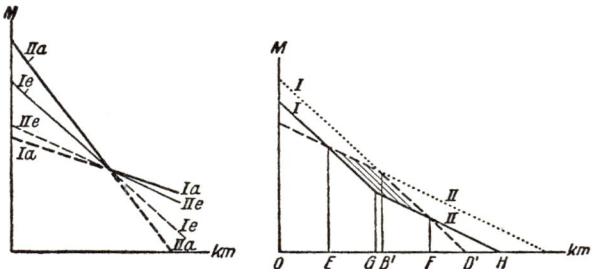

Fig. 9. Contradiction between figures 8a and 8e. Ia and IIa from 8a; Ie and IIe from 8e

Fig. 10. Comparison of rent per hectare in Thünen case (continuous line) and in its inversion (broken line)

arbitrarily, through historical accident or through tradition, that corn will be raised to the left; the planting of the individual farmer is thus controlled by his environment, which leaves him a choice only at the boundary line. Under these assumptions Figure 8a shows where the location of the boundary between corn (left) and potatoes (right) will finally be established.

But if the economic spirit is revolutionary rather than traditional; if each farmer doubts the whole basis of the customary agricultural methods; if he raises the question of the most advantageous choice of crops; he necessarily encounters the situation in Figure 8e. Yet it would be shortsighted for all farmers to the left of $A'B'$ (Fig. 8c) to change over suddenly from corn to potatoes, and all those to the right of it from potatoes to corn, because a

---

30. Figures 7e and 8e show the rent per hectare as a function of distance from a market, when the position of the boundary is given.

31. Ia and IIa from Figure 8a; Ie and IIe from Figure 8e.

larger rent was promised for the moment. Obviously that would mean disequilibrium. Now the solution in Figure 7 would hold, the boundary would have to shift toward the right, prices would fall, and, most important, all rents would decrease below the amount that had induced the farmers to change. Nor would the new situation be advantageous to all. The dotted line in Figure 10 shows the rent that enticed farmers to change crops (from Figure 8e); the continuous line shows the rent that turns out to be lasting after

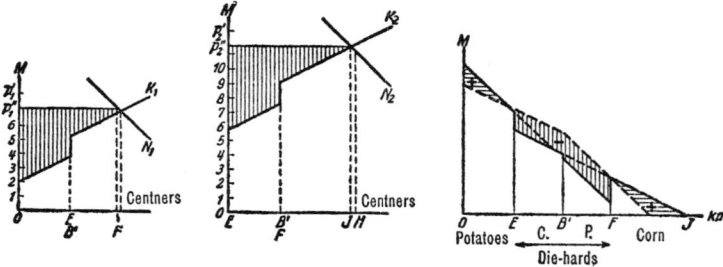

Fig. 11. Potato market (supply and rent of innovators, OE, and die-hards, B'F)

Fig. 12. Corn market (supply and rent of innovators, FJ, and die-hards, EB')

Fig. 13. Rent per hectare during transition. Broken line, former rent (from Figure 8e). Continuous line, rent during transition (from Figures 11 and 12). Horizontal hatching, gain in rent compared with the former condition; vertical hatching, loss

completion of the change (from Figure 7e); and the broken line shows the rent that prevailed before the revolutionary change (from Figure 8e). All farmers between E and F—sociologically speaking, the whole rural middle class or, more accurately, the entire region of moderate ground rent—will have lost rent (hatched area in Figure 10). Only a few of the richest farmers (between 0 and E) and the rural proletariat, and only on the soil at and beyond the boundary (between F and H)[32] will have gained.

Will the farmers between E and F, interested in preserving the traditional order, be able to obstruct the revolutionary method of planting by obstinately continuing to cultivate the original crop, giving up a merely transitory advantage in order to acquire greater rent in the end? The change to potatoes, profitable under all cir-

---

32. This agrees with our earlier calculation, that the commodity with the smaller yield per hectare is more profitably raised at the periphery of the cultivated area, the other near the market. The intermediate area, for which, as it now appears, an inversion of the Thünen order may be advantageous, was not considered in that discussion.

cumstances between 0 and E, and to corn between F and H, so lowers the price of both that the rents of the obstinate ones fall. Thanks to their better location, the rent of the innovators is larger than before, in spite of the lower price. As even this intermediate condition is more profitable to them than the old, and less profitable to the obstinate than the new [33] (see Figs. 11 to 13), it must prevail in the end.[34]

Thus we arrive at the conclusion that *in a dynamic economy Thünen rings must be formed, whereas in a traditional economy their reversal may hold equally well.*[35] The sequence of the rings cannot be proved in the traditional case as a necessary order, but only assumed as a possible principle of organization.

§3. ADJOINING FIELDS INSTEAD OF RINGS

Suppose that an equally large proportion of farmers everywhere change over to the new crop, whereas the rest keep to the traditional one; or, which amounts to the same thing, that each farmer plants an equally large area of his fields with potatoes. This can be most simply represented by having the two crops planted not in successive rings, but in adjoining sectors. A change in the width of the sectors causes a rotation of the supply curve about its intersection with the price axis. Since the enlargement of one sector necessarily occurs at the expense of the other, the supply curves must always be rotated in opposite directions. It is immediately apparent that this arrangement results in equilibrium only under special conditions. It is always possible, to be sure, to change the width of the fields in such manner that the rent at the periphery of cultivation, or near the market,[36] will be the same for both crops. But the rent is equal everywhere—and without this there is no equilibrium—in only two cases:

---

33. The new rent to the farmers between E and F is given approximately by the lower broken line in Figure 13. It is thus greater in any case than the transitional rent shown by the continuous line.

34. Corn will be planted in both cases only between G and B' (Fig. 10).

35. Of course this reversal is not desirable. It causes unnecessary freight, and less land is cultivated. A possible exception is the case where a commodity of greater yield per acre, but lower price, pays considerably less freight per mile.

36. In this case the fields are not only of different width, which would not be bad, but also of different length. Only when the crop with the smaller yield per acre (corn) is cultivated farther out can its rent by the hundredweight at market be greater than the corresponding rent for potatoes. And only when the rent per hundredweight on corn is *greater* is the rent per acre, because of the smaller yield per acre, equal to that for potatoes.

58   Part One. Location

1. With equal yield per hectare in terms of weight (Fig. 14),[37] a subcase to No. 18 in Table 2. The radial arrangement offers a possible solution only in cases 10, 14, and 18 of Table 2, because in the others, where $E_1 = E_2$, the remaining conditions impose a restriction on the production of one commodity. Or:

2. When the freight charges are inversely proportional to the yield per hectare. This must be distinguished from the picture we get when lines of communication leading out of a city pull the

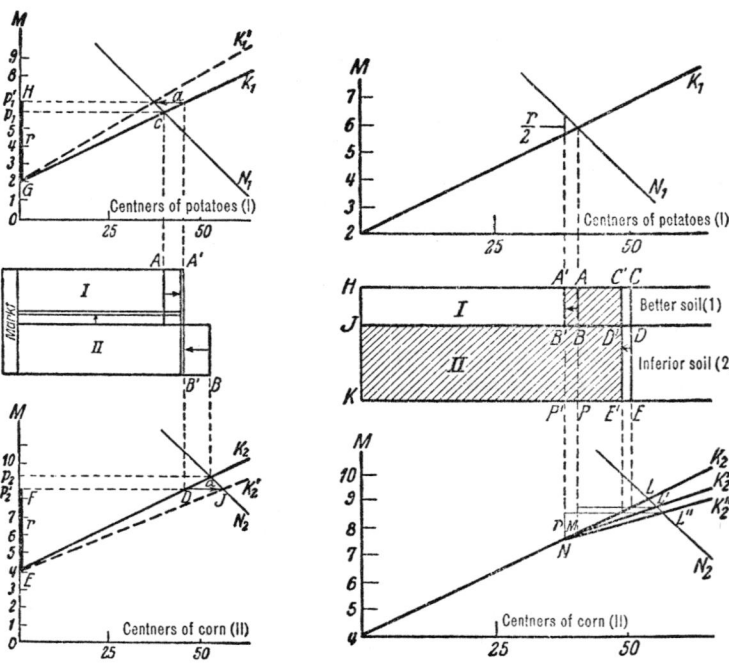

Fig. 14. Illustration of case 18 of the complete system

Fig. 15. Mixed cropping and rings

37. In Figure 14 the same physical yield per hectare is assumed for both I and II. First, let each of the two equally broad fields be extended in a direction away from the market (I as far as A, II as far as B) until at the periphery of cultivation the rent everywhere is zero. In order that rent at the market and the length of the fields shall be the same for both commodities, field II is broadened at the expense of field I (and K_1 rotated upward thereby, or K_2 correspondingly downward) until rent EF is equal to rent GH. Both fields then acquire automatically the same boundary, $A'B'$. (However, the length of the fields can now no longer be read off automatically from the supply curves K_1' and K_2', as was still possible with K_1 and K_2. To this end it is necessary to return to the original demand curves. where the points J, on K_2', and D, on K_2, give the field lengths.)

Agricultural Location

rings outward to such a degree that for a distance they are almost parallel to these lines. Here, however, unlike the case of our sectors, we still deal with actually rather than virtually separated zones. For it should be clear beyond any doubt that our sectors are only an especially convenient way of representing adjoining fields.

§4. Adjoining Fields *and* Rings

There still remains a situation in which sectors (in a schematic presentation) or actually adjoining fields (in reality) *partially* replace rings: where soil is of uneven quality.[38] Of course in those cases where a definite kind of soil, in comparison with another, is more fertile for *all* products in the *same* proportion, nothing is altered compared with the partition of soils of equal quality. Either the more fertile as well as the poor soil will be divided between the two crops (adjoining fields), or both will produce the same (rings).

Not so when soils are unequally suitable for different crops. Here we limit ourselves to one example. Suppose that everywhere one third of the soil is of quality 1, which produces twice the amount of potatoes as of corn. The remaining two thirds, of quality 2, uniformly produces equal physical yields per hectare for both crops, which are the same as the yield of corn from quality 1. Under these assumptions it is: (*a*) impossible, as long as both crops are cultivated, that the better soil should produce anything but potatoes, regardless of the distance from the market. For, as a little study of Figure 15 will show, the rent from potatoes grown on the better soil equals the rent that corn would yield on it (transportation costs of the physical yield of corn up to the limit for cultivation of corn, $C'E'$) plus the rent for half the physical yield of potatoes, calculated as freight up to the limit for potato cultivation, $A'B'$.

(*b*) It is impossible, furthermore, that the *depth of cultivation* on the better and the poorer soil should differ, so that to the right, say, of AB nothing more will be raised on the better soil. For since the better soil is always as suitable for corn as the poorer one, $ABDC$ will inevitably be planted with corn. This lowers the supply curve from ML to ML'. But since potatoes no longer yield a rent on the line AB, though corn does, corn growing pushes forward on

---

38. Any local variation in production cost for other reasons will have effects similar to those of variations in soil quality.

the better soil toward the left until at the new limit, $A'B'$, the same rent per hectare ensues for both crops because of the reduced cultivation of potatoes. Calculated per centner, the potato rent is only half that for corn, because the yield of potatoes per hectare is twice as large. This shift raises the supply of corn by the yield of the area $A'B'BA$, and the greater supply so lowers the price that the outermost limit of cultivation is moved backward from CE to $C'E'$. As a final result we have adjoining fields of the crops to the depth $A'P'$, which wholly corresponds to the differing soil qualities; and to the right of $A'P'$ we have a ring of production of the same crop.[39,40]

b. COMPREHENSIVE SOLUTION

We must now separate clearly the problems of location, which so far have interlaced, and consider in particular another important viewpoint: joint production in agriculture.

§1. THE LOCATION FOR AGRICULTURAL PRODUCTION

This problem, too, divides into questions respecting the location of the farm and the location of the products.

The problem seen from the standpoint of an individual farm is merely stated here and not solved, in order not to repeat [41] the reasoning already developed in discussing the choice of an industrial location. This problem is to find an area for production in such a region and of such a size, and so to place the farm therein, that the profit shall be as large as possible.

But on what part of the farm shall a certain crop—say, rye—be planted? In the absence of joint production it will be planted where it yields a higher rent than any other crop. But it is not a question of the rent from rye, or from single fields, but from the

---

39. The area for corn is hatched.

40. By a somewhat different train of thought T. Brinkmann, too, arrived at the conclusion that the whole scale from extensive to intensive cultivation is possible near a town (radial differentiation), whereas with increasing distance the choice is progressively restricted, poor soils are abandoned, and goods ones must be cultivated extensively (concentric differentiation). (" Die Oekonomik des landwirtschaftlichen Betriebs," *Grundriss der Sozialökonomik,* 1922, 7 Abt., p. 46.)

41. Only to this extent: Upon exact consideration (in contrast to p. 29, note 31) the question is no longer one of locating the farm so that the paths to fields for definite crops shall be as short as possible; for the intensity of cultivation of the individual fields depends upon the exact site of the farm (see the earlier objections to the point of minimum transport cost).

Agricultural Location

farm as a whole.[42] Thus a farmer cannot decide where to plant rye without deciding at the same time how he is to use his farm as a whole. There is room for rye only as it fits into the general production scheme (*Betriebssystem*), only as it promises the highest profit to the farm in the long run. One must be clear as to the consequences: In many fields rye might yield the highest rent provided the remaining fields were employed in a definite way (most favorable for the cultivation of rye in the particular field under consideration). Only in a few fields will the rent from rye still be highest even when every field is cultivated according to the over-all plan, in such a way that the profit from the farm as a whole is a maximum. But rye will not be grown everywhere that it yields the highest rent; and not everywhere that it is cultivated will it produce the greatest rent attainable from this field. Nor is it a question of the change in total rent attributable to this field, since such an imputation is impossible, for reasons given on p. 62, note 46.

Total profits alone are decisive; there are no additional criteria for individual crops. Even the production system (*Betriebssystem*) that would be most advantageous for the farm cannot be scientifically unequivocal, as a rule,[43] but can be determined only after experimentation; even then uncertainty would still remain, since innumerable combinations are possible and the choice among them depends in general upon irregular local relationships between supply and demand. Nevertheless, science can still be of service, as it is in the case of the industries.

The general distribution of farms seen from the standpoint of the economy as a whole will be discussed in Chapter 8. Joint production makes it difficult to determine where the whole of one crop will be produced—a main theme in one-sided solutions—as to determine the plan for the use of the land on an individual farm. The rye belts of the world, for example, cannot be fixed without determining the location of all other belts at the same time, and thus in the end the geographical distribution of the production systems of individual farms. In a rye belt, therefore, not rye as such yields a maximum profit, but a production system that includes the cultivation of rye. Rye will be grown wherever a production system favorable to it is more advantageous than any that excludes the cultivation of rye.

42. Industrial undertakings with joint production correspondingly add the returns from their various departments and from their various products.
43. Except with simplifications, as on p. 50.

§2. The Agricultural Production of a Location

Suppose soil qualities to be irregularly distributed and the markets with their ruling prices [44] given. Let the production at all but one location be given as well. It is required to find the production of this location. If it is a field, the cultivation of all other fields (including those of the farm concerned) must be given; if a farm, the cultivation of all other farms.

The cultivation of a field is not determined by what will yield the greatest profit on it, but, because of joint agricultural production, by what will yield the most profit to the farm as a whole. The same end will naturally be sought when plans for the use of its fields have to be formulated anew. These plans themselves depend upon market prices of location and supplies, and the composition and scale of output; upon the relative position of the various fields to the farm,[45] and of the farm itself to the sales market and to markets for the factors of production; upon the suitability of soil and climate, and not least upon the skill of the farmer; upon the advantages of mass production to the individual farm and to other farms (thus also upon what is cultivated by other farms in the neighborhood); and, finally, upon the disadvantages of one-sidedness already discussed.

Location theory can say no more on the subject.[46] It may, of course, investigate the way in which individual factors act by themselves, as has been done under (a). Their co-operation in simple cases is discussed by locational casuistics. But a systematic theory is impossible [47] because of the endless conceivable differences in situations and the complexity of most. Here, too, science can only indicate individual possibilities that deserve special investigation.

---

44. That this is true in practice because of the radically different market forms facilitates matters considerably in comparison with the problem of industrial location.

45. Cultivation would be arranged about the farm building also in Thünen rings if location alone mattered. The fact that land near a village is more expensive indicates that location plays a role even though in miniature, provided soil quality is the same.

46. Even a more precise characterization of the maximum is difficult. It would not be correct to assume, for example, that the partial derivatives of cost and receipt must be equal for every product. It is more likely that for a particular marginal combination the costs will be covered by the receipts, even when this is no longer true of every single product in the combination. This appears to have been overlooked by H. Marquardt in his otherwise excellent presentation (*Die Ausrichtung der landwirtschaftlichen Produktion an den Preisen* [Jena, 1934]. p. 80), and even by Schneider (*Schmollers Jahrbuch*, [1936], 213 ff.).

47. The Thünen procedure allows only an analysis of the influence of location, and at most a consideration of the additional effects of a few other factors. Its further

Unlike those of industry, however, mere calculations certainly do not suffice, because relationships are in part too difficult and, so far as they are determined by nature, still concealed from us. Only actual trial (which the great number and the small size of the interested farms make more easily possible) can help; indeed, since some effects show only after a long time, only extensive experience can give an answer.[48]

c. AGRICULTURAL AND INDUSTRIAL LOCATION THEORY: A COMPARISON

§1. DIFFERENT COMPETITIVE SITUATIONS

One of the main differences, at least in a brief comparison where certain industrial situations resembling the agricultural can be neglected, is the fact that in agriculture the number of production locations is larger, in industry the number of locations for consumption. Hence in agriculture producers group themselves around a consumption site; in industry, sites of consumption about a producer. The sales market for agricultural commodities is punctiform, whereas that for industrial commodities is areal. The latter is supplied by one or a few industrial, the former by many agricultural, enterprises. Thus the typical competitive situation for industry is *limited* competition; for agriculture, *free* competition. This means much less, however, than appears at first sight. What effect has it on the size of an enterprise, for example, that in industry the demand curve for the single firm generally falls, whereas in agriculture it is horizontal? At first it might be thought that the entrepreneur has an influence on the price; but his competitors can affect the size of his enterprise by alienating customers: partly through situation, partly through difference in product, and, when location and product are identical, partly through their mere presence. The individual farmer has no influence on price, but in return the size of his entreprise is independent of his neighbors. The size of his farm depends upon how much land, not upon what market, he controls. Geometrically this means that industry produces to the left, agriculture to the right, of the point of minimum average

---

extension is not to be thought of. One need only bear in mind how irregularly production costs vary from village to village and even from field to field in order to see immediately that there is no general procedure for deciding on an agricultural location, just as there is none for industry; and for the same reasons.

48. Marquardt shows why the more cautious and apparently reactionary farmers often fare better.

cost (Fig. 16),[49] or at that point if ground rent is included in the costs.[50]

But this apparent difference loses its significance when land is freely bought and sold according to economic motives (and only this case is comparable to the industrial). Here, too, the extent of a farm is limited by the tendency toward a maximization of the number of independent enterprises, which in this case is especially desirable.[51]

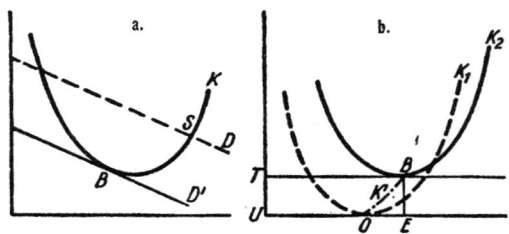

Fig. 16. Size of the producing unit in a) industry, b) agriculture

49. Neither excludes an optimal supply for the consumer, however, since the higher production costs may be more than compensated in the first case by savings in freight (reduction of the market area), and in the second by a fall in price (increased supply). To this extent the complaint of an industry that it suffers from excess capacity is irrelevant, for such excess capacity is in the interest of the consumer.

50. This is easy to understand. In Figure 16b let TB be the horizontal price line, K_1 the average cost, and OB the marginal cost curve. The firm will obviously expand at first beyond O to B, at the intersection of the marginal cost curve with the price line. But rent, $TUOB$, is a cost factor, appearing either as actual rent paid or as interest on the value of the land. Hence by its nature rent is not a differential but a price (see J. A. Schumpeter, " Das Rentenprinzip in der Verteilungslehre," *Schmollers Jahrbuch*, XXXI [1907]). The customary presentation, which makes it appear as a residual, is in reality only a calculation of the highest amount that a farmer can offer for the land. For nonagricultural uses there are other values, and still others for the rest of the land, and the price of land for industry as well as agriculture is derived from this competition of uses. Suppose this system to be such that a farmer obtains the area in question because he offers the most for it; then his cost curve must be shifted upward by the rent, whose total amount is fixed. B is the low point on the new curve, for no other amount of production can support such a high rent. Chamberlin used this new cost curve, K_2, to whose minimum point the demand curve is tangent, for industry from the very first. He regarded rent as a cost factor that is given from the beginning. Thus we find tangency of cost and demand curves a criterion of equilibrium in both branches of the economy.

51. A farm aiming at the minimum size necessary to its existence could add land as long as there were still larger farms (unless their size depended upon the special ability of their managers), merely because it produced larger rent and therefore could offer a higher rental or a higher price. Hence it would buy from neighboring farms the fields that were less favorably situated for them than for it.

The limitation works in a downward direction also: Even where division of the farm through inheritance is customary,[52] farms will be reduced only to a size actually necessary to support a family.[53] The maximization of the number of producers in both industry and agriculture is thus achieved in the same manner despite all formal differences: On the one hand, suitable location of their locational centers (plants, farm buildings [54]), on the other, the close approach of competitors, restrict the area (sales markets, farms)

52. The effects of a financial and a real division through inheritance must be distinguished. The former cannot render a farm incapable of existence if its value is correctly computed. One capitalizes what a farmer earns above what he would earn in an occupation without capital—as a skilled worker, say. A farm can carry that much indebtedness. Real division among the heirs works no harm either, if the share of the retiring heirs remains in the tenure of the farm or (in so far as the original farm produced more than enough to maintain a family) is used to improve or round out other farms. The evils of parceling out fields (which after all could have favored a co-operative spirit) are therefore not necessarily associated with real division. Trouble will arise, however, if land regularly becomes part of the dowry of a daughter who marries onto another farm. In considering free divisibility, finally, it is to be remembered that with improvements in agriculture and an increased demand, especially during the past century, with its great increase in population, smaller and smaller farms have become capable of existence. Real division around growing towns creates a wholesome transition from small farmers able to make a living, through commuters tied to the soil, to free industrial workers.

53. This is not extra-economically determined, as it were; it is not an independent variable at all, but means merely just enough land to afford a farmer's family, with or without outside help, the current agricultural equilibrium income. If this increases, the optimum size of the farm increases as well. On the other hand, the reverse is not necessarily true: When the most profitable size of a farm increases in the course of technical development (hitherto it has decreased for many crops; see H. Priebe, " Zur Frage der Gestaltung und Grösse des zukünftigen bäuerlichen Familientriebes in Deutschland," *Berichte über Landwirtschaft*, n. s., XXVII [1942], 523; A. Münzinger, *Bäuerliche Maschinengenossenschaft Häusern* [Berlin, 1934]), the rural income need not increase. The competition of independent farmers would cause it rather to fall, and so tend again to reduce somewhat the size of farms. The size that will maintain a family at any given time is set, therefore, in addition to the income that it is supposed to yield, by the other factors besides area on which this income depends: price relations, nature, technique, type of settlement, division of fields, law of inheritance, and so on. Farms of a few hectares, or even of less than one, that are near a market or situated in a fertile area can make an adequate profit from the most promising commodities (fruit, vegetables, medicinal plants, flowers, wine, tobacco, poultry. See Priebe, *loc. cit.*). The farm with a small income, not the small farm, should vanish! As the pay of rural labor at equilibrium should be adequate for existence, and interest on the value of the farm is additional, an unencumbered farm could be even smaller and still maintain a family.

54. Here the choice of a location must be considered not only in respect to the area of production (the farm's own fields and meadows), but also in respect to the situation of the sales market.

to the minimum necessary for existence (that is, to the equilibrium size, which cannot be reduced without decreasing the number of producers).

To return to the geometrical picture once more: As intruding competitors in industry restrict the sales area to a point where the demand curve shifts toward the left until it is tangent to the cost curve, so in agriculture they restrict areas of production until the cost curve, displaced upward and to the left by addition of the ground rent, is just tangent to the horizontal demand curve. This is the counterpart of the process described by Chamberlin and Robinson.[55] The only difference is that in industry, depending on the competitive situation, the cost curve is given and the demand curve variable, whereas in agriculture price is fixed and costs are variable. In either case, however, the variable curve is shifted for the same reason and with the same result, until it is tangent to the fixed curve. In short, we find in both industry and agriculture the two important forces that oppose one another and determine location: a tendency to maximization of the number of producers and maximization of rent.[56] The latter is well known. It remains to sketch briefly the former.

§2. The Common Tendency to Maximization of the Number of Independent Economic Units

The longing for an independent and established life in harmony with his nature is deeply rooted in man. The hope for an independent existence, more than any alleged material advantage, has won over the nineteenth century to the idea of economic freedom. This goal encouraged inventors, lured the pioneer into the wild West,

---

55. We can only touch upon certain complications. When farms grow smaller the rents of the owners increase and the income of the actual operator decreases. The former, because the fields in general now lie nearer the farmhouse and are for this reason more intensively cultivated, and probably also because of the smaller size of the farm. The latter, because the rent now goes entirely to the owner, and because a small farmer needs fewer unusual qualities. The average cost of the farm rises; its production falls as a whole, but increases per unit of area until the point is reached where any further diminution in the size advances the costs per hectare more than the proceeds; i. e., until the land rent ceases to rise. Then the agricultural equilibrium income is reached, for the rent could still increase if this were too high, and would have to fall if it were too low.

56. Even when a few other differences between agriculture and industry are examined (as in the first edition, page 55), they turn out to be of little weight, so that in both cases the problem of location is in all essentials the same, in spite of the different competitive situation and a few differences in degree.

drew those eager for great undertakings into the whirlpool of competition, and made unrestricted divisibility of the land appear rational to able farmer's sons.[57] It is hard to say whether or not these expectations were fulfilled, nor did the reaction,[58] the flight to economic security at the price of independence, fail to appear. The wide swing of the pendulum between security and freedom can be traced far back in the history of economics.[59] Again and again we find periods in which the successful strugglers limited the next generation's hope for independence by forcing them to join a guild, or obtain licenses, or by tying them to the land. And there were times when they prevented entirely the success of these aspirations through closed guilds and privileged monopolies or by severely restricting the transferability of farms or prohibiting new investments. This was followed by a thinning of their own ranks through competition or the elimination of the little man by the government. And finally, when self-confidence had broken down because of personal failure or *force majeure*, a flight to the protection of the more powerful followed, such as the transfer of free farms to great landed proprietors in the early Middle Ages, migration of artisans to the factories, flight to a cartel, to the right to a pension, and increasingly since the 1870's, to government security. After such periods, when the barriers between economic lords and serfs are open only in the downward direction, confidence returns again; social tension increases. Economically, too, men wish to live by their own wills and on their own responsibility, and a new tendency toward the maximization of the number of free economic units sets in.

---

57. Even poor districts often held tenaciously to this idea to permit the rise of the best qualified (H. Röhm, " Das bevölkerungspolitische und wirtschaftliche Gesicht des Dorfes Gruibingen 1838–1938," *Berichte über Landwirtschaft*, XXVI [1940], 430).

58. In 1882, 36 per cent of the German working population were independent. In 1933, 33 per cent; only the absolute number rose.

59 At the margin where men hesitated between dependent and independent occupations, an income was higher in this or that case according to whether the man was ready to pay the price of security or of freedom.

60. This often leads to violent social strife.

Chapter 6. Site and Reasons for Town Settlement

A town is a punctiform agglomeration of nonagricultural locations. Now the question arises, why there should be in any particular place: (1) an especially large enterprise, (2) a collection of similar enterprises, (3) an agglomeration of dissimilar enterprises. It is well to distinguish here between unrestricted agglomerations that could form anywhere, and those restricted to a particular locality. Moreover, from the first we shall avoid one way of answering these questions—mere enumeration of the good features of a location. These are not always essential to the choice of any particular spot, and when they are necessary, each by itself is inadequate. A seaport does not arise on every natural harbor. It must be proved, rather, why it is advantageous for some entrepreneurs to avail themselves of these favorable features.

a. REASONS FOR TOWN SETTLEMENT

§1. UNRESTRICTED AGGLOMERATION OF LOCATIONS (THE NATURAL SYSTEM)

Even though the earth had a perfectly uniform surface there would still be towns.

α. *Large Individual Enterprises*

The advantages of mass production of one commodity or the joint production of several would lead at some locations to the establishment of a greater assemblage of production: a factory. This may be so large, indeed, as to constitute a town by itself (Siemensstadt, Stadt des KdF-Wagens). (Gary, originally; Radford, Va., World War II; Oak Ridge, Tenn., and Hanford, Wash., atomic energy; Longview, Wash., lumber; Anaconda, Mont., copper smelting.)

β. *Agglomeration of Similar Enterprises*

1. ADVANTAGES OF NUMBERS AND ASSOCIATION

In some places a number of similar enterprises will establish themselves, partly because this increases the demand for each one individually since buyers like to purchase certain differentiated goods where they can compare different varieties, partly for the sake of those advantages which reduce the cost of all and which are summarized as external economies (large labor market, more efficient auxiliary industries, mutual stimulation, special fittings, and so on).[1]

2. ADVANTAGES OF SITE AND SOURCE OF SUPPLY

Production may also gravitate to one place because it is technically tied to an important source of the raw materials and intermediate products that it uses; or because it is technically tied to consumers, as is the case with craftsmen or merchants, for example. Or it may simply be attracted by a large labor market, a considerable local demand, contact with government agencies, traffic junctions, or the proximity of other towns. Such advantages, which are limited to a few places, occur also with natural uniformity, as we shall see later in the model of a simple system of economic areas. Locations like these are especially rare and at the same time especially favored in systems of equal structure (see pp. 130 ff.). The fewer possible market areas we assume, the larger becomes the number of goods whose markets around their possible locations is greater than is necessary for the mere survival of the individual firm.

3. INTERNAL COMPETITION

(aa) *Division of Local Demand.* All these advantages influence an enterprise established at a favored site, partly through lower costs and partly through increased demand. Such an enterprise can hardly be affected from outside, i. e., by neighboring competitors. Its production cost may be so low that another enterprise can survive only at a considerable distance. When the great demand comes chiefly from the location of the first enterprise itself, it is impossible for a distant competitor to attract part of it. In short, the Chamberlin process (see pp. 109 ff.), which depends on the tendency toward a maximization of the number of independent firms, cannot be carried on from outside against the favored enterprise. Instead, competition starts from within. When this leads to division of a town

---

1. See the excellent study of the town of Pirmasens by E. Schuster et al., *Monoindustrielle Agglomeration. Die Schuhindustriestadt Pirmasens* (Würzburg, 1940). In Pirmasens only shoe factories are agglomerated because, among other reasons, they completely exhaust the supply of every kind of labor available. That this is unusual another reason for association, and should be added to those discussed below on pp. 75–76 and 88–89.

among the various enterprises assembled there, the situation is fundamentally normal. Measured by the number of establishments (or enterprises), the agglomeration will become more intense the smaller the size of the firms in an industry at Chamberlin's point.

(bb) *Supplying the Same Market.* But what would happen if not the local demand is divided, but the demand from the market area in respect to which the individual enterprises enjoy practically no locational advantages over one another? Let N, in Figure 17, be the demand curve of the first enterprise to establish itself and K_1 its average cost curve. As an almost unrestricted monopoly, it sets

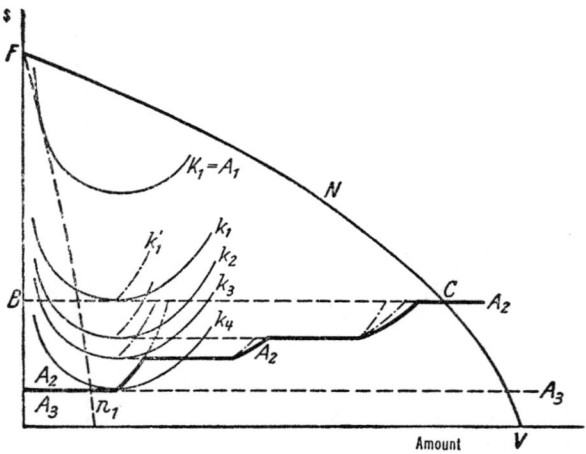

Fig. 17. Supply of the same market by several entrepreneurs

its price near Cournot's point. But a second and a third competitor appear. Is N still valid for all, or will it be broken into three partial demand curves? In other words, will the demand curve of the first firm be gradually rotated downward and toward the left, as in the Chamberlin process, until finally, as n_1, it is just tangent to K_1? Such a tendency might continue in a few firms because personal characteristics of the entrepreneurs, or advertising, etc., draw attention to the firm and are important in the particular case. But the more competitors there are, the flatter each partial demand curve becomes; that is, the more sharply demand reacts on each price change of a single firm. We are aproaching pure competition and shall have reached it when the partial demand curves become so flat that, in the long run, an enterprise offering its goods at a little above the equilibrium price can hardly continue to sell, whereas were it to cut the market price a little it would sell all that it could possibly produce.[2]

The partial demand curve, n^r, of a given firm, r, coincides at F and V actually, and throughout the remainder of its length practically, with the broken line $FBCV$, and where it deviates, it lies slightly to the right of FB and at first somewhat above and then somewhat below BC. In its last portion it is virtually identical with the aggregate demand curve.[3]

What is the shape of the supply curve? With the appearance of new competitors, external economies may at first lower the cost curve of the first enterprise from K_1 to k_1. Now workers of all degrees of efficiency crowd into the competing enterprises. Some of these firms can secure expensive sites near the railroad station, whereas others must be satisfied with cheaper but less favorable sites. Despite these differences all cost curves must be the same, if the productivity of the factors of production varies only with the degree to which the capacity of the plant is utilized and otherwise remains constant. The differences in the cost curves, as the figure shows (k_1 need not be the lowest one by any means), rest solely upon the varying ability of entrepreneurs to use their factors of production effectively.[4]

---

2. We can imagine the gradual increase in the anonymity of the individual firm by supposing that with a sufficiently large number of small enterprises a particular firm buys their products and retails them in the vicinity.

3. It would be meaningless to derive the aggregate demand curve by adding these partial demand curves, because they are not independent of one another.

4. Theoretically it might be expected that each entrepreneur would pay every factor of production according to its marginal product, and that this output would be the same whether the last unit of the factor were employed by the marginal entrepreneur or by a superior one. What more the latter was able to extract from it would have to be balanced by the disadvantages of exceeding the optimum size of the firm. Where the marginal worker (as seen by the individual firm) could be distinguished from other workers, all would have to be paid according to output, unless their greater output was due to their own skill rather than to their position in the factory. In so far as the former is true, it should make no difference, therefore, whether a good or a poor worker was employed, since each would be paid according to his productivity. In reality, the better enterpreneurs secure the better workers as well the better sites and pay them higher wages than they could get from the marginal entrepreneurs. The reason is that these workers need less supervision because of their personal characteristics, and that they make less demand per unit of output on the entrepreneur's time (indirect efficiency), so that through them he can achieve greater profits within the limits of his own ability. In its details the determination of wages is exceedingly complicated, of course, if labor is subdivided into groups, and only the qualitative and quantitative peculiarities of the efficiency of the individual are stressed.

The total cost curve is now constructed from the individual cost curves. Let the market price rise slowly. Each firm begins to operate when the price line touches its point of minimum average cost. If the price goes higher, it follows its marginal cost curve, k', up to its intersection with the price line. The discontinuous horizontal jumps of the aggregate supply curve show that a new factory has become able to compete. The smaller these jumps, that is, the smaller the optimum size of a firm in the particular industry, the greater the agglomeration of firms will be. The portions of curves between two jumps are obtained by adding all marginal cost curves, in so far as they lie to the right of the minimum average cost and within the relevant price intervals. From this it follows that every producer, after having entered the total supply curve, is represented in every portion of it. If all entrepreneurs were equally efficient the supply curve would necessarily be horizontal (A_3). This would exclude special profit *and would correspond to tangency in the Chamberlin process.* The agglomeration of factories would then be still greater; first, because the size of each would be less; second, because at the lower price the demand from the original market area would be greater; and third, because the area itself would be enlarged. The last two effects have been taken into account in our demand curve.[5]

4. HOTELLING'S CASE[5a]

Here would belong also that tendency toward agglomeration which is based on freight cost and which Hotelling[6] has tried to demonstrate. He assumed two competitors along a finite stretch (such as two ice cream vendors along a beach) with an inelastic demand. The location of at least one of the two is mobile, and the f. o. b. prices, which are uniform for all customers, are changeable. In setting his own factory price, every competitor assumes that the price of his rival is fixed. Under these assumptions Hotelling shows that the location which is most favorable from the standpoint of the individual firm does not coincide with the economically most desirable location of minimum freight cost. The location that would minimize freight cost would be at a distance of one quarter of the total length of the stretch from each end. In fact, however, each competitor finds it advantageous to move close to the other.

---

5. On the proliferation of factories in Pirmasens see E. Schuster *et al.*, *Monoindustrielle Agglomeration. Die Schuhindustriestadt Primasens* (Würzburg, 1940), p. 22.

5a. Section 4 has been translated from the first German edition, pp. 12–15, for insertion here where Lösch had omitted it to save space.

6. H. Hotelling, " Stability in Competition," *Economic Journal*, 1929.

The objections against this derivation [7] are that it is valid only under very unusual circumstances. The first group of objections concerns *unlikely behavior* of the rivals. First, it is hardly likely that one duopolist will assume that his rival will not react to his own actions. As soon as this assumption is dropped we find, as Palander has shown, "a pronounced tendency toward deglomeration." [8] If, for example, both duopolists act alike, the optimal location for each is one sixth of the length of the whole stretch from each end. Here is a second improbability: Why should the two duopolists act differently if all circumstances confronting them are identical for both? It is true that the more symmetrically the competitors are located along our stretch, the greater will be the profit for both of them together. But the distribution of this profit would be equally asymmetrical, and why should the competitor who finds himself on the short end be content with such a situation?

Symmetrical possibilities are rather more probable. Either we permit the first competitor to locate himself in the center from the very beginning, in which case the best thing his rival can do is to imitate him and do likewise; or else the first places himself asymmetrically on the stretch. Then the other will settle near him but on the longer end of the stretch. In the next round, however, the first will jump over him, and the two will dance around one another until they have reached the center. Or else both will start at the same time and place themselves simultaneously, either in the center or at any symmetrically located points on the stretch. In the latter case—and the central location is after all only the limiting case—the profit (of each one separately and of both together) will be everywhere the same, however unlikely this may sound. This follows immediately from the profit formula. *Consistently pursued,* Hotelling's case leads, *under his own assumptions,* to the result that it is completely irrelevant for both enterprises where they will locate as long as they are *located symmetrically.* (Hotelling himself considers symmetry merely " improbable," without excluding it by his assumptions.)

The result is valid only if both rivals assume in their price policy that they have to share the market. But this assumes a great lack of foresight and this is the *third* improbability of their behavior. Palander [9] shows that the interaction of two possible behavior pat-

---

7. The mathematics will be found in Hotelling, *op. cit.,* and in even more general form in Tord Palander, *Beiträge zur Standortstheorie* (Uppsala, 1935), pp. 232–235.
8. Palander, *op. cit.,* p. 394.
9. *Op. cit.,* pp. 237 ff.

terns will lead to continuous price fluctuations, and this is true even when the firms are still fairly distant from each other, but is certainly true when their distance from each other equals half the length of the stretch. Hotelling's formulas indicate that the price and the profit of that rival who moves nearer to the other will rise. Instead of increasing his price also and thus sharing the intermediate stretch with the aggressor, the duopolist attacked will find it more profitable after a certain distance to *lower* his price and thus either crowd the aggressor out of the market entirely or force him to lower his price. Hotelling does not consider this possible behavior. Such a price reduction means that the rivals will move farthest apart, until the critical distance has been reached, when an increase in price will again appear to be more favorable. The cause of this incessant fluctuation lies in the assumption that the rival will keep his price unchanged. This assumption drives both rivals beyond the stretch within which an equilibrium would exist, which is bounded by the end points and the quarter points of the stretch.

The second group of objections is directed against *unlikely circumstances*. First, Hotelling assumes a completely inelastic demand, which is a rare case. Hotelling told me he would agree that with an elastic demand there would be a tendency for the rivals to move into the neighborhood of the quarter points. I would go even farther: In the case of an elastic demand an enterprise will locate exactly at the quarter point if it selects an equilibrium point at all, since every other point lies asymmetrically in the market and thus limits demands and profit possibilities.

The situation changes, secondly, if more than two producers are assumed. Hotelling might salvage his argument for several competitors by abandoning the line for an area. On the other hand, for the line—and this is true also for a larger area—Chamberlin shows that more than two producers would spread out even under Hotelling's own assumptions.[10] The intermediate producers are all equally spaced from each other. If one of them moved nearer to his right-hand neighbor, for example, he would lose as much area to his left-hand competitors as he gains from the one on his right. Nevertheless, Chamberlin overlooks the fact that such an asymmetry might be profitable for him if it were an equilibrium position. But equilibrium exists now only if the rivals are equidistant. However, even independent of any considerations of equilibrium Chamberlin is correct: It is impossible that more than two entrepreneurs approach

10. E. H. Chamberlin, *The Theory of Monopolistic Competition* (Cambridge, Mass., 1936), pp. 194–196.

each other. A third producer who was located between them would always gain by jumping over either his rival to the right or his rival to the left. Only the producers at the ends of the stretch have an area one and a half times as great as that of the others. As long as they remain on the interior third point of the end portion of the stretch, none of the rivals has any incentive to jump over them and become an end man. To this extent one might speak of a tendency to an agglomeration toward the middle.

But even this tendency disappears completely if we drop the *third* restriction. Suppose we have an *endless* stretch—an assumption quite permissible if we are thinking of conditions on earth. In this case, each of the two competitors with a finite maximum delivery distance would gain by moving apart until there arose between them a completely unsupplied area. Even more appropriate for this earth would be the substitution of a circle on a sphere for our stretch. If one of the competitors remains in place while the other approaches him, the "back end" of his half of the circle will become larger and larger. But unlike the case where the rivals are situated on a plane stretch, the "back end" of his rival's part of the circle increases equally at the same time. Since according to the formula, however, profit increases with the difference of the two ends, and since this difference remains zero for every position, it follows that on a circle, the situation on a finite stretch, it is useless for one competitor to approach the other even if one is immobile.

Since Hotelling's "tendency to agglomeration" has created some *furore* and has led to considerable and fruitful discussions in which not all participants sided against Hotelling, it was necessary to scrutinize his interesting thesis in some detail. We conclude that under assumptions with even a slight degree of realism, no such tendency to agglomeration conditioned by freight cost exists.

γ. *Agglomeration of Different Enterprises*

4. AGGLOMERATION THROUGH INTERRELATIONSHIP

(aa) *Advantages of Numbers.* There are common advantages to producers in the agglomeration at one place of a moderately [11] large output, no matter of what kind. One of the most important

---

11. There is an optimum point beyond which confinement to a town tends to raise costs. The growth of towns is slowed on the one hand by the increasing disadvantages and cost of crowding, which manifest themselves particularly as traffic slowdowns and rising land prices, and on the other by the increasing disadvantages and cost of distance from places of work and from sellers of agricultural and buyers of industrial products. These costs, to be sure, have been shifted in part to the general public;

is the advantage of having a railway station, not to mention better streets and drainage, cheaper water and electricity, and a larger labor market.

(bb) *Advantages of Association.*[12] *First, under any given market situation*: The preference of consumers for combining small purchases or comparing various qualities of differentiated products is hardly less important for the formation of towns than for the existence of special business districts within a town and of department stores in these districts. The mere fact of their proximity not only lowers the cost of production, especially general costs, but at the same time increases the share of the demand.

Second, with economic fluctuations: It is advantageous for a place to harbor industries whose seasonal or cyclical variations do not coincide. Of course this alleviates not these fluctuations themselves, but their reinforcing secondary effects on enterprises that are directly concerned, such as local handicrafts and business.

Third, with structural changes in the economy: Structural changes in the economy are easier to cope with when a population has varied interests, activities, and characteristics. On such a soil, as List emphasized, ingenuity and adaptability flourish more readily and, in addition, the well-balanced culture that is not only admirable in itself but fruitful for independent and adaptation to new situations.

Fourth, more general reasons: The ablest members of all professions and trades which are not tied down to particular places, who therefore can live where they wish and are in general the bearers of a conscious cultural tradition, tend to attract one another and thus increase their achievements and their enjoyment of life.

(cc) *Advantages of Proximity, etc. First, for " city fillers ":* W. Sombart [13] drew an admirable distinction between " city founders " and mere " city fillers "; i. e., between occupations that establish cities and those that exist because a city is already there.[14] By ful-

for example, in the case of expensive railway terminals in metropolitan centers and of the expensive supply installations of suburban settlements, but also through the prevention of speculation in land. In order to cause large cities to spread out it would have been better, while there was still no municipal planning, to tax land speculation severely but without actually preventing it.

12. These, too, represent common external economies.
13. *Der moderne Kapitalismus*, I 5. A (1922), pp. 131 f.
14. This is a special case of the general difference between occupations that determine, and occupations that are determined by, location. In a rough classification the former generally include agriculture, mining, and some manufactures; the latter

filling a function for a smaller or larger surrounding area the former create claims on the outside world, so to speak, in return for which its commodities, and especially agricultural products, are brought into town. The latter work for the former or are otherwise tied to their locations: local trades, i. e., trades with a very small market radius; ancillary industries; but also certain finishing trades as well as complementary enterprises such as the textile industry, which gives work to the wives of the men employed in heavy industry. None of these would exist in the absence of the founding occupations.

Second, for "city founders": In one case "city fillers" rise to the rank of "city founders." It is advantageous in every economic region to have the market networks for individual goods coincide at one point, as we shall see later. This metropolis, to be sure, fulfills functions for the whole area, but its functions could be fulfilled also if the market networks were set down indiscriminately. Aside from the reasons previously given they will meet in one place because industries largely determined by consumption mutually create in this way the advantages of a large local demand for each other.[15] These advantages consist partly in the feasibility of more or larger firms, and partly in the fact that only thus does there arise a sufficiently large demand for many goods. This large demand has two causes, the size of the urban population and of the demand of individuals for individual goods which may amount to three times what it would be with an evenly distributed population. This will be shown later.

2. Chance Agglomeration

The pattern of the ideal economic region will show that location of different enterprises may coincide even when they derive no advantage at all from one another; when from their standpoint the coincidence is merely fortuitous. Seen from the standpoint of the regional system this agglomeration has three important causes: (1) orientation by a capital city, (2) orientation by main roads, (3) the relative distances of similar locations from one another. These relationships, which rest on the original distances between the original settlements, are such that only compartively few places offer possible

---

include their followers: handicrafts. service, trades, etc. But this is a very rough approximation only, which neglects reactions on allegedly independent locations. Nevertheless it is useful in planning the development of new areas.

15. This plays an important role, also, in the development of a downtown district (a "city"), which in general arises for essentially the same reasons as do towns and particularly capital cities within a country.

locations for industrial enterprises, which, therefore, necessarily gather at these points, especially where orientation by a capital city is added. Finally, the order of the regional system creates certain favored points, points where communication routes cross, that offer special advantages to different enterprises independently of one another.

δ. *Agglomeration of Pure Consumers* [16]

Corresponding to large single producers, there are large single consumers: royal courts and bishops' sees in earlier times, garrisons and administrative and educational centers today. The fact that certain institutions like fire departments, churches, schools, and places of entertainment pay, causes pure consumers, also, to collect in one place. This agglomeration of consumers is further favored by the advantages of association and situation. In short, almost all the reasons for the establishment of towns by producers are repeated.

ε. *Summary*

Even though the earth were a smooth and uniform sphere towns would still arise for numerous reasons. These agglomerations of locations would be partly fortuitous, when seen from the standpoint of those concerned though not from the standpoint of all, and partly the result of advantages they offered not from the participants. The advantages are divided into those of number and association,[17] and of site and supply. All may be subdivided into advantages of consumption, of sales, and of production. The latter divide into advantages of uniform and differentiated production, and finally into internal and external economies. At first all these factors favoring the establishment of towns act everywhere, but they concentrate at definite points as soon as the capital and the main highways are located. Under our assumptions, these may be located arbitrarily, at least in a single economic region. But once they have been fixed whether because of a historic advantage or by political act, there is no further room for arbitrariness as to where and why additional towns shall arise. Thus the general interdependence among all locations determines not only those points where the advantages of site suffice for agglomeration, but also where the other factors mentioned shall create towns, either singly or in co-operation.

---

16. According to Sombart (*op. cit.*, p. 142) most towns were consumers in the Middle Ages, whereas today they are, without doubt, chiefly producers.

17. Of course the advantages of number and association include those of site as well, but are not exhausted by these.

§2. Restricted Agglomeration of Location (The Historical System)

We have mentioned four factors besides chance that always determine the establishment of towns: numbers and association, site and supply. The latter does so only in the sense that it appears first during locational development, and then in turn attracts other enterprises. Historical reality, with its spatial differences in population density, topography, and natural resources adds another factor that operates only from an already determined place: *the traditional source of supply*. This concept must be defined in a wide sense. For producers proper it may include raw materials, water power, a favorable climate, or labor or capital that are already available. For transport it may mean a river valley as well as a river crossing; for the consumer, climate and surroundings. This raises no new problems. We have already learned from the discussion of the natural system of town formation that certain places may offer special advantages. The field to which this applies is now simply widened considerably. The difference is merely that under the natural system favored places do not appear until a location has been determined, whereas here intrinsic sources of supply are present first. In general such sources of supply limit the number of possible locations for a particular industry, but increase it for towns since the fortuitous coincidence of locations that is so important in the natural system is made more difficult.

It might be thought at first that site, too, is one of the historical factors. Closer scrutiny shows, however, that all the advantages of a historical site can be reduced either to those of the site itself or to those of a source of supply. Neither geologic nor geographic differences of any sort are necessary to create differences in the favorability of a site, or even to introduce site as a new factor. All that is new is, that in addition to location on the basis of consumers, manufacturers, and routes of communication, we have also location on the basis of sources of supply.

The great significance of these in the establishment of towns is this: they not only *influence* the location of rural towns and highways, but also *determine* that of the capital city and the main lines of communication, which in the natural system was left to free choice. Differences in the earth's surface ordain from the very beginning that for every town there is only one best site. They exclude all human arbitrariness in so far as it is unwilling to pay the price. But Part III will show that deliberate intervention may still be advisable.

b. THE SITE OF TOWN FORMATION

§1. LOCATION OF THE INDIVIDUAL TOWN

He who wishes to explain or determine the location of towns must constantly bear in mind two circumstances above all. First, all five reasons for their origin determine in general the place of their settlement: numbers and association, site and supply, and chance. These may work with or against one another. Only in rare cases will one factor alone be decisive. Second, towns as a rule are not merely agglomerations of locations of similar types, but above all of different ones. Thus the explanation will necessarily differ with the branch of industry or the kind of pure consumer.

α. General Determination of Site

The problem of location for the individual town is: Given all other towns, to find a site for this one. This is more difficult by far than to determine a location for a firm. For in the case of a town not only one but many locations are simultaneously variable. Furthermore, they are interdependent, so that the problem cannot simply be reduced to that other one: To determine the location separately for each industry in this part of the country, on the assumption that the town will arise where many of these locations approximately coincide. This might be acceptable, at best, as a very rough first approximation. A more precise analysis, in so far as economic considerations play any role at all,[18] cannot possibly disregard the interdependence of the locations of the various industries concerned. For example, each individual location within the area under examination may be favorable for a factory in different degree, depending on the exact site of the railway station. But the site of the latter depends again on the location of all the other industries in the district.

A somewhat more exact statement of the problem consists, therefore, in selecting a location for each industry for every possible combination of the other locations, and then choosing that site for the town in whose neighborhood most optimum locations (interdependence having been considered) are situated. Even this state-

---

18. Obviously they do not in the case of fortresses, administrative or religious centers, and the like.

ment would still admit arbitrary selection of locations that are not economically determined, but nevertheless economically significant. This problem is practically insoluble.

Thus, as in choosing a location for a single factory, nothing remains but to calculate roughly which among a few hypothetical sites for the town would attract most industries. The best that location theory can do is to suggest the locations to be examined. Important sources of supply, intersections of traffic routes, and the center of gravity of the polygon formed by the neighboring towns of similar function are such test locations. But one should not be deceived as to the gross inaccuracy of such a procedure. Even the excellent rule to fix the site of a town first in the economy as a whole, then within a region,[19,20] and finally at the place itself [20] does not usually help very much. For these three situations are of varying significance for different industries, and the advantages of one may compensate for the disadvantages of the others.

Thus we cannot avoid the fundamental difficulty in locating a town: We can neither neglect the interdependence of the locations of the firms directly concerned nor can we grasp it in its complexity. Even after exhaustive examination towns continue to be founded with fingers crossed, and the reason for the relatively small number of failures is the stickiness of the location system. The competition among possible locations is worse than imperfect. In earlier times, and particularly during the critical periods of first development, it was still further restricted by state privileges or municipal prohibitions.

β. *Special Cases*

Easiest to explain is the location of a town at a favorable point, which in this context means in particular natural resources, locations of pure large-scale consumers, and intersections of traffic routes. But again one must beware of regarding such obvious advantages as *sufficient* causes of an agglomeration of locations. If the splendid port of New York, for example, were on a remote island the city would consist of a few huts at the best and one of the competing ports, Boston or Baltimore, would take its place; or if necessary an artificial harbor would be built.[21] On the other hand, if the whole

---

19. More exactly, in the area enclosed by neighboring towns of similar function.

20. For a short description of all German towns see E. Keyser, ed., *Deutsches Städtebuch* (Stuttgart, 1939 and following years).

21. E. A. Kautz has minutely analyzed the limited significance of a natural coastal situation for the location of seaports in *Das Standortproblem der Seehäfen* (Jena, 1934), pp. 15, 33, and elsewhere.

East Coast hinterland were a desert, New Orleans or San Francisco would flourish despite the splendid Atlantic harbors. It might be mentioned incidentally that a good part of the business of New York has been directly attracted neither by such advantages of site as its harbor and the rock foundation for skyscrapers, nor by its closer proximity to American and West European industrial areas than any of the more southerly ports, nor by its situation at the terminus of the Erie Canal and of many railroads, etc., but by the advantages of numbers.

Consider first a few examples of cities whose existence seems to have been determined to a high degree by their location. The centers of states or of natural basins often have the advantage of being optimum transport points in a region that cannot easily be reduced by outside competition because it is protected by natural or artificial tariff walls. Such points are ideal locations for consumption-oriented industries [22] with an extended sales radius.

Leipzig, for example, possesses this advantage in double measure: It is the approximate center of the basin that is bounded by the Erzgebirge range, the Thuringian Mountains, and the Harz Mountains, all about sixty miles distant. It is also the central city of Germany; almost all of Germany lies within two hundred and fifty miles of Leipzig, or a comfortable day's journey, and conversely, nearly the entire area within that radius is German. A third advantage of its location is that the Berlin-Munich, Upper Silesia-Ruhr, and Hamburg-Prague-Vienna trunk lines intersect there.

Chicago possesses similar advantages. True, it does not lie at the center of the United States, but, more important, considering the unequal distribution of the population, it is near the center of population and production (measured by "value added"). In addition, there is its unique situation where the railway between New York and Minneapolis meets the steamship lines on the Great Lakes; and, less important, between the iron mines near Lakes Superior and Michigan and the coal of Pennsylvania. Paris, too, belongs in this group as center of the basin named after it, as do Breslau, Prague, Frankfort (midway between the most important European capitals and banking centers), and the encircled Addis Ababa and Madrid. The latter, though in the geographic center of Spain, lies away from the center of population and industry.

Places favored in another way by location are those where traffic

---

22. Industries, that is, in which location with respect to consumers is important.

23. On towns arising through damming of traffic see F. Ratzel. "Die geographische Lage der grosen Städte," *Kleine Schriften*, II, 446.

is dammed up by transshipment.[23] Points, that is, where lines of communication cross (pure situation), or traffic lines of different sort meet (situation at sources of supply as on a seacoast). Hamburg and Cologne owe much to this.

But the most significant special cases are those where choice of location is restricted by a source of supply. More important still than localities that are favorable to traffic, such as harbors, are those to which production must conform: above all sources of coal, a material that loses much weight in production. Since coal supplanted wood in smelting and ore has moved toward coal,[24] and since the substitution of steam for water power, favorably situated coal fields have become prominent among those regions that are studded with towns. Take, for example, England, where nearly all the large cities are concentrated in the coal districts, or the highly urbanized zone stretching from the coal of northern France and Belgium across the Ruhr and the lignite region through Upper Silesia and far on into Poland.[25] Examples of source-oriented consumption are health resorts, many university towns, religious shrines, and capitals.

But not much is proved by such examples. Dependence on source does not mean *unconditional* restriction to a source, still less to one particular source; for competing sources and other factors which affect town formation become relevant. Neither does it mean that all of the industries of a town are confined to this one source. Some are tied to the source of supply, since they depend in turn upon industries that are so tied. Others, however, find themselves in the town although not one of the forces that determine their location has its seat there. The site of a town can be explained satisfactorily in the end only by calculating its advantages over competing sites. This becomes even more obvious if the problem is to find the most advantageous location, not to explain its actual location, which is so often determined by past and fortuitous conditions.

---

24. Improvements in the technique of smelting have undermined this rule however, because the amount of coal required per unit of iron has been reduced. Furthermore, ore deposits have become more and more powerful locational attractions, as ores with less and less iron content have to be used.

25. The concentration of towns in Germany would have been even greater had coal not been shipped by rail over great distances, probably far below cost. The low long-distance rates for coal were one of the most important factors in location and, indeed, in the decentralization of former times. Electricity, too, which is cheaper to transport over short distances than coal, has recently had a dispersive effect.

§2. THE SYSTEM OF TOWN LOCATIONS

As towns are essentially agglomerations of locations of economic activities, the system of town locations is defined simultaneously by the general equations of location and the geometry of economic regions, which will be discussed later. The general location problem is the same for single industries and agglomerations of industries. In the case of the individual plant it differs only because fewer variables need be considered in selecting a site for a factory than for a town.

Chapter 7. Site and Cause of Belt Formation

We shall limit our analysis to belt-shaped areal agglomeration of locations of production (see pp. 10–11).

a. BELTS OF LOCATIONS PRODUCING IDENTICAL GOODS

§1. ADVANTAGES OF SPECIALIZATION

Consider the cotton belt, the corn belt, the wheat belt, and so on in the United States. These belts produce mainly the crop in question; or, which is not the same thing, most of the crop in question is produced there. Belts are formed for the same reasons as towns: the advantages of site, source, and scale.

Thünen showed more than a hundred years ago how different advantages of a site make it profitable to specialize in different crops in successive zones around a market, and here it will suffice merely to recall Chapter 5.

Among the advantages of a source of supply we included a special suitability of soil, of climate,[1] and of population for the production of a certain commodity. But it would be no explanation of the cotton belt, for example, to tell how its natural conditions favor the cultivation of "white gold." They might favor other branches of agriculture as well. Certainly it is not only here that cotton can be grown, for the necessary conditions occur elsewhere too, or at least could be provided; for example, by transplanting cheap Negro labor from the cotton belt. Only by comparison can it be proved that conditions here are exactly suited to the cultivation of cotton. Of course mere physical yields must not be compared, since these depend entirely upon input. Where but one crop is grown only the highest profits attainable per unit of area are really comparable.

Figure 18 provides an example. The profits from two crops, 1 and 2, on two different grades of soil, I and II, are compared. The technique of presentation is as follows:[2] Profit is greatest where

---

1. Differences in climate and situation determine agricultural location chiefly in the large, differences in soil in the small. See T. Brinkmann, "Die Ökonomik des landwirtschaftlichen Betriebs," *Grundriss der Sozialökonomik* (1922), Sec. 7, p. 91.
2. After A. Haase, "Die Thünensche Intensitätstheorie in graphischer Darstellung," in *Thünen Festschrift*, edited by Seedorf and Seraphim (Rostock, 1933), p. 202.

marginal cost equals marginal receipts. Geometrically this means that the tangents to the curves for receipts and cost per acre must be parallel. Or, since in the example the cost curve is a straight line, the tangent to e_1, for example at B, must simply be parallel to a. Then g_1 is the highest profit that can be achieved by crop 1 on soil I. On this soil $g_1 > g_2$, hence cultivation of the first crop will be more profitable, whereas the second will be more profitable on soil II.[3] If nature were the only location factor, the area of cultiva- for crop 1 would have to coincide with the area of soil I.[4]

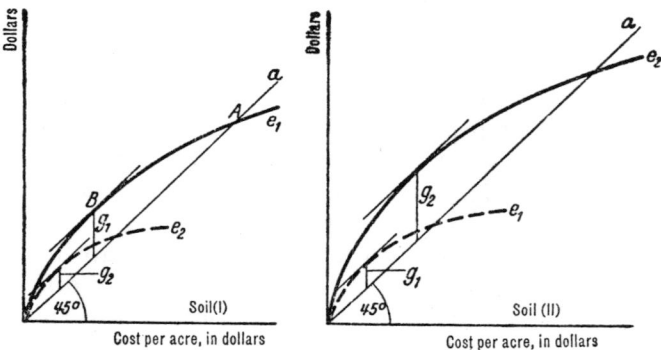

Fig. 18. Suitability of different soils for different products.
  a) Cost per acre, dollars;
  e) receipts per acre as function of cost, in dollars;
  g) profit per acre as function of cost, in dollars
  The subscripts refer to products 1 and 2 respectively.

The third cause for the establishment of belts is the advantage of numbers, which favors regional specialization particularly in staple products that are not raised for local need only. If every farmer in the United States were to devote a few fields to cotton, assuming that climate permitted, the cost of production would be considerably increased. To begin with he would be less familiar with, or less well equipped for, cotton growing, or at least his equipment would not be fully used. In short, the scale of production would be too small on the individual farm and production costs would rise accordingly. In addition there would be disadvantages unconnected with the individual farm. The radius of the supply

---

3. If product 1 were more profitable on both soils the situation would suggest application of the theorem of comparative costs. We shall return to this in note 46 on p. 252.

4. The figure eliminates the influence of site in assuming that the grower's price is the same everywhere. On pp. 87 f. site also will be taken into consideration.

Belt Formation

area for cotton gins and presses would have to be considered because of the small return in raw material per unit of area. Thus much higher freight costs would result. The whole sales organization would be more diffuse and less fully used. No single port in the country would ship enough bales to make profitable the loading machinery and efficient export presses that now exist in the two southern ports specializing in the shipment of cotton.

Similarly, every other belt has its centers: commodity exchanges, transshipment points, collecting stations, sales markets, research institutes, and so on. Other things being equal, profits decrease with distance from these centers, either because all shipments pass through them, or because with increasing distance their facilities can be enjoyed only with correspondingly greater difficulty. Thus production crowds around these centers,[5] whose existence may even depend on this crowding.[6]

If a belt has several such centers (and the competition of towns tends to maximize their number), we are, depending on their origin, not confronted by only one homogeneous belt. Thus, for example, one should distinguish the cotton districts around New Orleans, around Houston and Galveston, and around a few smaller ports. Of course this does not prevent the cotton belt, as far as the other reasons for its origin are concerned, from constituting a unit nevertheless.

But the forces which work toward the establishment of belts seldom operate without interference. Their influence is partly cumulative, partly compensating. A single example may suffice (see Fig. 19). If it were merely a question of site, and if the soil everywhere were thus of the same quality, I, product 1 would be cultivated about the point O up to the distance OC, but from there on up to OD product 2 would be grown. Now suppose, however, that from A outward the soil is of quality II, more favorable for crop 2. Besides the curves for the profit per hectare on soil I, g_1^I and g_2^I, we must draw in the corresponding curves g_1^{II} and g_2^{II} for soil II. For product 1, the second curve lies below the first; for product 2, above it. The profits per hectare are now equal at dis-

---

5. This is especially true of small enterprises, which depend more on external economies than do the larger ones.

6. This would be represented graphically in such a way that with scattered production the demand curve for the services of a center would not even touch its cost curve, let alone intersect it. As soon as production is spatially concentrated, however, the demand curve will be rotated upward about its intersection with the price axis until finally, with sufficient concentration, it will at least touch the cost curve.

tance OB, and B necessarily lies between A and C. The area for cultivation of the second product will not include the entire area, II, which is especially suited to it, yet it will push nearer to the market than it could if only distance mattered.[7,8]

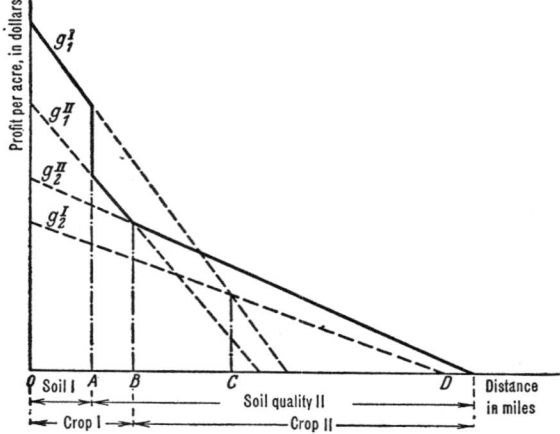

Fig. 19. Location of crops as a function of soil quality and distance

§2. Disadvantages of Specialization

There are forces at work, however, that prevent a region from specializing in one product. This difficult subject has already been so thoroughly analyzed that a brief summary will suffice for the

---

[7]. Hence the suitability of a location is decided not by site (quality of soil) alone, but also by situation (producer's price). With an adequate price a crop will be cultivated even on less suitable soil. A good example is the enormous increase in conifer plantations at the expense of deciduous trees since the rise of industrialization. Fir quickly produces the desired timber, and beechwood has been supplanted as a fuel by the cheaper coal. (See H. Koch *et. al.*, *Die Buche der Ostalb. Eine Standortuntersuchung* [Stuttgart, 1939], pp. 92 ff.) We have entirely disregarded above the fact that with the introduction of a new quality of soil into our example the market prices of both products necessarily change. This change would shift point B somewhat farther outward, but not so far as to make it coincide with C.

[8]. Other considerations, of course, favor the cultivation of a single crop in the vicinity of a town. Here predatory cultivation can be allowed for sooner than anywhere else, or counteracted with expensive fertilizers instead of by mixing or rotating crops (see Koch, *loc. cit.*, for forestry, which is subject to the same laws of location as agriculture). On the other hand, the cultivation of one crop far from a town is made possible by rotating or even migrating cultivation.

present purpose. The following presentation is based on the works of F. Aereboe and T. Brinkmann.[9]

The following arguments in particular speak against the cultivation of a single crop: (1) It makes only partial use of the soil, and in the long run requires a greater expenditure of fertilizer. (2) It leads to seasonal peak demands for labor, which can be overcome only by an increase in wages. (3) It stakes everything on one venture; the more economically self-sufficient a farm is, the less sensitive is it to fluctuations in costs and selling prices and the more easily can it adapt itself to permanent structural changes in the market. (4) It raises freight costs. (5) Moreover, strict specialization in one product is often technically impossible. Thus where wool is produced, mutton also is obtained; where manuring is required, fodder must be raised, and so on. For these various reasons a point is inevitably reached where the lowered costs due to increasing mass production are outstripped by the rising costs due to increasing specialization.

The resultant of the forces working toward specialization and diversification is a compromise. It is not the commodity that may appear at first sight to yield the greatest profit that is produced, but rather that *combination* of a *limited* number of goods that will turn out to be the most profitable in the long run. In general, but particularly far from a market where only a few crops may economically be chosen,[10] the combination will include, or, rather prefer products that, considered singly for the short run, can be cultivated with greatest profit. But this is not absolutely certain. It is impossible to offer a more concrete theoretical rule for determining the optimum combination than this general statement. From the innumerable possible combinations [11] the one that affords the greatest possible average profit throughout the planning period will be chosen.

Because of the frequent interdependence of marginal revenues this does not necessarily presume that for every single product in the combination *marginal costs* equals *marginal revenue,* but only that none of the many possible and infinitely small changes in the combination, embracing several products at the same time, will yield an additional profit.

9. F. Aereboe, *Kleine Landwirtschaftliche Betriebslehre* (Berlin, 1932).
T. Brinkmann, " Bodennutzungssysteme," *Handwörterbuch der Staatswissenschaften,* 4th ed., Vol. II; " Die Ökonomik des landwirtschaftlichen Betriebs," *Grundriss der Sozialökonomik,* 1922) , Sec. 7, pp. 27–124.
10. See p. 88, note 8.
11. This does not mean that any combination is possible.

Finally, it may be concluded that although the disadvantages of specialization do not actually prevent the formation of belts, nevertheless they prevent the production in these belts of only the single commodity whose name they bear.

b. BELTS OF DIFFERENT LOCATIONS

The areal agglomeration of different locations, which may be illustrated by industrial districts, has essentially the same causes that we have already encountered so frequently; the advantages of site and source of supplies, of scale and association. The advantages of site brings about industrial agglomerations independently of all natural inequalities. Even in the ideal economic district, as will be seen later, there are sectors that are especially rich in towns, because the main lines of communication can thus be used to best advantage. In the actual economy there are the additional advantages of situation at a source of supply and, above all, of these sources themselves. As the weight of coal does not appear in the finished product, coal fields are especially attractive to industry. It has already been pointed out that up to the World Wars almost all the large towns in England, with the exception of her seaports, lay in one of the coal regions.

Especially fertile soils also may attract industry, for a dense agricultural population offers a good location for enterprises that are strongly consumer oriented. Climate, too, plays no small role. Thus the northerly and southerly limits of the North American industrial belt were undoubtedly fixed in part by the fact that the climate beyond them was too strange to northwest Europeans, who composed the bulk of the immigation and of the industrial population up to the end of the nineteenth century. Similarly, the ancient Greek colonization appears to have been restricted to a climatically uniform region.[12] But even more striking is the intense agglomeration of populations along the seacoasts in antiquity, which resulted from the advantages of site and sources of supply. According to Gillman[13] colonization in Africa depended critically upon water supply. Not least in importance are the locations of men with special gifts, since the most favorable environments for industries is found in those places where an unusual intellectual activity has developed.

12. J. H. Schultze, "Zur Geographie der altgriechischen Kolonisation," *Peterm. Mitteilungen*, LXXXVII (1941), 7–12. With a map.
13. *Geographic Review* (1936).

The advantages of size and scale of production, finally, are likewise obvious. The more industrial production exceeds agricultural, the more do the same causes underlying the establishment of a city in an ideal system favor the development of industrial areas, which, because of the cost of land, transportation, and labor are often merely sprawling cities. But just as we found it impossible to offer more than a very general formula for a system of agricultural enterprises, so one should not expect a demonstration of how the location of industrial areas must necessarily be determined. There are usually plausible reasons in favor of certain regions, of course, and the better we know the possible factors and their effects the more certain it is that none of the factors operating in individual cases will be overlooked.

Chapter 8. The Problem of General Location Patterns

Certainly it is more than a mere coincidence that the theory of economic location has been almost entirely confined so far to the point of view of the individual firm.[1] As in price theory, the interdependence of all economic events was eliminated by simplifying assumptions, and the problem thus made susceptible of geometric treatment. But in contradistinction to price theory, the proof of the existence of a general equilibrium and of its conditions is of far less interest here. After the Walrasian equations had confirmed the belief of the Enlightenment that even an economy given over to competition will hover in equilibrium,[2] nothing fundamentally new seemed to have been added when this proof was complicated by the introduction of space and time. Later, when many had entirely abandoned that belief, there seemed on the other hand to be little sense in trying to prove for the particular what they had long been unable to see in the general: that there is a reason in things preserving them from chaos, and as a rule without any human assis-

---

1. Alfred Weber (*Ueber den Standort der Industrien*, P. I [Tübingen, 1909], pp. 200 ff.) has already described the reciprocal effect between the locations of various branches of the economy. He distinguished strata according to whether, like agriculture as the basic layer, they were more influencing or, like "central organizers" as the uppermost stratum, more influenced. According to Predöhl ("Das Standortproblem in der Wirtschaftstheorie," *Weltwirtschaftliches Archiv*, XXI [1925], 304) the systems of equations that determine the prices and distribution of production factors with respect to interdependence implicitly solve also the problem of location. E. Schneider ("Preisbildung und Preispolitik unter Berücksichtigung der geographischen Verteilung von Erzeugern und Verbrauchern," *Schmollers Jahrbuch* [1934]) set up price equations which take account of all locations. But all of them merely touch the problem: Weber's description has less application where the agricultural sector is smaller, as in rich countries or in those that import their food; and his explanation selects only *one* factor: the influence of locations for consumption. Predöhl treats actually only the problem of individual economic units, and Schneider assumes locations as given from the first.

2. It seems to me the chief contribution of classical and neoclassical theory to have proved on a simple model—no one can take everything into consideration—that when certain assumptions are guaranteed a free economy will work. Whether it will work in a desirable manner is another question, and here the classical proofs are no longer convincing. But such reflections must not shake our belief in the fundamental importance of the contribution just mentioned.

tance whatsoever. Once the self-confidence of thinking men that culminated in Hegel had been destroyed, the world founded on it was put out of joint socially, politically, and economically in turn. Because of his lack of belief in a pre-established harmony man believed that he himself must set things in order; but the more eagerly he went about it and the more planlessly he acted in opposition to the conditions of that harmony, the more surely was it destroyed. Today, when we are sensitive once more to the natural rhythm, it seems time to ask who, or what, really failed in the economic sphere during the years of decline: the rational and therefore natural order—or we?

It is not true that man must supply the world with an organizing principle! It already exists, though in human relations it functions unconditionally just as little as man acts morally of himself. The natural equilibrium of economics differs from the equilibrium of nature exactly as the moral differs from the mechanical. Nature works according to laws, but man acts according to his *idea* of laws. In other words, nature *must*, man *may*, act correctly. In order to do so he must have some conception of how he shall act. As to economic equilibrium this means that *in order to guide his activities he needs insight into the conditions of this equilibrium.* This is especially true for the lawmaker, since all others are bound by his precepts even though unable to perceive their rationality. What matters is that statesmen shall act correctly; the comforting assurance that all will come right of itself is no longer granted us. Actually they need plan little, but it is essential that this little be planned with enconomic insight.[3] Knowledge of the conditions governing the most general equilibrium is not enough today; it is necessary to know also how it works under conditions that are more nearly real. It is for this reason that time and space can no longer be neglected.

The following paragraphs will discuss the conditions of general equilibrium in space.[4]

---

3. The few great simple principles according to which the economy works basically, and the few more according to which it works desirably must be strictly observed of course; then there will seldom be need of interfering in details. This is the meaningful sythesis of restraint and freedom.

4. The center of gravity of theoretical economics is shifting once more: Emphasis was laid at first on a price theory that neglected time and space; then the theories of interest and business cycles introduced time; and now the third period has dawned, when space is seriously considered.

a. THE EQUILIBRIUM OF LOCATIONS

This is determined by two fundamental tendencies: the tendency as seen from the standpoint of the individual firm and hitherto alone considered, to the maximization of advantages; and, as seen from the standpoint of the economy as a whole, the tendency to maximization of the number of independent economic units. The latter is affected by competition from without, the former by industrial struggle within. The individual chooses his location in such a way as to achieve the highest profit as a producer, or the cheapest market as a consumer. But in so doing, as though it were a trick of the idea, he makes possible the existence of more competitors. They crowd into the market and reduce his living space until his advantage disappears. There is constant struggle between two forces; what is gained by the one is taken back again by the other.

The point where these forces balance determines location. This equilibrium, born of the interdependence of locations, can be understood only through a system of general equations of location. As soon as the conditions expressed by these equations have been fulfilled the struggle for space dies down, and when the equations are solved the locations themselves are determined.

We now present the general conditions of equilibrium that are valid for independent producers and consumers, for agriculture as well as for industry, and develop the *pertinent* equations briefly for the latter (Tables 3 and 4).[5]

Condition 1: *The location for an individual must be as advantageous as possible.* An entrepreneur therefore makes his choice within the whole district and within his market area in such a way that his profit, within the narrow limits still left by the general interdependence within the economy, shall be greatest.[6] With the same purpose in mind the farmer decides where he shall buy land, and where he shall place his buildings on it. Consumers select a location in accordance with the same principle.

---

5. In order to eliminate all extra-economic factors for the time being we assume that industrial raw materials are evenly distributed over a wide plain, in which the agricultural population also is evenly distributed and lives in a similar fashion. All industries and their production methods are assumed to be accessible to everyone. This simplifies the equations, yet alters nothing in the conditions that they formulate.

6. If all locations but one are thought of as given, everything in the equation for S_q^m, Table 3, is constant except the coordinates (x_q^m, y_q^m). The partial derivatives with respect to them then hold the condition that the location p_q^m will be chosen at the point of greatest profit (equation 1, Table 4).

Table 3. SYMBOLS OF SPATIAL ARRANGEMENT

Product No.	Place of Production		Market Boundaries	
	Site	Number	Abbreviations of their equations	Number
1	$P_1^1 (x_1^1 y_1^1); P_2^1 \ldots P_a^1$	a	$\alpha_1^1, \beta_1^1 \ldots \epsilon_1^1; \alpha_2^1, \beta_2^1 \ldots$	A
2	$P_1^2 (x_1^2 y_1^2); P_2^2 \ldots P_b^2$	b	$\alpha_1^2, \beta_1^2 \ldots \eta_1^2; \alpha_2^2, \beta_2^2 \ldots$	B
.				
m	$P_1^m (x_1^m y_1^m) \ldots P_q^m$	q	$\alpha_1^m, \beta_1^m \ldots \vartheta_1^m; \alpha_2^m, \beta_2^m$	Q
m	(Together)	n	(Together)	N
		$= \Sigma a + b + . q$		$= \dfrac{\Sigma A + B + . Q}{2}$

- Given

  $d^m = f^m(\pi)$ Individual demand for product m

  $\pi_q^m = \phi^m(D_q)$ f. o. b price ⎱ of product m at site q as a function of the total
  $k_q^m = \chi^m(D_q)$ Average cost of production ⎰ demand $D_q^m = \psi(f^m, x_q^m y_q^m, a_q^m \beta_q^m \cdot \cdot \epsilon_q^m, \sigma, \sigma_q^m \cdot \cdot)$.

  $S_q^m = D_q^m \cdot (\pi_q^m - k_q^m)$ Profit on product m at site q

  σ Rural population per sq. km.

  σ_q^m Urban population of the town P_q^m

  r   Freight rate

  m   Number of products

  G   Size of entire area

- To find   Number of Unknowns

  1. π_q^m Factory price of product m at location P_q^m n
  2. G_q^m Sales area of location p_q^m in sq. km.   n
  3. q^m No. of towns that produce product m   m
  4. x_q^m, y_q^m Coordinates of location P_q^m 2n
  5. $\alpha_q^m, \beta_q^m \cdot \cdot \epsilon_q^m$ Equations for the boundaries of the market area of P_q^m N

  Sum: $4n + m + N$

Now for the opposing tendency (see p. 8, note 8). Under the following three assumptions the number of independent enterprises is as large as possible, in individual industries and in the economy as a whole: *The locations must be so numerous that the entire space is occupied* (Condition 2). Furthermore, in all activities that are open to everyone *abnormal profits must disappear* (Condition 3). Thus, in production, prices must correspond on the whole to costs.[7,8,9] In consumption, so far as comparison is possible at all, the advantages must be evenly distributed.

This condition would be fulfilled when the individual voluntarily decided not to exhaust all possibilities of profit. Nevertheless, there would still be room for new competitors since the areas, as they developed under the existing conditions, could be made yet smaller without detriment to the profitability of the industries or farms already established. In addition, therefore, *the areas of supply, production, and sales must be as small as possible* (Condition 4), for only then has the number of enterprises that can survive reached its maximum. If still more farmers or entrepreneurs should now push in, all enterprises would become unprofitable. Independent self-employed producers always tend in general toward this point, for behind them is the inexhaustible reserve army of dependent employees, poised and ready to jump into any breach.[10,11]

---

7. It may happen as an exception that even the greatest possible number of producers will still leave the marginal entrepreneur a profit small but within these limits maximized: for example, when an area is larger than necessary for five entrepreneurs but not large enough for six. The situation is similar when, on the one hand, a place offers conditions so favorable for production that no external competition can approach closely enough to take away all profit, but, on the other hand, a competitor who has established himself in a place is unable to develop because his market is too small.

8. To these, of course, belong three sources of income that sometimes flow in an abundant stream. The entrepreneur's wage for his personal efforts, which falls with decrease in the size of the business until the income of the marginal entrepreneur is so small that the influx of entrepreneurs ceases; the payment of interest on his own capital; rent for the productive contribution of the land that happens to belong to him, which is limited in area, situation, and quality (in place of contractual rent).

9. This gives for each of the n locations an equation of the general form $\pi_q^m = k_q^m$, or like equation No. 3 in Table 4. A geometric explanation will be helpful. The market area that can be supplied from a location depends on the one hand on the shape of the demand and on the other on the shape of costs within the firm. Both are illustrated in Figure 16a; the total demand, D, within this market area as a function of f. o. b. price, and total production as a function of the costs, k. The curves intersect at S where costs and price are equal.

10. In geometric terms, a diminution of the area means a shifting of the demand curve toward the left. The limit of this diminution is reached when the demand curve is tangent to the supply curve. In Figure 16a, D' is the shifted demand curve and B the point of tangency. Equation 3 contains the first algebraic condition for the tangency of the two curves; the second condition is: $(\pi_q^m)' = (k_q^m)'$, or like equation 4.

11. It might appear at first sight that condition 1 is contained within condition 4, since the market area can be as small as possible only when the factory is so situated in it that the profit is as large as possible. But condition 4 relates only to the size of the area, independently of whether it's shape is appropriate; and conversely, condition 1 relates only to the shape of the area, independently of its size. For the location of all other firms, and thus the order of magnitude of the market area of the selected firm, is assumed to be given, whereas under condition 4 the distance between

For consumers, on the contrary, the space necessary for continuance of an individual enterprise is a minimum only in overpopulated regions.

Table 4. SYSTEM OF EQUATIONS I

	Condition	Pertinent Equation Equation which fulfills condition	Number of Equations
Maximum number of Producers	1. Maximum profit (so far as 2-4 permit	$\dfrac{\partial S_q^m}{\partial x_q^m} = 0; \quad \dfrac{\partial S_q^m}{\partial y_q^m} = 0$	2n
	2. Total area used	$\Sigma\, G_1^m + G_2^m + \ldots G_q^m = G$	m
	3. No unusual profits	$\phi^m (D_q) = \chi^m (D_q)$	n
	4. Area as small as possible	$\dfrac{\partial \pi_q^m}{\partial G_q^m} = \dfrac{\partial k_q^m}{\partial G_q^m}$	n
	5. Boundaries Indifference lines	$a_q^m = \pi_q^m + r_q^m \sqrt{(x - x_q^m)^2 + (y - y_q^m)^2}$ $= \pi_{q-1}^m + r_{q-1}^m \sqrt{(x - x_{p-1}^m)^2 + (y - y_{q-1}^m)^2}$	N
		Sum:	4n + m + N

Finally, Condition 5: *At the boundaries of economic areas it must be a matter of indifference to which of two neighboring locations they belong. They are indifference lines.*[12,13]

---

locations is variable. Hence for a given shape of the area, condition 4 is supposed to maximize the number of producers; condition 1, on the contrary, maximizes the profit of a given number of producers. For example, condition 1 ensures that once a definite number of producers has been reached the shape of the area on a uniform plain will be that of a regular hexagon; whereas condition 4 ensures that this hexagon shall be as small as possible. Profits would disappear also if rectangles were made sufficiently small. Nevertheless, the number of producers would be maximized only for rectangles, not in general. It is therefore required in addition that the shape of the area which is being reduced be economically the best.

12. For any given point (x, y) on the edge of the industrial market area (factory price + freight rate × distance) must be the same whether one buys from P_q^m or P_{q-1}^m. For the geometric form of the border see pp. 165 f.

13. Everything can be obtained from these five equations: size and limits of market areas, the situation of production locations within them and within the entire area, and f. o. b. prices. The equations from which possible exchange rates could be determined (Condition: equilibrium in the balances of payments) have been omitted from the system in the interest of simplicity. Thus it presupposes equal currencies, not only in the ordinary sense but in the strict sense to be employed on subsequent pages, which excludes also the creation of money by banks. Otherwise the price levels of the various bank districts would appear as unknowns instead of the exchange rates, which would then have to be determined in such a way that the balances of payment would be in equilibrium. We shall return to this in Part III.

The system of equations under discussion could be expanded still further. It might be desired to find, say, which source of supplies is used, and how efficiently; or the prices of land parcels and who receives them.

b. THE SEPARATION OF LOCATIONS

The preceding five basic conditions must be fulfilled if the spatial order of the economy is to have meaning and permanence, but they do not guarantee that the best locations for production and consumption will coincide. On the contrary, these general equations of location show that they may be separate.[14] *The best location for producers is not necessarily also the best for consumers.*

With free competition the best location for industrial production is also the most favorable for consumers of industrial goods, to be sure, and if centers of agricultural production could be regarded exactly as are those of industrial production, all would necessarily be in complete harmony. But this cannot be done. Unlike a city, a village is not the *center* of a market area, but merely *part* of a production area. Agricultural production cannot be concentrated as industrial can; dispersion and small size of its ultimate units are of the essence. Hence the fundamental contradiction remains: The best location for the production and consumption of industrial goods

---

14. The location of any given town in its role as production center may me represented by the coordinates (x, y) and as a center for consumption by (ξ, η). The first system of equations determines x and y, and ξ and η can be determined by a very similar one that will not be derived here, however, in order not to linger over extraeconomic matters. If we were to expect that $x = \xi$ and $y = \eta$ the system would be overdetermined. Consequently the best location for a town as a production site differs from its location as a site of consumption. Just as little do their supply and market areas coincide, except at the level of the economics of a self-sufficient town where otherwise the balance of payments between town and country would not be in equilibrium.

Nevertheless, the two locations of consumption and production are interconnected. If, in the equation for D_q^m the relation between D and (x, y) is supposed to be determined not only by varying freight costs from P to consumers but also by production costs, which in turn depend upon the situation of P with respect to its sources of supply, that is to say other towns and the open country, the best locations for producer and consumer are combined from the standpoint of the industrial entrepreneur. As long as an approach to the best location lowers labor costs for the consumer of agricultural goods more than it raises his freight costs, there will be more demand for his products. He will therefore leave the location that would be best for production if the optimum location for a producer as consumer were left out of account, for the latter location.

Something similar will occur in the case of a town that is a center of consumption. It, too, will approach an industrial location. Thus we obtain two new best locations for towns as producers of industrial and consumers of agricultural commodities, in the determination of each of which the other location was taken into account. Now the two locations may be nearer to each other, but still they do not coincide. Something similar can be shown for farmers as producers of agricultural and consumers of industrial goods.

by themselves is a great city, whereas the best one for the production and consumption of products of the soil alone implies an even distribution. This is confirmed by the distribution of populations in earlier times and today. *Formerly,* when the consumption of agricultural commodities outweighed that of goods produced by artisans, there were many small towns.[15] *Later,* when food made up only a part of living costs, even for the workingman, there was a tendency toward concentration in large cities. *Today,* thanks to improvements in transportation, the complete separation of locations has become a reality. Farmers, of course, find it difficult to live away from their farms,[16] but industrial workers are often faced with the question whether to live where they are employed, or whether the cost of commuting will be balanced by the lower living costs and greater intangible advantages of the country such as light and air. That it frequently is regarded as so balanced is shown by many workers who daily pour into industrial towns from the country, no less than by the rural and semi-rural suburbs of the large cities.[17,18]

c. CONCLUSION

The significant thing in our derivation is not that we can heave a sigh of relief at having as many equations as there are unknowns.[19] It was to be expected that among locations, as elsewhere in the economy, equilibrium would be possible under certain conditions, but it is important to be clear about these conditions.[20] For the

---

15. At that time agriculture could still constitute the determining basic stratum.

16. Yet sometimes they do. Many ranch owners in Texas pass the week ends in their town houses, but stay on their ranches during the week.

17. The cheaper becomes the automobile, the farther beyond the real suburbs does the commuting area extend. Distances over forty miles are not unusual in the United States. According to a Gallup poll, only about three per cent of American workers live in the immediate neighborhood of their places of employment, whereas 45 per cent commute either in their own cars or in car pools.

18. Another important example is the separation between places of employment and vacation resorts or places for retirement. Many persons move from localities of lower wages and living costs to those where both are higher, but where the *absolute* amount of possible savings is also higher, in order to spend these savings later in their places of origin and thus considerably increase their real value. This is the attitude, for example, of many who emigrated to America. Conversely, regions of lower wages and prices are less attractive to those who wish to spend their savings later in more expensive localities.

19. In the case or regional boundaries the equations themselves rather than the single variables have been counted, as an exception, among the unknowns (see Table 3, point 5).

20. In my opinion, systems of general equations of equilibrium like this one have no other significance. I consider it utopian to assume that they can be gradually

conditions of this, as of other economic equilibria, must first be validated, or at least respected, by the legal framework or by economic policy.[21] They are the basic principles of all governmental intervention where the restoration of equilibrium is concerned; and they form the framework within which measures for obtaining other public objectives must be kept if the entire economy is not to be endangered or incessantly regulated. Next in importance, after establishing that an equilibrium exists, is to show how it looks. The derivation of the equations [22] shows likewise which levers can be easily regulated if the need should arise.

As a matter of fact, most phenomena fall between these general economic principles of location theory and the empirical methods of the theory of the individual firm, which we can neither comprehend nor control by general principles or individual calculations. If only we had a method that combined the generality of equations with the clarity of geometrical figures! Such a combination would inevitably have weaknesses, of course, since in a strict sense it is impossible. But does not the path of science include many precarious emergency bridges over which we have all been willing to pass provided they would help us forward on our road? And so I hope that the theory of economic regions to be developed in the following pages will turn out to be a path into a rich but almost unknown country.

---

improved, and employed to solve practical problems more precisely than with our present coarse methods. After all, the physicist does not derive the law of freely falling bodies from a universal formula, nor the physician his remedy from a general formula for treatment. Still, see the gallant attempt of W. W. Leontief, " Interrelations of Prices, Output, Savings, and Investment. A Study in Empirical Application of the Economic Theory of General Interdependence," *Review of Economic Statistics,* XXIX (1937) , 109 ff., and later publications; and, more recently, that of H. Peter in *Finanzarchiv* und *Archiv für mathematische Wirtschaftsforschung,* 1941.

21. This is least true for condition 1, the fulfillment of which is ensured by the individual's self-interest.

22. These are the independent variables that affect equilibrium without its reacting upon them: in our case, for example, the size of an area, the direction of demand, the technique of production, and the level of freight costs.

PART TWO.   ECONOMIC REGIONS[1]

---

[1] The basic ideas for the following discussion have already been developed in my probationary lecture of 1936 before the Faculty of Law and Political Economy at the University of Bonn (" Wirtschaftsgebiete als Grundlage des internationalen Handels "), and also in my paper read before the Econometric Society at its 1937 meeting in Atlantic City (" The Nature of Economic Regions "). The English lecture was published in the *Southern Economic Journal*, V (1938), 71 ff.

THE THEORY of international trade has proceeded until now on the assumption that states are the most important, if not the only, economic units. It was argued, for example, that if Germany had to pay reparations to France the German price level would have to fall and that of France would have to rise in order to make the transfer possible. But no doubt it might just as well have been said that the price level between 10 and 20 degrees East longitude and 45 and 50 degrees North latitude would have to fall, and that between the Meridian of Greenwich and 10 degrees East longitude and 40 and 50 degrees North latitude would have to rise. In other words, it is highly improbable that the line dividing falling and rising prices coincides exactly with political boundaries. Even though it could be shown statistically that the German price index was falling, this would prove neither that prices had fallen everywhere in Germany nor that they had fallen only in Germany.[2] For instance, it is very unlikely that the coal mines in the then Polish Upper-Silesia would have been able to maintain their prices if German mines a few miles away had had to lower theirs. The fact that Upper Silesia constituted an economic unit would seem to be more important in many respects than the fact that it was politically separated from Germany. On the other hand, suppose large subsidy payments to flow from western Germany toward the east. In such a case the economic consequences would resemble those of war indemnities to a hair. Prices would necessarily fall west of the Elbe and rise east of it. Two economic regions would arise in the same country.

Of course no one any longer thinks of denying that political boundaries are also economic boundaries.[3] The preceding examples are meant to show only that there are economic regions within political boundaries and others again that extend beyond them.

This has not remained unnoticed, and a few writers on international trade, Ohlin above all, have endeavored to take it into account. Their investigations belong therefore in the small group

---

2. It is probable, rather, that price changes, which according to the old theory affect a particular country, really extend only to parts of it, but extend to neighboring countries as well. In the case of small or long and narrow countries like Canada and Chile this is immediately obvious, but it holds also for those whose shape is better rounded, as we shall see later (pp. 302 ff.).

3. To what degree they are so will become still clearer in the course of our inquiry. But the differences lie elsewhere, and are more important than the old cylinder-piston theory of the price level assumed.

of fundamental inquiries into economic regions.[4] Actually they altered little more than words; they began to speak of interregional, in addition to international, trade; and what had held for states now held also for regions. But the structure of these economic regions was not examined. To give but one example: The fallacious idea of a general price level was merely split into fallacious ideas of regional price levels. Yet even cursory examination of the nature of such a region would have shown that the price surface was much more like a hilly country than a calm lake. Certainly all that is included in an economic region must have something or other in common. But it would be premature, though it is a mistake that suggests itself in consciously logical procedures, to conclude from this that since prices are the central phenomena in all exchange processes, the best definition of an economic region would be a region throughout which prices are approximately the same. This definition is unsuitable, however, because there are no such regions; and even if there were they would be without significance and thus not worth our attention. In order not to fall into a similar error we shall proceed in the opposite direction and try to discover whether and how, under rational assumptions, an economic boundary can be expected to arise. Instead of starting from a preconceived idea we shall look first for actual differences, and not until then for their logical common denominator.

4. These inquiries have many different origins. Writers on location theory have provided a few of them (besides Thünen, Launhardt in particular, and recently H. Ritschl in his theory of the economic regions [*Kreise*], " Reine und historische Dynamik des Standortes der Erzeugungszweige," *Schmollers Jahrbuch*, 1927). The history of economics has contributed others; G. von Schmoller's economic stages— village, town, territorial, and national economy, " Das Merkantilsystem in seiner historischen Bedeutung," *Schmollers Jahrbuch*, 1884: also K. Bücher's home, town, and national economy, *Die Entstehung der Volkswirtschaft* (1st ed., 1893).

Among the works on economic geography that of W. Christaller is especially to be recommended, *Die zentralen Orte in Süddeutschland* (Jena, 1933); and " Raumtheorie und Raumordnung," *Archiv für Wirtschaftsplanung*, I (1941).

The American economists N. S. B. Gras (for example, " The Rise of the Metropolitan Community," in *The Urban Community* [Chicago, 1926], edited by E. W. Burgess), and R. D. McKenzie (*The Metropolitan Community* [1933]), among others, have written on the economics of large cities. Factual inquiries are much more numerous, but all suffer from a lack of the theoretical background. Ohlin's book was mentioned above because it has much in common with the writer's volume, at least in the goal set though not in the solution (C. Brinkmann to the contrary, in *Finanzarchiv*, 1940, pp. 210 ff.). It, too, endeavors to combine the theories of location, economic regions, and international trade. Yet in many respects, including its concise presentation, Alfred Weber's neglected essay on this subject seems to me more successful (" Die Standortlehre und die Handelspolitik," *Archiv für Sozialwissenschaft*, XXXII [1911], 667–688.

A. Economic Regions under Simple Conditions

Chapter 9. The Market Area

Among all the factors that can create an economic region we shall select the economic. We shall consider market areas that are not the result of any kind of natural or political inequalities but arise through the interplay of purely economic forces, some working toward concentration and other toward dispersion. In the first group are the advantages of specialization and of large-scale production; in the second, those of shipping costs and of diversified production.[1]

In the following derivation we start from radical assumptions in order that no spatial differences may lie concealed in what we assume: that economic raw materials are evenly and adequately distributed over a wide plain. Our area shall be homogeneous in every other respect as well, and contain nothing but self-sufficient farms that are regularly distributed. How can this starting point lead to spatial differences?

Let us select any one of these farms, and ascribe to its owner the wish to produce manufactured goods over and above his own needs. Will he be able to sell them? The savings due to mass production will favor his enterprise, whereas transportation costs will hamper it. How large will his market eventually be? Suppose his neighbors are of the same stamp and live similarly, so that the demand curve for one is typical of all. Let d, in Figure 20, be such an individual demand curve for beer. If OP is the price at the brewery, which is at P, those living at P will buy PQ bottles of beer.

---

1. As the advantages and disadvantages of specialization may be reckoned among the advantages of mass production, we contrast only these latter with shipping costs.

Farther away the price will naturally be higher by the amount of the freight, and the demand consequently smaller. Still farther away, at *F*, where Freight costs amount to *PF*, no beer at all can be sold. Thus *PF* will be the extreme sales radius [2] for beer, and total sales in this district will be equal to the volume of the cone that would result from rotating the triangle *PQF* on *PQ* as an axis (Fig. 21).

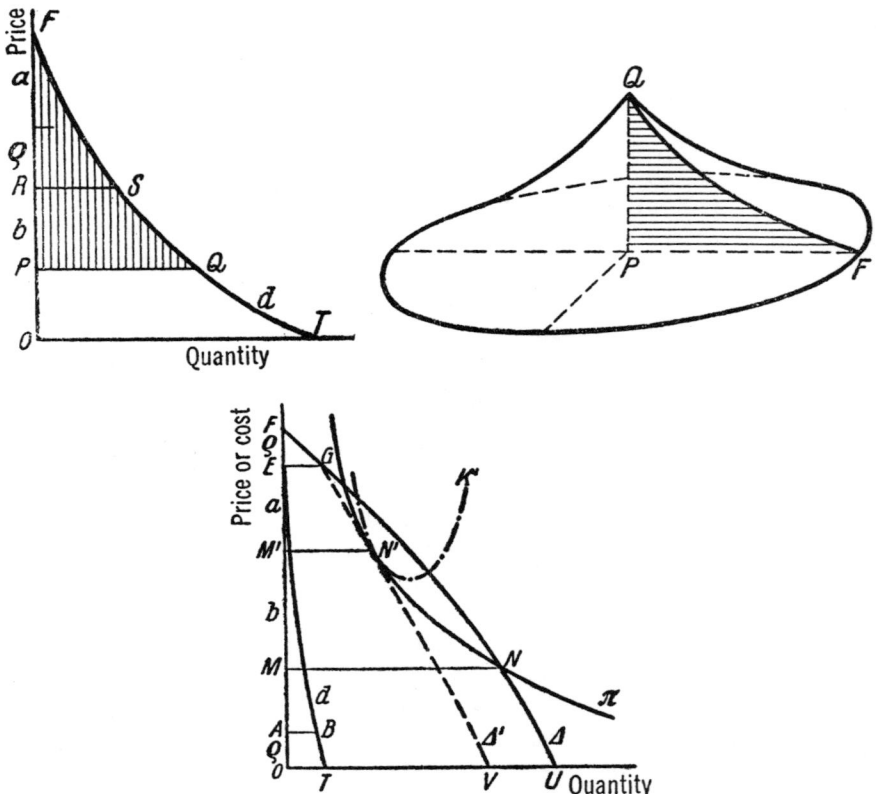

Fig. 20–22. Derivation of the demand cone (Fig. 21) and the market area from the demand curve for the product as function of distance (Fig. 20) and the cost curves (Fig. 22)

Its volume must still be multiplied by a constant that is given by the population density. The result is the total demand, *D*, at the brewery price *OP*.

2. Freight costs expressed in marks, not in kilometers. To reduce to kilometers it is necessary only to divide the value for *PF* by the freight rate per kilometer.

The Market Area

Expressed algebraically,

$$D = b \times \pi \int_0^R f(p+t) \times t \times dt.$$

where D = total demand as a function of f. o. b. price p;

b = twice the population of a square in which it costs 1 mark to ship 1 unit along one side;

$\pi = 3.14 \cdots$;

$d = f(p+t)$, individual demand as a function of price at the place of consumption;

p = price at the brewery;

t = shipping costs per unit from brewery to consumer;

R = greatest possible shipping cost (PF in Fig. 20).

The derivation is simple. The volume of a solid of revolution is equal to the area of the generating surface times the path of its center of gravity. Let the surface PQF in Figure 20 have the area F, and let the ordinate of its center of gravity (for P as the origin) be y_0. The center of gravity therefore revolves along the path $2\pi y_0$, and the area of the generating surface $2\pi y_0 \times F$, or

$$2\pi \int_0^R f(p+t) \times t \times dt.$$

(since according to the formula for the center of gravity

$$y_0 F = \int_0^R f(p+t) \times t \times dt).$$

Taking into account, finally, that the population density is $\dfrac{b}{2}$ we obtain the formula given above for D as a function of the brewery price p.[3]

Actually the brewery price is not yet given, however, as we have assumed thus far, but depends on the total demand. Thus the volume of the demand cone must be calculated for various arbitrary

---

3. It had already been given, as I discovered in the meantime, though in somewhat different form, by W. Launhardt (*Mathematische Begründung der Volkswirtschaftslehre* [Leipzig, 1885], p. 152) as well as by E. Schneider, following Launhardt (" Bemerkungen zu einer Theorie der Raumwirtschaft," *Econometrica*, 1935, pp. 79–105; E. M. Hoover (" Spatial Price Discrimination," *The Review of Economic Studies*, June, 1937, pp. 182–191); and in a wholly general form by G. Tintner (" Die Nachfrage im Monopolgebiet," *Zeitschrift für Nationalökonomie*, 1935, pp. 536–539).

brewery prices. The result can be drawn as a new curve, Δ in Figure 22, which gives total demand as a function of brewery price. In the same system of coordinates we draw also a so-called planning curve π, which gives the smallest average cost at which any given amount can be produced.[4] Only if the supply curve π, and the demand curve Δ, intersect can our farmer open a brewery. If they do not, beer cannot become a marketable product, because shipping costs are too high or the advantages of large-scale production too small. Every farmer will then have to brew his own beer as best he can. If the curves intersect at N, MN will be the total amount of beer that our farmer can sell. The longest market radius, or shipping distance, for beer in this case will be equal to the radius of the base of the demand cone with a volume $2MN \div B$, or simply to MF. And, like beer, every economic commodity has its own maximum shipping distance, beyond which it cannot be sold.[5,6]

---

4. This minimum can be reached only by a plant that has been built especially for this capacity. Its average cost curve touches the planning curve once, but otherwise runs to the right of it. Consequently the low point of the average cost curve for an individual plant lies to the right, below the point of tangency with π. However, a plant does not produce more cheaply than any smaller or larger one the amount that corresponds to its minimum average cost point, but only the amount that corresponds to its point of tangency. This point represents the capacity for which it was built. For since the point of minimum average costs already lies above the planning curve, another and larger plant would evidently be more advantageous. This is easily seen from the average cost curve, K' in Figure 22 for the capacity $M'N'$. The planning curve represents geometrically the envelope of the average cost curves for plants of various sizes. See E. Schneider, "Statische Kostengesetze," *Nationaløkonomisk Tidsskrift*, LXX (1932), Fig. 9, p. 423; J. Viner, "Cost Curves and Supply Curves," *Zeitschrift für Nationalökonomie*, 1930.

5. Weber (*Über den Standort der Industrien*, Pt. I [Tübingen, 1909], pp. 240 ff. and particularly p. 244; translated by C. J. Friedrich as *Alfred Weber's Theory of the Location of Industries* [University of Chicago Press, 1928]) treats this problem in essentially the same way, as an "agglomeration of originally evenly distributed small scale producers." The difference is, first, that this deduction is not correct, because it regards demand as independent of local price. Secondly, his (marginal) method is different, and less suited to the Chamberlin process. And thirdly, he does not employ this process. A further difference is didactic in nature: He starts with an unequal distribution of natural resources and introduces agglomeration later, whereas we proceed in the opposite direction.

6. As soon as there are several marketable goods their price relationships are different at different points and so are their receipt relationships as soon as their production sites agglomerate, and thus strictly speaking their demand curves are different, too. So, for example, the demand curve for beer differs for those near the brewery and for those at a distance. But however significant this may be, we must neglect it for the moment. See p. 143, note 10.

Chapter 10. The Network of Markets

a. CONTINUOUS DISTRIBUTION OF POPULATION

§1. SIZE OF REGION

The deduction so far would be relevant if economic regions were circular in form. But they are not. Even if our district were full of breweries lying so closely together that their sales areas touched, one or another farmer would still be tempted to start a brewery for himself. And he could do so. First, because all the corners between the circles would not yet have been fully turned to account; and second, because the size of the individual brewery could be reduced from MN, in Figure 22, to $M'N'$ without making the plant unprofitable.[1]

The corners can be utilized by pressing the circles together until a honeycomb results. As a consequence of this diminution in regional size the total demand curve Δ will be shifted downward.[2]

---

1. This procedure has become familiar for product differentiation through the work of E. H. Chamberlin (*The Theory of Monopolistic Competition* [Cambridge, Mass., 1933; 5th ed., 1938]) and of Joan Robinson (*The Economics of Imperfect Competition* [London, 1933]), but it holds just as well for differences in location. For those unfamiliar with the literature on the subject, Chamberlin's fundamental ideas will be briefly sketched: (1) With product differentiation (which here includes differences in the location of the seller) the demand curve for the individual seller is not horizontal, as with homogeneous products, but slopes downward. If, for instance, a seller raises his price, not all his customers will desert him. To some of them his product will offer advantages, such as convenience of location, that are worth even the higher price. (2) As long as the demand curve intersects the cost curve, surplus profits that attract competitors are possible. These will turn out differentiated products or, which is of special interest in the present context, will choose the location of their establishments in such a way that they are particularly convenient for some of the buyers. As a consequence of this loss of purchasers, the demand curves of the earlier enterprises will shift to the left until they are tangent to the cost curve and all surplus profits disappear. The tendency to the maximization of independent enterprises that underlies the process just described now reaches its limits. Small surplus profits may still remain, however, if an area is larger than necessary for n producers, but not large enough for $n + 1$. If $n = 1$, there is a monopoly which, of course, is restricted by latent competition that may become actual if the monopoly is exploited to the full. Then comes a struggle between the earlier and the later firms, one of which must finally succumb since there is not room for both.

2. With increasing curtailment in the size of a region, the point of rotation, G,

But the hexagon can be made even smaller, until the total demand curve Δ' still just touches the supply curve π. Then the market is full. If still another brewery were to be established, the market area would not be large enough for all, and the two curves would no longer be even tangent. If the longest possible sales radius R corresponds to the total sales MN, the shortest possible radius ρ [3] would correspond with the total sales $M'N'$; ρ also is characteristically different for different goods.[4] Figure 23 shows the transition for the same commodity from the largest to the smallest possible sales area.[5]

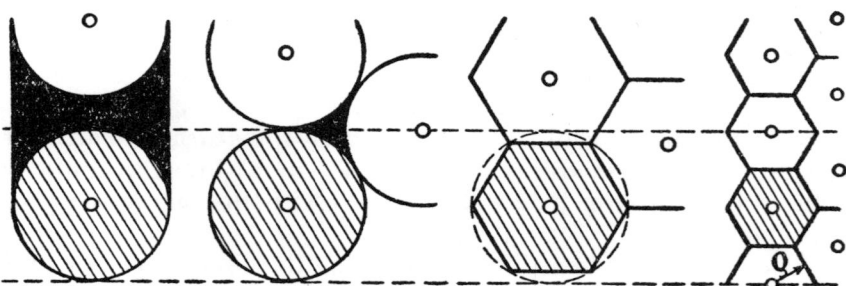

Fig. 23. Development of market areas from the large circle to the final small hexagon

§2. Shape of Region

Geometrically speaking there are two other possibilities for utilizing the corners between market circles: triangular or square economic regions can be imagined. But the hexagon has the advantage of being nearest to the ideal circular form. Consequently among all three possibilities the demand per unit of area is greatest with the hexagon.

---

moves upward on Δ. It is determined by FE, which is equal to the radius of the region at the time, expressed as freight costs. V, the lower end-point of the shifted demand curve, Δ', is determined by the fact that OV must equal the volume of a cone developed by rotating the surface $OABT$ about OT as an axis. OA again is equal to the radius of the region.

3. ρ represents the radius of the inscribed circle.

4. This we know from daily experience. Suppose one is to have a cake baked near home. Nobody would carry the heavy pan of batter across the whole town, even to the best baker. But no one would mind a long trip to leave a watch for repair with a skillful watchmaker, and one would go even outside the town to a medical specialist.

5. Diminution of a region is disadvantageous for the established entrepreneur, because his profits disappear; it is welcome to the newcomer because then there are more possibilities of making himself independent; and it is often advantageous for the consumer because although the price at the plant usually rises, the average freight costs fall.

Table 5. DEMAND AS A FUNCTION OF REGIONAL SHAPE

Shape of Market Region		Size of Demand[1]		
		Total	Per unit of area	
			of entire region	of region utilized
Large circle[2]		R²H 1.04720[4])	0.302 H	0.333 H
Small circle[2]	of equal area	r²H (2.598 − $\frac{r}{R}$1.575)	0.907 H − 0.550 H_R^r [3])	H − 0.606 H_R^r [4])
Hexagon		r²H (2.598 − $\frac{r}{R}$1.580)	H − 0.608 H_R^r [4])	H − 0.608 H_R^r
Square		r²H (2.598 − $\frac{r}{R}$1.602)	H − 0.617 H_R^r	H − 0.617 H_R^r
Triangle		r²H (2.598 − $\frac{r}{R}$1.690)	H − 0.651 H_R^r	H − 0.651 H_R^r

1. R = radius of base of original cone. (Largest possible shipping costs, PF in Fig. 20.)
   r = radius of the circle circumscribed about the hexagonal area of base removed (r < R).
   H = height of demand cone. (Individual demand at site of factory, PQ in Fig. 20. For the sake of simplicity it is assumed that the population density b/2 is 1.)
2. Large circle, radius R; small circle, radius 0.909r.
3. It is easily seen that this quantity is smaller than that corresponding to the hexagon if r is given the limiting values of O and R.
4. The highest value in the column concerned.

For the case of a linear demand curve[6] a more rigorous proof can be adduced. Let the ruling *QF* of the cone in Figure 21 be a straight line, and let the height *PQ* be equal to *H* and the radius of the base *PF* be equal to *R*. If the cone is cut by a plane parallel

6. This will be assumed more frequently, for it is not only an especially convenient assumption but an especially reasonable one. If *OF*, as in Figure 20, is the price at which nothing more will be sold, and *OT* the amounts that would be consumed if the good were free, then *OF* and a line parallel to it through *T*, and *OT* and a parallel line to it through *F*, will in almost all cases delimit the area in which the demand curve must lie. We now choose our scale in such a way that *OF* is equal to *OT*, so that these lines and their two parallels form a square. If we draw in this square all conceivable forms of demand curves and the diagonal *FT*, the resulting triangles and all portions of the possible demand curves lying within them will be congruent and symmetrical in resepct to *FT*. The sum of the deviations from *FT* is zero. The straight line *FT* is the average value of every possible form of demand curve. In all cases where no details are known about the actual shape of the demand, the linear form is the only well-founded assumption.

to the axis of rotation at the distance ρ, the volume [7] of the portion of cone cut off will be

$$V = \frac{H}{3}\left(R^2 \arccos \frac{\rho}{R} - 2\rho\sqrt{R^2-\rho^2} + 2.302632 \frac{\rho^3}{R} \log \frac{R+\sqrt{R^2-\rho^2}}{R}\right)$$

We now cut the demand cone through planes parallel to the axis in such a way that an equilateral triangle, a square, or a hexagon of equal area appears as a base. The volumes of the portions of cone remaining above are then proportional to the total demand for the market areas concerned. These volumes are calculated by the formula given above, and Table 5 shows the result. For comparison the cone is cut also by a vertical cylinder the base of which has the same area as the figures just edscribed.

The result is that the demand of the market area as a whole is greatest when this area is not curtailed at all. The demand of the curtailed sales area is greatest when it is circular in form. But per unit of area of the market region, the demand of the small circle, not that of the large circle, is greatest because in the latter case the average for the area is reduced by the small demand near the limits for shipment. The average demand in the small circle is obviously greater than in any polygon of equal area. But because circles leave empty corners, the demand per unit of the entire area in the case of the hexagon exceeds not only that of a square and a triangle, but even that of a circle. In other words, among all the possibilities of realizing the same total demand, the most land is required with a triangle, and the least with a regular hexagon. *The honeycomb is therefore the most advantageous shape for economic regions.*[8] The advantage benefits consumers as a whole,[9] whereas for the

---

7. Professor C. H. Sisam, of Colorado Springs, was so kind as to derive this formula for me. Arc cos is to be taken as an arc, not as an angle.

8. The regular hexagon is the most advantageous shape for a market area just as it is for the true honeycomb, but for not quite the same reasons. With the true honeycomb the ratio of perimeter to area must be especially favorable; with the market, the ratio of cone to area. In both cases the circular form would be best were it not for the empty corners. The result of these is that in one case the wax, in the other the demand, is not utilized to the full. Among all the possibilities of utilizing the corners, the hexagon retains most of the advantages of the circle. The size of the hexagon depends, of course, upon totally different factors.

9. So far we have proved only that the hexagon is superior to other regional shapes; nothing has been said about the best size of the hexagon. It remains an open question whether the Chamberlin process (incomplete utilization of the capacity of a region with a concomitant rise in price because of an increased number of competitors) is of advantage to consumers. In the proof given above, the producer's price could be regarded as practically constant in so far as the market areas differ only in form, not

individual producer the uncurtailed large circle would be most favorable. But because free competition results in the elimination of undeserved profits, it is a matter of indifference to the entrepreneur *how* his region is cut down. Yet the honeycomb shape contributes to the advantage of producers as a whole also, since it makes possible the largest number of independent enterprises.

It is easy to see from the table how great is the advantage of the hexagon. As compared with the other polygons, the advantage varies with r; it is greatest when $r = R$, where as it disappears entirely for $r = 0$. As compared with the small circle, it is almost independent of r. In the maximum case the demand in a hexagon is 2.4 per cent greater than in a square of equal size; always about 10 per cent greater than in a circle, if the empty corners are included; and at a maximum 12 per cent greater than in an equilateral triangle of the same area. The superiority of the hexagon over the square is least, and of no practical importance in many instances, its advantage being greatest in comparison with the triangle and the circle—at least when the individual demand curve is a straight line.

For curves of other form the advantage of the hexagon may be greater or less, but it changes to a disadvantage only in a few of those unusual cases in which demand increases with rising price. Compared with a linear demand, the advantage of the hexagon becomes greater, the more elastic the demand at the boundaries of the region, and smaller the more inelastic is this demand.[10] In the

---

in size. In judging the *reduction* of sales areas it is important to know, however, whether the average saving in freight will be greater than the increase in costs of production; that is, whether b, in Figs. 20, 22, and 41, will be exceeded by a. This need not always be the case. An entirely similar problem is posed in governmental organization. Not every simplifying of administration makes matters easier for the governed as well. If it is proposed, for example, to merge small administrative districts into larger ones, any possible economies in government must be weighed against traveling expenses for the citizens.

It is a somewhat different question whether these differences in expenditure are large enough to be statistically shown; that is to say, whether it can be decided from differences in nominal costs of the order of magnitude here considered, in which case the real costs will be greater. An analogous situation will be discussed in more detail below on pp. 327 f. in connection with free trade, and on pp. 490 ff. in connection with the cost of living. See also H. Schmidt, *Die wirtschaftliche Mengenteilung des nationalen Bedarfes eines Erzeugnisses* (Berlin, 1942).

10. In comparing the hexagon with the square, for instance, the boundary region is to be reckoned from the inscribed circle of the hexagon to the circumscribed circle of the square. The elasticity within the inscribed circle is less important for the comparison, and the elasticity outside the circumscribed circle is of no consequence at all.

first case, for example, the demand will fall rapidly with the distance from the production site, a fall that becomes increasingly greater as larger portions of the market area such as the corners of triangles lie relatively far from the center.

The size and shape of the entire region also exert an influence on the favorability of the honeycomb shape. Thus if the whole region is small in relation to the area of the individual market, or very irregular, wide departures from the shape that imply an enlargement of the region may become necessary if the whole region is to be fully utilized.

In summing up it may be said that the regular hexagon becomes more favorable as a regional shape the larger and more rounded-off the whole area, the more elastic the demand at the boundaries, and the more closely the necessary shipping distance approaches the possible one.[11]

b. DISCONTINUOUS DISTRIBUTION OF POPULATION

For every commodity the proposition holds good, that a market area with the form of a regular hexagon and an inscribed circle of radius ρ that is specific for this commodity, is necessary and sufficient to make its production possible. On the one hand, ρ depends upon the cost curve, which for the time being is assumed to be given; and on the other hand, upon the demand. This, again, can be traced back to two factors: The individual demand curve, whose influence we have so far been examining; and the consumers, whom we have for the sake of simplicity assumed to be equally and continuously distributed over our area. If this were so, ρ could have any value. But in reality the number of possible values of ρ is limited, because the population may be equally but not continuously distributed. Whatever the smallest settlements may be—single

---

11. I have found the hexagonal shape discussed in two places in the literature, though without adequate proof. First, by W. Launhardt (*Mathematische Begründung der Volkswirtschaftslehre* [Leipzig, 1885], p. 181), who assumed it only by way of example; and recently in the admirable book by W. Christaller (*Die zentralen Orte in Süddeutschland* [Jena, 1933]), who at least advanced a general though inadequate proof. According to Christaller the hexagonal arrangement of central sites has the advantage " that they are neither too few nor too many, and also that no districts are left without regular supply " (*ibid.*, p. 69). H. Haufe (*Die geographische Struktur des deutschen Eisenbahnverkehrs* [Langensalza, 1931], pp. 14 f.) finds hexagonal networks of transport lines most favorable for the uniform spherical surface of the earth because with them, though not of course with the triangles into which they necessarily divide, the relation of these lines to the regions they serve is advantageous; and because hexagons, like triangles but unlike squares, can cover the earth without a remainder.

Network of Markets

farms, hamlets, or villages [12]—they are separated from one another by certain distances that may be neglected only when they are small in relation to the market area. With most commodities, however, the situation and size of the original settlements exerts a considerable influence on the situation and size of the market area. This influence we shall now proceed to examine.

Let a be the distance between the smallest settlements A_1, A_2, and so on, which we have assumed to be farms. Again the most suitable shape of their area is that of the regular hexagon. Consequently their centers, where the buildings are set, lie at distances of a kilometers on straight lines that cross at an angle of 60° or 120°, not at right angles as on a square farm—a distribution that may be described as honeycomb scattering.[13]

---

12. For farmers as producers the advantages, for farmers as consumers the disadvantages, of scattered settlements may preponderate. Scattering shortens the distance from farm buildings to fields except with mixed cropping, but lengthens the distance from the center of the village and generally, also, from the town to the farm buildings or its fields. This affects the farmer in uncultivated country, not only as pure consumer but also as producer, in so far as he employs such outside aids to production as the help of neighbors, co-operatively owned machines, water power, electricity, coal, or artificial fertilizers, and in so far as he sells his produce. This variation in distance, the net effect of which depends upon circumstances, becomes more important: (1) *the greater it is*, as in the case of districts that are especially large because of limited or sporadic productivity in regions that are mountainous, wooded, or rich in lakes; or because wide areas are used, as on ranches in Texas; (2) *the heavier the road traffic is*, whether because of the size of loads, for example, with extensive fertilization or naturally high yields, or because the number of trips is larger (as with cattle, schools, churches, government offices, daily requirements—in so far as these cannot be cheaply produced in small quantities, as with goods needing a large market area; (3) *the higher the costs per mile* and the more they differ for villages as against more dispersed settlements. These differences, which were formerly more important than they are today, favored a scattering of the population if distances could be shortened at all thereby; and without question they are higher in areas whose settlements are widely scattered because roads are worse or more expensive and transportation on a small scale more costly despite the motor truck.

Thus the type of settlement that is economically most advantageous varies with circumstances; only the intermediate form, a sprawling village, generally combines the disadvantages of both kinds. Nor are the effects of recent developments by any means unequivocal; inventions like the telephone and the radio encourage scattered settlements, whereas the increasing interlacing of markets favors the establishment of villages. The issue is often decided by extra-economic considerations. In scattered settlements the greater vulnerability to attack by nature and by man must be taken into account, but above all the high price that is paid for greater freedom. Isolation does not suit most people and seclusion may easily destroy community life, for culture flourishes better in the stimulating life of not too large towns. See p. 28, note 31, and W. Christaller, *Die ländliche Siedlungsweise im deutschen Reich* (Stuttgart, 1937).

13. In Latin it is called *quincunx*, and in English *lattice*. The distribution is that

Let b be the distance between the small market towns B_1, B_2, and so on, as we shall call the smallest places where industrial goods are produced for sale. b corresponds to the diameter of the inscribed circle 2ρ of the market area, except that ρ is expressed in freight costs and b in kilometers or miles.

Let nV be the necessary shipping distance; that is, the greatest distance at which a commodity must be sold to make its production worth while. But this does not mean that all farms lying within this circumference will be supplied by the market town concerned, except where nV equals the radius of the inscribed circle. Nor can nV be simply identified with the radius r of the circumscribed circle of the hexagon, for often there are no settlements at all along the boundary, or at least in its corners. Thus with a discontinuous population, nV is independent of r and of ρ or $b/2$, respectively.

§1. Relative Positions of Settlements

We shall now examine the ten smallest market areas with respect to size and location. The smallest possible value for the necessary shipping distance is obviously the distance between the farms as long as we assume that production takes place on one of these, A_1 (settlement site), and not in a building erected between them for this purpose. The smallest possible value for the number of settlements supplied, however, including A_1 itself, is not 7, but 3. For it is conceivable that there is a product for which A_1, which develops into a market town B_1, does not need the entire demand of the 6 neighboring farms in order to recover its costs. It might share instead with the neighboring market towns B_2 and B_3 in supplying the needs of farm A_2, and similarly supply only one third of the needs of each of the farms A_3 to A_7 (Fig. 24). When these shares are added, market area 1 contains [the equivalent of] three fully supplied settlements. Its area, F, is $a^2 \cdot 3\sqrt{3} \div 2$, and the distance between market towns is $a\sqrt{3}$.

For the next larger, area 2, nV is still equal to a, but now the demands of neighboring farms are so shared among adjacent competitors that B_1 receives the entire demand of three neighboring farms, which together with its own makes four (Fig. 25). From this it follows that area 2 must be oriented differently from area 1. Its borders are not simply parallel to those of the latter. Consequently b also is now larger, namely $a\sqrt{4}$, though nV is still equal to a.

---

of the crossing-points of strips in a fence where one series is inclined to the left at an angle of 60° and the other is nailed over it at a similar angle toward the right.

Network of Markets

There remains yet a third area for which nV is equal to a, though it is the sole supplier of seven farms. Area 3 offers an example of a boundary line that runs through open fields without

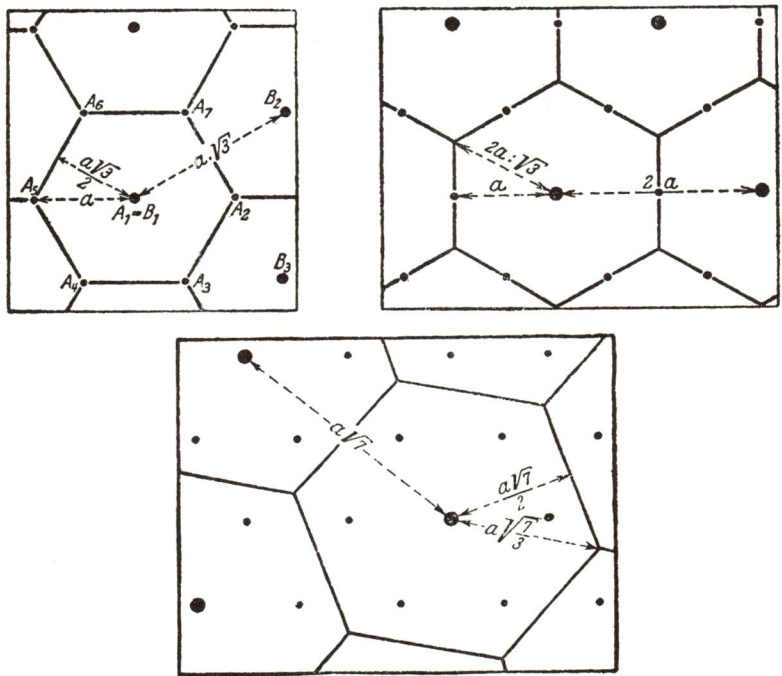

Figs. 24–26. The three smallest market areas

touching any settlement (Fig. 26). Though such a boundary has, therefore, no immediate economic significance, the survey is facilitated if we know how it runs. This border, again, is not parallel to the boundaries of the first two areas.

The three smallest market areas show three typical orientations at the same time (Fig. 27). Assuming that one of the straight lines on which the farms follow each other at distance a, is horizontal in the figure, the first orientation is such that the hexagon rests on one side (e. g., areas 1 and 5). In the second orientation it stands on one corner (e. g., areas 2, 4, 7, and 10)). In the third, it is inclined to a varying degree (e. g., areas 3, 6, 8, and 9).

Table 6 contains the most important measurements for to 10 smallest possible market areas. From it is derived an extremely simple relation between n, the number of settlements supplied, and b, the distance between the market towns that supply them. It is

$$b = a\sqrt{n}$$

Expressed in words: *The distance between two enterprises of the same kind is equal to the distance between the settlements supplied times the square root of their number.* Furthermore, the number of whole settlements included within a market area increases according to a definite law, as can be seen from Table 7.[13a] Finally, the size of a market area can be very simply calculated. It is always equal to $a^2 n \sqrt{3} \div 2$.

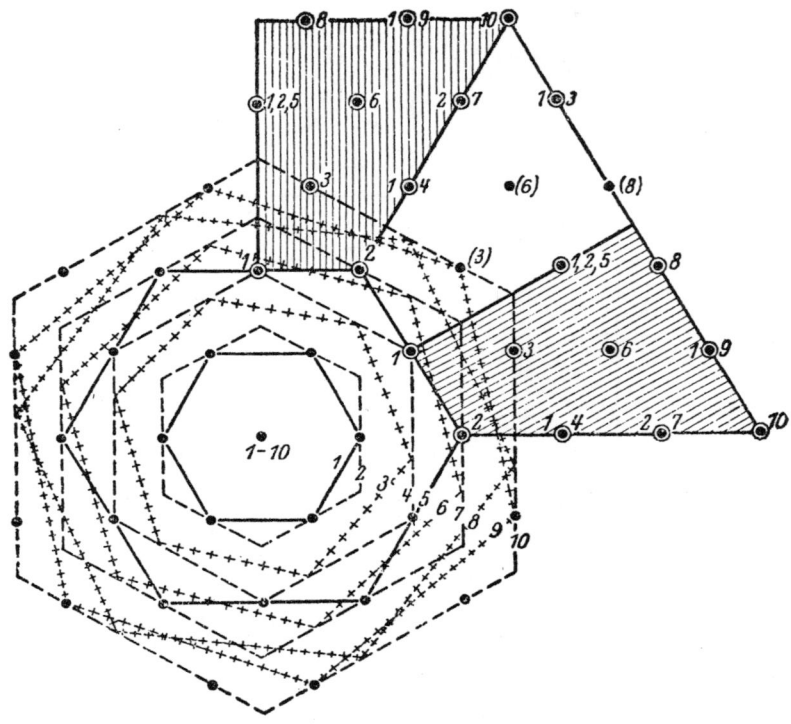

Fig. 27. The 10 smallest economic areas. The sectors containing many towns are hatched. Alternative regional centers are in parentheses. Simple points represent original settlements. Those enclosed in circles are centers of market areas of sizes indicated by the figures.

13a. August Lösch did not give the actual formula for this law by means of which n could be calculated for any desired market area. From inspection of Table 7, Professor Werner Känzig of the Department of Physics, University of Illinois, has kindly supplied the following general method of finding the number of settlements corresponding to the hth area. The general formula used by Lösch has the form $(k\sqrt{3})^2 + l^2 = n$, where n is the number of settlements. Let the number of the area,

Table 6. THE TEN SMALLEST POSSIBLE MARKET AREAS

Area No.	n	b	nV
1	3	$a\sqrt{3}$	a
2	4	$a\sqrt{4}$	a
3	7	$a\sqrt{7}$	a
4	9	$a\sqrt{9}$	$a\sqrt{3}$
5	12	$a\sqrt{12}$	$2a$
6	13	$a\sqrt{13}$	$a\sqrt{3}$
7	16	$a\sqrt{16}$	$2a$
8	19	$a\sqrt{19}$	$2a$
9	21	$a\sqrt{21}$	$a\sqrt{7}$
10	25	$a\sqrt{25}$	$a\sqrt{7}$

n = number of settlements completely supplied, including the point of supply. Those partly supplied are reckoned in terms of the equivalent number of fully supplied settlements.

b = distance between points of supply = distance between centers of areas = diameter of inscribed circle.

nV = necessary shipping distance = distance of seller from farthest still necessary customer.

a = distance separating original settlements.

Table 7. CALCULATION OF n

Area No.	n	Area No.	n
1	$(1 \cdot \sqrt{3})^2 + 0^2 = 3$	3	$(1\frac{1}{2}\sqrt{3})^2 + (\frac{1}{2})^2 = 7$
2	$(1 \cdot \sqrt{3})^2 + 1^2 = 4$	4	$(1\frac{1}{2}\sqrt{3})^2 + (1\frac{1}{2})^2 = 9$
5	$(2 \cdot \sqrt{3})^2 + 0^2 = 12$	8	$(2\frac{1}{2}\sqrt{3})^2 + (\frac{1}{2})^2 = 19$
6	$(2 \cdot \sqrt{3})^2 + 1^2 = 13$	9	$(2\frac{1}{2}\sqrt{3})^2 + (1\frac{1}{2})^2 = 21$
7	$(2 \cdot \sqrt{3})^2 + 2^2 = 16$	10	$(2\frac{1}{2}\sqrt{3})^2 + (2\frac{1}{2})^2 = 25$
11	$(3 \cdot \sqrt{3})^2 + 0^2 = 27$	15	$(3\frac{1}{2}\sqrt{3})^2 + (\frac{1}{2})^2 = 37$

for which the number of settlements is to be found, be called h. The problem is to find k and l.

First, find an integer m such that $(m+1)(m-2) < h \leq (m+1)(m-2) + 2m$. Call the expression $(m+1)(m-2) + 2m = h_0$. There are two cases:

a. If $h_0 - h \leq m$, then $k = \dfrac{2m-1}{2}$ and $l = \dfrac{2m-1}{2} - (h_0 - h)$

b. If $h_0 - h > m$, then

$k = m - 1$; and $l = (m-1) - (h_0 - h)$. —W. F. S.

The most important result of the preceding argument, however, is that with discontinuous settlement, the possible size of the market areas and the number of settlements they contain also grow discontinuously. This, again, makes surplus profits possible. For if sales in 32 settlements, say, were required to make a certain commodity profitable, area No. 13 with 31 settlements would be too small. But the next area is the unnecessarily large market area 14, with 36 settlements, so that sales must extend to 36 settlements. The demand curve would then intersect the cost curve instead of merely touching it, and surplus profits would thus arise in this industry.[14,15] Such moderate surplus profits are actually the rule, for it would be pure chance if the demand curve in its jumps should still "just touch the cost curve."

One more point must be emphasized. Not all the possible market areas need occur in reality. There may not be any commodity whose commercial production would be profitable for only three farms. Then area 1 would not exist. But conversely, every actual market area must be on the list of possible ones.[16]

14. As a consequence of this discontinuity in the size of areas the demand curve jumps if it is displaced toward the left by a diminution of area in the course of the Chamberlin process. With mere price increases, on the other hand, the demand falls continuously, if one moves up along the old curve, although a gradual price rise also eliminates settlements discontinuously at the shipping limits then prevailing. This apparent contradiction is easily explained: Before a place is suddenly and entirely eliminated from the sales area, its demand has gradually fallen to zero with the rising price; i. e., its elimination no longer affects total demand. Thus whether a market area is reduced by the approach of competitors, or by rising prices, are two entirely different questions. The discontinuity of settlements has an effect only in the first case because here, in contrast to the second case, the demand of settlements on the borders is not zero.

15. They may even soften the impact of business cycles with continuity of settlement. An oligopolistic struggle for the distribution of surplus profit may break out, a discussion of which is not warranted by the insignificant object of strife and the even distribution of chances. The solution of Frisch, Schneider, von Stackelberg, Möller, Zeuthen, Palander, and others can be adapted to the problem.

16. Among the first 10 cases the realization of Nos. 3, 6, and 8 seems to me especially probable. Here, in contrast to the remaining cases, no settlement is divided among several supply centers. Various circumstances are against such a partition. (1) It hardly occurs in administrative districts, and trade has a tendency to turn toward political centers as populous places. Political division is *possible*, however; one need only recall earlier conditions, when several lords had serfs in the same villages. (2) Division would create, not theoretically but practically, an unstable economic situation: three competing for *one* place! (3) If the settlements are single farms, division is wholly improbable. If it does not occur a no-man's-land arises between neighboring market areas with discontinuous settlement that makes oligopolistic market strategy even more difficult.

§2. Location at a Center of Gravity

A production site might be established *between* three settlements instead of *in* one of the original settlements. This we shall call location at a center of gravity. Compared with location in a settlement it has the disadvantage of no local demand worth mentioning, but the advantage of being nearer to the next sales points. Hence the smallest possible value for nV is $0.58a$ instead of a, as is the case with location in a settlement. Except for nV, however, the two possibilities show an astonishing agreement in respect to the size and situation of the market areas. Thus all but the last column of Table 6 is valid also for location at the center of gravity. On the other hand, the distribution of sales points within otherwise similar areas is essentially different. The question of whether one of the two locations is definitely superior must now be investigated. The criterion for superiority would be that the same number of places permitted a greater total demand.

Unusual demand curves may be imagined that actually favor one of the locations throughout; but if the straight line may be regarded as the average of all possible demand curves, it can be shown [17] that, at least for the 10 smallest areas examined, location at an original settlement entails a greater demand in half of the cases (areas 3, 4, 6, 7, and 9), and location at a center of gravity in the other half.[18] However, in those cases where location at the center of gravity is more economical, its advantage over location in a settlement is more pronounced than the reverse.

Thus whereas location sometimes appears more favorable in a settlement and sometimes at a center of gravity, if each is considered by itself it may be presumed that when everything is carefully considered location uniformly at either one site or the other is to be preferred on the whole for many reasons. (1) With a split location structure the number of industrial sites would increase, and consequently the advantage of a concentrated local demand would

---

17. The proof, though not difficult, is too long to be given here. In any case, it is unimportant for the development of our ideas.

18. Consequently it may happen that with appropriate location of a factory fewer places will provide a greater demand for the same commodity. This is possible with goods whose longest shipping distance is too short to make the demand at points on the borders of the large area felt, either strongly or to any degree, so that the more favorable situation of the remaining places in respect to the factory is decisive in the small area. With relatively short shipping distances other unusual features may appear, but their discussion would lead us too far afield.

decrease. This is especially true of economic capitals, which determine the sites of other locations, as we shall see later. (2) The splitting of towns would also bring about a splitting-up of transport lines. (3) With larger areas the advantage of one situation over another is negligible; with the smallest ones it is greatest for areas 1 and 3.

Above and beyond all this there is a number of practical reasons why the uniform pattern of locations will generally favor original settlements. (1) Industry first arose as a side occupation, or as production on a socage farm or in a village. (2) Location in a settlement assures better contact with consumers. (3) Lines of communication even between economically self-sufficient settlements are already in existence, but may have to be provided for locations at a center of gravity.

c. REGIONAL NETWORKS

We have seen that there is only *one* suitable shape for market areas, and only a *limited* number of possible sizes and situations. Because of the restricted number, the most favorable area is uniquely determined for every commodity.[19] One and the same area will usually be the market for several goods, since there are more products than regional sizes. But beyond the market area these goods need have nothing in common. In particular, they will generally realize sales of entirely different magnitude, even though local demand at the factory price is the same, since even with the same market area they will generally have different possible shipping distances. Indeed, one might almost establish the rule that goods having one of these three properties in common—market area, possible shipping distance, and necessary sales volume—will differ in respect to the two others.[20] Thus with a discontinuous distribution of population things are no longer as they are with a continuous distribution, where every product can be as unfailingly recognized by its area as the chemical elements by their specific weights. But now the forms can be deduced a priori in which the sale of all known goods and

---

19. With a discontinuous population the number of settlements, not the size of the area, must be as small as possible.

20. From this a few apparent anomalies follow. For example, even with the same local demand at the factory the total demand over a small region may exceed that throughout a larger one. This is easily possible when the product sold in the smaller area has a longer maximum shipping distance. The greater the possible shipping distance, the fewer settlements will be required to achieve a certain sales volume, for a long distance implies little sensitivity to shipment; that is, only an inconsiderable fall in demand with increasing distance.

Network of Markets 123

of all others still to come *must* take place. Market areas are no longer specially tailored for a single commodity, but the commodity takes the most suitable size from a fixed assortment. We can therefore continue our deductions without first considering the actual sales situations for the various goods. The actual must be contained in the possible.[21]

Market areas need no longer be classified according to goods, therefore, but according to size. Goods whose necessary market areas are equal are included in one class. Because of their shape the areas of the same size lie in immediate contact with one another, and form a honeycomb network that covers the whole area. Their centers, that is, the production sites for the *same* commodity classes, are all separated from one another by the minimum distances, 2ρ, and are distributed in regular honeycomb fashion. But how are production sites for *different* classes of goods situated with respect to one another?

---

21. What can be deduced need not be derived laboriously yet imperfectly from experience. Here I disagree with Euckens, *Grundlagen der Nationalöknonomie* (1940), p. 126. On the contrary, reason opens new possibilities that fructify daily experience.

Chapter 11. The System of Networks

a. THE GENERAL PATTERN

Market areas for the various kinds of goods resemble narrow-meshed or wide-meshed nets of hexagons that to start with can be thrown at will over our plain.[1] Despite the resulting confusion, every place would lie in the market area of every good.[2] Yet it is worth while to bring order out of this chaos by means of a few reflections.

First, we lay the nets so that *all* of them shall have at least *one* center in common. Here a metropolis will arise, with all the advantages[3] of a large local demand. Second, we turn the nets about this center in such a way as to get six sectors with many and six with only a few production sites (Figs. 28 and 29).[4] With this arrangement the greatest number of locations coincide, the maximum number of purchases can be made locally, the sum of the minimum distances between industrial locations is least, and in consequence not only shipments but also transport lines are reduced to a minimum. With discontinuous settlement, of course, only the networks of those market regions described on page 117 as lying obliquely can be rotated. Figure 27 shows that there are always two possibilities for their location. If, for example, a circle with the diameter of area 3 as radius be drawn about the central town, it will pass in the first quadrant through three settlements, which are thus possible locations for centers of the neighboring area 3. There is now a choice between the two outer settlements whose distance is likewise equal to the radius of the circle, or the middle settlement together with a fourth possible point at the proper dis-

---

1. With the limitation, already established, that their middle points coincide with original setlements, not with centers of gravity and certainly not with arbitrary sites.
2. The situation is wholly symbolic. We live simultaneously amidst many surroundings and cannot, without harm, neglect all others for the sake of one single preference.
3. This presupposes that in a number of branches the planning curve does not fall steadily. See Figure 48 and the accompanying text.
4. More places are indicated in Figure 29 than in Figure 28, which shows only the centers of the four smallest areas, whereas Figure 29 shows all regions.

The System of Networks 125

tance in the next quadrant—not with one of the other two, which are too near. Once network 3 is selected, the choice as to position of the remaining networks that can be rotated is no longer free,

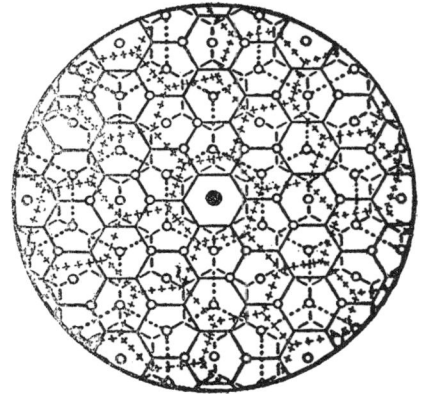

Fig. 28. Theoretical pattern of an economic landscape

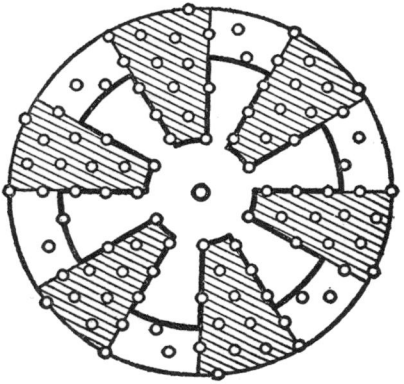

Fig. 29. Theoretical pattern of an economic landscape, but without nets

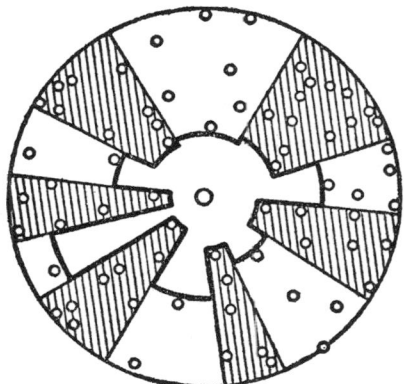

Fig. 30. Indianapolis and environs within a radius of 60 miles. (From Andree's *Handatlas*, 8th ed., p. 198.)

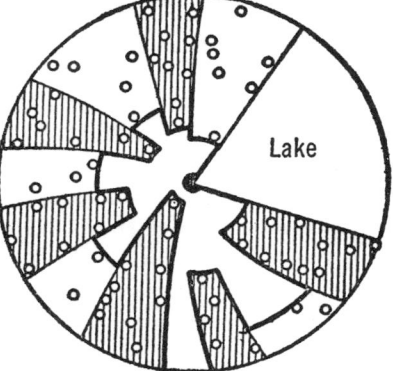

Fig. 31. Toledo and environs within a radius of 60 miles. (*Ibid.*)

provided the separation into sectors with many or few towns is to be carried through. Depending on the decision as to the position of area 3, the middle or two outer sectors in the first quadrant will contain but few towns.[5] The cogwheel-shaped immediate environs

5. The following consideration makes this clear: In Figure 27 the middle and lower sectors of the first quadrant are mirror images of one another in respect to possible

of the metropolis are also necessarily poor in towns, for only a few local goods can be produced with profit in its neighborhood.

Neither are the outlying environs, even within the same sector, uniformly settled. Some localities have no production of their own at all, whereas at other places the centers of several market areas of varying size coincide. Such agglomerations of locations, or "central sites," as Christaller so appropriately calls them, are found upon closer examination to be distributed with a certain regularity (Fig. 32). Smaller agglomerations can be found at distances of $\sqrt{3}a$, $3a$, and $2\sqrt{3}a$ from each other; many of medium size at distances of $6a$; and larger ones lie $12a$ apart.[6] Yet it is not true that when an equal number of areas have their centers at two places these areas themselves will be of equal size. Towns of the same size may quite possibly fulfill entirely different economic functions; that is, they can harbor entirely different industries. A smaller agglomeration generally lies about halfway between two larger ones. The size of agglomerations increases with their distance from the metropolis.

The greater the accumulation of industries the cheaper, obviously, are industrial goods on the average. Their wholesale price level is therefore lowest in the metropolis.[7] In the ring containing few towns, and somewhat farther out, industrial prices rise sharply until at last, with minor fluctuations, production sites again become so numerous that the local price level falls (unless the index is heavily weighted with goods having a very large sales area that can be purchased only in the metropolis and therefore become increasingly dear with rising freight costs).

If the entire regional system has the radius L, goods for which ρ is somewhat greater than $L/2$ can be produced only in the metropolis.[8] Even locations on the borders between two regional systems can no longer compete in such commodities. Consequently, at a distance of something more than $L/2$, no new competition arises for the metropolis. With a distance of something more than $L/2$,

---

locations. On the other hand, the distance between these pairs of possible locations is less than the radius of the circle on which they lie. Hence they are too near together, and a choice must be made between them. If a location in the lower sector is chosen, its mirror image in the middle sector must necessarily be relinquished. The possible locations in the two outer sectors, on the contrary, are separated by the proper distance.

6. The minimum distance between two production centers of any given size is $a\sqrt{3}$, and every center has at least one neighbor at this distance.

7. Living costs, on the other hand, which include agricultural products, rent, and extra expenses, and take retail markups into account, are highest in the metropolis, at least when fuel is disregarded for reasons discussed on p. 42, note 10.

8. Such a typical metropolitan function, for example, is bank clearing at the highest level.

The System of Networks

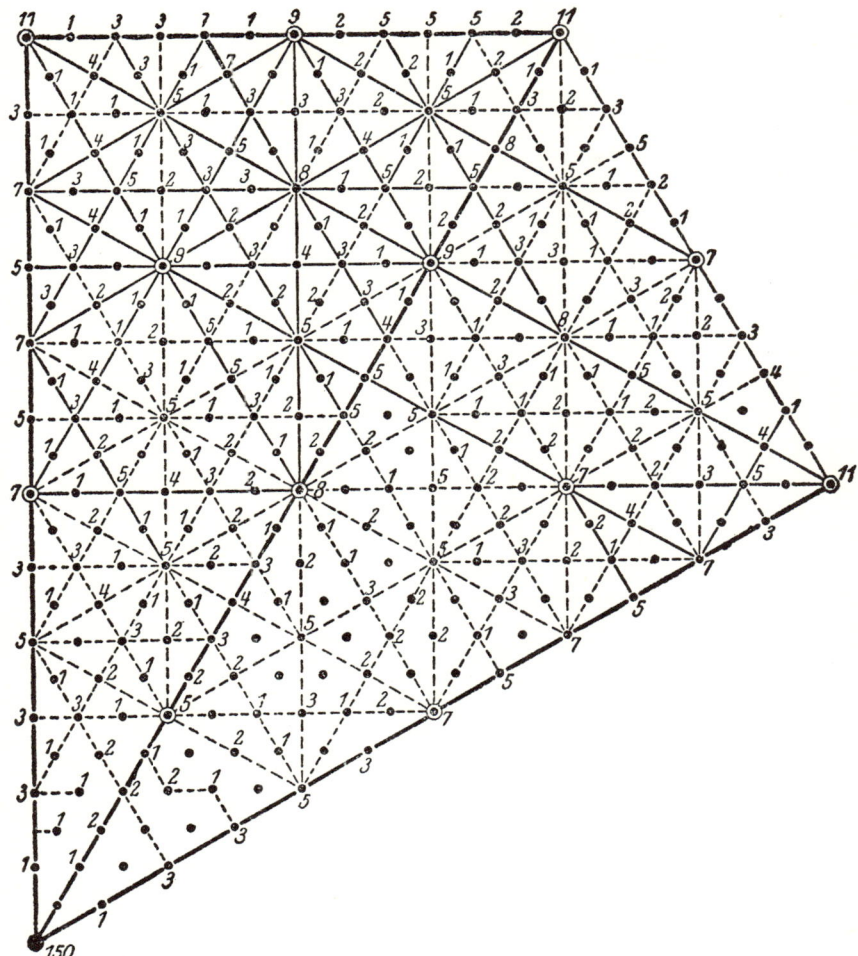

Fig. 32. The transport lines in the ideal economic landscape (one sector only).

The numbers refer to the number of centers which coincide in a particular point. In the middle of the landscape there are 150 centers of areas all of which are smaller than the landscape to which the pictured sector belongs.

The lines: The number of centers along the heavy lines is twice or more that along the broken lines; the number of centers along the thin lines is approximately one and a half times the number along the broken lines. The difference in traffic density between the left city-rich and the right city-poor sector can easily be seen.

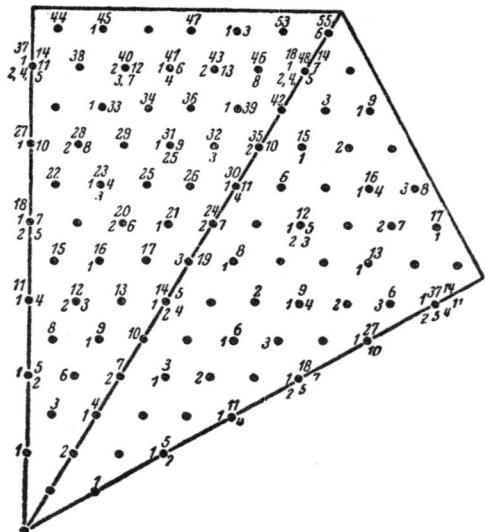

Fig. 33. Location of regional centers in the complete system. The centers bear the numbers of their region.

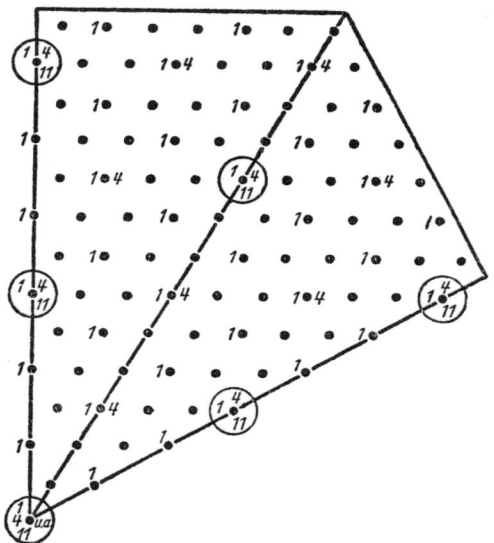

Fig. 34. Regions with equal structure. (1) $k = 3$. Every town controls two complete towns of the next lower rank. The numerals indicate regional centers with the same number as in Figure 33, from which this one was made by omitting all regions without a center and two complete places of next lower rank.

prices will thus rise again, since goods with a large sales radius become more expensive with increasing freight, and their (unilateral) price rise cannot be counteracted by local production. Thus from the metropolis to the boundaries of its region we find wholesale prices first low, then rising, then falling, and finally rising again.[9,10]

Finally, upon drawing in the principal lines of communication, we find that the busiest traffic (measured by the number of area centers per unit of length) occurs along the sectors. Thus twelve such main lines radiate from the metropolis;[11] i. e., six lines cross in it. Elsewhere in the region there are junctions of only two or three lines. Cross connections in the vicinity of the metropolis are theoretically not worth while and seldom exist in practice.[12] In sectors containing but few towns, the lines of communication are fewer and generally not well developed. In an over-all view, they spread out like a cobweb around the metropolis.

Order has now suddenly been brought into our market areas. The position of individual regional networks is no longer a random one, but follows from economic principles. Now we realize that there must be at least one metropolis, around which its market area and competing locations lie concentrically.[13] It is, so to speak, the

9. Instead of spatial price differences there are spatial differences in profits when a government enforces the same prices everywhere. For any individual product the " crater field " of price is then replaced by profit " cones."

10. This is *one* reason why it is generally meaningless to speak of the price level of a region; the dispersion of local prices around the average for the whole region is too great. The price cones and price funnels about single points of supply and production give rather the impression of a mountain range. We shall encounter the other reason later: not only the height, but also the change in prices varies locally too much. To conceal these variations by calculating their average would lead to error in many cases.

11. Eleven through railway lines run out from Berlin, for instance; from Paris, including branches within a radius of about 25 miles, exactly twelve; directly from London, twelve through highways. This orientation of main arteries toward the metropolis was noticeable after the incorporation of Austria and the Sudetenland into the Reich. Their main roads formerly ran toward Vienna and Prague, and good connections with the old Germany were often possible only by way of their own capital cities.

12. In endeavoring to travel by railroad around Munich or Nuremberg, say, one finds that this is possible only at a distance of some 50 miles.

13. Further important results are: six sectors containing few towns and six containing many are grouped about the metropolis; in its immediate environs a region having the form of a cogwheel remains free of towns; the towns show a honeycomb distribution, and are separated from one another by the same minimum distance; the main lines of communication meet in the metropolis; and so on.

industrial corollary of Thünen's "isolated state." We shall not apply this political concept to a situation that is at first entirely nonpolitical, but shall call this system of market networks, this highest phenomenon in the hierarchy of economic spatial arrangement, exactly what it is: an economic landscape.[14]

b. SPECIAL CASES

§1. MARKET AREAS OF SIMILAR STRUCTURE

It has already been mentioned that our series of market area includes all cases that are logically possible, though not all need exist in reality. They cannot exist, either because there is no product whose necessary market area is exactly as large, or because extra-economic factors—above all, political division into administrative units—influence spatial economic arrangement.

Political division is frequently carried out in such a way that a certain number of smaller regions are combined into a larger administrative district. In France, for example, three cantons make an *arrondissement* and three *arrondissements* a *département*. We shall therefore briefly examine regional systems in which every area includes k regions of the next smaller size.[15] All other regions that are possible according to our analysis will accordingly be disregarded.

If $k = 3$, say, Tables 6 and 7 show that regional sizes 1, 4, 11, 30, and so on may exist, but not 2 and 3, 5 and 10, and 12 to 29.

---

14. Economic empire, economic region, or economic area (in the narrower sense) would be suitable, especially if one recalls the original meaning of *regio* and *Gebiet*: an area of authority, according to Grimm's *Wörterbuch*. It is, in fact, the economic domain of the central metropolis. On the other hand, economic district, or province, emphasizes the lack of self-sufficiency that is generally encountered in reality. Geographers may object to the way in which I employ the word landscape, but I ask them to consider that it not only corresponds with common usage, but approaches very closely the true meaning of the word. In both cases the environs relate to a center— the beholder, or the metropolis. Only by way of these economic relationships do geographic peculiarities influence the region that has sprung out of pure space, as with R. Häpke's more general "economic landscape" ("Die ökonomische Landschaft und Gruppenstadt in der älteren Wirtschaftsgeschichte," in *Sozial- und Wirtschaftsgeschichte, Gedächtnisschrift für G. von Below*, 1928, pp. 82–104). On the other hand, the "industrial landscape" of E. Winkler, who, following the general usage of geographers, would orient all geography toward the landscape as its sole object, represents a geographical unit in which industry alone dominates ("Stand und Aufgaben der Industriegeographie," *Zeitschrift für Erdkunde*, IX, 597 ff. [extensive bibliography]. Also, E. Winkler, "Raumordnung der Wirtschaft," *Neue Zürcher Zeitung*, October 18, 1940; and in correspondence.)

15. These regions may also be pieced together from parts of others. Strictly speaking, therefore, the large region includes k centers of next smaller regions, which, however, are made up of parts of more than k such regions.

The System of Networks

For only region No. 4 is large enough to embrace three regions No. 1; only region No. 11 embraces three regions No. 4, and so on. Table 8 gives for a few values of k the most important data for the corresponding regions.

Table 8. REGIONS WITH HOMOGENEOUS STRUCTURE

Regional Size (actual)	Distance of the Centers from Each Other			Regional Size, Number in the Complete System		
	$k = 3$	$k = 4$	$k = 7$	$k = 3$	$k = 4$	$k = 7$
1	$a\sqrt{3^1}$	$a\sqrt{4^1}$	$a\sqrt{7^1}$	1	2	3
2	$a\sqrt{3^2}$	$a\sqrt{4^2}$	$a\sqrt{7^2}$	4	7	19
3	$a\sqrt{3^3}$	$a\sqrt{4^3}$	$a\sqrt{7^3}$	11	24	106
4	$a\sqrt{3^4}$	$a\sqrt{4^4}$	$a\sqrt{7^4}$	30	81	?
5	$a\sqrt{3^5}$	$a\sqrt{4^5}$	$a\sqrt{7^5}$	77	?	?
6	$a\sqrt{3^6}$	$a\sqrt{4^6}$	$a\sqrt{7^6}$	?	?	?
7	$a\sqrt{3^7}$	$a\sqrt{4^7}$	$a\sqrt{7^7}$	?	?	?

a = distance of the original settlements. k = number of next smaller sub-areas. The number under the radical sign is at the same time the total number of settlements in the region concerned.

Figures 34 to 36 show how much simpler the spatial picture is than in the complete system of regions. This simplicity is gained by some sacrifice of economy, to be sure, since it seems certain that the necessary market areas of many goods have sizes that do not appear here. Such goods have unnecessarily large markets in a simplified system.[16] Nevertheless, such a simple landscape has something

---

[16]. Hence it is not correct to regard the special case where $k = 3$ as "the" arrangement according to the principle of most efficient supply, as does Christaller, *Die zentralen Orte in Süddeutschland* (Jena, 1933), pp. 63–85. Furthermore, the chance fact that when $k = 3$ all places lie symmetrically with respect to each of the six through lines and hence no thickly and thinly settled areas appear, has misled him into establishing a different arrangement on the "communication principle" ($k = 4$). In this arrangement the greatest possible number of important places lie on main lines of communication. But this is true anyway (see Fig. 32), especially in a complete system of market regions. The communication principle was one of the axioms by which the final position of regional networks was determined. In our economic landscape both this principle and the principle of supply are therefore united. It would disrupt logical geometrical development if one were to suppose that cheapness, rapidity, frequency, and extent of communication over long distances could create a special locational advantage that would result in more industries being established

attractive about it, and above all it is probably the most that can be attained today by conscious planning. Adapted to individual cases it forms, furthermore, the very basis for the new organization in the East.

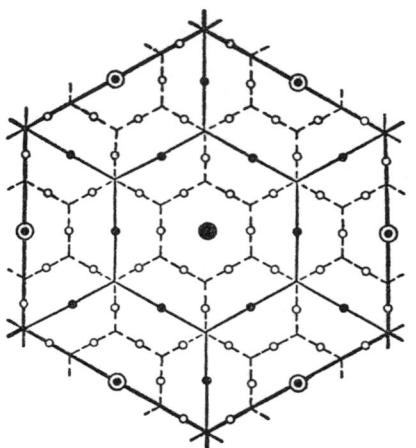

Fig. 35. Regions with equal structure. (2) $k = 4$. Every town dominates three complete towns of next lower rank. In contradistinction to Figure 34, regional boundaries and, instead of one sector, the whole interior of the landscape have been drawn.

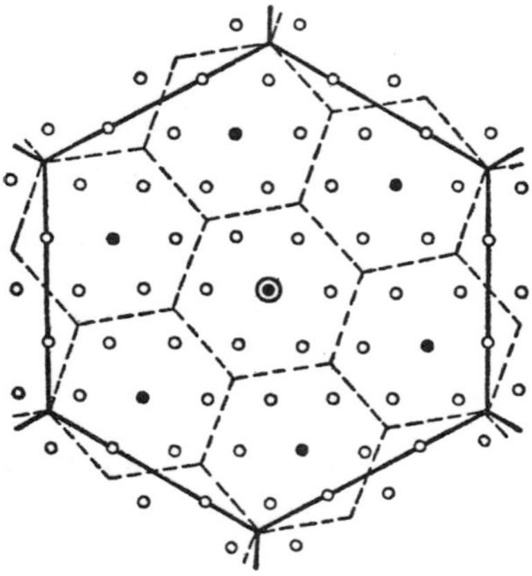

Fig. 36. Regions with equal structure. (3) $k = 7$. Every town dominates six complete towns of the next lower rank.

---

than otherwise would be the case; partly because they could manage with smaller regions, partly because these regions would be narrower in the direction of the communication line and therefore broadened at right angles to it.

Whoever wishes to take all this into account must either incorporate it in the general location equations or content himself with a partial geometrical presentation. In any case, he has to forego the advantages of a *complete* geometrical presentation. For the same reason we did not consider, among other things, the fact that in the role of important consumers towns mutually distort their own market regions. For instance, the smaller towns are displaced excentrically in their regions toward the larger, as is rightly considered by Culemann in his planning ("Zur Stadtplanung in den neuen deutschen Ostgebieten," *Raumforschung und Raumordnung*, 1941, pp. 100–230). With larger towns it is supposed that the local demand and the demand from the environs can be met by separate regions; this justifies the assumption that the market region for a given product will be as large as in smaller places.

The special case $k = 7$ is called by Christaller (*op. cit.*, pp. 84–85) a structure based on the administrative principle. He aptly characterizes it by the fact, first, that no place is divided among several administrative districts (as is often the case, of course, with twin cities like Ulm and Neu Ulm, or Kansas City, Missouri, and Kansas City, Kansas); secondly, that the market regions of the places in question are cut up as

§2. Square Market Regions

We have already found the second best market region to be the square.[17] In utilizing demand it frequently is not much inferior to the hexagon and has the advantage of simply drawn boundaries, but also the disadvantage of longer roads. In the square, too, the relation between the number of settlements, the size of market areas, and the distance of their centers is extremely simple. If a be the minimum distance separating the original settlements (which is perhaps 5 per cent less with a square than with a honeycomb distribution) and n the number of settlements in a market region, the size of the region is $a^2 n$ and the distance of its center from the nearest rivals $a\sqrt{n}$—exactly as in the honeycomb shape. The smallest

---

little as possible by political boundaries. For these conditions $k = 7$ is, in fact, a possible solution; $k = 13$ would be another. In the first case, however, the regional boundaries are not as Christaller has drawn them, but as they appear in our Figure 36. Christaller's figure is possible only because he departs from the most rational distribution of the original settlements. Besides, the political principle does not contradict the economic principle, as he believes; rather, a few of the possible market boundaries are at the same time possible political boundaries.

The complete regional system considers all principles at once. Whenever only the smallest possible market areas of similar structure are taken into account despite their slight flexibility (as is often done in practical spatial planning for the sake of simplicity), each of the three smallest regional types is especially advantageous from a different standpoint. Thus $k = 3$ is really the best solution according to the supply principle, because under these circumstances it still provides the largest assortment of regions; $k = 4$ is the best according to the communication principle, and $k = 7$ according to the political principle. In this sequence the central sites become less numerous and larger and the whole system, of course, cruder and more rigid. Yet although Christaller has limited himself to these special cases, his inquiry is the best that I know in all the literature on the subject, and at the same time a distinguished example of research in economic geography. It has visibly influenced planning in the East (see, for example, *Reichskommissar für die Festigung deutschen Volkstums. Stabshauptant. Planung und Aufbau im Osten* [Berlin, 1941], 7. *Hauptdorfbereiche bei Kutno*).

That not only the subject, but also the manner of its presentation, fit so perfectly into our own system is the more remarkable in that the present system was developed without knowledge of his.

17. Thünen assumes it as an example (*Der isolirte Staat in Beziehung auf Landwirtschaft und Nationalökonomie* [Hamburg, 1826; Schumacher-Zarchlin edition, Berlin, 1875], Vol. II, Pt. II, §4, p. 11), and C. Culemann (" Aufbau und Gliederung gebietlicher Bereiche als Aufgabe räumlicher Gestaltung," *Raumforschung und Raumordnung*, 1942, pp. 249–256) recommends the rectangle because, unlike the hexagon, through lines of communication do not cut up small regions and thus disturb local traffic, but run tangent to them. Nevertheless, either long detours often result or else, as in many cities, diagonal streets are subsequently laid out, so that the regions are cut up after all.

regions include 2, 4, 5, 8, 9, 13, 16, etc., settlements, thus increasing in size rather quickly as in the honeycomb form. Here, too, there is a choice as to how a few regions (Nos. 3, 6, 9, etc.) shall be placed, and with proper positions sectors are likewise obtained that are rich or poor in towns; four per quadrant in all. However, they are con-

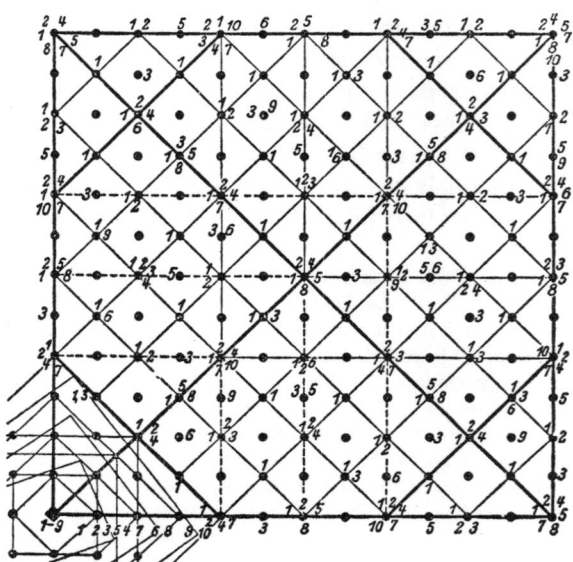

Fig. 37. Part of a square economic landscape. Upper right quadrant. The central site of the landscape and the ten smallest regions surrounding it are in the lower left corner. The original settlements bear the numbers of the ten smallest regions whose centers they are. Comparison with Figure 32 shows the difference between quadratic and hexagonal arrangement. In the former up to eight, in the latter up to twelve, routes run together at one point. The angles at which they meet are 45°, 30°, or a multiple thereof. Thus right-angled intersections occur in the hexagon also, and oblique-angled in the square.

siderably less pronounced than in the hexagon—one more reason why square regions are less economical. Figure 37 shows the shape and the distribution of the centers for the 10 smallest regions.

The cut shows the most important lines of communication as well. In the larger places four through lines intersect; in the smaller, two. But although two square road networks that are turned 45 degrees in respect to one another are superimposed, most connections in the honeycomb road network are obviously shorter (Fig. 32).

Chapter 12. The Network of Systems

a. THE RELATION OF LANDSCAPES TO ONE ANOTHER

In comparison with the size of our plain, even the largest necessary market area may be small. The landscape is not smaller than this largest market region, for this would mean abandoning without cause the production of goods with a large necessary shipping distance. But the landscape will hardly become larger, for this would mean that all places farther away than L (see p. 126) from the

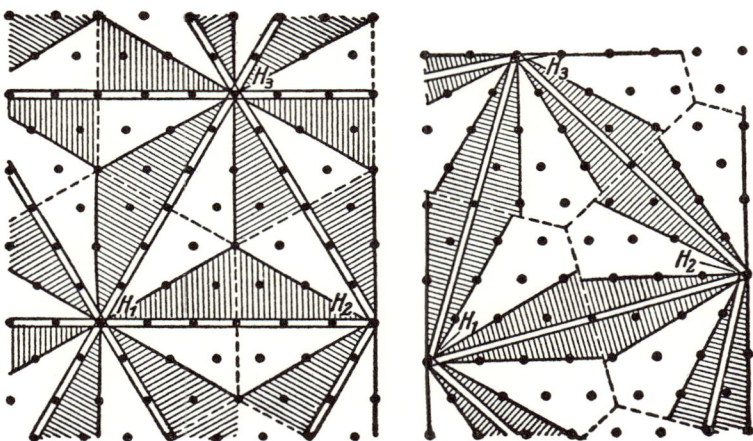

Figs. 38 and 39. Location of landscapes in respect to one another. Double lines: connecting routes between large cites. Broken lines: landscape boundaries. Hatched: sectors with many towns

metropolis H_1 would have to give up without reason the establishment of a second metropolis, H_2. In these distant parts the advantages of agglomeration of producers at H_1 are no longer noticeable, since they buy nothing more from there; secondly, the difference between sectors rich and sectors poor in towns and the advantages of communication associated therewith disappear progressively. Hence a second metropolis arises at a distance of $2L$ from the first, and so on, until finally the entire plain is filled with landscapes.

When these have become numerous enough, they assume the

shape of regular hexagons. But it is still undecided how the sectors with many towns in the various landscapes lie in respect to one another. Figures 38 and 39 give two possible solutions. The first has the advantage that the trunk lines of communication, between H_1, H_2, and H_3, run straight as a string, and yet along the route containing the largest number of towns. In the second case, only a few towns lie directly on the main lines, but many lie within a relatively short distance to the right or left of them. It might be thought at first that the position of the largest market region would determine the boundaries of the entire landscape, but the demands of communication are much too imperative for them not to predominate over it.

b. THE BOUNDARY REGION

All industries find at least one location in every landscape. Only those goods with a necessary shipping distance, ρ, that is not much greater than $L/2$ are produced at more than one place. If ρ lies between a little more than $L/2$ and somewhat more than $L/3$, all further locations will be on or near the boundary (at the most a distance of $L/3$ away from it), and their market areas will generally encroach upon the neighboring landscape. But even with goods for which $\rho < L/3$ it is impossible that the network of their market regions should end exactly at the boundary of the landscape. Empty corners always develop. Once in a while, and especially at a corner where three landscapes meet, a factory erected on the boundary can piece together an adequate market region from the empty corners of neighboring landscapes. Should the corners be too small for this, one of those situations arises again in which market regions can be somewhat larger than necessary and moderate excess profits become possible, which are particularly large in those cases where $L/2 < \rho$. To summarize: if ρ is less than $L/3$, first of all boundaries will be transgressed; if ρ lies between $L/3$ and $L/2$, some transgression of boundaries and some excess profits will result; if ρ is considerably larger than $L/2$, excess profits arise.

	0	⅓	½	⅔	1	
Center	These producers supply only the domestic market			These producers export also[1]		Boundary
	These consumers buy only domestic goods			These consumers import also		

1. Only these, on the other hand, can also be displaced by foreign competition. Thus where a landscape boundary is at the same time a customs frontier these producers alone are interested in protective duties if they fear a competitive struggle.

The effects of landscape boundaries can be more easily surveyed if they are arranged not according to the shipping distance of goods, but according to the locations of those concerned.

The area within which consumers are affected by boundaries is thus larger than the corresponding area for producers; that is, the region dependent on imports is larger than that participating in exports. Of course, this says nothing as to the relative size of imports and exports, though it may, nevertheless, be concluded that more persons buy from abroad as consumers than export in their capacity of producers. If imports and exports are equal, the individual consumer imports less on the average than the individual producer exports.

c. RESULTS

Upon closer examination, many more regularities could be extracted from our system of market regions, but as the assumptions of our analysis are seldom completely fulfilled in reality there would be little profit in pursuing it to the last detail. The findings so far have been surprising enough: an area from which our assumptions have actually wiped out all differences can be divided on purely economic considerations into regions that do not represent simply homogeneous logical constructs, but form, if the expression be allowed, an organic whole.

First we discovered simple market regions surrounding every center of consumption or production in the form of a regular hexagon. Second, for every group of products a net of these market regions was found. And in the third place, a systematic arrangement of these various nets appeared. This self-sufficient system is the ideal type of an economic landscape, or economic region in the narrower sense. Finally, such landscapes are distributed throughout the world like a network and in accordance with definite laws.

B. Economic Regions under Difficult Conditions

So far we have derived economic regions simply as functions of distance, mass production, and competition. It must not, of course, be expected that we shall now consider all the factors thus far neglected, in order to derive a theory that fits reality. This sounds good, but is humanly impossible. Were we to try, we should either end up with equations and be forced to give up observation (visualization) and application, or else deal with an infinite number of individual cases without general validity. We shall therefore discuss the effects of only a few interesting changes from our assumptions (Chapters 13 and 14), and then give conversely a more realistic picture of economic regions, though without endeavoring to fathom all their causes (Chapter 15). No simple rule for the application of theory to practice should be expected, since that is more than science is able to give. There art and venture begin.

Chapter 13. Some New Factors

a. ECONOMIC DIFFERENCES
§1. LOCAL DIFFERENCES IN PRICE[1]
α. *Within the Same Market Region*
1. POSSIBILITIES OF GEOGRAPHICAL PRICE POLICY

Three possibilities are open to the entrepreneur—for only his price policy will be discussed here. He can adapt his prices to the individual case (**A**); or keep them so rigidly fixed that all buyers pay the same f. o. b. price (**F**) or the same c. i. f. (or "delivered") price (**C**).[2,3] Depending on his policy, his prices will differ on the average and from place to place. We shall now examine how they are set, how high they are, and how they affect the entrepreneur himself and his customers. In order to do so we must first free ourselves completely from the notions of traditional price theory, which regards demand as though it were concentrated at one point.

(aa) *Preliminary Study* (1): *Local and Distant Individual Demand—A Comparison.* Among other factors the extent and variability of the demand of its consumers (in various places) will depend on the geographic price policy of a firm. For the sake of simplicity we shall start once more from the assumption that individual demand is linear, and the same for all individuals.

---

1. Those who dislike mathematics may skip §1 up to p. 167. The principal results are these: (1) Spatial price differentiation makes it possible to decrease the size of market areas still further. Hence it is enforced by the tendency toward maximization of the number of independent enterprises, though it eliminates again the profits from differentiation. (2) Differentiation is generally contrary to the interests of nearby consumers. (3) The most advantageous differentiation is generally not so great as to be damaged by resale. (4) Uniform f. o. b. prices would be more favorable to the consumer as a rule.

2. This should not be confused with the irrelevant technical question of whether the carrier collects the freight from the buyer or the seller; that is, whether or not it appears on the bill.

3. There are several combinations and variations of this. For example, the creation of zones with equal prices (**A** + **F** or **A** + **C**) or calculation of the freight from a fictitious location (basing-point system). The meaning of **A**, **F**, and **C** should be kept in mind in what follows.

Let d_0 in Figure 40 be the individual demand with regard to the delivered price. It is the same for all buyers, whether they live close to or far from the factory, since it relates to the price actually paid by each; i. e., to the local price prevailing at the destination. The demand curve of a customer in the neighboring place with respect to the f. o. b. price is d_1. This demand curve, d_1, lies below the demand curve d_0 by the vertical distance i, which is the unit freight cost from the factory to the neighboring place. d_1 is valid only for all customers at a particular distance since it is based on the factory price, which represents the net payment to the manufacturer and which varies with distance, but which is of no particular

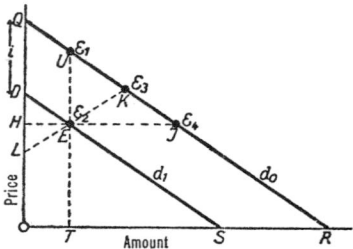

Fig. 40. Comparison of individual demand with respect to the c. i. f. price (d_0) and with respect to the f. o. b. price (d_1), the latter as seen by a buyer in a neighboring town. Vertical distance i between d_0 and d_1: unit freight from factory to neighboring town.

interest to the purchaser. We assume that prices have already been determined. Let a vertical line, UT, intersect d_0 at the level of the uniform c. i. f. price. It will cut d_1 at the level of the distant f. o. b. price. Let a horizontal line, HJ, intersect d_0 and d_1 at the level of the uniform f. o. b. price. The corresponding c. i. f. price then lies on d_0 vertically above the intersection with d_1. A straight line, KL, bisecting UJ for reasons to be given later, cuts d_0 and d_1 at the level of the differentiated f. o. b. price (policy **A**). The corresponding c. i. f. price lies on d_0 vertically above the intersection with d_1.

From this it follows that with **C** the seller pays the whole freight, with **A** half of it, and with **F** no freight at all. As as consequence the individual market under **C** is everywhere equally large; under **F** it declines, independently of the level of the unit price in the neighboring place, by an amount proportional to the freight. The same is true of **A**, except that the amount is lost is always half as large as under **F**.

Geographic differences in the elasticity of demand are more difficult to determine. The elasticity in U is $\epsilon_1 = UR \div QU$; in E, $\epsilon_2 = ES \div DE$; in K it is $\epsilon_3 = KR \div QK$; in J, $\epsilon_4 = JR \div QJ$. Since $QU = DE$, and $UR > ES$, $\epsilon_1 > \epsilon_2$. Corresponding comparisons give:

$$\epsilon_1 > \epsilon_2 > \epsilon_3 > \epsilon_4$$

In words: (1) The individual demand in respect to the c. i. f. price is more elastic than the individual demand as a function of the corresponding f. o. b. price ($\epsilon_1 > \epsilon_2$).[4] This is true of every price policy for one and the same place, and for any demand curve; not, like the following propositions, for the linear only.

(2) If f. o. b. prices for increasingly distant places differ by total freight costs (**C**), ($\epsilon_1 > \epsilon_2$) falls;[5] if they differ by only half these costs (**A**), or not at all (**F**), the elasticity of the demand in respect

---

4. The reason is that a certain percentage change in the f. o. b. price causes a smaller percentage change in the corresponding c. i. f. price, whereas the absolute change is the same in both (see E. M. Hoover, "Spatial Price Discrimination," *Review of Economic Studies*, June, 1937, p. 183, note 1). Since the same effect is produced by a smaller percentage change in the c. i. f. price, the elasticity in respect to it is greater.

An exactly corresponding situation holds when a market center is surrounded by a supply region—for milk, say. The same change of price in the town affects the distant seller more strongly, because his net receipts are smaller by the amount of the freight costs. Therefore his supply in respect to the c. i. f. price is more elastic than in respect to the f. o. b. price (contrary to Hoover, *op. cit.*, p. 191). Besides explaining the profound areal effect of even a small shrinkage in the radius of the supply region, it also explains why agricultural supply reacts so strongly on world market prices, particularly in distant overseas countries, and within these countries in their outlying parts. Here we meet a further difference between agriculture and industry. In the former, supply, in the latter, demand, is especially elastic in respect to the c. i. f. price. Hence changes in demand in the former, in supply in the latter, influence the c. i. f. price relatively little; as, conversely, demand in the former (because of the fixed need for food) and supply in the latter (because of fixed costs) react less upon it. Thus price drops should exert an equilibrating effect in agriculture by increasing demand less than they decrease supply, whereas in industry they should decrease supply less than they increase demand. But the market price is a c. i. f. price in agriculture only; in industry, on the contrary, it is an f. o. b. price. Consequently the producer pays the freight in the case of agriculture, the consumer at least half the freight in the case of industry.

In regard to the f. o. b. price, the demand of the customers of industry, and especially of mining, is also less elastic, though it is nevertheless elastic enough, particularly at the boundaries of the market area (except under **C**). At any rate, a cyclical decline in demand, especially as it is greater here, must, depending on the geographical elasticity relationships, lower unregulated market prices in heavy industry and mining more than the market prices of agricultural goods. Only the excess supply of those overseas marginal farmers who are really bankrupt but generally subsidized, and the reduction of supplies by industrial combinations, often lower agricultural prices more.

5. Except, perhaps, with goods that are not strictly comparable.

to current f. o. b. prices *increases* with the distance ($\epsilon_2 > \epsilon_3$; $\epsilon_2 > \epsilon_4$), the more rapidly the smaller the difference in f. o. b. prices ($\epsilon_3 > \epsilon_4$).[6] This holds true for a comparison between different places.

(3) In respect to the c. i. f. price, demand becomes continuously more elastic with increasing distance from the production site than in respect to the corresponding f. o. b. price (with increasing distance from the factory the superiority of ϵ_1 over ϵ_2 becomes greater and greater): under **C**, because the elasticity in respect to the current f. o. b. price, which corresponds to the constant c. i. f. price (ϵ_2), falls absolutely according to proposition 2; under **F** and **A**, because the elasticity of the demand in respect to the current factory price rises with distance, though less than in respect to the local price. This is plausible because $\epsilon_1 > \epsilon_2 > \epsilon_3$ and $\epsilon_1 > \epsilon_2 > \epsilon_4$.[7] Thus ϵ_2 increases absolutely, but decreases as compared to ϵ_1.[8]

(4) Elasticity in respect to the c. i. f. price increases with it ($\epsilon_1 > \epsilon_3 > \epsilon_4$) in all places, so that at a distance even small changes in the local price may elicit a greater reaction on the demand under certain circumstances than large changes in the vicinity of the factory.

(bb) *Preliminary Study (2): Local and Spatial Total Demand—A Comparison.* A comparison of the demand at the location of a factory alone with the demand throughout its whole market area is but a comparison between individual and aggregate demand. The demand of n fellow-townsmen of the manufacturer is equal to n times the demand of any one of them. It is different, except with **C**, when these n buyers are distributed over the entire market area. To anticipate the result: *The regional demand is smaller, and*

---

6. Proof: If d_1 is continually shifted downward it will intersect UT nearer and nearer to its (i. e., UT's) lower end, and HJ nearer and nearer to its (i. e., HJ's) upper end; that is to say, in the former case demand reacts more and more feebly on the rapidly falling factory price, and in the latter case more and more strongly on the factory price that is not falling at all.

7. If J is taken as any arbitrary c. i. f. price unconnected with E, $\epsilon_1 > \epsilon_2 > \epsilon_4$ can be interpreted also as follows: With the same sales (associated f. o. b. and c. i. f. price) the demand in respect to the c. i. f. price is ($\epsilon_1 > \epsilon_2$); on the contrary, if the prices are by coincidence equal, it is more elastic at the same place in respect to the f. o. b. price ($\epsilon_2 > \epsilon_4$).

8. This is true even though with increasing distance the same change in the factory price causes less and less percentage change in the local price. Proof for **F**: In calculating ϵ_1 and ϵ_2 the denominator is the same $(QU = DE)$. If d_1 is shifted downward, the denominator in the new calculation of the elasticity decreases in both cases by the same absolute amount. But only with ϵ_1 is the numerator increased by the same amount (Fig. 45: $\epsilon_1 = P_2L \div AP_2$; $\epsilon_2 = p_2K \div Bp_2$ [where $Bp_2 = Ap_2$]. New calculations: $\epsilon_1 = P_2L + P_7P_2 \div AP_2 - P_7P_2$; $\epsilon_2 = p_7J \div Cp_7$ [where $p_7J = p_2K$ and $Cp_7 = AP_2 - P_7P_2$]).

generally also more elastic, than the local demand. In both cases, elasticity increases as a rule with price and distance.

The regional demand is smaller: If there are n persons in P (Fig. 21), their demand (urban demand) will be $n \times PQ$, other things being equal. But if the same persons are evenly distributed over an area with the radius PF, around P, the demand of each with price policy **F**, and generally with **A** also, will be smaller than PQ (rural demand). If the straight-line demand curve is taken once more as the average of all possible shapes, we can even say by how much the rural demand falls short of the urban demand: It amounts to one third of the urban demand.[9] For since the volume of a cone equals the area of its base times one third its height, the demand at any one point in the circular area would amount on the average to $PQ/3$, and at n points to $n \times PQ/3$. Now we see why the metropolitan demand $(n \times PQ)$ is so much more attractive to industry than the rural demand: It is not only, and not always, the greater number of consumers that attracts, but also the demand of each, which is about three times greater in the limiting case; that is, when the actual sales radius is equal to the possible one. But competition reduces the size of the area considerably, and it is precisely the boundary zones, which have the smallest demand of all, that are eliminated. In the remaining area the individual demand is still smaller on the average than PQ, but generally, and above all with **A**, considerably larger than $PQ/3$.[10]

---

9. If, on the other hand, the demand curve is concave upward, the demand of country dwellers (compared with that of a person living at the factory site) will be less than one third, and if the individual demand curve is convex, more than one third, of what would correspond to their numbers.

10. A few factors, neglected until now, modify this result. Affluence, or at any rate population density, decrease with distance from a town. For since farmers living away from the city pay double freight—in the manufactured products that they buy and the agricultural products that they sell—either their income will be smaller or their farms larger than in the vicinity of a town. But even with the same income and at the same price, especially if this is high, the individual buys fewer and fewer urban goods with increasing distance from the town; for his demand depends upon price relationships as a whole, and these shift more and more in favor of rural products. Consequently the individual demand curve is rotated more and more toward the left about its intersection with the x-axis. The sales cone cannot then be constructed from the individual demand curve, but must be constructed from a special one that falls more abruptly as prices increase. Because prosperity and the desire to buy decrease, the rural demand throughout the entire region amounts to still less than one-third that in the town. Only the decrease in population density counteracts this: More farmers with a more even distribution then live near the town, where their demand is still relatively large. Since for all three reasons demand in the boundary zones is particularly small, their elimination raises the rural demand to a comparatively high degree, though perhaps absolutely not much above one third of the urban demand.

The regional demand is more elastic. Strictly speaking, this statement holds only for the average form of the straight-line demand curve; but it is therefore valid for the majority of conceivable, if not actual, cases. It is a rule of thumb. It seems plausible because a rise in price, for example, diminishes not only the individual demand (the height of the demand cone), but also the number of buyers (the radius of its base). Of course the average height of the cone (which is the relevant magnitude so far as total demand is concerned) is decreased by less than its maximum height (which represents the individual demand at the center of the region). It is therefore necessary, at least for the average case in which the demand is linear, that rigorous proof of the statement be given. It is offered herewith for the case where the market region is restricted by nothing but transport costs. In this case curve Δ in Figure 41 represents the total demand.[11] Now let d be the individual demand at the site of production, D the total demand throughout the sales region, and R the unit transport costs, borne by the consumer, from the production site to the boundaries of the region (the highest freight) at the factory price p; and let d', D', and R' be corresponding values at price p'. Then $D \div D' = \pi R^2 d/3 \div \pi R'^2 d'/3 = R^2 d \div R'^2 d' = d^3 \div d'^3$, since with a straight-line demand curve $R' = d'R \div d$. If $p > p'$, $d < d'$; $d \div d' > d^3 \div d'^3$; $d \div d' > D \div D'$. If $p < p'$ then, on the contrary, $d \div d' < D \div D'$. That is, the regional demand increases with falling prices and decreases with rising prices more sharply than the individual demand at the factory site; in short, it is more elastic in respect to the factory price.[12]

To give an example: with a linear demand $D \div D' = d^3 \div d'^3 = R^3 \div R'^3$. That is, the regional demands at various factory prices are related as the cubes of the maximum freights. If, for instance, the factory price is raised by half the highest freight, the regional demand will fall to 1/8, but the individual demand to only 1/2. A similar proof could be brought for the case in which the market

---

11. The following symbols, however, do not refer to Figure 41.

12. In still more general terms: The smaller the necessary area the weaker is the effect of a price change on the total demand. When the area becomes a point, as with a town, the demand is therefore least elastic. Consequently outlying demand is more elastic than local, and foreign demand more elastic than domestic, which is of importance in examining the transfer problem. It is interesting to understand the other side of the situation also. The lower the price, the more does a change in regional size affect demand, as is readily seen from curves Δ' and Δ in Figure 41. But the smaller the region the more effective is its change, even with a high price. In the limiting case, point concentration, G coincides with F, and the effect of a division of the town among several producers is percentually the same at every price.

Some New Factors

area is restricted by competition (Δ″ in Figure 41 corresponds to this).

As for the relation between the price and elasticity, total demand, exactly like individual demand, is more elastic the higher the price (always assuming a linear demand). This is easily seen from the

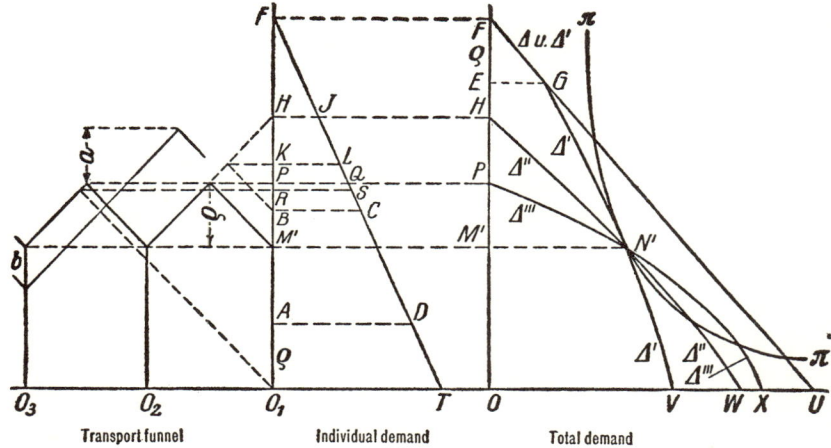

Fig. 41. Various types of total demand curves

OU   Volume of cone resulting from revolution of O_1FT about O_1T as an axis
OV   Volume of truncated cone resulting from revolution of O_1ADT about O_1T as an axis
OW   Volume of truncated cone resulting from revolution of O_1RST about O_1T as an axis
OX   Volume of truncated cone resulting from revolution of O_1PQT about O_1T as an axis
Δ   Greatest possible total demand as a function of factory price
Δ′   Demand within the circumscribed circle ρ $(=M'P = O_1A = EF)$ as a function of factory price [13]
Δ″   Total demand as a function of factory price when price and distance of competitors are given
Δ‴   Total demand as a function of factory price when price at areal boundaries is supposed always to be OP
OM′ is the price, ρ the size of the area, which together result in equilibrium. The shipping distance, that is, the circumference beyond which no more demand is supposed to come to O_1, does not reach the value ρ with every factory price.

equation $D \div D' = R^3 \div R'^3$, if it is recalled that consecutive equal absolute (and even more so percentage) price increases diminish R successively more and more. So much for the elasticity of curve Δ.

---

13. From factory price *OE* upward this restriction in regional size has no further influence on the extent of the total demand. Hence Δ′ coincides with Δ from here on.

The matter is exactly the same if the radius of the market area cannot be greater than r (or ρ in equilibrium), regardless of what the possible shipping distance R may otherwise be (curve Δ', Fig. 41). We let R increase slowly; that is, we let the price fall. As long as $R < r$, the given boundaries are irrelevant. But when R becomes greater than r, an increasingly large part of the possible demand will not be realized because of the restriction of the region; i. e., for this reason, too, total demand will become less elastic the lower the price.[14]

If, on the other hand, it is not the maximum distance of the boundaries of a producer's market, but the distance and the prices of competitors that remain constant (curve Δ''), this situation, too, provides an additional reason why elasticity should increase with price. In Figure 41, O_2 is the location of O_1's nearest competition, which limits the highest f. o. b. price obtainable by O_1 to O_1H; that is, to the equilibrium price, p, and the corresponding doubled shipping distance 2ρ. At any given price, O_1B, the extent of sales obtainable, BK, is equal to half the difference between the actual and the highest possible price $(BK = BH \div 2)$. Again it is true that an equal percentage rise in price shortens the sales radius percentually more the higher the price. For the higher the price absolutely, the shorter absolutely is the sales radius. Now since this is already shorter than under the conditions of curve Δ, it follows that the elasticity of curve Δ'' increases the factory price even more rapidly than that of Δ.

Finally, the elasticity of demand in respect to distance itself is interesting; that is to say, in respect to transport costs. The number of persons living at a certain distance from a factory $(c2\pi r)$ increases in the same proportion as the distance (r). The elasticity of the individual demand in respect to transport costs, on the contrary, rises with distance, as can be seen from Figure 40 if one thinks of the x-axis as passing through H and thus obtains the elasticity of d_0 in respect to the freight drawn into the figure from H upward. The elasticity coefficient of the total demand in respect to distance may, for the first reason, be low or even negative, but for the second reason it increases with distance.

On the other hand, the elasticity of the total demand is independent of population density, since this influences total demand to the same degree at all price levels.

---

14. One may say also: The smaller the region the less the elasticity of the total demand. Yet it cannot fall below the elasticity of the individual demand, but only reach it in the limiting case if the whole region coincides with the manufacturing site.

(cc) *Geographical Price Discrimination.* With price discrimination the seller asks of each buyer the factory price that will yield the highest profit. Where it does not involve too much trouble, price policy **A** is therefore the best. Now how is the most favorable price to be found at any given time?

1. *The Size of Price Differences.* The factory price of an isolated enterprise influences its sales and, conversely, marginal revenue does not equal price. Hence the equilibrium condition also does not hold in its limiting form (marginal cost = price) but only in its general form (marginal cost = marginal revenue). In this case price discrimination is most advantageous when this condition is fulfilled for each single buyer, not only (as with **F** and **C**) for all buyers together.[15] Marginal revenue depends upon the strength and elasticity of demand, and both in turn depend upon distance. Everything is to be related to the f. o. b. price, for the entrepreneur is interested only in the effect of the price he receives, not that which the buyer pays.

Now let

t = freight per unit from factory to buyer

P = delivered price $[P = f(n)]$

p = factory price $(p = P - t)$

n = individual demand at delivered price

ϵ = elasticity of demand in respect to delivered price

$$\epsilon = -\frac{P \times dn}{n \times dP}, \text{ i. e., } \frac{\text{percentage change in quantity}}{\text{percentage change in price}}$$

c = marginal costs.

Then marginal revenue is:

$$\frac{d(Pn)}{dn} - t = \frac{P \times dn + n \times dP}{dn} - t = P - \frac{P}{\epsilon} - t$$

Marginal revenue equals marginal costs when $P - t - (P \div \epsilon) = c$. Hence it follows that the most profitable factory price is $p = c + (P \div \epsilon)$, or $p = c - nf'(n)$; or, more correctly, since no quantities containing p remain on the right side of the equation,[16]

---

15. Only in the case of a prescribed market area is the marginal condition not necessarily fulfilled at the point of greatest profit. See Lösch, "Geographie der Preise" (in preparation). On the contrary, total revenue ≥ total costs must always be a second condition.

16. The derivation is E. M. Hoover's ("Spatial Price Discrimination," *Review of Economic Studies,* June, 1937, pp. 182–191).

$$p = \frac{\epsilon c + t}{\epsilon - 1}$$

Obviously the factory price is not the same for all buyers, but depends upon t, ϵ, and c. We shall now discuss the influence of these three factors on p, using the simple first formulation

$$[p = c + (P \div \epsilon)].$$

Distance.[16a] The greater the distance of the customer from the factory, the greater, *ceteris paribus*, is the factory price which he has to pay. p increases with t when ϵ and c are constant. ϵ does not remain constant as a rule, but increases with distance exactly as t. (See the preceding section on this point.) While p rises with increasing t, it falls with increasing ϵ. Whether p rises and falls with distance therefore depends on the relation between ϵ and t.

What are the conditions under which p will rise with distance? Let A_1 be nearer the factory than A_2. p_2 will then be greater than p_1 if

$$\frac{\epsilon_2 c + t_2}{\epsilon_2 - 1} > \frac{\epsilon_1 c + t_1}{\epsilon_1 - 1}$$

From this it follows that

$$\frac{\epsilon_2(t_1 + c) + (t_2 - t_1)}{\epsilon_1(t_2 + c)} < 1$$

But $\frac{t_2 - t_1}{\epsilon_1(t_2 + c)}$ is necessarily smaller than 1. The remainder of the inequality will be less than one if $(\epsilon_2 t_1 + \epsilon_2 c) < (\epsilon_1 t_1 + \epsilon_1 c)$. But $\epsilon_2 c$ is, as a rule, greater than $\epsilon_1 c$. If the inequality is to hold, t would have to show a greater percentage increase than ϵ. But this is highly improbable, since ϵ can become infinite while t always remains finite. If in the absence of better information we assume a straight-line demand curve as the average shape, ϵ will increase more rapidly than t. That is, the very shape of the demand curve makes it unlikely that p will increase with t. But, in addition, even in the few cases in which p might increase with t as far as demand is concerned, it can actually happen only in the still fewer cases where A_2 can be prevented from buying through A_1 rather than directly from the factory. *It follows that the factory price will fall with distance as a rule.*[17,18,19]

16a. The subsections "Distance," "Elasticity," and "Marginal Cost" have been translated from the fuller version of the first German edition, pp. 96–98.

17. This is shown in Figure 42 as follows: If p and ϵ are variables but c is held constant, then $p' = \frac{\epsilon c}{\epsilon - 1}$ is a rectangular hyperbola which, for $\epsilon > 1$, lies entirely

Some New Factors

Elasticity. The more elastic the demand the lower is the factory price that must be paid. This statement is absolutely valid for constant t, and usually holds also for $t = f(\epsilon)$. If demand is very elastic, the factory price virtually coincides with marginal cost: the hyperbola $p' = \phi(\epsilon)$ approaches its asymptote $p = c$. The price cannot fall below marginal cost. Yet if $\epsilon < 1$ this would have to be the case. It follows that the equilibrium point must lie on the elastic stretch of the demand curve.[20]

within the first quadrant. Its asymptotes are $p = c$ and $\epsilon = 1$. Since $t = f(\epsilon)$, $p'' = \dfrac{t}{\epsilon - 1}$ represents a family of similar hyperbolas with the asymptotes $p = 0$ and $\epsilon = 1$. Finally, $p = p' + p''$. For $\epsilon > 1$, p' falls with increasing ϵ. Consequently p'' must rise at least as much as p' falls, if p is to increase with ϵ. But p'' can increase with increasing ϵ only if even small increments in ϵ raise the corresponding hyperbola greatly, that is, if t increases very rapidly. Figure 42 shows furthermore that with constant ϵ the factory price will increase less with distance the greater is ϵ. For $\epsilon > 2$ the factory price increases by less than the freight. This follows from Figure 42 and from the equation

$$dt = \frac{t + d_t}{\epsilon - 1} - \frac{t}{\epsilon - 1},$$

which is fulfilled for $\epsilon = 2$.

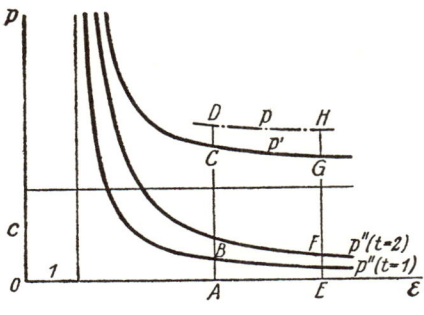

Fig. 42.

18. Since the excess profits of the nearer entrepreneur are greater, therefore, than those of the more distant ones, the former have a greater influence on the choice of location than would correspond to their demand, to say nothing of their numbers—a further reason for the concentration of industry in large cities.

19. This is not only rational but also realistic. One need think only of the many instances in which a product has a uniform price, or in which the seller pays at least part of the freight.

20. The left branch of the hyperbola $p' = \phi(\epsilon)$ is limited by $p = c$ in the upward direction and by $\epsilon = 1$ toward the right, and it always goes through the origin. With a negative elasticity the price is thus positive, but it is too low. For $0 < \epsilon < 1$, the price becomes a subsidy payment. This would make marginal revenue, which for $0 < \epsilon < 1$ is negative, positive again. As production increases, total costs rise and subsidy payments fall. Hypothetically speaking, production is expanded in this case until marginal cost equals the marginal savings in subsidy payments. For $\epsilon < 1$ the

Marginal Cost. The higher the marginal cost the higher is the factory price which the same buyer must pay. How does a change in c affect the spatial price dispersion, i. e., the dispersion of the factory prices which are established for *different* distances? Since p' changes proportionately with c, while p'' is independent of c, a change in c affects $p = p' + p''$ more the greater p'/p'' is. Since this fraction increases with distance, an increase in marginal cost raises the factory price for distant buyers more than for near-by customers. Thus an increase in marginal cost reduces spatial price differences and a decrease widens them.[21] As the reduction in the market area that is made possible by price differentiation raises cost, and thus diminishes spatial price differences, it brakes itself.

Example: We now apply the results to the characteristic case in which the individual demand is linear, and offer first an algebraic solution. From the demand equation, $p + t = - [(b/a)n] + b$,[22] it follows that $\epsilon = (p + t) \div (b - p - t)$ and hence, according to the formula for the factory price $p = \frac{1}{2}(b + c - t)$. Since b and c are given, p falls as t rises. For two different places we get $p_1 - p_2 = \frac{1}{2}(t_2 - t_1)$. *Thus with a linear demand schedule the factory price falls with distance, and by half the freight.*

As for the geometrical solution, d_0 to d_2 in Figure 43 are individual demand curves in respect to the f. o. b. price in three places, B_0 to B_2, separated successively from one another by the distance i. B_0 is the site of the factory. The marginal revenue, u_0', is easily derived from the demand curve d_0 by drawing the line AN' in such a way that N' bisects ON.[23] The curve for marginal revenue

---

equality of marginal revenue and marginal cost means minimization of losses rather than maximization of profits. The equality of marginal cost and marginal revenue is therefore only one equilibrium condition; the other is that there must be a true profit maximum.

21. I doubt that the intensification of spatial price differences that has been repeatedly noticed during a depression requires an explanation as complicated as that given above, or even admits of it. A general reduction in costs acts differently from a partial decrease, for which alone our analysis is valid. H. W. Singer ("A Note on Spatial Price Discrimination," *Review of Economic Studies*, October, 1937, p. 77), who attempted such an explanation, based his argument solely on the improbable case that ϵ is constant.

22. Where p, t, and n have the meaning given above, and b/a and b are the parameters of the particular straight-line demand curve.—W. F. S.

23. Proof: General equation for the linear demand curve: $y = -\frac{b}{a}x + b$; for the total revenue curve, $R = (-\frac{b}{a}x + b)x$; whence by differentiation is derived the marginal curve, $R' = -2\frac{b}{a}x + b$. (For a geometric proof, see J. Robinson, *The Theory of Imperfect Competition* [London, 1934], p. 32—W. F. S.)

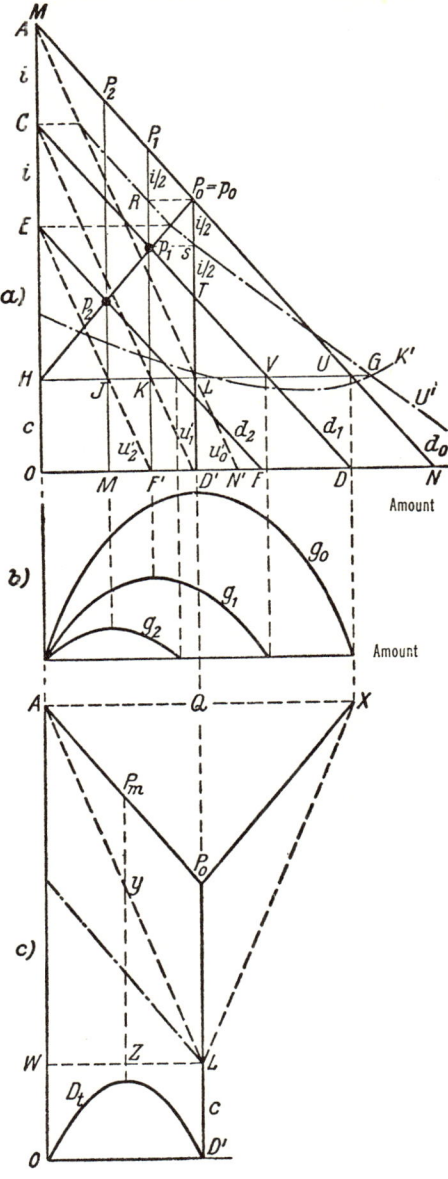

Fig. 43. (a) Three individual demand curves with respect to f. o. b. price as function of distance from site of factory. (b) Corresponding total revenue curves. (c) Corresponding transport cones.

as a function of total sales, U', is derived from the individual marginal receipts by horizontal addition. This intersects the marginal cost curve, K', at G. Here marginal costs equal marginal revenue; hence it is the point of highest profit. The points of intersection of HG with the individual marginal revenue curves give the optimum amounts that will be shipped to each place. The factory prices, p_0, p_1, and p_2 (which, incidentally, all lie on the straight line HP_0) can be read off from the corresponding demand curves. Finally, the corresponding delivered prices, P_0, P_1, and P_2, lie on d_0.

It is easily seen that these prices differ by $i/2$. According to a well-known theorem P_0L, for example, is equal to $AH \div 2$ and $p_1K = CH \div 2$. Since $AH - CH = i$, $P_0L = p_1K + i/2$, and so on. Furthermore, it is clear that *for every place the price lies halfway between the variable direct costs and that price at which nothing more would be sold;* that is, where the elasticity of the gross profit in respect to the amount sold is equal to 1 (for example, $Vp_1 \div p_1C = 1$). If one were to try to dispose of a larger or smaller amount, the gross profit from the buyers concerned (that is, receipts less *variable* costs) would be smaller in both cases (Fig. 43b).[24,25]

All this is made especially clear by the traffic funnel in Figure 43c, where the symbols are the same as for the corresponding lines in Figure 43a. $D'L$ is marginal costs, assumed to be constant for the sake of simplicity; LP_0 is the monopoly profit from home buyers, and P_0A the line of c. i. f. prices. ALX would be a cross section of the traffic funnel if no monopoly profit were taken but a uniform factory price at the level of the variable costs were asked. AP_0X is the funnel with monopolistic prices. If one unit were sold at every point on the line OD',[26] the area $OWLD'$ would represent variable production costs, the triangle WAL transport costs, and the triangle LAP_0 the gross monopoly profit without deduction of fixed costs. Or, from a different standpoint, the quadrilateral area WAP_0L is the amount paid by buyers over and above the variable costs of production. One third of it goes for freight paid by the buyers themselves, one third for freight paid by the shipper, and one third for monopoly profit.

---

24. Construction of the curves for gross profits assumes that the single buyer exerts no influence on marginal costs.

25. A similar but somewhat simpler diagram is given by J. Robinson, *op. cit.*, p. 183. Mrs. Robinson treats also a simple case of curvilinear demand curve.—W. F. S.

26. The sales radius, which would be represented in the demand cone by the highest possible freight, *may* be shown in this so-called traffic funnel also by the greatest amount sold per buyer—the line OD'.

The three triangles of equal area into which the quadrilateral is divided correspond to these amounts.[27]

Now of course the same amount will not be sold at every point on a radius of the market area, even when it is assumed that the buyers are evenly distributed. On the contrary, the sales, d, per buyer fall from OD' to zero with the distance from D'. On the other hand, the number, $n2\pi t$, of buyers (n per freight unit) at a certain distance (measured in transport costs, t) increases proportionately with distance. From this follows the equation for total sales at a certain distance: $D_t = d \times n2\pi t$. With a linear demand $t = -\frac{b}{a}d + b$. Therefore $D_t = -\frac{n2\pi b}{a}d^2 + n2\pi bd$. This is a parabola, with its vertex at the point $(a \div 2/ab\pi n \div 2)$ as drawn, with the ordinates shortened, in Figure 43c. It follows that if R is the radius of the market area, the combined demand of all the consumers at the distance $\frac{R}{2}$ will generally be of the greatest importance, whereas the total demand of nearer and more distant consumers will decrease symmetrically.[28] Consequently the monopoly profit, $YP_m = LP_0 \div 2$, is at the same time the average profit per unit, and the total monopoly profit is equal to this quantity—no longer multiplied by WL, however (and thus no longer equal to the triangle ALP_0), but multiplied by the content of the area enclosed by the parabola D_t and the line OD'. It is assumed here that the market area is not encroached upon from without.

2. *The Limits of Discrimination.* Besides the normal shape of the demand curve there is still another reason why the price at the factory is rarely higher for distant buyers (A_2) than for those near by (A_1): otherwise it would be advantageous for A_2 to purchase

---

27. The profit triangle is LAP_0. Thus profits decrease with distance exactly as do agricultural rents. However, the farmer gets the same rent on each unit, which therefore differs only among different farmers, whereas the profit of the industrialist varies with the location of the buyer.

28. It is now clear why competition is so keen at their boundaries when market areas are reduced by competition: most of the demand of factories which themselves are located in small places is here. If areas are curtailed but little, here is one of the reasons why foreign trade also decreases with distance. In Germany, powdered and broken pumice has a market area limited only by freight, and linoleum a market area that is limited in certain directions only by freight; because all the former is produced in one single district and the latter made chiefly in but a few factories. In 1938 the most frequent shipping distance by rail was about 300 to 375 miles for the former and about 375 to 430 miles for the latter, or, in accordance with theory, almost exactly half the maximum (about 750 and 800 miles respectively).

through A_1.[29] Conversely, the factory price for A_1 can exceed that for A_2 only by the freight, f, from A_2 to A_1 at the most; else A_1 would order through A_2. As for the c. i. f. price, P_1 can be above or below P_2 by f at the most, and similarly the extent of fluctuation for P_2, when P_1 is given, is equal to *twice* the freight between the two places; whereas the difference between P_1 and P_2 can be equal to the *single* freight at the highest.

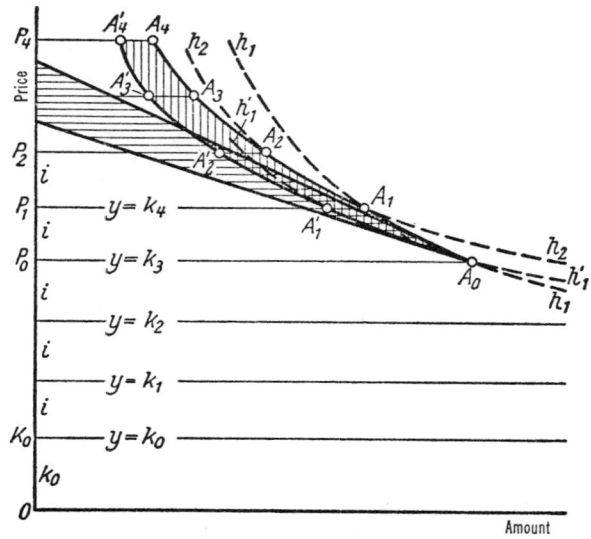

Fig. 44. Geometric solution of limits of price differentiation

How must the demand be constituted in order that factory prices, differentiated irrespective of the possibility of intermediate trade, shall never differ by more than the freight? We shall discuss this question only briefly because it is rather difficult, and because it is important only for those demand curves that differ widely from the average, as will be seen later.

Geometrical Solution: Let k_0 in Figure 44 be the marginal costs without freight at the factory site B_0; $(k_1 = k_0 + i)$ the marginal costs including freight for delivery to the place B_1; $(k_2 = k_0 + 2i)$ for delivery to B_2, twice as far away; and so on. For purchasers at B_0 let OP_0 be the price that yields the highest profit, and P_0A_0 the amount sold to each buyer at this price.

---

29. It must be remembered, however, that interrupted hauls are more expensive than direct hauls.

Some New Factors 155

First: How must the individual demand curve d look in order that the factory price shall be the same for all buyers wherever they may be, despite the tendency to discrimination? So far we know only one point on d: A_0. We draw through A_0 the rectangular hyperbola h_1, whose asymptotes are the y-axis and the horizontal $y = k_0$. As the product $x(y - k_0)$, which represents profit, is the same for every point on this hyperbola, d must touch the hyperbola at A_0, and otherwise lie to the *left* of it. Else OP would not be the most advantageous factory price for a buyer at B_0. Next we draw through A_0 the rectangular hyperbola h_1', whose asymptotes are $x = 0$ and $y = k_1$. If d and h_1' touch at A_0 and if d lies otherwise to the *left* of h_1', a greater profit cannot be obtained at B_1 with any other delivered price than OP_0. The factory price for B_1 is, therefore, lower by f than that for B_0. The condition that would have to be fulfilled if the delivered price in B_1 is to lie above OP_0 is that d must pass above A_0 and to the *right* of h_1'. Hence not h_1', but a hyperbola with the same asymptotes and lying to the right of it, would touch d. If the point of tangency were between $y = k_3$ and $y = k_4$, it would be advantageous in shipping to B_1 for the entrepreneur at B_0 to absorb part of the freight. The condition under which B_1 would pay all the freight is that the point of tangency must lie on the line $A_1'A_1$. The nearer it is to A_1 the greater is the profit from buyer B_1. Thus, between $y = k_3$ and $y = k_4$, d must lie within the vertically hatched area, and in such a way that no hyperbola of the group defined by the asymptotes $x = 0$ and $y = k_1$ touches it anywhere else than at $y = k_4$. Similarly two hyperbolas can be drawn through A_1, of which the steeper, h_2 (asymptotes $x = 0$, $y = k_1$), limits the farther course of d toward the right. The flatter one is superfluous, since the left limit for d is given by the flatter of the hyperbolas passing through A_1' (asymptotes $x = 0$, $y = k_2$). If the construction is carried further a cornucopia-shaped area, vertically hatched in Figure 44, is obtained, within which d must lie if the factory price is to be independent of distance.[30] To this is added, as a second condition, that d must lie within this area in such a way that the ordinates of the points of tangency of the profit hyperbolas must differ by exactly the freight.

Second: If the factory price is to rise with distance, the cornucopia must be more steeply inclined above $A_1'A_1$, as can readily be seen. Then h_1 and h_1' still constitute the extreme limits above A_1'

---

30. All demand curves that rise above the upper limits (A_0, A_1, A_2, and so on) lead to greater, and all that fall beneath the lower limits ($A_0, A_1', A_2', \cdots$) lead to smaller, price differences than would correspond to the freight differences.

and A_1, and they are steeper than h_2 and h_2'. In this case, therefore, the elasticity of the demand in respect to the delivered price must fall with distance more slowly, if at all, than in the preceding case. This we have already seen on page 149.

Third: If the factory price is to fall with the distance of buyers, the cornucopia, and with it the demand curve, obviously must be less steeply inclined. This means that with a rising price the elasticity of the demand is increased relatively quickly. A subcase deserves special attention. Suppose that the group of hyperbolas determined by the asymptotes $x = 0$ and $y = k_1$ touched the demand curve halfway between $y = k_3$ and $y = k_4$. This would mean that the delivered price would rise with increasing distance by only half the freight, and that the price at the factory would therefore fall by the same amount. It could easily be shown [31] that the limits of the cornucopias in this case would be straight lines,[32] the steeper one of which would have the equation

$$y = -\left(\frac{y_0 + \frac{i}{2}}{x_0}\right)x + 2y_0 + \frac{i}{2},$$

whereas the equation for the flatter one would be

$$y = -\left(\frac{y_0 - \frac{i}{2}}{x_0}\right)x + 2y_0 - \frac{i}{2},$$

where $x_0 = P_0 A_0$ and $y_0 = K_0 P_0$. The scope of d is horizontally hatched in Figure 44. In this case among others the demand curve itself can be a straight line. Conversely, it is true that *when the demand curve is a straight line the entrepreneur always pays half the freight.*[33]

Algebraic solution: From the formula for the factory price there follows as the c. i. f. price for B_1,

$$P_1 = \frac{\epsilon_1 c + \epsilon_1 t_1}{\epsilon_1 - 1}$$

and for B_2,

$$P_2 = \frac{\epsilon_2 c + \epsilon_2 t_2}{\epsilon_2 - 1}$$

---

31. The proof is omitted in order not to overburden the text with mathematics.
32. This is strictly true only when f is very small. Otherwise at least the points of intersection of the branches of the hyperbolas lie on a straight line.
33. Strictly speaking, he does not pay half the freight, which represents variable costs that the buyer must make good in any case, but he foregoes profit or compensation for his fixed costs to the extent of half the freight.

Let B_2 be farther away from the factory than B_1. If P_2 is higher, the condition under which the delivered price will not differ by more than the freight is $P_2 - P_1 \leqq t_2 - t_1$; or, if $t_2 - t_1 = i$,

$$\epsilon_1 (c + t_1 + i) \leqq \epsilon_2 (c + t_2) + i$$

It will be found that, among others, the elasticities resulting from a straight-line demand curve fulfill this condition.

3. *Application (Dumping, Overlapping Areas, Basing Point)*. *Dumping*, or factory price discrimination in favor of more distant buyers, need not by any means imply invasion of an outside market. There exists rather a desirable form of dumping in the more remote part of an undisputed home market, as we have shown.

An *overlapping of areas* in the case of homogeneous products, that is, dumping in the market area of a competitor, on the other hand, is often a sign of disintegration or panic, or a result of megalomania, and to this extent concerns more the psychiatrist than the economist. At the least it is an outcome of a thoughtless disregard of distance.[34] In America especially there have been many complaints about such cross-hauling. The Federal Trade Commission has calculated that in 1928–29 it caused unnecessary freight in the cement industry, for example, amounting to some 20 per cent of the total production and marketing costs.[35] Exact analysis shows, however, that quality differences are often involved; or that where statistics are broken down according to large areas of localities we are dealing with only apparent cross-hauling, and in reality with " small boundary trade." The cross-hauling proper that remains is often quantitatively negligible. It has been said in justification of cross-hauling that it is necessary in industries with high fixed costs

---

34. Perhaps because a producer is not sure of his costs, is not acquainted with neighboring buyers or shippers, wishes to continue accidental business relations, enjoys exceptional freight rates that are much too low, or in transactions within the concern does not worry over distances. A certain amount of cross-hauling could, however, be avoided only if production were more mobile. Such unavoidable cross-hauling would occur when the sites of those producers or consumers chiefly concerned cannot handle a sudden falling off in production, or sudden great demands such as the threat of a bad harvest or extensive construction. Fundamentally, market areas shift temporarily, and under certain conditions a market area may even become a supply area. This may lead, as a precaution, even to normal orders going in part to distant shipper in order to be sure of them in case of peak demand. All this is confirmed by the findings of the *Baustoffleitstelle* and the *Dienststelle* (formery *Büro*) *für Transportordnung*.

35. T. K. Urdahl and L. J. O'Neill, " Operation of the Basing Point Provisions in the Lime Industry Code," *NRA, Division of Review, Work Materials No. 65*, 1936, pp. 75 f.

in order to assure an adequate volume of business,[36] and even that with falling marginal costs it may lead to a drop in domestic prices.[37]

But these arguments overlook the fact that, especially within the same country, reciprocal dumping inevitably develops from unilateral dumping, and that none of the participants therefore receives additional orders, though all incur additional expenses. That dumping should be answered by dumping is only psychologically, not economically, necessary. It would be more advantageous to employ a part of the freight costs that dumping must absorb to prevent foreign dumping into the home market, instead of invading another market.[38]

As unlimited dumping leads only to pressure on prices and all-round losses, the *basing-point system* attempts to replace it with regulated, or limited, dumping. The simplest of its many forms is that in which all factory prices are the same and the freight from the basing point to the buyer is added to all. Producers outside the basing point therefore charge their customers more or less than the actual freight, according to circumstances. Only thus in the limiting case can all producers compete at the same price for every buyer (quality rather than price competition). They will not do so in reality, of course, if, in the case of unfavorably located customers, they had to absorb more freight than would correspond to the profits from near-by customers plus the share in the fixed costs (m). In addition, the permissible freight absorption will sometimes be still further limited by agreement. If the same factory price is to hold for all customers wherever situated, the freight at most from factory to basing point can be absorbed (h). In other agreements, the absorbable freight will be fixed at a percentage of the factory price (z).[39] In any case, the maximum degree of permissible dumping with the basing-point system is automatically established for every place in the area of a competitor; and, except at the geographical boundaries of any area that can be won at all by dumping,[40] it will

---

36. G. Seidler, "The Control of Geographic Price Relations under Codes of Fair Competition," *NRA, Division of Review, Work Materials No. 86*, 1936.

37. G. von Haberler, *Der Internationale Handel* (Berlin, 1933), p. 229; (English ed., 1936), p. 309.

38. This is one reason why international dumping does not necessarily presuppose the protection of high domestic prices by duties. Moreover, the most advantageous price discrimination is generally such that it does not pay, in any case, to re-import cheap exported goods.

39. G. Seidler, "The Control of Geographic Price Relations under Codes of Fair Competition," *NRA, Division of Review, Work Materials No. 86*, 1936, p. 33.

40. *As to the size of an area supplied at all:* If h is the maximum degree of dumping technically possible under the basing-point system alone (freight from factory to

be smaller as a rule than the whole absorbable amount in the limiting case of profit plus fixed costs. Thus it is true that *the basing-point system restricts but does not prevent unreasonable dumping into a foreign area. On the other hand, reasonable dumping within the home area will be prevented,* though in varying degree according to the construction of the basing-point system.[41]

(dd) *Uniform Prices.* Uniform prices are less advantageous for

---

basing point), unassociated with price policy A; z the degree granted by agreement; and m the degree economically possible (profit plus average fixed costs), then the seller will be willing to ship anywhere, with uniform f. o. b. prices, if m and z are at least equal to h (the highest value of h in absorbed freight will be reached only on the extension of the factory basing-point line beyond the latter). If m or z is smaller than h, not even the basing point itself will be supplied. With a straight mileage tariff in a uniform transport area the market area will then be bounded by a hyperbola. This includes the basing point when m and z lie between h and $h/2$; it becomes a straight line that passes halfway between factory and basing point when z is equal to, and m at least equal to, $h/2$, or vice versa. Conversely, if m or z is smaller than $h/2$, the hyperbola includes the factory site. In the latter case, however, not only will no freight be absorbed; more will be taken in than when freight is charged as of factory (so-called freight advantage: see, for example, Möller, *Weltwirtschaftliches Archiv*, 1943, p. 91, Fig. 1). With a sliding-scale tariff [involving lower mileage rates for longer hauls.—W. H. W.] the hyperbolas close to ellipsoid curves (G. Mecklenburg, *Der Gütertransportaufwand der Deutschen Eisenindustrie*, Hannoversche Dissertation [1941], p. 27).

On the size of an area supplied to special advantage: Besides the area that a factory not situated at the basing point is willing to supply at all, that part of an area that it will supply with more profit, and that other part that it will supply with less are of interest; or, more accurately, that part that it will supply at higher or lower prices than when freight is charged from the factory. The dividing line passes halfway between factory and basing point if the price policy in both places is the same; that is, if they either charge the same uniform f. o. b. price or if both discriminated starting from the same level. Prices will be higher via the basing point at the site of the factory, and vice versa.

On the other hand, if equal prices are charged from the basing point and discriminatory f. o. b. prices at the factory, the area in which charges via the basing point result in higher f. o. b. prices is widened (provided $z, m \geqq h$). Only in an ellipsoid area in which the basing point itself lies excentrically is an f. o. b. price policy more advantageous. The ellipse becomes larger when the starting price with discrimination is higher than the uniform basing-point price, and smaller in the opposite case. In short, with shipments toward the basing point the seller, with shipments away from the basing point the buyer, pays more freight than with rational dumping. Hence in the one case revenue, in the other, demand, decreases more rapidly with distance.

41. With a uniform basing-point price, producers at the basing point cannot differentiate their factory prices at all according to the distance of buyers. Producers who are not situated at the basing point do not discriminate directly away from the basing point, but toward the basing point they discriminate too strongly against neighboring buyers. (The c. i. f. price falls with distance from the factory instead of rising, though more slowly than would correspond to the actual freight.)

the seller unless they considerably facilitate sales promotion and business calculations. Uniform factory prices (**F**) and uniform delivered prices (**C**) must be distinguished. The buyer pays the freight in the former case, the seller in the latter. Nevertheless, it makes no difference to the seller (in the average case of linear demand) which of the two uniform prices he selects, so long as his sales area is determined by competition and not, say, by governmental authority. The size of his sales area and thus the number of independent enterprises as well, no less than the size of their profits, will be the same in either case.[42] Sales and the average factory price will also be equal. All this is true whether, from the standpoint of the individual firm, the tendency toward maximum profits predominates; or whether, from the standpoint of the economy as a whole, the tendency toward maximization of the number of independent business units predominates;[43] in other words, whether sales areas are chosen as advantageously as possible, or as small as possible.[44]

(ee) *Geographic Price Policy and Competition.* The competition of old and of new enterprises, that is, efforts to expand, or to begin an independent existence, must be sharply distinguished. The former finds its geographic limits; the latter is virtually as unlimited as the reservoir of those who would like to make themselves independent.

1. *Competition by New Enterprises.* We have developed the various possibilities of geographic price policy for the case where an arbitrary market area is at the disposal of an entrepreneur. The tendency to keep the area of the individual enterprise as small as

---

42. Thus **C** is possible not only with goods for which freight plays no role. The elimination of too distant buyers is caused with **F** by the price, with **C** by the refusal of the entrepreneur to deliver.

43. See section *ee*.

44. This is because the aggregate demand curve and the aggregate marginal revenue curve are identical with **F** and **C** for both the uniform and the average f. o. b. price. My "Geographie der Preise" advances the difficult proof. The intersection of the marginal revenue and marginal cost curves determines the most favorable uniform price. In Figure 45, an amplification of Figure 40, if P_0 is the uniform f. o. b. price, and P_3 the uniform c. i. f. price, DP_0 will determine the sales and TP_3 the f. o. b. price and the marginal revenues in the individual localities (points of intersection with d_0, d_1, and d_2, and u_0', u_1', and u_2' respectively). EP_1 gives the discriminatory factory prices for the case where aggregate sales are as they are with **C** and **F**. The marginal revenues from all buyers are the same (Q, R, S) only with A; with **F**(M, R, W) and **C**(N, R, T), on the contrary, they are partly too high and partly too low to permit an equally advantageous exploitation of the demand, and thus an equally large profit.

Some New Factors 161

possible prevails only in an open market. It was assumed in Chapters 9–12 that the limit had been reached when the area was so diminished that the demand curve at a uniform factory price was tangent to the cost curve. With any further decrease the enterprise would no longer cover its cost, unless it adopted the expedient of spatial price discrimination; that is, unless it demanded different

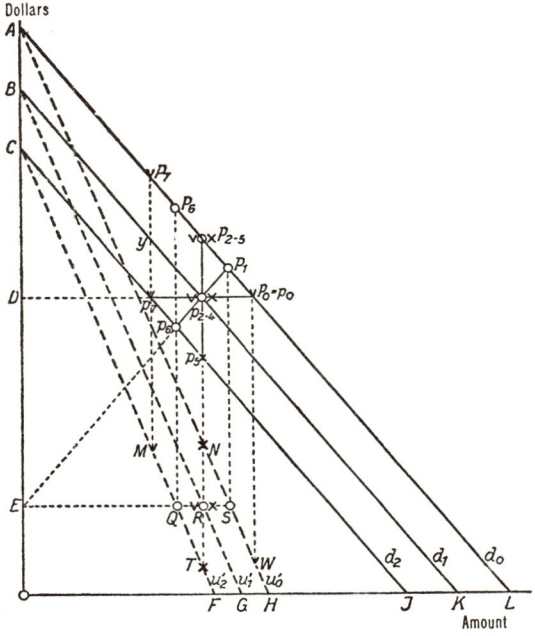

Fig. 45. Comparison of price discrimination (O), uniform f. o. b. price (V), and (X) uniform c. i. f. price

factory prices of its customers according to their distance. This brings in additional revenues. These do not always permit a further reduction in the market area. Such a reduction becomes more and more possible, however, the greater the necessary market area and the greater, therefore, the possibilities for freight absorption.[45] Thus

45. To determine the smallest market area and the most favorable price therein, the marginal cost curve is no longer made to intersect the current highest marginal revenue but the lowest possible one, and thus the one that is valid for the smallest possible number of places. It need not be the lowest absolutely, if in such a small area total revenues are below total costs throughout. This is less common with **A**, and in addition the chances that a low marginal revenue curve here would be intersected by the marginal cost curve are rather better because the former, though mathematically identical with the curves for **C** and **F**, is significant for a larger area. With

where the tendency to multiplication of independent enterprises is in full operation *it compels geographic price discrimination*.[46]

2. *Competition by Existing Enterprises.* How does the approach of competition affect price policy: (*a*) at the boundaries of the geographic area supplied, and (*b*) in general?

(a_1) Will the compactness of areas be destroyed by dumping; or (a_2) will the price be lowered by competition to variable costs, at least on the boundary? Or (a_3) will competitors leave to each other the contributions of marginal buyers to profit, or at least to fixed costs? Or (*b*) will they nevertheless pursue a policy in respect to the general level of their prices that can never lead to a stable equilibrium of their prices and their markets?

Here I can only set down my answer—not give reasons for it. (*a*) The tendency toward maximization of the number of independent enterprises forces the entrepreneur with sufficient insight at the boundary also toward price discrimination in the manner indicated. (*b*) Furthermore, it generally leaves but little room for a strategic price policy as developed by W. Launhardt,[47] H. Hotelling,[48] T. Palander,[49] E. Schneider,[50] and others with respect to freight costs, at least for duopolists.[51] With adequate insight there usually exists a definite equilibrium. If many act irrationally, equilibrium will be

---

A smaller areas are therefore possible than with **C** and **F**, where among a host of identical marginal revenue curves one lying higher than with **A** will often be decisive. There would be so much to say in explanation here that I refer once more to my forthcoming "Geographie der Preise." Only this need be said here: That marginal revenue curves should be identical is entirely consistent with the fact that the total revenue curves with **A** lie uniformly higher.

46. If the tendency to a multiplication of independent enterprises compels price discrimination, this in its turn encourages an increase of competition—either local or distant. In the former case, more firms share the same area; in the latter, the area will be still further reduced until in both cases profits have disappeared despite price discrimination. Local competition need not prevent price discrimination itself. It is enough that by cutting into sales it raises production costs so high that profits are consumed. Price discrimination occurs even though its purpose is thus thwarted. The areal diminution provides a typical example of monopolies almost without teeth, that may practice price discrimination in their areas and yet be unable to make excess profits, because the areas that they control absolutely are too much restricted from without.

47. W. Launhardt, *Mathematische Begründung der Volkswirtschaftslehre* (Leipzig, 1885), pp. 161 ff.

48. H. Hotelling, "Stability in Competition," *Economic Journal*, 1929.

49. T. Palander, *Beiträge zur Standortstheorie* (Uppsala, 1935), pp. 231–253, 370–394.

50. E. Schneider, "Bemerkungen zu einer Theorie der Raumwirtschaft," *Econometrica*, 1935, pp. 90 ff.

51. With geographical dispersion each has perhaps half a dozen competitors, and thus has a moderate influence on each individually.

deferred, whereas knowledge and legal encouragement of the right behavior will lead more quickly to a stable and rational outcome.[52] This will be discussed under β.

52. Concerning a_1: Dumping in a neighboring area would be countered or, still better, averted, so that the aggressor in particular would rather diminish and destroy his own profitability once the endeavor to establish new plants is wholly effective. If all dump, then of course the necessary minimum size of market is increased, but so also is the chance of still invading them by an abandonment of dumping. Only in competition with different goods, therefore, not with homogeneous ones, is it rational to absorb freight.

Concerning a_2: The following holds true for price discrimination. As the aggregate marginal revenue curve is shifted to the left with the diminution of an area, its intersection with the marginal cost curve also moves toward the left. According to whether the new point of intersection is higher or lower than the old, the new factory price at the geographical boundary will be higher or lower than before. In the new equilibrium the average costs, which generally rise with decreased sales, exceed the factory price at the geographical boundary. Here the price lies between average and marginal costs. Marginal costs are, of course, still equal to the marginal revenue. But this says only that variable costs, not necessarily all the fixed costs involved as well, are covered by the revenue in the boundary zone. Indeed, this certainly will not be the case, and the deficit will be just made up by the surpluses in the vicinity of the factory. The "exploitation" of districts near the factory and dumping in those at a distance compensate one another. Together they make it possible to decrease the necessary market area far more than without price discrimination. The diminution proceeds until the average costs are so high above the factory prices prevailing in the boundary zone that the deficit in fixed costs is only just covered by the surpluses in the interior.

Concerning b: How are a stable price and market to be found? The matter is not so simple that one need only advise that half the freight be added to the costs. For the costs depend upon the size of the area also, and this is still unknown. Following the example of Walras with his "prix crié par hasard" in a one-point market, would it not be possible to start from a boundary accidentally held between areal markets? Each would then determine the most favorable starting price on the basis of his costs and his share of the demand (Δ' in Figure 41). Whoever was cheaper than his competitors because of this starting from an arbitrary boundary would as a rule have to move the boundary back until prices were equal there. It is improbable either that the cheaper seller should retreat of his own accord, or that the boundary (like price in the Walrasian market) should be jointly changed. Each, rather, would eagerly hope for a market area of the most advantageous extent, no matter whether or not his competitors were located in it; whether he would therefore have to drive them from the market or share it with them. According to this boundary, as he imagines it, he sets his starting price, only to find that he has begun with too large an area, since his competitors will underbid him before he reaches that boundary. Each one, therefore, has higher costs and smaller revenues than he calculated, so each generally lowers his sights as to the desirable market area and usually raises the price. Each gropes his way toward the equilibrium point where boundary and boundary price coincide. Is there only one such boundary and boundary price? The curve of delivered prices at the boundary for all boundary points on the line connecting "I" and "II" at which "I" can aim, cuts the corresponding curve for "II" only once if the boundary price changes monotonically with shifting of the boundary—which upon closer examination appears to be the rule. When each stops struggling and cannot expect more than mere existence where there is a strong tendency to independence—stable equilibrium reigns.

2. EFFECTS OF GEOGRAPHIC PRICE POLICY

(aa) *Effect on Density and Agglomeration of Locations.* With **A** the most profitable market area is larger, that necessary to existence equal to or smaller than with **F** or **C**. Hence, in industries to which there is free entry, *locations will often lie closer together with price discrimination* than with uniform prices.

The effects of price policy on the agglomeration of locations in favored regions are harder to assay. First, as to the locations of the *originators* of the policy: With **A**, and still more with **C**, the profits from neighboring buyers are higher than those from more distant ones. Consequently the former weigh more heavily in the choice of a location than would correspond to their demand, to say nothing of their number—one more reason for the concentration of industries in large cities. Most important are the effects of the basing-point system: Plants situated at a basing point enjoy an unlimited market area. Nowhere can they be undersold, nowhere can they lose; but their goal is the highest profit. When the point of lowest c. i. f. costs does not coincide with the basing point they move, like all plants, toward it.[53] The more evenly all competitors in a market area share the demand, the more nearly do the points of least c. i. f. costs for all coincide. They agglomerate until some costs of production rise so much because of the concentration that some plants migrate to another point of agglomeration. Only when industries voluntarily concentrate in a smaller market area (which will generally be more advantageous) does there arise a tendency to disperse from the basing point, and to settle more densely the farther they scatter. Whether dispersion or new agglomeration is the final result, *migration from the basing point is probable.*[54]

For the *buyers* in the industry whose price policy is under con-

---

53. Here is a striking example of Weber's theory that until now has passed unnoticed by its adherents. An enterprise with a given output (quota), a given body of buyers who can nowhere be lost to cheaper competitors, and a particularized demand (since delivered prices are stationary) can actually choose a location by means of the isodapane diagram, especially when the prices of many production factors are geographically leveled by rate schedules and stabilized. The minimum transport need not be at the site of consumption. It is not true, therefore, that a tendency necessarily develops to move from the basing point to the point of consumption in order to save freight, which the customer pays anyway. It depends upon whether or not the freight on raw materials is increased thereby.

54. According to A. R. Burns the capacity of the iron and steel industry from 1916 to 1931 rose more rapidly outside the basing point, Pittsburgh (*The Decline of Competition* [New York, 1936], p. 341).

sideration, the advantages are reversed. They may be attracted to or toward the cheap basing point or (with policy **A** and especially **F**) the production site, but this is likely to be overshadowed by a host of other factors. Policy **C**, like the basing-point system, eliminates not only the influence of the producer's location on prices, but also the influence of prices on the location of the consumer. Within the sales area chosen the good concerned becomes ubiquitous. Buyers agglomerate less at the production site; but whether they will then disperse or concentrate more thickly somewhere else remains undecided. To set uniform delivered prices is to eliminate the most important regulator of a rational spatial arrangement.

(bb) *Effects on Producers and Consumers.* A comparison with price discrimination shows that **A** almost always results in higher profits and, with free entry, a greater number of independent enterprises.[55] Thus it is more advantageous for the entrepreneur, whereas **F** always results in lower c. i. f. prices, and so on the average favors the consumer.[56] Only distant consumers fare better with **A**, and better still with **C**, because here freight is absorbed; those living near the factory, on the other hand, pay higher prices (see Fig. 45). With the basing-point system and with policy **C** much waste through cross-haulings is likely,[57] which raises prices.

β. *Price Differentials among Different Market Areas*

If factory prices and freight rates with policy **A** or **F** are the same for all production centers, as we have assumed so far, their sales areas are equilateral hexagons and their boundaries straight lines. If the freight rates (straight mileage tariffs) are different, the sales areas are irregular polygons and their boundaries are arcs. If factory prices are different, the sales areas are irregular polygons and their boundaries are hyperbolic arcs.[58] Practically, this is perhaps the most

55. A. Lösch, *Geographie der Preise* (in preparation).
56. One may be undecided whether to interpret this to mean that the demand curve of a certain area in respect to the average c. i. f. price is lowest with **F** and highest with **C**. Consumers are more heavily overcharged with **A** and **C**, but also they are *prepared* to pay more.
57. Especially, also, within the district around a basing point in which producers are located and in which in the transport system is already subjected to heavy strains.
58. This is easily seen, even without algebraic proof. To points on the boundary it must be a matter of indifference from which of the neighboring production centers they order. The constant differences in factory price must therefore be compensated by an equally constant and opposite difference in freight. But the geometric locus of all points whose distances from two given points differ by a constant amount is a hyperbola. In so far as prices are lowest in the metropolis, the hyperbolas lie with

important case. Finally, if both factory prices and freight rates are different, the sales areas are irregular polygons, and their boundaries are curves of the fourth degree.[59] The boundary lines become still more complicated if the straight mileage tariff is replaced by a graduated tariff.

The situation is entirely similar for regions of agricultural supply except that they are, so to speak, the mirror image of industrial sales areas. If the boundaries of the latter are projections of sections of price funnels, agricultural boundaries originate in the intersection of price cones. Again the case of equal freight rates, but different prices at the centers, is the most important one. Figure 46 shows the price cone for three places, A, B, and C, and above S the industrial mirror image. In exactly the same way that B, as an industrial place, would be excluded from sales if the price there were equal to the price at A plus the freight costs from A to B, it would be prevented from supplying agricultural products if the price at B were equal only to the price at A less the freight from B to A.[60] Just as the line DG'' forms the upper limit of industrial production, so DG is the lower limit for agricultural production at the price in B. The larger a town, the higher the market price of agricultural products in it. Assuming that the population of A doubled, the price of milk, say, would have to rise above AD in order that the milkshed could increase at the expense of town B. B, too, would experience a price increase, but by a smaller absolute amount because its population has remained the same. Consequently the branches of its bounding hyperbola will be more compressed: it carves out for its own needs [61]

---

their vertices toward the center of the areal system. Moreover, they intersect in such a way that their foci lie about in the middle of the areas that they enclose. For then then demand is greatest.

59. W. Launhardt has already shown this (*Mathematische Begründung der Volkswirtschaftslehre* [Leipzig, 1885], pp. 157 f.). T. Palander has given a detailed derivation (*Beiträge zur Standorttheorie* [Uppsala, 1935], pp. 223–230. See also his Fig. 193, p. 363). Moreover, A. Schilling ("Die wirtschaftsgeographischen Grundgesetze des Wettbewerbs in mathematischer Form," *Technik und Wirtschaft*, XVII [1924], p. 146) introduces in addition market boundaries ("isostants") between a point and an economic front, which likewise are conic sections—ellipses, parabolas, or hyperbolas. They do not arise geometrically as with competition, between two points by the intersection of price funnels, but by the intersection of a price funnel with a plane representing the c. i. f. price, which rises from the economic front outward by the amount of the freight costs.

60. Unless B were on a traffic route that connected A with its hinterland.

61. A. Predöhl ("Die örtliche Verteilung der amerikanischen Eisen- und Stahlindustrie," *Weltwirtschaftliches Archiv*, XXVII, 239–292, and 314*–329*) has described the corresponding industrial case. As long as B (Chicago) does not fully meet the local demand for steel, A (Pittsburgh) will supply the rest and, being the marginal producer determine the price until Chicago produces enough, and more than enough,

Some New Factors

a smaller area of the milkshed supplying *A*. The milkshed of *C*, a still smaller town, lies within that of *B*. As there are other towns lying beside *B* and *C*, their supply areas actually will not extend up to the circular arcs, but will be already bounded by further branches of the hyperbolas.

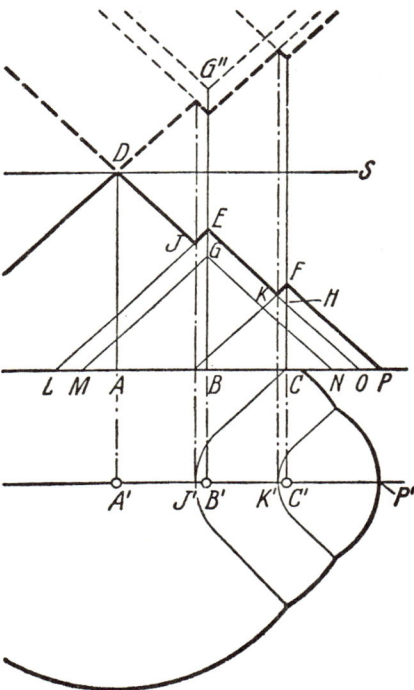

Fig. 46. Price cones for agricultural products around towns *A*, *B*, and *C*, and, above the *s*-axis, their industrial mirror image

It is different with price policy **C**. If every producer of a standard-sized product asks a uniform c. i. f. price, different, however, from that of his competitor, the cheapest producers would extend their sales areas in all directions up to the most advantageous sales radius. Farther out they will refuse deliveries, even though they are cheaper than their competitors.[62]

---

for local demand at the Pittsburgh-plus-price. Then the price will drop in Chicago and it will have its own sales area.

62. No diminution of areas occurs in this case. The competition of those already established reacts on the competition of new entrants in such a way that it affects the particular individual rather than the number of competitors—until the new entrants change to policy **A** or **F**, which are more profitable for them.

§2. Local Product Differentiation

Although spatial price discrimination enables market areas to become very small, spatial product differentiation counteracts this effect. Only a few goods are homogeneous when produced in different places.[63] As a rule they satisfy jointly a number of requirements that do not exactly coincide. Not even the main requirement need be the same: thus, independent of price, a car is a necessity in one place and a pure luxury elsewhere; to say nothing of the way in which it meets needs with various models, for example, or satisfies minor needs, as with seats that can be thrown back for sleeping. The character of an article, among other things, is a function of its production site, and conversely. It is designed in accordance with the cost and demand relationships prevailing there. The demand that it is intended to meet generally comes from the immediate neighborhood of its production site, though not exclusively as with homogeneous goods. The boundaries of its sales area no longer coincide with those of the neighboring production sites. *The market areas overlap.* For even though the majority of buyers lived near the factory and its product conformed to the requirements of the neighborhood,[64] there would still be individual purchasers farther off who for various reasons preferred just this type of article to one manufactured in their own vicinity. Migration is not the least important contributor to this. Often enough migrants are pioneers of exportation.[65] So common taste creates about every factory a circle of buyers that overlaps in space the sales areas of similar products.[66] The individual nature of a product thus works

---

63. The difference may lie in the type of retail business rather than in the goods themselves. Retail trade margins, and with them the price for the same product, vary according to the type of business. In the more expensive shops one pays for the possibility of making a number of other purchases at the same time, for their better equipment with all that this implies, or for the certainty of receiving high-quality, tasteful, or fashionable goods, and so on.

64. Not necessarily the most immediate neighborhood, if the factory is in a small place. For in an unrestricted area most of the demand would then come from a medium distance, according to Fig. 43c.

65. In the United States this tendency is counteracted by the extremely high tariff on the one hand, and by the extremely low price of domestic mass-produced goods and transportation on the other. Without them this "melting pot of the nations" would hardly have been able to bring about uniform production so quickly. It is interesting to observe the effect of similar factors in Germany: strangulation of foreign trade, "Volks" radios, the Volkswagen, directed consumption, cheaper travel through "Strength through Joy," and so on.

66. Something similar occurs also in the cultural field, and is perhaps at the root

both for and against a manufacturer: for him because he can invade the field of his competitors in spite of freight costs; against him because, in spite of his more favorable freight position he cannot keep the competition of similar goods entirely out of his home area.[67] The more unique an article is and the fewer substitutes it has, the less does it have its market entirely to itself.[68] But for the same reason its market area is very much larger than if all its buyers lived in the same place.[69] How many sales areas overlap may be realized from the great variety of goods carried by retail dealers.

Entrepreneurial activity also can be understood spatially. Small improvements extend the home sales area at the expense of competitors and make it more concentrated. New or greatly improved goods capture their market at the expense of all old goods together. Thus the development of the automobile took place at the expense

---

of the described phenomenon. The more local, national, or even racial cultures surrender their peculiar character; the more wide differences give way to harmless nuances that practically exhaust themselves in different dialects, a few idiosyncrasies in customs and costume, and the fading memory of a different past; the more do regions of influence of different cultural centers overlap. They were separated as long as the differences were real, and would be separate again if these differences vanished entirely; but in this intermediate stage they overlap.

67. It is hard to say, threfore, whether product differentiation takes the edge off competition, as is so often asserted. It seems to me that it intensifies competition for the efficient and protects the inefficient. Sensible though it may be to have real differences, it is senseless if not harmful when inefficient producers are able to maintain themselves through insignificant variation in product or even through adulterations that the customer can hardly detect.

68. Hence the markets for raw materials and semifinished products overlap less than those for finished products, because they are still relatively amorphous and so can often be standardized. In addition, freight costs are more important for the former in relation to the producer's price, so that for this reason alone overlapping is restricted to a narrower border region. With high-quality goods everything often depends upon specific properties of the raw material, which then is ordered from a great distance even though ordinary grades may be plentiful enough. Thus hundreds of German places can supply clay, but only one can furnish the clay needed for the making of highly fire-resistant products.

In the case of finished products, and especially of consumer's goods, the small standard goods in daily use that are distributed from small centers with fairly compact sales areas must be distinguished from more expensive goods in which the possibility of choice and subtle differences are valued, and which therefore can be stocked only in larger places with less sharply circumscribed sales areas. See, for example, C. Zimmerman, " Farm Trade Centers in Minnesota, 1905–1929," *University of Minnesota, Agricultural Experiment Station Bulletin 269*, 1930, p. 16.

69. An extension of the sales area at the expense of competitors or of other goods can thus occur in many and very different ways: (*a*) by displacement outward of its farthest boundaries; (*b*) by extension of the actual sales area within these boundaries; (*c*) by larger sales in the original area, partly to old and partly to new customers.

not only of the railroads but also of the manufacture of pianos, beverages, and so on. Later, when a new product has become an economic success, imitators will share its market area. If, on the contrary, this was too small even for the first entrepreneur (i. e., if he could not make the demand and the cost curves intersect), he counts as one of the pioneers who failed. Between the one market of the entrepreneurial genius and the rigidly circumscribed areas of enterprises that produce standard goods,[70] development moves back and forth.

§3. THE FREIGHT RATE

With public enterprises, monopoly freight rates often aim only for certain services at the greatest profit;[71] with others, at covering the costs;[72] while a third group is deliberately subsidized. The prevailing German railway tariff offers examples of each. A graduated tariff is not essential to any of the three principles. Only the extent of the graduation shows which is in question.[73] As far as location is concerned the most important case of a subsidy in Germany is certainly long-distance transport of coal. It breaks up agglomerations around coal fields, which the increasing use of machinery and exhaustion of the forests had encouraged during the past century.[74] Something similar is true for important raw materials.[75]

But only competitive tariffs follow general rules. Next to a drop in the level of freight rates to about 1/10,[76] differential railway rates

---

70. For example, steel, cement, bricks, coal, salt, sugar, and so on. Even here, to be sure, there are exceptions. Certain furnaces, for instance, utilize the caloric content of certain kinds of coal better than others. To this extent there is still some overlapping. But the cores of the sales areas of the various coal fields are distinct.

71. Especially with busy stretches, moderate distances, small shipments, and expensive goods (see note 77). In these cases the competition of the motor truck enters.

72. The significance of fixed costs for a railroad is generally much overestimated, and the height of the marginal costs therefore underestimated. With fully employed equipment every traffic increase must raise costs almost proportionately. It is generally impossible to justify cheap special rate schedules of wide applicability with low marginal costs. I shall discuss this subject in more detail in another book.

73. When, in 1924, the cheapest railway kilometer for the cheapest commodity was about 1 per cent of the most expensive kilometer for the most expensive commodity, the one was obviously subsidized and the other profitable.

74. W. Sombart, *Die moderne Kapitalismus*, II (1919), 1143 ff.; III (1927), 98 f., 122.

75. Other things being equal, the use of machinery must nevertheless decrease with the distance from coal, and so must the production of low-quality mass-produced goods with distance from raw material; on the contrary, the importance of poorly paid labor of high quality must increase.

76. W. Sombart, *op. cit.*, II, 345. P. Schulz-Kiesow, *Die Eisenbahngütertarifpolitik in ihrer Wirkung auf den industriellen Standort und die Raumordnung* (Heidelberg, 1940), p. 25.

Some New Factors 171

according to product [77] and distance constituted the most significant change for the location pattern since the exit of the horse and wagon, which, like the autotruck, charged freight essentially in proportion to weight and distance.

α. *Local Differences in Tariffs*

1. GRADUATION ACCORDING TO DESTINATION

Suppose that goods are to be shipped from one place, B, to others at various distances. The elasticity of the volume of traffic with respect to the freight rate will rise, first with this rate, and second with length of haul.[78] For the second reason a monopolistic enterprise lowers the freight rate for long hauls. The spatial freight discrimination of a graduated tariff corresponds to the spatial price discrimination for the goods.

Figure 47, together with Figure 20, will serve as a proof. For the sake of simplicity assume that only a single customer lives at each place. If OP (in Fig. 20) is the price at the factory, the volume of traffic to each outlying point would be PQ (in Figs. 20 and 47) if the seller paid the freight or if the freight rate were zero. The volume of traffic is zero when the product of distance times freight rate is equal to or greater than PF (in Fig. 20). Thus the farther away a place is, the lower is the freight rate that suffices to prevent all traffic. If e_0, e_1, e_2 (Fig. 47), and so on, are demand curves for shipment to increasingly distant points, they become flatter and flatter in this order and so more and more elastic for the same freight rate. That graduated tariff (i. e., the particular set of freight rates for transports over different distances) which maximizes the surplus of receipts over variable costs (PR) (Fig. 47) [79] is easily

---

77. From the standpoint of maximizing profits what matters is transportability of goods, not their value. Salt can stand higher freight charges than furniture, although it is much cheaper by the pound. The reaction of consumers as well as of the producer is important: whether new production sites will be established and distances shortened thereby because of an increase in freight rates.

78. Elasticity depends, in sales areas, upon the willingness of buyers to pay the price demanded; in supply areas, upon the chances of profit to the seller. According to Lenschow the types of goods produced by the Negroes in British East Africa pay more freight than those produced by the white inhabitants, because the same profit means more to the Negroes and it is harder for them to susbtitute other possibilities.

79. This is the exact meaning of the saying that railways exact as freight "what the traffic will bear." The lower limits of the freight rate are the variable costs. The rate is not arbitrarily fixed above this level, but in such a way that the surplus for the individual case shall be as large as possible. The total surplus must be at least equal to the fixed costs, otherwise the whole industry will be unprofitable.

obtained by the customary procedure: In Figure 47 draw *RS* parallel to *PQ* and halve the segment of the demand curve lying between *RS* and the *y*-axis. The graduated tariff will lie on the line *RA* connecting these points.

The effect of the graduated tariff upon the size of the necessary market areas differs. For short distances the graduated tariff lies above, for long distances below, a tariff proportional to distance. If,

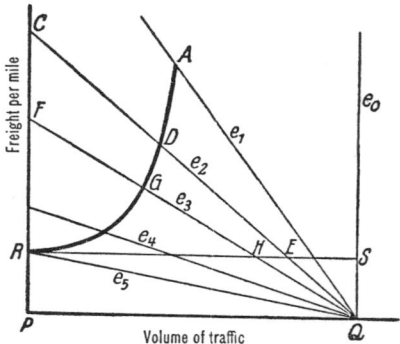

Fig. 47. Similarity of price differentiation for goods and spatial freight differentiation through zonal tariffs

under free competition, the latter just covers the costs, the tariffs intersect at a greater distance than if, with a monopoly, a tariff proportional to distance gave the same total profit. The effect of a graduated tariff on the size of the necessary market area depends upon whether, for shipment to the boundaries of the necessary sales area with a tariff proportional to distance, the graduated tariff lies above or below the tariff proportional to distance. If it lies above, and all local prices are therefore higher and the regional demand is accordingly less than with a tariff proportional to distance, the necessary sales area will be larger with a sliding-scale tariff. But if the sliding-scale tariff lies at the critical point, considerably below the tariff proportional to distance, a smaller sales area may suffice. Hence it cannot be said a priori whether a graduated tariff encourages [80] or discourages industrial concentration. The influence of a sliding-scale tariff on the possible shipping distance (which it naturally extends) must not be confused with its influence on the

---

80. M. Keir insists that it does. ("Economic Factors in the Location of Manufacturing Industries." *Annals of the American Academy of Political and Social Sciences*, 1921, p. 90.)

necessary shipping distance, an influence which is usually [81] decisive in itself. As freight costs increase but slowly over long distances with a sliding-scale tariff, large areas arise in which the superiority of one particular producer depends merely upon small differences in the c. i. f. price. This is enough when products are homogeneous. But even slight product differentiation leads to an unstable equilibrium and extensive regional overlap.[82]

In a few cases the freight rate *increases* with distance. This is true, for example, of firms that make deliveries by their own motor trucks. If their customers are more than a day's trip away, the cost of delivery is increased by overtime and lodgings.[83] The effects are the reverse of a sliding-scale tariff.

2. GRADUATION ACCORDING TO POINT OF ORIGIN

A tariff graduated according to the point of origin can be thought of by imagining that various means of transportation radiate out from different points, or that the same carrier grants special rate schedules to certain places, or that the difference is due to the nature of the goods transported. For instance, with the same rate per ton, a rich ore pays less freight per unit of yield (unit of useful content) than a poor ore.

What is the relation between the sales areas of two places that ship the same product under different freight rates? In general two things may be said. First, the product with the lower tariff cannot be entirely excluded from sale, whatever its factory price may be. Even though it is displaced at its own production site by another article that can be made much more cheaply, with a sufficiently large possible sales area a point is nevertheless reached at some distance where the delivered price of the product paying the lower rate falls below that of the other.[84] Second, the sales area of the place with the higher tariff will be surrounded by that of the other. It is naturally smaller the higher the freight rate and the higher the factory price. It may shrink to a mere point and, in contrast to the other area, disappear entirely.

---

81. With mining outputs the actual and the possible shipping distances may perhaps coincide. The sales area for Rhenish pumice stone, for example, is limited only by the freight, not by direct competition.

82. See T. Palander, *Beiträge zur Standortstheorie* (Uppsala, 1935), p. 365.

83. As the result of a fairly good investigation J. Schmitz calculated that this point is reached for the brewing industry at a sales radius of about 47 miles. (*Das Standortproblem in der deutschen Brauereiindustrie*, University of Cologne dissertation, 1930, p. 61).

84. See the figures in Palander, *op. cit.*, p. 228.

β. *Level of the Freight Tariff Schedule*

We come now to the case where the tariff is raised or lowered, not for single points but for all.[85] If the freight level falls, the possible size of sales areas is increased, but the minimum necessary size is decreased.[86] For the lowered freight lowers the c. i. f. prices, and as a consequence there now comes from the original sales areas a demand that is greater than necessary. *Lowered freight rates permit smaller sales areas.*

There are several reasons for the prevalent belief that reduced freights extend markets. First, an erroneous one: The possible shipping distance is regarded as equal to the reasonable one. For the possible shipping distance the following propositions hold true: [87] The shipping distance in kilometers is inversely proportional to the freight rate; the sales area and the sales are inversely proportional to its square.[88] But that this enormous effect of lowered freights can never be actually exerted is easily seen from the fact that it benefits competitors also, and the cheaper competitor more. His sales area expands, chiefly at the cost of his more expensive rivals,[89,90] a few of whom may be driven completely from the market. But this is not the end result, for now profits appear that induce the establishment of new factories, and these finally cut down sales areas.

---

85. On goods with a large necessary shipping distance the sliding scale tariff operates in many respects as a general lowering of the rate schedule.

86. For example, the automobile has increased the possible sales radius of retail business almost tenfold, but certainly not the economic sales radius.

87. See D. Lardner's century-old *Railway Economy* (London, 1850), p. 14. W. Launhardt's paradoxical conclusion, that lower freight rates increase sales areas greatly (*Mathematische Begründung der Volkswirtschaftslehre* [Leipzig, 1885], p. 152) but supply areas hardly at all (*ibid.*, p. 177), rest upon the fact that in Thünen's case the *number* of consumers (i. e., the population of a town) is constant, whereas with industrial sales it can be increased *as long as competition is not considered*, and is in fact increased in the case of monopolistic industries. An example is the extension of rural mail delivery with motorization. See Heberle's beautiful maps in *Weltwirtschaft*, 1934, p. 15, and for the opposite opinion, C. Pirath, *Die Grundlagen der Verkehrswirtschaft* (Berlin, 1934), p. 73.

88. In contrast to price policy F the possible sales with A are thus increased fourfold, and with C to infinity. Of course a *general* lowering of freight does not increase sales so much as the individual demand curve might lead one to expect.

89. Similarly, the sales area expands for goods that are cheaper to produce but more expensive to ship (Fig. 3). Agricultural materials, for example, are more frequently processed at some central location.

90. Launhardt (*op. cit.*, p. 160) wrote that with improvements in communication the more expensive product loses " the most effective of all protective tariffs, the protection of bad roads." Hence protectionism rises with the lowering of freight rates. Conversely, an increase in freight rates benefits the more expensive producers because

The new competition, however, may now have to arise " **within** "—that is, at the location of the cheap factories—because **immobile conditions of production are now more important than freight.**[91]

In such a case the sales area would retain its increased size, but more factories would share the same market. To this extent the lowering of freight rates really does further the concentration of production,[92] especially where the supply of labor is favorable.[93]

The cheapening of transportation has likewise extended the market areas for similar goods, because here the actual approaches the possible shipping distance. (A sociological parallel would be a widening of the circles between which marriages occur.) This intensifies true competion, just as overlapping markets for similar goods intensify senseless competition.

One more exception to our thesis is possible. Suppose there are two methods of manufacturing a certain product, of which one is cheaper only with very large sales. The planning curve would then divide into two branches, π_1 and π_2 in Figure 48; it is broken. Suppose further that at the old freight rate even the entire possible

---

freight becomes more important in relation to production costs. The guiding maxim of medival road policy, "The worse the roads the higher the profits," thus benefited inferior producers only. Their business prospered under the protection of inconspicuousness and seclusion.

Launhardt has formulated this double effect of cheaper freights with classic brevity. Reduction of freight rates decreases the importance of distance. " Mastery over space has been extended, and all activities that were hampered in their development by spatial restrictions have been broadened and advanced in consequence; on the other hand, all that required the protection of isolation have been curtailed and enfeebled " (*ibid.*, p. 206).

91. Local characteristics are now more sharply developed. Thus the effects of a lowering of transport costs are by no means only leveling.

Agricultural production is affected in the same way by lower freight rates, resources like soil quality, climate, or cheap labor gaining in significance as compared with site. The intensity of agriculture decreases on land near cities. In the nineteenth century many scattered and rather unproductive mines closed down and mining was concentrated at the cheapest deposits; this contributed to the agglomeration of the iron industry, which once had flourished in many places. The great general lowering of rail and ocean freights, together with special reductions for long hauls and raw materials, made it the general practice at that time to obtain many raw materials from the most favorable sources. If the natural productivity of a soil becomes thus more important the lower the freight rates, then, conversely, the location of a country plays a smaller role the richer it is by nature.

92. As for the effect on consumption, lower freight rates diminish price **differences** and with them also differences in supply, as, conversely, a reduction of shipping space in wartime again increases spatial differences in supply.

93. On the other hand, the artificial leveling of wages nowadays raises the importance of even low freight rates.

sales area has been too small to make cheap mass production possible. Δ_1 has not intersected π_2. But with a lowering of the freight rate, sales in the old area, as well as the possible area itself, are greatly increased. Now Δ_2 intersects π_2, and cheap mass production becomes profitable. Now, too, the area can be decreased again until Δ_2' is tangent to the curve π_2. It is now possible, though not necessary, that the new area is larger than the old.

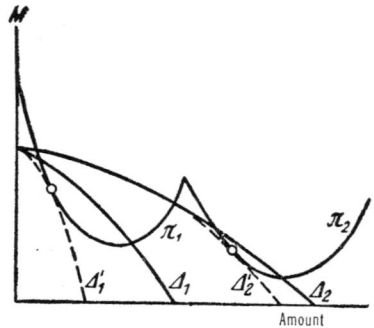

Fig. 48. Effect of new large-scale economies on size of market area

The extraordinary reduction in transportation costs during the nineteenth century has most probably had this effect in general,[94] but it must not be forgotten that two phenomena were then working together: first, improvements in large-scale production (π_2 supplants π_1 at a certain volume of production); and second, improvements in transportation and communication (Δ_2 replaces Δ_1).[95] Had not

---

94. An increase in population or, more accurately, in buying power, acts in this respect like a lowering of freight rates. This explains in particular the fact that businesses are larger in cities than in rural areas, not smaller, as one might at first be led to expect since the urban demand curve is generally steeper and therefore touches the *old* cost curve at a point characterized by higher price and smaller sales. For this reason, on the other hand, the reduced demand in wartime often favors the small producer.

A further reason why many prices are lower in cities may be that cities attract a number of the most skillful entrepreneurs, who find it possible to employ their capabilities to the full only in large cities; either (when they are especially skillful in production) because they lower the cost curve, or (when they are especially skillful in advertising) because they shift the demand curve to the right—both of which lead to a lowering of prices.

95. They belong to the six great events that have revolutionized locations during the nineteenth century: (1) increase in population; (2) monopolies based on inventions; (3) the change from wood and water power to coal; (4) the exhaustion of smaller sources of raw materials through a sharp increase in production; (5) further mechanization; (6) lowering of freight rates. These factors favored the following locations, though they partly counteracted one another: coal deposits (3, 5); large and

the two coincided (which certainly was not mere chance), the fate of those worlds in miniature whose unquestioned center was a princely residence, a small rural town, or often only a manor house, would not have been fulfilled so soon. At it was, most of their central functions were transferred, perhaps all too quickly, to the potential centers of larger areas.[96] This generally brought down the price of centrally produced goods, but at what cost! The world in miniature, which had been so clear to the understanding, so easy to survey, fell in ruins. The "province" became part of a greater whole that in its wide expanse was at first much more difficult to grasp, much more abstract. The attitude toward life did not broaden in step with this technical expansion.[97] This was true not only in quiet corners remote from the metropolis but, much more important, in the metropolis itself. The unmanageable specialization in central functions impeded not only their close touch with the rural areas, but their mutual fructification as well. Individual functions were fulfilled more cheaply and more and more practically—which of course was the reason for this rearrangement—but society as a whole suffered at first an increasingly thorough uprooting. The great drop in freight rates tore the towns away from their regions. In America especially, every-day goods are frequently ordered from fantastic distances, because of small differences in quality, or in order to circumvent the seasons: potatoes from Idaho, lettuce from California, cabbage from Texas, flowers from Florida.[98] Here it may

cheap sources of raw materials (4, 6); cities (1, 5, 6); supply of labor (6); arbitrarily selected sites (1, 2). See, for example, W. Sombart, *Der moderne Kapitalismus*, I 5. A (1922); II 3. A (1919); III 1. A (1927). O. Schlier, *Der deutsche Industriekörper seit 1860.* Tübingen, 1922. H. Ritschl, "Reine und historische Dynamik der Erzeugungszweige," *Schmollers Jahrbuch*, 1927. P. Schulz-Kiesow, *Die Eisenbahngütertarifpolitik in ihrer Wirkung auf den industriellen Standort und die Raumordnung* (Heidelberg, 1940).

The expansion of many markets in the nineteenth century was itself part of a greater chain of developments that was, however, not free of reverses. Beginning with specialization (handicrafts on socage farms and in villages), continued by urbanization (guilds against rural crafts), and accelerated by mechanization (factory against crafts), it ended with the double-edged victory of mass production (large against small enterprises) that results here and there in a reduction in the size of markets (controlled markets and autarky).

96. The subordination of a once independent center to a *larger* one, or of a dependent center to a *different* main center, affects the central upper stratum most severely, for with it the changes in either location or function are greatest.

97. Or accepted it only in externals. Röpke has much that is just to say against this rising "cult of the gigantic."

98. See, for example, E. A. Duddy's investigation of this subject in respect to Chicago: "The Physical Distribution of Fresh Fruits and Vegetables," *University of Chicago, Studies in Business Administration*, Vol. VII, No. 2.

be asked whether food grown in the very soil on which we live may not agree with us better, and the most recent investigations tend to favor this view.

To summarize the purely economic effect of lower freight rates: Though in general they reduce the size of economic areas, under certain conditions they increase their size.[99] A reduction in freight rates affects only the size of individual towns, however, not their geographical distribution. For the variety of possible market areas remains unchanged by lowered freight rates as long as the distribution of farms is unchanged. Only the individual products are now associated with areas of another size. Only the distance between *their* production sites is altered,[100] whereas the possible sites for factories remain as before. Hence the economic function of towns changes with changes in the cost of transportation in so far as entirely different goods are now sold in the market areas whose centers they are; but the possible market areas themselves and the situation of their centers remain as they were.

b. NATURAL DIFFERENCES

§1. LOCAL DIFFERENCES IN PRODUCTIVITY[101]

We now dismiss the assumption of a uniformly fertile plain, and take into account the fact that nature favors human endeavor unequally from place to place. Production, cultivation, or acquisition is possible, according to the manner in which she co-operates: manufacture or building when nature supplies only resources (industry); cultivation when man, on the other hand increases natural fertility (agriculture); and collection when the desired products are already present (mining, fishing, and the like).

The kind and degree of nature's co-operation may vary from one place to another in the most irregular way, or in conformity with some rule, or may be entirely uniform over wide areas. The frequency of the first situation causes many to despair of any spatial

---

99. If it is desired to encourage industry in an outlying district where conditions of production are not especially favorable, it follows that (except for raw materials) incoming freight rates should not be lowered; but (where freight decrease reduces the size of one area) the rates *within* it, or (where freight decrease increases the size of the area) *from* it to the rest of the country, should be lowered.

100. Large losses or gains may occasionally be caused by the shift: losses, if necessary sales areas increase in size, for then the concentrated industries suddenly appear overcrowded; gains, if necessary market areas grow smaller, because it always requires some time for the influx to fill vacancies in thes branches.

101. Their economic significance has been worked out with the greatest care by E. W. Zimmermann, among others, in *World Resources and Industries* (New York, 1933).

economic pattern. The irregularities of nature do indeed interrupt the uniform development of landscapes. But they need not destroy it entirely, since all the organizing forces combine against the separate chaotic ones. For instance, even if soil quality differed radically from field to field its use would not show the same mosaic confusion; the differences would be modified here and there by the effects of equal distance from a market, by the establishment of belts, and so forth. But even if these were of no great moment and farming and the rural population were irregularly distributed, a superstructure of rural towns and larger settlements would nevertheless spring up *and remain separate despite everything,* which, in spite of all distortion, would still form a pattern, and which would orient themselves toward the metropolis and the great lines of communication.

Regular changes in natural conditions are obviously much less disturbing,[102] and by good fortune they are both common and important. One need only recall the climatic changes associated with latitude, or the fairly uniform variations in the lines of equal precipitation over wide stretches of the earth's surface. Precipitation is of definite importance in the United States, for example, where it decreases from east to west; or in southwest Australia, where it decreases toward the interior. Natural gradients such as these can be found even in zones that appear economically uniform. Thus harvest time in the American cotton belt varies (or shifts) with fair regularity from early July in the south to the end of October in the north.[103]

If interruptions of the sort first described cause a certain irregularity and those of the second group cause inequalities of the spatial economic pattern, the interference to be discussed now does not appear at all as such over wide areas. Thus there are extensive regions of more or less equal fertility close to others with a wholly different level of productivity, as when a mountain chain rises suddenly from a plain. If plain and mountains are extensive enough, two regions may arise that exhibit great regularity within themselves but which are characteristically different.[104]

---

102. In Weber's words, they influence the choice of a location continuously, like freight costs, not alternatively, like local advantages that occur without transition.

103. As possible supply areas for cities are extensive today, they often include regions with entirely different harvest dates for the same crop. For instance, New York gets oranges and grapefruit from Florida, from Texas, and from California at different times.

104. Such regions developed in the lowland indentations about Paris, Cologne, Münster, Leipzig, and Breslau. The centers for the corresponding interlocking high-

Here we are interested, first, in these differences and, second, in the conditions at the border. First, are market areas in the fertile [105] region smaller or larger, and are the towns more numerous or larger than in the poor region? The answer and the reason for it are the same as those for the consequences of a general reduction in freight rates: It depends upon whether there are fundamentally different kinds of mass production, between which no transition is possible. If they exist, the market areas on the fertile soil may possibly be more extensive and the towns larger. If they do not exist, or if they are profitable even on the poor soil, then the market areas will be smaller [106] and the towns more numerous on the rich soil.[107]

---

lands are Trier, Kassel, Prague. See Blum, "Deutschland und Südosteuropa nach Rückgliederung der Ostmark und der Sudetenländer, verkehrspolitisch betrachtet, *Zeitschrift für Verkehrswirtschaft*, XVI (1939), 1–31.

105. The difference between small and large holdings of land, between proximity to and distance from the center of a landscape, between peace and war economy, and often between greater and lesser population density, is equivalent to that between more and less fertile soils. On a more fertile soil the agricultural population is always denser and (which is not the same) the villages larger (since a small acreage is enough for the agriculturist the distance to the fields nevertheless remains tolerable). Large villages make possible more or cheap production of goods that are bought from nearby than do smaller villages.

106. They are smaller the more closely the necessary shipping distance approaches the possible one. For sales areas on poor soil contain relatively much land but a small demand. A sales area in a thickly settled region need not even be large enough to have the same demand as that of the more thinly settled one. Since the demand in a smaller sales area, other things being equal, is less elastic (as has already been shown), a firm in a populous region can always cover its costs despite further curtailment of the area by raising prices. Conversely, however, the sales areas in the thinly settled region are not large enough to result in the same demand at the same factory price as sales areas for the same goods in the other region. They, too, may be curtailed, and an adequate demand nevertheless be achieved by a lowering of prices.

Figure 49 resolves this apparent contradiction. r_1 and r_2 are demand curves in a thickly settled region (R), a_1 and a_2 in a thinly settled one (A). The necessary demand in A is DE. The demand curve r_2 would result in R in the same demand, DE, at the price as in A. But the corresponding area would be larger than with the curve r_1, which lies to the left of it and which results in BC, the minimum demand necessary in R. The same thing holds true when sales areas in A are compared with those in R. It follows that the prices of industrial goods in the towns of a thinly settled region will be somewhat lower. Conversely, the prices of agricultural products in the towns, and perhaps even average rural ground rents, will be somewhat higher than in a thickly settled region; first, because freight rates are higher on account of the less intensive use of the means of communication; second, because the agricultural supply area for the towns is larger since they are more populous; and, third, because that supply area itself is less fertile.

107. Moreover, goods may appear here for which there would not be an adequate market in a thinly settled region, even with full exploitation of their possible shipping distances.

Some New Factors

This does not mean a difference in size, but only in distribution of the population. Other things being equal, the number of inhabitants will obviously be greater on fertile soil.

Second, if a factory lies on the border, the size of that part of its sales area extending into the rich or the poor region respectively will depend on the relative size of markets in the region concerned. If the markets are large in the poor and small in the rich region the real hinterland of the factory, measured by areal extent, will lie in the former. But in their economic value both regions are about the same. Because of their irrational shape, such border areas are on the whole somewhat larger than interior areas. If sales areas in the rich region are larger, it is uncertain whether a factory on the border will attract sufficient demand from the poor region to produce on the larger scale of the fertile region.

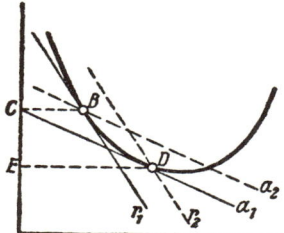

Fig. 49. Comparison of market area in thickly settled and thinly settled regions, with equal cost curves

Still another case of natural differences of an areal kind is important. Imagine a large region, A, and a small one, B, wholly similar in natural features but separated by a wide uninhabited region like a mountain range, a desert, or a body of water, or by high customs duties in A. The essential assumptions are the differences in size and distance. Two further assumptions are economic in character. First, the planning curve must have a break, as in Figure 48. Thus there must be two different production methods: large-scale and small-scale production. Second, only B must be too small for mass production. Under these conditions A is the indicated location for a large plant.

B may constitute part of its sales area, but enterprises can never be situated in B and supply A as well. According to the assumptions, a large-scale enterprise in B cannot depend upon B alone for its support. In A, however, it is too expensive by the amount of the freight compared with a local large-scale business, even if there are no customs duties. But a large enterprise would be able to maintain itself in A, either if A were an adequate sales area or if its costs were less than those of the small firm in B by more than the amount of the freight.

The situation would suffice to make the United States the classic land of large-scale enterprises, even without its fantastic customs duties.[108] Of all the European countries, Germany most nearly approaches it today as a large economic area.[109] The decisive factor is less the size of a population than the national income. The other European countries would lie within the market areas of many large American businesses if they did not "protect" themselves by customs duties.[110]

Uniformly operative natural factors will be more important in general for agriculture, irregular factors for industry and mining. But the influence of nature plays a significant role in all branches of the economy in the formation of "districts" and "belts."[111] This has both advantages and disadvantages: disadvantages in so far as it encourages urbanization and causes an irrational distortion in the shapes of market areas; advantages in so far as the external economics that result when similar production is concentrated in one place need not be purchased by carrying out part of this production under unfavorable natural conditions.[112]

§2. Local Differences in Accessibility

Among the purely economically conditioned deviations from our initial scheme it should have been mentioned that a transport surface (i. e., an area within which transportation between any two arbitrary points is always possible over a direct route) does not exist. The limited number of roads and railways lines, of railroad stations and

---

108. Essentially similar conditions make large cities the favored sites for large-scale businesses. The metropolis corresponds to the United States, provincial towns to the European countries, and the open country to the ocean.

109. Written before the autumn of 1939, but retained in the 1944 edition.—W. H. W.

110. See A. Lösch: *Selbstkosten- und Standortverschiebungen von Genussgütern nach dem Krieg als Ursachen von Zolltendenzen* (Berlin, 1934) (*Zwischenstaatliche Wirtschaft*, edited by H. v. Beckerath, Heft 4).

111. S. W. Wilcox, Chief Statistician of the Bureau of Labor Statistics in Washington, D. C., told me that an attempt to divide Illinois into areas of similar production showed a surprising agreement with geological structure, which went so far that regions where corn was grown for the market, for example, were associated with a formation different from those where it was used as fodder.

112. It would be so, for instance, if all kinds of soil were evenly mixed everywhere.

harbor facilities, can be ascribed to their high fixed cost if to nothing else. Thus, in reality, transportation is not possible between any two given points over any desired route, but only between a few so-called transport points and over a few so-called transport lines. Still, the number of these points and lines varies with the means of transportation.[113] It is large in the case of wagons and motor trucks,[114] smaller in the case of railways,[115] and smallest in the case of airplanes and ships. Their position results [116] essentially from

113. For the laws according to which transport is distributed among the various carriers, and the relative size of their loads, see A. Lösch, "Die Leistung der Seeschiffahrt," *Nauticus*, 1941, pp. 326–336.

114. The narrow-meshed network of highways, with stopping places wherever desired, approaches a true transport surface more closely than the wide-meshed railway lines. This feature of motor-truck transportation is especially important in its competition with the railways and in the development of locations. If, in addition, the characteristic tariff schedule (according to straight distance and weight, not sliding-scale or according to value) is taken into consideration, the most important results of motorization can easily be deduced. In so far as it *lowers* freight costs it favors places with low production costs, as does any decrease in freight rates. In so far as it *equalizes* freight rates it works to the disadvantage of "favored points," as already shown. Thus no simple answer can be given to the disputed question of whether the motor truck has a centralizing or a decentralizing effect. It facilitates access to *and* from newly developed and unfavorably situated places, for example. On the one hand, metropolitan competition can now break into remote corners and destroy local industries. According to both German and American experience this seems to be true of retail trade especially. (See A. Erlenmaier, "Die Bedeutung des Kraftwagens für den Standort in Produktion und Handel," *Zeitschrift für Verkehrswissenschaft*, XII [1934]; and C. E. Lively, "Growth and Decline of Farm Trade Centers in Minnesota, 1905–1930," *University of Minnesota, Agricultural Experiment Station, Bulletin 287*.) On the other hand, favorable production conditions may attract industries to formerly inaccessible places once they have been opened up by the motor truck. (For examples see Erlenmaier, *op. cit.*, p. 94; and Palander, *op. cit.*, pp. 352–360.) In a similar manner the construction of railways once benefited outlying sources of labor. (See O. Schlier, *Der deutsche Industriekörper seit 1860* [Tübingen, 1922]; and P. Schulz-Kiesow, *Die Eisenbahngütertarifpolitik in ihrer Wirkung auf den industriellen Standort und die Raumordnung* [Heidelberg, 1940].)

As for superhighways, the *Autobahnen* of Germany, they resemble railroads in that the number of their junction points is limited. Hence in comparison with ordinary highways they save more time the greater the distance between starting point and destination and, obviously, the nearer both lie to the *Autobahnen*. Lines of equal time-saving run like arrowheads toward the destination. The angles are considerably more acute in the case of the *Autobahnen*, to be sure, than they once were with the railways; i.e., the latter signified a much greater revolution of communication. See the highly interesting maps of C. Pirath, "Auflockerung und Ballung im Lichte der Reichsautobahnen," in *Volk und Lebensraum*, edited by K. Meyer (Heidelberg, 1938), pp. 262, 269.

115. Three out of four German communities are without railway station!

116. As a reaction, of course, there is a tendency to concentration along a few well-developed traffic routes, especially with expensive railway installations.

our ideal system of market areas; that is to say, from transport requirements proper—as long as disturbances brought about by nature are absent.

α. Transport Lines

Natural obstacles divert transport lines according to the law of refraction, which is valid far beyond the sphere of economics.[117] Man subjects himself to it by choice (after all, it is merely the economic principle applied to a special situation); nature (light and sound) by necessity. Here is a significant identity between a law of nature

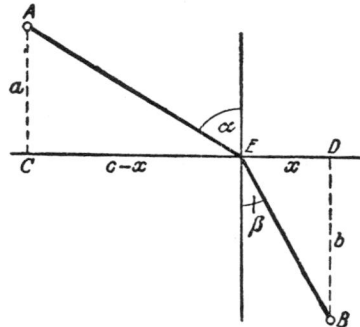

Fig. 50. The law of refraction

and a law based on reason, which shows clearly enough that the economic principle is not merely a human invention and does not simply correspond with the attitude of a particular epoch.[118] It runs through the history of natural science as *lex parsimoniae*: the principle of simplest means or least resistance; as the hypothesis that natural events reach their goals by the shortest route.[119]

Suppose that a product is to be shipped as cheaply as possible from A to B (Fig. 50). North of the coastline CD, which is equally

---

117. I have already referred to this in my review of Palander ("Beiträge zur Standortstheorie," *Schmollers Jahrbuch*, 1938). In the meantime appeared the detailed and admirable account of H. von Stackelberg, "Das Brechungsgesetz des Verkehrs," *Jahrbücher für Nationalökonomie und Statistik*, CXLVIII, 680–696.

118. On the contrary, it embraces the behavior of some men in almost all situations, and the behavior of almost all men in some situations: when desire and aversion are strong (one wants to attain a definite end or avoid it as far as possible—pursues every advantage or high aim; husbands his powers; avoids the unpleasant). It is otherwise when we live everything instead of separating means and ends; when we rejoice in the game; surrender ourselves completely—only those can do so who are free of desire and filled with love. There are two worlds, and we are wanderers between them.

119. Others of our results, too, have their counterparts in nature. What, after all, are the often sharply separated feeding grounds of various animal families and species,

favorable everywhere for landing, the cheap ocean freight, f_a, is in effect; south of it, the high rail freight, f_b. The transport costs per unit for the distance $\overline{AE}$ will then be $F_a = f_a \sqrt{a^2 + (c-x)^2}$; and for EB, $F_b = f_b \sqrt{b^2 + x^2}$. $F(x) = F_a + F_b$ is a minimum when $F'(x) = \dfrac{(x-c)f_a}{\sqrt{a^2 + (c-x)^2}} + \dfrac{xf_b}{\sqrt{b^2 + x^2}} = 0$. Hence $f_b \sin \beta - f_a \sin \alpha = 0$, or $\dfrac{\sin \alpha}{\sin \beta} = \dfrac{f_b}{f_a}$. This determines the site of the harbor E. If the distance per unit of time is substituted for the distance per unit of freight in this formula, the formula for the refraction of light and sound will be obtained.

Suppose, thirdly, that an officer has to lead his troops from A to B with the smallest possible losses, and the severity of the enemy's fire in the two zones is related as the freights in the example above. He will choose route AEB. In short, the formula for refraction is universally valid when two unequally favorable zones have to be crossed with the smallest expenditure, whether of time, money, blood, or the like. The most important application of the law of refraction is probably the case where a cheap transport line such as a railway or a navigable river cuts a more expensive transport surface like a dense network of roads.[120] The angle β, within which transportation to and from the railway takes place, is easily calculated. Since in this case AE in Figure 50 coincides with CE, and α is therefore 90°, $\sin \beta = f_a \div f_b$. Another application of the formula is the construction of railway bridges over broad streams. The higher the construction costs the more will a bridge deviate from the main direction of the tracks in order that the crossing may be made as short as possible.

The law of refraction naturally covers more difficult cases as well. Refraction by lenses, too, has its counterpart in economics. For the solution, it is completely irrelevant whether the hatched area in Fig. 51 is a biconcave lens and the problem is to project a beam of light from H in such a way that it will arrive at N; or whether H is Hawaii, the hatched area the isthmus of Central America, and N is New Orleans, and instead of a beam of light being projected a

---

if not the market areas of man? Plant species also have their necessary and typical distance, as a consequence of the struggle between an individual impulse to spread and the tendency to maximize the number of independent existences familiar to us from economic analysis. I doubt that the fundamental principles of zoological, botanical, and economic location theory differ very greatly.

120. Palander (*op. cit.*, pp. 337 ff.) gives an admirable presentation of the combination of means of transport. ((The minimum condition on the left side of the equation on p. 337, however, should read $x \div \sqrt{a^2 + x^2}$, not $x \div a$).

load of pineapples is to be shipped to New Orleans as cheaply as possible. The greater the refractive index of the lens—that is, the more it resists the passage of a beam of light—the more will the beam be deflected (path I instead of path II). Exactly so, were there no Panama Canal today, would a connecting railway be chosen between Pacific and Atlantic ports that would be more southerly the higher the rail tariff in comparison with the ocean freight. At

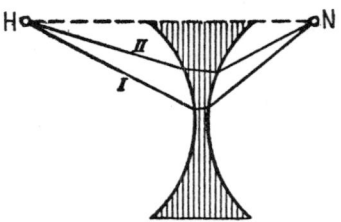

Fig. 51. Schematic representation of efficient route from Hawaii (H) to New Orleans (N) via Panama Canal and possible Nicaragua cut

present the problem is stated thus: Whether the cost of a canal through Nicaragua would be repaid by the shortening of the sea voyage. Other things being equal, the higher the cost the shorter would a cut have to be; in other words, the greater would be the superiority of the Panama Canal over one running through Nicaragua. In this case a decision can be reached without appeal to the law of refraction, because there are only two practical alternatives. Where there are more, which cannot all be thoroughly explored, the right choice can be made only with the help of this law.

But an important limitation of the law of refraction must be added here. Its nature is essentially similar to Launhardt's and Weber's geometrical figures: it assumes that the points between which transportation is carried on are definitely fixed and few in number—in the present case only two. Hence the objections to the earlier figures are substantially valid against the law in question. However, the objections are less important here because transport lines, with which we are now dealing, are considerably less numerous than transport points. In the case of ocean traffic between the east and west coasts of America, for example, it can be said, despite the numerous harbors and innumerable points of departure and arrival, that in the neighborhood of the Central American isthmus at least there are only one or two transport lines. But if the traffic of the west coast of South America with Europe and with the east coast of North America is added, there will be several lines, and for each one a somewhat different situation of the Panama Canal would be more advantageous. Since it would not pay to have a special canal for each transport line (quite apart from the fact that the choice of locations is severely limited for technical reasons), the location of the present cut is a compromise. The higher the fixed costs of overcoming an obstacle to traffic and the greater the number of transport lines that have to surmount it, the more does the law of refraction lose in significance. It cannot be applied to a group of transport lines, that is, to importing *areas*. In such cases, gateways must be regarded as like any other industrial undertaking; their location will be so chosen as to reach an adequate market.

β. Transport Points

Among transport points the nodal points are of special importance. They are more favorably situated in respect to freight than mere stopping places. We have already seen that the mechanical model for determining the optimum transport point comes to rest only in them. This is why they are preferred locations for industry and trade. Among nodal points those primarily determined by nature (bottleneck cities) are of outstanding importance. Unlike other nodal points, they cannot be by-passed by technical means, though others will not be by-passed for economic reasons. They are literally gateways that must be passed through. The particular barrier—a mountain range, a river, an unbroken coastline—may be provided by nature or may depend partly on economic factors. The expensive means of transferring goods, say from a ship to a railway, or of surmounting obstacles (bridges, tunnels) presuppose a relatively large supply area, and thus are to be found at a few points only.

The classic example of a " pass city " is Vienna (and at the other end of a long curve in the Danube, Bratislava,[121] as a threefold gateway leading into the Bohemian and Hungarian basins, and into south Germany. The narrower the pass and the more important the market lying behind this natural gateway, the nearer to it will industries with large necessary sales areas establish themselves, other things being equal; but they will pass through it only when there is a larger market on the other side.

---

121. Budapest, on the contrary, is a gateway not for river traffic on the Danube, but for traffic crossing the Danube. (See Blum, " Deutschland und Südosteuropa nach Rückgliederung der Ostmark und der Sudetenländer, verkehrspolitisch betrachtet," *Zeitschrift für Verkehrswirtschaft*, XVI [1939], 1–31; and Schneefuss, in *Lebensraumfragen europäischer Völker*, edited by K. Dietzel et al. [Leipzig, 1941], p. 659.)

A special problem arises when the barrier separates not only different markets [122] but different means of transportation as well. In such a case the pass city is at the same time a transshipment point, and if the pass is fairly long it will be situated as near as possible to the end where the more expensive means of transportation begins. Hence if a seaport is on a navigable river it will lie as far upstream as possible.[123]

Palander [124] has shown how much larger the hinterland for a river port is compared with that for a seaport. It must not be assumed, therefore, that the choice of the natural harbor to be developed and the question of how far upstream it shall be situated are two separate problems. It will not do to select a hypothetical location (in the wider sense) by means of the law of refraction, say on a conventionalized coastline where the possible seaports have been indicated, and then choose the actual location (in the narrower sense) as far inland as possible. There is only one single location problem, and it cannot be solved in stages. The position of the hinterland, the destination of the shipments, the contour of the coastline, the cost of harbor installations, all must be considered simultaneously in a general calculation that covers a few selected sites.

Transport points play an important part in the formation of market areas. If, for instance, wheat growers supplied wheat consumers directly, there would be a chaotic plethora of market areas, the shape and situation of which are the harder to imagine because the deficit and surplus regions of wheat are widely separated geographically. Transport points simplify this situation so greatly that only through them can it be grasped. Every railway station in a wheat belt is a collecting point in miniature. Each is surrounded by its small supply area, and the receipts of each farmer are equal to the uniform unit price at the collecting station less the cost of transporting the wheat there. The nodal traffic points are the collecting places of the railway stations. A larger supply area surrounds them, and the price at each stopping place is equal to that at the

---

122. This holds true for smaller market areas, whereas a gateway merely constricts larger ones. In general, therefore, countries separated by mountain chains are economically less closely integrated. This in itself is a sufficient reason why Württemberg and Baden, for instance, do not constitute a single economic area. Mountains make Chile an independent economic region; her share in the foreign trade of Argentina amounts to but a small percentage.

123. This is especially important when the possible supply radius is not much longer than the necessary one. Furthermore, port installations are cheaper on a river.

124. *Op. cit.*, p. 349.

Some New Factors 189

superior nodal point less the freight. The collecting stations for these collecting stations, finally, are the few great ports that export wheat. In each the product of an enormous hinterland is assembled. Only these great gateways can give rise to great delivery regions in place of the small supply areas. Furthermore, they simplify the spatial price system. All prices at the subordinate collecting stations are determined by a single price at the port and the freight to it.[125]

If this uniform price falls, the hinterland of the port becomes smaller and more fragmentary. Smaller, because in the region of the farthest nodal points or " whistle stops " the cultivation of wheat would be no longer profitable; more fragmentary, because even in the nearer part of the hinterland individual farmers, who are especially far from the railway, or own poor soil, or lack ability, will now give up. The important function of price in the ordering of spatial relations is unmistakable.

The sales area for wheat is simplified in like manner. To be sure, simplification does not go so far that only one exporting port for wheat in the whole world supplies one single importing port. In such a case everything would be perfectly clear: one single area would be confronted with one single supply area and there would be a single world price for wheat, which could be chosen at either the export or the import harbor, since it would differ only by the freight.

But it is not quite so simple in reality.[126] Even if we neglect the product that is locally consumed, several supply areas are related to several consuming areas. Almost every exporting port ships to

---

125. When wheat is traded between places, local prices differ exactly by the cost of shipment; otherwise they may differ by less. In such cases considerable local price variations may exist without any movement of goods. If A and B supply C, the price in A may be above or below that in B by as much as the freight, and yet no trade will take place between them. This does not mean that the difference can fluctuate within these limits as long as A and B have a surplus. Since price fluctuations always originate at the central collecting station, they must be exactly the same for all subordinate places. *Gateway points fix spatial price differences rigidly,* for permanent surplus as well as for permanent deficit places. Prices in A and B always differ, therefore, by the difference in freight from A to C or from B to C. Otherwise one of the two places would be excluded as a source of supply. Only when A and B supply two different and unconnected places can the price in A be higher or lower than that in B by almost the amount of the freight to B, and vary arbitrarily within these limits, without one of the places being driven entirely from the market. The actual frequency of fluctuations in the price differences between two places is due not only to frictional difficulties, but also partly to slight product differences and partly to the fact that many places sometimes have a surplus and sometimes a deficit.

126. See the section on the " World Market " in Chapter 23, *b*, §4.

several importing ones, and almost every importing one receives from several exporting ports. This is an unusual situation. We should expect several consumers to order from one producer, or several producers to supply one large consumer. Does this strange overlapping of areas, as it is found, for example, in the wheat market, depend solely upon differences in the product, or can it be explained in some other way?

Suppose the prices in all ports of exportation to be given. Then in principle a small importing port can obtain wheat of the same quality from only *one* exporting port, for only to the few importing ports on the borders of the sales areas of two exporting ports is it a matter of indifference whether they supply the one or the other, or both. But suppose that the import needs of one of these border ports are very great, and cannot be met at all by a single exporting port, or only when the import price rises. Such an importing port

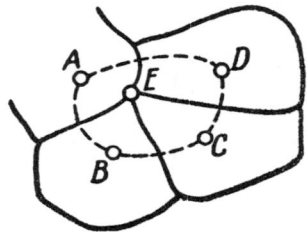

Fig. 52. Effect of gate cities on market and supply areas. *A, B, C,* and *D* are export ports with separate sales areas. *E* is a large importing port, whose supply area is endorsed by a broken line.

(Liverpool, for example) is not only a border point for the sales areas of several ports, but at the same time the center of a supply region on whose borders lie those exporting ports that, among others, supply the great importing port. The same exporting ports can supply in common only such importing ports as lie on their common boundary. But it seldom happens that more than two sellers share more than a corner of their sales areas.

With these considerations we have shown an important and remarkable effect of the gateway points: They can of themselves create a state of imperfect competition between millions of independent producers and millions of independent consumers. This is expressed by the fact that to large buyers on a border it is not a matter of indifference (as it is to small buyers) how much they buy from each sales center on the border of whose areas they lie. As an example, England and Peru buy wheat from Canada, the United

States, Argentina, and Australia. But whereas it would make little difference if Peru were to get its entire supply from Argentina, the whole spatial price structure would be radically altered if England were to try the same thing. For England buys over-a third, Peru only an insignificant fraction, of the combined amounts exported by the countries mentioned. The share of the various surplus regions in English imports is uniquely determined in equilibrium.

Thus the characteristic effect of gateway points is twofold. First, they create a few great supply and sales areas. Second, when one or another of these turns out to be especially large they cause a strange overlapping. With a standardized product, however, the sales areas will only touch, but supply and sales areas will in this case overlap! (Fig. 52.)

c. HUMAN DIFFERENCES

§1. DIFFERENCES AMONG INDIVIDUAL ENTREPRENEURS

As the planning curve of a less capable entrepreneur lies above that of an abler one, the necessary extent of his sales area and his producer's price are generally greater, which can easily be deduced from a graph. The unskillful one could not maintain himself if there were enough capable ones. This is probably true in old established trades, because in order to succeed the head of an enterprise need only good average abilities such as approach those most often found, since human characteristics seem to be distributed along the Gaussian frequency curve. Very good and very bad entrepreneurs should be relatively uncommon in these branches, and the regional size should be about equal.

In pioneer industries, however, where a rather infrequent combination of characteristics is required, less able entrepreneurs may also find a place, though they are still above average. Will the abler producers be content with small sales areas and leave large markets to the less skillful, who could not otherwise exist? The outcome is as though all entrepreneurs were competing in the same market: The well qualified extend their sales areas until at the boundaries, which now extend farther outward than need be, the price is equal to that at the boundaries of the necessary sales areas of their less skillful neighbors. Consequently the actual, though not the necessary, sales areas of the ablest will be larger than those of the others.[127]

---

127. As the capabilities of a leading entrepreneur can extend his sales area in general, so the special abilities of his regional sales representative can expand it greatly in a certain direction.

In a literal sense they are the ones with the larger sphere of influence. Since they prefer great cities as locations wherever possible, their sales areas will be often, and perhaps usually, above the average in size for this reason alone.

§2. DIFFERENCES IN NATIONAL CHARACTER

The character of a people expresses itself also in the way in which they organize their economic life. But such national differences interest us here only in so far as they operate spatially—which presupposes that the various races and nationalities are not thoroughly intermixed. Where consumption is still rigidly determined by a common way of life (that is, where it represents a meaningful group of needs similar for all), tribal, national, and racial differences, like all differences between regionally confined groups, are of great economic importance from a spatial standpoint. Then the boundaries of a tribe or nation are at the same time the boundaries of regional networks for whole classes of goods. Not much is altered when in cosmopolitan periods customs and usages relax and become more similar. But even when they do, and advertising and fashions of the day instead of established custom attempt to determine consumption, not all boundaries are obliterated. Many customs are determined by the character of a landscape, by its history, and perhaps biologically too,[128] and can be changed only slowly or not at all.[129] Thus a native born entrepreneur can judge more accurately what compromise with the prevailing fashion will be possible. His solution and his advertising will correspond more closely with the national or tribal character, and up to a certain point national boundaries will still remain economic boundaries.

[128]. Heredity and landscape affect national character in part directly, in part through tradition, which also is largely determined by historical chance. For the influence of landscape see W. Hellpach, *Geopsyche* (5th ed., 1939).

[129]. Conversely, one of the most striking phenomena to a European visiting the United States is how little its great regional differences have been transmuted into differences in character and custom, and hence in consumption, even though the subtle variations are greater than appears at first sight. One gets the impression that the American is nature's master and shapes it, rather than allowing it to shape him. This imposing uniformity (as Ratzel has put it) is one of the sources of America's wealth. If there were as many cultural differences there within the same space as in Europe, cheap mass production would be finished. Earnings at least would fall, though psychic income need not. Incidentally, it is just this economic and cultural uniformity that makes the strong political position of the individual states so little dangerous to the Federal Government. Nevertheless, even in the United States the heyday of the regional is only beginning.

Some New Factors 193

But *production*, too, is largely influenced by the individuality of producers, even when they do not work exclusively for their own needs. What is produced will naturally depend in great measure upon the special skill of a people, though it cannot be said simply that they will produce that which relatively they know best.[130]

Characteristic skills must not be invariably regarded as given a priori, since, for example, they often require a suitable task for their development. Thus the parsimony of nature will spur some peoples on, but discourge others. It is by no means objective criteria alone that decide what a location is suitable for, since different peoples will develop it differently. They react differently to their human, as they do to their natural, environment. The diversity of production of a people is determined by how far they can resist a general leveling. The more they can do so, the less will they specialize one-sidedly in goods for a larger market.[131] They will neither simply accommodate themselves to an unfamiliar demand nor be satisfied with goods that are fashionable elsewhere.[132] Such loyalty to the native and indigenous has enormous advantages,

---

130. For further details see pp. 226 ff. and 236 ff. Ability varies among the citizens of different places, especially among those of larger and smaller towns. The former often work faster, the latter better.

131. The real meaning of European colonial policy was chiefly to enforce specialization.

132. It is hardly possible to overestimate the degree to which a too sudden or too great concentration of production may uproot an established way of life, or how trade may alienate a people from their soil. Foreign in place of domestic wood in the construction of furniture, fruit that has never been seen to ripen, clothing that might do for a different climate, travel among cultural surroundings for which one is not prepared, a thousand things that are possible against the background of a cosmopolitan attitude—when all this suddenly breaks into the life of a people, it is difficult to judge calmly which of the new economic possibilities will suit it. For there is little sense in ordering a multitude of goods from afar simply because they are cheaper or more attractive, as long as one has not found in some way or other a place in one's world pattern for their individuality, their origin, and their producer. One's horizon must widen with the expansion of markets. But it would be far from right to hold that this expansion of markets intrudes upon a people like fate from without. They themselves decide whether it shall take place at all; it depends on them whether they are ready for it.

Of course it would be as fallacious to prevent the concentration of production as to hasten it. The enormous increase in our wealth since the dawn of capitalism was only possible because we were willing, on the whole, to accept standardized products instead of individual ones. America went further in this respect, and that is one reason why she has more goods. For Europe there lies dormant a great and dangerous possibility of quickly becoming rich again after the war, even though only on the surface.

far transcending the diminution in economic risk,[133] for it is conducive to a more harmonius development of human nature. The individual will have to specialize everywhere, but it makes a great difference whether in his sphere [134] there are only associates who specialize in the same field, or whether he is surrounded by men who live for him the *other* possibilities that he has had to forego—that is, whether his horizon constitutes a complete whole.[135]

Tribal and national characteristics show also in the conduct of business. There is not nearly enough attention paid to how much not only individuals, but tribes and nations [136] as well, vary in such characteristics as timidity or daring, discretion or rashness, a liking for tradition or for innovation, a conservative or a flexible mind, thorough or superficial training, stability or frivolity, and to how strongly these differences dominate the character of their economies: the objects produced, the size of their undertakings, the relation between an entrepreneur and his workers, the mobility of labor and capital, the strategy of monopolists, location, resistance to crises, and so on. All these depend not only upon the individual entrepreneur, but also upon the environment in which he works as well as upon his environment in a spatial sense, since the intimacy of economic relations generally decreases with distance.

When an explanation was sought for the fact that the economy of Württemberg withstood the great depression of the 'thirties especially well, the discussion occasionally touched upon these matters. But many explanations did not get near enough to the root of the matter. The poverty of the region in natural raw materials was certainly a piece of good fortune in this instance. But the balance of the economic structure, as shown in the diversity of production and particularly in the happy combination of industry and agriculture, and again in the dispersion of industry and landed

---

133. The expansion of markets gained at the price of specialization also tends to diminish risks (see E. Willeke, *Von der raumgebundenen menschlichen Arbeitskraft* [Jena, 1937], p. 113), but this rarely suffices to compensate for the increased risk connected with specialization itself.

134. This broadens with improvements in transportation, though not necessarily at the same rate.

135. For the development of a cultural individuality a landscape must therefore be large enough to constitute a world in miniature, yet at the same time small enough to be more or less understood by its intellectual leaders.

136. For national types of entrepreneurs see W. Sombart, *Der Bourgeois* (Munich, 1913), pp. 170–193, 266–281); K. Wiedenfeld, *Das Persönliche im modernen Unternehmertum* (Leipzig, 1920); and R. Michels, *Wirtschaft und Rasse. Grundriss der Sozialökonomik* (2d ed., 1923), Vol. II, Pt. 1.

property [137] resulting from free divisibility and deliberate policy [138]—these were not due to chance. Whoever considers thoroughly the particular nature of the products and production; the highly valuable specialties that can be made only by unusually well-trained and adaptable workers who like to tinker and experiment; whoever considers the energetic yet sound business policy that clings to easily understood and controlled conditions and to enterprises seldom exceeding the capital and labor resources of one family [139] (just as Württemberg itself in many respects resembles a large family which has contributed greatly to the easing of social tension and encouraged the use of native products) —whoever considers all these factors will see clearly that national character has influenced this economy to

137. Well described by G. Stockmann, "Grundlagen und Krisenfestigkeit der württembergischen Industrie," *Deutsche Zeitschrift für Wirtschaftskunde,* I (1936), 281-298. See also the great atlas of P. Hesse et al., *Landvolk und Landwirtschaft in den Gemeinden von Württemberg-Hohenzollern (Kartenwerk)* (Stuttgart, 1939); and several contributions in *Weltwirtschaft,* 1934, No. 11/2.

138. Ever since 1848 the *Zentralstelle für Gewerbe und Handel* (the present *Landesgewerbeamt*) fulfilled certain functions of a regional planning office in an exemplary manner, more recently under the farsighted leadership of Ferdinand von Steinbeis.

139. According to 233 official American studies, the largest enterprises are seldom the cheapest; it is generally the medium-sized and often the small ones (G. J. Stigler, *American Economic Review,* June, 1942, Pt. 2). As for agriculture in Württemberg, the number of farms that are too small is apt to be overestimated (see above, p. 65, note 53). The net market return (money receipts less expenses) in 1934 amounted in Baden to 155 reichsmarks per hectare, in Württemberg to 145, in Hanover to 124, in Schleswig-Holstein to 88, and in Pomerania to 73. Large farms were more common and most natural yields larger in the same order, but this was achieved by a greater outlay for machinery and artificial fertilizers. "The economic efficiency of an area under cultivation increases as its size decreases." (H. Priebe, "Zur Frage der Gestaltung und Grösse des zukünftigen bäuerlichen Familienbetriebes in Deutschland," *Berichte über Landwirtschaft, Neue Folge,* XXVII [1942], 585.) Though higher money return per hectare does not entirely compensate for the thicker settlement of regions containing small farms (the net return per person principally engaged in agriculture was 300 reichsmarks in Württemberg and 400 in Pomerania), the difference almost vanishes when it is taken into account that on a peasant farm an especially large number of workers are employed, such as children or old people, who are not fully efficient. (G. Isenberg, "Die Tragfähigkeit des deutschen Ostens an landwirtschaftlicher und gewerblicher Bevölkerung," in *Struktur und Gestaltung der zentralen Orte des deutschen Ostens* [Leipzig, 1941], p. 13.)

In any case, depopulation of the Swabian villages would affect the vitality of industry itself through the loss of the qualitatively irreplaceable younger generation (Bosch himself, typical in so many ways, came as a peasant boy from the Swabian Alps) and would altogether sap the energy of the whole region, which springs psychically and economically from the fertile proximity of man and nature. Even without such a depopulation much is taking place in Württemberg that some day may change favorable into unfavorable conditions.

an extraordinarily high degree.[140] The Swabian economy cannot be entirely grasped without an understanding of Swabian philosophy, which has probably formulated this national character in the most apt way.[141]

d. POLITICAL DIFFERENCES

Countries and economic regions do not necessarily coincide. It lies with the state as an independently governed society, and hence in the final analysis with the people themselves, whether or not it shall be entirely self-sufficient economically; that is, whether its outer economic boundaries shall coincide with its political boundaries, or whether deliberate state interference shall remain limited to arranging the economy in such a way that, once set going, it shall continue on the whole by itself.[142] In the latter case many economic boundaries will extend beyond its frontiers. Between these two clear-cut extremes there is naturally an infinite variety of less well defined economic policies,[143] but we shall limit the following paragraphs chiefly to the second limiting case, because it allows recognition of the minimum extent of political influences on the formation of economic areas. The discussion will be preceded by a comparison between purely political and purely economic regions.

§1. STATES AND ECONOMIC LANDSCAPES: A COMPARISON

α. *Similarities*

1. States and economic landscapes each have a capital toward which their subdivisions and main traffic routes are oriented.[144]

2. Both kinds of capital are located as centrally as possible,

---

140. E. Preiser (*Die Württembergischer Wirtschaft als Vorbild* [Stuttgart, 1937], p. 79) justly praises it for having disarmed the most damaging criticism of capitalism by its relative invulnerability to crises, its spatial arrangement, and its social harmony.

141. See H. O. Burger, *Schwabentum in der Geistesgeschichte* (Stuttgart, 1933).

142. It is not quite accurate to speak of rules of the economic game set up by a state. For in the economy the individual (though not all individuals together) can do about as he pleases without disturbing its functioning, which is not true of a game. A free economy is rather constructed precisely in such a manner that it functions as a whole, no matter what the individual may do. The most important exception to this statement concern monopolistic tendencies, which must therefore be supervised or checked.

143. Thus it is only a question of convenience whether to regard free trade as normal and state interference as a disturbance, or to begin with state planning and show the workings of economic forces within this given framework. Similarly, the actual intermediate condition may be derived from either free competition or monopoly.

144. This explains the odd fact that frontiers of the German states are often language boundaries without being tribal boundaries. The border between Bavaria and Württemberg is an example. The Swabians just over the line speak a dialect tinctured with

taking into consideration the location of competitors and the fact that their functions are not demanded in a uniform manner throughout the whole area and that local locational advantages are not everywhere the same.

3. The tendency toward equal size is common to both states and economic landscapes. This we have already shown for economic areas. For states the reader is referred to Ratzel, who, in his great *Politische Geographie,* ascribes to the notion of equilibrium the fact that neighboring states in competition with one another struggle toward equal size.[145] In this mutual pressure and thrust the peculiarities of the central position are the same in both cases; it is as powerful in strength as it is threatened in weakness.[146]

4. The size of states and economic landscapes, of administrative districts and market areas, depends in great measure on the development of transportation and production techniques. In every case the size must be at least such as to assure existence; that of economic landscapes and market areas through markets, that of states and administrative districts through power. If they exceed this size there arise the rich entrepreneur and the mighty state. The former can afford to be generous, the latter magnanimous.

5. The boundaries of states and economic landscapes cut through regular market networks, which results in economic losses.

6. Boundaries have the function of separating the various orders. Enclaves and exclaves are politically and economically unprofitable.

7. The influence of centers always grows less toward the periphery. The capitals and their immediate surroundings differ more sharply from each other than do the border regions. Just as we have seen market areas on the borders of economic landscapes that did not belong exclusively to either of the adjoining orders, and just as the border zones of individual market areas are most easily lost to competitors, so a political boundary region is most endangered. Furthermore, administrations on either side of a frontier co-operate in many ways (joint river commissions, for example); there are sundry overlaps, such as customs exemptions; and diverse privileges granted to the neighbor state, as when the border-control formalities are performed in the neighboring country's frontier station (see Ratzel, *op. cit.,* p. 487).

Bavarian because they are oriented toward Munich both politically and culturally; this is especially true of teachers and clergymen, who are so important in the evolution of a language.

145. F. Ratzel, *Politische Geographie* (Munich, 1897), p. 221.
146. *Ibid.,* p. 282.

Thus political and economic areas have their most important principles of organization as well as many properties in common. Because of this structural similarity it is no wonder that states and economic regions frequently overlap; at least in the sense that their political and economic capitals coincide, that political boundaries are at the same time boundaries of many market areas, and that many market areas and administrative districts, or at least their capitals, are identical.

β. *Dissimilarities*

1. Political frontiers are more rigid than economic boundaries. They are not so easily changed.

2. Political frontiers are wider, so to speak, than economic boundaries. States, like oases, are separated as in a great desert by customs duties, laws, language, a sense of community, insecurity,[147] and destiny. Economic boundaries separate only through minute price differences.

3. Political frontiers are more sharply defined than economic boundaries. To be sure political boundaries, too, may be belts rather than lines,[148] particularly when they depend upon natural features. But the influence of the center grows less toward the border in both cases. Nevertheless, the overlaps and transitions are disproportionately more common in economic landscape boundaries. There are profound reasons for this. On economic boundaries there live individuals, small units that make a gradual transition possible and are at the same time concrete units that "collide in space" and to whom distance therefore means something. On political frontiers two organizations meet, and often two nations—large and in certain respects abstract units, for whom distance changes little or nothing. It has been truly said that patriotism draws no distinctions within, but sharp limits without.[149,150] Economic boundaries change as profit changes. With political boundaries, ideas or the people change, or

---

147. Especially since the two political principles that are so important to world trade—balance of power and differentiation between war and peace—were abandoned after World War I. (See W. Euken, "Staatliche Strukturwandlungen und die Krisis des Kapitalismus," *Weltwirtschaftliches Archiv*, XXXVI [1932], 297–321, particularly p. 309.)

148. See Ratzel, *op. cit.*, p. 451; and J. Sölch, *Die Auffassung der "natürlichen Grenzen" in der wissenschaftlichen Geographie* (Innsbruck, 1924), p. 26.

149. W. Sulzbach, *Nationales Gemeinschaftsgefühl und wirtschaftliches Interesse* (Leipzig, 1929).

150. Thus List's program was an eminently patriotic one: railroads in the interior, and tariffs at the border to protect infant industries.

at least the organization for the sake of which the individual sacrifices something. Hence economic ties are very much looser and weaker than political ties. Between economic landscapes transitional areas are possible which derive no advantages from definite orientation toward one or another order. Between states, on the contrary, the individual must choose.

4. The goals of economic landscapes and states are different. If those for states are arranged in a descending order as follows: continuance, power, *Kultur*, prosperity, this order must be exactly reversed for economic areas. Entirely different sides of human nature are expressed in the political and economic orders.

γ. *Political and Economic Boundaries*

In certain respects the boundaries of economic landscapes have exactly the same effect as political frontiers, even though the two are of opposite nature. The former resemble a seam, the latter a cut, through the elaborate maze of market networks. Both have the same effect, however. Both break up the regular meshes, which are then replaced by relatively uneconomic types of areas. In order to minimize this disadvantage there is a tendency to reduce the length of boundaries, first by making political and economic boundaries coincide wherever possible, and second by making states and economic landscapes as large as possible. Fewer economic landscapes may be able to maintain themselves within a given area, therefore, than if there were no frictions at the boundary.

On both types of boundary the regular areal network shows gaps, which are filled in by irregular areal forms. In other respects, however, the two situations are as different as those of two men with entirely different starting points and destinations who meet along the way. On economic landscape boundaries the tendency prevails to *close* unavoidable gaps wherever possible; on state frontiers, to *open* avoidable gaps wherever possible. It is characteristic of economic landscape boundaries that they offer a particularly favorable location for the centers of market areas that fill in these gaps and thus extend across the boundary. It is characteristic of state frontiers, on the contrary, to hamper the crossing of boundaries by market areas (that is, the filling in of gaps); to create new gaps in a market network where none exist [151] (for a boundary can pass directly

---

151. In the extreme case a whole state is cut out of the market area to which it belongs because of its situation. The entire state becomes a market by itself, an artificial gap, whose existence is assured by protective tariffs and made profitable by a national industry that prospers in their shadow.

through an economic landscape); and with certain exceptions to discourage industries from settling near a boundary, where in fact they often have a market in one direction only.

This explains, too, why after a shifting of political frontiers the new border regions so often become depressed areas. Not only must they transpose their economic activities; they must curtail them as well. This devastating effect of boundaries would be still more apparent if they did not so often pass through regions that would be thinly settled in any case (such as mountainous frontiers), or through regions (such as those along river boundaries) that by nature are especially thickly settled, so that the population density in the latter case appears normal anyway and in the former is attributed to the parsimony of nature alone. But when a boundary opens up gaps and keeps them open—that is to say, prevents their closure by industrial enterprises on the boundary—the result, so far as no multiplication of the interior market can be achieved by regrouping (which is also relatively uneconomic), is greater excess profits but almost always a poorer supply for the consumer.

Why do political boundaries exert this effect? The secondary phenomena that are usually associated with them are to blame. First, they are almost always customs boundaries as well. But tariffs are like rivers, which separate their banks economically more than would correspond to their actual width.[152] Second, they are often national frontiers also. Differences in language, in requirements, and in national character have the same effect as customs duties. Third, they are administrative boundaries, which means on the one hand that public contracts are only reluctantly awarded beyond the border, and on the other that business traffic, to the extent that it is associated with official traffic, as is especially common among country folk, does not cross the border. Fourth, border regions are regions of danger, for special consideration must be given to military requirements even in time of peace, and in war they are the most seriously threatened areas.

§2. Economic Areas as Basis for the State

We shall begin our investigation by sketching at least the influence of an economic area on the state, and conclude with a more minute analysis of the inverse relationship. It need hardly be men-

---

152. Thus tariffs are equivalent to a lengthening of transport routes. The lengthening depends partly upon the tariff level and partly upon the way in which duties are collected (a frontier can be crossed only at certain designated points). The effect of a railway line that cuts through a town is similar.

tioned that the often divergent interests of individual businesses within a state determine its policy and size to a rather large degree. The safeguarding of profits in the long run postulates the participation of business leaders in politics.[153] The safeguarding of the power of the state in the long run demands that a state make the economic interests of the citizens its own. Exports and, when necessary, imports are protected if possible by conquest, by command, or by treaties in regard to tariffs, special trade privileges, and so on. History shows how closely the destiny of states is connected with that of their domestic economy. Italy lost her commanding economic position in the Roman Empire, which depended upon wine and olive oil privileges, and her political pre-eminence as a result, when she gradually permitted the legions to supply themselves and when she gradually emancipated the provinces with respect to these and to important industrial goods.[154] And the sway of the Italian commercial cities came to an end when the old trade routes to the Orient were deserted upon the discovery of a sea route to the East Indies. The nature of the British economic landscape has favored the creation of the British Empire in a particularly clear-cut manner. Size limitations force islands to make the most of their limited areas, while at the same time their position offers them the compelling advantage of far-flung contacts.[155] This explains the difference between British and German imperial development. As ocean freights are so low, and no place in England lies much more than about 60 miles from the sea, she is as closely connected with other maritime countries throughout the entire world as Germany is with the adjoining countries of Middle Europe. The great difference between land and ocean freights sets much narrower limits for the Continental emipres than for those oriented toward the sea.[156]

The simpler and more uniform are economic interests within a state,[157] the clearer and more productive is the adjustment of politics

---

153. The degree of participation naturally varies. If in the course of time all lose interest (free trade), an individual entrepreneur or an individual people have less reason to enlist political power in the service of economic interests, but the temptation to do so increases.

154. See M. Rostovtzeff, *Gesellschaft und Wirtschaft im römischen Kaiserreich* (Leipzig, 1930), 2 vols.

155. See Ratzel, *op. cit.*, pp. 356 ff.

156. Next to its ideological and racial homogeneity, the fact that its economic distances are much shorter than its geographic is undoubtedly the most important cause of the tenacious cohesion of the British Empire. (See A. Lösch, " Die Leistung der Seeschiffahrt," *Nauticus*, 1941, pp. 326–336.)

157. For examples see A. Predöhl, " Staatsraum und Wirtschaftsraum," *Weltwirtschaftliches Archiv*, XXXIX (1934), 1/12, p. 3.

to economics. It would have been of great economic advantage to the Confederate States of America if they had succeeded in creating a union of their own. Their free-trade policy would have been approved by all their citizens, and would therefore have been able to pursue a definite course. But since the protectionist industries of the North and the free-trade cotton growers of the South live in the same country, American policy vacillates between moderate and exorbitant protective tariffs according to the outcome of elections.

§3. Coincidence of Political and Economic Boundaries

A political frontier is an economic boundary also when by nature it is hard to cross. This is regularly true when it exists for significant reasons such as natural or national (racial) barriers especially. Seas, lakes, and broad rivers keep many smaller market areas from further expansion, exactly as do mountain chains, deserts, or language barriers.[158]

Though it is often said that streams connect rather than separate their banks, this is so only for trade over long distances, which is cheaper, though not quicker, than if the stream were solid land. But there is no doubt that on the opposite bank the sale of many goods with short or even medium shipping distances is made extraordinarily difficult, and the more so the wider the river and the fewer therefore its bridges. Since states aspired to natural obstacles as boundaries until the awakening of national consciousness in the nineteenth century, and since these often separate peoples as well, many, if not most, of today's political frontiers are also natural boundaries for the smaller market areas. This is particularly true for retail trade and artisans, but much less true for factories.

The coincidence of political and economic boundaries in " great spaces " (*Grossraum*) is desired and mutually conditioned. The leading state delimits regions of influence geographically in such a way as to include wherever possible those economic conditions that it believes important for its existence, and to this extent accommo-

---

158. This refers to natural boundaries. Such a border need not make *all* trade impossible, nor does every natural obstacle have to be turned into a political frontier. Thus a natural boundary need not by any means include only what is homogeneous. It is sufficient that the state enclosed be strong enough to maintain itself by reason of its size and economic structure and the suitability of its border for military purposes. In my opinion Sölch asks too much of natural boundaries in his otherwise admirable work (J. Sölch, *Die Auffassung der " natürlichen Grenzen " in der wissenschaftlichen Geographie* [Innsbruck, 1924]).

dates itself to the economy. On the other hand, it shifts the necessary foreign trade as much as possible to easily safeguarded markets, and here the economy has to adjust itself to the policy of the state. Only when that which is important for existence coincides more or less with that which can be defended has the development of a great space (*Grossraum*) succeeded.[159]

§4. Transformation of Economic Areas by State Boundaries[160]

Larger market areas are always transformed along political frontiers, and all areas are changed where the borders represent merely man-made obstacles to trade. We can classify these changes into: first, destruction of locations or their removal away from a boundary, which in the absence of disturbing influences together create the border wasteland; and second, removal of locations across the border.

α. *The Border Wasteland*

What has already been sketched in comparing political and economic boundaries may now be supplemented.[160a] Figure 53 shows at the left a few typical situations at the border of economic landscapes; at the right, at the border of two countries. The relative position of the regions on either side of the landscape varies, depending on their size and other factors. Since they are oriented toward different centers, they do not necessarily dovetail with each other. The political boundary, on the other hand, necessarily cuts through the regular networks of market areas unless it happens to coincide with an economic boundary.

---

159. When it is economically profitable. See p. 339, and Lösch, *Wesen und Nutzen wirtschaftlicher Grossräume* (in preparation but never published). The provision of important means of defense obviously will never be *wholly* guaranteed. Some raw material obtainable only beyond the frontier may suddenly acquire significance, or an invention may be made there that may be more threatening than any lack of raw material, which often can be made synthetically or for which a substitute can frequently be found. There will never be absolute safety in any region smaller than the earth itself. It must also be considered that as the space grows in size more defensive measures are needed and more means of defense provided, for larger empires have to reckon with more powerful adversaries. The development of one great space starts that of another. All depends upon which increases more rapidly—the need for the means of security, or their supply.

160. For transformation within states especially through the enormously important transport policies, see below, pp. 345 ff.

160a. The rest of this paragraph and the next four paragraphs are from the first German edition of *Die räumliche Ordnung der Wirtschaft*, which were omitted from the second edition to save space.—Ed.

We shall discuss first the individual possibilities. Area 1 remains unchanged, because the economic boundary by itself has no effect whatsoever. Area 12, on the other hand, will be divided, because the political border reduces the demand from the other side of the border and because the total demand therefore ceases to be sufficient. The size of the neighboring areas will thus increase. Areas 4, 5, 16, and 17 remain unaffected. Between areas 2 and 3 parts of market areas are situated whose sources of supply would lie on the other

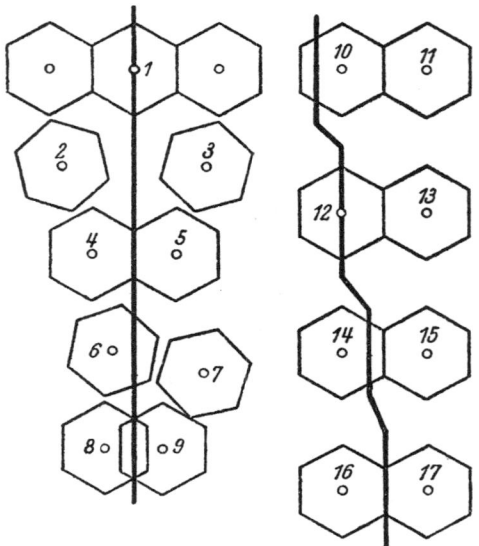

Fig. 53. Economic and political borders

side of the border if the market networks could expand farther without interference. Depending on the size of these "splinter" areas a "corner" area will arise, which, because of its uneconomical shape, will extend far in the upward and downward directions in order to lead to a sufficiently large sales area, provided that the other areas and the possible sales radius permit this extension. If the splinters are small, areas 2 and 3 will expand. The same is true also of areas 6 and 7.

It is different with areas 10 and 14, whose corners are also cut off by the boundary. Area 10, to the right of the border, and area 14, to its left, now face an insufficient demand. They will therefore (at least at first) be divided among the neighboring areas which expand correspondingly. Areas 8 and 9, which overlap, are also too small when taken by themselves. But they can be consolidated into a fairly large new market area whose center will lie on the boundary of the economic landscape. The situation is similar to that of areas 2 and 3 though more clear-cut. So much for the temporary solution of the typical situations.

These derived areal extensions do not last in all cases, however. By changing the shapes of the areas and by a movement of the locations, additional areas may be created here and there, particularly along the economic landscape boundary, and most probably at corners where three such landscapes meet,[161] because splinters of neighboring landscapes can be used to a much larger extent than would be the case where three countries meet.[162]

Wherever the odd pieces are not sufficient for a new market area, the old area remains enlarged. The sizes of the areas along the border and within it are equalized only if the surplus is sufficiently large for all sales areas of the good in question to move into the next higher size class, but too small to permit an increase in the number of areas. This is especially probable for goods with a large necessary sales radius.

In other respects state and economic boundaries have the same result: The market areas in their vicinity are larger,[163] and therefore less numerous.[164] The seam at the boundary gives more or less the impression of a wasteland, in so far as it is less thickly populated and many products can be obtained only from a distance or not at all.[165] Prices are higher, partly because more freight on the average is added to the factory price and partly because there is less competition. Boundaries cause economic losses, and double boundaries, economic and political, mean doubled losses.

---

161. Such triple corners are surrounded by a region of especially numerous overlapping and atrophied market areas. But, as the pieces of three regions may be consolidated, more enterprises can exist here than at any other point along the border.

162. The enterprise locating at the border will select that side of the border where the empty space is larger; or, if it is not much smaller, where higher tariffs compensate for the smaller size.

163. E. H. Chamberlin shows the same thing for a boundary beyond which there are no more markets (*The Theory of Monopolistic Competition* [Cambridge, Mass., 1936 edition], pp. 195–196.)

164. Adjustment in the size of the region between a boundary seam and the interior of an economic landscape takes place only when the surplus is large enough for all sales areas of the product concerned to rise to the next higher order of size, but too small to permit further increase in the number of areas; that is, especially in the case of goods with a large necessary shipping distance.

165. This is true also of economic landscapes where the necessary sales distance is not much less than half the radius of the landscape, without the possible sales distance reaching it.

All these consequences, distortion of areas, expansion of areas, and dead corners, are disproportionately more prominent on political frontiers. Since these, unlike economic boundaries, lower the demand from remnants of areas beyond them, and since they often entirely prevent market areas from extending beyond them, industries occupying gaps are still less common and market areas still larger. The number of unobtainable products is greater, too. For example, the effects of tariffs are felt most in the boundary seam and less toward the interior. The boundary itself, which in economic landscapes is the location of many enterprises that occupy gaps, is most deserted in the case of states; for, when half the demand comes from an adjoining country despite the political frontier,[166] it is definitely more advantageous as a rule to move production there. Exceptions referable to unusual circumstances will be discussed in the statistical section.

The effect of political frontiers naturally depends entirely on the kind and size of the barrier that they set up against trade; but under otherwise similar conditions, products with small necessary shipping distances are hardest hit. First, any given tariff rate has a more adverse percentage effect when low freight charges are added to the purchase price than when these charges are high. Second, there must be added to the customs duties all the annoying formalities at the border, which cause many small enterpreneurs to give up all foreign trade. A third, and especially important, factor is the technically necessary limitation of the number of border crossings. The resulting increase in distance between a seller and his customers is relatively greatest when the latter are near the border.[167]

β. Shift of Location to an Adjoining State

Suppose that country B is large enough for several plants of a certain sort, but that in country A there is a place, O, with conditions so advantageous for production that the entire branch of industry is concentrated there and some of its firms supply country B. If B were to introduce a high tariff that nullified the special

---

166. This demand originates from an area considerably larger than half the necessary sales area.

167. The tariff on retail goods, which typically have a short sales distance, is calculated from the high retail price; that on wholesale goods from the much lower middleman's price. This makes no difference to the ultimate consumer if the retail margin on either side of the border is the same percentage of the purchase price inclusive of tariff.

advantages of O in so far as sales to B were concerned, the firms in question would migrate from A to B.[168]

Suppose, again, that in one branch of industry very small and very large enterprises were technically possible, and that one or the other was more profitable according to the density of population. Suppose that a few of the large enterprises in thickly settled country A had formerly helped to supply adjacent parts of thinly settled country B also. But suddenly B sets up a high tariff. Suppose that the internal demand in B is not great enough for very large enterprises though adequate for very small ones, and that since they are no longer exposed to competition from large enterprises across the border, small enterprises spring up like mushrooms. Whereas, in the first example, a long-established enterprise would migrate, in the second, only a newly established one would move across the border. Canada [169] provides classic examples of each, as does also the shifting of industries after the partition of Austria-Hungary.

A country poor in capital may be well adapted to the working up of raw materials found in it, but foreign capital may be frightened away by uncertain political conditions and unpredictable expropriations. The country is doubly harmed: it loses openings for its labor because foreign entrepreneurs finish the material abroad,[170] and it is further exploited through high risk premiums.

γ. *Economic Width of a Boundary*

Let S be the radius of a rounded-off state and L the radius of an economic landscape. The lengths of the two are decisive. If S is shorter than L, consumers throughout the entire state may under certain circumstances be able to order goods with relatively large necessary shipping distance ($\rho > S$) from abroad. If S is equal to L, then, as in the case of an economic landscape, all consumers who are more than $S/2$ away from the capital will order from abroad. If S is greater than L, imports may, under certain circumstances, be limited to a narrow border seam. Similarly for the producer. If S is shorter than L, all producers may be able to export. If S equals

---

168. See Palander, *op. cit.*, p. 331, Fig. 83 and text.

169. See H. Marshall *et al.*, *Canadian-American Industry. A Study in International Investment* (New Haven, 1936).

170. For example, almost all Venezuelan petroleum is refined on the neighboring islands of Curacao and Aruba, in the Netherlands West Indies. Once built, such enormous installations can be moved only with the greatest difficulty, though in the meantime Venezuela has developed into one of the best-governed countries in the world. Of course, ocean steamers could not penetrate to the oil wells in any case.

L, only those at a minimum distance of $2S/3$ will do so. If S is greater than L, only a few producers in a very narrow border seam may, under certain circumstances, export.[171]

From this reasoning a number of conclusions may be drawn. But first it is well to remember that we have excluded all natural differences that would tend to increase the extent of foreign trade. For this reason our conclusions are minimum expectations, since some differences will always exist in fact. Second, we have excluded any state intervention. For this reason, our conclusions would be the maximum that could be expected. Since the effects of our two assumptions go in opposite directions, our conclusions show a sort of average picture of what is to be expected.

(1) The width of a boundary is the same for all economic landscapes, but different for states. (2) The effect of an economic boundary is felt halfway to the center; that of the political frontier of a large state only in the boundary seam, and of a small state possibly as far in as the capital itself.[172] (3) In both cases the economic influence of a boundary declines toward the interior, but is greater the greater are the necessary sales areas.[173]

§5. Political Economic Areas

These are economic areas that exist only because there are states, and hence, as a rule, coincide with these states. Most important is the area over which an economic order based on politics extends. It is quite conceivable that every state may have its own special principles of economic organization. In the face of such fundamentally different political beliefs the world-wide acceptance of capitalism during the nineteenth century was by no means a foregone conclusion.[174]

---

171. When state frontiers are farther away than economic landscape boundaries, agricultural products also are artificially diverted from their natural markets. This is hardest for the farmers concerned, but affects those economic landscapes as well that have been deprived of their natural boundary zones. Even a large state benefits only to a limited degree from this diversion. Because of increased agricultural supplies the per capita income of the inhabitants of its central economic landscape is higher than if state frontiers and economic boundaries coincided; but the per capita income in the boundary seam, and that of all citizens of the state taken together, is lower. The costs of a boundary thus appear in agriculture exactly as in industry.

172. Foreign trade is therefore more important for small countries than for large.

173. Consequently more large industries than small are interested in tariff policies.

174. H. von Beckerath, " Politik und Wirtschaft," *Schmollers Jahrbuch,* LVI (1932); " Politische und Wirtschaftsverfassung," *ibid.,* LVI (1933), 258–276.

The second profound effect that may originate from a country is the creation of a single economic landscape embracing its entire area. Just as it is advantageous for such a landscape to rise to statehood, so the damage is at least reduced when a state develops into an economic landscape. This assumes three things above all: first, that political boundaries represent a great artificial barrier to trade; second, that the administrative structure of a state is of great economic importance; third, that the greatest possible extent of an economic landscape is not very much smaller than that of the state.

Furthermore, individual households and firms in the same state share a common political fortune. We have learned perfectly what a deep influence this may exert upon the level, the source, and the stay of capital imports.[175] It is wise, also, to direct the export of capital in accordance with political alliances; and this has been widely practiced even during the liberal era, if only because investment in the territory of a possible enemy is risky.[176]

But even market areas for goods proper are not unaffected by political situations. It is only necessary to recall the political boycott, or it converse, a preference for domestic goods for patriotic reasons. The lessons of 1871, 1918, and 1933 show how greatly national victory or defeat can exhilarate or depress entrepreneurs in the state concerned and lead to an upswing or a decline in the *national* economy. Wars also have an aftereffect on subsequent business cycles. They raise birth waves, and when these have been transformed into waves of marriages and in the labor supply they cause cyclical variations in the economy. At least it was so in Germany.[177] Population waves, and thus business cycles, vary characteristically in amplitude from one country to another, since the immediate effects of wars cease abruptly at frontiers.[178]

In the fourth place, a state may represent a politically created sales area for goods that would not be in demand at all, or not in this state, or not only in this state, or not everywhere in this state,

---

175. Of course the destiny of the state, with which the national economy is so closely associated, is in many respects nothing but a higher or lower import duty on capital. It determines the risk premium that is to be added to the interest rate.

176. A form of risk against which there is no insurance.

177. A. Lösch, " Bevölkerungswellen und Wechsellagen," *Beiträge zur Erforschung der wirtschaftlichen Wechsellagen Aufschwung, Krise, Stockung*, edited by A. Spiethoff, Vol. 13 (Jena, 1936).

178. Similarly the domestically conditioned reluctance of American industry to make investments in 1937, or an armament boom with a throttling of foreign trade, had effects that reached at first almost to the borders.

without pressure from above such as tariffs, taxes,[179] regulations, or freight rates. It must be clearly understood, however, that only a few customs duties, etc., have such effects. In the case of public works state boundaries are generally the boundaries of the possible supply area also.

There still remain to be mentioned those exceptional cases in which economic areas created by a state, not merely controlled by it, do not coincide with the state itself. Currency, tariff, and political unions need not coincide. There are customs, currency, and legislative frontiers that include only parts of states, and others that embrace several states. Consider, on the one hand, customs and mint unions or the identity of many German and Austrian laws after World War I; and on the other hand, internal customs duties, significant today principally in trade between a motherland and her colonies, or as an anachronism still to be seen in the vicinity of Paris,[180] the regional validity or significance of many laws, and so on.[181]

Finally, in many respects the state is only apparently or temporarily a homogeneous economic area. The power of a common monetary system to create regions is normally but slight, as will be seen in Part III. The opposite experience during the inflation period and since the last crisis was exceptional. Most tariffs, too, do not even approach the creation of a national market, or even a network of purely domestic market areas. As a rule they curtail only the tips of areas that extend over a boundary. Moreover, there will be pointed out below some further limitation of the old thesis that production factors are less mobile internationally. If it was wrong formerly to underestimate the importance of political factors in developing economic areas, we should not forget today, on the other hand, that this is, after all, but one influence among several.

---

179. The method of computing taxes affects, for example, the construction of automobiles.

180. These were reduced in 1941 in order to improve the food supply.

181. W. Sulzbach gives a good presentation in "Der wirtschaftliche Begriff des Auslands," *Weltwirtschaftliches Archiv*, XXXII (1930). For the many trade barriers between individual states in the United States see *Works Progress Administration, The Marketing Laws Survey, Comparative Charts of State Statutes Illustrating Barriers to Trade Between States* (Washington, D. C., 1939).

Chapter 14. Further Restriction of Market Areas

In the preceding chapter the various effects of individual factors were examined. This chapter will discuss all the different factors that work together toward the same end: to limit the extent of market areas. It is a question of the greatest importance, for many will doubt whether today's low freight costs are of sufficient consequence to restrict markets effectively.

In addition to freight there is another restraining influence: competition. But where freight costs are of little importance, competition by itself would hardly influence the limitation of market areas and the distribution of production sites. Locations would not have to maintain a certain distance from one another, and all market areas would overlap everywhere. Even competition can exert its limiting effect only by way of freight, or other factors that operate similarly. Here it is immaterial whether these factors work by raising prices to the consumer or by lowering the profits of the producer.[1] For the sake of simplicity we shall limit the discussion to the former.

(a) *Transport costs.* The freight rate sometimes increases with distance, and naturally a point is soon reached where the demand is zero. In such cases the argument that freight costs are insignificant falls to the ground. One thinks here of retail stores, laundries, breweries, and the like that deliver by motor truck or messenger boy. With increasing distance from a producer the density of habitations and the demand of individual customers drop, partly because outside of large cities the density and buying power of the population decrease and partly because, even with a constant freight rate and for all the reasons still to be given, both this particular producer's proportionate share of customers and the inclination of individual customers to buy become smaller. As a consequence the time of the motor truck or of the messenger boy is less and less efficiently employed with increasing distance, and there remains only a choice

---

1. In the latter case, revenue cones appear in place of price funnels. Curves for equal gross receipts were probably first used by V. Furlan, " Die Standortprobleme in der Volks- und Weltwirtschaftslehre," *Weltwirtschaftliches Archiv*, II (1913).

between charging distant customers for delivery or abandoning delivery beyond a certain point. Costs resembling freight have the effect of higher freight rates. Among these are, in particular, insurance and the deterioration of goods in transit—not during loading and unloading, since these are fixed costs.

(b) *Time costs.* These are disadvantages that arise not so much from the overcoming of distance as from the time that this requires. In this category belongs the time lost by the housewife in making her purchases, no less than the time that elapses between the ordering of goods and their delivery. The monetary cost of time appears in various guises: as interest on the sum invested in goods in transit; as an additional charge for quick delivery; as the cost of larger inventories to the retailer, for whom a distant factory is not a reserve warehouse in the same measure as one that is near by; or as loss of business if goods cannot be delivered in good time.[2]

(c) *Selling costs.* The cost of sales promotion increases with distance. The time of a commercial traveler cannot be so profitably employed, for example, when buyers are thinly distributed, and similarly a newspaper advertisement draws a smaller response. Furthermore, one must understand one's market, and keep well informed on current trends. This often happens automatically when a market is near, but involves costs in the case of more distant ones. Branches and representatives cause additional expenditures, and the outlay for postage, telephone, and travel is also greater.

(d) *Business risks.* Risks generally increase with distance. Far too little attention is paid to this fact, but it will receive concrete proof in the statistical section. Long distances make it difficult to get reliable information on the credit and needs of buyers, as well as on the legal methods to be taken in respect to payment should these become necessary.[3] This fact in its turn is used to their advantage by a less desirable class of buyers.

(e) *Idiosyncrasies.* Most products are adapted to the characteristics of their own limited markets—to climate, habits, income, and so on. Thus the demands of a more distant neighborhood are not so easily met.

---

2. Quick delivery plays a role especially in the case of fashionable articles. It may even determine location, as E. M. Hoover has shown in his admirable study of the shoe industry, *Location Theory and the Shoe and Leather Industries* (Cambridge, Mass., 1937), p, 176.

3. According to German law, payment has to be made at the domicile of the buyer unless another place has been stipulated in the contract.

(f) *Extent of business.* Even though the spatial expansion of a business entails no particular costs, nevertheless such costs arise after a certain point, when the physical plant of the business has to be enlarged as a consequence. This factor does not become operative immediately with plants that work to the left of the point of minimum average costs, but with continued expansion it makes itself felt eventually.

(g) *Hindrances to trade.* Sooner or later the sale of most goods encounters governmental barriers. In the Middle Ages especially there were countless road taxes, excise taxes, and customs duties to be surmounted, and since the 1870's the weight of such restrictions has been increasing again.

(h) *Disinclination and incompetence.* The difficulties of the entrepreneur increase with the growth of his sales, and particularly with the distance of his customers. How many, for example, give up foreign trade because of the formalities associated with it! Moreover, a lack of ideas and imagination in most entrepreneurs precludes more distant connections.

Thus, over and above its immediate costs, distance plays a role in everything that is individual and that presupposes thorough knowledge and confidence—a role that men often neglect to their cost. Even when more distant buyers are no longer served directly, but through distributors or branches, these can only mitigate the effect of distance, not remove it. This effect is evident, indeed, far beyond the sphere of economics. It is more difficult to hold large or misshapen empires together, and as a rule it can be done only at the expense of native individuality. Even the proportion of Catholics in Europe decreases, by and large, with their distance from Rome.[4,5]

There is a strong inclination to disregard the laws of distance, and for a long time this tendency was esteemed as progress. Trade was no longer regarded as determined by such immediately experienced realities as local and regional relationships, but by abstract ideas, universal principles, guiding maxims, or general laws, that

---

4. Not their proportion in a single place, but their proportion among the people of each individual but not too narrow ring. Similarly, Mecca and Medina lie at the geographical center of the Mohammedan world.

5. In the field of sociology compare: the sphere of marriage, migrating supply areas (examples in *Bevölkerungsbiologie der Grosstadt*, edited by E. von Eikstedt [Stuttgart, 1941], p. 242), and the distribution of students. The percentage of persons subject to punishment often decreases with distance from the center of a city, and so on. (See R. D. McKenzie, *The Metropolitan Community* [1933], p. 185.

met the needs of any one place only very roughly. They did away with a great deal of narrow-minded whimsey, but at the same time with much that had grown to be of solid value. It will be shown in the statistical section that this contempt for distance caused great losses, economic and otherwise, for the saying of Saint Thomas Aquinas on *inclinatio rerum in proprios fines* [6] still holds true.

---

6. The tendency of things to stay within their own limits.

Chapter 15. Economic Regions in Reality [1]

a. SPATIAL ARRANGEMENT

The two preceding chapters considered separately the various causes or the various effects of the same phenomenon. It is now necessary to combine the results of both methods of study and draw a complete picture.

§1. MARKET AREAS

When we drop the assumption of a uniform plain, the simple market and supply areas assume irregular shapes and sizes because of the natural, personal, and political differences already mentioned. Furthermore, market areas for the same product overlap, since it is seldom finished in exactly the same way, and each area is fringed out in consequence. Nevertheless, our original simplifying assumptions often seem to be more or less fulfilled, and in such cases our theoretical findings will hold without much change. A few examples will be offered in the statistical section.

§2. REGIONAL NETWORKS

Since market areas for the same product overlap, as has just been said, strictly speaking they can no longer be compared with a network. They are more like an irregular layer of pieces of slate, carelessly flung down. The essential properties of a network are usually retained, however, and hardly a single chart of market areas represents them otherwise. But there is another modification of the network that is of great importance. We assume that networks would cover the whole plain, though in reality their extent is more or less restricted and we speak then of districts and belts, according to whether only production sites or their market areas as well are circumscribed as to space. Such a concentration may be based on external economies or depend upon the limited scope of natural or political factors. This is especially clear when these factors them-

---

[1]. Based in part on my lecture, "The Nature of Economic Regions," *Southern Economic Journal*, V (1938), 71.

selves create certain market networks. Yet it is not necessarily true that these extra-economic factors and their economic result coincide. Cotton is not grown wherever it will thrive, nor is it always spun where it is cultivated.[2]

§3. REGIONAL SYSTEMS

Economic landscapes, the highest and most complicated form of economic area, differ most of all from the simplified theoretical picture. It is simply impossible to arrange all the irregular and often spatially bound networks in such a way that they will have at least one common center. Actually there is no longer an economically self-sufficient economic landscape, nor is there a metropolis in which all industries are fully represented. And this is not all. In fact, one might imagine, and perhaps even discover, a few cases where economic landscapes exchanged their specialties exclusively by way of their capitals.[3] Under these circumstances every economic landscape would still be as compactly organized as in our ideal system. However, it would be better then to speak of economic districts, or economic provinces, because these words express more clearly the fact that we are no longer dealing with independent, economically self-sufficient units. In reality, not only do entire districts depend on other capitals for certain specialties;[4] for many goods, small places that otherwise depend completely upon neighboring larger towns are centers of extensive market areas that reach far beyond the home district, and may even include the whole world. Again, whereas every regional system has a large town for its center, every large town is not the center of such a system. Many large mining towns, for example, can hardly be said to fulfill an economic function for their environs.[5] From such specialized large towns the

---

2. Spinning mills in the United States are concentrated in the eastern part of the cotton belt.

3. One of the two most important functions of the central town is then to establish connections with the remaining economic landscapes. The other is trade with its own economic landscape.

4. O. Schiller ("Die Landschaften Deutschlands," *Allgemeines Statistisches Archiv*, XX [1930], 24–41) even goes so far as to maintain that in Germany only the following cities are more or less autocrats in their economic landscapes: Berlin, Stettin, Königsberg, Breslau, Munich, Vienna, and Stuttgart.

5. Hence they often show extraordinary fluctuations in population. The gold-mining town of Cripple Creek, in Colorado, for instance, had 45,000 inhabitants in its heyday, and only 4,000 in 1930. But after the depreciation of the dollar the old mines became profitable once more, and the population rose quickly to 7,000. (C. Goodrich *et al.*, *Migration and Economic Opportunity* [Philadelphia, 1936], p. 271.)

major cities of districts are distinguished by the diversification of their production, or at least of their trade, which provides abundant connection with their environs.

Amid all the chaos of reality a basic pattern of economic districts is nevertheless unmistakable. These differ from the ideal economic landscape in one important point: they are not self-sufficient. They coincide with it in so far as they are established on the same principles—the advantages of a large local demand and traffic density.

These principles suffice to call economic landscapes into being, as we have already seen in the theoretical derivation. But, second, the hierarchy of markets may depend also upon the hierarchy of administrative areas. Third, it may originate in natural or national factors of an areal nature as does a region of agricultural monoculture (cultivation of a homogeneous product) or a racial manner of life (homogeneous consumption).[6] Thus cotton growing determined for a long time the spatial organization of the economy in the American southern states. The supply regions of 15,000 cotton gins, which cleaned the cotton and removed the seeds, were superimposed upon the producing areas of the individual plantations; above these came the wider-meshed network of presses;[7] above these, again, the 500 oil mills; then the transport points; the collecting depots, where the cotton is sorted and stored; and, at the top, the two principal export ports with their enormous supply regions.[8] The arrangement of the networks of the distributing trades was largely patterned after those of the all-controlling cotton production. (*Ibid.*, p. 190.)

---

6. In the last case the networks of market areas for a whole series of goods are of similar extent; not accidentally, but because these goods represent a meaningful combination. This is enough to delimit an entire group of economic landscapes, if not from one another then at least from without.

7. As a heavy press costs about $50,000, it would not pay the individual cotton gin, with an average yearly output of only 1,000 bales, to buy one. A profitable press will take care of the output of some 30 gins and has a supply region of perhaps 50 miles' radius, as compared with less than 10 miles for gins. These provide an interesting example of the stickiness of a once firmly established location pattern. Formerly the supply region for cotton gins had a radius of roughly 5 miles, but with their improvement and with better roads the most advantageous size of the supply area increased. But this more advantageous size of the supply area is realized only in the new cotton area west of the Mississippi River, where individual gins work up on the average one third more cotton than those in the old cotton area. (E. S. Moulton, " Cotton Production and Distribution in the Gulf Southwest," *U. S. Department of Commerce, Domestic Commerce Series No. 49* [Washington, D. C., 1931], p. 46).

8. Only the cotton of the Southeast is spun near by, as a rule, which gives rise to many small supply regions.

Regional substrata like this are to be found almost everywhere, but they are not always of equal importance. Their importance is inversely proportional to that of market areas that do not fit into the economic landscape pattern. In south Germany, for example, these substrata are of the highest importance, as Christaller has so convincingly shown.[9,10] In the Ruhr, on the contrary, it is difficult to find any at all.[11] According to the regularity of spatial organization, a regional substratum will be regarded as the essence in one case, whereas in another it may be thought irrelevant and left entirely out of consideration. However suitable a regional point of view may be for many areas, it would be difficult and profitless to attempt the complete subdivision of a large country into economic landscapes.[12]

Finally, economic and political or cultural landscapes share essential features in their structures. All have a central point, for example. In fortunate cases their central points coincide, and then there arises one of the world's great centers of power.

§4. Summary

We have found three main types of economic regions: simple market areas, regional networks, and regional systems. Or to impress the matter more clearly we may speak of markets, belts, and districts.

---

9. W. Christaller, *Die zentralen Orte in Süddeutschland* (Jena, 1933), pp. 165–251.

10. The economic capitals Frankfort, Nuremberg, Munich, Zürich, Strasbourg, and, at the center, Stuttgart, are very evenly distributed.

11. Unless, like Schlier (*op. cit.*, p. 37), one combines the regions of influence of the rival Rhenish-Westphalian centers, thus obtaining a larger economic lanscape that is split through the center. On the other hand, see Isenberg, " Zur Stadtplanung in den neuen deutschen Ostgebieten," *Raumforschung und Raumordnung*, 1941, pp. 141 f.

How clearly the supply regions for individual partial centers can be separated is seen in the simple example of the twin cities St. Paul and Minneapolis. Even when their economic functions in general are at all similar, the regions they control are clearly distinguished. The hinterland of Minneapolis stretches toward the west, whereas the more easterly St. Paul commands the east. (See M. L. Hartsough, *The Twin Cities as a Metropolitan Market* [Minneapolis, 1925], p. 13. The case of Leeds and Bradford is similar. (Stamp and Beaver, *The British Isles* [London, 1937], p. 573.)

12. Yet, according to K. Haushofer (" Grosstadtprobleme der Monsunländer," *Archiv für Bevölk.*, 1942, p. 268), Japan is made up entirely of cells having about the same shape, and the size of a district; small river drainage basins with urban centers " that fit together like the cells of a honeycomb." And Isenberg (*op. cit.*, p. 266) found an astonishingly regular substratum for the most dissimilar parts of Germany. Even a good many disturbances may not greatly change the regularity of the structure. (J. Umlauf, " Der Stand der Raumordnungsplanung für die eingegliederten Ostgebiete," *Neues Bauerntum*, 1942, p. 287, map of the *Regierungsbezirk* Posen.)

The members of this series become, in that order, increasingly complicated, increasingly self-sufficient, but, unfortunately, increasingly uncommon too.

On the one hand we have simple supply or market areas—very simple indeed, manifestly real, and wholly dependent upon trade. The systems of market areas or districts are the antithesis. Their structure is anything but simple. In the ideal case of a " landscape " they are wholly self-sufficient, but seldom can they be found so distinct. Many goods remain outside every such system. And whatever systems we find overlap still more than simple markets. A clearly defined economic landscape is a piece of good fortune rather than a natural subdivision of a state. Nevertheless a substratum resembling an economic landscape is to be found almost everywhere below a maze of market areas, though developed to different degrees.

Between the simple market area and the complete economic landscape comes the network—that is, the totality of all market areas for the same product. The network itself, or at least its heart, is often compressed into a narrow space. Such belts, or zones, of homogeneous production or consumption arrest our attention, but they should not be confused with economic landscapes. The economic landscape is a system of *different* markets; an organism, not merely an organ.

b. ON A CHAOTIC INTERPRETATION

No doubt the spatial economic pattern about us contains enough illogical, irregular, lawless features. But I refuse to put the whole emphasis on this lack of order. No matter how widely a chaotic interpretation may be confirmed by the facts, it is not only unworthy but dangerous. Unworthy because there is also a reality of reason, upon which incomparably more depends in the long run than upon the reality of the factual. Dangerous because our idea of reality is one of the factors that shape the future. Had only obstacles to the operation of logical and natural forces been emphasized and fostered at the dawn of capitalism, this would never have been able to complete its great achievements. It needed no planning; indeed, could despise planning as a " disturbance," since it believed in the great principles of its time and lived in accordance with them. It rose with belief and declined with unbelief in its own order. In the face of a belief in an orderly progress or, more accurately stated, in its possible functioning, chaotic facts automatically lose their significance. This belief is based on nature and reason when it can no longer depend on the facts. From them it creates the model for an order that may originate only as a result of it.

The roots of anarchy? There is a chaos that arises from doubt and despair, a parasite upon order when it reminds us of the temporal nature of all human ordering, even though occasionally it may fructify order. But there is another sort of chaos, which is really nothing but order in disguise. Thus the bewildering individuality of various places and events in space may arise merely because each consists of a special combination of different orders—geographical, geological, political, racial, religious, and so on—which interfere with one another and cause tensions but do not destroy each other's roots. The economic sphere is simply added to the many other spheres of life that overlap, neither dominating nor merely tolerated.

PART THREE. TRADE

A. Description of Equilibrium

Chapter 16. Six Cardinal Problems of the Division of Labor and Their Interrelations [1]

OUR THEME is the combination of man, work, and place. Seen from the standpoint of man it is the problem of the occupational and spatial division of labor. Often enough, however, we do not start with ourselves, but wish to know what combination will be best for an enterprise or a country. For this reason, only the following six questions together will cover the subject completely (see Fig. 54).

These are already more or less familiar to us in another form:

1. The problem of choice of an occupation.
2. The problem of the cooperation of men in an enterprise.
3. The problem of selecting a place to live (the emigration problem) and of the distribution of populations.
4. The problems of urban sociology.
5. The " chamber of commerce " problem (the developmental possibilities of a town).
6. The traditional location problem.

We thus place in a broader context the sixth problem, the main one considered hitherto.

---

1. Here we discuss only the nature, not the cause, of the division of labor. In the final analysis the cause would be our old familiar trio: site, supply, and volume; that is, natural differences in and advantages of mass production or, as Ohlin and Iversen express it, a lack of mobility and divisibility. A historical treatment would have to take developmental stages into account as well. E. W. Zimmermann (*Foreign Trade and Shipping* [New York, 1918], pp. 40 f.) has hit upon the distinction, very pretty in itself, that because of developmental differences world trade today still definitely follows latitude, whereas in the future, when only climatic differences remain, it will have to follow longitude—a concept upon which is based the idea of establishing world economic areas. It forgets, however, that site and volume also lead to trade. Furthermore, the concept of supply must be broad enough to include human capabilities also.

The preliminary answer to all six questions may seem very general at first, or even naïve. It amounts in each case to a maximization (of production, of utility, of financial return, and so on) that is felt to be self-evident. We endeavor to make the most of every situation. But it will soon be realized that all more exact

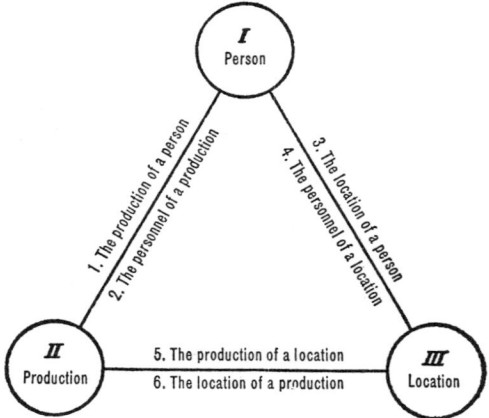

Fig. 54. Schematic representation of the six basic questions of the division of labor

and detailed solutions, which interest us much more, can be derived from this general solution only by abandoning full understanding of the situation. The mathematical determination of the optimum transport point, for example, is infinitely more impressive as a solution of the location problem but also incomparably less accurate than the statement that an entrepreneur, all things considered, will establish his enterprise at a place that he likes best. We shall do well to recall from time to time the limited validity of our precise formulas, in order not to overlook the fact that they merely help us in arriving at a decision; in themselves they do not provide one.

Even the most carefully considered conclusion is only an experiment after all. It is like shooting when we are neither certain of the target nor able to test how close we have come to it. In the last analysis, of course, we say that we have been aiming at the highest utility, and many believe themselves able to measure it. But to balk at words would be petty. Utility may signify the general good as well as personal happiness, and efforts may be directed toward it either from a sense of duty or by inclination.[2] And yet— we have agreed upon a vague word that any critic will be able to pick to pieces! The real difficulty in all measurements of utility

---

2. But in every case only such efforts as accord with the economic principle in the sense developed on p. 184, note 118.

lies in the fact that we have no idea of what "utility" actually is. Often we surmise its meaning, to be sure, but frequently enough we decide upon one of two mutually exclusive courses, not because it seems preferable, or because it makes no difference to us, but because something or other must finally be done. Every choice naturally gives the impression that the greater utility has been selected. But why, then, is there so often pain at having to forego one possibility after another preferable one has been chosen? We should not feel this distress if the case were merely one of deciding between two and four units of utility, as between two coins. Here we meet an obstacle so fundamental that we cannot circumvent it by the little trick of "indifference curves." In reality these curves do not avoid the concept of utility, but merely conceal it. The shape of utility curves can be reconstructed from them. Indeed, they presuppose a better knowledge of utility than do the ordinary decisions of mankind. For one may prefer one object to another that costs the same without being able to say how much more utile it seems, but the value of a combination of foods cannot be equated with that of another combination without a very exact idea of their utility. Choice becomes especially difficult in the neighborhood of the equilibrium of marginal utilities.

We must not deceive ourselves (and we do well to remember this when we are in danger of being too sure of our results) by the thought that with the introduction of the concept of utility we have firmly founded our science in the unknowable; and yet no other course remains if we wish to pursue it. Though we know that in the end we always must act with our fingers crossed, through a curious yet wholly reasonable quirk in our nature we seek for the meaning of the single act, and for the higher order into which all events fit.[3] We act as though we understood the purpose of life, and hence could classify routes according to the speed with which they lead to its goal. We interpret economic activities as if they aimed at the highest utility, reading into them a rational design that may be lacking in reality.

But why should not such a basic construct as the physical concepts of force and mass have at least the merit of providing a foundation for an intellectual edifice of preliminary truths, which, like *all* that we think and believe, is not eternal, but with which we can live for a time? What distinguishes science from idle talk is not the *nature*, but the *breadth*, of its foundation, and the *consistency* of its structure.

---

3. We cultivate science for no other reason than that we cannot live without interpreting the world as best we can.

Chapter 17. The Six Cardinal Problems of the Division of Labor Discussed Individually

a. THE OCCUPATION OF A PERSON

What does any given person produce? Official occupational guidance should assign to each one the activity in which he could best serve the interests of the state. But as long as the state allows free choice in the matter *everyone selects the occupational that he likes best among those available to him.* In so far as his liking depends upon earnings, there are two ways of deciding on an occupation. One is the marginal view, as it corresponds to the Walrasian method of describing equilibrium.

§1. THE MARGINAL VIEW

The marginal approach would be valid if "labor" could be subdivided into homogeneous subgroups. The members of each subgroup would be equally good at every occupation. This does not mean, however, that their physical productivities need be comparable. When such homogeneous groups exist, the following equilibrium conditions hold true: (1) The members of a particular homogeneous subgroup are distributed among the various industries in such a way that their wages are everywhere the same. This automatically also gives the answer to the question just put. (2) The members of the different groups will be employed in such numbers in any particular industry that their marginal products are proportional to their wages. This also answers the next question.

The assumption that persons can be divided into groups within which they may be regarded as interchangeable units simplifies the problem greatly. But in reality it is improbable that even two persons would be equally productive in one and the same activity, or that their productivity would differ in the same proportion. This means the impossibility of a marginal approach that would answer our question summarily for whole groups of persons. But the marginal principle could be applied to individual persons provided they were units large enough to influence wages in the various activities. For then a person would divide his working hours among

Table 9. INTERNATIONAL TRADE

1	2						3a						4b						5c	6d					
Commodity	Objective Productivity (World record = 1)						Hourly Production (Unit)						National Prices with Economic Self-sufficiency						Exchange Rate	Potential Prices with Free Trade (Shillings)					
	A	B	C	D	E	F	A	B	C	D	E	F	A	B	C	D	E	F		A	B	C	D	E	F
Country I	1.0	0.8	0.7	0.2	0.6	0.1	10	8	7	2	6	1	1.00	1.25	1.40	5.00	1.66	10.00	1 reichsmark = 0.5 shilling	0.50	0.60	0.70	2.50	0.80	5.00
Country II	0.8	1.0	0.4	1.0	0.1	1.0	8	10	4	10	1	10	1.25	1.00	2.50	1.00	10.00	1.00	1 shilling = 1.0 shilling	1.25	1.00	2.50	1.00	10.00	1.00
Country III	0.9	0.3	1.0	0.2	0.3	0.1	9	3	10	2	3	1	1.10	3.33	1.00	5.00	3.33	10.00	1 dollar = 0.4 shilling	0.40	1.30	0.40	2.00	1.30	4.00
Country IV	0.9	0.2	0.3	0.2	0.9	0.95	9	2	3	2	9	9.5	1.10	5.00	3.33	5.00	1.10	1.05	1 franc = 0.9 shilling	1.00	4.50	3.00	4.50	1.00	0.95

a. Calculable when the hourly production of the record producer is given.

b. Internal prices are expressed in the national monetary unit (Table 9) or, for individuals, in hours (Table 10). In the former case the national hourly wage must be given, which requires merely an assumption as to the amount of money in circulation, before absolute prices can be calculated. The exchange ratio, that is, the price system, is determined as in the latter case, by the amount of time employed in production. To simplify the comparison, monetary circulations are so chosen that equal physical productivity is rewarded with an equal number of monetary units in every currency.

c. The exchange rates and wages at which equilibrium should prevail. Since demand curves are not given, their values can be chosen arbitrarily, subject to the following limitations: (1) That each country or each person can produce something for the market; otherwise no equilibrium can exist, because either the exchange rate or the hourly wage of the persons concerned has to fall sufficiently to bring them into the trading system. (2) That individual countries are either so small that none of them can satisfy the world demand for certain goods individually (when the situation is exactly as it is with individual men) or so large that they are able to produce more than one commodity for the world market. Table 9 is restricted to the latter assumption. For individual persons, however (Table 10), it is assumed throughout that no individual can satisfy the whole market for a certain product, or that one can produce several goods at the same time. (Because of the narrow compass of the table, occupation B, in which only worker βII is engaged, seems to be an exception). He limits himself, on the contrary, to the most lucrative occupation, and the hourly wage of all in the same occupation must naturally be in proportion to their product. Thus, unlike the exchange rate, it cannot be fixed at will within the limits of conditions 1, but must be such that efficiency wages are equal.

d. Calculated by multiplication of columns 4 and 5. The prices of goods that are actually produced are emphasized by boldface type.

Table 10. INTERPERSONAL TRADE

1[a] Commodity		2[b] Objective Productivity (World record = 1)				3[c] Hourly Production (Units)				4[d] Production for Self-consumption (Hours per unit)				5[e] Hourly Wage (Cents)	6[f] Potential Prices with Division of Labor (Cents)			
		A	B	C	D	A	B	C	D	A	B	C	D		A	B	C	D
α	I	1.0	0.8	0.5	0.6	2.0	0.8	50	6	0.50	1.25	0.020	0.16	70	35	87	1.4	12
	II	0.8	0.5	0.4	0.6	1.6	0.5	40	6	0.60	2.00	0.025	0.16	60	37	120	1.5	10
	III	0.7	0.3	0.4	0.2	1.4	0.3	40	2	0.70	3.30	0.025	0.50	49	35	163	1.2	24
β	I	0.2	1.0	0.75	0.4	0.4	1.0	75	4	2.50	1.00	0.013	0.25	83	206	83	1.1	21
	II	0.5	0.6	0.2	0.4	1.0	0.6	20	4	1.00	0.16	0.050	0.25	47	47	78	2.3	12
	III	0.3	0.4	0.3	0.3	0.6	0.4	30	3	0.16	0.25	0.033	0.33	33	55	82	1.1	11
γ	I	0.8	0.5	1.0	0.5	1.6	0.5	100	5	0.62	2.00	0.010	0.20	110	68	220	1.1	22
	II	0.4	0.2	0.8	0.2	0.8	0.2	80	2	1.25	5.00	0.012	0.50	88	110	440	1.1	44
	III	0.5	0.5	0.6	0.5	1.0	0.5	60	5	1.00	2.00	0.016	0.20	66	66	132	1.1	13
δ	I	0.7	0.8	0.8	1.0	1.4	0.8	80	10	0.70	1.25	0.012	0.10	100	71	125	1.2	10
	II	0.3	0.5	0.7	0.9	0.6	0.5	70	9	0.16	2.00	0.014	0.11	90	150	180	1.3	10
	III	0.9	0.5	0.3	0.9	1.8	0.5	30	9	0.56	2.00	0.033	0.11	90	50	180	3.0	10

a. Group α includes all those persons who subjectively produce most in occupation A. The same hold for β and B, and so on. Within groups the persons are arranged according to their objective production in the occupation concerned (I–III).

b. The physical output of αI in occupation B, for example, is 80 per cent of the world record, held by βI. The output of αII in occupation A is 80 per cent of the record, held by αI.

c. Compare *a* in Table 9.
d. Compare *b* in Table 9.
e. Compare *c* in Table 9.
f. Compare *d* in Table 9.

these different employments according to the principle by which the group, so to speak, directs its members into the individual branches. But since the individual does not usually exert this influence on wages, he devotes his *entire* time to the trade that yields him the largest return, though not in money alone. Thus, with few exceptions, the marginal approach fails with individuals as it does with groups.

Table 11. COMPARATIVE EFFICIENCIES (COMPARATIVE ADVANTAGES) OF THE COUNTRIES[a]

	Country I						Country II					
	A	B	C	D	E	F	A	B	C.	D	E	F
I	100	100	100	100	100	100	125	80	175	20	60	10
II	80	125	57	500	167	1000	100	100	100	100	100	100
III	90	37	131	100	50	100	112	30	250	20	30	10
IV	90	25	43	100	166	950	112	20	75	20	99	95
	Country III						Country IV					
	A	B	C	D	E	F	A	B	C	D	E	F
I	111	265	70	100	200	100	111	400	232	100	61	10
II	89	333	40	500	333	1000	89	500	133	500	101	105
III	100	100	100	100	100	100	100	150	233	100	30	10
IV	100	66	30	100	333	950	100	100	100	100	100	100

[a] Calculated from column 2 of Table 9.

§2. The Principle of Comparative Cost

In my judgment the choice of an occupation follows the principle that the earlier theory of international trade developed for determining the international division of labor: the principle of comparative cost. As a matter of fact, for reasons that will be given in discussing the fifth problem, this principle is applicable in general only to persons, not to countries. As it is more familiar to us in its unwarranted application, however, a comparison of the phenomena that correspond to each other in the two cases may be of interest.[1] But first the application of this principle to more complicated cases must be examined in greater detail than it has been in the literature heretofore.[2] Although it is incorrect to do so, we base the discussion

---

1. Of course its application to the division of labor among individual persons is not new. See J. D. Black (*Introduction to Production Economics* [New York, 1926], pp. 129 ff.) and G. von Haberler (*Der internationale Handel* [Berlin, 1933], p. 100; English edition [1936], pp. 130–131). But so far it has not been carried through accurately or exhaustively enough.

2. The following is based upon my article on comparative cost, "Wo gilt das Theorem der komparativen Kosten?" *Weltwirtschaftliches Archiv*, July, 1938. (The

on trade between countries because the theory will be familiar to most readers only in this connection.

α. *Development of the Principle*

Consider first only two countries. So long as the number of products also is limited to two, what each country specializes in can be unequivocally determined in the usual way from differences in comparative cost. If there are several products we can only give for each country the order in which they must enter international trade. Only with the help of the additional principle of fair settlement of the balance of payment (p. 298) is it possible to decide which goods in the series are imported and which are exported. If the products are arranged in order of their comparative advantage beginning with the good in which country I has the greatest comparative advantage over country II, country I will export all goods above the dividing line and import the remainder.[3] With several products and more than two producers, the sequence of comparative advantages must be determined separately for each pair of countries. When II is its partner, the order of comparative advantage of country I differs from what it is when III is its partner. If there is trade in both directions between two countries, I and II, for example, which now is no longer necessary, the interchange need not extend to all products even when freight costs are disregarded. On the contrary there are then two dividing lines as a rule; one below the exported product for which country I has the smallest comparative advantage over II (line 1), and one above the corresponding product exported from II (line 2). Line 1 must of necessity lie above line 2. Again the lines are determined by the condition that the balance of payment must be in equilibrium. But if the lines for only one pair of countries are available, it is certain only that I imports everything under line 1 but not that it exports everything above it. Similarly, II imports everything above line 2 but does not export everything below it. Hence it remains un-

---

erroneous changes introduced by the editor are here corrected.) An elementary knowledge is assumed.

3. The dividing line can be determined only if absolute prices, i. e., the price level, as well as relative prices implied in comparative cost are given. The change in the price level has the function of restoring equilibrium in the balances of payments. With a gold standard the price levels are moved back and forth until the direction and magnitude of the absolute price differences suffice to bring the international accounts into equilibrium without defaults or involuntary credits. Only this mechanism transforms the possible (comparative) into real (absolute) cost differences in sufficient numbers and in order of their magnitude.

The Six Problems Discussed Individually

decided what goods enter into trade between the two countries. Only for commodities lying between the two lines is it true without limitation that both countries will import them from other countries. As for exports, even this incomplete knowledge is impossible. It is not known what products will be exported, or in what order their chances of exportation are greatest.

Tables 11 and 12, calculated from Table 9, will serve as an illustration. There happens to be only one dividing line for trade between I and every other country, but in all other cases there are two. Consider the trade between countries II and III (column 4,

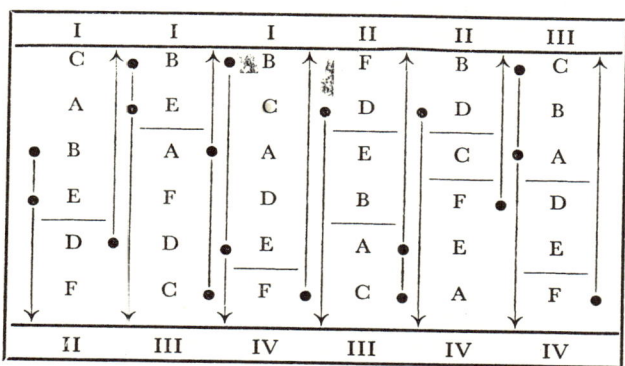

Table 12. ORDER OF COMPARATIVE ADVANTAGES^a

a. Products are arranged in descending order of advantages, taken from Table 11, for the upper row of countries as compared with those in the lower row. The dots and arrows indicate products and the direction of exchange between two countries.

Table 12), for example. Line 1 lies between products D and E, line 2 between B and A. Of the products above line 1, country II exports food D to country III but not food F, although in II its comparative advantage as compared with country III would be still greater. But in comparison with country IV it is smaller, with the result that not only the two products B and E, lying between the dividing lines, but also F, above the upper line, will be imported by both countries from a third.

We summarize what may be concluded from a simple knowledge of comparative cost in the three cases (two countries—two products; two countries—many products; and many countries—many products): In the first, the textbook example of theory, there is a unique line separating imported and exported goods. In the second, the necessary sequence in which goods enter international trade can be determined, from which follows the hypothetical proposition that if the dividing line were given it would sharply separate imported and exported products. The third case provides the half-knowledge that if there are any dividing lines at all, goods on the farther side of the line would all be on the list of imports but would not exhaust it. From this follows the little that is definitely known about the trade relationships between any two countries: That they do not exchange the goods between the dividing lines but import them from this and other countries. Whereas everything is known in the second case, once the dividing line is given, in the third case even the lines separating two countries provide only partial information as to what takes place between them. For a full knowledge of the trade between even two countries we need, in addition, the dividing lines between the two in question and all others. Thus in the case of several goods, and even more so in the case of several countries. it is very hard to determine what a country will export; this cannot be decided from comparative cost alone, without the additional principle of the fair settlement of balances of payment; and with more than two countries we require a knowledge of the trade of the other countries as well.[4]

β. Application of the Principle of Comparative Cost to the Choice of an Occupation

Now compare trade between countries and trade between persons, in order to see what concepts of interpersonal trade correspond to those with which we are already familiar from international trade (Tables 9 and 10). For this purpose we must proceed as though the principle actually could be applied to foreign trade. A scale of relative productivity can be set up for a person exactly as for a country (column 2).[5] From these proportionality coefficients and

---

4. The matter may be expressed in this way also: The principle of comparative cost is valid between two countries, but it is impossible to determine by a comparison of costs between these two alone what they will exchange with one another, in which direction, and with what probability. Other countries and the rate of exchange so interfere with the system as to make it possible to say in advance only that the order in which goods are exchanged between two countries, which is fixed by the size of comparative advantages, can be interrupted but not jumbled.

5. The following derivation assumes that efficiency remains constant. I have endeavored to show elsewhere that the principle of comparative cost holds at the margin also when, as with factory workers, efficiency varies with employment in the firm. (" Wo gilt das Theorem der komparativen Kosten? " *Weltwirtschaftliches Archiv*, July, 1938, pp. 50-52).

the absolute output of one of the producers in a unit of time (column 3) the national price system before entrance into international trade can be calculated (Column 4 of Table 9 contains in addition the absolute level of prices in domestic currencies, and thus involves a further assumption about the quantity of money). In exactly the same way, the goods that the individual produces exchange in proportion to the working time spent on them (Table 10, column 4).

In both cases, finally, we need a rate of exchange to convert the domestic unit of account (reichmarks, hours) into a foreign unit in which all domestic prices are then comparable. For countries this international unit might be, for example, the pound sterling or gold; for individuals it is the standard currency (say reichsmarks). This exchange ratio fixes the relative height of the domestic price level. It is familiar to us in international trade as the rate of exchange, and the hourly wage in interpersonal trade corresponds with it almost to a hair.[6] Just as a national unit of value like the reichsmark can be converted into an international unit like the pound sterling by means of the exchange rate (Table 9, column 3), so the personal unit of value, the hour, can be converted into the general unit, the reichsmark, by means of the hourly wage (Table 10, column 5). The level of the exchange rate depends upon reciprocal demand, and should bring this into equilibrium. As with countries, so with individuals; the sum of their debits must equal the sum of their credits; that is, their balance of payments must be in equilibrium. And in the absence of a knowledge of demand relationships the rates of exchange in both cases can be assumed arbitrarily only within certain limits.[7] They must always be such that no product is excluded from interchange; otherwise equilibrium would not prevail. The producer with a rate of exchange that was too high would lower his rate, or his wage demands, as the case might be, until even he could produce at least one article more cheaply than the others.

And now we come to the sole difference, a difference in degree. In the international division of labor an article can be produced in several countries if none of them alone can wholly satisfy world demand. Conversely, countries may be so large that they are able to export more than one product. The latter is not generally true

---

6. The sole difference is that the exchange rate does not give the international wage for a working hour directly, but only after the introduction of an intermediate link (the hourly wage in national currency).

7. See G. von Haberler; *Der internationale Handel* (Berlin, 1933), p. 102; English edition (1936), p. 133.

of persons. The demand for most goods is so great that no one individual alone can fully meet it, much less engage in several occupations at the same time.[8] Thus in setting the *hourly* wage in Table 10 we must be sure not only that each worker can engage in one trade, but also that the efficiency wage corresponds for all equals in a trade. Thus whereas farm laborer III in Table 10 receives an hourly wage of but 66 cents and farm laborer I is paid $1.10, they are rewarded exactly according to their productivity. The wage for one unit and the price for one unit are the same everywhere, no matter what person or what country supplies the unit. If we had assumed for countries also that no individual country could by itself satisfy world demand, we should have had to take into account, in determining the exchange rate, the condition that prices of the same commodity must be equal in different countries. Efficiency wages and international prices correspond to each other.

To elucidate this perfect correspondence further we shall now discuss the effect of a few disturbing elements, the main subject of the theory of international trade, under simple assumptions in interpersonal trade. Suppose that a man is willing to work for a very low hourly wage, which correspond to dumping by a country. Several different jobs are offered him; everyone attempts to employ him, and the demand exceeds his capacity for work. He finds that he can ask a higher hourly wage and still be fully employed. As his demands increase he eliminates more and more possibilities, until his wage demands at last are so high that his efficiency in but one single trade corresponds to it. This one he chooses. In the same way international cut-throat competition, too, finally reaches its limits and its legitimate place. However, with a very large country it takes longer to reach the point where the demand for its goods exceeds productive capacity and drives its exchange rate upward, until the foreign demand for its still remaining special products can be satisfied by the domestic supply of hours of work required to produce them. Sooner or later this point must be reached. Hourly wage and exchange rate will finally become so high that the balance

---

8. There are exceptions; for example, among sparse populations. There the hourly wage is so adjusted that the sum of the activities possible at this wage just fill the working time of a man. Consider the versatility of the rural artisan, or the combination of innkeeping with agriculture; a sharp separation of occupations would be undesirable in rural districts. Secondly, the wish to be continuously employed forms one of the main reasons for the existence of the farmer-workman. Because of its fluctuations industry cannot employ labor constantly throughout the year, and agriculture is carried on, therefore, as a side line. Hence the difference between personal and international trade is one of degree only.

of payments is equalized in both cases; that is, the national or personal supply of working hours times their price (= export) is equal to the demand for foreign goods (= import).

Another example of the difference in degree mentioned above: In order to pay debts out of current income, a country must lower its prices, and this increases its export surplus, partly through increased exports and partly through decreased imports. An individual (a wage earner), on the other hand, does not generally have to lower his price in order to increase his " export," since he exports his entire production anyhow and exerts no influence on its price. He cannot raise his income by undercutting, but only by working more hours. Of course the normal way of achieving the necessary export surplus is for him to cut down his expenditures, which again requires no lowering of " domestic prices." A typical example of transfer by a simple shift in buying power without change of price! It is based upon the relative insignificance of the individual in the whole economy.

The table summarizes this one-to-one correspondence between international and interpersonal trade

INTERNATIONAL TRADE	INTERPERSONAL TRADE
Rates of exchange	Hourly wages
International prices	Efficiency wages
Barter terms (relation of export to import price)	Real wages (relation of wages to prices of goods)
National price system	Relation of time spent per unit
National price level	Wage level
Gold import	Hoarding (hiding money in a stocking)
Capital export	Saving (depositing money in a bank)
Export = import	Earnings = purchases

The question, upon what does a rational choice of an occupation depend, may therefore be answered to this effect in so far as it depends on earnings: upon the native aptitude of a person; upon the price he can get, and upon the length of the workday. These determine the highest hourly wage that will just ensure his full-time employment. Thus the choice of an occupation does not depend simply upon aptitude but upon how much it will bring in and how much employment it will provide. This formulation is especially valid for the case of a limited monopoly, which enables one to engage in several activities and to influence their prices. As long as full-time employment in *one* occupation is possible, the matter may also be put in this way: That occupation will be chosen which pays the highest hourly wage considering aptitude and efficiency wages. The parallel with international trade is complete.

What a country will eventually export or a person produce in his occupation depends, with given comparative advantages, upon the exchange rate that each achieves in equilibrium. Both will specialize in what, compared at this exchange rate, they can produce at least as cheaply as others. *Thus exchange rate and hourly wage have exactly the same function.*

But the choice of an occupation does not depend entirely on money income, as we have been assuming up to now, or even upon the utilities that this income will buy. On the contrary, to these more or less variable utilities there must be added all those imponderables that are associated with various occupations and usually appear as fixed utilities (or disutilities). For a man aims at the highest total utility, not at the highest purchasable utility, but the general principles for making his decisions are the same for the utility calculus as for the money calculus. When engaged in several trades at once, he will work at them and apportion his time among them until the utility per time unit is the same at the margin for all activities and equal to the marginal cost (measured in disutilities or in other utilities relinquished). The principle of comparative cost, too, is probably applicable to the utility calculus, even though with difficulty.

b. THE PERSONNEL OF AN INDUSTRY

§1. THE PERSONNEL OF AN OCCUPATION

What have the members of any given occupation in common? First, this: that despite all difficulties they are equal to the demands made upon them. This may presuppose a certain minimum of aptitudes that is more or less rare, depending on the kind and quality of work.[9] In any case this common characteristic (at least as far as native ability to perform the jobs is concerned) is not restricted to members of a particular occupation. The particular ability may be found outside the occupation to a greater or lesser degree. It can therefore be at most a necessary characteristic, which, moreover, hardly need be mentioned. It is never a sufficient characteristic. Is not the relevant question for the members of an occupation how quickly the job can be done, rather than whether it can be

---

9. It may even presuppose a definite type of man. The dextrous textile worker, for example, tends to be an extrovert, the steadier mine or foundry worker an introvert (W. Mitze, *Die strukturtypologische Gliederung einer westdeutschen Grosstadt* [Leipzig, 1941]). A distinction should be drawn, of course, between how much this is a cause of the choice of a trade and to what extent it is a result.

done at all? What is the exact meaning of the formula that says there are found in an occupation all those who are "relatively most productive" in it, or who are "comparatively superior"? In no case can it mean those who *objectively* produce most in it as compared with other persons. A bank president will not change places with a bootblack because he excels him in polishing shoes, as well as in banking. But neither can the formula mean those who come nearest to the world record in this special occupation; that is, those who are *subjectively* most skillful in it.[10] In Table 10, for example, α II chooses occupation D, where his output is 60 per cent of the world record, not occupation A, where it is 80 per cent, for the simple reason that, considering the pay in both, his hourly wage is greater in D. Or, more obviously, a banker may be a superb messenger but a second-rate bank president. Yet he earns more as a president when he multiplies his output by the efficiency wage.

But what else can the phrase "comparatively superior" mean? As in international trade, it can be applied only to two producers. If their relative productivity in various occupations is arranged in series, each will choose an occupation on that end of the series which is more favorable for him. Exactly what this is can be determined only if the equilibrium wage of *all* producers is known. Then it will appear that all who choose a given occupation have in common only that they earn most in it and that this occupation, when compared with any given persons in another occupation, is on that end of the comparative series which is more favorable for them. The formula for comparatice advantage, so clear in simple cases, is both obscure and incomplete in complicated ones. *In any case, it is not necessarily the most skillful in any ordinary sense who gather together in an occupation,*[11] but those whose productivity in it is at least so great that it earns them, and them alone, the highest hourly wage at the prevailing piece wage.[12] Or, stated

---

10. Except, perhaps, in the case of two men only, where "most skillful subjectively" is the same as "comparatively superior."

11. This leads to doubts whether Schumpeter is correct when he sees in special aptitudes for definite functions the origin of class differences. (J. A. Schumpeter, "Die sozialen Klassen im ethnisch homogenen Milieu," *Archiv für Sozialwissenschaft*, 1927, pp. 1–67, particularly p. 58.) Only when wages are paid by time rather than by output is it true that with rational selection no one performing a definite task is sufficiently qualified for a more highly paid one. See p. 240.

12. What follows from this for the choice of an occupation by women? That women are as efficient as men in many occupations was once an effective argument in the feminist movement. But it was sound only when wages were paid according to time, not to efficiency. Otherwise it is irrelevant in the choice of a suitable occupation whether the absolute output of women is equal to that of their male associates. The

still more generally, when one leaves the money for the utility calculus: As against outsiders, *the members of any given occupation have only one thing in common:* they find their highest satisfaction in it.[13]

A few examples will perhaps clarify this point. Among all workers in occupation D (Table 10), δI is most and αII least skillful. Hence their hourly wages are $1.00 and 60 cents respectively. If the wage for piecework should fall from 10 to 8.5 cents per unit both would leave the occupation because they could earn more elsewhere (δI in C, αII in A). Or again: A rise in the piece wage in occupation B from 78 to 84 cents will attract not only worker βI, who is unexcelled in this trade, but the moderately skillful βIII also. It is thus impossible to say in advance who will be the marginal worker when wages rise. It need not even be the one who is least efficient in this occupation; indeed, the most skillful worker may only now enter the occupation because he has nevertheless earned more until then in another; and it is even possible that the most efficient worker will leave an occupation because in the future he will earn more elsewhere. The marginal worker in an occupation is therefore one whose hourly wage in another most nearly approaches his earnings at the occupation in question. Or, in brief: *The marginal producer is not the worst, but the most unwilling producer.*

Although workers in every employment can be arranged in order of productivity, this does not exclude the fact that there are persons engaged in other employments who could be included in this one, not only at the end of the productivity series but anywhere along the scale, some of whom could be drawn in by higher wages.[14]

---

most lucrative occupation for a woman is at the same time necessarily one in which she is comparatively superior to all men who pursue another one, and perhaps even absolutely superior to some of them; the latter, however, is not necessary. On the contrary, an activity in which a woman surpasses all men may earn her less than another in which she is absolutely inferior to all men. Hence " typical women's occupations " can be described only as the ones in which those who earn the most are generally women. These women are comparatively superior in it to all men; that is to say, they do this work relatively better than they would do " men's work." But it would not be to the advantage of all women who might be comparatively superior to men in this occupation to enter it. The relation between aptitude and the choice of an occupation is by no means so simple.

13. That is, the highest satisfaction possible for them under existing conditions.

14. Thus the wage in a given employment does not depend upon the productivity of the least efficient though still necessary worker, but upon how many believe it most advantageous to specialize in such work at this particular wage within a given wage structure. From this must be distinguished the case in which the productivity of the marginal worker is reduced, not because of his personal inefficiency but for reasons

The entrepreneur is interested chiefly in the wage per unit [15] of output, the worker only in his hourly wage. Mistaken kindness toward labor has made the latter into *the* wage; that is, the price of the worker's output. Payment by time instead of by output has revolutionary results: With a piece wage there are no " better paid " occupations, because there is no basis for comparison. The wage for making a coat cannot be compared with that for making a pair of shoes. Uniform hourly wages for tailors and cobblers do not exist when they are paid according to output.

The picture changes when wages are paid according to fixed hourly wage schedules. Many who would have earned more at their former occupations under free competition are driven into more lucrative ones, where they are still worth the higher wage despite their lower productivity. And all who would have earned less under free competition are driven into less lucrative occupations as long as they are sufficiently productive there to earn the established wage. The others join the ranks of the unemployed. Only wage schedules make marginal workers economically significant; that is, marginal in the sense of the least productive workers, not in the sense given above of those that are readiest to leave or to enter an occupation. Only in the case of wage schedules is it correct to say that all those engaged in a more lucrative occupation are objectively more productive in it than all in less lucrative ones. The situation differs fundamentally from barter, where it need not be true that those who objectively or subjectively excel in a task will actually perform it also. When wages are determined in a free market that occupation will be chosen that will lead to the highest earnings when efficiency and piece rates are taken into account. With an hourly wage schedule that occupation is chosen in which output times the piece rate is at least equal to the established hourly wage and which offers the highest hourly wage of all. (This is true only when wages are determined in a free market.) Of course, it is not necessary that output times the piece rate should equal any of the existing time rates. This will then result in the army of unemployed that muddled philanthropists are never tired of creating.

---

connected with the organization of the firm; for example, because the firm has exceeded its optimum size or is being run by a marginal entrepreneur whose incompetence impairs the work of his employees. Though the marginal view has become impossible from the standpoint of the individual person, it remains valid from the standpoint of industry. It will continue to attract a mixed group of persons of all degrees of efficiency until the value of the marginal product equals the wage paid for it.

15. Except in so far as production results in costs that depend simply upon the lapse of time or upon the duration of the production process. Then he also is interested in work tempo and hence in the hourly wage of the individual worker.

§2. The Personnel of a Firm

Who works at the production of a given commodity? At bottom the answer is the same as that to the question discussed in the preceding section, except that here it is even more manifest that highest utility rather than, say, similar characteristics, leads persons into the same firm. This follows from the multiplicity of occupations represented in a firm; all that has been said previously holds true for members of the same occupation, but we must at least touch upon an additional point. The preceding analysis implied that in free occupations all persons produce independently as master craftsmen, dealers, or farmers. At the least it implied that the combination of workers in firms does not affect their productivity. Whenever this assumption is not valid the choice of an occupation does not depend upon different efficiencies in themselves (which in many occupations are not even conceivable), but upon different *possibilities* for production, which depend on combinations with other factors of production possible at any moment. These are a function of the degree of utilization of the capacities of a plant at any given time. Thus the choice of an occupation by employed workers depends still less upon mere aptitude than does that by the self-employed. On the contrary, the common output of persons in different occupations, as represented in a factory, is also a function of the price of their products *and the technical possibilities at any one time for developing aptitudes.*

c. THE LOCALITY OF A PERSON

Where does any given man produce? This time we shall invert our customary procedure and trace our answer step by step from special to more general solutions.

§1. The Locality of Employed Workers

α. *Equal Nominal Wages*

All popular views on a person's choice of location agree on one point: the principle of interlocal equalization of the wage level. Only against this background is it possible to understand the shocking opinion of the American Department of Labor given to the NRA, which declared local wage differentials economically unjustifiable. This view could be defended on two assumptions, of which one is not given in reality and the other is not desirable.

1. There is in fact a dangerous modern tendency toward the inter-local equalization of nominal wages. Its supporters are those who are either unwilling or unable to perceive differences in places and things, and in this and in other matters follow what others do without considering reasons for and against. They follow the highest nominal wage as though it were a magnet. These persons, who consider only the money wage, tend to equalize it everywhere if they are sufficiently numerous.

2. If the " iron law of wages " held, an individual would work where he found a livelihood, and all together would be located so that as many persons as possible could live on this planet.[16] But as the number of people, unlike the number of firms, does not tend to reach the maximum number possible, labor, like land, receives a scarcity rent; that is, the workman earns more than his cost of reproduction. Like every entrepreneur, he will consequently seek a location where his profit will be greatest. In both cases profit is the difference between receipts and variable costs, both of which are functions of location.[17] With persons variable costs are not only the expenses necessary to mere existence (as little as expenses in a firm go only for the maintenance of capital goods), but also such additional expenditures beyond mere existence as keeping fit for work with better food, work clothes, carfare, and so on. But like everyone in a limited monopolistic position the individual is free to choose his location in such a way that his gain accrues not chiefly in money, but more directly in some such natural form as a more agreeable climate instead of higher wages. From this it follows most emphatically that nominal wages can never be equalized interlocally any more than they can be equalized among occupations. Man wishes to maximize his total utility, not only his monetary return. But interlocal equalization of total utilities requires interlocal inequality of nominal wages; that is, of wages for piecework, since the hourly wage varies in any case for different persons, as we have seen.

β. Equal Real Wages

It will be objected, however, that only real wages for piecework are supposed to be equalized. But that again is not correct. For the individual the difficulty of comparing real wages interlocally

---

16. *Mutatis mutandis* this statement holds also for firms, in so far as they are subject to an " iron law of profits."

17. Only in statics is profit the difference between the receipts and *total* costs, because here, otherwise than in dynamics, the probability is that fixed costs too will be recovered.

might be overcome. The type of work is generally different in different places, and when his place of residence has to be changed with a change in his place of work a man becomes completely unsettled. The price system, and accordingly his consumption pattern, changes from place to place; in many localities he will be unable to procure goods to which he has become accustomed because their possible sales areas do not extend that far.[18] But in so far as his marginal utilities change with relative price and with his environment he will voluntarily [19] adapt himself to local custom, which R. Wilbrandt [20] ingeniously derives from the local marginal utility, which is largely fixed. Thus the individual, though not necessarily a statistician, could in principle compare the utilities purchasable in various places.

But our total satisfaction does not depend solely upon what we can buy in various places with the income available at a given time. For besides purchasable goods unique things that are without price influence our location; those individual characteristics of places and people that cannot be interchanged, all those imponderables of production and consumption that often mean incomparably more to us than the economic process proper. For this reason potential real wages for the same worker, unlike the wholesale price for the same product, may differ from place to place by more than his travel costs.

γ. *Equal Satisfaction*

We wish to maximize neither our money wage nor our real wage, but our total utility. This, too, differs interlocally for individuals by far more than traveling expenses, for it makes an enormous difference whether we were born in a place or have to move there. Migration means relinquishing much that, like friends, can be replaced only after a long time; or never, like one's native place. We cannot take landscape and people with us. And seldom do we become as attached to new surroundings as if we had grown up

18. In his admirable study L. B. Zapoleon ("International and Domestic Commodities and the Theory of Prices," *Quarterly Journal of Economics* XLV [1931], 443) expresses the opinion, however, that local differences in the style of living nowadays show more in the relative amounts in which goods and qualities obtainable everywhere are bought, than in the existence of different products that can be obtained only locally.

19. On the other hand, those local differences in custom to which one adapts oneself simply in order not to seem queer can no longer be included in the concept of real wages.

20. R. Wilbrandt, *Vom Leben der Wirtschaft*, P. I (Berlin, 1937).

The Six Problems Discussed Individually 243

among them and were wholly a part of them. Hence the same wage and other identical circumstances provide a newcomer with less utility than they give to a native with the same characteristics. In the marginal case, therefore, utility differs interlocally for individuals by traveling expenses plus the loss of one's home.[21-24]

Are there any other universally valid interlocal differences in utility? If all persons were alike, and if they chose what they recognized as an improvement over their present activities, total utility would again differ interlocally at most by traveling expenses and compensation for the loss of one's home.[25] But as no interpersonal utility comparison can be drawn, or even a comparison of the utilities of the "same" person at different times [26]—because, to put it plainly, the concept of utility is nothing but a chimera—spatial comparison of utilities, to say nothing of equalization, is impossible in any sense at all.

21. Thus as long as familiar conditions continue to exert their charm and expenses make removal difficult, freedom of movement will not lead to limitless agglomeration.

22. If a person could divide his working hours and his free time among several localities, equalization of his local marginal utilities (after deduction of traveling expenses and loss of his home) would constitute the condition of equilibrium.

23. Hence the utility that must be offered a worker in order to induce him to change his place of employment increases, at first slowly, with the distance of the new location from his original home (as long as this can be retained); then at one jump, a little more (change of dwelling in the same place); then suddenly and considerably (with removal to another town); and finally again more slowly, until there comes an abrupt rise at the border of a district or country. (See K. Philip, *Finanspolitik* [Copenhagen, 1942], p. 354.)

24. We may go a step further and assume that individuals are not free to choose a locality, but are placed by the government where they will be most useful to it. Then there are no longer limits to the interlocal differences in personal utility. Instead, the individual is so situated that in no other locality would his public utility be greater by more than the traveling expenses.

25. For this reason labor is less mobile than goods. Goods begin to move when price differences are *equal* to the cost of transportation. Migration, on the contrary, does not take place until local differences in utility are *greater* than travelling expenses. Only a modern gypsy can apply the same rule to goods and to himself. But differences in the mobility of stable persons, gypsies, and goods are evidently differences in degree only, even where movement between countries is concerned. Whoever starts with the assumption that labor is internationally immobile is dealing with a limiting case.

26. Utility for the individual can be compared between localities at a given moment, when he really is one and the same, provided we interpret his choice of locality as though he had decided in favor of the greater utility. But interpersonal utility comparisons are something entirely different. This would be an interpretation of a formal principle of explanation as an actual force, which does not become any more real because men believe in it and calculate real wages and set up wage schedules in conformity with it. Worship does not transform an idol into a god.

8. *Conclusion*

From all that has been said it follows, first, that the objective criteria for human choice of a location vanish more and more as our model approaches reality until, in the limiting case of the individual, no choice remains. In the end not much remained of the simple conformity to law of the voluntary spatial distribution that we deduced at the beginning from special assumptions. It is to be suspected that the original precision was achieved by impossible assumptions. This shows the great psychological difference that exists when we pass from the general to the particular instead of from the particular to the general, as we have done here. When we proceed from the general to the particular even the special case has significance against the background of the general, in that it gives a more exact solution for certain conditions. When we start with the special case it is soon covered over by the more general solution, and then appears merely as an error on the road to truth.

Secondly, as universally valid spatial differences in utility do not exist in a free economy, there is also no limit for spatial differences in nominal or real efficiency wages. All wages remain unique and incommensurable in space, and thus offer no criterion for the spatial distribution of persons. Only where interlocal wage differences are felt similarly by a sufficiently large number of persons can one-way migration result, which in turn may, under certain circumstances, lead to uniform wage differentials. (See below, Fig. 91.)

Only one general principle can be established for the choice of a location by the individual. *He will select it so that nowhere else does he feel enough better to make up for the cost of moving and, if necessary, the loss of familiar surroundings.*

§2. THE LOCATION OF AN ENTREPRENEUR

An entrepreneur, too, wishes to maximize not his profit in terms of money but his utility. For this reason his profits, like the wages of the worker, vary irregularly from place to place. But as there is no " iron " law of wages, though there is a tendency toward an " iron " law of profits,[27] and since, therefore, entrepreneurial incomes are especially sensitive to location; [28] and, furthermore, as an entre-

---

27. In other words, wages may lie arbitrarily above the minimum of existence, but an entrepreneur's profit cannot exceed the enterpreneurial income by an arbitrary amount without bringing counteracting forces into play.

28. That is, through the wrong choice of a location it can fall below the minimum

preneur, unlike a worker, is generally tied more closely to his branch of industry and, naturally, even more closely to his own factory, *the choice of a location by the individual entrepreneur is more restricted and that of entrepreneurs as a group more calculable than is the case with workers.* Only when conditions in an industry or the capability of an entrepreneur allow relatively large monetary gains, or when the location of entrepreneur and enterprise or factory can be separate without disadvantage, is there wider scope for free personal choice of a locality.

Finally, as for the connection of a choice of locality by persons and by enterprises, it is easier for an adequate number of potential workers than for potential entrepreneurs to make the sacrifice that would permit the establishment of a factory in the locality of their choice. (See, for example, the southward migration of the American textile industry.) On the other hand, migration from country to town offers examples enough of men following factories either voluntarily or of necessity, so that generalization in respect to one practice or the other is impossible. On principle, the location of men and factories are interdependent.

d. THE OCCUPANTS OF A LOCALITY

Who occupies any given locality? The answer depends, first, upon what is meant by "locality." The word may have a vague or a precise meaning. It may be understood as a group of locations [29] whose number can be increased, like New York, or one single spot [30] like Macy's.

---

of existence more easily than can the income of a worker, especially as an entrepreneur's mistake cannot be so easily remedied, since the migration of factories is incomparably more expensive than that of persons.

29. In a double sense: (*a*) an agglomeration of areas through artificial increases in a vertical direction (multistory buildings), (*b*) a horizontal agglomeration of areas that are not employed for agricultural purposes.

30. Of course even this is still not wholly precise. The extremely difficult problem of size of the individual lot remains, which recalls the problem of "product differentiation," and the difficulty of determining precisely what a "product" is. One might think of using a legal criterion, such as the unit of possession. This would be correct if the question were in what way the possession of a given piece of ground could be made to yield the greatest possible total return. But a discussion of basic principles must not employ such an institutional pons asinorum. Or one might assume infinitely small plots of ground together with a prohibition of sabotage; that is, no one would be allowed to withhold his land as the "key piece," but would have to surrender it to the highest bidder. In this case, however, the question of the production or occupants of such an infinitely small plot would have no sense, since it would be useful only in combination with adjoining plots. But not only can a given area be combined in

According to circumstances the inhabitants of a locality have to be compared among themselves, or with strangers; in the former case the comparison is directed toward similarities, in the latter toward differences. "People," on the other hand, might be divided into pure consumers, persons with a fixed income, whose only problem is to spend it in the most favorable locality; the others, the producers, on the contrary, have this one thing in common, that their *incomes*, too, depend upon their choice of location. For the pure consumer, therefore, the problem amounts to finding the best residence; for the producer, to finding the best combination of business place and residence.

§1. LOCALITIES IN THE WIDER SENSE

For the most usual case, in which residence and place of business coincide, the solution is this: *There are gathered together in one locality all those* [31] *who achieve their highest utility there*, even when loss of a home and traveling expenses are subtracted if necessary.[32] This holds not only for settlements but also for larger

---

endless ways with other areas for the same purpose; different men and different products do not always compete for exactly the same combination or areas. This means that the assumption that the prices of all remaining lots remain constant becomes impossible, and we can say nothing more about the occupants or the production of one locality *alone*, but can only determine the distribution of persons *in general*. Thus our subject cannot even be discussed unless all rivals compete for *the same* combination of areas, however this combination may be determined. Such a combination we call a locality in its more restricted sense.

31. Their number in turn affects the utility of the individual (e. g., through the level of rents and wages).

32. The explanation for a certain collection of people in a particular place cannot be found in special common characteristics of its inhabitants, any more than special characteristics are an explanation of why a given group of people belong to a particular occupation or a particular firm. Such characteristics might become prominent either through a process of selection or through mutation. Furthermore, any given characteristics are not found in a particular location only, nor are they the only ones found there. The really revelant question is: why are special characteristics used at all, and why are they used in just that particular place? With these limitations the most recent inquiries into the metropolitan type of person are really valuable. (W. Hellpach, *Mensch und Volk der Grosstadt* [Stuttgart, 1939]; E. von Eickstedt, ed. *Bevölkerungsbiologie der Grosstadt* [Stuttgart, 1941]; W. Mitze, *Die strukturtypologische Gliederung einer westdeutschen Grosstadt* [Leipzig, 1941]; K. V. Müller, " Siebungsvorgänge bei der Bildung von Grosstadtbevölkerungen," *Archiv für Bevölkerungswissenschaft*, 1942, pp. 1–26.)

All studies agree that an especially large number of gifted persons migrate to cities; similarly, those who move into cities are predominantly gifted. But on the other hand, even less well-rounded personalities succeed better in urban specialization.

areas such as economic landscapes, countries, and continents. Since under rational conditions all those assemble who find their highest utility here it follows that there is good reason for the special attitude toward space that binds these persons together, such as love for a native place, a feeling for economic landscapes, and national pride. Only when an unreasonably large fraction of the total utility is attributed to one of these geographical divisions may the exaggeration be condemned as the outcome of local patriotism, particularism, or chauvinism.

§2. Localities in the Narrower Sense

Who gets a location in the narrower sense, a site? *He who is prepared to pay most for it.* This has two implications: First, with prevailing price relations the individual in question finds his highest utility *here.* Secondly, at the price paid for this site he *alone* finds his highest utility here. Thus ground rent is a price [33] whose function is to exclude all but one from this locality.

For entrepreneurs the mechanism may be imagined as follows: costs, excluding the price of the lot, are given for each; so are the revenues of all locations, as well as the prices of all locations except the one in question. The locations can then be arranged for each entrepreneur in order of the total utility that they will afford him. If the location to be disposed of is to be at the upper end of the series, that is, if it is to assure at least the same utility as the next best, its price must not exceed a definite calculable amount.[34] The price may even have to become a subsidy, especially if the revenues to be obtained from this location do not even cover the remaining costs. The various entrepreneurs may now be arranged in order of the highest price that they are ready to pay for the location in question. The one at the upper end gets it.

When we try to compare the highest bidder with the others, just as when we attempted to compare the personnel of an occupation with others, we find no further characteristics that would serve to distinguish him. For example, he need not be the one who achieves the highest gross profit here (proceeds before deduction of the cost

---

33. Wherever rent appears as a fixed " differential " the willingness to pay the price is limited merely by certain objective factors such as differences in freight or in natural yield; thus, the theories of site rent and of rent based on differential soil fertility show differences in the prices of lots only for certain simple cases.

34. That is, the amount that anyone is willing to pay for a certain place depends upon the price at which another site will afford him a greater total utility.

of the lot). Despite a smaller gross profit he may obtain a total utility so high that he outbids all the others.

When we attempt to compare, for the highest bidder, the chosen location with the competing localities, no criterion at all appears save highest utility. The locality selected need not offer him the highest gross profit (before subtracting the cost of the lot); this may be greater elsewhere, yet provide a smaller net profit because of a disproportionately greater outlay for space. Yet even the net profit may be higher somewhere else, for it does not by itself determine total utility.

In our model of economic regions, in which we restricted ourselves to monetary calculations and assumed that the competition was sufficient to exclude money profits, the mechanism is in principle the same. The price of a site will rise until all but one would produce there at a loss.[35] The rising price of land shifts the cost curves upward, which reduces profits just as much as when the demand curve is shifted toward the left by reduction in the size of a territory. The one that remains is generally a farmer, since except for a few central points industry would operate everywhere at a loss, and so would be able to pay only a negative price for land. In our theoretical deduction the problem of the price of land did not appear, because we neglected industry's need of space, arguing as though industrial production could be concentrated at a point. But as factories are included among the objects that jostle one another in space, local variations in the price of land cannot be overlooked. They are included among the factors that distort our regular hexagon.

e. THE INDUSTRY IN A LOCALITY

§1. LOCALITIES IN THE WIDER SENSE

α. *The Correct Solution*

The firms in a locality have this one thing in common: their entrepreneurs find their highest utility there. But as the influence of an entrepreneur on the choice of a locality for an enterprise is limited, especially when profits disappear under pure competition, and as with many corporations locations are determined exclusively by profitability rather than by any sort of personal utility, a some-

---

35. This does not hold with the utility calculus. But then money profits can no longer be excluded, for the returns to the entrepreneur need no longer be equal. The case then amounts to a normal one.

what narrower formulation will bring out the essential point more clearly: *In any given locality everything is produced for which neighboring competition leaves room.*[36] It is the difficult task of those authorities who must plan and develop cities or countries to decide which particular industries should locate in a particular place. The practical procedure may be imagined about as follows: First, the chief production advantages of the locality in question, and next the main cost factors for the various enterprises are determined, from which appear the industries for which the local cost advantages will be most advantageous. So much for supply.

As for demand, it would have to be determined which were the industries whose nearest competition was unusually far distant, and whether the intermediate demand would be adequate. If both favorable production conditions and a satisfactory distance from competition exist, an undertaking of the type considered would have a good chance. Cases are much harder to find in which neither favorable conditions for production nor a particularly favorable competitive position are manifest, yet where an enterprise might nevertheless succeed in the end against neighboring competition.[37] The most difficult thing of all is to discover how the industries that are to be attracted will themselves reciprocally alter the bases of calculation; particularly at what price level the final equilibrium will be reached.

Whether neighboring production sites will leave room for a new factory depends upon more than competition from similar firms. As a rule the product of one locality differs in quality as well as packaging and the like from similar products of other localities. On the whole it is a somewhat different and characteristic article obtainable only there, and the real question is whether it can hold its own against all other possible similar or entirely different goods that consumers would otherwise purchase. Whether the individuality of a locality can be maintained, whether the products peculiar to it will find an adequate market, whether it can obtain the consumer's goods peculiar to it at such prices that a sufficient number of people will remain attached to it—these are the questions that must be answered.

---

36. That is, everything for which the planning curves and demand curves at least touch. The cost of the particular site in the locality must be included in the planning curve.

37. Hence the question is not necessarily one of lower costs than in neighboring localities but of sales adequate to cover them.

β. *The Traditional Solution (The Principle of Comparative Cost)*

1. THE INDUSTRY OF A COUNTRY

This classical location theory is not wrong, but it is always employed in the wrong way. The theory tried to explain the sort of production that localities, economic landscapes,[38] or countries will specialize in.[39] It *could* explain what is produced by persons.[40] The main reason why the theory of comparative cost can hardly ever be applied to countries is their spatial extent. The theory of comparative cost treats countries as points, and believes it has done all that is necessary when it has taken "the" freight costs *between* countries into consideration. But in many cases these are equal to zero, whereas up to the frontier they almost never are. This degradation of countries to points facilitated the erroneous theory of their economic uniformity.

Such uniformity does not exist in two respects that are fundamental here: (1) Under the assumptions of the classical theory, which was supposed to be independent of political differences, countries have no comparative advantages apart from those of their inhabitants and localities (and of the larger units, enterprises and economic landscapes at most); nor have their inhabitants and localities any advantages in common that would distinguish them from the rest of the world. For on the one hand people and the gifts of nature vary from place to place. These are the differences on the side of supply.

On the other hand, demand varies in different places and not least the demand from abroad.[41] Distance plays an important role here. One need only recall the different situations relative to a

---

38. Depressed areas whose workers do not wish to migrate (see p. 326, note 13) should change over to something wherein their greatest comparative advantage lies. See A. Robinson's review of S. R. Dennison's *The Location of Industry and the Depressed Areas* (Oxford, 1939) in *Economic Journal*, L (1940), 26.

39. The solution of the problem is this: Every country specializes in the goods that it can produce comparatively more cheaply.

40. Only in extreme cases can the theory be applied more or less to countries also; perhaps when these are small, widely separated, and very dissimilar islands, and differences in the size and utilization of enterprises do not play too important a role. It was probably not by chance that the theory originated in England.

41. The classical demonstration proceeds as though the problem for every country in respect to every product were only to choose between no market area at all and the largest possible market area: the world. This oversimplification of possible market areas is on a par with the oversimplification of possible locations: choice is restricted to a few countries. The difficulty of deciding on a location in an infinite continuum is avoided by dividing it into a finite number of discontinua.

foreign country of a site located at the frontier and of one in the interior of a country. This location relative to one frontier influences decisively the chances of export, even when trade between two countries has to pass through practically but one gateway in each: Antwerp to New York, say. Even then the freight costs to the domestic harbor, which are added to the ocean freight, are often higher, and always as different as can be for individual points of origin and destination. Because of these local variations in supply and demand absolute prices and comparative advantages differ everywhere.

(2) It was explained in the preceding section why absolute prices for the same goods, and price ratios for different goods within the same country, vary from place to place. It must now be added that the movement as well as the level of prices varies in different localities. In other words, there are no uniform national price levels that change abruptly at the frontier. On the contrary, international migration and international trade connect domestic and foreign prices, especially near a frontier. A fundamental though tacit assumption of the application of the theory of comparative cost to countries is not given in reality.[42] The transitory possibility of an independent central bank policy cannot alter this in the long run.[43]

But this means that countries simply do not show the economic uniformity postulated by the principle of comparative cost; hence it is illogical to apply the theorem to them.[44-46] The problem of determining the production of a country must be solved in some other way.

42. This subject is treated at greater length in my article, " Wo gilt das Theorem der komparativen Kosten? " *Weltwirtschaftliches Archiv,* July, 1938, pp. 48 f.

43. The long-run processes are unjustly neglected today. Only they obey laws that together constitute a functioning and meaningful whole. Studies of short-run processes are useful within their limits, but are so overvalued at present that the situation borders on decadence and dissolution. Keynes, of course, brilliant as always, has broken a lance in their defense: In the long run we shall all be dead. But that is just brilliant bluff. In the first place, it is not true of peoples as a whole; and secondly, it often does not hold for individuals either, since in general a long period means not more than a few years.

44. There are still other objections. For example, it is practically and theoretically impossible to estimate the cost of an article that is not produced in a country at all, yet the principle assumes that it is known. See Lösch, " Wo gilt das Theorem der komparativen Kosten? " *Weltwirtschaftliches Archiv,* July, 1938, p. 51.

45. Except for certain practical purposes, such as disproving the popular prejudice that countries poorly endowed by nature have a more difficult time in international trade. Since this prejudice regards countries, though incorrectly, as units the principle

2. THE EXPORT INDUSTRIES OF A COUNTRY

It was characteristic of the theory of comparative cost that it could answer simultaneously the two questions of the industry of a country and of its export industries. For since it regarded countries as points everything that they produced would naturally be exported. But for us the answers to these two questions are distinct. Knowing what industries will be profitable in a country tells us very little about what that country will export or import. Only when we can find a new answer to this question will the theory of comparative cost have been entirely replaced.

Under the assumptions of the theory of comparative cost, which were more or less fulfilled at the time it was developed, countries from an economic standpoint are completely arbitrary constructs to be used as a frame of reference. Thus nothing remains but to determine, first, the production of all locations without regard to political frontiers, then to draw in these frontiers and consider their effects upon the size of the market areas. Then all goods whose market areas are intersected by frontiers are export goods if the production center lies within the frontier, and import goods if it lies beyond. The same is true of supply areas.[47] This is the solution of the second problem that the theory of comparative cost has set itself.[48]

---

is perfectly suitable for its refutation. And so long as no theory existed that could take account of the inherent multiformity of differences within a country, the principle of comparative cost had its place even in the theory of international trade.

46. At best the theorem might still be applied to locations in the narrower sense. Here net profit per unit of land would have the same function as the wage per unit of time has in the case of persons. Nevertheless, this way of looking at the matter is unnecessarily complicated.

47. The smaller the country, the larger the proportion of all domestic market areas that will be cut by the border. Consequently the relative importance of international trade diminishes with the increasing size of a country. For example see J. H. Herberts, " Importance du commerce extérieur dans l'économie française," in *L'Activité Économique* (Paris, 1937), p. 6.

48. According to B. Ohlin (*Interregional and International Trade* [Cambridge, 1933]) a country specializes in goods requiring factors of production with which it is relatively best endowed. This may or may not be true. (See p. 30, note 33, and pp. 248 f.). That local variations in the scarcity of factors of production is not a necessary or even sufficient condition for the exchange of goods can be seen, on the one hand, from our model of economic areas in which trade is carried on despite an equal distribution of productive resources; on the other hand, there will be no trade between two islands differing in nature and separated widely enough, despite all price differences. Ohlin overemphasizes supply, as though demand were less important. Yet he would then have to consider also the prices of raw materials and supplies for he does not think basically in terms of space.

Consider for a moment the regional network for one single product. When individual markets are small but countries large it is clear that some of the regional centers will lie within and others beyond the border. In other words, the same article will be both imported and exported, though in different parts of the same country. On the other hand, if the market areas are large in comparison with countries and if their centers are perhaps even concentrated in a narrow space, as is true of many natural resources, certain countries will be typical exporters and others typical importers of the product concerned.

§2. Localities in the Narrower Sense

The solution of the problem of the personnel of a locality, *mutatis mutandis,* applies here also. *A locality in the narrower sense goes to the enterprise that is willing to pay most for it.* This can be visualized by assuming that all settlements and their industries are given, with the exception of one. Somewhere in the network of settlements, therefore, a gap is to be filled, and the question is, what industries can squeeze in here and, inseparable from this question, precisely where shall they be situated.[49,50]

First, each possible place is systematically examined to see what industries would be profitable if land were free.[51] The net profit that it will yield under this assumption shows the highest rent that the indsutries in question will be able to pay for the place under consideration. This amount will be negative for most industries; neighboring competitors leave them no room at all. The few industries that yield a positive return will generally show a profit at sites that lie close together at the center of the free space, or even overlap. Industries compete for these favored sites, and not all that could exist with free land will continue to be profitable when competitive bidding begins to increase land prices and to raise costs. Thus the number of industries exceeds the number of available sites at first,

---

49. It cannot be emphasized strongly enough that the frequent separation of choice of region, choice of locality, and choice of site is not tenable in a strict sense, however useful it may be pedagogically. For of what use is a favorable locality if it offers no good sites? The problem of location must be solved at *one* stroke.

50. We thus go outside the most rigid formulation of the problem, since we do not assume the prices of all lots except one as given (in conformity with the procedure in section d, §2, but only the prices of all except a few. This broader formulation makes the processes still clearer.

51. In practice one will have to be content with rough calculations for several likely locations. An exact scientific solution for a concrete case is generally impossible.

for with free land many enter the race that come to grief with an increase in the price of land. Prices are raised in such a way that finally but *one* buyer remains for each site. Even with relatively few sites and competitors the determination of this equilibrium price presents a difficult mathematical problem (calculus of variations). No simple solution exists for the problem of who shall acquire individual sites and at what price, and who shall be completely eliminated.

This is true even though we have not even considered the fact that revenues, in turn, also depend on the final result, especially on the related ultimate determination of the prices of the factors of production, on the exact location of the railroad station, of the road system, and so on. The revenues at various locations are as much a function of the lines of communication as the reverse. Finally, there remains the difficulty that different industries never compete for exactly the same sites, but for overlapping ones. This shows the great complexity of the problem. There is no simple method of determining the industry that will finally settle in a locality. All that can be given in a few words are the conditions that the victorious enterprise must satisfy: It must not only be more profitable at the particular site than anywhere else; it must also offer more for this site than the other competitors.[52]

Tables 13 and 14 give a very simple example of the method for determining who is to acquire a piece of ground and at what price. They show competition by three industries, a, b, and c, for two sites, I and II. The winners are industry a, which acquires site II at a price of 4, and b, which gets I at a price of 2. Industry c, on the contrary, loses out even though it shows relatively high gross receipts. It is interesting that site I should go to industry b even though industry a would be still more profitable at the purchase price. Table 13 shows that at price 2 for site I industry a achieves a net profit of 2 on it, whereas industry b achieves a net profit of only 1. Nevertheless industry b alone fulfills the condition that not only is it more profitable at the site obtained than anywhere else, but also that it is the highest bidder, since industry a prefers site II.

---

52. Thus within certain price limits there is a bilateral monopoly. See R. Triffin, *Monopolistic Competition and General Equilibrium Theory* (Cambridge, Mass., 1940), p. 172.

The Six Problems Discussed Individually 255

Tables 13 and 14. EXAMPLE OF DETERMINATION OF THE PRICE OF LAND

Competition among three enterprises, *a*, *b*, and *c*, for sites I and II

Price of Site	Net Profits of Enterprise Less Cost of Land on Site					
	I			II		
	a	b	c	a	b	c
0	4	3	2	7	1	4
1	3	2	1	6	—	3
2	2	1	—	5	—	2
3	1	—	—	4	—	1
4	—	—	—	3	—	—

Table 14

Price of Site		a	b	c
I	II	Chooses Site		
1	1	II	I	II
1	2	II	I	II
1	3	II	I	I or II
1	4	I or II	I	I
2	1	II	I	II
2	2	II	I	II
2	3	II	I	II
2	4	II	I	—
3	1	II	—	II
3	2	II	—	II
3	3	II	—	II
3	4	II	—	—
4	1	II	—	II
4	2	II	—	II

f. THE LOCALITY OF AN INDUSTRY[53]

§1. INDUSTRIES IN GENERAL

α. *The Regional Basis*

Industrial locations are usually not distributed at random, but group themselves in economic landscapes with a metropolis as a center and a general distribution of the remaining towns that is favorable with respect to communication lines (see Chap. 11).

β. *Rules of Thumb for Special Agglomerations*

Strictly speaking all locations are interdependent. No one location or location factor can be called leading and the others dependent. The location system, like the solar system, hangs free

---

53. Summary of the most general conclusions of Part I.

in space, so to speak, nowhere suspended and held together only within itself. In practice, however, those natural factors to whose sources production is necessarily bound have special weight as a rule: arable land, natural resources, valleys, harbors, and climate. The most important of these are the factors whose occurrence is on the one hand limited and concentrated and to which, on the other, a relatively large amount of economic activity is tied. Natural resources, for example, rank above soil. There still remains the choice among several possible sites of these resources, but in many cases the proximity and superior quality of several natural factors is so strikingly combined that such regions may be regarded with high probability from the first as cardinal points in the location system.

Other production centers, whose locations are not unconditionally bound to natural resources, in the extreme case those that by nature are strongly consumer oriented, are more or less attracted to this leading concentration or at least located with respect to it. The resulting aggregation of populations finally results in large-scale enterprises such as would have been impossible with more equal distribution. The extent, importance, and proximity of these favored localities determine whether only regional centers will arise in them, or whole regional systems more concentrated than elsewhere, though often concentrated to the point where they can no longer be recognized. It is mainly the need of space for agriculture that prevents complete concentration of industrial production and of trade in a few places. For this reason even the urban population is much more uniformly distributed in predominantly agrarian countries. As soon as the important group of agricultural consumers is widely distributed the advantages and disadvantages of distance begin to play a role for many industries. Their concentration breaks up, which in its turn causes other branches of industry to follow them. In the language of economics: The more the market networks expand, the greater becomes the distance between the centers of individual markets.

We shall neglect historically determined inconsistencies, though in practice they are temporarily very important. The Chinese mineral deposits, for instance, would have led to a much more intense concentration of the population if the economic development of the country had not been so backward. But a respect for history must not be carried to the point of contempt for logic. Here we are interested in the rules of thumb for logical distribution, not for the distribution that has actually occurred. Examples will be offered only if they permit a logical as well as a historical explanation.

The importance of source is obvious in the distribution of populations in both Europe and the United States.[54] Why is the population of the North American continent concentrated in the northeastern part of the United States?[55] The most important reason is the *climate:* too cold in the North, too hot in the South,[56] too dry in the West. Then the *soil:* on the whole it is poorer in the West than in the Middle West and the East, and often below the requirements for grass, not to mention grain.

Climate, soil quality, and man co-operated to produce the result. In the South some of the soil is very good even today, an example of the fact that a natural factor alone is of no great significance. *Natural resources* are not unequivocally on the side of the Northeast, though they may give it a slight advantage.[57] Its situation in respect to communications, on the contrary, is unusually favorable. It lies nearest the industrial areas of Europe,[58,59] has the best harbors,

54. We combine discussions of the distribution of people and of their industries.

55. The boundaries for the rectangle of dense population are about as follows: a vertical line west of Iowa; in the east, the ocean; a horizontal line through Montreal to the north and another through Washington to the south (somewhat further south for the agricultural population as a whole. See Fig. 64).

56. The hotter the climate the less dense must be the agricultural population with the same soil, the same crops, and the same plane of living, and the larger, therefore, the individual farm. Even when the heat does not affect natural fertility it prevents the intensive use of the soil that is possible further north, though these differences must not be exaggerated. In the United States, of course, it is not so much the agricultural as the industrial population that is concentrated in the Northeast. This is due partly to historical reasons. The feudal system in the South and, after its collapse, the aftermath of the Civil War, which manifestly broke the backbone of the South, did not favor any extensive influx. But a more important reason was that most of those who did come in were accustomed to a northerly climate, in which they were more efficient and, perhaps most important of all, in which they felt better. In this case the influence of climate probably makes itself felt through consumption rather than through production.

57. In the South (ore and coal) and near Duluth (ore; coal as a cheap return freight) iron and steel could be produced more cheaply, but their relation to the market is so unfavorable that factories cannot reach their optimum size, at least near Duluth. See A. Predöhl, " Die örtliche Verteilung der amerikanischen Eisen- und Stahlindustrie," *Weltwirtschaftliches Archiv,* XXVII (1928), 286 ff., 329*.

58. Which includes the *fortuitous* advantage that when immigrants arrived from Europe over the shortest route they landed in the Northeast and at first remained there.

59. Even though certain freights to Europe are now the same for all harbors on the East Coast despite the different distances, the time costs such as interest can still be saved over the shorter northern route.

and the waterways of the Great Lakes. Of course artificial measures—like the politically rather than economically determined discrimination of freight rates to the disadvantage of its great rival, the Mississippi Valley—have strongly emphasized the natural advantages of the Northeast.

The belt of strikingly dense population that stretches slightly southward from the English industrial areas across northern France and Belgium, southern Holland, the Ruhr, central Germany, Saxony, Upper Silesia and the neighboring parts of Bohemia and southern Poland, into northern Rumania and the Ukraine, where it turns

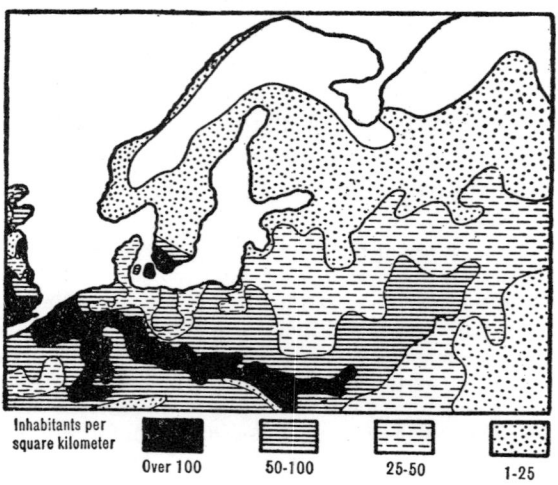

Fig. 55. Population density of northeastern Europe, about 1930. (After Goode and others.)

toward the northeast in the Donets area,[60] is chiefly attributable to the presence of natural resources, particularly iron and coal. But the fertility of the soil on the northern edge of the German Mittelgebirg Chain and the Carpathian Mountains also plays a part, especially in the areas of black soil.[61] So does a naturally favorable

---

60. It is really astonishing, and further proof of the attraction of large aggregations, how regularly the population density falls off with distance from this belt, especially toward the north. In the south the pattern is distorted by, among other things, a second densely populated belt that runs up the Rhine Valley and continues on the other side of the Alps down to the tip of Italy (See Fig. 55).

61. According to Haufe this belt was very thickly settled even before the days of industrialization (*Die Bevölkerung Europas* [Berlin, 1936], Map 1). On the relative locations of industry and especially productive agriculture to one another, see O. Schlier, "Regionale Statistik," *Weltwirtschaftliches Archiv*, LIV (1941), 292.

situation in respect to communications, for example, with London, the lower Rhine, and central Germany.

Be it repeated that, strictly speaking, this is no explanation of reality, because it omits not only historical factors but also the whole interdependence of economic forces. But as a first approximation, and above all in the face of such extensive regional differences,[62] it is useful to put the most important factors into the center of the picture even though they are not the sole effective ones. The idea was not to provide a complete derivation of a rational choice of location. The result is not conclusive, though it is probable. Such limited rules of thumb are more important in practice than scientifically exact emphasis on boundless interdependence.

§2. THE INDIVIDUAL INDUSTRY

α. *In General*

The individual agricultural and industrial enterprises are of such size and so distributed in space that the total number of independents, and in this context the income of every individual, is maximized. Accordingly a single good is *produced in as many localities as possible.*[63] The solution might be visualized in some such way as this. A network of market areas small enough to allow no profits, at least to a marginal entrepreneur, is placed over a region. It is shaped and placed in such a manner that the demand for the individual is, nevertheless, as large as possible.[64] (See pp. 94 f.)

β. *The Individual Enterprise*

1. THE GENERAL SOLUTION[65]

Corporations erect a factory where it will yield the *greatest profit*

---

62. The more we get down to single localities the more important do the other factors become.

63. This is true only for given techniques. Technical progress may bring out the opposite tendency—to decrease the number of producers.

64. The choice of a locality by an industry depends upon maximization of the producers, the choice of an industry for a locality upon maximization of the ground rent. The first tendency determines the regional network for a product when the site and size of the networks for all other goods are given. The second regards the networks themselves as given, and determines their relation to one another.

65. I have disproved elsewhere the solution given by the theory of comparative cost: "A factory chooses that locality where the comparative advantage for its type of production is greatest." (" Wo gilt das Theorem der komparativen Kosten? " *Weltwirtschaftliches Archiv,* July, 1933, pp. 50 f.)

(if market conditions show monopolistic elements), or at least where it can just continue to *exist* with a normal return on the capital invested (pure competition). Such a location is objectively unequivocal. Individual entrepreneurs may choose another location, since they are not concerned with money profit but with the *greatest total utility*. The scope for this subjective choice of a location is objectively limited, since at most it may cost profits and the entrepreneurial wage.[66]

Monopolistic profits are possible chiefly in five cases: (1) When the amount offered is limited. (2) When the number of producers is limited. (3) When even with free entry their number is small relative to the size of the market, so that new entrepreneurs can enter only discontinuously. (4) When the market areas cannot be reduced exactly to the smallest necessary size because of the discontinuity of the original settlements. (5) For those entrepreneurs who are more skillful than the marginal producer.[67]

But in all cases where entry into an industry is free, where the number of possible enterprises is large, and development goes on smoothly, the pressure of potential entrepreneurs always tends toward the elimination of profits and a condensation of locations accordingly. In this case an enterprise is established simply where it can exist. Its existence depends primarily also upon the location of neighboring enterprises that compete either for sales or for factors of production. If a new bank, say, is to be founded, a gap in the already existing bank network must be found that will assure an adequate supply area of deposits on the one hand, and an adequate market area for bank credits on the other.

2. SPECIAL CASES

A few special solutions that have dominated the past literature are valid only in the rare cases in which their very restrictive assumptions are fulfilled.

1. A factory chooses the locality with lowest freight costs. This assumes that production costs are the same everywhere, and also that the number and demand of consumption centers are unchangeable. If their number is variable the total freight or the average

---

66. True in a free economy. For a planned economy the statement must read: An enterprise will be established where it can best serve the interests of the government.

67. In a strict sense (1) and (2) are rents that depend upon natural or artificial scarcity; (3) and (4) profits due to indivisibility; and (5) an entrepreneurial wage (F. Machlup, "Competition, Pliopoly and Profit," *Economica*, 1942, p. 164).

freight would be lowest when sales remained limited simply to the producing locality. If the number of consuming localities is fixed but their demand is variable, one of two localities may still show the lower total and average freight; but only because the demand from remote points is too small to be of any importance. A shifting of the location in their direction might increase their demand so much, and need decrease so little the demand of places that now become more distant, as to make the new location more favorable in spite of its higher freight costs. Indeed, the increased demand might lower costs so greatly that the price might fall even in the deserted location. Finally, the first condition for location at the point of least freight cost, namely that production costs are equal at different locations, is seldom fulfilled even in times of uniform prices and uniform wages.

2. A factory chooses the locality with the lowest cost of production.[68] Obviously this is true only when shipping costs and personal contact with the customer play no role. In this rare instance all factories of the same branch of industry collect in this one locality. It should be said at the same time, however, that local costs are never constant but depend in turn upon their power of attraction. Localities with favorable cost curves naturally exert a special drawing power, but it cannot be emphasized strongly enough that much depends also upon their position with respect to one another and to consumers. The final list of locations need by no means contain the localities with lowest cost of production.[69,70]

3. A factory chooses the locality with lowest delivered price (production costs + freight on the finished product). Weber and Palander have been principally occupied with this case, of which one-sided production or transportation orientation constitute only limiting cases. All the objections already brought forward under (1) and (2) apply to it. The assumptions of this solution are fulfilled only under exceptional circumstances.

68. Unlike the case of pure production orientation discussed on p. 23, these include also the freight on raw materials and supplies.
69. Suppose a mine is to work an especially rich vein. The main problem of this individual enterprise is as follows: Is there a sufficiently large uncontested territory (do supply and demand curves intersect)? But for the mining industry at large this does not yet settle the question. The particular mine may be profitable, but perhaps the total number of entreprises could be increased if all mines were so distributed that instead of this single mine, two others, perhaps less rich and so profitable only *alternatively* with this one could be worked.
70. In agriculture, too, pure transportation or pure production orientation are obviously marginal cases and interdependence, on the contrary, is the rule. Neither the best nor the nearest land need be cultivated.

g. CONCLUSION

The division of labor is determined by the two great principles, necessity and inclination. By necessity when producers (person or enterprises) can just barely exist, but in turn should be as numerous as possible; by inclination when a fixed number of producers attempt to maximize their utility. In the first case the income of the individual is constant and the number of income recipients is variable; in the second the situation is reversed. However, the variable should always be maximized. Now as a rule the number of individual producers (workers) at any one time is fixed, that of producing combinations and their leaders (enterprises and entrepreneurs), on the contrary, always variable; that is, the constant number of producers can be collected into a smaller or larger number of groups. If Malthus were right, if man, like the lower animals, continued to multiply so rapidly that each individual would be just able to exist,[71] there would be no such difference. But because man restrains his multiplication his income rises above the minimum of subsistence (profits from work), and there is scope for his inclinations. It is precisely the employed rather than the independent producers that are free within these limits to choose a location. In contrast to these, the smaller number of independents can be increased at will from the great reservoir of the employed. Their lot therefore resembles that of enterprises. Their choice of a location is decided more by necessity than by inclination, and there is a perpetual tendency to eliminate again the entrepreneurial profit, which would allow some degree of freedom to the entrepreneur also. There is more an " iron law of profits " than an " iron law of wages." Any entrepreneurial profits that appear nevertheless, may be attributed for the most part to the same cause as the " profits from work "; the limited multiplication of man. Thanks to this, man can place himself largely as he likes in the great spatial division of labor, whereas enterprises necessarily tend at least to seek gaps.

---

71. Of course the minimum of existence of a nation lies above that of its individual citizens, for certain necessary functions cannot be performed by persons who are only just able to exist.

Chapter 18. Price Gradients [1]

In a free economy the spatial division of labor is guided by geographical price differences. In equilibrium these often constitute regular gradients of three types: (1) The price in any part of a single supply or market area differs from the central price at most by the costs of distance. The resulting price cones and price funnels make up the *market gradient*. (2) If a commodity is produced at the same time on several levels of an economic landscape hierarchy, that is, in localities of different size and rank, a *landscape gradient* may arise among central prices in these localities. (3) Price differences occur also between different economic landscapes in localities of equal importance: a *world gradient*, of which national and continental differentials represent sectors.

Landscape and world gradients apply to goods of different producers; market gradients affecting industrial products apply to goods of the same producer. All these differences are at most equal to the costs of distance in the broad sense, which also includes trade margins. Even within the limits of these differences all prices are uniquely determined; each is such that the conditions of locational equilibrium are fulfilled.

---

1. Here it is possible only to sketch what is discussed at length in my *Geographie der Preise* (in preparation) and *Zur Beurteilung des westöstlichen Preisgefälles* (unpublished monograph).

B. *Disturbance of the Equilibrium*

The theory of trade has two tasks; First, to explain the principles of the division of labor and, second, to show the mechanism by which they prevail against disturbances.[1] The first task has already been discussed in the preceding chapters; the second will be taken up in the following one.[2]

---

1. I dismiss as insoluble a third traditional task; to calculate the gains from international trade.

2. The most important results are summarized in my article, " Eine neue Theorie des internationalen Handels," *Weltwirtschaftliches Archiv*, 1939. But only the detailed presentation offered here will provide a complete understanding.

Chapter 19. Self-Regulation

a. TRANSFER OF PRODUCTS DURING SHORT-RUN DISTURBANCES (THE TRANSFER PROBLEM)[1]

A change in the division of labor even between two localities only, eventually alters the whole system through movements of prices. The effects of a temporary disturbance are substantially exhausted by shifts in income, fluctuations in the volume of employment, changes in the place of employment but only seldom in that of residence, and a rearrangement in the flow of goods and of capital. In short, the size and composition of the balance of payments change, but the locational pattern as a whole is unaltered. Everything connected with these price fluctuations (how they come about, what form they take, their locality, time, direction, extent, and effect) is among the most important topics of the theory of international trade. We shall discuss here these aspects of price fluctuations for the most important subjects and the spatial constructs that are used as a frame of reference in international trade.

§1. Individuals

Let us start with very simple conditions. Suppose the demand for the work of the cobbler Jung increases because he has joined a large club, the members of which now favor him. He will ask a slightly higher price, if not because he is anxious for profits then at least because his work has become more irksome because of the longer hours. On the credit side of his balance of payments, the value of his " export " increases; first, because he commands a higher price; second, because he works longer hours; and third, because he now finds it advantageous to give up much of the work that he used to do about his home and to repair shoes instead. The situation corresponds to the diversion of production from a domestic market to exports in international trade. On the debit side, the value of

---

1. Here it is my purpose to explain the new fundamental ideas, whereas my theory is presented more compactly but systematically more completely in my article, " Die Lehre vom Transfer—neu gefasst," *Jahrbücher für Nationalöknonmie,* CLIV (1941), 385–402.

his "imports" increases. First, for the reason just mentioned of a simple shift in production. He will no longer paint his garden fence, for example, but will have this work done for him. Second, because with his larger income he can afford more. Whatever remains he will deposit in the bank. In other words, he will expand his capital export. The prices of most of the goods that he buys will hardly increase, because on the whole his customers or his competitors will now buy less of those articles on which he spends more; besides, the amounts are so dispersed as not to affect prices.

Of course he may be more free with his money, less careful about his purchases, shopping in more expensive stores and there paying higher prices even when they do not correspond to better quality. The landlord may have the best chance to profit from his increased prosperity by raising his rent. Our cobbler now lives in an atmosphere of prosperity: He asks higher prices, pays more rent, spends more freely, and deposits more in the bank. The opposite of all this applies to his competitors, though to a much smaller degree, since their loss is divided among many. The cobbler nearest to Jung will be most severely affected, since even club loyalties weaken with distance.

One day a new tax bill arrives unexpectedly and puts to Jung the same problem that Germany had with reparations: A unilateral transfer must be made. His "import of goods" and his "export of capital," both of which he will decrease with a sigh, will most likely bear the chief burden; he will spend less and be able to save less. But in addition pressure will be exerted upon the whole level of high prices that surrounds Jung. Forced by necessity, he will again buy more carefully; he will bargain with his landlord, and reduce his prices somewhat, in order to recover at least a part of the tax. In short, Jung will pass through a deflationary crisis. This crisis will be aggravated if other cobblers should now join the club [2] in order to take away the customers that Jung had just gained, and until the tax has been paid he may even be worse off than ever—until at last everything is as it was in the beginning.

Thus does the mechanism that is familiar to us only on a large scale operate in miniature, and with different emphasis. We shall now examine it once more and in greater detail for larger economic units than the individual.

---

2. If this does not work, and the loss of customers has to be regarded as permanent, one or another of the cobblers a few blocks from Jung will move away in order to gain more customers. Here we embark on the combination problem, to be discussed later.

§2. FACTORIES

Suppose that a Stuttgart shoe store A suddenly orders 1,000 marks' worth of shoes, which it formerly ordered from a local seller B, from B_1, located in a smaller place such as Tuttlingen. The additional demand for shoes from this town will raise their price, partly because the Tuttlingen firm has to fear only imperfect competition, but perhaps also because its production can be expanded only at increasing cost. By offering higher wages, it will attract additional workers away from other local enterprises. If this does not suffice, further wage increases will enlarge the supply area of commuting workers at the expense of neighboring factories, and wages will finally rise so high that labor will be attracted from a distance. This in turn will raise rents. The building boom that results will increase the pay of masons and other artisans. Vegetables and milk will become dearer because their supply area has to be enlarged; in brief, the local price level will rise. It is of fundamental importance, and of the very essence of the theory presented in these pages, to have an exact idea of the further course of such a local price change.

α. Price Waves and How They Spread

We can distinguish a direct and an indirect spread of a local price change. Distant customers of and sellers to the firms involved will be directly affected; the prices of competitors and those of other goods will be affected indirectly. The direct spatial spread of a local price inflation (hatched in Fig. 56) is retarded by freight costs and neighboring competition. However, the effects of the inflation on the region controlled by its point of origin are twofold. The higher price of its own products narrows their market area (in Fig. 56, for instance, from radius $B'_1G'_1$ to $B'_1G'_2$), and the higher prices of imported goods widen their supply area (for example, from $B'_1D'_1$ to $B'_1D'_2$), always to the advantage or disadvantage of neighboring competitors. The increase in prices does not operate uniformly throughout these market areas. Though for all goods it is relatively greatest in the "last" production locality, this "last" locality is the central point (B'_1) for the area for export; and the border (D'_2, for instance) for the import area, which happens to be the location where no freight costs (which need not rise concomitantly) are included in the price.

The indirect spatial extension of a local increase in prices goes further. At first it is transmitted to the adjoining competitors of B'_1. If B'_1 enlarges its supply area at the expense of B'_2 by raising prices, the scarcity of imports will raise prices in B'_2 also, though not quite so high as in B'_1, since the special cause operating there is absent. B'_2, on its part, now constitutes a new "focus of infection" for localities that B'_1 can no longer affect directly. In addition the price inflation is transmitted to other goods, not only through the producers selling to B'_1 but also indirectly through its customers, who spend more money for other things after B'_1 increases the price of its shoes.

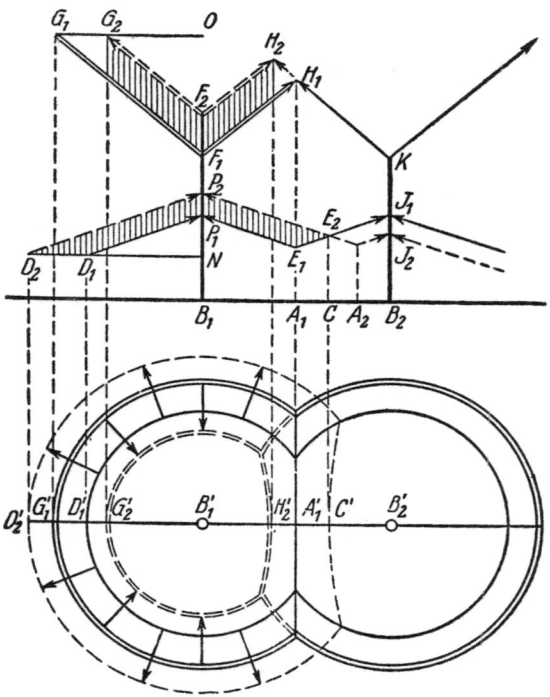

Fig. 56. Effects of a price inflation on market areas

β. *The Direction of Price Waves*

Price waves always move away from their point of origin. Each consecutive temporal and spatial link in the chain of purchasing-power transfers is necessarily farther removed from the starting point than the preceding one. For a recipient of increased purchasing power will turn it to better account in a direction away from the source (Tuttlingen, in our example), where prices have not yet been driven upward. And those factories affected by the falling-off of purchasing power in Stuttgart will endeavor to dispose of their goods in the opposite direction from that city, because nearer Stuttgart they encounter the still stronger price-cutting competition of B.

γ. *The Damping of Price Waves*

As the price change widens, its intensity diminishes for four different reasons.

1. DECREASING INFLUENCE OF THE POINT OF ORIGIN

Not only are the supply and market areas of a locality B definitely restricted by freight costs and other factors, but within these areas business connections with B *as a rule* grow closer the nearer it is approached. Although it happens occasionally that B receives important imports from remote points,[3] so that an inflation at B can jump directly to distant localities such as coal or ore fields, purchases and sales nevertheless decrease with distance. Because cases like these are especially striking their importance is apt to be overestimated.

Analyze the expenditures of consumers in any given locality, and see how large a proportion goes to local activities (builders, retailers, artisans, teachers, newspapers, beverages, and so on). The next largest part goes for goods from the near vicinity, the radius of which naturally varies with the size of the town (greens, potatoes, milk, eggs, firewood, brick, stone, and so on). Another portion of its supplies comes from a greater hinterland (cattle for slaughter, fruit, butter, flour, furniture), while many industrial goods whose share of the total expenditure may be small come from all parts of the country, and only a small remainder of agricultural and industrial products is imported from the world at large.[4] The truth of this

---

3. But only to export them again in the products of local factories—a type of finishing trade.

4. B. Barfod (*Local Economic Effects of a Largescale Industrial Undertaking* [Copenhagen and London, 1938], p. 44) calculated that in Aarhus 45 per cent of consumption expenditures (dwelling up to 85 per cent, clothing 30 per cent, food 25 per cent) was retained as *local* income. According to Isenberg (" Zur Stadtplanung in den neuen deutschen Ostgebieten," *Raumforschung und Raumordnung*, 1941, p. 137), in a German agricultural region up to 60 per cent of the expenditures of those who are not farmers will become *regional* nonagricultural income again. This he calls the "intraregional expenditure quotient." For economic regions in which industry and agriculture are intermixed it would have to be considerably higher. According to the same author (*ibid.*, Vol. 6, p. 18), 29.3 per cent of *German* productive workers were employed in 1939 for local requirements, 27.3 per cent in agriculture and forestry, and 27.1 per cent in remaining industries (grouped according to regional, national, and world markets). If the rest (public services, wholesale trade, and communications) is divided among these groups it proves to be true on the whole that the demand of a locality decreases absolutely with distance.

becomes still clearer when it is realized that the market area around B grows as the square of the distance from B. If this is divided into rings of equal area it will be found as a rule that with incrasing distance a constantly diminishing fraction of the product of each ring is sold in B, and a constantly smaller proportion of its purchases are bought from B. This is obvious for one and the same product, and especially for the exports of B. It is true also for the imports of B, since the increasing distance from B even smaller localities can carve out for themselves constantly growing supply areas from the region that supplies B, and since home consumption rises with falling producers prices. But the statement holds also for any group of products. It follows that the effects of a price change diminish gradually with distance from its point of origin.

2. INCREASING ABSORPTION OF A CHANGE IN PURCHASING POWER

Assume that A, in Fig. 57, is the man who has ordered the additional 1,000 marks' worth of shoes from B_1. C, E, G, and so on, and C_1, E_1, G_1, and so on, are consumers, and the rest are producers of one product each: B, of shoes; D, of bread; F, of butter, and so on. Suppose that a unit of each product cost initially 1 mark. Now let A disturb the equilibrium. Let the chain of trade connections be as in the figure. Thus D, the baker, for example, would have supplied C and perhaps E also, but he would have supplied neither A nor F. Such a selective chain is the rule in reality where imperfect competition prevails.

By paying 1,000 marks more to B_1, A pays out that much less as a customer of B. In order to win a substitute buyer, B reduces his price to one half. At this price a new customer C buys from him the 1,000 shoes that were not taken by A. Since C now buys 500 marks' worth more from B than formerly, he must diminish his purchases from D by an equal amount. But in order to sell his 500 units of bread, D will offer them to E at the reduced price of 80 pfennigs instead of 1 mark. He need lower his price less than B—and this is the point—because his loss of sales amounts to only 500 marks; not to 1,000, as with B. E buys 375 units at 80 pfennigs each for 300 marks, while C, for whom the reduced price also holds, buys 125 additional units of bread; which, to simplify the argument, would reduce the value of his purchases from D, despite the lower price, by only the 500 marks already mentioned. D's loss is reduced thereby from 500 to 200 marks. And so on. So much for the spread from B, the center of the price depression.

Now for the center of the price inflation B_1. As the demand for his shoes suddenly increased, B_1 raised his price to 1.5 marks. C_1; whose income has not gone up, will no longer buy 1,000 marks worth as before, but only 500 (so that B_1 will sell 667 units to A and 333 units to C_1), and use the remaining 500 marks for the goods of D_1, which so far have not risen in price. By joining D_1's long-established customers with an additional 500-mark demand, he drives D_1's prices up also, though by less than A was able to do with his additional purchasing power of 1,000 marks from B_1, and so on.

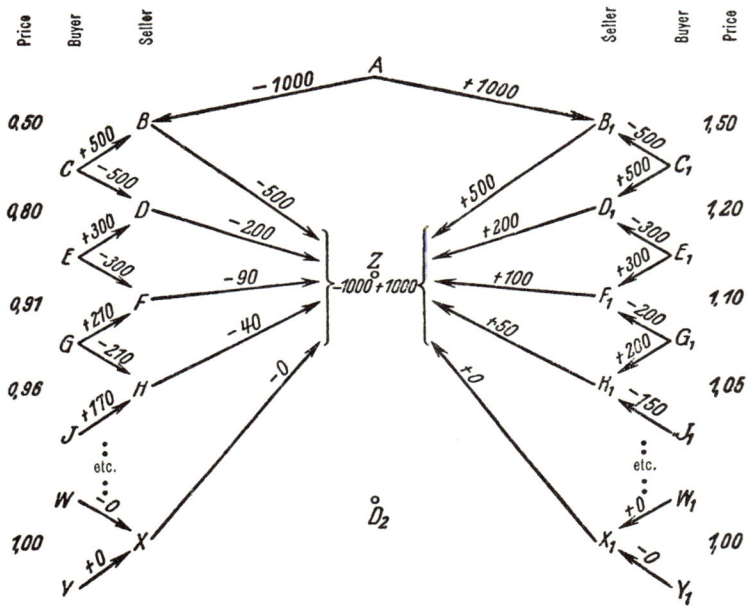

Fig. 57. The spread of price changes. (Complete transfer in goods and an elasticity of demand greater than 1 are assumed.)

In this way it comes to pass that with distance from the center of origin both the fall in purchasing power and prices (starting with B) and the increase in purchasing power and prices (starting with B_1) will *flatten out*.[5]

5. This conclusion is reached under the most probable assumption for these conditions: that the elasticity of demand is greater than unity. If the elasticity everywhere were equal to 1, B or B_1 would suffer all the loss or gain all the profits no matter how they set their prices. If B and B_1 each are several producers competing with one another, an elasticity of demand of less than unity is conceivable; (if each represents but one producer, an elasticity of demand of less than unity implies that he failed to

3. THE DISSIPATION OF PURCHASING POWER

So far we have assumed that the shifted demand of A fell entirely on seller B, who in turn could gain only one new customer C as a substitute. But in reality A will reduce his purchase from *several* sellers, and B will gain several new customers.[6] Thus the reduced demand will affect the individual seller less and, in addition, he need not lower the price so much to dispose of his unsold goods. This dissipation increases in geometrical progression, whereas the distance from the origin of the disturbance increases only in arithmetical progression. The price change therefore dies out in space even more quickly than we should have had to assume from the foregoing argument.

4. THE INCREASING TRANSFER OF GOODS

The three causes thus far described cause a price wave to flatten out with increasing distance from its origin because it *divides*. In so far as a more and more extensive transfer of goods takes place, as the two price waves approach one another, they flatten out because they *disappear*. This will be described below.

5. *The End of the Price Waves*

Whereas local price differences are very great in the first economic period, the fall in prices widens and flattens out in the succeeding ones. It must be remembered, however, that so far as the causes of this phenomenon (discussed under 1 to 3) extend, the sum of the increases or decreases in purchasing power remains the same, even though it is divided among more and more persons by partial shifting. This is the law of the conservation of purchasing power. Thus, though the total fall in purchases from B, say, was 1,000, he suffers a loss of only 500 marks and through a price cut shifts the further loss of 500 to D, who in turn absorbs 200 marks of it and passes on a loss of 300. The sum of the amounts absorbed $(500 + 200 + 90 + 40 + \cdots)$ is exactly 1,000. The shift from

---

set his price at Cournot's point). In this rather improbable case the movement of prices may be exactly the reverse of that described in the text: upward with B, downward with B_1. At best B could shift the entire loss to D; at the worst, B_1 would have to transfer all the profits to D_1, until at last profits and losses reached Z and were equalized there. The effect of a combination of different elasticities is still more complicated and, for a general discussion, still less interesting.

6. Here we speak of dissipation *within groups* of buyers and sellers, whereas in 2 dissipation between (individual) buyers and sellers was discussed.

income period to income period is to be distinguished from this shift from person to person. If in the second period A were to buy his shoes again from B as usual, the latter would nevertheless have received 500 marks less in the first period with which to buy leather from Z. B's loss therefore consists in the curtailment of his purchases from Z, and once he has dealt with this loss the storm has passed him.[7,8] But now the cloud hangs over Z.[9]

The disturbance would be carried over from one income period to the next and continue to claim new victims, were it not gradually dissipated in two different ways. The *compensatory* absorption about to be described must not be confused with the damaging absorption already discussed. The latter reappears again and again, and if the other did not intervene (that is, if we dealt with a closed economic system) it would come to an end only with a general and uniform price reduction in the region in which the purchasing power has fallen. The former is final. The manner in which it appears first, though not most frequently, is this. B_1, for example, with his increased income, wishes to buy from Z exactly what B had to give up because of his reduced purchasing power. In this case Z's prices remain unchanged. But such a prompt agreement between increased and decreased demand is hardly to be expected.[10] As a rule there would start from B as a producer not only the series of price drops illustrated; from him as a consumer with 500 marks' less purchasing power there would start also a corresponding series of price drops that is not shown in the figure. The same would be true for D, with his 200-mark reduction in purchasing power, and so on. Buyers B, D, F, H, and so on, would pass on together to Z a purchasing power reduced by up to 1,000 marks; not directly, of course, but through chains of intermediaries. Z must exist some-

---

7. Thus B has shifted when he has sold 500 marks' worth more of merchandise to C, even though at a loss, and bought 500 marks, worth less from Z. Then he enters the next production period with exactly as much purchasing power as he had in the preceding one. Unless part of the loss in purchasing power still affects one of his customers, the transfer is over as far as he is concerned.

8. In the case of single disturbances, therefore, we deal with a true wave, not simply with a price gradient.

9. Here two situations must be distinguished. The drop in purchasing power shows again at an increasingly distant place during every new economic period, but within one and the same period its effect is exhausted as soon as all goods have been sold, even though in part at reduced prices.

10. It is still more improbable that B_1 should obtain his increased requirement directly from B. As a general rule B would endeavor to dispose of his stock by trading with a third person, and B_1 would try to replenish his in the same way.

where, however; that is, there must be one or several places where diminished and increased purchasing power balance one another without altering prices.

Besides this there is still another possibility, more probable at first: That D_1 and F_1, with their combined additional purchasing power of 300 marks, will become new customers not of Z, but of D, in place of E. The series will then stop with D and the price drop will no longer reach F, H, and so on. Consequently their demand from Z will not decrease, which equalizes Z's loss of an additional demand from D_1 and F_1 previously assumed. In other words, these two simultaneous possibilities of a link between chains of price increases and price decreases mean that those who gain in purchasing power, either as a simple result of its shift (through Z) or after a preceding price change (in the case of D, for instance), demand what the persons with reduced purchasing power have given up. Both are typical examples of the real transfer, which is achieved when decreased and increased purchasing power meet somewhere.

The spatial distribution of these two forms of transfer is important. At first those persons or places with decreased purchasing power dp and those with increased purchasing power ip may be so far apart that no equalization occurs at all. But as the waves of purchasing power spread dp and ip move closer together. At first only their largest supply and market areas overlap slightly, and the shift in demand from ip to dp of those few in the region of overlap Z can influence their prices but little. Consequently only a slight real transfer occurs at first at sharply altered prices. Gradually the overlaps increase and dp and ip even move into each others' areas, so that a direct real transfer develops at prices that are very much less changed. At last dp and ip coincide with Z, and the final transfer is completed at unchanged prices. With time, that is, as the waves of purchasing power spread, the localities between which the real transfer takes place approach one another, the transfer increases in extent, and the prices at which it occurs depart less and less from the normal ones.

The territory involved in the real transfer does not as a rule coincide entirely with the areas of increased and decreased purchasing power, but lies necessarily within their borders. *The real transfer takes place between parts of areas with decreased and increased purchasing power.*

§3. Economic Landscapes

The economic connections of an enterprise are not the same in all directions; on the contrary, it is generally situated in an economic landscape toward whose center it is oriented. This is not without influence on the spread of price waves. Although the movement of prices always remains especially pronounced about its origin, the central points of economic landscapes reflect local changes anywhere in the hinterland relatively early and strongly; on the one hand, via the whole area; on the other, the movement jumps from these central points to those of neighboring landscapes, which thus are exposed not only at their borders but at their centers as well. That is to say, they are exposed throughout.[11]

This important function of economic capitals, the transfer of price fluctuations (of a cyclical nature also) to their economic landscapes or, conversely, from these to the rest of the world,[12] becomes still more clear when it is recalled that the final money transfer takes place as a rule through central banks, not directly between those concerned. If, therefore, there is any logic at all in the substitution of simplifying spatial constructs for the individuals who are really the ones affected by disturbances of trade, these constructs should certainly be economic regions [rather than countries].

§4. Countries

Do disturbances in economic relations always exhaust themselves in the described effects on those first concerned and by spreading through the channels of their originators' business connections, or are special phenomena *added* when payments have to be made across national boundaries? We must now examine the significance of political boundaries for the overcoming of temporary disturbances

---

11. This is really a special case of Huygens' principle, according to which every point in a wave may become the center of a new wave.

12. Individual industries in a landscape will of course also maintain direct connections with the outer world, and a machine factory, for example, will feel a cyclical revival in other regions more by way of industrial areas or its particular circle of customers than through the capital of its own region. This is even more obvious where there is no organized landscape at all. When a town has but little connection with its landscape, a local improvement in its economy cannot spread through the region but must be dispersed here and there. This need not mean its complete dissipation, for the arming of a fort, say, may at first chiefly benefit one single factory somewhere in a region of heavy industries; but it does mean an irregular geographical distribution, which of course may suffice to rob it of the cumulative cyclical effect which otherwise would occur in the course of interregional trade.

of equilibrium; not their significance for the equilibrium itself, since that has already been discussed. In so far as countries coincide approximately with economic regions, either fortuitously or by compulsion, what has already been said of them holds here also. Has the state as such, not as an economic area, additional significance?

α. *Currency*

Differences in currencies are the first important characteristic of international trade. Differences in monetary *policies* will form the subject of the next chapter; here the question is whether differences in the *fundamental construction* of currencies alter the transfer mechanism. But first we shall separate from this problem a more basic one.

1. THE SIGNIFICANCE OF THE FACT OF CREDIT CREATION FOR THE TRANSFER

Since large payments are almost never made directly, but generally through banks, we could have asked long ago what is changed in the process of transfer so far described when banks create credit. But this question has been postponed in order to discuss it together with the influence of a modern monetary system on transfer.

Suppose the monetary system were such that on the basis of the money generally acceptable between debtors and creditors (gold or other international means of payment, bank notes or deposits with the central bank for trade within a country) a *greater* amount in not universally accepted money [13] (bank notes and bank deposits in international, bank deposits also in domestic trade) could be created that would circulate only within the central area of the debtor's or creditor's bank. Then a debtor might pay a foreign debt in money, but not necessarily in internationally accepted money, so that the creator of the local money would still face the problem of procuring the rest of the international money. In this case the final transfer described above is preceded by a preliminary transfer, the results of which are later nullified by a reaction.

(aa) *Preliminary Transfer.* The preliminary transfer is brought about by a further price movement, which is added to that caused by a shift in purchasing power.

---

[13]. I shall call a medium of payment that is valid only within a spatially or otherwise restricted group "local money."

First: **Shifting of the Price Level.** An additional and general price drop, somewhat sharper about its source, however, will occur in the area of those banks that have received the amount to be transferred in credit money, whereas they themselves have to remit in monetary reserves.[14] There is first the local bank, which receives the amount in its own deposits and pays it out again in money serving as regional means of payment.[15] Another is the regional bank, which has to change its deposits into notes; finally, the central bank, which receives notes and has to pay out gold. Suppose a unilateral payment of 1,000 marks has to be made from Stuttgart to Paris. And suppose that in Germany gold is not the only medium of payment but that there arises on it a superstructure of, say, twice as many notes, on the basis of which a tenfold amount of deposits will be created. If the Reichsbank sends 1,000 marks in gold to Paris it must collect twice as much in bank notes by raising its discount rate (assuming that only the minimum reserves are kept at all times). The credit basis for the Bank of Württemberg, which sent 1,000 marks in notes to Berlin, has shrunk even more. It must reduce the amount of deposits by 10,000 marks, either by raising its rediscount rates or by direct curtailment of credits. Consequently prices in Württemberg fall ten times more than if there were no deposits, and in Germany twice as much as if there were no bank notes. This true shifting of the price level occurs only with credit creation; that is, with a hierarchy of different kinds of money, whereas in a region with a uniform currency the price waves started by a shift in purchasing power *necessarily* suffice for transfer.[16]

Second: **Effects up to the Due Date (Immediate Partial Transfer).** The change in relative price level will not go so far, however, for it is counteracted by the increasing export surplus that it is supposed to bring about. But gold shipments exceed nevertheless what would be required merely to cover the price waves. Thus, if only 50 marks

---

14. If some time passes between the creation of the deposit and its disposition, there arises the additional problem of whether the banks will intervene in the transfer with short-term loans of the idle amount. In this way the debtor's bank could counteract the local deflation that he has caused, and the creditor's bank could anticipate the local price inflation. But this would be wise bank policy only when it was certain that the owner would not first dispose of his deposit; that is, if no further transfer threatened.

15. For example, a transfer of reserves with the local Federal Reserve Bank from one commercial bank to another within the same Federal Reserve District.—W. F. S.

16. Not only money rates, but all prices must have at least the same *tendency*; not merely some, as with price waves. In this case the change in the price level is a reality instead of only a fictitious average, as with price waves.

in gold were sent to France, on the basis of which 1,000 marks in deposits would be created there and destroyed in Germany,[17] 950 marks' worth of goods would still have to be transferred. But this is impossible at this price level as long as the two price waves are still in the neighborhood of Stuttgart and Paris. On the contrary, Germany can pay punctually only if more than 50 marks in gold go to France. In anticipation of this the Reichsbank raises its discount rate, which immediately lowers the German price level up to the frontier. For opposite reasons the Bank of France will just as quickly force a general increase in prices. Whereas the price waves approach one another slowly, the areas of falling and rising price levels meet almost instantaneously (at least with neighboring countries). This causes a rapid and considerable transfer of goods, which probably takes place chiefly in the border regions. We shall disregard the capital movements that also are released and assume that 700 marks in gold and 300 in merchandise are transferred at first, which must be paid when the German payment comes due.

Third: Effects After the Due Date (Early Total Transfer). Although the disturbing payment has now been completed, the transfer is by no means finished. For the price shifts still continue: the price waves because they are still too far apart to neutralize one another entirely, and the relative shift in price levels because there are still 700 marks in German gold in France. As long as the change in the German relative to the French price level persists, the German export surplus will continue beyond the original due date. But now it must be paid by France in cash since the 1,000 marks have long since been paid, partly in gold and partly in goods; that is, all but 50 marks of the German gold flows back from France, price levels return to their former height,[18] the German export surplus dries up, and after a further 650 marks' worth of goods has been shipped the transfer of goods appears completed.

(bb) *The Final Transfer.* But the price waves started around Paris and Stuttgart by the shift in purchasing power are still on their way, and approach one another. Even during this process they are partially equalized, and completely so when they meet, as has already been described. This levelling off of increased and

---

17. Thus a gold shipment to this extent has no further influence on prices in addition to that of the transfer of purchasing power.

18. Only mathematically is the French price level slightly higher than before because of the continued increase in the amount of money by 1,000 marks; and vice versa for the German price level.

Self-Regulation 279

decreased purchasing power represents the genuine transfer of goods that takes place in any case, whereas a preliminary transfer, which must be sharply distinguished from it, is *added* only with a certain type of monetary system.[19]

(cc) *The Reaction.* Thus 950 marks in goods were transferred twice: the first time as the result of the change in relative price levels, the second with the neutralizing of the price waves. Thus there is *one* transfer *too many*. If France orders an additional 1,000 marks' worth of German products when one of the two waves crosses the frontier, she would have to pay partly in gold and partly in goods, and finally up to 50 marks in the former and 950 in the latter. Hence exactly as much French gold flows temporarily into Germany as she lost of her own gold in the beginning, except for those 50 marks, which cover the price waves; this gold movement alone is not reversible, because the price waves are not. Thereupon the German price level rises above the French by as much as it was below this before. So in the final settlement the exact mirror image of the original preliminary transfer is repeated. Later the whole process is again undone. Although technically necessary with credit creation (when it resulted in redeemable local money), in a deeper sense it was superfluous. The preliminary transfer and the subsequent reaction cancel out, and neutralization of the waves of purchasing power remains the sole essential feature in the entire transfer.

2. THE SIGNIFICANCE FOR TRANSFER OF THE EXTENT OF CREDIT CREATION, AND OF DIFFERENCES IN CURRENCY

(aa) *Various Possibilities in the Construction of Currencies.* Where local money has but little international means of payment as cover (as with credit creation), or none at all (as with paper currencies), payment on the due date offers a special problem for the debtor as well as for the debtor country, which is solved by the preliminary transfer. We shall now compare it for the whole scale from complete to zero cover, always under the assumption that the

---

19. Additional local money must be created, which is redeemable in generally accepted money. The local money must be *additional*, at least in part; it must not simply replace international money. The additional money must be local money. The creation of more generally accepted money has different effects. The local money must be redeemable, otherwise there arises no necessity to destroy it. Though not necessary, it is usual for this creation of local money to take place in the process of credit creation.

currencies of debtor and creditor countries are similarly constructed and that the reserve ratio, like the exchange rate, is strictly maintained.

Suppose once more that 1,000 marks are to be sent from Stuttgart to Paris. (I) If transfers are made in hoarded gold and the receiver hoards it in turn, no price fluctuation will be necessary.[20] (II) If the local money is 100 per cent covered by gold in both countries, but this time the amount owed has to be withdrawn from circulation, both price waves due to the shift in purchasing power will be started; the immediate payment, however, will likewise be made at first almost entirely in gold, into which the local money accumulated by the debtor can be converted without further trouble. (III) If there is a 10 per cent bank-note coverage behind deposit money and the bank notes in turn are fully covered by gold, we have the typical case of intranational trade, already described above, also in international trade. Now the local money can no longer be simply converted into gold; on the contrary, gold shipment reacts tenfold on the amount of deposits. To the extent of 10,000 marks the creation of local money must be reversed in the one country and brought about in the other. A shift in the price level takes place in addition to price waves. Perhaps 200 marks will now be transferred in goods, and only the remainder in gold. (IV) if the gold cover of the notes is only 50 per cent a gold shipment of 800 marks will change the amount of notes by 1600 marks and the amount of deposits by 16,000 marks. Price levels will shift still more than in the preceding case, because the remainder that is paid in gold has twenty times the effect on the monetary circulation. Whereas in the first case 1,000 marks were transferred in gold, in the second almost 1,000, and in the third at least 800, it is now perhaps 700 marks. (V) With a pure paper currency no monetary gold will be shipped; on the contrary, the 1,000 marks will have to be sent entirely in goods up to the due date. Moreover, there occurs the greatest shift in price levels that can accompany the transfer of this amount.

Decreasing reserve ratios or, which amounts to the same thing, increasing the creation of local money, therefore means a growing risk that this creation will have to be temporarily reversed.[21] There

---

20. This is immediately true when gold flows from the hoard of the debtor to that of the creditor. If it flows from the hoard of one to that of another bank of issue it is true only when both neutralize the effects of the shift in purchasing power by their credit policy.

21. It is therefore no meaningless caprice of the currency mechanism when countries

is but one alternative: a fluctuating exchange rate. Then the relative change in prices takes place through this instead of directly.[22,23]

As paper currencies are conceivable also without credit creation and as fluctuations in the price level, either directly or through the exchange rate, are especially pronounced with paper currencies, their causes must lie even deeper than we have been assuming until now. They consist in currency differences in the widest sense; that is, in the fact that all, or at least the created, means of payment of the one banking area are invalid in that of another bank.[24] Thus there

---

with low reserve ratios have to resign themselves to wide price fluctuations. This is the natural drawback of their extensive creation of credit.

22. This would not contradict in the least our assumption of a fixed reserve ratio. For whether the amount of local money, and with it the price level, is lowered by one tenth because of a gold loss of 10 per cent of the reserve, or whether the price of gold, expressed in local money is raised by one tenth (for a 10 per cent depreciation can mean only this) so that the physically diminished gold reserve will regain its former nominal value and the amount of local money can thus be left unchanged, the actual reserve ratio is the same in both cases. We must accustom ourselves to the idea that the individual features of the old-fashioned gold standard, such as fixed reserve ratios and exchange rates, do not necessarily go hand in hand. (See my article, " Die Lehre vom Transfer—neu gefasst," *Jahrbücher für Nationalökonomie*, CLIV [1941], 395, note 1). Paper currencies too (no reserves) may be accompanied by fixed or fluctuating exchange rates.

23. The difference appears especially in the difficulties of transfer. When a creditor country buys nothing from a debtor country in spite of an enormous drop in the exchange rate, the latter cannot pay if the debt exceeds its gold supply, but its economy goes on as though nothing had happened. With fixed exchange rates, on the other hand, the debtor country will be bankrupt, not only externally, but also at home because of the severe deflationary crisis. It is clear that the cause of transfer difficulties lies in sales alone. With dissimilar currencies they appear earlier, to be sure, and the *smaller* the reserve ratio, the greater are their secondary deflationary effects because the fewer the installments that can be paid at first out of the supply of international means of payments, the more the gold drain alters the amount of local money. The more inflexible the reserve ratio, here more quickly the secondary effects begin to appear, but they are avoidable with variable exchange rates and thus not to be ascribed to the currency difference itself. Only for fixed exchange rates does F. W. Meyer (*Der Ausgleich der Zahlungsbilanz* [Jena, 1938], p. 111) correctly make the distinction that the gold cover may be insignificant for restraining the creation of money but that for international payments, on the contrary, its size must be appropriate to the gravity of the disturbances. Moreover, even with the old-fashioned gold standard, thanks to fluctuations between the gold points, price fluctuations will be replaced at least in small part by fluctuations in the exchange rate, an advantage that would be abolished by international clearing through BIS (Bank for International Settlements), as W. Sulzbach has emphasized (" Der wirtschaftliche Begriff des Auslands," *Weltwirtschaftliches Archiv*, XXXII [1930], p. 75).

24. Hence one must think here not only of the bank notes of various countries, but also of differences within countries. For instance, the notes of Federal Reserve Banks in the United States are returned to the issuer when they reach another Federal Reserve

is a slow transition between gold and paper currency. *The greater the supply of international means of payment (gold cover), the smaller are price fluctuations at first and the greater the movement of gold, and vice versa* (Table 15).[25,26]

Table 15

	Construction of Currency				Preliminary Transfer by	
		Gold cover of notes	Note circulation	Deposits (fractional) reserves by notes)	Gold movement	Price movement
I	Gold currency	Excess	Yes	Immaterial	Decreasing	Zero
II		100%		No		
III		100%				Increasing
IV		99–1%		Yes		
V	Paper currency	0			Zero	

These differences lose some of their significance, however, since in all cases even the preliminary transfer must be made in goods. As a consequence price changes are more lasting the smaller they are; that is to say, it takes all the longer for the great stream of gold to flow back again. The sole remaining difference between transfer with dissimilar and similar currencies is that with the former (paper currency) the transfer takes place immediately in goods, whereas with partial (gold currencies) or complete similarity (intranational trade or a world currency) it is distributed over a longer period.

District. This was the case also with the notes of the Bavarian and Württemberg banks of issue. The deposit money of a bank is invalid outside the circle of its customers. Conversely, the circulating media of different currency systems may have equal value in practical dealings. Thus American bills, and to some extent Canadian as well, are usually accepted at face value throughout a rather wide zone along the border, and the coins, in particular, of both countries are so similar that they can be used in slot machines on either side of the line.

25. Poor nations that can afford only a small gold cover therefore do well to go over to "free" rates of exchange, which render the wide price fluctuations considerably less harmful.

26. There is a second and different reason, based only on frictional difficulties, why price fluctuations are smaller with a high gold cover. As the shift in the prices of goods and the reaction of foreign trade to it require time, whereas nominal transfer must take place immediately, in all cases the largest part of the payment, neglecting short-term captital movements, will be transferred at first in gold until the transfer of goods begins. But approximately the same gold movement has less effect with a higher than with a lower gold cover. For this reason a high gold cover is more favorable with fixed exchanges.

The shift in price levels in the first case is therefore sharper and shorter, in the second weaker but more lasting. In brief, *the more uniform the currency, the more slowly preliminary transfer in goods takes place.*[27]

(bb) *Creditor and Debtor Countries Have Differently Constructed Currencies.* When the degrees of cover are unequal, the actual shift in price levels and the effect on each country, varies with the degree of cover.[28] Table 16 shows, first, what we have already seen in the last section: That the higher the gold coverage with one participant in a transaction, or even with both, the larger the portion of the resulting payment through gold movement alone.

Table 16. TRANSFER WITH DIFFERENT RESERVE RATIOS

	1		2	3		4
	Note Coverage in Gold, %		Gold Shipment, Marks from A to B	Price Fluctuation %		Price Difference B over A %
	A	B		A	B	
1	10	10	200	−20	+20	50
2	10	40	260	−26	+ 7	44
3	40	10	300	− 8	+30	41
4	30	50	490	−16	+10	31
5	40	40	500	−12	+12	28

Explanation: Column 2: The order of magnitude, but not its gradation, is arbitrary.
Column 3: A total note circulation of 10,000 marks in each country is assumed. Deposits are supposed to be nonexistent. Country A and Country B are supposed to be equally large.

The table shows further that when only one of the participants (cases 2 and 3) has a greater coverage than in the comparison case (1), price fluctuations are smaller for him, and greater for his partner, than in case 1. A high reserve ratio gives the same gold flow a smaller effect on prices than a lower ratio.[29]

---

27. In our former example it took place slowly outward across the Württemberg frontier, because reichmarks were valid on both sides. Beyond the national frontier it took place quickly, because of dissimilarities in currency.

28. Temporary differences in the full utilization of note coverage resemble lasting differences in it. These differences may be unintended. With a 50 per cent gold coverage in each of two countries the shipment of 1,000 marks in gold may cause a change of 2,000 marks in the amount of notes in one if it is on the upswing, in the other of hardly 1,000 if it is in a depression.

29. This among other things explains the slight reaction of prices in gold movements in the United States and France, where the actual, if not the legal, gold coverage of notes is very high and, in addition, deposits in central banks have to be partly

It forms a cushion against the effects of cyclical changes originating abroad and of international capital movements. It moderates deflationary crises and inflationary upswings, though in return it prolongs them. Indeed, it even mitigates the deterioration of the barter terms of trade of the debtor (that is, his increased cost of imports compared with his exports). For we do not get the same result when we interchange the reserve ratios of debtors and creditors (compare cases 2 and 3). If we were to assume that in case 2, as in case 3, 300 marks in gold had been shipped, and that prices therefore fell in A by 30 per cent and rose in B by 8 per cent, so that in comparison with case 3 only the roles of A and B had been interchanged, the end result would still not be the same. In contrast with the original situation ($= 100$), in case 2 the prices in A would stand at 70 and in B at 108, or 54 per cent above those in A; in case 3 at 92 in A and 130 in B, or only 41 per cent above those in A. If equilibrium prevails in case 3; that is, if the price difference is just enough to cause 700 marks' worth more exports from A to B, which together with 300 marks in gold is exactly equal to the amount of the debt; then the export surplus in case 2 would necessarily be more than 700 marks. The price change therefore went too far; less than 300 marks in gold would suffice to compel the remaining transfer of goods. Nevertheless the gold shipment is large enough to raise prices in B by 44 per cent above those in A, instead of by only 41 per cent as in case 3.

Interchange between a country with paper [30] and one with gold currency takes place according to the rules that prevail with different reserve ratios. Gold shipments are reduced to a minimum.[31] We have already discussed the different price fluctuations.

Of course these differences are only temporary. (1) The larger

---

covered by gold. The great accumulations of gold in these countries are not explained thereby, since according to the table it is not the creditor whose actual coverage is far above that of its debtor (Case 2) who receives large shipments of gold, but the one that has a debtor also with a high coverage (Case 5). In addition this gold should flow back to the country whence it first came.

30. Here fixed cover excludes an exchange stabilization fund consisting of monetary gold, which with variable reserve ratios moderates price level changes even when the country formally has a paper currency.

31. The same is true when paper currency is associated with variable exchange rates. If the debtor country has a gold currency, whereas in the creditor country the price rise includes also the commodity gold, gold will flow temporarily to the latter from the debtor country and from other countries as well. Conversely, when the debtor country has a paper currency, so that its price fall includes that of gold too, commercial gold will flow into the creditor country and into other countries with a fixed gold price.

the gold shipments and therefore the smaller the price and commodity movements at first, the longer will these movements persist before the preliminary transfer has been completed entirely in goods. *Thus higher note coverage does not decrease the necessary transfer of goods, but merely distributes it in time.* As a result, the terms of trade of the debtor remain unfavorable longer, the less they deteriorate at first because of large gold shipments. This means however, that the same quantity of goods can be transferred at lower cost on the whole when the transfer is distributed over several economic periods. *Thus higher note coverage lowers the cost of preliminary transfer.* (2) This is not of much importance, of course, as long as these costs are made good in the reaction. But with different constructions of currency this need no longer be invariably the case. Consider once more situations 2 and 3 in Table 16. With the preliminary transfer the terms of trade of A deteriorate more (price difference 44 per cent) than they improve in the reaction (price difference 41 per cent).[32] Accordingly, the statement that higher note coverage decreases transfer costs has a truer meaning than would appear at first sight. In the final judgment it should be remembered, however, that the higher note coverage, too, had to be accumulated at some time, with transfer losses or the foregoing of transfer gains. When this process, which has generally occurred far in the past, is taken into account also, it turns out that *in the final analysis the construction of a currency is immaterial for the transfer.*[33] If the past is disregarded, however, the possibility cannot be rejected that despite the cost in interest of a large gold

32. A and B must be imagined as interchanged in case 3 of the table since we are supposed to be dealing with the same participants as in case 2, only with transfer in the other direction.

33. In common with Lutz, F. W. Meyer ("Devisenbewirtschaftung als neue Währungsform," *Weltwirtschaftliches Archiv*, XLIX [1939], 415–471) has skillfully defended the thesis that the gold standard could no longer function today because, among other things, countries often endeavor to sterilize the effects of gold movements out of cyclical considerations. In other words, they act as though their reserve ratios were considerably higher. Now although this results in larger gold shipments, most of the gold, even with protracted unilateral payments, soon flows back again to the debtor, whose prices compared with those of the creditor and in contrast with the prevailing view, need fall less than if gold movements could affect the credit structure (see Table 16). Basically it remains true nevertheless that the construction of a currency (and the sterilization of gold movements means only a supplementary change in this construction) is immaterial for the transfer in the final analysis. A policy of sterilization becomes dangerous only when it attempts also to neutralize the shift in purchasing power proper (not only its multiple effect on the credit structure); that is, when it tries to prevent the origin of the waves of purchasing power that bring about actual **transfer**.

reserve, price fluctuations and transfer costs hit poor countries very much harder than rich ones.

(cc) *Summary.* With different monetary standards (that is, when there are various local monies that are only partially covered by international means of payment), even those wholly unconcerned in a transfer (the entire debtor and creditor country) co-operate at first with the individual economies concerned (debtors and creditors) in making the transfer. The central bank of the debtor must make the necessary international money available on the payment date, and with a fixed reserve ratio this can be done only if it recalls or devalues a certain amount of its local money. Both courses release part of its international money, one by decreasing the amount of local money to be covered, the other by increasing the value of covering international money. Both provide it, in addition, with more international money by reducing prices in the region where its local money circulates compared with those abroad, thus increasing the export of goods. Compared with the second (additional exports), the first source of gold (freed cover) flows more abundantly the higher coverage, especially its own. With fixed reserve ratios the creditor bank *must* support these endeavors of the debtor bank. All these events are repeated in the opposite direction during the reaction and leave no permanent effect.

3. APPLICATION OF THE NEW THEORY

Our train of thought carries such wide implications, yet corresponds so little with the traditional view, that it may be good to apply it to a few important examples.

(aa) *Do International Obligations of a Part Mean Injury to the Whole?* Does Stuttgart, in our preceding example, reduce the foreign exchange for the whole country by its payment abroad? Does it shift the costs of transfer to others? The old theory of international trade, which regarded the preliminary transfer as the sole and final one, would have to answer in the affirmative. Unquestionably it is the function of an increase in the German discount rate to expedite the transfer by drawing in also those who are not concerned in it; that is, all those within the sphere of influence of the Reichsbank, not only those situated in the Stuttgart wave of falling prices. It worsens the barter terms of trade also for those who either have already shifted their share in the loss of purchasing power to others or who, with a uniform currency, would have had nothing at all to do with the transfer. But we now know that this deterioration is only temporary, and that it will be compensated later by an equally great improvement. The contributions of non-participants in the transfer are not permanent. The whole is not burdened by the acts of individuals.

(bb) *The Results of Transfer Aid for Those That It Favors.* In contrast to the situation where Paris and Stuttgart lie within an area in which the same simple metal currency is valid and nothing occurs, therefore, save the final transfer, *additional* price fluctuations appear in Stuttgart also. The smaller the sphere of influence of the central issuing bank, the sharper are these fluctuations. If Württemberg had still had its own issuing bank and had sent gold directly to London, the rise in the Württemberg discount rate would have been much greater than in that of the Reichsbank, because the same amount of gold would have meant for little Württemberg a disproportionately greater loss than for the whole country. Compared with this situation (case *A*), the co-operation of the entire country (case *B*) has *moderated* the price fluctuations in Württemberg.[34] Hence in case *B* prices in Württemberg are higher, and in the rest of the country lower, than in case *A*. As a consequence it takes longer for Württemberg to achieve the export surplus required even for the preliminary transfer. The co-operation of the entire country does not relieve Württemberg of the preliminary transfer,[35] but facilitates this transfer in so far as it helps to spread it over a longer period of time. Prices in Württemberg have to remain lower for a longer time, though the decline is less. Nevertheless, even in case *B* they are still below German prices as a whole: (*a*) because of decreased purchasing power, and (*b*) because of a restriction in bank credits consequent upon the decreased circulation of notes due to this decline in purchasing power. This restriction in bank credits is *in addition to* the general national restriction, which is associated with a reduction in the gold reserve.

(cc) *The Extent of the Preliminary Transfer.* For various reasons the preliminary transfer does not assume the proportions of the final one.

1. It does not take place if debtors and creditors make early arrangements in anticipation of payment, which unintentionally

---

34. Unless similar disturbances started simultaneously in all parts of the country. As a rule, however, the larger the currency area (at least until it includes about half the world), the more of these will be opposite and compensatory.

35. For so far as deposit money exists such a preliminary transfer still remains to be carried out between Württemberg and the remainder of the country.

provide the debtor bank with additional foreign exchange until the date of settlement.[36] If we disregard capital movements because they merely postpone the problem, the debtor must bring about an export surplus of the size of the payment. This may be done by decreased buying (his imports), as when he keeps a smaller stock on hand; restriction of his enterprise; relinquishment of plans to enlarge his factory, and the like; and by increasing his exports. The former lowers wages and the prices of imported goods; the latter, the prices of the debtor's products.

In expectation of payment the creditor also will make certain arrangements. He will install new machines, hire workers, and order an addition to his building. This will raise somewhat the prices of his imports, and local wages in particular, even before the actual payment. Thanks to this anticipatory behavior on both sides there is, on the one hand, a German export surplus in consequence of the mere shift in purchasing power; for example, because the debtor restricts among other things his purchase of goods that formerly were imported into Germany.[37]

On the other hand, price waves begin their course, which is accompanied by a gradual transfer of goods, even before the transfer of cash is to be made. It is important to note that this need not necessarily be a *final* transfer; that is, an *equalization* of increased and decreased purchasing power. As we have already seen, the movement of the waves of purchasing power is nothing but the result and cause of a lasting transfer of goods. It might be called an "advancing wave transfer." As soon as the wave of price reductions, or probably in this case merely its forerunner, has passed the national frontier, the transfer of goods is to this extent completed for *Germany*, although the final equalization may not occur, perhaps, until later, and far from the frontier, in Lorraine or even deeper in France. So far as shifts in purchasing power and price waves caused a final transfer of goods across the German frontier, a certain amount of money is already available on the date of payment, and to this extent a "preliminary transfer" is superfluous.[38]

---

36. Applied to our former example, the preparation for (Stuttgart) or expectation of (Paris) a transfer of cash increases the supply of foreign exchange in Berlin, and only with the remainder of its demand for foreign exchange does Stuttgart raise the rate of exchange for the franc until it reaches the upper gold point.

37. In countries that specialize in the production of one or a few goods, as is often the case in South America for example, a falling off in the demand for one of these exports may automatically cause a decrease in imports. See H. Backe, *Um die Nahrungsfreiheit Europas* (Leipzig, 1942), p. 75.

38. Strictly speaking, therefore, even in a final transfer of goods one must distin-

2. The preliminary transfer can be replaced to a certain extent by short-term *capital movements*. These not only postpone the transfer problem temporarily, as followed from the classical view, but obviate the (strictly speaking) superfluous preliminary transfer. This is desirable because of the unfortunate secondary effects of shifts in the price levels. The following types of credit have this result: (1) Those based on a shift in purchasing power or the waves of interest to which it gives rise. The credits must expire as soon as the reaction would have set in. In so far as this serves to discharge the credits (at most up to half the debt), the preliminary transfer becomes superfluous. (2) Credits between central banks, except when not only is the preliminary transfer thereby avoided but the effects of waves of purchasing power are compensated in addition. Otherwise preliminary transfer would not be avoided, but merely postponed. In our example either the credit must not exceed 950 marks, else the Reichsbank would be able to bring the 1,000 marks withdrawn from circulation in Stuttgart back into circulation by granting an equal amount of new credits; or the 1,000 marks can be credited in full if Berlin withdraws them from circulation and sterilizes them, and Paris, nevertheless, pays them out to the buyer.[39] The credit must expire as soon as one of the two waves of falling prices passes the German frontier, thus providing an additional amount in foreign exchange of 1,000 gold marks.[40] (3) Partial crediting of the debt through the creditor (payment by installments). With continuing payments a preliminary transfer is necessary only until the first price waves have reached the frontier.[41] Then the yield of foreign exchange from the passage of price waves beyond the frontier is sufficient to make good the current transfer

---

guish: (1) between a mere "advancing wave transfer" and a final equalization of increased and decreased purchasing power (concluding, or final, transfer of goods in the narrow sense); and, (2) in both cases between such a transfer within and beyond currency boundaries.

39. Example: obligatory clearing credits. See my article, "Die Lehre vom Transfer— neu gefasst," *Jahrbücher für Nationalökonomie*, CLIV (1941), 400 f.

40. This recalls the procedure employed with the reparations payments, except that then the tribute money collected by the Reichsbank did not have to be sterilized—upon which everything depended.

41. If payments are repeated at sufficiently short intervals the waves become a continuous price drop. The price differential around health resorts during their season, for example, is of this type. The *high* prices in such places result not only from the influx of purchasing power, however, but also from the fact that their season is very short. It is also important that production for their own consumption, like that in towns populated by *rentiers* is comparatively small, so that their supply areas have to be greatly extended during the season.

of cash. From this moment on the regions that are not concerned are eliminated again from the transfer mechanism. The reaction does not follow, of course, until payments have ceased. Unlike those described, such credit movements, which are due to the discount policies of central banks, are not a substitute for but only a special form of the preliminary transfer.[42]

3. If some waves of purchasing power pass beyond the German frontier after the due date, but before all German gold has returned, an appropriate amount of gold serves to pay for the German exports which have increased with that passage. To this extent the export surplus thus disappears because of the relative change in the price level. The *interference* subsequently reduces the extent of the preliminary transfer of goods, and consequently also the reaction.[43]

(dd) *Is the Transfer Aid Necessary?* When the legal or economically advisable reserves are fully used in the creation of notes or deposits, the bank authorities cannot chose whether or not to co-operate in the preliminary transfer. With a reduction of the reserve they *must* raise the discount rate. If, on the other hand, the reserves are sufficient, so that both central banks can sterilize [44] the gold movements, the situation is exactly as with a purely metallic currency: The preliminary cash transfer is not, nor need it be, associated with any sort of transfer of goods. It is accomplished simply out of the excess reserves, and the circulation of money is decreased only by those means of payment that are withdrawn from circulation when the debtor accumulates the amount to be paid.

It is not quite so easy to judge the absence of the transfer aid when only the creditor, but not the debtor, can sterilize gold movements; that is, when these lead to a fall in the debtor's price level. This drop results in a smaller export surplus than if prices in the creditor country had risen at the same time. Consequently a larger

---

42. See "Die Lehre vom Transfer—neu gefasst," *Jahrbücher für Nationalökonomie*, CLIV (1941), 391 f.

43. See my article "Um eine neue Transfertheorie. Zur Verteidigung der alten Lehre durch Fritz Meyer," *Jahrbücher für Nationalökonomie*, 1943, pp. 23–25, a reply to Fritz Meyer, "Eine neue Transfertheorie?" *Archiv für Wirtschaftsplanung*, I (1941), 171–180.

44. It is only reasonable to prevent a shift in price levels by foregoing a change in the discount rate, but not to prevent price waves by open market operations. Moreover, it would be a mistake to believe that the effect of an influx of gold on purchasing power can *always* be compensated by issuing government bonds instead of bank notes. If the economy wants more money, credit will be created to the limits of possibility, the bank discount rate will rise and attract foreign money, more gold will flow in, and it will become increasingly difficult to counteract its effects by issuing more bonds, because the prices of previous issues have fallen.

part of the preliminary transfer will consist at first of gold, and a smaller part of goods, despite a sharper drop in prices. The sterilization policy of the creditor hurts the debtor through the unfortunate effects of such a particularly great and lasting fall in prices. In the case of large sums the severity of the price decline, and with it the success of the preliminary transfer depends essentially upon whether or not the central bank of the creditor provides transfer aid.

(ee) *Whom Do Transfer Costs Affect?* The advance of both waves of purchasing power is associated with shifts in prices, and hence in incomes, that are partly their result and partly their cause. We shall call them "transfer costs" and "transfer gains." As for the two parties chiefly concerned, two cases must be distinguished: (1) If debtor and creditor are pure consumers, that is, if we deal with payment without an immediate offsetting payment, the effects of a transfer are exhausted by a temporary fall in prices where the debtor reduces his purchases, and a rise where the creditor buys more. All purchases become cheaper for the payer and dearer for the payee. *The debtor makes a transfer gain, the creditor suffers a loss. Their suppliers are affected in the opposite way.* (2) It is different when those principally concerned are themselves producers and a debt for goods is to be paid, as was assumed in connection with Fig. 57. Then it is probable that *the debtor will bear a transfer burden.* For he has bought at a higher price from the creditor B_1, though more cheaply from his former supplier B, as set forth above, and he will reduce his own prices in order to raise the additional amount. Conversely, the creditor will make a transfer gain, which will be limited, however, by the fact that his increased demand makes the services of his workers and sellers more expensive. The change in the selling prices of those chiefly concerned diminishes, though in small measure, the losses or profits of their sellers in so far as these in turn buy from them. Even for those chiefly concerned, this business connection means too little for the change in purchasing power of their workers and sellers to be noticeable at first. With time, of course, both will shift part of their loss or gain in purchasing power to others in the manner already described, thereby diminishing their disadvantage or advantage. At the same time, though to a smaller degree, the price movement will be passed on to the regular customers of those chiefly concerned, which increases their transfer gains or losses.[45] The remainder taking part

---

45. The severity of the repercussions varies according to how closely and elastically business is connected with the source of the movement. It is probable that their strength will decrease with distance from it.

in the advancing wave transfer will be less affected by the losses and gains the farther removed they are from the points of origin, for price changes decrease with distance, as we have seen. But it is not true that all those in the region of a wave of rising prices will make transfer gains and all those in other regions will undergo transfer losses. If the environs of Paris and Stuttgart are divided into rings those buyers in every ring about Stuttgart who made the advance possible will gain, and the sellers who have to force the advance will lose. Conversely around Paris. Now as almost everyone is both buyer and seller, he makes transfer gains only when he loses less by the cheapening of his own goods than he gains through the cheapening of other goods. This is the case with Stuttgart in all except the two innermost rings, which include the debtor and his suppliers, since the transfer costs decrease from ring to ring and buyers thus gain the higher transfer costs from the ring preceding their own, whereas sellers bear the lower costs of advance to the next ring. The sum of these net gains, which decrease with distance, is equal to the loss sustained by the suppliers of the debtor.

The situation at the German frontier remains to be clarified. Buyers in the German frontier ring gain from Germans, that is, from sellers in the preceding ring, whereas sellers lose to Frenchmen, that is, to buyers in the French frontier ring. Thus in the German frontier ring, as in all others, there is a transfer gain, but for Germany as a whole a transfer loss results, though it is not very great because the frontier lies far away from Stuttgart.[46] In contradistinction to political frontiers, no income shifts appear at all on economic frontiers, where the two waves of purchasing power meet, because here the final settlement is completed without changes in price.

One more significant error in the old theory remains to be corrected. In so far as the creditor buys simply what the debtor has relinquished, the transfer of goods was thought to succeed through mere transfer of purchasing power without change of price. This argument disregards the importance of distance. In Fig. 56, page —, let B_2A_1 be the radius of the former supply area of the debtor, and let B_1A_1 be the same for the creditor. Because of the transfer of purchasing power, prices fall in B_2, whereas they stiffen in B_1. The new price cones are hatched. The region between A_1 and A_2, which formerly supplied B_2, does indeed fall to the creditor;

---

46. The old theory recognized only this loss at the frontier, and overestimated it because it was equated with the loss of the seller in the innermost ring. Moreover, it confused the losses during preliminary transfer, later made good, with the final losses.

but only at one single point C is the price received by the seller still the old one.[47] To the right of it the sellers lose, to the left of it they gain, exactly as we have concluded in general for regions with a loss or gain in purchasing power.

(ff) *Significance of the Size of a Country.* All bank customers, and especially those of the central bank, constitute a transfer community, since means of payment circulate among them that are invalid with outsiders. The smaller such a community is, the more is it at first affected by a transfer, but because of the compensatory effect of the reaction this fact can be of consequence only as a result of frictional difficulties. For it is not countries or service areas of banks that take part in exchange and are affected in the end by its mechanism, but individual economic units. Geographic differences prevail eventually against movements that for technical reasons are at first nationwide [see (bb)].

(gg) *Depreciation.* Like a change in the discount rate of the central bank, a change in the exchange rate affects an *entire* country even when caused by only a part of it. Suppose that upon repayment of a large loan by a Berlin firm to a London banking house, the Reichsbank prefers depreciating the exchange rate by 20 per cent to a sharp increase in the discount rate. As soon as the preliminary transfer has been completed the exchange rate goes up again to its former level, and even higher during the reaction. If the Reichsbank wished to maintain the lower rate, German prices would have to rise instead. When through depreciation one aims merely to avoid such price fluctuations, it is wrong to adhere forever to the lower rate of exchange.

Let us compare exchange depreciation to facilitate transfer with the results of a depreciation to revive the economy. If a 20 per cent depreciation is assumed in both cases, the price levels will eventually rise by 20 per cent in both. But what will happen before matters have gone this far is decidedly different. (1) According to *extent:* With transfer the price level rises in the reaction by as much as 40 per cent, but with a depreciation for cyclical reasons never by more than 20 per cent. (2) According to *direction:* With transfer the calculated price average falls at first because of the wave of lower prices, and again later when the reaction subsides (from 40 to 20 per cent above the old level), whereas with a cyclical revival

---

47. Only when the supply in A_1 is very large, so that the shift in demand is expressed solely by the fact that B_1 and B_2 are now supplied in different proportions, will no price change occur.

and without the necessity of a reaction, the price level always rises continuously. (3) *Geographically:* The manner in which the rise of the price level is accomplished is the same in both cases, to be sure, yet instructive enough to be examined more closely in the case of a depreciation for cyclical reasons. Depreciation lowers domestic prices at first compared with those abroad. The foreign, and with it the total demand increases; so, too, do prices therefore in both domestic and foreign currency. But they do not rise uniformly. As a rule, though not necessarily, the smaller exports were before depreciation relative to domestic sales, the less important will be the increase in foreign demand and the less prices need rise in consequence. For this reason the price rise, and with it the revival is regionally quite different at first, but with time it is diffused from the region and the branches of business first affected, to all equally. At last, if we disregard secondary cyclical effects, all prices except interest rates will rise in the same proportion as the rate of exchange has been lowered.

This second phase is hard to demonstrate in concrete cases, because it appears so late that new events distort the picture again. The first phase, however, is well shown by the example of the American depreciation. In 1935, as compared with 1932, the year preceding the depreciation, the prices of such typically domestic goods as fuel and furniture rose least, the former by $4\frac{1}{2}$ per cent.[48] Industrial goods of which a few were exported rose more: e. g., textiles by 29 per cent. The greatest increase was shown by agricultural products with a high export quota; cotton, for example, of which more than half the crop is exported, rose in price at New Orleans by 87 per cent.[49] The still greater increase in the case of wheat, almost none of which was exported, was caused by failure of the harvest.[50] Measures to limit the acreage under cultivation also played a role, though not a decisive one.

Hence depreciation benefited most America's great depressed area, the cotton-raising South which, conversely, had been hardest hit earlier by the depression. The situation of the cotton grower was naturally communicated to the prices of the goods he used, but not in such a way as to change them immediately and uniformly throughout the whole United States; on the contrary, they reacted most strongly first at the seat of the cause. Thus up to 1932 the retail prices of food had fallen 33 to 37 per cent below those of 1929

---

48. See *U. S. Statistical Abstract*, 1936, p. 299.
49. *U. S. Department of Agriculture, Agricultural Statistics*, 1936, p. 83.
50. See S. E. Harris, *Exchange Depreciation* (Cambridge, Mass., 1936), p. 341.

in the individual census regions comprising the main industrial belt: New England, Middle Atlantic, East North Central. By comparison, they had fallen in the cotton belt, i. e., the South Atlantic, East South Central, and West South Central States, by 35 to 39 per cent. Conversely, in the industrial area in 1935 they were 15 to 20 percent and in the cotton belt 20 to 22 per cent above those of 1932.[51]

The same result emerges in a comparison of the cost of living for workers in six cities of the industrial area (Boston, Buffalo, New York, Philadelphia, Chicago, and Cleveland) with those for six in the cotton belt (Atlanta, Houston, Memphis, Mobile, New Orleans, and Savannah). Between 1929 and 1932 they fell 20 to 26 per cent in the industrial area, to 22 to 27 percent in the cotton belt, and rose 3 to 6 per cent in the former in 1932–1935 and 4 to 10 per cent in the latter.[52]

It must not be forgotten, however, that the export quota merely determined the rate at which the prices of various goods eventually adapted themselves equally to the depreciation. With transfer, the price average adjusts itself in the described manner more slowly and among regions less uniformly. The fault lies with the wave of lowered prices, which is added to the true shift in price level and changes the arithmetical average.

First, it is clear that the original price fall relative to other countries in the part of Germany affected by loss of purchasing power (spreading outward from Berlin in our example) is greater by the effects of this loss. But even within the Berlin economic area there are differences. In the first place, the prices of the repaying industries decline. Even later, when the price drop is being transferred to other businesses, a difference remains compared with the debt-paying branches. The change in local prices depends, therefore, entirely on the industries of the place concerned: those primarily affected by the lower prices, those only moderately affected, or those that are wholly untouched. The price level of the Berlin area does not fall evenly, but by separate drops here and there.

Even within the market areas of the industries particularly affected the price drop is not uniform. As a rule, production costs in the industries concerned have to fall more sharply (though not equally in all branches) than shipping costs, which also depend upon sales in other businesses. Consequently prices drop by the

---

51. Calculated from *U. S. Bureau of Labor Statistics, Retail Prices, Serial No. R 384*, pp. 8–9.

52. Calculated from *U. S. Statistical Abstract*, 1935, p. 298. Original data from the Bureau of Labor Statistics.

largest percentage at the site of production and less sharply on the borders of the market area; because freight, which has hardly decreased, is an important factor there. In addition, the whole wave of lower prices eventually draws away from Berlin and flattens out as it hits other places.

Finally, instead of paying attention to these local differences, let us compare the calculated average for the economic landscapes of Germany regardless of the causes of its change. Although German prices as a whole fall at first compared with foreign prices, those in Munich rise at once compared with those in Berlin, if we regard Berlin as representative of the part of Germany affected, and Munich as representative of the temporarily unaffected part; that is, not yet reached by the wave. Gradually the depreciation, which for no reason at all has lowered Munich export prices also by 20 per cent, leads by way of the resulting export surplus and decline of imports to the restraining rise in the price level that has been described above. Penetrating from the frontier to the interior of Germany, it equalizes again the fall in the exchange rate for the whole country in so far as this is not actually affected by the ebb in purchasing power originating in Berlin; and later, during the reaction, more than equalizes it. This last difference in price levels persists, even though between changing regions, until the wave has receded from Germany.

From all this it follows that repayment of a foreign loan first raises and then lowers the German price level *on the average*; but that *within* Germany, within its great economic areas, within individual small market areas, and even within single enterprises something entirely different takes place.[53] The difference is not merely a matter of subtle variations; they go so far that Munich will reverse what started in Berlin. This example shows what a great number of differences the concept " general price level " conceals. But, to return to our starting point, it shows above all that a depreciation due to a transfer works quite differently from a depreciation to revive the economy.

Fluctuating exchange rates present the transfer theory with yet another difficult problem: The two waves of purchasing power seem no longer equivalent in value terms; how, then, can they equalize one another? Suppose 1,000 marks originally equal 1,000 francs. But because of exchange depreciation the German debtor has to pay

---

53. Something very similar is to be seen in meteorology. Within widespread weather conditions every street and every square in our German cities often maintains its own entirely distinct climate, which shares with varying intensity in a change of weather.

1,100 marks for 1,000 francs. On the other hand, with the higher exchange rate that results from the passing of the ebb in purchasing power across the border, 1,100 marks might now correspond perhaps to 1,300 francs. An ebb in purchasing power of 1,300 francs and a tidal wave of only 1,000 francs would then meet in France.

But as a rule events do not occur in this way. The fate of the true Stuttgart ebb in purchasing power of 1,000 marks and of the additional Stuttgart exchange loss of 100 marks is different. The ebb is locally limited, whereas the corresponding increase in purchasing power [54] among exporters, who export more, and importers, who import less, is distributed throughout all Germany and raises the price level everywhere.[55] Exchange profits and losses are similarly distributed spatially and the Stuttgart loss is generally indistinguishable from the others. It is decisive that the small waves of ebb and flood that arise everywhere in Germany because of the altered exchange rate equalize one another more easily than do the general rise in level and the local Stuttgart ebb. Only at first, when the great wave has just begun its course, do the ebb and the excess purchasing power that is not yet absorbed through higher prices, equalize one another. The greater part of the ebb, hower, will reach the national frontier. The small exchange waves, on the contrary, cancel out within a short distance unless the Stuttgart disturbance is unusually severe. Thus the essential processes in the transfer are the same with fixed and fluctuating exchanges.

(hh) *Does It Make Any Difference in What Currency a Debt Is Payable?* Whether in that of the creditor or the debtor? It is obviously immaterial for the countries concerned whether the creditor or the debtor starts the fluctuations in price level or exchange rate in the process of changing one currency into another. With a fixed exchange rate it makes no difference to either, but with variable rates the one that makes or receives [56] payment in foreign money bears the exchange loss.

---

54. It does not leave Germany, as would be the case with a fixed exchange rate through the shipment or the destruction the money.

55. *On the average* it does not rise, if the ebb is also taken into account.

56. This is improbable, however, for who would desire payment in a currency that he does not wish to spend? But so far as the statement holds, and it holds especially for foreign deposits in banks, it is true that fluctuating exchanges hinder international capital movements because of the exchange risk involved. With paper currencies, therefore, special reasons are added to the general reasons why capital is less mobile than within countries. But on the whole one can agree with Ch. R. Whittlesey (" Internationale Kapitalbewegungen bei gebundener und freier Währung," *Weltwirtschaftliches Archiv* XLIV [1936]) that the restraining effect of free exchanges on the international movement of capital has been greatly exaggerated in the past.

(ii) *Unilateral Waves of Purchasing Power.* A local upswing can release a flood of purchasing power to which no ebb corresponds anywhere. As in the normal case, goods are drawn into the center concerned without necessarily having to be paid for by a corresponding increase in exports. Payment may be made out of hoards, for instance. A still more striking example is the sudden and often fantastic increase of prices in newly discovered gold fields. A great and unexpected local augmentation of purchasing power appears, with which the local production of goods does not keep pace. Trade with the outside world must first be established. In the beginning it is very much harder and more expensive to import goods than to export gold. As the flood of purchasing power is not equalized by an ebb it is gradually distributed rather uniformly throughout the world, and may lead to a world-wide boom. For otherwise than with a normal transfer, prices will rise everywhere and permanently.

(kk) *Equalization of the Balance of Payments.* Price movements are never necessary for mere equalization of the balance of payments, because since every claim must be paid, deferred, or canceled, it is always equalized. Only when the equalization is to be brought about in a certain way, that is, otherwise than through deferment or default, may it become a problem. With identical currencies even such a fair equalization still comes about automatically; since, for example, if the export (that is, the income) of an individual decreases, he must necessarily restrict his purchases correspondingly or, if he can, part with some of his savings. For the equalization of payments between transfer communities, on the contrary, it is not enough that the individual fulfill his obligations since his payments, which with similar currencies would suffice, are now made in local money as a rule,[57] and must first be converted into generally accepted money by special measures. Thus only with different currencies does the principle of a fair equalization of the balance of payments constitute an ordering, even though but temporarily effective, force.

(ll) *Comparison with the Old Transfer Theory.*[58] The difference between the two views appears clearly in the different

---

57. For an exception see p. 288, note 37.

58. See my critical discussion of it ("Eine Auseinandersetzung über das Transferproblem," *Schmollers Jahrbuch,* LIV [1930], 1093–1106 [typographical errors corrected in LV, 192]; its defense by F. Meyer ("Eine neue Transfertheorie?" *Archiv für Wirtschaftsplanung,* I [1941], 171–180); and my reply ("Um eine neue Transfertheorie. Zur Verteidigung der alten Lehre durch Fritz Meyer," *Jahrbücher für Nationalökonomie,*

significance attributed to the first and second price movements that arise during transfer—the waves and the shift in level. The old school itself is divided into two camps, one of which holds that under certain circumstances only the second price movement, due to changes in the discount rate, makes the transfer possible,[59] whereas the other is of the opinion that even the first price movement, due to the shift in purchasing power, merely facilities transfer while, on the contrary, the mere shift in purchasing power would usually suffice.[60]

Both camps have confused the preliminary and the final transfer. The shift in purchasing power (which of course generally leads to price waves even when creditors now wish to buy in addition what debtors forego) does indeed suffice for the *final* transfer. For the success of the *preliminary* transfer in goods, however, an artificial shifting of the price level is necessary, but its effects are later annulled by a reaction. The advocates of the old school thought statically, and neglected space. For them the results of a loss of purchasing power, and of a rise in the discount rate, were, equally, a lowering of the " price level." They had no real notion of the movement of a change in purchasing power in space and time. They could not recognize, therefore, the fundamental difference between the preliminary and the final transfer, which is ultimately caused by the varying strength and proximity of the two price movements. The crests and troughs of the two price waves are too ill-defined and too far apart to result in the rapid transfer of goods that with different currencies is required to complete the transfer of money. Only for this reason does there occur the preliminary transfer of goods, which can be brought about only through a shift in the price level. The prompt effect of a discount policy, and especially [61] of the exchange-rate mechanism, depends, besides their influence on the movement of capital, upon the fact that they bring the two opposite regions nearer together by jumps, since in point

---

1943, pp. 19–28). Agreement with the new theory has predominated so far. For example, see E. Schneider ("Der Raum in der Wirtschaftstheorie," *Jahrbücher für Nationalöknonomie*, CLIII [1941], 727–734.

59. In the transfer debate I, too, agreed with the first group on this point.

60. For details see my article, " Eine Auseinandersetzung über das Transferproblem," *Schmollers Jahrbuch*, LIV [1930], 1103.

61. Against the advantage of fluctuating exchange rates that the movement in the prices of goods occurs automatically and without loss of time, fixed exchanges have the advantage that the discount policy very quickly affects short-term capital movements so that the somewhat slower effect of a changed discount rate on prices can be awaited.

of fact shifts in the price level extend uniformly at first to the national frontier.[62]

Because the central bank cannot wait until the wave of purchasing power reaches the frontier it simply anticipates the effects of this, in so far as they are of importance to *it*, by changes in the discount rate, for *these* effects are the same in both cases: Goods flow mainly from the border region,[63] in a broader sense, of the one country into that of the other. Even with a shift of the general price level the international equalization is thus completed at the border, to which are then added domestic transfers between the interior and the border region.[64] But apart from this, price waves and the shift in price level operate in an entirely different manner both spatially and chronologically, and therefore fulfill different functions in the transfer. Most advocates of the old theory regarded the preliminary transfer, associated with the shift in price level, as the final one and greatly overrated the importance of monetary factors in consequence. But even when the theory recognized the decisive significance of the shift in purchasing power associated with price waves, a lack of any spatial vision prevented the recognition that the final transfer must be complemented by a preliminary one.

β. *Tariffs* [65]

Customs duties aggravate the price fluctuations necessary to the completion of a transfer. They obviously do so when, as in the United States, they are newly introduced for this express purpose, to prevent the flow of goods from a debtor country. But even old customs duties have this effect since they so restrict the volume of trade that, despite a higher elasticity in demand,[66] a greater price movement must occur to bring about any given absolute change in foreign trade. What customs duties mean to commodities trade,

---

62. The principle is the same as that according to which the change in purchasing power is equalized. Furthermore, its equalization is more important the nearer the ringlike trough of the purchasing power loss and the ringlike crest of the influx of purchasing power approach one another in space, or the deeper or higher they are from the very first.

63. Goods with a large necessary shipping distance, and small countries, are exceptions.

64. The direction in which these domestic transfers move is the reverse of that taken by price waves. They begin at the border and progress gradually toward the interior.

65. It follows from our theory that customs duties affect the frontier zone most and that their effect is least in the interior.

66. Compare the discussions on pp. 141 and 147 on the relation between elasticity and distance, the effects of which resemble those of customs duties.

political risk means to international movements of capital. One could easily imagine a tariff policy that would not make transfer more difficult, but rather facilitate it by simply taking the place of discount policy. If the receiving country lowers and the paying country raises its duties, the effect takes the place of a shift in the rate of exchange or in the price level.[67]

γ. *Summary*

Reviewing our results, we find that *transfer across political frontiers generally calls for greater price movements than a corresponding transfer within a country.* This is due to the following causes:

1. Customs duties and direct prohibition either limit the range of goods that may actually be transferred, or limit at least the effect of price movements themselves on such goods as enter into foreign trade.

2. With partial or complete differences in currencies (which among countries are usually pronounced), brief but acute shifts in the price level are added to price waves.

3. Payer and payee in international trade are apt to be farther away from one another than in domestic trade. But the wider separation of regions with decreased or increased purchasing power, or even higher or lower discount rates, allows a presumption as to the smallness of their trade, so that greater changes in the price level are required to achieve the same preliminary export surplus for which smaller changes would suffice with more extensive trade connections.

4. Usually the movement of labor and capital meets with greater obstacles, which will be discussed below. It must therefore be replaced by a movement of goods.

5. The use of credit, which moderates price fluctuations, is more uncommon and unpredictable in international trade. On the other hand, a sudden big withdrawal of short-term credits that gives rise to price fluctuations is more frequent. However, a large part of these sharper price movements is fully compensated later by a reaction.

---

67. Export or import premiums are another substitute.

§5. Other Extra-Economic Spatial Patterns

When a Berlin firm has to pay 1,000 marks in Paris this is what actually takes place: Prices fall in the area of decreased purchasing power around Berlin, and rise in that of increased purchasing power around Paris. Decrease and increase of purchasing power together with price shifts advance on the average farther from their point of origin with every income period, until finally they meet somewhere, partly as a result of price shifts and partly without them. Then the transfer of goods is complete; [68] that is, an export surplus from the region of lower to that of higher prices to the full extent of the payment to be transferred.

These are the facts, beyond which it is a purely arbitrary matter or a question of interest to what greater whole the movement of prices and goods is to be imputed. As a citizen the Berlin merchant has lowered the average of German prices; as a Protestant he has lowered prices in a Protestant as compared with a Catholic region; as a dweller on the right bank of the Rhine he has reduced prices there in comparison with those in countries on the left bank; and as a German, in comparison with those of the Latins. His action disturbs every circle in which he moves, but it lowers the statistical average of prices only in those that are predominantly within the region of decreased purchasing power. Only when Germany as a whole fulfills this condition should one speak of a fall in German prices; in reality they fall at first only around Berlin. And only when the center of the price drop is predominantly within German frontiers should the German price drop be regarded as *the* essential phenomenon.

Now it is not very likely in most international transactions that any given price wave will include one country *completely* and essentially *alone*. This might perhaps be true if international trade were carried on between the central points of large rounded-off countries. In reality, however, the average German and the average Frenchman, for example, is separated by more than half the distance from the center of his country.[69] Thus the price rings that develop around

---

68. Two transfer effects are combined, one of which moves *forward* from Berlin whereas the other, as if anticiapting its arrival, moves *backward* and toward the Berlin effect. In other words, goods to the value of 1,000 marks move in constantly new form towards Paris, to which, however, they have already been delivered in advance by its environs, which in their turn borrow them again from their neighbors, and so on until the shipment from Berlin reaches the last of these.

69. It is probable that the locality involved in international transfer in a circular and evenly populated country with a radius of r is not its center, but a point about

his home will very soon cross the frontier of his country in a particular direction, even before they have reached its center. Nevertheless, it is at least probable in the case of sufficiently large and rounded-off countries that the *greater* part of the inner region of most concentrated shift in purchasing power will lie within the same country, and that the *greater* part of this country will be affected only by the wave of purchasing power that originates within its own frontiers.

Regions of import and export surplus can be delimited in the same way. One thousand marks' worth more of goods flows to the side on which Paris lies across *every* line between Berlin and Paris—whether it passes midway through the region of increased or decreased purchasing power, or to the west of places that actually order more from Berlin and thus over political frontiers as well. This would be a truism only if 1,000 marks' worth more of goods were really sold from Berlin directly to Paris. But the statement holds absolutely, and thus even if Berlin and Paris have no business connections at all. That this is so can easily be seen in Fig. 57, p. 271. Any desired line can be laid through it. As long as B and B_1 do not lie on the same side, the side of B_1 has a passive trade balance of 1,000 marks. In general: *Across any arbitrary line between two places, one of which makes a payment to the other, more goods flow toward the receiving place to the extent of the payment.*

§6. The Globe

So far we have been following the waves of purchasing power spreading out from Berlin and Paris only in longitudinal section, as it were; that is, only in so far as they lie on direct lines (BB_1 in Fig. 58). For this reason they meet at one *point Z*. But the Berlin wave of lower prices runs not only to the West, where it meets the tidal price wave from Paris, but also eastward (PQ), northward, and southward. If the amounts involved are small it is dissipated here in open space. This merely reduces the problem of its fate to insignificance, however, instead of solving it. What happens when not a thousand, but a thousand million marks are transferred? The decrease in purchasing power rolls onward, farther and farther around Berlin. Long after equalization has occurred in the West,

---

$0.7r$ away from this (with an evenly distributed population a circle with a radius of $0.7r$ divides the population into halves). Hence the point directly concerned lies eccentrically. Large areas of its own country are farther away from it than neighboring parts of other countries.

approximately in Belgium, and normal prices prevail once more in Berlin, the unequalized portion of the ebb is still on its way, its strength scattered but still undiminished, among Eskimos, Negroes, and to the ends of the earth. In spite of all dispersion it cannot be lost until it encounters the flood tide somewhere. Where does this happen?

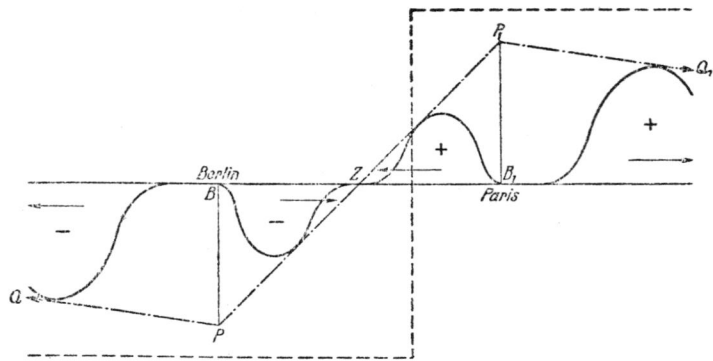

Fig. 58. World-wide price waves

If all conditions were perfectly uniform throughout the whole world the locus of the points of final equalization would be the great circle passing halfway between Berlin and Paris, on which lies Z also, among other places. Here the final equalizing transfer would occur, in so far as it had not been carried out before flood and ebb had arrived at the great circle. They reach it first at Z, between the two capitals. Then the point of each final transfer runs along the great circle in both directions around the world [70] until the last transaction has taken place at the antipode to Z. Thus waves of purchasing power are propagated from the center of decreased and that of increased purchasing power, each over half the world, not to disappear smoothly and completely until they reach the juncture of these halves.[71]

---

70. Its velocity is somewhat greater than that with which waves of purchasing power are propagated.

71. The strength of the waves, represented in Fig. 58 by the line QPP_1Q_1 on which the various crests lie, diminishes most rapidly on the shortest connecting line between B and B_1, most slowly on the longest connecting line. The broken line represents the shift in price level.

b. REDISTRIBUTION OF THE FACTORS OF PRODUCTION WITH LONG-RUN DISTURBANCES
(THE COMBINATION PROBLEM)

§1. Equalization by Migration

So far we have discussed adjustment to temporary disturbances: the transfer problem. Now we come to the effects of final shifts: the combination problem; that is, the problem of new spatial combinations of labor, capital, and land.[72] Such final shifts in supply and demand may be due to changes in taste, the exhaustion or discovery of resources and countries, protracted unilateral payments, increased tariffs, different rates of population increase, technical advances, and so on. Disturbances like these manifest themselves in persistent deviations of wages or interest from the former equilibrium levels.

Examine Fig. 57 once more. If A had shifted its demand from B to B_1 permanently rather than temporarily, a lasting price differential between the two places instead of temporary price waves would have arisen. Hence prices would have remained permanently lower in the region of decreased purchasing power, and permanently higher in that of increased purchasing power. So much for the transfer mechanism. If everything were to be reconciled to its effects, a new equilibrium would be reached as soon as a complete final transfer of goods had been achieved, which would be repeated in every income period to the extent of the shift in purchasing power.

But the permanence of the price shifts causes a redistribution of productive forces: It alters the location pattern. In the area of decreased purchasing power (particularly around B) not only money wages but, in so far as imports become more expensive, real wages as well decrease; conversely, they rise in the area of increased purchasing power. Because this shift appears to be permanent, labor migrates away from B toward B_1.[73] As a consequence of this migration, interest, which had originally gone up because the debtor restricted his borrowing and his bank raised the discount rate, now falls around B and rises around B_1. Capital movements follow the migration of labor, which temporarily presents the region of de-

---

72. It could be called also the "redistribution problem," or the problem of the spatial redistribution of productive forces.

73. In so far as the differences are now found great enough to compensate for the inconvenience of a change of locality itself, and for the disadvantages associated with increasing distance from one's birthplace.

creased purchasing power with an additional transfer problem. The solution of the transfer problem is price movement; that of the combination problem, migration.

Like the movement of goods, migration need not occur directly between B and B_1. If the same work earns 50 pfennig in B, 60 in D, and 70 in F, much of the migration will occur by many workers in B moving not to unfamiliar F, but to neighboring D, and only those who are crowded out there will go on to F. So it was, for example, with migrations of labor during the past century. Native Canadians moved to the United States or opened up their own west, western Europeans supplanted them in eastern Canada, and migrants from eastern Europe took their places in western Europe.

The outward migration removes the pressure of the shift of demand from B. The supply of its goods falls and prices and wages rise again, though perhaps not quite to their former level. As a rule the smaller scarcity in B (because of the desertion) and the greater scarcity in B_1 (because of the crowding in), as well as the smaller marginal productivity of the land, will prevent a return to the old prices. The new situation is characterized as little as the old by an interlocal equalization of wages, for reasons already advanced. Hence, not much is known about it. In most cases all that can be established is that migration takes place away from regions of falling wages and toward those where wages are rising, though it cannot be said in general where incoming migrants are from or whither outgoing ones are bound. It is certain, however, that distance plays a role in both cases.[74,75] Neither can it be stated in general by what the new state of equilibrium is to be recognized, except for individuals. See what has already been said in Chapter 17.[76]

A renewed equalization of interest rates also, at least up to the costs of distance and the risk premium, is to be expected only within the same market area, whereas between financial centers they can

---

74. Naturally it is known in a general way that with complete freedom to migrate men will go places that please them most, or to those where they can at least gain a livelihood, and industries to places where they can make a greater profit or at any rate cover their costs. But in this connection such knowledge is *too* general.

75. For examples see the maps in *National Resources Committee, The Problems of a Changing Population* (Washington, D. C.,1938), pp. 93 ff.

76. Save when interlocal utility differences are similarly felt by a sufficiently large number. Then, perhaps, there will be with wages, as with prices of goods, some scope within which they can vary from place to place without causing greater migrations. In such cases one may speak of an upper, or inward, migration point and a lower, or outward, migration point for local wages, though not with the same precision as in the case of homogeneous goods.

be equalized at most temporarily, and even then only if capital has moved between them. Later, interest may vary arbitrarily between them again, as prices between markets for goods, by twice the costs of distance; indeed, because of subjectively different estimates of risk, by much more. In short, it is not correct to say that migrations continue until wages and interest are everywhere equal once more. They need be equal in neither the old nor the new equilibrium.

§2. Results of Migration

It is possible, though not necessary, for the movement of factors of production to substitute for the movement of goods.[77] As experience has shown, in fact, migrations are followed very often, if not generally, by shifts in demand [78] toward the emigrants' country, so that an increased export of products occurs in addition to the migration of productive factors.[79] It is generally recognized that emigrants remain faithful customers of the mother country and introduce its exports to other countries besides. Similarly, loans are used generally, and often by stipulation, to buy in the homeland of the lender. Such threefold movements of men, goods, and capital in the same direction are actually the rule in colonial history. The choice for overpopulated countries, therefore, is not " whether to export men or goods," but whether to export only goods, or men as well. In the latter case export is substantially facilitated, of course, and the real question is whether or not one is ready to pay the price for this assistance; that is, a loss in population.

Every autonomous change of location such as shifts in rural population or the removal of a factory from B to B_1, raises a question that is important even in a free economy, and really vital in national planning: How much *further* migration of craftsmen, subsidiary industries, and so on from B or to B_1 will this cause? Strictly speaking, we deal with a disturbance of the local balance of pay-

---

77. The opposite is much more common, movements of goods taking the place of movements of factors to a certain extent, as Ohlin has so well shown.

78. Strictly speaking, it is not so much that there is a new demand at first for goods from the emigrants' country, as that part of the emigrants' demand and part of the demand created by exported capital is *retained* by the emigrants' country. What is new is merely that this demand now comes from abroad, and hence leads to export.

79. The more so since the prices of exported goods may very well rise. For on the one hand emigration reduces the supply of goods produced in the emigrants' country, and on the other increases the demand for them from the immigrant country, as has already been set forth above. That is, the supply curve is displaced toward the left and the demand curve perhaps toward the right, so that the new equilibrium price may easily be much higher.

ments, which is settled by means of the entire mechanism that such a disturbance sets in motion: by lower prices and changes in occupation as well as by migration. How much later migration will actually take place depends upon many things: It may even happen that nonagricultural enterprises are crowded out of B_1 and develop in deserted B instead. Or B may at least hold its own if those who remain behind would rather earn less or change their occupations than migrate. If these possibilities are excluded, the extent of further migration depends upon how much of their income those who were left behind have received from those who migrated (a per cent) and how much from elsewhere (b per cent). The remainder of their income consists of consumption of their own products or exchange among themselves (c per cent). Hence $a + b + c = 100$. The emigrants may continue to buy something from their former suppliers (α_1 per cent), who depend to the extent of about $(a + b)$ per cent on foreign exchange income. Consequently there remains $100(\alpha_1 + b) + (a + b)$ per cent; the rest likewise migrates elsewhere. Conversely, the farmers that have migrated to B_1 raise the number (determined by $a + b$) of artisans already present $(\alpha_2 + b) \div (a + b)$ times (the latter at first derive a per cent after the influx α_2 per cent of *their* original income from the farmers).

If α_1 and b are zero, which often is approximately the case, everything finally leaves B. The absolute number is then especially easy to calculate. If it is desired to know, for example, how many artisans a given number of farmers support (that is, how many they provide with the craftsmen's equilibrium income less the consumption of their own products of these workers and their exchange with one another), it will be known how much farmers spend for the products of craftsmen, and how much of it these earn (10,000 marks).[80] Furthermore, let c (the proportion of the artisan's income spent locally) $= 60$ per cent. Then $a = 40$ per cent $= 10,000$ marks, and consequently $a + c = 100$ per cent $= 25,000$ marks.[81] If an average artisan earns 5,000 marks, five artisans will emigrate.

---

80. According to B. Barfod (*Local Economic Effects of a Large-scale Industrial Undertaking* [Copenhagen and London, 1938], pp. 21-38) wage payments and local purchases by the firms involved do not increase the local income to the same degree, but by only about 70 per cent.

81. The multiplier is then $100 \div 40 = 2.5$. That is, every mark of original income that craftsmen derive from farmers raises their income by a further 1.5 marks through trade among themselves to a total income of 2.5 marks. Not that the total national income has increased by that much (Keynes's error). A rise of one mark in original income in B_1 results only in an additional 1.5 marks of the total national income being shifted there, just as those remaining there are not simply unemployed but are

§3. Interference with Migration

α. *Consequences*

Ever since the days of the classical writers the smaller international mobility of labor and capital has been so overemphasized that with few exceptions [82] the problem of the combination of the factors of production has been practically excluded from the theory of international trade. Haberler, for instance, says hardly a word about it. Assume first, for the sake of argument, that the classical writers were correct and that international migrations are especially difficult. What follows from this in respect to trade and the international division of labor?

1. ARE INTERNATIONAL WAGE DIFFERENCES GREATER?

Comparison between Places: It is uncertain whether differences in efficiency wages (and only these can be geographically compared) are increased or decreased by migration. Wages rise, to be sure, where workers leave and fall in the places to which they migrate. If it were certain that migration occurred only from places of low to those of high piece rates, wages would become more nearly equal interlocally, the easier and therefore the more common migration becomes. But the money wage, or even the real wage, may be lower at the destination of the migrant because he wishes to increase not his purchaseable, but his total utility. In this case, wage differences would be increased by migration.

Comparison over Time: In a region of decreased purchasing power, wages not only tend to fall in comparison with a region of increased purchasing power, but tend to fall absolutely also, in comparison with previous wages. Matters remain thus as long as frictional resistance or the prohibition of migration prevent a fresh distribution of labor.[83] Of course migration must not be expected

---

unemployed only at their former site, in their former trade, and at their former wage. Moreover, it is unnecessary to calculate the multiplier as the sum of an infinite series, as is easily seen, or even to think of it as originating in this way, as do Barfod (*op. cit.*, pp. 39, 51) and the author of " Zur Stadtplanung in den neuen deutschen Ostgebieten " (*Raumforschung and Raumordnung*, 1941, pp. 100–230). In other respects both articles are excellent.

82. For example B. Ohlin, " Die Beziehung zwischen internationalem Handel und internationalen Bewegungen von Kapital und Arbeit," *Zeitschrift für Nationalökonomie*, II (1930), 161–199.

83. Here we deal with restrictions on migration for police, military, or political reasons. Those that are economic in nature will be discussed in the next chapter.

to restore wages completely to their old level, as has already been said, for even in equilibrium they may fluctuate between the upper and lower migration points. The possible extent of the fluctuation is greater, however, the more difficult the migration, and with complete prohibition it may be of any size whatsoever. Thus the greater the restraints that migration encounters, the less need (not " must ") wages be brought back to their former level by migration. On the contrary, it must be *presumed that after interference, wages differ more from their earlier level, the smaller the extent of migration.* Hence the degree of the mobility of labor permits conclusions only on the extent to which wages differ in time, not on the extent to which they differ in space—the very question in which we are most interested in the present connection.

2. ARE INTERNATIONAL MOVEMENTS OF GOODS GREATER?

Do political boundaries obstruct the flow of men in favor of the flow of goods? We have already seen that trade in goods may be heavy because migration is extensive, as well as because it is slight. Thus the international flow of goods need not be greater just because international migration is less extensive than domestic.

3. WOULD POOR CONTRIES BE DEPOPULATED WITH FREE MIGRATION?

The classical economists held the view that obstructions to international migration raise the principle of comparative cost to a predominating position, according to which even poor countries (that is, those with only comparative and no absolute advantages) could compete in international trade.

We shall explain the identical facts in our own way as follows. Even locations that are handicapped in some respects may be competitive if they can balance their disadvantages against advantages of another sort. Thus if their production costs as a whole are very high they can still be protected against competitors by a cushion of freight costs. Or if only some are very high these may be offset by economies in other directions. For example, if the services of land are very expensive—and the classical writers had this situation chiefly in mind—their competitive position will not be affetced as long as some men are ready to work for appropriately low wages.

Why are there such men? In the first place, they may feel that a greater abundance of free goods compensates for a scarcity of purchasable goods. They would prefer to be here even though born elsewhere. A second group would migrate were it not that the advantages of other localities would be wiped out by the disadvantages of traveling to them. Their misfortune lies in having been born here. For both these groups the prevailing wage is the equilibrium wage, even though it may vary from place to place; that is, it procures them all the utilities they can possibly get. A third group, finally, is made up of those who are prevented from migrating by police regulations, or by those inner restraints that may prevent us from doing what we have recognized to be right, even though migration would be to their best advantage. Only for a part of this third group is it true, therefore, that countries create artificial wage differences and lower the incomes of their citizens through an enforced choice of location.

Thus countries more scantily endowed by nature would be populated even though international migration had not been made especially difficult. Indeed, they would be settled even though migration cost nothing at all. But of course they would be more *thinly* settled. Improvements in means of transportation and the easing of international migration would encourage the depopulation of unfavorably situated localities and the agglomeration of population at the more favored sites.

β. *Reasons for Obstructing Migration*

Even had the classical writers been correct, it follows from what has been said that the results of difficulties in the international movements of the factors of production are neither sufficiently important nor characteristic enough to justify preserving the strong and unique position of international trade in the theoretical structure.[84] But were the classical economists correct at all? Is it not true that in their time, and throughout the reign of their theory, no particular obstacles to international migration existed, though there might have been hindrances to migration within countries? Often enough national frontiers *created* no special difficulties for migration, but merely adjusted themselves to these. In fact, countries even promoted migrations through their customs duties. Do such special hindrances as prohibition of migration or love for the fatherland operate any differently in principle from the usual curbs: cost of travel and the law of diminishing returns? Even if there were no frontiers at all, the whole population of the earth would not collect in regions that possessed " absolute cost advantages " for

---

84. For the solution of the transfer problem, for example, though not for its origin and extent, the degree of mobility is completely irrelevant.

one or another branch of industry. That which the classical writers extolled as the fundamental characteristic of the international division of labor is neither as characteristic nor as important as they believed.

§4. Comparison with the Transfer Problem

The economy adapts itself to brief disturbances by movements of products; to long-continued disturbances by movements of productive factors. The former is a sales problem, the latter a problem of location. Both goods and migrations move from a region of decreased to one of increased purchasing power. Both are impeded by expense and other obstacles associated with any change of place, by goods as well as by men. With transfer, migration, and with the new distribution of productive factors, any movement of goods, is of secondary importance. The purpose of transfer is to bear the consequences of a shift in demand; that of redistribution is to avoid them.

c. WHAT REMAINS OF THE CLASSICAL THEORY?

The solution of the three fundamental problems of international trade by the neoclassical theory is partly incomplete, partly untenable, and partly inaccurate. A solution of the combination problem has not been undertaken. To answer the question of the international division of labor by the theory of comparative cost seems indefensible. And the transfer problem is treated inaccurately and, in important points erroneously.

To mention only the most essential points: The statements about the form and spread of price movements prove to be incorrect when carefully examined. First, these do not occur in their *essential* features as a uniform rise and fall, like the rise and fall of a water level. Even when such a phenomenon appears temporarily with a difference in currencies, it and all its consequences are necessarily compensated in the end through a reaction, a fact that has been completely overlooked so far. The *necessary* price movements take rather the form of a wave, rolling forward from its point of origin or, with lasting disturbances, of a gradual price gradient. Second, the regions over which these necessary price movements extend do not usually coincide with political areas. Consequently it is to be expected that prices in different parts of the same country will shift in opposite directions.

The classical view, which interpreted countries as units,[85] was an important achievement for its time, but it touched reality only in part and even there only as a first approximation, a rule of thumb. Within certain spatial and chronological limits, it was right with respect to the movement of the price level of a country as a whole. In cases where the source of the disturbance was not too far from the center of the country, it described the change in price level accurately for the period preceding the reaction. But even within these limits the price level after all is only an average of organic differences, among which the wider movements predominate at first, though the smaller but essential movements prevail in the end. Everything depends upon separating price waves from real shifts in the price level, for their functions are entirely different. Transfer is understood neither theoretically nor in practice if the two are confused.

Currency policy will be guided by wholly new principles as soon as it frees itself from the obsolete view. This saw only an *incomplete phenomenon*, whereas the new theory views the *whole process*. The classical writers explained what took place *on the average*, but now it is necessary to show what happens in *detail*. As physics now investigates with profit the minute occurrences underlying the broad general laws of classical mechanics, so economics will be rewarded for pushing beyond mere calculated averages to the meaningful differences of reality. For of necessity we shall have to acquire a more accurate knowledge of these the more we guide economies away from a natural and toward a consciously planned development. If economic policy were to stop at the attractively simple interpretation of the classical writers, it would resemble a hat manufacturer who made hats of *one* size only, to fit the *average* head.

As is the case with price levels, gradual rather than abrupt transitions appear upon examination also for different currency systems, varying mobility of productive factors, natural differences among

---

85. The reasons for this view are easily seen. There was a wish to derive principles at first from simple cases that were at least roughly applicable to English conditions. Working with whole countries offered the one possibility of verifying these principles statistically. Finally, *the results for whole countries were of greater interest than those for their parts*; first, because practical decisions on such problems as free trade or protection depended on these findings; second, because the main interest of the classical writers was not in individuals or parts, or even structure, but solely in the functioning of the whole. They differed from their opponents, who also emphasized the whole, only in the fact that these latter could not understand how the whole could be built on the utility instead of on the sacrifices of the individual; on his freedom rather than on his restraints.

countries, and the determination of what goods will enter international trade. Real, vivid individuality replaces the outmoded subsidiary assumption of uniform mass phenomena. As a consequence countries can no longer be regarded as economic units. We now think of them in all their diversity and expanse rather than as mere points. We take space seriously.

Chapter 20. Regulation from Without

The advantages of a free economy operating under ideal conditions lie in self-determination of the individual and self-regulation of the whole or, briefly, in freedom and equilibrium.[1] But, say its opponents contemptuously,[2] this need not be reasonable; it may be "any kind of equilibrium." There is this much truth in what they say: it remains to be proved whether a free economy also provides, as a third advantage, the greatest possible social product. Its critics might reflect, however, that economic freedom is a good in itself, and as such constitutes a part of the national income.

This is the first reason why judicious regulation from without ("intervention") *may* be advantageous in principle. But, though a free equilibrium may not be the best possible one, it is not therefore arbitrary but reasonable after its fashion *if only men act in accordance with nature and logic.* The automatic spatial organization of the economy, for example, shows a quite acceptable pattern on the whole, even from extra-economic standpoints, but now and then *the result can be improved by intervention.*[3] A second type of meaningful regulation from without attempts not to create a situation better than that arising from the free play of forces, but to bring this situation about *at a lower cost;* that is, to facilitate adaptation. Direction should therefore operate more accurately, or at least more promptly, than self-regulation.

---

1. In a developing economy mere functioning takes the place of equilibrium.
2. J. M. Keynes, for example ("Nationale Selbstgenügsamkeit," *Schmollers Jahrbuch*, 1933, p. 82).
3. For even perfect functioning of the free play of forces guarantees only that everyone will achieve his greatest attainable utility for every given constellation of the other forces. It does not guarantee that the general welfare, or perhaps even the welfare of each individual, cannot be increased *under certain circumstances* by a judicious alteration of the grouping from without. This should be possible, especially when unwholesome forces are able to participate in the free play. On the other hand, not many cases can be imagined in which an unwelcome situation could develop from the perfect co-operation of *wholesome* forces.

a. REGULATION OF THE TRANSFER OF PRODUCTS (THE TRANSFER PROBLEM)

§1. Obstruction of Adaptation

Disturbances in existing trade relationships generally lead to price changes or migration. The former plays the chief role in temporary, the latter in lasting, disturbances. Both are annoyances today. Men are almost as ready to prevent transient adaptations as they are to prevent permanent shifts. In the transfer problem opposition is concentrated at two points.

First, the associated *changes in the price level* are held to be undesirable. We know, indeed, that they are not necessary, and that they can be obviated by appropriate measures. Certainly those measures customarily employed accomplish their purpose only imperfectly. The sterilization of gold movements in particular, to which we shall return later, moderates shifts in prices, to be sure, but at the expense of the other participant. If not only the unnecessary changes in price level but also the essential price waves are compensated, and if this occurs on both sides, the transfer of goods is actually made impossible.

Secondly, the *movements of goods* associated with transfer are objected to. If a country pursues the senseless policy of obstinately preventing the successful handling of greater, even though transient, disturbances (reparations, for example), through continuous increases in tariffs, it may start a movement of the factors of production themselves. Men and capital desert a country that is protected or especially affected by customs duties, since both suffer from their effects. If these effects are felt very much less in the protected country it may come either to increased immigration (United States) or to capital imports (Canada), according to whether wages or interest rates are high. Immigration into a country with high tariffs will be mainly composed of such factors of production as seek employment in protected industries, whereas emigration will be recruited from the remaining parts of the economy that have to bear the burden of the duties.

§2. Facilitation of Adaptation

α. *By Monetary Policy* [4]

1. THE MONETARY STANDARD

Monetary policy is the chief method employed by countries to facilitate short-run adaptations; that is, partly to avoid the shifts in price level, which are later annulled by the reaction in any case; and partly to avoid their secondary effects. Secondary effects are those associated with the particular form, not with the essence of the event. For instance, whether prices or exchange rates fall, the chief effect is the same—an export surplus. The weary road of deflation, however, has an undesirable and unnecessary companion phenomenon that is avoided by the easy path of devaluation: a direct fall of prices has a depressing effect, and may lead to a cyclical downturn. To this extent even short-run fluctuations are still influenced by a policy decision that was made far in the past—a decision as to the monetary standard.

A purely local standard (paper currency) leads, in the form of fluctuations in the rate of exchange, to short but severe price jumps; an approximation to a world currency (gold standard with a high gold coverage), on the other hand, leads to small but protracted shifts in price levels. With perfect mobility this difference would be of no importance. In practice, however, wide price fluctuations are disadvantageous in themselves, especially when they result directly and not as fluctuations in the exchange rate. It must be considered further that with a low gold coverage the reaction may not compensate entirely for the transfer costs, whereas with a high gold cover uncompensated transfer costs arose once at the time when they were being accumulated.

Furthermore, the high gold cover means loss of interest, though it has the advantage over a paper currency that the preliminary transfer is largely completed through capital movements—a result of the discount policy that is necessarily associated with functioning of the transfer mechanism under a gold standard. Finally, gold countries attract more foreign capital, as we have already seen.

It is very difficult to balance these advantages and disadvantages

---

4. We start with an old-fashioned gold and paper currency; thus the exchange rate and the gold cover will be fixed in the one, and fluctuating in the other. We say that the currency policy will remain within the system when only one factor is changed; for example, when with a gold currency the coverage is freed, or with a paper currency the rate of exchange is fixed. We shall speak of a new system only when both factors change.

at all, and impossible to compare them in a way that is universally valid. The result depends almost entirely upon the particular case and upon individual opinion. This is precisely why there is some scope for "regulation from without." In my judgment there is always a majority of reasons in each situation for preferring one or the other monetary standard. To adhere as completely as possible to a world currency facilitates the preliminary transfer, impedes the transmission of foreign economic fluctuations, and permits more reliable calculation.

But only rich countries can afford these advantages, for they require a great store of gold and exceptional renunciation of credit creation as we see it realized in the United States. For poor countries, on the other hand, and especially those with great disturbances in the balance of payments, a paper currency is incomparably more suitable than a gold currency with low coverage. If a high coverage were always more advantageous (for which there seems much to be said at first) it would of course repay a poor country either to borrow gold or at least to accumulate an interest-bearing fund of foreign exchange. No doubt only psychological inhibitions or undervaluation of future advantages as compared with present sacrifices stand in the way. It is true, furthermore, that a high gold coverage develops its full advantages only in company with a small extent of credit creation. But as this would mean other disadvantages for a poor country, a paper currency probably remains advisable.

It is obvious that in the intermediate case of moderately prosperous countries a combination of the two extremes, in the form of a paper currency with a stabilization fund, is best. Price fluctuations will generally be avoided as long as the fund lasts. In so far as they cannot, they will at least occur in the relatively harmless form of fluctuations in the exchange rate.

2. MONETARY POLICY WITHIN THE SAME STANDARD

Within what limits is an independent policy possible? That is, how far can central banks influence fluctuations in prices or in the rate of exchange, or replace them with other movements?

(aa) *Gold Standard.* Case 1: A central bank may exceed the legal coverage. As long as it has a free gold reserve (which will be especially large during depressions because of the reduced note circulation), it can proceed as though the prescribed coverage were greater or less. When gold movements occur it need not set the discount rate so that the quantity of notes is changed exactly as the legal reserve ratio (normal discount rate). On the contrary, it can call in fewer notes with an outflow of gold, issue more with an influx, than would correspond to the legal reserve ratio (discount rate below normal). In the former case the transfer mechanism operates as though the notes had to have a high gold coverage: price fluctuations are smaller and gold movements larger. In the latter case the reverse is true. In both instances, however, the gold reserve dwindles. This policy is limited by adherence to the legal coverage.

On the other hand, a central bank can also call in more notes with an outflow of gold, and issue fewer with an influx, than would correspond to the legal reserve ratio (discount rate above normal). Then in the former case price fluctuations are wider and gold movements smaller than if the legal ratio had been exactly maintained. In the latter case the reverse is true. This policy encounters no legal limits, but only the elastic economic limit of the damping effect of deflation.

Now the debtor country will keep the discount rate below, and the creditor country above, normal. They will thus sterilize the gold movement; that is, prevent it from affecting the price level. The gold movements will, of course, be increased thereby. Conversely, the debtor country will reinforce the effects of the smaller gold movement on prices with a discount rate above normal, and the creditor country with one below normal. But this is only rarely intended. Thus the sterilization of gold will facilitate the preliminary transfer of goods, that is, will distribute it in time; the enhanced effectiveness of gold will accelerate it.

The secondary effects on short-term capital movements will accentuate the difference between these various possibilities in the case of gold movements, and weaken them in the case of price fluctuations. When gold is sterilized fewer credits flow from the creditor country to the debtor country; this necessitates a still greater flow of gold. With increased effectiveness of gold the discount policy brings about still wider movements of credit, which reduces the already small movement of gold even more.

In the first case, on the other hand, the otherwise slight shift in price level will be accentuated, in the second the otherwise considerable shift will be moderated. Thus the various possible central bank policies are even more important to the central bank itself than to the economy. They affect gold movements more than price movements. The effects of gold sterilization differ most from those of a normal discount policy when the legal reserve ratio is low; conversely in the opposite case. A policy of sterilization is therefore more important for poor debtor than for rich creditor countries, though at the same time more difficult.[5]

Unilateral sterilization moderates one's own price fluctuations at the expense of the other participant (Table 16). Co-operation by central banks would be more sensible, as has often occurred with exchange control (though there is no necessary logical connection between the two). The central bank of the creditor permits the central bank of the debtor to postpone settlement of international accounts until the waves of purchasing power have crossed the frontier, and the debtor bank has received thereby the necessary foreign exchange. In order for the waves to start it is essential that the debtor bank collect the amount in cash from the debtor, and that the creditor bank pay it over to the creditor at first with created money.[6]

Case 2: Fixed rate of exchange with arbitrary coverage.

Case 3: Fixed coverage with arbitrary exchange rate. These two additional possibilities may be merely mentioned. In case 2 the debtor can use his whole supply of gold before changing his price level. In case 3 the movements of gold and of the exchange rate occur simultaneously.

(bb) *Paper Currency* offers corresponding possibilities for manipulation; there are thus no clear-cut distinctions compared to a gold currency. As in case 2, the central bank, for example, can maintain a foreign exchange reserve, whose function corresponds to that of a free gold reserve. If it is exhausted, the bank can lower prices by means of its discount policy rather than permit a fall in the exchange rate, whereas a price rise might be limited by a legal limitation on the amount of fiduciary note issue.

---

5. If the cover is relatively high, as in the United States, and scope for the creation and limitation of credit therefore correspondingly narrow, it does not make much difference whether the discount rate is above or below normal. In contrast to the Reichsbank, the member banks borrow so little from their reserve banks that these have to engage in open market operations in order to influence the circulation of money, because their discount policy would not be effective enough.

6. During the war, when the control of foreign exchange greatly hindered passage of the waves across the frontier, they widened out eventually to a rise of the price level in the creditor country. See A. Lösch, " Die Lehre vom Transfer—neu gefasst," *Jahrbücher Nationalöknonomie*, CLIV (1941), 400 ff.; and " Die neuen Methoden der englischen Handelspolitik," *Weltwirtschaftliches Archiv*, LIV (1941), 337; also the witty article by F. Meyer, " Eine neue Transfertheorie? " *Archiv für Wirtschaftsplanung*, I (1941), 174 f.

3. CHANGE OF THE MONETARY STANDARD

The preliminary effects of slight disturbances can be accelerated or moderated by a suitable monetary policy. Within certain limits, for example, the central bank can act as though its monetary standard were different; or it can really alter parts of it. With *extensive* disturbances in a fixed currency this behavior "as if" (case 1, above) leads so promptly to the legal limits, and partial relaxation through a loss of the gold reserve (especially in poor countries) so promptly to the actual limits (case 2), that only two choices remain: either to relinquish all further attempts at management and let the sudden change in the price level jar the economy, or to change the basic structure of the currency by temporarily or permanently freeing the rate of exchange also.[7]

England made an important and fortunate decision in 1931, when she stopped the drain of extensive short-term credits by devaluing the pound and risking its repute, instead of throwing the country into the prescribed deflationary crisis in an excess of conscientiousness, as did the German government of that period. Of course, such a change of front may also have secondary effects upon capital movements that are similar to those of discount policy. If devaluation serves only to make a domestic inflation possible, as was the case in France in 1936, and if its limits therefore cannot be foreseen, the resulting flight of capital results in constantly new devaluations. One single step within the frame of the gold standard is then replaced by the transition to freely fluctuating exchanges.

All these measures have this in common: They do not encroach upon the freedom of the economy. Not so with exchange control. Hence with a systematically liberal attitude exchange control is resorted to only when the monetary standard cannot be altered because of psychological reasons. Conversely, if with a paper currency only *slight* disturbances are to be overcome, it may be advantageous to stabilize the exchange and the coverage; that is, to go on the gold standard.

In brief, rich countries will prefer a pure gold standard in the event of slight disturbances, poor countries a pure paper standard in the face of grave disturbances (see Section 1). As the disturbances increase with a gold standard and decrease with a paper standard, first a partial (Section 2), and in extreme cases a complete, change to another monetary standard becomes advisable (Section 3).

7. In case 3 an attempt will be made to damp the wide fluctuations in the rate of exchange by using *all* gold at first; that is, making the cover also variable.

β. *Tariff Policy*

A tariff policy can be imagined that would facilitate a transfer by taking the place of changes in the price level or the exchange rate, and forcibly bringing about an import or export surplus. But even a tariff policy that seeks to obstruct a free adjustment to disturbances may be sensible under certain conditions. Together with a suitable discount policy it might, for example, attempt to replace the movements of goods that otherwise would occur during the preliminary transfer by capital movements; because, together with the reaction, they represent an avoidable disturbance of production.

§3. Improvement of the Result

α. *Objectives*

1. *Higher Business Profits.* A monopolist increases his profits by adapting his price to the elasticity of supply or demand, and by differentiating it wherever possible for each individual customer. A country achieves the same end by centralized control of its foreign trade. The high cost of the increased administrative machinery reduces these advantages from the very first, and they vanish as other countries follow suit. In a world of foreign trade monopolies, some countries at least are worse off finally than they would be under free trade. Then the time is ripe for it, and a new cycle begins.[8]

2. *Full Employment.* A boom seems to be doubly endangered from abroad. (*a*) The changed balance of trade (increased imports, decreased exports) leads during preliminary transfer to partial reversal of the cyclical creation of credit, at least under an old-fashioned gold standard. (*b*) A depression abroad affects the country

---

8. Thus the complete antithesis to free trade is not merely protective tariffs, but a system of import and export duties or other regulatory measures aimed at a flexible exploitation of marketing possibilities. I suggested such a system in 1930 for the relief of Germany's transfer burdens (" Eine Auseinandersetzung über das Transferproblem," *Schmollers Jahrbuch*, LIV [1930], 1093–1106. Typographical errors corrected in vol. LV, p. 192). At that time Germany would still have had a temporary advantage, but in later years it has become questionable whether the German gains from trade were actually increased by this policy. (H. S. Ellis versus Meyer: " Exchange Control in Germany," *Quarterly Journal of Economics*, vol. LIV, no. 4, Pt. II). Today even F. W. Meyer, who in 1939 still regarded exchange control as " the only possible lasting solution " (" Devisenbewirtschaftung als neue Währungsform," *Weltwirtschaftliches Archiv*, XLIX [1939], 453), accepts our objection advanced above and admits its " validity in time " (" Zum Europäischen Währungsproblem," *Bankarchiv*, 1941, p. 443).

through a lowered demand, cut-rate exports, withdrawal of credits, and also in purely psychological ways. Attempts are made to remedy the situation (under *a*) by restricting imports that are cyclically unimportant and, if this does not suffice to equalize international accounts, by cheapening exports through devaluation or by export subsidies; or (under *b*) by excluding fluctuations in the international economy to a certain degree through a reduction and control of foreign trade.

Now it is, of course, actually desirable in a normal upswing that credit creation is slowed down in good time (under *a*), whereas protection against economic fluctuations originating abroad is complete only when foreign trade (including capital movements) is absolutely prohibited—and even then waves of optimism and pessimism continue to cross the frontier (under *b*). The better the protection, naturally, the higher its cost—which consists in relinquishing the advantages of free trade. Furthermore, protection against outside influences is of value only when management of the economy succeeds in avoiding domestic cycles. If it does not (and account must be taken of the fact that normally the familiar causes reappear, though in different form), the forces making for an upswing operate more strongly in an isolated national economy. But then, on the other hand, a depression can no longer be shifted abroad. It follows that control of foreign trade guarantees full employment only under special conditions, such as the German rearming.[9] Finally, it remains to be seen which is more favorable to economic development: uninterrupted business activity or, figuratively speaking, the rhythm of day and night that has prevailed in the past.

3. *Autarky*. The direction of foreign trade may also pursue political aims: to assure one's supply by changing over to sources within the sphere of influence, by stockpiling of strategic materials, or by protecting home production; and, on the other hand, impeding the supply of the enemy by interfering purchases or by the prohibition of exports. This requires regulation not only of the extent of foreign trade, as with a liberal monetary policy, but also of its origin and composition.

---

9. Again F. W. Meyer, otherwise one of the shrewdest defenders of exchange control, has generalized unique situations without dealing with business-cycle theory, and has applied them to large economic areas as though this were a matter of course. (See his " Devisenbewirtschaftung als neue Währungsform," *Weltwirtschaftliches Archiv*, XLIX [1939], 415–471; and " Die Sicherung der autonomen Wirtschaftsentwicklung im Bereich der Aussenwirtschaft," *ibid.*, LIII [1941], 321–369, particularly p. 364.)

β. *Methods*

In the management of the balance of payments all the means of self-regulation, and three new ones in addition, are available: direct regulation of prices (by tariffs and subsidies, regulations and agreements), of amounts (quotas, purchase agreements), and of values (import: foreign exchange licensing; export: restrictions on the use to which foreign claims can be put; compensation transactions).

The old methods have been refined and technically developed; for example, prices are permitted to fluctuate only vis-à-vis foreign countries, and price discrimination is employed in accordance with market condition. But above all, the controlling authorities can largely determine the methods they wish to use. In particular, they will rarely make use of a direct lowering of domestic prices.[10]

γ. *The Course of Managed Transfer*

Lack of space prevents repetition of what I have shown elsewhere for each single phase of transfer: That despite interesting differences in details *the essential process with free and managed equalization is the same.*[11] In both cases final transfer takes place by the equalization of waves of purchasing power, whether these appear as price waves or, with price control, as waves of employment. In both cases final transfer must be preceded by a preliminary transfer, and the chief medium in both is the movement of money, goods, or credit, even though these may differ partly in their importance and in their reasons. In both cases, finally, the results of this preliminary transfer, which are in many respects alike, are again eliminated after completion of the final transfer.

b. REGULATION OF THE DISTRIBUTION OF FACTORS OF PRODUCTION (THE COMBINATION PROBLEM)

Here, too, economic policy may wish to expedite and facilitate the results of the equilibrium mechanism (§2), or to change them. Either the new situation is to be even more advantageous than it would be without interference (§3, or, conversely, everything is to

---

10. For details see A. Lösch, " Die Lehre vom Transfer—neu gefasst," *Jahrbücher für Nationalökonomie*, CLIV (1940), 401; and " Die neuen Methoden der englischen Handelspolitik," *Weltwirtschaftliches Archiv*, LIV (1941), 312–348.

11. " Die Lehre vom Transfer—neu gefasst," *Jahrbücher für Nationalökonomie*, CLIV (1941), 394–402. This fact is overlooked by all those who do not understand how to apply price theory to the new forms of currency and foreign trade, and hence with much ado seek for errors in the theory instead of in themselves.

remain as it was, or at least particular new developments are to be prevented (§1).

§1. Impediments to Adaptation

α. *Preservation of Old Connections*

The economic is distinguished from the natural landscape by its more rapid change. This may go so far that an entire economic landscape dissolves: fields are abandoned, industries find better locations, and people leave. Forces are always at work endeavoring to prevent such changes, especially in those fortunate cases where economic landscapes originally coincided with cultural and political landscapes. A large part of the modern struggle is a result of the disintegration of old or the formation of new combinations and the attempt to prevent this.

The wish to leave everything unchanged often leads to strangely vague aims: the preservation of England's role in world trade, the protection of the American South, and the like. In the latter case, for example, there may be meant the people, the land, or industries, all of which together determine the character of the South at any given time. The wish to help would mean, then, an attempt at any particular time to join together two or even all three of these factors: people and landscapes (" Its population must be preserved to the South "); men and occupations (" Our cotton growers must be helped," perhaps by transplantation to the more fertile cotton fields of Texas); or nonagricultural enterprises and economic landscape (" Let us promote the textile industry of the South "). And at worst, a unique historical combination of people, land, and production is supposed to be preserved in its entirety: the original people at their original occupation on the original site (" The Negro, the South, and cotton belong together ").

The *means* toward these ends are compulsion, payment, and education. Compulsion: prohibition of the migration of men and enterprises, of the closing down of old or the establishment of new enterprises, of the limitation or expansion of cultivation, or of any change of the place of employment or the individuals employed. Payment: principally in the form of duties or direct subsidies. Education: schooling itself, and modernization of all sorts, perhaps the consolidation of farms, and the introduction of new industries.

What are the *results*? In the case of a forcible overcoming of old backwardness, unquestionably an increase in welfare. In other cases, at least an increase in the national or the social income,[12] though only one of them at a time and at the expense of the other. Men can be prevented from moving to places or occupations that they would prefer, even though they produced less physically and would therefore be worse off in a material sense. Or they can be spared migration under conditions in which they are unhappy, though materially better off. In the latter case, however, it must be considered whether out of respect for emotional loyalties an unreasonable situation is to be endured forever which the younger generation, in the absence of such a powerful incentive, would perhaps gradually abandon.[13]

Enforced perpetuation of an originally profitable combination of interests, and the perfect preservation of old conditions in particular, creates a museum, which, like all such institutions, requires large sums for its maintenance.[14] As soon as the breaking up of old combinations is economically justified, every attempt to obstruct it means a sacrifice. A sacrifice, however, that may be vindicated now and then by the fact that it helps to preserve the political and cultural existence of an economic landscape for a while even though it has passed its economic prime. Those who have to bear the burden in this case are the inhabitants, who, prevented from migrating, are forced to put up with a lower standard of living. In the long run they are also politically endangered thereby. If it is a case merely of a depressed area within a country, the prosperous areas generally bear the cost. This is not always a wise policy, even when the importance of extra-economic causes is freely admitted. It would often be much better to facilitate the breaking up of an old combination of land, people, and economic activities and seek

---

12. I define national income as the quantity of physical goods, and social income as the amount of psychic utility. Neither can be measured, though it is possible to speak of their increase or decrease, if changes at any one time occur in but *one* direction. The individual is interested only in the amount of utility, the state chiefly in the quantity of goods. Social and national interests may conflict. Of what use to a country at war is a number of contented philosophers, when it needs steel for its cannon? In times of peace, though, one would rather see happy people than so much useless activity.

13. I am thinking of the poor farmers in the Appalachian mountains, who live on a miserable soil and near the minimum of subsistence, generally have many children, and yet refuse to migrate.

14. The cases are very different where men cling so tenaciously to their economic landscapes and their occupations that they are ready and able to make a *voluntary* sacrifice solely in order not to lose their connection. This solution, born of loyalty and reason, is often thwarted, to be sure, by the doctrinaire attitude that finds it sensible to equalize wage rates, fixed prices, and tangible property taxes, thus creating many new depressed areas everywhere.

systematically for a new and vital one; that is, to promote adaptation rather than to obstruct it.

β. *Prevention of New Combinations*

The prevention of particular new combinations is not quite so bad as the retention of everything without change. There are two methods of warding off the corresponding influences coming from abroad: Making international commodity movements more difficult may hinder a redistribution of productive factors within a country, while interference with international migration may impede their redistribution between countries.

1. TRADE BARRIERS

A lasting change in foreign trade may result in undesirable dislocations of domestic production, which can sometimes be avoided by tariffs and so on. These changes may be undesirable:

1. If consumers gain less than producers lose. This amounts to an objection against the argument for free trade. To the best of my belief, it has been proved so far only that the division of labor (that is, free trade) between two persons raises the *physical* income of each when their abilities in the production of two goods are comparatively different. A larger amount of both products is then available to each of them. If there are several goods, physical amounts can no longer be compared as soon as even a single good is consumed in smaller quantities under free trade than under autarky (which is conceivable). But for the individual his *psychic* income, not his physical income, is relevant. In the most simple basic case this also must speak for the advantage of the division of labor, if we consider only the utilities to be derived from consumption and neglect the pleasure or tedium of work. When these are taken into account, cases could be found such as that in which a man specializes so unwillingly in an occupation for which he is particularly well suited that he does not feel compensated for the greater disutility by the utilities of increased consumption that it makes possible. Despite the possibility of physical enrichment no exchange will then take place. It is different with more than two persons, and those who gain utilities through cheap imports need no longer be identical with those who must change over to a production of exports that may not be so agreeable to them.[15] Then there is

---

15. While it is certain, of course, that they earn more (in terms of utility) at this new occupation than if they had continued at their old one (otherwise they would not

nobody in the economic mechanism who can balance the consumer's rent of the one against the disutilities endured by the other, and it may happen that the free play of forces will compel a change-over even though the disutility is greater than the rent.[16] This balancing (which, as pointed out before, is in any case very problematical), that is, this choice between free trade and protective tariffs, is thus a purely political decision. But even though the proof that free trade increases the social product degenerates into mere presumption, as it does even with Haberler,[17] it is nevertheless probable, and the moral argument for free trade remains unshaken: That only those who fear no sort of fair contest can possess an unfailing self-assurance. *The one certain advantage of free trade is freedom itself.*

2. There are still a few good extra-economic reasons for preventing the greater specialization of productive forces by means of customs duties and so on: (*a*) because in the end it is more advantageous for a people to develop their capabilities in many directions;[18] (*b*) because materials for defense must be produced at home, in so far as they cannot be procured from reserves or from spheres of influence abroad; (*c*) because it may be politically undesirable to have foreign countries profit more by free trade than the home country.

3. It will often be useful to change an abrupt redistribution into a more gradual one through sliding-scale customs duties.[19]

2. PROHIBITION OF MIGRATION

As with free trade, freedom of movement would unquestionably

---

change), it is not certain whether they are better off than if they could have continued at their old occupation under the *former* conditions.

16. Furthermore, a few consumers may even pay higher prices under free trade because the new sources of supply, which are cheaper for the majority, are remote from them. Who will compare this with the advantage of the favored ones? " If we do not make the assumption of equal capacity for satisfaction, we are precluded from asserting that the repeal of the Corn Laws tended to increase the general welfare." (L. Robbins, *Economic Journal*, 1938, p. 636.) Only in extreme cases do subjective judgments virtually coincide.

17. G. von Haberler, *Der internationale Handel* (Berlin, 1933), p. 162; English edition (1936), pp. 221 ff.

18. Naturally this argument is true only within certain limits. Complete autarky would condemn almost any people to poverty and impotence.

19. In most cases, of course, a tariff to help over a period of adaptation, like an infant industry tariff, will be most likely to benefit a nation as a whole only if new enterprises would be profitable even though they themselves had to bear the cost of a changeover or of development. (For exceptions see von Haberler, *op. cit.*, pp. 207 ff.; English edition, pp. 281 ff.)

be advantageous to an individual in a given initial situation only if he alone were allowed to move. If all were to migrate, a man would have to consider that even though he adapted himself to a new situation as well as was possible, it might still be less advantageous for him than the old. It follows from this that even governmental influencing of migration may *under certain conditions* increase the general welfare, but this would have to be proved in every individual case. The prohibtion of migration in particular is a method, though an imperfect one, of preventing a redistribution of productive factors that are undesirable for a country. For instance, if too many dissimilar people were to assemble in a country with complete freedom of movement, it would be sensible to restrict the immigration of members of certain nations and races, as the United States has done, though perhaps it was already too late. The result is, of course, that instead of the excluded productive factors, their products attempt to break in, just as, conversely, productive factors may sometimes be attracted to a country when their products are excluded.

Finally, provided that only one of the two factors has immigrated, a country that fights the entry of goods as well as of men or capital risks an outflow of the complementary factor. If, for example, the United States were to prohibit further immigration from Europe, North American capital would flow toward South America, to cooperate there with the diverted stream of men, though perhaps under less favorable conditions.

§2. The Facilitation of Adaptation

α. *Defects of a Free Choice of Location—in Reality*

One of the chief defects in the choice of a location as it is made in practice is inadequate knowledge of the facts, the difficulty experienced by individuals in drawing conclusions therefrom, and the interferences in putting them into effect. Now for an example of each of these *frictional difficulties*.

There is no lack of national price averages, the most important signposts in all economics. But there are almost no maps to show their local variations, as differences in barometric pressure, say, are shown on weather maps, though they would be of great assistance in choosing a location. I offer the first such for nonagricultural enterprises in the statistical section. A central bureau to furnish particulars on especially desirable and easily opened up locations, would be still more important than information on single locational factors.

Furthermore, location theory has made no real advance in the past thirty years, that is, since the time of Alfred Weber. The practical man therefore lacks scientific tools that would facilitate the solution of his location problem. Still, the answer can be found only by systematic trial, as was set forth in an early chapter, and thus can never be found for all times. All that can be expected of even systematic examination is an approximation. But suppose that a better location has been found. Removal to it encounters difficulties, many of which would have been unavoidable by any means. Our buildings, our living, our customs, our whole way of thinking, in fact, are still adjusted to a settled and immobile way of life.

A second major reason why the location actually chosen differs from the ideal lies in the *entrepreneurial profit*. Its frequent appearance prevents a result which theory leads us to expect: that only those undertakings survive, though really more by good luck than by good management, that are properly situated. He who makes a good profit can afford a poor choice of location since he pays for it not with his every existence, but only with part of his possible profits.

One more reason will be sufficient: the *accident of an early start*. There are two sides to this. Once a factory has been erected it cannot easily be moved. Even when the starting point has been wisely chosen, the location will be overtaken sooner or later by new developments; yet unfortunately it cannot be simply abandoned. For example, railroads still suffer today from the heritage of the stagecoach: the narrow gauge. The choice of a location may not only become accidental; it may have been so from the very beginning. In either case not only will the site of the enterprise directly affected be not quite right, but also the sites of all others that are closely connected with it and adjusted to it because of its size or its earlier start. When the file leader is in the wrong place the whole company is improperly drawn up.[20]

The accident of an early start is especially important in colonization. The first settlers naturally establish themselves near the harbor at which they arrived, because the interior has not yet been opened up. Seen from the standpoint of the history of the development their choice of a location is wise, but it is wrong in respect to the final outcome. That is, it has the unfortunate end result that the country is never settled uniformly. An unduly large part of the later immigrants will also settle near the harbor (New York), not only because

---

20. Thus a whole industry may be poorly located, yet its individual units may be unable to seek more favorable sites if external economies play an important role.

of an unconquerable fear of venturing farther, but even after careful consideration: The market is here, in the Far West the wilderness.[21]

To summarize: the actual locational pattern deviates from the ideal principally because the basic assumptions of a free economy—knowledge, mobility, and competition—are only imperfectly given in reality. As a consequence production is carried on in the wrong place from the first, or at least in the course of development.

β. *Furtherance of the Regulating Forces*

A very sensible location pattern can be achieved and most of the specified unfavorable conditions avoided even without governmental planning down to the very last detail. A few simple measures that tend to order space in the large will suffice. These are measures which lead the individual to subordinate himself in a sensible way to the whole, even when only his own interests are his immediate motivation. First we shall briefly sketch the general nature of these measures (1), and then their concrete form in respect to an objective that is especially important today (2).

1. *Organizing Factors.* The realization of knowledge,[22] mobility, and competition is the basic formula of all liberal economic policy, and we indicate some of its consequences for spatial organization. Knowledge of the facts essential to a choice of location should be disseminated. These can be systematically established for places and nonagricultural enterprises far more completely by government bureaus than they could possibly be by private persons. The next step would be to make available to entrepreneurs the scientific means for evaluating these facts, through institutes or individual investigators that would perform the necessary calculations for them.

---

21. In Uruguay settlement proceeded from Montevideo. There most of the immigrants and a large part of the population in general have collected. (W. Mädje, *Uruguay, Volkwerdung und landwirtschaftliche Erschliessung eines überseeischen Einwanderungslandes* [Berlin, 1941], pp. 34-35, 39.)

22. The work of F. von Steinbeis is an admirable example of the efficacy of knowledge. His great achievements were in large part an outcome of the fact that he disseminated information in Württemberg that stimulated imitation of representative foreign products, and propagated information abroad that encouraged the purchase of Swabian products. This he did through expositions; educational trips; directories; technical schools; provision of foreign machinery, samples, and skilled workers; direct consultations; advertisement, and so on. He wisely regarded production and sales as of equal importance. (See F. von Steinbeis, *Die Elemente der Gewerbeförderung, nachgewiesen an den Grundlagen der belgischen Industrie* [1853]; and J. Häring, *Entwicklung und Aufgaben des württembergischen Landesgewerbeamts,* University of Munich dissertation, 1937.)

Secondly, the mobility that the entrepreneur needs in order to act according to the results of this investigation should be facilitated. In particular this would include lowering the cost of a change in location through special rates, a matter of special importance during the early days of settlement, when all locations are occupied experimentally and changes are frequent. There is a lack of mobility today in wages and prices,[23] and a failure of supply and demand to react promptly to their changes. Otherwise even a slight decrease in prices would necessarily help a structurally depressed area if it were in close contact with the environment on all sides. Exports and the consumption of home products would increase, men would leave, and new enterprises would come in. Finally, encouragement of the tendency for the number of independent economic units to increase in itself stimulates competition.[24]

2. *Factors Making for Dispersal.* Three of these are of special importance: (a) *The costs of distance and agglomeration.* There is reason to suspect (see pp. 396 ff.) that the economy underestimates the former, and communities the latter.[25] Proper knowledge of their importance, their correct assessment, and their burden, would result in considerable improvement. Enterprises would be careful to keep at a suitable distance from one another,[26] and communities to restrict their growth (see p. 75, note 11).[27] The natural *striving* for *independence* should be encouraged wherever large profits appear. Instead of being concentrated in a few great enterprises that are sensitive to changing situations, production would be divided among a greater number of medium-sized or even small ones. (c) Since

---

23. Not because of, but in spite of, the greater fixed costs. See p. 505, note 12.

24. Conversely, free competition itself favors this tendency to increase, whereas in a controlled economy the cost of mere information about, and subordination to, control measures is often too high for small businesses. In addition to this (competition by entry into the field), for competition of the already existing businesses see *Der Wettbewerb als Mittel volkswirtschaftlicher Leistungssteigerung und Leistungsauslese,* edited by G. Schmölders (Berlin, 1942). Special attention is called to the contributions of Eucken, Böhm, and Miksch, and to p. 196, note 142. For the sake of completeness it should be remarked that nationalization, or even the strict supervision of private monopolies, proves under certain conditions to be a solution that cuts both ways. Public monopolies are even harder to evade; they can crush potential competitors still more easily, need be less afraid of interference from above, and feel less often the cost-lowering lash of the struggle for profits.

25. I have been commissioned to investigate this in greater detail.

26. There are enough examples of spontaneous decentralization. See Z. G. Dorner, "Die Wahl des Standortes für Industrieanlagen und das Prinzip der Rationalität," *Journal der ungarischen Statistischen Gesellschaft,* XIX (1941), 41, 45.

27. A good mayor is proud of the *government* of his city, not of its growth.

such a large part of the national income has come to be spent by the government even in peacetime, an administrative center offers many locational advantages. *Self-government* by states and communities in all matters that do not absolutely have to be finally decided by the central government therefore has a decentralizing effect.[28]

3. *Control by Geographic Price Differences.* As a free economy is in general controlled by prices, so is its spatial organization controlled by local differences in costs of production, prices, and incomes. These are the levers through which all the factors mentioned above operate.[29] Every individual faces special geographic differences whose controlling influence is attuned to his exact location more finely than any planning could be. Thus there arises a meaningful geographic division of labor that may not be the best possible, but that in any case takes into account the suitability of men and soil no less than the significance of their location and the direction of their needs. If geographic price differences were to be abolished,[30] or even merely frozen, they would soon have to be replaced by *complete* spatial planning, which would face the enormous task of taking into account the effects of thousands of locations upon one another—something that only the play of changing prices has so far been able to do successfully for any length of time. It would make more sense, instead, to increase geographic price differences, until they corresponded in general with the actual differences in cost.

γ. Anticipation of the Result

The state can shorten the costly groping of an uncontrolled economy toward equilibrium by acquiring an idea of how it is likely to turn out, and then encouraging an appropriate develop-

---

28. With the distribution of industries among small towns, many would, of course, cease to be vacation resorts. The Ruhr was the price of the Rothenburg idyll. The question is whether decentralization reduces the need of vacations more than it does the possibility of vacations.

29. So much in the economy is unique, and not comparable with anything else. Only in special situations that resemble laboratory conditions do comparable features come together, and they are then treated in the same way. Thus identical products command the same price in the market, no matter in what uncomparable places and at what uncomparable costs they are produced. Markets are therefore the strategic points in the economic activity, from which all irrational activity is guided.

30. Many deficiencies in the spatial organization of the German economy after World War I resulted from an endeavor to abolish geographic price gradients through erroneous policies respecting wages, taxes, and the price of land. Many new depressed areas were created in this way, and many urban agglomerations extravagantly encouraged.

ment. We single out discovery of the economic suitability of a location as especially important. First, the most significant advantages of the area under examination are investigated.

1. *Labor.* In mining regions female labor is cheap, and textile industries might therefore be profitable. In overpopulated agricultural countries casual and irregular part-time work (such as seasonal work) is poorly paid; therefore home weaving or the manufacture of toys or cigars might be possible.[31] With the eye of genius, von Steinbeis recognized that for Württemberg highly skilled labor was the most important location factor, systematically developed it, and then selected industries accordingly. Without this official encouragement the economy of Württemberg as a whole would hardly be in such sound condition today.

2. *Soil.* Natural resources that are worth developing should be discovered, and the suitability of arable land determined.

3. *Savings in Freight.* Here many suggestions can be made. (*a*) Shipping weight can be reduced to advantage by foundries, mill, oil and sugar refineries, distilleries, tanneries, wool processors, waste converters, and the like. (*b*) In the case of goods with comparatively high freight costs, such as vegetables, fruit, meat, milk,[32] bricks, crockery, furniture, repairs and other local needs, artificial fertilizers, fuel, and so on, local production can replace imports. The typical program for colonial industries is based on this possibility.

4. *Sales.* With truly national consumer's goods, the advantages of close contact are apparent.

The first incomplete indications appear somewhat in the manner given, but they must be thoroughly investigated with a combination of location and market analyses in the manner indicated, that will bring to light locational openings. The economy can avoid many disastrous experiments, though not all, by prompt governmental investigation.

§3. Enhancement of the Result

In the third place, the state can compel certain new combinations, and here its intervention becomes truly creative. This is a rational course when the measures adopted aim at achieving for a given

---

31. H. Metzdorf, "Raumordnung und Agrarpolitik," *Vierteljahrshefte zur Wirtschaftsforschung,* XVI (1941–42), 119.

32. For information on California see G. Pfeifer, *Die räumliche Gliederung der Landwirtschaft im nördlichen Kalifornien* (Leipzig, 1936), p. 40.

nation, area, or industry, by constructive combination, a result greater than would be possible with the free play of forces. It is impossible, of course, to give a complete account, but we can discuss briefly a few possibilities that are of special interest in the present connection.

α. *Advancement of a People*

A people can be made more prosperous, first, by fuller utilization of resources already present: by education; the encouragement of progress; better distribution of national income and national wealth; more normal distribution of the population; a more reasonable proportion between working hours and free time; elimination of much harmful, inferior, and useless production; regulation of production and consumption in order to encourage easier and more complete success of the economically rational; and so on. Second, by increasing these resources at the expense,[33] or at least with the help, of other nations. Here belong plundering, subjugation (reparations, enslavement), expulsion (from the home country or from foreign markets), development (education of backward peoples and opening up their territories), exclusion of competing peoples, and duties that are borne by foreign countries or at least improve terms of trade.[34] We select for discussion three stages of spatial expansion.

1. *Colonies.* These broaden the view, offer new problems, give those who crave adventure an outlet for their activities, and may be of military importance as well. But what is their real economic value?[35] Plundering of a country and its people and exhaustion of the soil may provide great temporary gains, but a harsh, precipitate seizure removes valuable possessions accumulated by man and nature over long years. The flow of taxes and the advantages of cheap goods, labor, and land last longer, either because of a natural surplus or because of an artificially created market condition (monopolistic demand—supply extorted by high head taxes). It is more fitting

---

33. See J. J. Spengler ("The Economic Limitations to Certain Uses of Interstate Compacts," *American Political Science Review*, XXXI [1937]), who believes that all state intervention that does not merely help economic laws to prevail can achieve results only at the cost of other countries.

34. G. von Haberler, *Der internationale Handel* (Berlin, 1933), pp. 215 ff.; English edition [1936], pp. 290 ff. A. Lösch, "Ein Auseinandersetzung über das Transferproblem," *Schmollers Jahrbuch*, LIV (1930), 1093–1106 (typographical errors corrected in LV, 192).

35. On the question whether colonies save foreign exchange see the first edition of this book, pp. 221 f. On varieties of colonial trade policy see von Mühlenfels, *Weltwirtschaftliches Archiv*, LVII (1943).

and apparently more profitable also to develop colonies, though it is more risky in the long run *when the drive for profit and for power subsides.*[36] Certainly the return to capital and the incomes of the colonies are at first higher than at home, but how often has the time soon come when blood and money have been lost for the mother country: lost either to foreign peoples and new conquerors or by succumbing to the temptation to strive for independence. Thus investments are stolen, expropriated, or dissipated. Europe has already lost untold billions by helping in the development of the rest of the world, including its own competitors—more, perhaps, than it ever gained from this development.

As for these benefits, did it matter *who* did the colonizing? If free trade, peace, and the principle of the open door prevailed it would be practically immaterial, from the standpoint of economics, who governs a colony. Not quite, however, for its officials would still belong to the governing nation and consequently many official purchases would go to the mother country, not only because of sentiment but also because of the many and varied reasons of greater "nearness." Again, her colonists would have the advantage of a common language, and so on.

In reality, free trade does not exist, but preferential treatment of the goods of the mother country. Nor does the principle of the open door prevail; on the contrary, home capital and colonists of like race are favored.[37] Finally, perpetual peace does not prevail, but rather the possibility of wars.

Thus colonies increase emigration and exportation from the mother country, and improve its supply conditions. Trade and migration follow the flag.[38] If colonists themselves bear the cost of their government this is certainly advantageous, and may be so if they need subsidies.[39]

36. One-sided development amounts in the end to predatory cultivation. The raising of one single product, for example, has ruined wide stretches of African soil. (G. Lenschow, "Struktur und Probleme afrikanischer Kolonialwirtschaften," *Weltwirtschaftliches Archiv*, LIII [1941], 597 ff.

37. Consequently it is difficult for small nations with large colonial possessions to develop them as quickly as can large nations with but few possessions overseas.

38. This has also been proved statistically through the exhaustive investigations of C. Gini ("Trade Follows the Flag," *Weltwirtschaftliches Archiv*, March, 1938), though the exceptions to this rule are important. In any case, the share of colonies in the foreign trade of the mother country has increased considerably almost everywhere in comparison with 1913. (*Statistisches Jahrbuch für das Deutsche Reich* [Berlin, 1938], p. 148*.)

39. W. Sulzbach ("Der wirtschaftliche Wert der Kolonien. Die Zukunft des Kolonialproblems," *Deutscher Volkswirt*, 1926, pp. 300 ff., 334 ff.) is overly skeptical on this point.

If colonies overseas are to guarantee the economic independence of the mother country even in time of war, a navy becomes necessary. Most of the colonial powers in western Europe lie closely adjacent, whereas their oversea colonies are far away and promiscuously intermingled. With a few limitations in favor of France, Spain, and Italy, it is not true, therefore, that in defending its possessions against an aggressor a single colonial power would enjoy the advantage of shorter distance from its center of operations, as would be the case if every colonial possession surrounded the mother country. But when no other factors compensate for a difference in naval strength, it follows that only the strongest sea power, and consequently only one *single* colonial power, is really sure of communication with its overseas possessions in case of war. This one was England as long as she continued to maintain a navy equal to the two next largest together. For every rising industrial country in Europe there remained only the choice between allying itself with England or defeating her, since an unsettled rivalry would entail the constant danger of being cut off suddenly from essential overseas resources.

Concessions combine the advantage of colonies with a saving in government subsidies. In order to obtain and keep them, military power is needed in addition to diplomatic finesse, just as in general the promotion of foreign trade is essentially a political task.[40]

Colonies of emigrants continue to offer advantages to the former motherland long after they have become independent, for a common language, similar customs, and many personal ties favor trade with it.

A good part of Europe's prosperity is based upon her American offshoots, her Asiatic concessions, and her African colonies.[41] Up to World War I the great powers could compete for the size of their shares in these advantages, but in the course of this competition the object of dispute itself became smaller. More and more the *common* interest of the European industrial nations, preservation of their hegemony *in general*, demands consideration. Day by day it becomes clearer that they must abandon the vital principle of European special treatment or at least of the open door, if their armies and navies continue to neutralize one another. Not that the independence of colonies, the crumbling away of concessions, the separation of the American countries, and particularly the rise of new great powers, are merely the result of the decadence of

---

40. In special cases, of course, political weakness may in itself favor exports. Sombart traces the adaptability of the German economy in the past century to it, and others the increase of Germany's trade with China since 1918.

41. The association of capitalism and imperialism was not essential, though profitable.

European might. Though the course of events could not have been wholly arrested, it could at least have been delayed.[42] It is small comfort that overseas industrialization benefited Europe also, that it increased the purchasing power for her goods, and at most merely changed the commodity composition of the exports: more machinery instead of finished goods, more quality goods instead of mass-produced articles.

It is true that the proportion of overseas trade to the total trade of Europe changed but little immediately after World War I. In 1910 38 per cent and in 1930 40 per cent of all European imports came from overseas, while in 1910 as well as in 1930 31 per cent of European exports went to countries outside Europe (*Statistisches Jahrbuch,* 1931, p. 95*). Power and welfare are not absolute, however, but relative to that of others. They diminish in Europe, even though they may increase absolutely, when countries outside it grow powerful and rich still more rapidly.[43] European foreign trade has declined proportionately, though not absolutely. In 1910 Europe's share in world imports was 66 per cent and in 1930 59 per cent; her share in world exports declined from 60 per cent in 1910 to 53 per cent in 1930.[44] This means that the world outside Europe carries on increasingly more trade with itself.[45] No longer do all roads

---

42. It is said that the *situation* has changed for Europe. But the decisive factor is the changed *reaction* to this situation, which is no longer so logical and so decisive as formerly. See A. Lösch, "Die neuen Methoden der englischen Handelspolitik," *Weltwirtschaftliches Archiv,* LIV (1941), 338 ff.

43. In contradiction to the otherwise excellent presentation of O. Veit, "Industrialisierung und Welthandel," *Wirtschaftskurve,* 1936, pp. 349–361. It would be to the interest of European countries together to limit the exportation of certain patents, machinery, and books, as well as the emigration of skilled labor to, and the admission of students from, particular countries; that is, to prevent Europe from being pushed back into the position of a teacher. Yet the threat to European export must not be exaggerated. Certain advantages of situation (as compared with North Africa and the Near East, for instance), of resources (research, highly skilled labor, tradition, coal and iron), and of mass production (in so far as this is chiefly based on her own great markets) cannot be taken away from Europe at all for many years, or only by fantastic tariffs. This is also Alfred Weber's opinion ("Europa als Weltindustriezentrum und die Idee der Zollunion," in *Europäische Zollunion, edited by H. Heiman* [Berlin, 1926]), who sees consumption-oriented industries endangered most, labor-oriented industries less, and material-oriented industries least. On Europe as an agricultural location see G. Pavlovsky, "Zur Frage der räumlichen Ordnung der Landwirtschaft," *Internationale Landwirtschaftliche Rundschau,* Vol. XXXIII, No. 1 (1942), p. 351.

44. For a more detailed statistical analysis see W. Scholte, "Zur Frage der sogenannten 'Enteuropäisierung' des Welthandels," *Weltwirtschaftliches Archiv,* Vol. XXXVII, no. 1 (1933).

45. Even within Africa World War II is said to have developed a considerable trade. South Africa became the most important supplier as far north as the Equator. Enter-

converge on Europe. The world threatens to shake off its leadership, and Europe is becoming more and more just one continent among others,[46,47] yet finds this to be right!

2. *Large Economic Areas.* Their economic value (for their military-economic value, see p. 202) depends upon whether they represent what is left of a world empire or are composed of smaller areas; that is, whether they originate analytically or synthetically. In the former case, the results are disadvantageous in almost every respect; in the latter, it depends on the individual case. To what extent the advantages of free trade materialize is contingent on whether hindrances to trade increase or decrease on the whole; that is, on whether a large economic area is formed by the increase of restrictions on trade with the outside world or by the reduction of internal trade restrictions. In addition it is essential to distinguish the country at the geographical center whose market areas are most expanded by the removal of internal barriers, from the frontier regions whose markets above all are curtailed by the increase of outward barriers. The connection between the formation of a large economic area and the stabilization of economic development is not so simple as has been represented by some of those with no knowledge of cyclical relations.[48]

Certainly the economy will be less disturbed by political tensions at the center of the area than on its edge. In the monetary field it is possible to replace the shipment of international money by the less expensive clearing;[49] also, most motives that used to lead to exchange control between parts of the large area will perhaps disappear.[50] Economic planning will be facilitated, since internal

---

prises supplying local need appeared everywhere and more and more raw materials from overseas are worked up on the spot. Industry continues its spread, and world trade necessarily loses in importance thereby.

46. The loss of England's dominion over world trade around the middle of the nineteenth century is now followed by Europe's loss. See K. Wiedenfeld, " Raumgebundene und raumunabhängige Wirtschaft," in *Raumüberwindende Mächte,* edited by K. Haushofer (Leipzig, 1934), p. 274.

47. This may have undesirable repercussions on the other continents also. As a domestic economy cannot function without a strong government, so the world economy cannot function in the absence of a leading power or group of powers.

48. For this I must refer to my forthcoming work, *Wesen und Nutzen wirtschaftlicher Grossräume.* See also pp. 322 f.

49. This has always been done within the sterling area. (A. Lösch, " Verrechnung und Goldwährung—ein Vergleich," *Die Bank,* August 21, 1940.) To this extent the Keynes plan offers nothing new.

50. For the rest, the monetary standard within a large economic area is partly a matter of no consequence, and partly raises the same problem that would exist also

disturbances will be eliminated by pacification and external ones by isolation, especially in the central region of the area and to a smaller degree also on its borders. More than this cannot be said in the space available, but even so it is clear that the advantages of large economic areas depend upon many conditions, and that the vision of genius is required to recognize in what situations their creation would be profitable.[51]

3. *Unions.* A people can further increase its wealth not by forcing preferential treatment from others or laying claim to leadership, but by uniting with them as an equal. Then all customs duties among them will disappear as a rule, even though only gradually.[52] Vigorous industries push their market areas far into an adjoining country, whereas weak ones are thrown back from the frontier or succumb entirely.

The advantages of unions are, first, that all goods are brought from the cheapest place. Second, the wider markets enable particularly small countries to take full advantage of the economies of mass production in a good many industries.[53] Thus not only

---

without the formation of such an area. I hope to throw light on these questions in my *Theorie der Währung.* [*Weltwirtschaftliches Archiv,* LXII (1949), 3–88.]

51. The first large economic area was carved out by England from the pre-existing world economy. (A. Schlie, *Die britische Handelspolitik seit Ottawa* [Jena, 1937]. A. Lösch, " Die neuen Methoden der englischen Handelspolitik," *Weltwirtschaftliches Archiv,* LIV [1941], 312–348.

52. The abolition of tariffs was incomparably easier a hundred years ago, when the German *Zollverein* was formed, than it is today, because most industries still had very short sales radii. In the main, therefore, only enterprises near a frontier suffered from the competition of an adjoining country. After a union has been formed, prices will drop more sharply in the country with higher duties. First, because the prices of imported goods will be perceptibly reduced; and, second, because the resulting import surplus (= loss of purchasing power) depresses domestic prices.

53. From a definite price onward (the highest delivered price at the former frontier) the demand curves of those enterprises with the lowest delivered price at the frontier fall less after union than those of neighboring competitors beyond the border. Then it may even happen that, after the Chamberlinian operation has been undertaken, the new point of tangency between the demand and cost curves lies lower when the latter is not broken (as in Figure 48). This is shown in Figure 59, where N' is the new demand curve and P' the new equilibrium point. The market area within the frontiers of the old state may be curtailed or extended, but the sales *must* extend into the other member of the union if prices are to fall. In Figure 60 the limits of the market area before the formation of the economic union are represented by a continuous line, those of the new one by a broken line. If Eastland had previously collected duties of a height DJ, the market of A in Eastland would be bounded by CDE if deliveries could be made directly to every point, and by FDG if only through the customhouse B. If HK represents not a customs border but a narrow river with a bridge at B, the eastern market area would be bounded by the arc HJK.

has everyone in either country free access to the cheapest sources of supply in both countries, but many goods can be produced more cheaply than before. The advantages of mass production are added to those of free trade.[54]

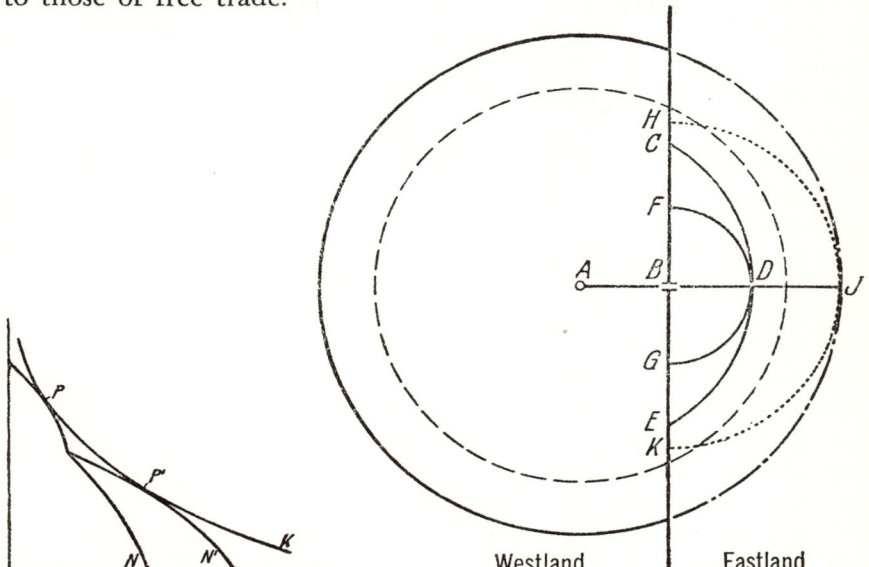

Fig. 59. Possible effect of customs union on demand and price

Fig. 60. Reduction of market areas by a tariff

---

54. These necessarily outweigh the disadvantages of a possible deterioration in the relation of import to export prices, such as easily occurs when small countries are able to produce their export goods more cheaply, whereas their increased demand is apt to make imports more expensive (if it affects them at all). These countries gain less per unit through free trade, but because by specializing they can produce and exchange greatly increased quantities, they gain more in all.

For the following train of thought it suffices to consider countries as units. Suppose that in ten days of labor America produces 200 cars and 200 chemicals, and that Germany produces 10 cars and 15 chemicals in ten days under the assumption that the United States is surrounded by a tariff wall. But let German production be 100 cars and 150 chemicals if the United States should change over to free trade. The exchange ratio of cars to chemical can thus fluctuate between 10 : 10 and 10 : 15. If the United States pursues a protectionist policy, the barter terms of trade will be in the neighborhood of 10 cars to $10\frac{1}{2}$ chemicals. With American free trade and the resulting German mass production, it will change to around 10 cars to $14\frac{1}{2}$ chemicals.

With American protection the United States thus gains $\frac{1}{2}$ chemicals and Germany $4\frac{1}{2}$ chemicals. Germany therefore gets the lion's share. With American free trade the United States exchanges 145 chemicals for 100 cars, thus gaining 45 chemicals compared with their no-trade situation. Germany gains only 5 chemicals, on the other hand, since she could produce 100 cars in the same labor time as 150 chemicals. The lion's share of the gains from trade *per unit* goes to the United States.

But what difference does it make to Germany that she can buy her cars in the

If Eastland is more thinly settled than Westland and migration is unrestricted, the population in the two countries will become even, other things being equal. This is easily said, but how strongly it influences social customs and attitudes! In Westland, for example, almost all the trips of daily life become longer. It is farther to the fields, to neighbors, to the baker, to the town hall, to the city. Individual villages disappear entirely, whether or not they are overtaken by the wilderness,[55] and some of the towns are reduced in importance; the whole hierarchy of central places is slowly thinned out. People voluntarily leave certain occupations, or marginal producers are forced out by the impatient. Average productivity rises, at least in agriculture, and the question now is whether this will exceed the increase in the costs of distance. Only where there are no possibilities for large-scale production (see p. 175 and pp. 179 f.) will efficiency and the size of markets decrease also. But in all other cases people widen their horizons, become healthier, more open-minded, more self-confident, but perhaps also more awkward, more sluggish, less sociable. The towns draw nearer to nature since they spread out more, yet, being less numerous, become unfamiliar again to many inhabitants of the country.

In Eastland all is reversed. Such a revolution in the modes of settlement and living requires much capital. In Westland it is not replaced or destroyed, and is newly invested in Eastland.[56] Furthermore many traditions are lost in Westland, and must arise again in Eastland.

β. Furtherance of a Country [57]

Is it enough to remove the evils associated in reality with the

---

United States for not much less than she could produce them for herself, provided she specialized in car production and free trade prevailed, compared with the fact that she can now exchange ten times as many cars although at a less favorable price? Even though the German barter terms of trade (per unit) have deteriorated, her gain from free trade (namely, 125 chemicals: $150 - 30 + 5$) is incomparably greater than the American gain of 45. (Of the gain of 125 chemicals, 120 are due to increased productivity which free trade, compared with autarky, makes possible, while 5 chemicals are due to the gains from trade proper. Expressed in chemicals, the productivity under autarky would be only 30.) [Translated from the first German edition, pp. 196–197.]

55. Instead of many villages becoming too small for local industries.

56. Thus, by increasing the amount of capital the Italian policy of the Hohenstauffen Emperors was a precondition to settlement of the East. See Dannenbauer, in *Festgabe für Haller*.

57. For many years its territory rather than its people was the main interest of a state. The emigration of hundreds of thousands of citizens caused no concern, but the state was ready to make war over every square mile of land. It is more understandable that the main interest of young countries should be in territory or, under certain

free choice of a location? That is, is it merely a question of creating the conditions under which reality comes nearest to the ideal result of the free play of forces without a long detour (§2)? Or does even this ideal case still show defects?

1. RESULT AND DEFECTS OF A FREE CHOICE OF LOCATION— IN THE IDEAL CASE

It is impossible to state in detail how the spatial order of the economy would appear in the ideal equilibrium of freely operating forces. We cannot solve the general equations of location, but we know the equilibrium conditions that they express and, as a first approximation, their geographic pattern as well. After all, this provides a general impression of a spatial order whose principal features one can accept: organic arrangement of economic landscapes with a favorable mixture of town and country (if man but desire this); regard for the suitability, but also for the geographic position, of land and peoples; equal use of all space by as large a number as possible of separate and economically independent units;[58] protection of the producer against excessive competition, and of the consumer against exorbitant prices; a larger national income; and, to crown the whole, equilibrium in spite of freedom.

Indeed, the most important result of this book is probably the demonstration of the surprising extent to which free forces operate favorably. But there are shadows in the picture, too. The mechanism is not guaranteed to work toward the welfare of the individual as *correctly* understood, or adequately toward the highest common good. First, it respects all human wishes sight unseen, whether these are wholesome or unwholesome. It assures the best supply of opium as of milk, and takes note of a desire for the metropolis just as it does of a love for the soil.[59] In short, as soon as sound

---

conditions, the people living in it *at any given time*. Here the people belong among the variables, whereas under α it is the land.

58. The decisive advantage of the free location is that it permits economic units to be independent without subsidies. But it guarantees neither the greatest production nor the lowest costs of production. On the contrary, the national income may be raised at the expense of the social income, by forcing persons to work in places or at occupations where they may be less happy but produce more in physical terms.

59. If men were indifferent in this respect, as in our simple scheme, the free play of forces would bring about a fairly regular distribution of settlements of various size, which would be somewhat denser only along lines of communication. Thus abnormal agglomerations are due only to man and to natural differences, not to the economic mechanism. Even the unsatisfactory living conditions in these agglomerations are chiefly the result of an injudicious use of income, not of an increase in the price of land. (A. Spiethoff, *Boden und Wohnung* [Jena, 1934], pp. 90, 109.)

instincts are lost it makes the influencing of the human will not superfluous but necessary. Education, propaganda, and pressure have to take over the function that habit used to perform.

Second, the free market mechanism works much more toward the common good than is generally supposed, though with certain exceptions. It offers hardly any protection against disturbances of the equilibrium in nature, or against the ruin of beautiful landscapes. Moreover, an economically advantageous location may be unfavorable from a military standpoint. But it would be wrong to conclude from this that economic considerations are irrelevant; that in doubtful cases, and thus in effect always, the military point of view should prevail and simply assign locations to each economic unit. In the first place, economically and militarily desirable locations often coincide. For example, it is favorable from a military standpoint if large places do not lie close to a frontier, since they can then be more easily protected. But the free play of forces works in exactly the same direction under the influence of political frontiers. As a rule the various economic implications of a political frontier greatly curtail market areas in an adjoining country, and most places with a central function therefore keep a certain distance from the border. The most important exceptions are supply-oriented activities such as ports, which, however, even a decree could move to another place only with difficulty.[60] In the second place, even in the interest of defense the economically best location is actually abandoned only in urgent cases, because every such removal lowers economic efficiency in case of war.

Finally, the free play of forces guarantees the economically best result only in a static state. In a developing economy it is wasteful to introduce every technical improvement immediately and to order the moving van instantly with every shift of the best location. To anticipate the common misconception: the waste does not lie in the fact that the old discarded machinery was still perfectly good, or that removal was carried out at a loss. As long as production is cheaper with old machinery than with new, even though perhaps ignoring depreciation—that is, as long as the old has real economic (not technical) value—it will not be discarded at all.[61]

Similarly with a change of location. A location will be aban-

---

60. Most of the large Canadian cities, for instance, lie surprisingly near the American border. This is mainly because of climate and the natural routes of communication.

61. This has been shown with the utmost clarity by G. von Haberler, *Der internationale Handel* (Berlin, 1933), pp. 138–139; English edition (1936), pp. 183 ff.

doned only when it does not produce cheaply enough even though the cost of all installations has been completely written off. The difficulty lies elsewhere: the new machinery and the new location are more advantageous only *under certain assumptions.* In the calculations a definite length of life or a definite, and generally shorter, amortization period is assumed for the better machinery and the newly erected plant. If the new machinery is replaced by still better, or if the new location is changed again before the end of this period, the calculation was *wrong.* In retrospect, it turns out that considering their *actual* length of life the new machinery and the new location did not produce by any means so cheaply as had been assumed originally, because future improvements had been anticipated incorrectly or not at all. If the future had been known, the old factory often enough would never have been sacrificed to the first improvement. One would have waited until a second improvement, still greater in comparison with the original condition, had arrived. Not to be able to wait, always to want the best machines at the moment (not only technically, but economically best), to react instantly to every change in locational factors, merely decreases profits in some cases, but in others it means real private and social loss. The latter is more probable the less superior is the second machine or the second location to the first.[62]

2. RESULTS FOR SPATIAL PLANNING

We have found two compatible aims of a sensible location policy: to help bring about the results of a free economic mechanism (§2), and to modify them. To bring them about when they are reasonable in themselves and not fully achieved without help only because of frictional resistance (lack of knowledge and mobility). To modify them, first, when even in the absence of frictional difficulties these results represent not the most advantageous economically, but a historically conditioned situation, either because they still depend upon accidents in past development (the first start), or are in danger of being refuted later by the incalculable future. To modify them, second, when the utility calculations of the individuals upon which the economic result was based are acceptable in their own interest

---

62. Hence it is not at all unreasonable for large firms to buy up new inventions without using them. One might even imagine a tax on progress that had to be paid by everyone who improved his machinery or location, and that would be refunded if the supposed improvement turned out to have been precipitate. Such a tax would increase the national income and be a guarantee against overhasty development. As a tax on location it would discourage removal without retarding progress.

(abnormal individual cases or mass phenomena) or in the general interest (perhaps because of insufficient allowance for natural, aesthetic, military, or future interests).

What is to be done in the individual case cannot be stated in advance. Politics must determine the order of importance for the various aims.[63] Like medicine, economics can only provide the means. These can be classified according to the gravity of the intervention (restraints, prohibitions, lures, orders); according to its cost (compulsion, payment, education), its extent (an individual or an inclusive plan, the latter of which may be for a locality, a district, a country, or an empire). Here we distinguish with respect to the moment; that is, according to whether economic policy forms the locational system from its very beginning or whether it intervenes only later in an already existing system.

(aa) *Spatial Organization in Old Countries.* In adapting an existing order to the ideal there is a choice between altering it abruptly and ruthlessly, or guiding it gradually toward the desired form by influencing its further development. The supreme ideal is the welfare of the country. This is hard to define, but there is a series of generally accepted goals that serve this end, and in the interest of brevity I have drawn up in tabular form a hierarchy of means to these ends (Table 17).[64,65]

---

63. It balances special interests, for example, in the competition for water by households, agriculture, power stations, industry, and communications (see Heiser, *Raumforschung und Raumordnung*, 1938, pp. 31–36). Final decisions must be made by those who venture, not by those who balance one argument against another.

64. It was a difficult task, not only because different means serve the same goal, but also because the same means may serve different goals. This would be clearly shown by a large chart, but Table 17 seems to me to be the next best method of presentation. It should be added in general that methods of the same rank often favor one another, though this is not always indicated in the table. I have also included certain methods about which I entertain grave doubts (followed by an asterisk), if they are in use. Unfortunately there was not space for either criticism or comments. As the starting point is in reality the actual, not the ideal, pattern of a free economy, methods discussed in §2 have been repeated in the table.

65. On planning in Germany within the 1938 borders, see, for example, H. Muhs, "Die Raumordnung vor neuen Aufgaben," *Raumforschung und Raumordnung*, 1938, pp. 476–480 (programmatic); W. Fischer, "Die Organisation der Raumordnung," *ibid.*, 1938, pp. 225–229 (organization); K. Brüning, "Über die Bearbeitung von Raumordnungsplänen," *ibid.*, 1941, pp. 6–12 (working methods); F. Kann, "Grundsätze für die Bereinigung des deutschen Dorfes," *ibid.*, 1942, pp. 386–394 (rural reorganization); G. Isenberg, "Der Umfang und die Auswirkungen der ländlichen Neuordnung in Deutschland," *Deutsche Verwaltung*, 1942 (planning the optimum size for a farm); W. Puttkammer, "Forderungen der Raumordnung an die Standortauswahl," *Raumforschung und Raumordnung*, I [1937], 358–364 (location policy); *Raumforschung und*

Table 17. SYSTEM OF METHODS FOR REGIONAL PLANNING

Method for	No.	Goal	Attained by	Method for	No.	Individual Methods (continued)
A	A	More healthful life	I–IV	a h x y	3	Proper cost allocation (see p. 137[5] footnote 000, and p. 238)
B	B	Higher earnings	V–VII	a c n v	4	Closed regions[1]
C	C	Fostering of *Kultur*	u v w z	a y z	5	Regions to be promoted
D	D	Military protection	a r s t	a	6	Graduated tariffs for coal and raw materials
		Methods		a c t	7	Separate zoning of residential and industrial areas
A	I	Life nearer to nature	a–c	b w	8	Preference to local people and firms
A	II	Easier life	d z	b c	9	Ownership of homes
A	III	More secure life	f g i x	b c	10	Ownership of land[2]
A	IV	More independent life	h	c	11	Easy access to nature[3]
B	V	Conservation of productive powers	d m–p	d	12	Forestation of remote land
B	VI	Increase of productive power	n p–r	d	13	Consolidation of agricultural land
B	VII	Better utilization of produtive power	d f i–m	d	14	Reversion of land to nature*
			x y	d	15	Interchange of migratory workers*
		Auxiliary Methods		d w	16	Consolidation of supply and market areas[4]
D I	a	Decentralization[22]	1–7	d	17	Maintenance of adequate inventories
I	b	Intimate contact	8–10	d	18	Consolidation of railway lines on outskirts of towns
I	c	Recreation	4–7, 9–11	d	19	Remove large railway and industrial installations outside towns
II V VII	d	Avoidance of unnecessary roads	12–19	f	20	Specialization in nonagricultural enterprises*
VII	e	Avoidance of traffic jams	52	f	21	Full-time employment* (see p. 164, footnote 1)
III VII	f	More assured basis for business planning	20–22	f	22	Consolidation of landed property*
III	g	Adequate size of enterprises	23–26	g	23	Obligatory licensing for new enterprises*
IV	h	Encouragement of small enterprises	1, 3, 27/29	g	24	Merging of old enterprises*
III VII	i	Elimination of unprofitable nonagriculutural enterprises	25/6	g i	25	Elimination of submarginal enterprises*
VII	k	Encouragement of old nonagricultural enterprises	27/8, 30	g i	26	Discontinue subsidies
				h k l	27	Decrease costs[5]
				h k l	28	Increase sales[6]
VII	l	Introduction of new nonagricultural enterprises	27/8, 31/5	h	29	Break up large enterprises
				k	30	Improve quality
				l	31	Survey possibilities of technical improvements[7]
V VII	m	Prevention of damage	36/7, 46	l	32	Test economic suitability of locations (p. 239)
V VI	n	Soil conservation	4, 37/40			
V	o	Water conservation	37, 41	l	33	Take over preliminary risks[8]
V VI	p	Control of climate	37, 42/4	l	34	Compulsory locating of monopolies
VI	q	Increased productivity	45/6	l	35	Encourage enterprising persons[9]
D VI	r	Regulation of size of population	47/8	m	36	Organize simultaneous and general advance[10]
D	s	More self-sufficiency*[22]		m–p	37	Promote[11] woodlands and thickets*
D	t	More protected settlement	7	n	38	Soil conservation[12]
C	u	Protection and planning of labor	49/50	n	39	Soil improvement[12, 13]
C	v	Preservation of nature	4, 51	n	40	Increase amount of land[14]
A C	w	Spatial communities	2, 8, 16, 53	o	41	Regulate supply and use of water[15]
III VII	x	Diversification of business possibilities	3	p	42	Influence precipitation[16]
VII	y	Full use of public installations*	3, 5, 27	p	43	Influence warmth[16]
				p	44	Utilize industrial gases*[17]
C II	z	Encouragement of poor regions	5, 34	q	45	Education
				q m	46	Rational basis for setting wages[18]
		Individual Methods		r	47	Influence natural increase of population[23]
a h	1	Encouragement of independence		r	48	Influence migration[19]
a w	2	Autonomy of units of manageable size		u	49	Protect national monuments
				u	50	Foster pattern of settlement
				v	51	General partial protection of nature[20]
				e	52	Separate local and through traffic[21]
				w	53	Encourage obvious central points

(1) Closed to new nonagricultural enterprises, building (urban parks, good farm land), cultivation (danger of wind erosion), alteration (preservation of wild life, etc.). Zoning is in general an important measure in the organization of space. (2) For example, by free divisibility. (3) Thus permit no factories, warehouses, squares, etc., to intrude on the edge of a town between the residential quarter and the open country. (4) By accurate calculation of the costs of distance (see pp. —— ff.), organization of the market, protection of a region, exchange of customers; knowledge of neighboring associates, and promoting the maintenance of inventories. (5) With small enterprises: promote small-scale technique (small motor, for instance); tax advantages. With old nonagricultural enterprises: rationalization of the enterprise and the industry (standardization, regulating the working up of national resources); foreign models; cheap raw materials (geological research, reclamation of waste). With new nonagricultural enterprises: reduction of freight and taxes and other rewards for an adaptable choice of location. (6) With small enterprises: development of a demand for quality, public orders. With old enterprises: dissemination of knowledge of their existence (by common

advertising) and their quality (by expositions). With new enterprises: public orders, curbs on importation. (7) Encourage research, publish the results; instruction, advice, study of foreign achievements. (8) Infant industry tariffs, temporary tax exemption, establishment of public installations (roads, electricity, water, railway station). (9) For example, admit political and religious refugees (Huguenots). (10) Important in fighting many pests. (11) Protection against wind and erosion, equalize precipitation, sanctuaries for insectivorous birds (A. Seifert, *Die Heckenlandschaft* [Odal, 1942], pp. 323–333). (12) Protection against drifting and erosion (woods, hedges, protective planting, and perhaps prohibition of plowing), against leaching (suitable fertilizers), and against building on good arable land. (13) Irrigation and drainage. (14) By dikes, clearing, and improvement. (15) For example, requiring licenses for large consumers, equalization of peak demands for various regions. (16) Encourage rain: forestation, facilitate evaporation from open water (slow and shallow flow), rainmaking by cannon fire and seeding clouds. Prevent rain: clear forests, rapidly flowing or deep water, cause rain to fall over the sea, eliminate the rainy season (the plan to widen the English Channel, which is supposed at the same time to moderate the climate of northeast Europe. See A. Jaumann, " Gelenktes Klima," *Deutscher Volkswirt.*, 1942, pp. 972–974), hail rockets. (17) Locate industry to windward [sic]; keep exhaust gases (carbon dioxide, iodine) in the country with ventilators (Kaserer, *Berichte über Landwirtschaftl*, n. s., Vol. XXVIII). (18) For example, time rates, not piece rates, for the finishing of expensive products that are easily spoiled (investigations of *Refa*). (19) For instance, *increase immigration by indenturing*,* attract by free land for settlement (United States), expectation of independence, tax exemption, supplying of public service (dwellings), beautifying of landscapes, and so on. (20) Protective animals, protective planting, protection of picturesque landscapes as distinct from protection of whole regions (closed areas). (21) Also in urban traffic. Direct through traffic past center of town. (22) Parallel where possible by the size of the locality and enterprise. The best relation of agglomeration and dispersion from the standpoint of aerial defense varies. (23) See, for example, F. Reichert, *Das Gleichgewicht der Geschlechter im Heiratsalter* (Berlin, 1942).

(bb) *Spatial Organization ab ovo.* If the development of a young country were left entirely to the play of free forces, the vivid pictures of unbridled land grabbing would be repeated in all its magnitude and cruelty, with all its unprecedented achievements and

---

Raumordnung; and many monographs. Valuable data for reorganization are provided by the District Maps of the Reichs Bureau for Spatial Organization, which indicate statistically and descriptively the economic structure of individual districts and permit comparisons among them. (See *Erläuterungen zu den Kreisübersichten für das Wirtschaftsgebiet Niedersachsen* [Oldenburg, 1941].)

Kann (*Raumforschung und Raumordnung*, 1941, pp. 361–365) illustrates the reorganization of a village on the basis of an ideal. Furthermore, Bohnert (*ibid.*, 1943, pp. 79–84) has developed careful plans for a rural reorganization of Württemberg (for my objections see pp. 65, 66 f., 115, 195, 234, and elsewhere), though they are much too radical. For an example of modification of an old industrial location system that was established in the first place largely by planning, the reader is referred to the plan for the spatial organization of Württemberg (*Raumforschung und Raumordnung*, II [1938], 13 ff.). Most of its proposals result directly from a comparison of the real with the theoretical pattern; for instance, the plans for through highways, consolidation of farms, and a more even distribution of population and industries. For this purpose the regions where more, or fewer, or the already existing number of inhabitants seemed desirable were outlined on maps. The most important preliminary study consists, as theory indicates, in establishing gaps in production in regions that were to be more thickly settled.

War damage facilitates reorganization. In England especially the war gave a mighty impetus to the order of spatial planning, and three commissions published reports: *Royal Commission on the Distribution of the Industrial Population (Barlow Commission) Report*, (Cmd 6153) (London, 1940), which deals with industrial decentralization; the *Scott Report* (Cmd 6378), which considers the development of the open country; and the *Uthwatt Report* (Cmd 6386), unnecessarily radical, concerned with the nationalization of building land. A special Ministry of Town and Country Planning was established. For a discussion of regional planning in other countries see the *Barlow Report*, pp. 288 ff.

incalculable waste. The century of freedom thought that this wild behavior was curbed by hidden laws; the century of order believes that such laws must first be given.

In many respects it may be enough to establish the conditions under which a free economy functions by an act of the state. However, problems arise in the first settlement of a country the solution of which is best undertaken from the first by more farsighted planning rather than by the costly and often shortsighted play of free forces. The practical solution still remains incredibly difficult. It certainly does not suffice to create *some* sort of Utopia by force. What has to be done is to organize the economy even more efficiently in space than if it were left to itself.

First: Influencing the Start. If a country is being newly, or more thickly, or differently settled, the historical progress of its settlement influences the subsequent outcome. How can that short first period of stormy development be prevented from dominating unduly the following period of quiet growth? Furthermore, how can the possible neglect of extra-economic considerations be prevented when land is being occupied for the first time?

[a] *The Plan.* The first and greatest difficulty is to get a clear idea of the *concrete* goal. We know only its general outline: The economy must be kept within its limits, but within these limits it should be helped to attain its greatest efficiency. The concrete problem now is to discover the economically ideal size, distribution, and employment of the population of a given country, and what corrections in this picture are demanded by national health and national defense.[66]

---

66. The "investigators of space" school ("*Raumforscher*") tend to devote their real interest to these corrections, and to distrust a priori the locational pattern that results from economic principles. As soon as the emphasis is a little less extreme and the theory of the economics of space is interpreted, as by H. Weigmann ("Standorttheorie und Raumwirtschaft," in *Thünen Festschrift* [Rostock, 1933], pp. 137–157), say in the main as simply a *general theory of* positions, in which the corrections then receive their rightful place, one can thoroughly agree with them. See F. Bülow, "Gedanken zu einer volksorganischen Standortlehre," *Raumforschung und Raumordnung*, I, 385 ff.; G. Schmölders, *Wirtschaft und Raum* (Hamburg, 1937); H. Weigmann, *Politische Raumordnung. Gedanken zur Neugestaltung des deutschen Lebensraumes* (Hamburg, 1935); and others. In our sense, also M. Pfannschmidt, *Standort, Landesplanung, Baupolitik* (Berlin, 1932).

Actual knowledge of a real area is the mainspring of research. It is the best guarantee that investigation will be directed toward actual possibilities instead of losing itself in a mere play of the intellect. He who does not wish to pursue science may content himself with this experience alone. But how, then, can he compare the

We shall first eliminate the question of the optimum size of the population of a country.[67] I have shown elsewhere (*Was ist vom Geburtenrückgang zu halten?* 1932, No. 2, pp. 19–24) why it cannot be determined within wide limits, either practically or even theoretically. On the other hand, it is not impossible, but merely expensive, to estimate approximately how large a population must be to permit a certain desired material standard of living. The facts that must be known are the same as those required to determine the best employment for and distribution of this population; that is, the natural conditions of production and the traffic routes in the various parts of a country; the cost curves for the most important products (including the output of trade and transport) as well as the approximate demand as a function of distance with various population densities; and the range of foreign competition. With this knowledge as a basis the most advantageous situations for central towns and the principal locations for their systems of satellites, as well as the main lines of the traffic network, can be ascertained with fair accuracy. Then a locational system is obtained that corresponds more or less with our ideal (Figs. 28 and 29).

Though achieved by scientific means, the result is not absolutely correct, but merely a sound presumption—the best that can be done toward deriving guiding principles for a policy. Nothing more is to be expected, for the attempt has presumed, in fact, to solve the general equations for location. But as these are insoluble even by science itself, the practical man can only try to solve them with

"space of experience" with "mathematical space"; that is, the starting point of research with its result, as a scientific approach of equal rank? For the practical significance of the theory of space see W. Christaller's excellent article, "Raumtheorie und Raumordnung," *Archiv für Wirtschaftsplanung*, Vol. I (1941). Compare H. Meinhold's review of the first edition of this book in *Die Burg* (Krakau, 1942), p. 360. He who speaks about experience wants to convince those of like mind, but he who deals with the measurable aims to convince all by his arguments. It is another matter when, at the completion of his work, an investigator's findings for which he has paid dearly are announced with passionate enthusiasm. Another matter, too, when he who actually shapes space blends the ponderable and the imponderable into one artistic whole.

67. In this case, advancement of a *country,* it would be determined not by the highest per capita income but by the highest total income, which would presuppose a somewhat larger population. From a military point of view one would even have to say the highest *surplus* total income; that is, all income that is above the subsistence level and could therefore be used in case of war or renounced. The latter means that the labor concerned would be freed for military service. In case of war the total available excess income is augmented when capital goods are not replaced, and by other possibilities which temporarily increase the efficiency of the war economy. A. Lösch, *Was ist vom Geburtenrückgang zu halten?* [Heidenheim, 1932], Heft 2, 7th Exkurs, pp. 67–72.)

vision, sound instinct, and rules of thumb that can be derived partly from the conditions that these equations express and partly from the special location theory and from our knowledge of the structure of economic areas. The resulting prototype for the economic organization of space, obtained in this crude yet only possible manner, must now be corrected by the policy maker if he wishes to attach more importance to certain extra-economic principles.

In specific cases that are of practical importance today the situation is so simple that it is relatively easy to sketch out a plan; as when a predominantly agricultural country is to be settled anew,[68] and benchmarks for the structure of the settlement can be taken from an old agricultural region where conditions are similar and whose system of locations came about by the free play of market forces. Then it may be hoped that the copy also will stand the crucial test of functioning by itself as soon as it is left alone. Exact imitation, of course, is neither possible nor desirable; every new plan is a creative act. Larger farms can be laid out,[69] the superstructure of nonagricultural enterprises changed,[70] a definite system

---

68. Or is to be entirely reorganized, as in the planning of the newly acquired eastern territories. For this see the important general directions of the Reichs Commissioner 7/II (rural development) in *Reichskommissar für die Festigung deutschen Volkstums, Stabshauptamt, Planung und Aufbau im Osten* (Berlin, 1942), pp. 68–70; and 13/II (planning and formation of towns) in *Raumforschung und Raumordnung*, 1942, pp. 68–73. See also the interesting instructions of March 25, 1942, on the treatment of special cases (which corresponds entirely with theoretical expectations) by J. Umlauf, "Der Stand der Raumordnungsplanung für die eingegliederten Ostgebiete," *Neues Bauerntum*, 1942, pp. 281–286, which contains an excellent survey; the compilations, *Landvolk im Werden*, edited by K. Meyer, 1941, and "Struktur und Gestaltung der zentralen Orte des deutschen Ostens," *Reichsarb. für Raumforschung*, 1941; and the extensive bibliography in *Raumforschung und Raumordnung* and in *Neues Bauerntum*.

69. It is safer to plan in such a way that all incomes shall be larger than in the older country.

70. In an old agricultural region almost every nonagricultural enterprise has its typical lowest-order location: in the small village (blacksmith), in the large village (dairy), in the small town (veterinarian), in the county seat (slaughter house), and so on. Within the 1938 borders of Germany in 1933 there were 62,000 smiths, 12,000 dairies, 7,500 veterinarians, and 527 slaughter houses in about 50,000 communities, of which 46,000 had populations of less than 2,000. Depending on its nature, every pursuit, therefore, requires a population of different average size. But these figures do not necessarily provide benchmarks for a new settlement if the number of customers varies greatly in consumption habits from region to region. In planning the start, moreover, it is impossible to change the size of a population (especially upward) that a given nonagricultural enterprise will need according to its development, desired income, consumption standard, and so forth. In this case the typical location of a particular business may be a community of higher function, unless all villages are planned to be

of areas selected (see pp. 130 ff.), or special industries providing for distant needs can be planned. The more one departs from tried conditions, however, the less easily can the mutual repercussions be grasped. Just as the interdependence of prices can be controlled only as long as they are not too distant in fact and in time from the freely developed world of prices, so it is with the interdependence of locations. In the long run no planning is a match for thousand-fold universal interdependence.[71]

But so far we have a concrete spatial plan in its main outlines only. We know where we wish or expect towns and traffic routes to arise, and how large and of what sort farms, enterprises, and settlements will be or should be.

Before we proceed to put this plan into effect we must realize that it has three great weaknesses: (1) Erroneous results: When the actual economy attempts after its fashion to solve the equations for location by continuous trial and error, and thus is able to take into account much more completely the interdependence of all factors, our incomparably more superficially derived plan may prove to be partly or wholly wrong.[72] It may happen, too, that the planned cultural landscape upsets the equilibrium of the natural landscape and that this cannot be restored as planned; for example, the water economy may become unbalanced. (2) Erroneous assumptions: Even when the plan was originally good it may become antiquated by unforeseen development. (3) Gradual putting into effect: The plan shows the final goal, but settlement of a country seldom takes place in a moment. During the state of transition the population distribution will differ entirely from its final distribution,

---

larger than in the older area. According to circumstances a wholly different system of districts may become necessary. A solution must be found that will keep enterprises *alive* in the interest of the producers, and *within easy reach* in the interest of the consumers. The latter determines the largest size of the market area, the former the minimum number of its inhabitants. (See J. Umlauf, " Der Stand der Raumordnungsplanung für die eingegliederten Ostgebiete," *Neues, Bauerntum,* 1942, p. 284.) The locating of nonagricultural enterprises whose necessary sales radii extend beyond the planned area is a risky business. Unlike smaller ones, these cannot be guaranteed survival by keeping competition out unless they are monopolies or enterprises supplying the state.

71. The same situation appears in the modern formation of artificial landscapes, where there is as little departure as possible from the condition of free equilibrium in natural landscapes. (See Schwenkel, *Forschungsdienst,* 1943, pp. 120–123.)

72. Of course it is saved from this fate largely because a precise scientific choice of location is impossible in any case, considerable scope often remains for personal opinion, and *all* locations are made obsolete sooner or later by development even though the existing state of affairs is protected for a time by the law of inertia.

and the problem now is to correct the inevitable initial anomalies and guide the country to the final condition as planned.⁷³

Two important principles emerge from these three restrictions on the applicability of our plan: (*a*) As long as the desired condition is neither attained nor tested, all installations should be regarded as provisional and kept as mobile as possible. The log cabin, not the stone house; light luggage, not complete household equipment; the path, not the highway, are the signs of the pioneer. (*b*) As the correctness of the plan can be only presumed, not proved, even in the most favorable case, its realization in the sphere of economics should not be attempted by force, but only by light pressure. If the real economy resists the planned settlements despite their advantages, the plan should not be forced, but reconsidered; the more so because force generally demands subsidies. But the desire is to provide settlements that in time will be capable of independent existence; everything else goes against the pride of the settlers. Planners should never forget that some day their creations must undergo the crucial test of independent existence.⁷⁴

[*b*] *Implementation.* The methods by which the state can carry out its plan may be divided into those through which it cannot help influencing the organization of space, whether it has a plan or not; and those others that it is free to employ or not. To the first belong:

Laying out the administrative network: Administrative centers, and particularly the capital, are points of crystallization for trade

---

73. See Isenberg for migrating developmental enterprises (*Raumforschung und Raumordnung*, 1941, p. 150).

74. Where this rigid test is lacking (extra-economic plans or points of view), an increased responsibility is placed on the planner not to let his power degenerate into despotism. For as freedom means *freedom* for the false also, so planning includes power to do the senseless. Here is an example from my own experience that could hardly have turned out worse if the settlement had grown entirely without plan. In a small town where a few steps used to take one into extensive woodlands and fields of waving grain, one must now pass through miles of ugly human projects before seeing the beauties of nature spread out before him once again. The most beautiful spots have been fenced in for particularistic or even extralocal purposes, or actually destroyed. Forest glades gently inclining to form a noble amphitheater have been converted into rubble pits and leveled off to make a concrete stadium. Edges of woodland have been cleared to gain a few yards of space, and are now a horror to the eye and the forester equally. (See O. Feucht, *Waldrand, Stadtrand, Strassenrand* [Schwaben, 1941], pp. 489–496). In short, a spot in the heart of nature that was once suited to residence and the storing up of reserves of health is now so transformed as to waste them. If man is surrounded by bungled instead of a few perfect things, if he does not keep the symmetry of nature constantly before his eyes, he will be destroyed himself in the end.

and industry. The situation and central point of a system of economic areas may even be first determined by a political act—namely, the founding of the capital; our ideal case of a uniform plain is the best example of this. There are many instances of the attraction exerted by a capital. Thus Stuttgart, a capital, has far outstripped Cannstadt, though the latter is more favorably situated from the standpoint of traffic; and even after industrialization the towns in Württemberg that are seats of higher administrative units (*Oberamtsstädte*) have generally remained the economic leaders of their districts. Where government plays such a minor role as it does in the United States, on the contrary, political central points have seldom succeeded in rising to the position of economic central points as well. The country is ruled from Washington, a city of officials. Springfield, the capital of Illinois, is a village compared with Chicago, the economic center, and the same disproportion exists between Albany and New York. Where the administrative network really does play a role as a nucleus of crystallization,[75] it may be important not to choose a permanent capital in the beginning, since this would have to be in the vicinity of the place first settled and would distort the whole spatial arrangement. It would be better to move the capital step by step toward the interior as opening up of the country progressed.

Laying out the traffic network: In our ideal economic region a main traffic route had to be arbitrarily established in addition to the capital, before the *position* of the system was unequivocally determined. Indeed, an economic region owes it very *origin* to the advantages of a capital and busy main traffic arteries. It is for this reason that the laying out of administrative and traffic networks is such a powerful means in the spatial policy of the state. As soon as the main traffic arteries and their tariff schedules are given, the rest of the economic region, the feeder lines and the rural towns, can be established.

By thus providing a framework of capitals and main highways *before*[76] actual settlement the state has already exerted a powerful

---

75. Points of crystallization have almost always been extremely important in colonization. Thus the development of the United States was "a steady process of radiation outward from central points of settlement." (*The Trading Area System of Sales Control, A Marketing Atlas of the United States* [International Magazine Company, New York, 1931], p. vii.

76. On maps showing the distribution of population by ten-year intervals since 1850 (G. H. Smith, "The Population of Wisconsin," *Geographic Review*, 1928, pp. 402–421) it is easy to see how a few rather large villages without a hinterland arose at first in the wilderness of central Wisconsin, from which the surrounding country was settled in the course of time.

influence on the spatial order of the country.[77] In addition there is the surveying and division of the country, which only appear to be purely technical matters.[78] The state *cannot* escape these tasks. It is at liberty to decide whether in addition it wishes to supervise the completion of this framework by private initiative. In so doing it would act on one of two principles: It would either encourage or restrict private initiative.

Encouragement of private initiative: The bolder resolve is to facilitate decisions that have been freely arrived at. The result represents an approximate solution of our equations for location.

---

77. Compare the following description of the settling of western Canada, where of course the railroads were built by private enterprise. " *Urban centers* were created in direct relation to the railroads and the convenience of elevators for grain shipment, e. g., approximately eight miles apart with loading platforms four miles. These centers became distributing points for supplies." " *Larger centers* flourished at divisional points located approximately 110 to 130 miles apart, depending on accessibility of water and the efficiency of engines, at which engines and crews were changed. *The largest centers* were dependent on the location of branch lines and junction points, of terminal points, and the stimulus to population afforded by government buildings, educational facilities, and wholesale houses." (H. A. Innis, *Problems of Staple Production in Canada* [Toronto, 1933], pp. 96–97.)

For the economy of many colonies the railroad running from the chief port into the interior was the backbone of development, which was essentially limited to the supply region tapped by this road. For an example see G. Lenschow, " Struktur und Probleme afrikanischer Kolonialwirtschaften," *Weltwirtschaftliches Archiv*, LIII (1941), 571–626; and *Kolonial Rundschau*, Vol. XXXIII. Cross connections between these railroads to the interior were hardly profitable at first because of the small amount of domestic trade. Later it often proved unfortunate that not even a uniform gauge had been provided.

78. The rectangular division of land in the United States favors a latticelike arrangement of the traffic network. Yet I do not understand clearly to what extent the unrestricted seizure of land by the first wave of settlers, the squatters, predominated, and how widely government sale of lots of regulation size through the Land Office prevailed; that is, when later surveying simply confirmed the actual situation and when it determined this in advance. According to the classic account of Friederici the actual end result depended upon whether the squatters who occupied the land or buyers who wished to get possession of it won in the end. Then, too, the tendency to give everyone an equal amount of land, with or without payment, came into conflict with the enormous allotments to individuals or companies (not always with the condition of later subdivision among settlers). In New England complete new settlements were planned with considerable success, in the South with but little; in the West everyone lived for himself. In any case, it is important that the organization of new states took place according to plan. (G. Friederici, *Der Charakter der Entdeckung und Eroberung Amerikas durch die Europäer*, III [Stuttgart, 1936], 187–191, 256–324, and especially 301. F. J. Turner, *The Frontier in American History* [New York, 1921]. Meynen and Pfeifer in *Lebensraumfragen Europäischer Völker*, edited by K. Dietzel [Leipzig, 1941], II, 278–292. Pfeifer, *Geographische Zeitschrift*, 1935, pp. 138–158, 361–380.

The entire plan of the state is thereby put to the test. As explained in §2, encouragement consists in the promotion of all ordering and especially of all liberating forces, but, in the settling of new countries, above all in anticipating the result. Here a *preliminary* determination of possible locations for settlement and their opening up through public installations (water, power, traffic connections) facilitates choice by colonists and entrepreneurs.[79] Correction of the preliminary rough plan by the introduction of finer details occurs only with time, when free initiative no longer needs to be encouraged.

Restriction of private initiative: The free choice of a location is subject to certain pressure from the beginning, since it cannot simply ignore the existence of artificial traffic routes, administrative centers, and other locations already established. In order to protect the public interest with absolute certainty and otherwise to provide for necessary corrections in the results of a free organization of space, the common will of the citizens is influenced also by measures of the nature indicated in Table 17. When applied to a new country they are appropriately changed, and they perfect the result in comparison with mere self-regulation.

Second: Influencing Later Movement. With the conclusion of settlement the location system has grown less fluid. The stage of experimentation is over, the best location seems to have been found, at least for the settlement as such, and above all the settlers have begun to be less foot-loose. The huts of the first arrivals give way to permanent structures, and with roads the community spirit grows stronger. Migration becomes less frequent, more difficult, and less desirable. At the same time the tasks and possibilities of a public location policy decrease, but the little that remains must now be carried out even more energetically. Desirable migration encounters more obstacles and therefore needs greater assistance. At the same time, and partly for the same reasons, less migration is desirable.

---

79. The settlement of whole regions at a time has the advantage that public installations are immediately profitable. Such a settlement may be established also by special private settlement enterpreneurs like the "locator" for the settlement of the East in the Middle Ages, who founded whole villages according to plan (D. Haenelt, "Lokator in der mittelalterlichen Siedlung," *Neues Bauerntum*, 1942, pp. 404–405); by great landholders, railroad companies, colonizing co-operatives, and land speculators in the United States; by trading estates in England, which rent out whole factories.

If the agricultural advantages associated with a low population density do not outweigh the nonagricultural disadvantages, long-protracted settlement may even end in incomplete settlement (Alaska?).

With increasing capital investment the consideration that not every apparent improvement in location will prove advantageous in the end grows more important. As workers become more deeply rooted there is much to be said against their transplantation, which, moreover, generally means urbanization.

γ. *Encouragement of an Industry*

Again the principal methods are education, payment, and compulsion.[80] Only through education can the whole economy be promoted together with the particular industry concerned.[81] Compulsion, as practiced by mercantilists, for instance, where the state provided workers and customers to young industries, means disguised payment, borne in this case by those who had to deal with the industry in question. Overt payment appears in the form of lost subsidies (direct subsidy and protective tariffs) or of productive subsidies (infant industry or temporary tariffs). The latter are designed to help out in a passing emergency. Thus the tariff to protect German automobile and film production in the 1920's was economically justified later, when they were actually able to hold out against foreign competition with the introduction of the small automobile and the sound film. After these changes in the structure of demand the German market was no longer wide open to the cheap products of American mass production, even without tariffs.[82]

c. THE PRACTICAL VALUE OF ECONOMIC THEORY

We have found economic theory valuable to economic policy in three respects: It shows forth the assumptions, the functioning, and the results of equilibrium for the model of the economy desired at a given time. It is the business of policy to achieve the basic forms of the model and make good the assumptions under which it operates.[83] In addition, it can intervene in the progress of the economy (and

---

80. See also K. Schiller's comprehensive systematization of the innumerable measures employed in one single branch of the economy: *Marktregulierung und Marktordnung in der Weltagrarwirtschaft* (Jena, 1940).

81. The amazing possibilities are shown by the example of the Württemberg linen industry, which Steinbeis developed in the 1860's from a decayed to a model industry.

82. See A. Lösch, *Selbstkosten- und Standortverschiebungen von Genussgütern nach dem Krieg als Ursachen von Zolltendenzen* (Berlin, 1934), pp. 112–114 (*Zwischenstaatliche Wirtschaft*, edited by H. von Beckerath, Heft 4).

83. Certainly the most important attribute of an economic system is not that it shall function justly from every point of view, but that it shall function at all. The equilibrium price is at first more important than the just price!

here the quarrel between deists and theists will be recalled) —though the correct policy almost always begins at the roots, and not with consequences. Finally, theory need not await the slow and inaccurate operation of the economic mechanism, but can anticipate the results by reasoning. We found an important example of this in the planning of locations. Thus thought and action go hand in hand, from first to last.

But—and this is the most serious objection—the theoretical model of the economy is so simple that it does not fit the intricate conditions of reality at all. The answer must be divided into two parts. First, when the purpose of theory is to show how the simple fundamental thoughts implied in the attitude of a period shape even its economy, nothing further is required. The great rules of thumb for practical affairs are derived from such simple cases.

Second, however, with time (that is to say, with the aging of a period), science refines the model as much as the current state of thought permits, and only with this elaboration does the idea come fully to life. Finally the realistic refinement is lost in details, understanding of the model as a whole is lost, and the period comes to an end.[84] For there is a limit to our understanding, and this is where theory reaches the height of its development with its most important achievement by deriving from conditions that can be immediately understood propositions that, as dogmas, give a clue to the mastery of much more intricate cases. Theory is not useless because it simplifies; it is useless only when it does not simplify down to the essentials, or simplifies more than necessary.

This is certainly true: What pure theory describes holds only under its simple assumptions. For this reason it is so difficult to explain by pure theory what has historically developed. Here descriptive [85] theory helps out, to be sure, but it too has its limits. Yet

---

84. Where could this be better shown than in the history of philosophy? The beliefs of the Enlightenment were brought to a climax by Hegel, who made the last great attempt to understand the world rationally. A comprehensive system based on a simple idea! His system was the backbone of its time, the background against which even belief in an economic or a political equilibrium must be viewed. As the individual sciences broke away from the system and philosophy set them free and itself began to specialize in logic and epistemology, so that no one remained who had a complete view of the whole, the fate of the period was sealed.

85. In the sense of A. Spiethoff, *Die allgemeine Volkswirtschaftlehre als geschichtliche Theorie. Festgabe für Sombart* (Munich, 1933), pp. 79 ff. [The German is "*auschauliche Theorie*" as distinct from "*reine Theorie.*" "*Pure theory* rests on the foundation and the validity of an ideal type, 'descriptive' theory on the basis and validity of a picture of reality." (*Ibid.*, p. 82.) —W. F. S.]

wherever something new is being created, and thus in settlement and spatial planning also, the laws revealed through theory are the sole economic guide to what *should* take place. It is no different in physics. The size of an irregular boulder cannot be determined by the general laws of physics, though the stone must have originated according to them. The strength of a wall, however, or the plan for a machine, can be calculated in accordance with these laws.

Not in explaining that which has grown, but where man himself is the creator, lies the real sphere of applicability for the laws of nature and of economics that he has discovered.

PART FOUR. EXAMPLES

THEORY may be compared with reality for various ends, according to the sort of theory held. If it is to *explain* what actually is, the examination attempts to discover whether it started with a correct idea of its subject and arrived at an explanation that not only seemed possible but also corresponded with reality. On the other hand, if theory is to *construct* what is rational, its assumptions may still be tested by facts, but not its results. Its author can discover from an examination of the facts whether he has built on adequately broad experience; whether he has taken all objective or subjective essentials into consideration. His procedure resembles the preliminary work of an architect, who cannot lightly neglect the characteristics of a site, the laws of nature, and the wishes of the owner. But a comparison with existing structures will not show whether his blueprints are accurate; in our case, that is, whether the theoretical structure has been properly erected. For the existing structure may be as faulty as the projected one. Whoever tries nevertheless to do so, whoever anxiously submits the results of his thinking to the judgment of the existent, that is, to tradition, shows little confidence in his own reason.

No! Comparison now has to be drawn no longer to test the theory, but to test reality! Now it must be determined whether reality is rational. In any case this, and not verification of theory, is the purpose of the following investigations. In undertaking them I have attempted more to suggest how strong the forces of order really are than to intensify, by enumerating contradictory case, the discouraging impression of chaos under which we have suffered too long. If we are unable to alter such cases, they arouse only bitterness and despair. It is my desire to reinforce in my readers the conviction that a rational economic order is not only conceivable, but realizable.

Long enough has our science considered indiscriminately [1] everything that *is*, even where the problem has been not to explain but to construct. To be useful, of course, economics must investigate the effects of typical attitudes as well as the possibilities for bold ones.[2] But it would degenerate into a contemptible or even destructive science if it were to consider tolerable and degenerate mass phenomena in the *same* way simply because both are common and

---

1. Most radically, perhaps, through a widespread tendency in the United States, and most dangerously through Keynes, whose *General Theory of Employment, Interest, and Money* (London and New York, 1936) is really based on phenomena of decadence in the economy.

actual. For the lack of confidence in reason it must not choose reality for its judge. It should not, to its own destruction, maliciously collect all those cases in which ivory-tower theorists have been wrong without considering that, otherwise than in the natural sciences, this sometimes speaks more against reality than against theory. In a word, it must not become a science that describes chaos instead of preaching order.

For reasons already alluded to in the preface to the first edition, my investigations deal primarily with North America. The advantages offered by the United States as an area for observation need be recalled only briefly.[3] For extensive comparisons between theory and reality we must, in the words of Haberler, break theory down into theorems on the one hand, else it will exceed the energy and means of one single investigator. On the other hand, we shall do well to select clear and simple conditions even when dealing with reality. The enormous area [4] of the United States, with a uniformity of geographic, political, and economic conditions that seems extraordinary to European eyes, aids our purpose. Furthermore, tradition has but little weight, and until recently there was a deeply rooted belief in reason and liberty.

As investigations on the economics of space are still relatively few and scattered despite an awakening interest in all countries, it was important to assemble as much material as possible, and I have therefore drawn to a considerable degree upon foreign writings in addition to my own extensive studies.

---

2. Like that of Alfred Marshall, in his brilliant discourse on national socialism, "The Social Possibilities of Economic Chivalry," *Economic Journal*, 1907, pp. 7–29 [reprinted (with minor alterations) in *Memorials to Alfred Marshall*, edited by A. C. Pigon, Macmillan, 1925, pp. 323–346.]

3. T. H. Engelbrecht has already acclaimed them (*Die geographische Verteilung der Getreidepreise in den Vereinigten Staaten, 1862–1900* [Berlin, 1903], p. 4).

4. It would be a mistake, however, to think that distance plays but a subordinate role in Europe as compared with the United States, for the shorter distances there are offset by higher costs and a greater density of population. Between Berlin and Stuttgart there are more things upon which the imagination can linger than there are between New York and Kansas; and more people, with all their various characteristics, are crowded in between the two German cities and withdraw the south from the immediate interest of Berlin.

A. Location

Chapter 21. Locations of Production

a. UNIFORM DISTRIBUTION

§1. Nonagricultural Enterprises

Where the assumptions underlying our theoretical derivation of economic regions are more or less fulfilled, or variations are of merely local significance, market areas for the same branches of business should resemble even-meshed networks. Their centers, the locations, would then be uniformly distributed over the earth. The location problem for an enterprise that was about to be established would then be simply to find a space in the existing arrangement large enough to assure survival.[1] On the whole the distribution of most economic enterprises seems to correspond to this pattern, despite all differences in detail.

A map of the banks in Iowa (Fig. 61) will serve as an example of such a distribution. Although the picture as a whole is doubtless correct, I am not sure that the locations of the banks within each of the 99 counties is accurately shown. I have therefore introduced Figure 62, an enlargement of the outlined northwest corner of Figure 61. Here the distribution of the locations, including those of nonmember banks, is accurately indicated. If one does not emphasize individual cases, but is content with a general impression, the tendency to uniform distribution is clearly recognizable in both figures.[2]

Similar examples exist in the literature in large numbers. As a

---

1. See the description by W. G. Holmes of the choice of locations by the American cement industry after discovery of the Portland process. " Cement mills began to spring up in a variety of places which were advantageous distribution points. Each was designed to serve a domain of its own. ... During the years following, mills have been built at vantage points between the older locations, further dividing the market, until to-day there are but few ' holes ' large enough to support a mill of economical size." (*Plant Location* [New York, 1930], p. 17.)

2. See also the distribution of banks in the United States in 1910 (Paullin and Wright, *Historical Atlas of the United States*, Map 154).

final example, Figure 63 is a map of the great European fairs. We are accustomed to regard the fair in our own district as something unique and, in a way, without competition, but the map shows that it, too, has its rivals and that they endeavor to rub shoulders on

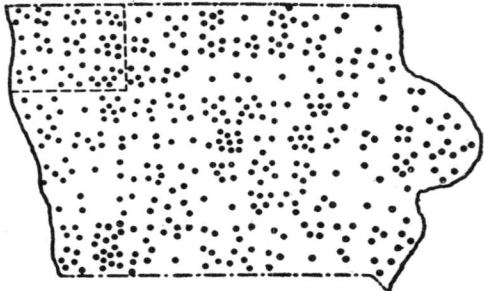

Fig. 61. Member banks of the Federal Reserve Bank of Chicago, in Iowa, on January 1, 1926. (*University of Chicago, Bureau of Business Research, Bulletin 17*, 1927, Map 5.)

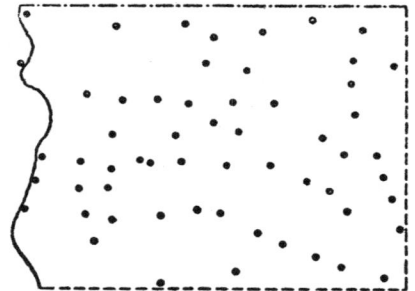

Fig. 62. Bank locations in the nine northwest counties of Iowa outlined in Fig. 61. (From information contained in Pocket Maps of Iowa [Rand McNally and Co., Chicago, 1935].)

every side with their neighbors. Variations are much more noticeable, of course, with such a small number of cases, and the distribution of the more numerous cattle markets, shown on a map in the same article,[3] is more regular. The reader is referred also to maps of the Russian tractor stations, dairies in Iowa,[4] American cotton gins,[5] and daily papers in Indiana.[6]

3. A. Allix, "The Geography of Fairs," *Geographic Review*, 1922, pp. 532–569.
4. H. H. McCarty, *Manufacturing Trends in Iowa* (Iowa City, 1930), p. 28.
5. E. S. Moulton, "Cotton Production and Distribution in the Gulf Southwest," *U. S. Department of Commerce, Domestic Commerce Series No. 49* (Washington, 1931). p. 56.
6. *U. S. Department of Commerce, Fifteenth Census, Census of Distribution, I, Retail Distribution*, p. 69.

I refer further to the distribution of American branches of Ford, of sawmills, cement and furniture factories, railway repair shops, the building industry, abbatoirs, mills, bakeries, printing establishments, ice cream plants, brickyards, breweries, and hotels; but above all to the distribution of trade and crafts, mechanics and artisans, and finally to the basic network of farms. In all these cases and despite all geographic differences the pattern is dominated not by the concentration and overlapping of market areas, but by their dispersion and separation.[7] Still, it is more important to establish the general significance of these locational types than to enumerate individual cases.

Fig. 63. Principal European fairs, 1921. (After A. Allix, "The Geography of Fairs," *Geographic Review*, 1922, p. 503.)

For this purpose I have investigated the distribution of selected nonagricultural American enterprises (Table 18). Branches with more than 1,000 factories in 1929 furnished exactly one half by value of the nonagricultural production. Its share in the production and consumption of various nonagricultural products was established for each state separately. The census (*U. S. Department of Commerce, Fifteenth Census of Manufactures, 1929* [Washington, 1933]) provided the basis for determining production, but a cruder method had to be used for consumption. As with few exceptions, such as beverages, perhaps, the consumption of the goods investigated would show only minor geographic differences, it was assumed that the

---

7. Sometimes this holds only for part of the locations. Thus French sugar refineries are either distributed throughout the beet-growing district or, in so far as they refine cane sugar, concentrated at three ports of entry. Similarly with gristmills. Some German cement works are scattered throughout central and southern Germany, whereas others concentrate near coal mines. Consider also the locations for natural and artificial carbonated waters.

Table 18. SIGNIFICANCE OF REGIONAL PRODUCTION IN THE UNITED STATES

Industries with more than 1,000 plants. Classification for 1929

	Industry	Number of plants	Production value added in millions of dollars	Of total production the following percentage was produced in			Consumption of surplus regions in per cent of their production	Production of deficit regions in per cent of their consumption	See note a
				Surplus	Self-sufficient States	Deficit			
1	2			3	4	5	6	7	8	9
1	Artificial stone............	2,438	59	32	49	19	56	58	86
2	Ice cream................	3,150	172	39	45	16	78	53	86
3	Planing mills.............	4,849	258	37	50	13	62	48	86
4	Bakeries.................	20,785	789	40	42	18	60	83	84
5	Beverages................	5,154	167	57	28	15	35	56	80
6	Artificial ice.............	4,110	171	47	42	11	56	34	80
7	Railway repair shops......	1,851	669	43	33	24	51	48	79
8	Newspapers and periodicals	11,524	1,347	48	28	24	54	52	78
9	Foundries and machine shops	8,605	1,753	66	25	9	61	26	73
10	Furniture................	3,778	522	59	25	16	51	36	71
11	Structural steel...........	1,482	232	68	7	25	57	46	71
12	Boxes...................	1,249	134	61	21	18	51	38	70
13	Abattoirs................	1,277	461	52	12	36	40	54	69
14	Potteries.................	1,749	213	59	17	24	46	43	68
15	Confectionery............	2,021	178	69	14	17	54	35	68
16	Printing and publishing....	12,712	740	54	18	28	41	47	68
17	Dyes....................	1,063	235	72	12	16	53	32	66
18	Natural stone.............	1,881	135	61	12	27	36	44	65
19	Canneries................	2,997	288	49	24	27	25	17	63
20	Butter...................	3,527	111	57	19	24	33	18	62
21	Grist mills...............	4,022	180	41	44	9	15	23	60
22	Electrical machinery and apparatus...............	1,802	1,329	78	13	9	45	17	57
23	Book binderies...........	1,108	72	66	14	20	33	31	56
24	Men's clothing...........	3,691	461	74	17	9	38	16	54
25	Woven goods.............	1,888	443	79	8	13	39	21	52
26	Shoes...................	1,341	451	74	15	11	30	17	48
27	Automobile parts..........	1,154	681	73	11	16	26	23	46
28	Wood products...........	12,915	854	79	10	11	27	16	42
29	Women's hats............	1,293	98	84	—	16	29	21	40
30	Jewelry..................	1,536	98	81	—	19	23	23	38
31	Women's clothing.........	8,082	775	76	1	23	14	26	35
32	Silk goods...............	1,491	319	85	12	3	24	4	35
33	Spinning and weaving mills	1,281	626	79	1	20	15	23	33
34	Furs....................	2,855	101	79	9	12	14	15	32
35	Cigars and cigarettes......	1,636	710	82	8	10	9	12	25
36	Turpentine...............	1,183	26	96	—	4	8	4	11
	Total		15,858	65	18	17	ca. 39	ca. 30	60

a. "Regionally" (that is, in the producing state) there was consumed (production of the self-sufficient states + local production of the deficit states + local consumption of the surplus states) in per cent of the total production. For the method of calculation employed see Table 19.

share of any single state in the consumption of individual goods would in the case of all goods be equal to its share in the national income.[8] Samples showed that using the share in retail sales would have given substantially the same result. If consumption was not more than 20 per cent above or below production, the state concerned was placed in the self-sufficient group. If consumption was more than 20 per cent below production, it appeared as a surplus state; and if consumption was more than 20 per cent above production, the state was entered as a deficit state. The results for all the investigated nonagricultural enterprises together are reproduced in Table 19.

Table 19

	Percentage share of total		Regionally consumed production as per cent of total production
	Production[a]	Consumption	
Surplus region............	65	25	25
Regions of self-sufficiency...	18	18[b]	18
Deficit regions............	17	57[b]	17
	100	100	60[c]

a. From columns 4 to 6 of Table 18.
b. Approximate values.
c. The difference from 100, in this case 60, would correspond to Florence's "coefficient of localization." (PEP [Political and Economic Planning], *Report on the Location of Industry* [London, 1939], p. 291.)

Thus 60 per cent of all production was consumed in the state that provided it.[9] When the nonagricultural enterprises presented at the end of Table 18, which lower the average considerably, are omitted, it will be found that enterprises 1 to 25, including 70 per cent of the production investigated, sell 70 per cent of it locally. This is far more than might have been expected from the usual descriptions of the concentration of industry. For example, 74 per cent of all shoes are made in New England and Missouri, to be sure, but local

8. Represented with sufficient accuracy for our purpose by wages and salaries in nonagricultural enterprises, and by agricultural cash income.
9. According to O. Schlier's enumeration something over 60 per cent of European industries also are wholly or in large degree consumption oriented—which is to be understood merely as a description, not as an explanation. (*Aufbau der europäischen Industrie nach dem Krieg* [Berlin, 1932], pp. 50 f.)
Isenberg estimates that in diversified regions 60 per cent of the income from nonagricultural enterprises is spent for the nonagricultural net output of the same economic landscape. ("Zur Stadtplanung in den neuen deutschen Ostgebieten," *Raumforschung und Raumordnung*, 1941, pp. 136 f.)

consumption in surplus regions and local production in deficit regions should not be neglected. The New England states and Missouri themselves buy nearly one third of their own product, so that, together with the 26 per cent of shoes produced in the rest of the United States, about half of all those manufactured are made and sold in the same state after all. But as the share of regional sales grows so does the share of the self-sufficient regions. Then not only do the surplus in surplus regions and the deficit in deficit regions grow smaller, but these two extreme groups lose significance in favor of the intermediate group. Small market areas obviously begin to predominate. The importance of these small market areas and the portions of market areas lying near a factory respectively has been greatly underestimated in the past. We conclude: (I) *The production and consumption of most goods lie closer together.*[10]

To this conclusion it may be objected: (1) That it is neither astonishing nor generally true, since in order to limit the number of nonagricultural industries investigated we have selected the half of industry with most factories, and thus probably also with an evident spatial distribution and the shortest sales distances. But in the first place it is immediately apparent from Table 18, column 2, that there is virtually no relation between the number of factories and the strength of regional connections. Thus the difference in the number of the widely dispersed factories producing artificial stone and the number of closely concentrated plants producing oil of turpentine is relatively small. Second, even in the case of the many industries with only a few hundred factories, perfect dispersion according to our standard must still be technically possible. Third, the significance of such enterprises with less than 49 factories, which technically prevents perfect dispersion since there are only 49 states [counting the District of Columbia], is very small. Fourth, and more important still, our measure of dispersion can no longer be applied

---

10. One has only to realize how much of the money spent by the inhabitants of a county town, say, where conditions are relatively easy to survey, is spent there (from 6 to 20 or 30 per cent according to F. Rechenberg, *Das Einmaleins der Siedlung. Richtzahlen für das Siedlungswesen* [Berlin, 1940]), or at least within the county. Expenditures for housing, retail purchases, local government, newspapers, personal service, workmen, beverages, electricity, gas, water, fuel, furniture, and such agricultural products as flowers, green vegetables, eggs, butter, milk, potatoes, meat, and so on, certainly make up more than half of the total. Even a world capital like Berlin with its enormous environs carries on more than half of its trade, calculated by weight, with the province of Brandenburg. (*Ausschuss zur Untersuchung der Erzeugungs- und Absatzbedingungen der deutschen Wirtschaft. 1. Unterausschuss. 2. Arbeitsgruppe. Das Wirtschaftsleben der Städte, Landkreise und Landgemeinden* [Berlin, 1930], pp. 94 ff.)

to them. For even when a product is made in only a few factories, these may be so regularly distributed in relation to the demand that their dispersion is as perfect as in industries with thousands of factories.[11] Only their market areas are relatively much larger. Thus our criterion includes only industries with short sales distances, even dispersion of factories, and general distribution of products. In addition there remain many industries that fulfill the last condition but not the first, and these too correspond completely with our theoretical picture. We may therefore conclude: (II) *The production of most goods is rather evenly distributed in respect to their sale.*[12] Finally, there are many nonagricultural enterprises such as cotton gins whose market network is both narrow-meshed and regular, but even so they cannot pass our test because their spatial distribution is limited. As these cases are exceptional our attention is drawn to the following rule: (III) *The market networks for most*

11. It might be thought that nonagricultural enterprises with but few factories, and in general firms that supply the whole United States equally, would choose their locations near the population center or, better still, the center of consumption. According to my calculation, based on the method of the United States Bureau of the Census, the center of gravity of retail sales in 1929 was somewhat to the east of Indianapolis. The more distant environs of this point, by which I mean the states of Illinois, Indiana, Ohio, Michigan, and Kentucky, do indeed contain a number of unusual types of factories. Of 45 industries with less than 25 factories, 11 were represented here in disproportionate number, among them those making matches, cardboard, bicycles and motorcycles, engraved articles, and other products. Yet this is not particularly impressive. It seems more important that an especially large number of firms with nationwide sales are found in this area. An excellent example is offered by the great soap factories in Cincinnati, which lies near the center of gravity of retail sales. From this point they supply the whole country with certain kinds of soap. As freight is a highly important item for the manufacturer of soap, and the sources of supply are favorably situated, this location appears to have been especially well chosen. Other examples from this region are the automobile industry in Detroit and the refineries of the Standard Oil Company in Chicago. It must not be forgotten, however, that in calculating the center of gravity of retail sales, distance is expressed simply as an air line, and traffic routes and freight rates are therefore overlooked. When these are taken into account it seems very possible that Chicago, so favorably situated in respect to traffic routes, is the real beneficiary of the location at the center of gravity. West of the Mississippi freight rates are much higher, and Canada has been omitted from our calculation. If these two most important factors are considered, the gravitational center of retail trade would have to be shifted toward the Northwest, that is, toward Chicago. If this is so, the gravitational center of consumption would exert extraordinary powers in the development of locations. In fact, the states around Lake Michigan, with Chicago as their central point, were the only ones in the northern part of the country in which the number of places of employment increased instead of decreasing in 1919–1929 (T. E. Thompson, *Location of Manufactures, 1899–1929* [Washington, 1933], pp. 50 ff.).

12. Not, however, in respect to mere area, since the population density is very uneven.

nonagricultural enterprises are widely spread out in space. " Belts " disturb our theoretical economic geometry much less than " districts " do, for example. This greatly strengthens the impression that *the spatial distribution of most nonagricultural enterprises corresponds very well, after all, with our theoretical model.*

(2) A second objection might be that the *Census of Manufactures,* upon which our investigation is based, does not cover all nonagricultural production. Enterprises with an annual production of less than $5,000, auxiliary production of retail shops, the building trades, most handicrafts, small mills, and so on, are not included. But presumably just these correspond especially well with the rule: Small market areas, regular and wide distribution and dispersion. When it is considered further how well agriculture, trade, banking, many personal services, and a great part of public administration fulfill at least the last two criteria, in addition to industry, there remain to be mentioned, besides the exceptions found everywhere, only such typically irregularly distributed branches of the economy as mining. *Most locations of economic activity in general within the individual branches of the economy in the United States fit well into our simple theoretical picture.*

(3) It might be urged in the third place that the fact that production and consumption in a state are equal still does not prove that a large part of its products is not exported and a large part of its consumption imported. For instance, the two most important wood-producing regions in the United States, the Northwest and the Southeast, supply one another because the former produces only soft and the latter principally hard woods. Yet experience shows that specialization and overlapping seldom go so far. As a rule a whole scale of qualities is produced everywhere, so that at most their ranking differs from place to place. And even though the sales radii are often very long, those regions near a market are nevertheless of most importance because of the thinning out of markets with distance, which will be discussed later. On the other hand, a difference between production and consumption may be only apparent and due to the fact that, though income or retail sales may be good average measure of consumption, they may not always be so in the individual case. On the basis of such a calculation the South would have a surplus of artificial ice and the North would have to bring it in, whereas it is perfectly clear in this case that the requirements of the South are above, and those of the North below, the average. Accordingly this third objection should lose much of its significance when everything is taken into consideration.

(4) In the fourth place it might be objected that the proportion of products consumed in the home area depends essentially upon its size. One hundred per cent of the world's products is consumed "domestically," 95 per cent of the production of the United States is so consumed, and 60 per cent [13] of that of the individual states, whereas virtually none of the production of an individual worker is consumed by this worker himself. A percentage of 60 is not high in itself, therefore, but only when it is recalled that in the United States almost a whole continent lies open to every producer, at low freight rates and without the encumbrance of tariffs or cultural or language barriers, and that most of his sales are restricted nevertheless to such a comparatively small area as a single state.

Although none of the four objections discussed has proved decisive, it cannot be denied, of course, that despite its extent our investigation of half of American nonagricultural production is after all only an incomplete means of determining the site of every single location and its market—an impossible task for one investigator alone. Consequently this study provides a strong presumption rather than a rigid proof of an agreement between reality and the essential features of the theoretical outline.

Table 20. EMPLOYMENT PER 1,000 INHABITANTS

	East Prussia	Wuerttemberg	Ruhr	Reich
Building industry	30	32	26	38
Other local requirements	30	32	39	32
Supplying district needs	26	30	31	24
Nonagricultural substructure	86	94	96	94
Dependent on raw materials	1	3	126	21
Supplying distant needs	12	147	39	92
Nonagricultural superstructure	13	150	165	113
All nonagricultural enterprises	98	244	261	207

This holds true for Germany also. According to the valuable enumeration of Isenberg [14] the number of employed in crafts and

---

13. In the individual states, which differ considerably in size, the relation between size and self-sufficiency, at least as far as nonagricultural production is concerned, is upset especially by the fact that the large states are mainly agricultural whereas the small ones, where a real need for outside products would be expected, have many different industries.

14. To be found in part in "Die Tragfähigkeit des deutschen Ostens an landwirtschaftlicher und gewerblicher Bevölkerung," in *Struktur und Gestaltung der zentralen Orte des deutschen Ostens* (Leipzig, 1941), p. 29.

industry required to supply the needs of their landscapes is large, but in single regions differs surprisingly little (Table 20). Together with inns and retail trade (in the Reich 13 and 29, respectively, per 1,000 population), they represent the greater part of the regional nonagricultural substructure (see p. 219). The importance of the Württemberg export industry and the attraction of the Ruhr coal fields is clearly shown in the table, whereas in East Prussia hardly a nonagricultural enterprise exists with the exception of the regional substructure.

§2. AGRICULTURE

At first sight the distribution of North American farms seems very uneven, if not highly irregular. In the Northeast industry preponderates decisively, whereas the rest of the country is usually described as largely or predominantly agricultural. Thus in 1930 the proportion of farmers in Rhode Island made up 2 per cent of the population, but in Mississippi 68 per cent. For the whole United States the average was 25 per cent. If an even distribution of agricultural and nonagricultural enterprises were desired throughout, 25 per cent — 2 per cent = 23 per cent would have to desert other pursuits for agriculture in Rhode Island, for example, whereas the remaining 77 per cent could remain at their former occupations. In most of the states, however, a much smaller fraction of the population would be affected by the change; in 10 states less than 5 per cent, in 29 less than 15 per cent, and more than a quarter in 5.[15] Hence, with but few exceptions, deviations from the normal ratio between the agricultural substructure and the nonagricultural superstructure would not concern nearly so large a part of the population as appears at first sight.

The basic agricultural network itself is still more uniform and still more important. Its density results from the ratio of the farming population to the land, not to the rest of the population.[16] East of the Mississippi River, at least, where most of the population is to be found, these differences are much smaller than with the

---

15. Highest in Mississippi (43 per cent), Arkansas (35 per cent), and the Dakotas (32 per cent).

16. On the other hand, the value of agricultural land seems to be influenced more by the ratio of the farming population to the total population than by the density of the former. Values rise with proximity to large cities and reach their highest level over a wide area in the industrial regions of the Northeast, and its westerly continuation in the fertile lands in and about Iowa. Individual variations depend mainly on differences in the quality of the soil. See the very detailed map in *U. S. Department of Agriculture, Value of Farm Land and Buildings per Acre, Based on 1930 Census.*

Locations of Production

ratio of agriculture to the economy in general. The difference between Rhode Island and the state of Missouri, for instance, shrinks from 1 : 34 to 1 : 2. Above all, the transitions are much more gradual and regular, so that differences within single economic landscapes can often be neglected. On the whole, the agricultural population thins out from East to West on the one hand, and from the center toward the North and South on the other (Fig. 64).[17]

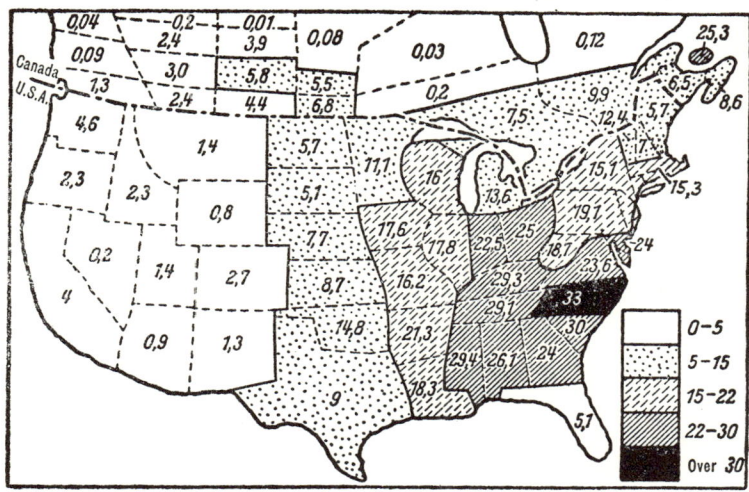

Fig. 64. Agricultural population per square mile in North America (United States, 1930; Canada, 1931). *Statistical Abstract of the United States* and *Dominion Bureau of Statistics, 7, Census of Canada, 1931, Census of Agriculture.*

As a consequence, the highest density is found toward the east central part of the country, in the tobacco state of North Carolina. Many causes work together in detail,[18] but by and large the effects of two fundamental influences are clearly apparent: climate and proximity to a market. Toward the North the cold, toward the South the heat, and toward the West a dry climate are unfavorable

17. But in the industrial area it is still far above the average, though the proportion of farmers to total population there is particularly small. Conversely, almost all the states in the arid region of the West have a farming population above the average, but its distribution is exceptionally sparse. For all states in which less than 40 per cent of the population are farmers that is, for three quarters of the states, the rule holds that the density of the rural population is less the higher its proportion of the state's population.

18. In the comparatively thickly settled South, for example, the slight inclination to migrate; families with many children; low wages, which hinder the replacement of men by machinery; and many other factors. However, we cannot go into details here.

to more intensive agriculture. Similarly, distance from the most important inland market increases in all three directions.[19]

Finally, the typical size of a farm east of the Mississippi River does not vary too greatly, so that this important region is rather regularly studded with farms.[20]

b. UNEVEN DISTRIBUTION

§1. Nonagricultural Enterprises

When nonagricultural enterprises occur in only a few irregularly distributed places, the question arises more readily, of course, why just this or that location was chosen. An answer, too, is more readily found. There is almost always a strikingly important factor that is frequently raised to the sole determining cause or, conversely, watered down by over-careful writers through the addition of every other conceivable locational influence. No wonder, then, that there exists an abundant literature on the location of the iron, steel, chemical, machine, glass, clock, mining, shipbuilding, and other

---

19. Whereas only the density of American agriculture has been derived here from climate and proximity to a market, H. Engelbrecht ("Der Standort der Landwirtschaftszweige in Nordamerika," *Landwirtschaftliche Jahrbücher*, XII [1883], 459–509) made an almost neglected attempt to explain its *nature* by them in accord with Thünen. Indeed, certain connections are unmistakable. Theoretically, a crop must be grown nearer its market the higher its natural yield per hectare. In the industrial Northeast (the New England, Middle Atlantic, and East North Central States), which in 1930 included 57 per cent of the population, the ratio of important crops grown there to the total American production in that year was higher the larger their yield per hectare.

Relation of physical yield of various crops to the proportion of total production of the U. S. supplied by New England, Middle Atlantic, and East North Central States

	Yield per hectare 100 kg	Share of the Northeast %
Cotton	1.7	0
Rye	8.0	21
Wheat	9.4	27
Oats	11.5	37
Corn	12.8	39
Hay	32.0	41
Potatoes	73.8	47

20. See O. E. Baker's map: "A Graphic Summary of the Number, Size and Type of Farm, and Value of Products," *U. S. Department of Agriculture, Miscellaneous Publication No. 266* (Washington, 1937), p. 6.

industries,[21] whereas but little has been written on scattered mills, breweries, cigar factories, lime kilns, brickyards, and even banks and handicrafts. The significance of regular and irregular distribution is exactly the reverse, in the literature, of what it is in reality.

Concepts like production orientation or transport orientation merely describe a location; they do not explain it. The reasons that actually motivate an entrepreneur explain, to be sure, though they do not always convince; an exact calculation of the most important possibilities would be convincing but extraordinarily difficult and, strictly speaking, impossible.

To these two circumstances, that uneven distribution has been overemphasized in the past and that its true reason demands special study in each case, there is added a third: Generalizations can hardly be made, because the situation varies from industry to industry. For all three reasons we abandon any idea of presenting the subject and refer to the extensive literature, of which T. Palander [22] gives an excellent review.[23]

Changes of location offer a striking and important problem for nonagricultural enterprises with irregular agglomeration. It corresponds with shifts between town and country or large and small cities in the case of evenly distributed nonagricultural enterprises. It is easier to discuss such migrations of industry than to give reasons for their original locations, because as a rule they are more clearly and rationally motivated. Furthermore, one can rely upon exact calculations in comparing the new with the old locations. In recent decades there have been several such migrations on a large scale; for example, the mass migration of the American cotton industry to the South, the slower shifting of iron and steel production in the United States and in Germany toward ore deposits, the decided preference of English industries for central and southern England, and others.[24] In the first case many old enterprises were actually

---

21. Incidentally, even the metal, machine, glass, paper, and leather industries of Central Europe are on the whole rather widely dispersed. See the maps in Meyer's great *Hausatlas* (Leipzig, 1938), pp. 26 ff. For the iron industry, see Buchmann in *Die Standorte der Eisen- und Stahlindustrien der Welt* (Berlin, 1927), p. 17.

22. Tord Palander, *Beiträge zur Standortstheorie* (Uppsala, 1935), pp. 408–416; see also " Literatur über Standortfragen," *Arbeitshefte zur Reichsplanung*, Heft 5 (published by Amt des Siedlungsbeauftragten, 1935).

23. For a lucid description of the locations of larger groups of nonagricultural enterprises see M. Pfannschmidt, *Raumordnungs- und Siedlungsfragen. Handwörterbuch der Betriebswirtschaft* (2d ed., Stuttgart, 1939), pp. 1270 ff.

24. Another American example is the partial migration of the shoe industry from New England toward the Middle West, so well described by E. M. Hoover in *Location Theory and the Shoe and Leather Industries* (Cambridge, Mass., 1937). An unpub-

closed down. In the two others, the new factories were attracted to the new location. In the first two cases the most important direct causes were economies in production; in the third, apparently, savings in sales costs. Deeper causes were the aftereffects of the American Civil War or World War I or, in the case of the iron industry, the exhaustion of better ores or the discovery of more suitable methods that made profitable the utilization even of poorer ones.

The freeing of the slaves and the prostration of the entrepreneurial spirit in the defeated and ruined South after the Civil War created an army of cheap labor that became still more attractive after the increase in power of the trade unions in New England, the former center of the cotton goods industry. In addition, some freight costs were saved in so far as the finished product remained in the South.[25] In addition there were lower taxes and building costs and cheaper power, and in general a relative price drop in the South due to the tariff. Finally, the invention of air conditioning made the South independent of the New England climate, whose humidity is so particularly suited to cotton spinning. Many old established spinning and weaving mills therefore closed down, in Massachusetts especially, to reopen in the South after new enterprises had proved their ability to survive there. The share of the cotton states east of the Mississippi in the total production rose almost uninterruptedly, from 6 per cent in 1880 to 56 per cent in 1929. Conversely, the share of Massachusetts fell from 38 per cent to 15 per cent.[26]

The North American iron and steel industry advanced slowly from eastern Pennsylvania through western Pennsylvania and Ohio to Chicago. But of course the shift was not nearly so violent as in the case of cotton mills. The share of Pennsylvania fell only from 58 per cent in 1890 to 35 per cent in 1929. The migration took place slowly because the ores from Lake Superior were so cheap

---

lished Kiel dissertation by M. Peeters (*Das Standortbild der belgischen Wirtschaft und die Möglichkeiten einer Raumordnungspolitik*) contains an interesting chapter on the possibility of a migration of industry from the center of Belgium to newly opened coal fields in its northern part. In so far as that country exports, it would then have a large market directly across the street, as it were, thanks to the southward migration of English industry.

25. Even though the actual saving in freight costs may have amounted to but 5 per cent (L. G. MacPherson, *Railroad Freight Rates* [New York, 1909], p. 54), together with all additional costs such as insurance, interest, and so on, it may have run to two or three times as much.

26. See also A. Predöhl, "Die Südwanderung der amerikanischen Baumwollindustrie," *Weltwirtschaftliches Archiv*, XXIX (1929), 106–159; 66*–80*.

to ship and so rich at first that it paid to transport them more than 1,200 miles to the coal of Pennsylvania.[27] But with a decrease in their iron content, with the increasing importance of scrap metal (abundant in Chicago) ever since the discovery of the Siemens-Martin process, and with fuller utilization of coal, the advantages of production in the Middle West, and especially in Chicago, became more and more evident. To this was added the advantage of close proximity to a growing market—a decisive factor in the opinion of Predöhl.[28] Thus coal approached ore, partly at the beginning and partly at the end of the water route. For good maps see *Wirtschaft und Statistik*, 1942, p. 306.

In Germany, too, the movement was toward ore before World War I, when the Thomas process[29] made the rather low-grade minettes from Lorraine usable,[30] and more recently because it became necessary to move toward sources of even lower-grade ores like those of central and southern Germany. As in Gary, near Chicago, so in Hennigsdorf, near Berlin, proximity to a large scrap metal and sales market was eventually turned to good account.[31]

As for the movement of English industry toward the South (except Wales), and especially toward the London area, several reasons in addition to climate and landscape have been advanced to explain it. On the one hand, the importance of the great southern centers of consumption and of the placing of government orders has increased even further with the decline in foreign trade. On the other hand, electrification has facilitated separation from the coal fields of southern Wales and northern England. Besides this there is the movement of the iron industry away from coal and toward ore.

27. Before the war 3 tons of Lorraine ore were required per ton of pig iron, but only 1½ tons of American ore.

28. " Die örtliche Verteilung der amerikanischen Eisen- und Stahlindustrie," *Weltwirtschaftliches Archiv*, XXVII (1928), 286 f.

29. Technical developments have caused changes in location again and again, particularly in the iron industry. In the Middle Ages it sought a combination of ore, wood (charcoal), and water power, and moved on when forests or ore deposits had been exhausted.

30. The advantage of the Lorraine iron foundries over those of the Ruhr lay in lower production costs and closer proximity to the markets of southern and western Germany.

31. See F. S. Hall, " The Localization of Industries," *U. S. Department of Commerce, Twelfth Census of Manfactures, 1900*, Pt. I, pp. 190–214; H. Schumacher, " Die Wanderung der Grossindustrie in Deutschland und in den Vereinigten Staaten," *Schmollers Jahrbuch*, 1910, pp. 451–482; and Buchmann *et al., Die Standorte der Eisen- und Stahlindustrien der Welt* (Berlin, 1927).

These migrations away from coal and the seacoast together with the long-run decline in coal exports,[32] and in part the exhaustion of good fields,[33] did more than the great depression to create the distressed areas of South Wales, Durham, West Cumberland, and Scotland,[34] and the doctrinaire rejection of a regional wage reduction delayed recovery. In the London area, on the contrary, the labor unions were not so strong. In addition, the distressed areas, adapted until then to export, had very poor traffic connections with the markets of the interior.[35] Since 1939 the greater danger to the southeast from the air has reversed the direction of migration.

§2. AGRICULTURE

Agriculture, too, shows many cases of striking unevenness in the geographical distribution of production. I mention only the formation of belts and of Thünen rings, which spread around northwest Europe throughout the entire world on a large scale,[36] around many cities,[37] and in rudimentary form around villages and individual

---

32. Prestige exports went to half of the world, but each coal district supplied mostly that part of Europe lying nearest in respect to freight. Thus the coal of South Wales competed in Italy to the South, and that of Newcastle in Scandinavia to the North with diminishing results against German coal, especially after the general strike [1926]. Furthermore, the growing importance of oil and water power affected the export of British coal, which was of fundamental importance for the lowering of import freights on bulk goods.

33. British mines, for example, are said to be three times as deep as American on the average, and to have longer galleries. (J. Lubin and H. Everett, *The British Coal Dilemma* [New York, 1927], p. 130.)

34. See H. J. von Schumann, *Standortsänderungen der Industrien in Grossbritannien seit dem Kriege* [Langensalza, 1936]; J. Uhlig, " Die Notstandsgebiete Grossbritanniens," *Wirtschaftskurve*, 1938, pp. 63–80; the Barlow Report, *Royal Commission on the Distribution of the Industrial Population (Barlow Commission)*, Report (Cmd 6153) (London, 1940); and others.

35. Thus the commissioner for the distressed areas was right in advising that they produce mainly for their own needs, and buy domestic products whenever possible. (*First Report of the Commissioner for the Special Areas* [London, 1935], p. 80.) Though it is difficult for countries to shift part of their burden of unemployment to other countries because of doubtful methods and foreign reactions, the attempt may succeed within a country. (See C. Hasenclever, *Arbeitslosigkeit und Aussenhandel. Eine theoretische Studie, insbesondere über die Wirkung von Zöllen auf die Arbeitslosigkeit*, Kiel dissertation, 1935); and especially G. von Haberler, *Der internationale Handel* [Berlin, 1933], pp. 190 ff.; English edition [1936], pp. 259 ff.)

36. H. Backe, *Um die Nahrungsfreiheit Europas* (Leipzig, 1942), p. 57.

37. H. v. d. Decken has shown for the supply area of Hamburg, from an examination of which Thünen had derived his theory, that on the whole his theory is still valid, though natural and human differences are more strongly in evidence today because of

farms as well.[38] I have borrowed an excellent example of this from a painstaking investigation by Müller-Wille (*Die Ackerfluren im Landesteil Birkenfeld*, Bonn dissertation [Bonn, 1936]). He points out first that in the eighteenth century the common fields of a village were clearly still cultivated more and more extensively outward from the village (manured land, open pastures, open woodlands, and woods). "With increasing distance from the economic center, the village, the constructive force that developed a cultivated landscape from a natural landscape lost its intensity" (p. 63). Today the increasing degree of intensiveness has further blurred the differences. But where distances are considerable, as in the Birkenfeld area, arable land is still divided in two: the inner field *J*, with a three-year rotation of crops and more frequent application of stable manure, and the less often fertilized outer field *A*, with a five- to six-year rotation, in which the heavy beet is omitted entirely and oats, with a smaller natural yield per hectare, or clover, with a smaller outlay, are substituted.[39] Müller-Wille was able to show clearly for the village of Georg-Weierbach the role played by distance, in addition to certain differences in the quality of the soil. On a map he connected all those fields to which the farmers said it required the same time to haul a load of manure. These lines he called "manure-isochrones" (Fig. 65). The longest time to a field within the area *J* was 50 minutes, to a field within area *A*, 2 hours. Thus twice as many loads could be carted daily to *J*, and heavier loads as well, since *J* was lower, as could be carted to the more distant *A*. In addition to the *time* required for hauling, the

---

lower freight rates. ("Die Thünenschen Kreise und Wagemanns Alternationsgesetz," *Vierteljahrshefte zur Wirtschaftsforchung*, XVI (1941–42), 220–232.) The physical return per acre falls with distance, partly because cultivation becomes less intensive and partly because high yields (potatoes), achieved through the large-scale employment of cheap labor, are diminished by increased investment to reduce potatoes to schnapps. Thus intensiveness may be great or small irrespective of distance, or may even differ at the same distance (extensive cultivation of grain and intensive production of butter in the fourth ring lie *beside*, not *behind*, one another). That intensiveness should fall in regular waves (Wagemann's "law of alterations") is therefore not convincing.

38. "There is a much greater compulsion to organize fields in rings around a production site than around a consumption site." (H. Müller-Miny, *Die linksrheinischen Gartenbaufluren der südlichen Kölner Bucht* [Leipzig, 1940], p. 58.) See also H. v. Thünen, *Der isolirte Staat in Beziehung auf Landwirtschaft und Nationalökonomie* (Waentig edition, Jena, 1921), pp. 98 ff.

39. Otherwise than with the location of production rings around a town outlay plays a role when they encircle a village, because the fraction of the same total expense represented by the cost of hauling varies with the distance of the fields from the village.

relative *cost* was greater for *A*, because the ascent put more strain on animals and carts. These considerable differences resulted in *J* being cultivated by three-field rotation and *A* by five-field, which requires less fertilizing. Hence E. Seyfried (*Versuch einer planmässigen Wirtschaft und Siedlung in Württemberg* [Heidelberg, 1936], p. 58) correctly proposes that where less can be raised on outlying land because of its distance, the establishment of new settlements in the form of hamlets *between* the existing villages be considered. For disadvantages see the end of note 12, page 115.

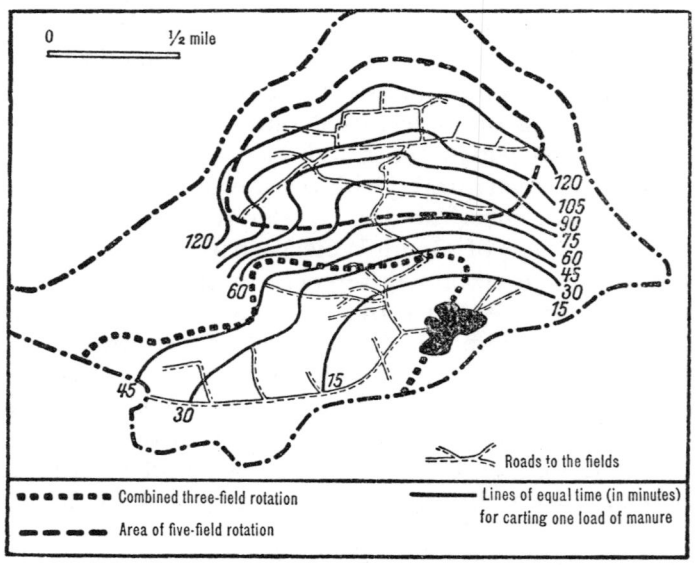

Fig. 65. Rotation of crops as a function of distance from a village. (After Müller-Wille, *Die Ackerfluren im Landesteil Birkenfeld*, dissertation, Bonn, 1936, p. 89.)

Seyfried's book contains numerous maps also (Figs. 2, 6, and 8) that show very clearly how with distance from Stuttgart, the undisputed center of an economic landscape, population density falls on on the whole, the proportion of persons engaged in agriculture rises, and the size of agricultural enterprises increases, just as theory would lead one to expect. Villages grow smaller on the average, or at least less common, and in remote areas become individual farms.

c. NATIONAL BOUNDARIES AS FACTORS IN LOCATION

Max Weh has published an interesting investigation of industry on the German-Swiss frontier (*Die Landesgrenze als Standortfaktor, untersucht an der oberbadisch-schweizerischen Grenzindustrie,* Basle dissertation [Bonn, 1932]). He distinguished propitiously between the reasons that led Swiss entrepreneurs to move their enterprises or branches to Germany, and the reasons for establishing them precisely in the border region. During the past century the decisive factor in most cases was the saving of German customs duties. This was shown, for example, after the entrance of Baden into the German *Zollverein,* and after Germany's adoption of a protective tariff in the late 1870's, by a blossoming-out of industry in Upper Baden; and shown less strikingly after World War I, when several Swiss branch plants were moved from Upper Alsace to the frontier zone of Baden. In a few instances (Wybert, for example) the German patent laws also resulted in removal. All these were defensive measures, intended not to expand production but to retain a market. (E. Waldschütz, *Die Schweizerischen Industrieunternehmungen im deutschen Grenzgebiet,* Frankfort dissertation, 1928, p. 24.)

An additional advantage, in earlier days perhaps the most important, constituting even a temptation to " aggressive establishment of new firms," was the cheap labor of the Black Forest. It remains an open question, however, whether some of these workers, as migrants across the border, would not have been available on the Swiss side as well. It is worthy of note that whereas since the end of the nineteenth century factories were usually moved to Germany, the enterprises themselves remained in Switzerland. For this there are two groups of reasons.

First, there was a saving in taxes, since the tax burden was lighter in Switzerland. This saving amounted to about 5 per cent of the sales in 1926–27; Weh even mentions a case where the Swiss tax amounted to 20 per cent and the German tax to 63 per cent of the net profit.[40] Consequently even the management of a few enterprises that were originally German was moved to Swiss soil.[41]

---

40. Incidentally, the tax burden, an important factor in location, varies greatly from place to place even within Germany. In 1930–31 the *extra charges* on land taxes in Prussian municipalities fluctuated between 100 per cent and 600 per cent, and on capital taxes on nonagricultural enterprises between 200 per cent and 3200 per cent (" Beitrag zum interlokalen Steuerbelastungsvergleich," *Vierteljahrshefte zur Statistik des Deutschen Reichs,* 1932, No. 4, p. 123). Other examples are provided by K. Brüning, " Beispiele über Auswirkungen der Ländergrenzen auf Verwaltung und Wirtschaft," *Niedersachsen im Rahmen der Neugliederung des Reiches,* II (Hanover, 1931). 44–59. His book is a mine of information on the effect of internal German boundaries upon location.

41. On the other hand, Weh mentions only *one* German branch enterprise in the Swiss frontier zone. Apparently the Swiss market is too small for most branches of industry, or the protective tariff is not high enough to make its evasion advantageous.

A second group of reasons gives at the same time an explanation for the establishment of branch enterprises in the frontier zone, which is so unfavorable from the standpoint of freight charges. In this case a branch could be managed from the home office, Swiss key personnel employed, and contact with Swiss financial backers maintained. In addition there was the lower wage on the frontier in earlier days, while direct dealings with local administrative officials might prove advantageous also. Names like Maggi, Wybert, Suchard, Villiger, and those of many important textile, chemical, and metal enterprises in particular show that these frontier industries were by no means negligible exceptions (see also Chap. 25).

Studies on the importance of the Canadian-American border in the choice of a location strengthen this impression.[42] American investments in Canada amounted to four billion dollars in 1933; more than half the Canadian production of motor vehicles, rubber goods, electrical appliances, and other products was in American hands. But of course many of these American branches would have been established in Canada even if it had been a part of the United States. A large number of the firms questioned declared that it was the proximity of the market that made them decide to go to Canada. By this they meant not only savings in freight and time, but also closer contact with the development of the market and a greater possibility of conforming to Canadian taste. There is hardly a doubt that still other American firms would move northward today if tariff barriers were to be abolished, to take advantage of the lower wages and lower prices of raw materials and land in some parts of Canada. For it must be realized that although the cost of nonagricultural production is higher today as a rule in Canada than in the United States, this is chiefly a result of artificial restriction of the market.

On the other hand, however, many of the branch enterprises would never have been established in the absence of a political frontier. In the first place, Canadian tariffs were raised partly for the express purpose of attracting American branches (Marshall *et al., op. cit.*, p. 201). Conversely, Canadian industry resisted higher tariffs for the same reason, because they feared that for which the lawmakers hoped. The importance of the frontier is further shown by the fact that of more than 1,000 American-owned Canadian factories, approximately 9 per cent are in border towns and 32 per cent in Toronto, which is virtually on the line. Why, for example, should

---

42. The statements in this and the following paragraph are from H. Marshall *et al., Canadian and American Industry, a Study in International Investment* (New Haven, 1936).

American automobile manufacturers have branches in Windsor, only a few miles from Detroit, if it were not for the international boundary? Seventy per cent of the firms questioned replied, quite superfluously, that the tariff had influenced their decision to establish branch factories in Canada (*ibid.*, p. 199). But more than the Canadian duties are involved here. In addition, Canadian branches enjoy tariff preferences within the British Empire. Forty per cent make use of this and supply the Empire from Canada, the Australian market in particular. Finally, branch factories escape not only paying tribute to the Treasury, but national feeling as well. Once the border is behind them they enjoy the protection of the Canadian tariff, and profit also by the advertising of native products in general [" Buy Canadian! "]. Of course the American invasion is not equally active in all fields. In the textile industry, for example, it is of little importance, partly because of English superiority but partly, too, because the individual enterprise in the industry is relatively small.

Unlike the case of Switzerland and Germany, it is less common for enterprises that would be located in the smaller country to be moved to the larger one because of the border. No doubt the reason is that Canada is still too undeveloped and dependent to excel the United States in many nonagricultural pursuits, whereas the Canadian market is large enough and susceptible enough of development to attract the superior American industries and the great stream of capital that seeks investment. Nevertheless, there are converse cases. One is the dairies on the American side of the border. As the American ad valorem duty on butter was much higher than that on milk, especially in the 1920's, whereas with milk the freight was more important, the farmer on the Canadian side found it more profitable to send his milk to the United States, where it was made into butter near the line. Only at a certain distance from the border did Canada ship butter rather than milk.

When the great influence of the Canadian-American border on the choice of locations for nonagricultural enterprises is borne in mind, the opposition of economic interests to a union with the United States is easy to understand. In 1937, to be sure, the Canadian Prairie Provinces examined the question whether a customs union with the United States would be advantageous for them. The industrial center of the Middle West, especially Chicago and Minneapolis, lies nearer to them and therefore, because of its greater market, could supply many goods more cheaply than could the factories of Ontario or Quebec. So far the calculation is certainly accurate. In the absence of a boundary line most of Alberta, Saskatchewan, and Manitoba would be partly included in the market areas of neighboring American centers, although the tariff on important products is not very high in any case; only 7.5 per cent on agricultural machinery, for example. Furthermore, the advocates of union with the United States can point to Nova Scotia. If the international boundary cuts off the Prairie Provinces from their cheapest source of supply, it also separates Nova Scotia from the best market for its chief exports, wood, fish, and coal—namely Boston, which is very much nearer to it than either Montreal or Quebec.[43] The extensive migration of industry is attributed to this artificial limitation of the market area by the American tariff, and the increase in living costs brought about by the Canadian tariff. Assurance of a Canadian market does not compensate for the loss of an American market.[44]

Yet an examination of maps of the market areas for Canadian and American wheat (p. 421) shows immediately that the Prairie Provinces would gain a cheaper source of supply at the price of a poorer sales market. The Canadian wheat belt would risk its preferential position in respect to British imports for the difficulties of the American wheat areas, which no longer dominate any significant importing market. The same reasons that induced the agricultural West to consider union would necessarily cause the industrial East to reject it. As we have already seen, a great many of its industries owe their very existence to the frontier.[45]

A peculiarity of the Canadian-American border seems to be the locational pattern of the frontier cities. The American tariff laws permit each American "tourist," that is, one who has been abroad for at least two days, to bring in free of duty each month for personal use goods to a total value of $100. Canada also has now a similarly generous and reasonable arrangement, by which certain specified

43. American coal is cheaper between Winnipeg and Montreal.
44. See Gras, "Regionalism and Nationalism," *Foreign Affairs,* VII (1928–29), 454–467; also *The Jones Report on Nova Scotia's Economic Welfare within Confederation* (Halifax, 1936?).
45. There is much talk, too, of a cultural similarity between the two countries. But the European observer who arrives in Victoria from Seattle, say, or in Ottawa from Washington, or in Montreal from New York, is impressed by the different atmosphere. Life suddenly seems more placid, more orderly, more like that in Europe. And that the United States would defend the Dominion in case of need is the exact opposite of a reason for their union. This would lose Canada the help of England without this being necessary to secure that of the United States. In short, we should do better to compare the relation between the two countries not with that between Germany and Austria, but with that between Germany and Switzerland: a good yet reserved neighborliness.

goods to the value of $100 may be brought in duty free every three months. At the time to which the following statistics refer this was not yet in effect, but because of the extensive traffic across the border it was relatively easy to smuggle in small things like clothing or tobacco. It might therefore be assumed that certain articles known by everyone to be substantially cheaper in the neighboring country would appear with unusual frequency in the retail trade of places along the border. This is actually the case. Anyone strolling through the streets of a small Canadian border town is amazed at the number of fur and china shops, of tailors and jewelers. Signs in show windows explain: "Canadian prices are lower on blankets, furs, knitted ware, English china, linens." The stroller will be struck, also, by the many hotels, where Americans pass their forty-eight hours if they must. Other kinds of business he will miss entirely.

In order to get an exact picture of retail trade along the border I compared sales in the large Canadian town of Windsor just opposite Detroit with those in near-by London, Ontario, which is about as large, though farther inland. The retail sales per capita in Windsor in 1930 were as follows, expressed as percentages of the corresponding sales in London (calculated from *Dominion Bureau of Statistics, Seventh Census of Canada*, 1931, Vol. X, *Retail Trade*):

Dry goods	55 per cent	
Tobacco	65 per cent	
Millinery	70 per cent	Cheaper in the United States
Shoes	73 per cent	
Metal Goods	81 per cent	
Total sales	96 per cent	
Jewelry	132 per cent	
Custom-made clothing	160 per cent	Cheaper in Canada
Furs	355 per cent	

The differences are still more striking between Niagara Falls, Ontario, and Guelph, which is about as large but some 60 miles from the frontier. The per capita sales for the former, expressed as percentages of those for the latter, were: tobacco, 33; shoes, 51; women's clothing, 43; men's clothing, 131. The same difference between women's and men's clothing appears when the border town Sarnia, Ontario, is compared with Stratford, which is exactly equal in size but situated about 60 miles inland: women's clothing, 55; men's clothing, 230. The explanation is that cotton is largely employed for women's wear and wool for men's, and that the latter is cheaper in Canada and the former in the United States. Thus a coat made of English cloth that would sell in Windsor for $55, say, might cost as much as $85 in Detroit, just across the river. Furthermore, northern Canada provides very cheap furs; and Canadian duties on diamonds and English porcelain are not so high as the American. This explains the extensive purchases in Canada by Americans.

Conversely, Canadian women prefer to buy their clothing, shoes, and hats in the United States for the additional reason that they regard English fashions as outmoded. The men, on the other hand, bring in mainly American cigarettes, since they cost one fourth less though normally subject to very high duty. If such conditions are peculiar in degree to the Canadian-American border, they are more or less typical in kind of all frontiers.

Chapter 22. The Location of Towns

The ordering forces of the economy operate everywhere, but only when they work relatively alone is it possible to see whether reality corresponds in some measure to our theoretical results. The assumption that we are dealing with a landscape of natural uniformity in which settlements are established more in accordance with economic than with political viewpoints, more in conformity with the needs of the modern economic system and unhampered by the past, is perhaps nowhere so perfectly realized as in the American Middle West. Especially is this true of the rich agri-

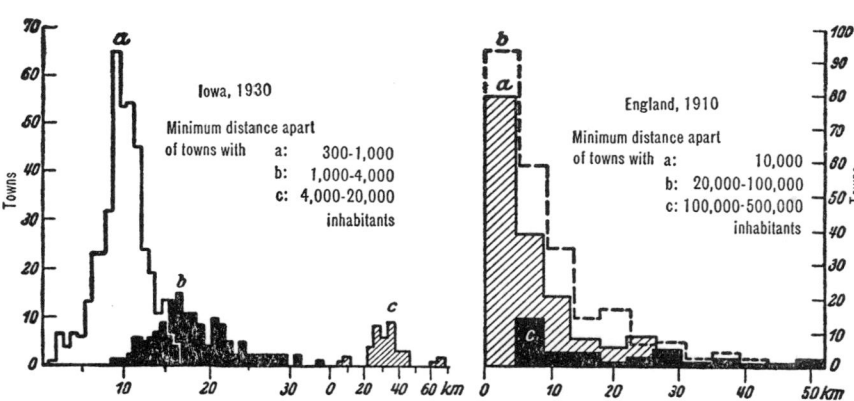

Fig. 66. Distribution of towns in Iowa, 1930, by size and distance from one another (see Table 21)

Fig. 67. Distrubtion of towns in England, 1910, by size and distance from one another (see Table 23)

cultural state of Iowa, which is about the size of England. There are a few mineral deposits in Iowa, to be sure; the terrain is not perfectly flat everywhere, but often somewhat undulating and in some places even hilly; the quality of the soil varies and with it the value of land, the size of farms, and the kind of crop raised. Yet all these differences are unusually small. Nature's impressive uniformity is reflected not only in agriculture, but indirectly also in the dispersion of industry, which in the main supplies the neighboring farmer or processes what he produces (H. H. McCarty, *Manu-*

facturing Trends in Iowa [Iowa City, 1930]). It might therefore be expected that at least our most general findings on the distribution of settlements would be confirmed in Iowa.[1]

If one measures in Figure 32 the minimum distances [2] separating the common centers of a given number of areas, for example those between the points upon which from three to five regions center,[3] an especially frequent [modal] value will be obtained about which the less common ones are grouped. Thus for every size of town there is a typical, though not even theoretical unequivocal, distance.

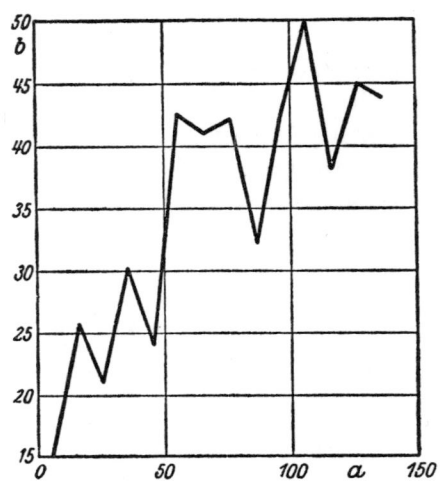

Fig. 68. Increase in distance between towns west of Chicago. a) Distance from Chicago in millimeters (1 mm = 4.95 km). b) Distance separating towns of 1,000–4,000 inhabitants, in millimeters.

But even if the maximum distance were, theoretically, uniquely determined, nothing more than a frequency curve could be obtained statistically, since the theoretical assumptions are only approximately realized. It is to be further expected that the dispersion will increase with the size of towns, because the number of observations grows smaller with increasing size.

I have measured the minimum distance separating towns in Iowa

---

1. Though it is true that many towns in the Middle West were planned by the companies that opened up the country, sharp competition has eliminated all the unfavorable locations.

2. That is, the distance in each case to the *next* point of equal value.

3. Because the section represented in the figure is small, there would be too few examples if the centers of three, four, or five regions were each measured separately.

Table 21

FREQUENCY DISTRIBUTION OF TOWNS IN IOWA, 1930

Airline distance from next equally large or larger town on the map
Pocket Maps of Iowa (Chicago, Rand McNally, 1935)

Distance in mm. (1 mm. = 0.85 km.)	Number of Places with 300-1,000 Inhabitants	1,000-4,000 Inhabitants	Distance in mm. (1 mm. = 0.85 km.)	Number of Places with 4,000-20,000 Inhabitants
1	2	3	4	5
0- 1	0	0	0- 5	0
1- 2	1	0	5-10	1
2- 3	7	0	10-15	2
3- 4	4	0	15-20	0
4- 5	7	5	20-25	0
5- 6	6	0	25-30	4
6- 7	13	1	30-35	8
7- 8	23	1	35-40	6
8- 9	32	0	40-45	9
9-10	65	0	45-50	3
10-11	53	1	50-55	3
11-12	54	1	55-60	0
12-13	45	2	60-65	0
13-14	24	6	65-70	0
14-15	19	5	70-75	1
15-16	11	6	75-80	2
16-17	13	7		39
17-18	7	9		
18-19	5	13		
19-20	0	15		
20-21	1	11		
21-22	1	11		
22-23	0	8		
23-24	1	4		
24-25		10		
25-26		9		
26-27		5		
27-28		2		
28-29		5		
29-30		2	Distance in cm. (1 cm. = 8.5 km.)	Number of Places with 20,000-100,000 Inhabitants
30-31		2		
31-32		2		
32-33		2		
33-34		2	6	7
34-35		2		
35-36		0	0- 5	0
36-37		2	5-10	5
37-38		0	10-15	4
38-39		0	15-20	2
39-40		1	20-25	0
	415	15		11

Table 22. DISTANCES SEPARATING TOWNS IN VARIOUS PARTS OF THE UNITED STATES

Airline distance from the next equally large or larger town on the map. M. Jefferson, "Some Considerations on the Geographic Provinces of the USA," *Annals of the Assoc. of Am. Geogr., VII, 3-15*

Distance in mm. (1 mm. = 4.95 km.)	Number of Towns with 1–4,000 Inhabitants in					Number of Towns with 4,000–20,000 Inhabitants in			Number of Towns with 20,000–100,000 Inhabitants in		
	Illinois Indiana Ohio	Iowa Missouri	East Texas Black Belt	East Texas Remainder		Illinois Indiana Ohio	Iowa Missouri	East Texas[a]	Illinois Indiana Ohio	Iowa[a] Missouri	East Texas[a]
1	2	3	4	5		6	7	8	9	10	11
0– 1	7	2	0	0		28	0	0			0
1– 2	143	5	9	2				7	8	2	
2– 3	111	51	12	4		70	8				
3– 4	60	52	18	5		68	9	4	20	2	0
4– 5	20	64	17	8			22	4			
5– 6	4	18	8	12		42			23	2	2
6– 7	2	10	1	7			8	11			
7– 8		1	1	14		5		9	9	2	2
8– 9			1	6			1	1			
9–10				1			3				
10–11				2				0	1	1	0
11–12				1							
12–13				0				0			
13–14				1				2			
14–15				1							
15–16											
16–17											
17–18											
18–19											
19–20											
	347	203	67	64		213	51	38	61	14	4
Average distance	2.9	4.3	3.7	6.3		4.8	6.6	8.8	8.8	14.9	19

a. A few towns have distances greater than 20 mm.: in column 8, one 25 to 26 mm.; in column 10 three 22–23, one 25–26, and one 26–27 mm.; in column 11 one 22 to 23, two 23 to 24, and one 30 mm.; Furthermore, in Illinois, Indiana, and Ohio there are six towns with 100,000–500,000 and three with 500,000–2,500,000 inhabitants and an average distance apart of 22.5 or 62 mm. In Iowa and Missouri there are two towns of the first group (distance 55 mm.) and one of the second group. In Texas these towns were not counted.

The Location of Towns

of different size-classes,[4] and have obtained clear-cut frequency curves for them (Fig. 66 and Table 21). The results are very good, too, for a group of other prairie states, Illinois, Indiana, and Ohio, even though here the irregularities are greater (Table 22). Comparison of this group with the two states lying just west of them, Iowa and Missouri, shows how the decrease in population density westward results in an increase of the typical distances separating towns. This is still more clearly shown in Fig. 68. I have assembled the places with 1,000 to 4,000 inhabitants[5] in a strip running westward from Chicago for some 400 miles, that is, about to the western boundary of Iowa, and about 80 miles wide, its northern edge being a prolongation of the northern boundary of Illinois and its southern edge lying an equal distance south of Chicago. These places were arranged in groups according to their distance from Chicago, and the average minimum distance from places of equal or larger size was then calculated for each group. It is manifest that this increases with distance from Chicago. But it can be further seen that in Iowa, about 50 to 140 millimeters on the map from Chicago, the average distance is at the same time the typical one when this state is considered by itself—further proof for the uniformity of conditions there.

Variations in the typical distance between towns in two neighboring districts suggest differences in fertility. Thus the curve for the small towns in the Texas cotton area had two peaks. This is because a strip of fertile soil, the Black Belt, runs across the state, and the towns on it lie twice as close together as elsewhere. English towns are separated by typical distances of their own (Fig. 67 and Table 23).

Here only the table is given; its interpretation will come later. Several other examples are to be found in the literature, though to the best of my knowledge none have been statistically verified. According to K. Bücher (*Die Entstehung der Volkswirtschaft* [1st ed., 1893], p. 49) there were in Germany at the close of the Middle Ages a round 3,000 places with city privileges, which in the south and west were separated by four to five hours' travel, and in the north and east by seven to eight.[6] All in all, a regular distribution of towns throughout the world is extraordinarily common.

---

4. For the method of defining the class limits see p. 434, note 7.

5. According to the map of M. Jefferson, "Some Considerations on the Geographic Provinces of the USA," *Annals of the Association of American Geographers*, VII, 3–15.

6. For the distribution of large villages in Hungary see L. deLagger, "La plaine hongroise," *Annales de Géographie*, X (1901), 44. See also Neupert's beautiful map of Mecklenburg (*Raumforschung und Raumordnung*, 1941, p. 64), and the honeycomb dispersion of markets in Westphalia (W. Christaller, *Die ländliche Siedlungsweise im deutschen Reich* [Stuttgart, 1937], p. 169).

Table 23. DISTANCES SEPARATING ENGLISH TOWNS, 1910

Airline distance from the next equally large or larger town on the map. M. Jefferson, loc. cit. See also Fig. 67.

Distance in mm. (1 mm. = 4.35 km.)	Number of Places with			
	"10,000"[a]	20,000-100,000	100,000-500,000	500,000-2,500,000
	Inhabitants			
1	2	3	4	5
0- 1	79	92	0	
1- 2	38	58	13	
2- 3	20	33	4	
3- 4	8	13	4	
4- 5	5	16	1	
5- 6	9	9	2	
6- 7	3	7	5	
7- 8		2	1	
8- 9		4	2	
9-10		2	1	2
10-11			1	
11-12			2	
Total..........	162	233	39[b]	4[c]
Average distance..	2.1	2.6	6.5	14.5

a. Unfortunately the size-class of the towns in column 2 is not clearly indicated on the map. Because of its small scale, not all the places of this class in the industrial areas were clearly recognizable.

b. Three of these were separated by distances of 16–17 mm., 20–21 mm., and 33–34 mm.

c. Among these there was one place with a distance of 12–13 mm. and one with a distance of 24–25 mm.

B. Economic Areas

Chapter 23. Simple Market Areas

The United States is particularly well suited to an examination of market areas. There they can be observed under a lens, as it were, for distance means less than in Europe whether measured psychologically or in terms of money. Again, the spirit of its people is especially favorable to mass production, so that market areas are generally larger than in Europe. There is a whole series of useful investigations on this subject, mainly by the Department of Commerce, schools of business, individual scholars, economic institutes, and planning boards.[1] Their methods differ. The most useful seems to me the utilization of business books and of statistics of freight traffic, as well as the direct questioning of consumers in areas of retail trade. On the other hand, the atlases produced at great expense by a few advertising firms among others, but in one case even by the NRA itself, which are supposed to indicate the " natural trading areas " of the United States, are hard to employ scientifically.[2] The principles for such a partitioning (traffic conditions, the region in which newspapers circulate, sales radii for retail businesses, turnover, number of inhabitants, income levels, and so on), and the products for which it is supposed to hold true (groceries, or even retail goods in general) are too numerous for such " market areas " to have any precise meaning.

---

1. At the federal level: National Resources Planning Board (formerly the National Resources Committee).

2. The regional atlas published for great department stores by the J. W. Thompson Company (*Retail Shopping Areas* [New York, 1927]) is still fairly useful. The towns in which large department stores are situated are shown on a map, and boundaries between them drawn in such a way that the distances from them to each of the neighboring centers is the same. But this procedure considers only transport costs, not differences in price or variety, or competition by smaller department stores.

a. THE SIGNIFICANCE OF DISTANCE FOR THE
INDIVIDUAL ENTERPRISE

§1. Erroneous Estimation

What is the result of these investigations? All agree on one point: Many manufacturers as well as wholesale and retail dealers have expanded their market areas excessively. *They ship too far at a loss.* The geographic marginal cost exceeds the marginal revenue. " Many manufacturers permit field sales operations to penetrate too far into unprofitable territory." [3] " Many small manufacturers have made the error of seeking national distribution at great expense only to find that a greater volume of business at much smaller cost could be secured within a few miles of the plant." [4] " Too much territory is being covered. It seems practically certain that a greater profit could be made within a restricted territory." [5] " The broad generality, that distributors should warehouse a reserve stock for retailers within a radius of economical distribution and convenience of service is generally followed. In the striving for sales volume it has been easy to lose sight of the sales expense attaching to sales made beyond the economical radius of distribution." [6] In Germany, "A calculation of individual cost items . . . showed that many beer storehouses that had been established to lengthen the sales radius did not repay their high cost, because of their small turnover." [7]

What causes the loss in sales to too distant buyers? First, too high shipping costs.[8] Williamson investigated a grocery store in a metropolis that delivered to homes free within a radius of almost seven miles. The yearly turnover of a quarter of a million dollars just about corresponded to the demand of families living within

3. International Magazine Company, *The Trading Area System of Sales Control. A Marketing Atlas of the United States* (New York, 1931), iv or v.

4. W. F. Williamson, *The Retail Grocer's Problems, U. S. Department of Commerce, Distribution Cost Studies, No. 5* (Washington, 1929), p. 14.

5. This in the wholesale dry-goods trade, where freight is supposed to play a subordinate role! *Problems of Dry Goods Distribution, U. S. Department of Commerce, Distribution Cost Studies, No. 7* (Washington, 1930), p. 2.

6. J. W. Millard, *Analyzing Wholesale Distribution Costs, U. S. Department of Commerce, Distribution Cost Studies, No. 1* (Washington, 1928), p. 2. (This refers also to wholesale trade.)

7. H. Fezer, " Brauereien als Rationalisierungsexempel," *Deutscher Volkswirt*, 1942, pp. 1038–1040.

8. Freight costs are more apt to be disregarded: (a) the lower the average total freight in relation to the factory price. According to Mellerowicz (*Frankfurter Zeitung, Wirtschaftsheft 8*, p. 8), it amounted in the United States to 4 per cent for textiles, 10

approximately half a mile, which shows the disproportionately long distances traveled by the delivery car. More than a third of the trips were made to deliver a single order. The average value of an order was hardly three dollars, and out of this an average of twenty-one cents went for the cost of delivery. At the periphery of the area these costs must have been considerably higher, since several deliveries could less frequently be combined because of the smaller number and greater dispersion of customers. For three quarters of the sales were made within about two miles of the store, whereas only one quarter of the demand came from the rest of the market area, which was six times larger.

But not only shipping costs rise with distance; the *selling* costs proper rise as well. Thus in a typical grocery house the costs dependent on distance were found to be as follows:

Selling Cost Dependent on Distance as Percentage of Total Cost [a]

Shipping Costs		Other Selling Costs	
Freight	10.1	Car and traveling saleman's expenses	6.2
Packer	3.1	Advertising	0.2
Packing material	0.1	Postage, telephone, telegrams	1.5
	13.3		7.9

a. J. W. Millard, *The Wholesale Grocer's Problems, U. S. Department of Commerce, Distribution Cost Studies,* No. 4 (Washington, 1928), p. 11.

per cent for shoes, 24 per cent for grain, 34 per cent for coke and salt, 42 per cent for milk, and 51 per cent for natural stone. (*b*) The lower the freight per ton-mile relative to the factory price (see column *c* of the following table for Germany).

	a	b	c	d	e	f
Building stone (Brandenburg).............	7.90	16.80	213	20	8.1	F
Lignite (Rhenish briquettes)...............	12.85	12.50	103	10	3.9	6 B 1
Soft coal (Rhenish-Westphalian egg briquettes)................................	17.—	12.50	74	10	3.4	6 B 1
Lump limestone (Ruedersdorf)............	21.50	16.80	78	20	5.2	F
Portland cement (Berlin)..................	31.80	16.80	53	20	4.1	F
Potatoes (yellow)g........................	42.70	13.10	31	20	3.6	G
Potash fertilizer (40% loose)g.............	51.80	4.10	8	5	0.9	11 B 1
Pig iron (cast III, Oberhausen)...........	63.00	16.80	27	20	2.5	F
Rye (German loading station).............	175.50	25.60	15	30	1.5	D
Wheat (German loading station)..........	201.10	25.60	13	30	1.3	D
Lead (f. o. b. German source)............	299.20	25.60	9	30	0.9	D
Cotton (standard middling, Bremen)......	738.10	27.40	4	30	0.4	21 S 1
Electrolytic copper (Hamburg)............	762.70	36.20	5	40	0.5	B
Cotton yarn (No. 20, Augsburg)..........	1,970.—	40.30	2	50	0.2	A
Tin (Banka, Hamburg)..................	3,216.70	40.30	1	50	0.2	A

(*a*) Shipping price in reichsmarks per ton (*Statistisches Jahrbuch für das deutsche Reich* [Berlin, 1938], pp. 322–329). (*b*) Railway freight per ton per

From this it follows that it is the worst possible business policy to canvass outlying areas intensively and to absorb the freight to them. It is somewhat better to pay the freight on orders received from them even without canvassing, and best of all not to solicit business in these areas at all and to charge at least half the freight to the customer. An investigation of costs in the confectionery business showed how little is earned by distant sales.[9]

Table 24. SELLING COST AND DISTANCE

(All figures: percentage of total sales)

Distance of Customer in Miles	Sales According to Distance Zones						Selling Cost											
							Total						of which direct selling cost					
	I			II			I			II			I			II		
	G	A	B	F	C	D	G	A	B	F	C	D	G	A	B	F	C	D
To 500	95	80	71	94	77	73	26	24	18	31	24	27	11	10	3	14	4	13
500-1000	5	16	18	6	16	21	29	27	19	41	25	36	8	9	4	21	5	16
1000-1500		1	4		2	6		29	20		32	32		6	6		11	13
1500-		2	7		5	0		27	19		25	50		6	4		5	19

Distance of Customer in Miles	Selling Cost						Profit (Estimate[a])					
	of which Freight											
	I			II			I			II		
	G	A	B	F	C	D	G	A	B	F	C	D
To 500	3	3	1	4	2	1	−1	5	6	0	− 2	7
500-1000	11	7	4	8	4	6	1	−1	8	−11	− 3[a]	3
1000-1500		12	3		4	6		1	7		−20[a]	5
1500-		12	3		4	18		2	7		− 3[a]	−11

a. Weighted average for almost all firms in the industry.

The six factories listed in Table 24 are divided into two groups, a seventh (*E*) having been omitted because it delivered to but *one* distance zone. Group I evidently operated on the principle of only accepting distant sales without soliciting them. Their selling costs hardly increased with distance, and what slight rise there was depended entirely upon a steep rise in freight costs, while, with

---

500 kilometers (15-ton cars). (*c*) *b* as percentage of *a*. (*d*) Freight for each additional 10 kilometers in pfennigs per ton. (*e*) *d* as *pro mille* of the price at 500 kilometers. (*f*) Class of freight rate or special rate respectively (1943). (*g*) Calculated from the average delivered price.

9. *Distribution Cost Problem of Manufacturing Confectioners, U. S. Department of Commerce, Distribution Cost Studies, No. 10* (Washington, 1931), p. 12.

the exception of B, less was spent on advertising. To make up for this, B charged all freight beyond the first zone to its customers. Group II went after distant sales vigorously, as may be seen from its direct selling costs. A calculation of profits showed that the policy of the first group was the correct one.

Analysis of the selling costs of an important dry-goods factory and wholesale house in Kansas City showed again that the ratio of selling costs to sales generally increases with distance.[10] The expenses of traveling salesmen in particular paid off less the farther from from the home plant was the district to be canvassed, or the nearer

Table 25. RELATION OF SALES RADIUS TO COST IN CERTAIN WHOLESALE TRADES

Cost as percentage of sales[1]

Sales Radius in Miles[2]	Radio[4] All costs	Groceries[5] All costs	Dyes[6]	Hardware[7]
			Expenses for salesmen	
- 75	15.1	8.3	4.4	4.6
75-150		9.2	4.3	5.1
150-250	16.0	11.7	5.6	4.6
250-500		10.0	7.3	4.4
500-[3]	18.6	13.0	9.1	4.9
U. S. A.	19.3		7.1	5.9
World	21.7		4.2	4.2

1. Weighted average of almost all firms in the industry.
2. Every zone contains all firms whose farthest shipping distance falls within the particular zone.
3. Firms that deliver within a radius of more than 500 miles but do not deliver over the entire United States.
4. Source: *U. S. Department of Commerce, 15th Census of U. S. Wholesale Distribution, Radio Sets, Parts and Accessories* (Washington, 1932), p. 25.
5. Source: *Idem, Wholesale Distribution, Groceries and Food Specialties* (Washington, 1933), p. 77. (Wholesale houses with annual sales of between $100,000 and $300,000.)
6. Source: *Idem, Wholesale Trade in Paints and Varnishes* (Washington, 1932), p. 32.
7. Source: *Idem, The Wholesale Hardware Trade* (Washington, 1933), p. 50 (No. 1).

it was to competition. As a rule both these factors coincide in distant areas. Table 25 gives additional examples, taken from the fifteenth census. It may happen occasionally, of course, that with extension of a market area fixed costs decrease faster than direct costs increase, but obviously this is not the rule.

The dry-goods firm in Kansas City provided some highly interesting information also on the increased business risk that accompanies distance (*ibid.*, p. 33). Although it was more strict

---

10. *Problems of Dry Goods Distribution, U. S. Department of Commerce, Distribution Cost Studies, No. 7* (Washington, 1930), p. 32.

about extending credit to distant customers, the proportion of accounts overdue to the total number outstanding was greatest in the outlying areas.

The far-reaching effects of this underestimation of distance, even under the more restricted spatial conditions in Germany, are graphically shown in Figure 69. In a certain region where an absurd interpretation of free divisibility permits every child to

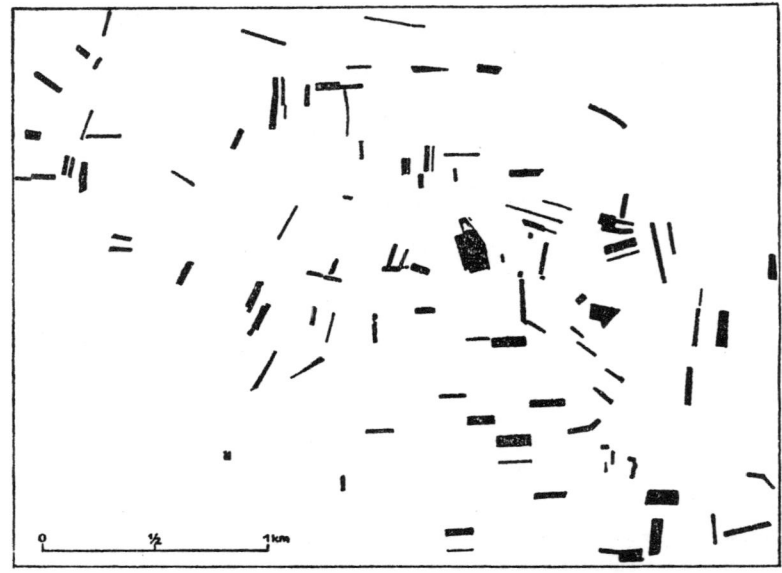

Fig. 69. Parceling of fields on a farm in the Administrative District of Herrenberg. Thirty hectares divided into 162 parcels, with a total distance from the farm of 206 km. Buildings are on the largest parcel. (After Münzinger, *Bäuerliche Maschinengenossenschaft Häusern* [Berlin, 1934], p. 9.)

inherit his share of every parcel of land, "more than one-third of the working day of the peasant is spent uselessly . . . simply to overcome the distance to individual places of work"[11]—and this included much time uselessly spent on the farm itself. (A. Münzinger, *Der Arbeitsertrag der bäuerlichen Familienwirtschaft* [Berlin, 1929], p. 826.)

Nor will planning ensure that the costs of distance are not neg-

---

11. Even with rounding off of the land, these ways would not disappear completely: They correspond to the time spent by factory workers in going to and from work. This should have been considered by Münzinger in his comparison in *Raumforschung und Raumordnung*, 1940, pp. 395 f., as well as the fact that they work in their own home and gardens, lose earnings during a depression, and have traveling expenses.

lected. Thus many small mills, handicraft enterprises, and factories are supposed to have been closed down in Russia in 1928 in favor of a few large plants with overextended supply and market areas. The villages often seem to be too large, and the distance to the fields unnecessarily long in consequence.

All these examples indicate that the economic significance of distance has often been underestimated in the past, even by businessmen themselves.[12]

§2. CONSOLIDATION OF AREAS

When distance is neglected, economic areas overlap; that is, they are too far extended on the one hand, and shot through with holes on the other. Consolidation reduces them to a smaller and more compact but more profitable whole.[13] Such an experiment to restrict the sales area was made in the United States by a wholesale hardware house. It decreased its *market area* (and from our standpoint unfortunately, its assortment also) each by one third. The area thereupon formed a compact whole, in which this firm was superior to its outside competitors. As a consequence of this voluntary restriction sales dropped off, but profits increased by one third! [14]

During World War II the consolidation of areas was facilitated in Germany on a large scale partly through the influence of this book. An exchange of customers or even simple shortening of sales radii was imposed on breweries and other nonagricultural enterprises—not, of course, in order to increase private profits, but to lessen the demands on transportation, which after all is but the economic side

---

12. So much so, indeed, that two leading entrepreneurs in hardwares expressed completely contradictory views to me on the influence of distance upon their business. One held that it played no role at all in the choice of a location; that he absorbed the freight, which after all amounted on the average to only 2 per cent of his sales, and therefore was able to compete on equal terms in any part of the United States. He declined to export merely as a matter of convenience and to keep his business within limits where it could be supervised. The other entrepreneur, who produced exactly the same articles, found freight so important that it wholly determined the location of his enterprise and the extent of his business connections. See also p. 157, note 34.

13. Strictly speaking, three objectives are sought: (*a*) To make areas more compact. (*b*) To round them off more. (*c*) To center them on their economic centers. Of course the last aim cannot always be achieved; for example, not for farmlands when the village is the center of settlement. Remaining exclaves are improved, at least in shape and size. There is much to be said against a *complete* rounding off of lands. See, for instance, p. 115, note 12.

14. J. W. Millard, *Analyzing Wholesale Distribution Costs, U. S. Department of Commerce Distribution Cost Studies, No. 1* (Washington, 1928), pp. 11 f.

of private advantage. Only with insurance companies were costs supposed to be lowered at the same time.[15]

Cartels have long been familiar with "protection of an area." An excellent example of the improvement of *supply areas* is provided by milk deliveries to Berlin, which formerly were made from distances as great as 457 miles.[16] The idea of consolidating areas of agricultural production originated with Thünen[17] over 120 years ago, and grew with Münzinger's proposal of co-operative agriculture[18] through the change in use caused by the war to a difficult change in ownership. The consolidation of regions inhabited by commuters is most difficult and doubtful, because it causes many hardships and is often equivalent to an encouragement of migration into towns.[19]

b. DESCRIPTION OF MARKET AREAS[20]

§1. SIZE

Since most theorists are even less accustomed to think in terms of space than the practical man, it will not be superfluous to offer

---

15. Though the German insurance centers are scattered, all the companies insure everywhere, which resulted in an excess of representatives, agencies, and regional offices (Rath, "Der Raum als Kostenfaktor in der europäischen Privatversicherung," *Wirtschaftsdienst,* 1942, pp. 938 f.), but had the advantage that the risk was distributed. During the war this scattering proved to be advantageous, especially in the case of mortgage credit, since otherwise one single bombing attack might have wiped out a good part of the collateral. To this extent the nature of insurance differs widely from that of businesses that deal in tangible goods. Rath takes into account only those factors that *favor* areal consolidation, but his material would be well worthy of consideration for such a purpose provided it is really typical. (*Organisationsform und Wirtschaftlichkeit im Versicherungswesen* [Leipzig, 1942].) So far as I am aware, no practical measures have as yet been taken.

16. H. Backe, *Um die Nahrungsfreiheit Europas* (Leipzig, 1942); maps, p. 207.

17. *Der isolirte Staat in Beziehung auf Landwirtschaft und Nationalökonomie* (Waentig edition, Jena, 1921), pp. 108–113.

18. *Bäuerliche Maschinengenossenschaft Häusern* (Berlin, 1934).

19. For its possibilities and difficulties see M. Eckardt (or *Landesplanungsgemeinschaft Sachsen*), *Die Hauptströme der Pendelwanderung in der sächsischen Industrie,* 1940, Pt. I, pp. 15–17. For a thoughtful discussion see Siebrecht, *Wirtschaftskurve,* 1942, pp. 235–241.

20. Enterprises without market areas are very uncommon. In the main they are businesses that are "oriented toward passers-by" (R. Schmidt-Friedländer, *Grundzüge einer Lehre vom Standorte des Handels* [Prague, 1933], p. 101), and live off passing traffic rather than the vicinity. I do not include here those businesses that supply larger recurrent necessities such as furniture, better clothing, and so on, and would have to occupy a central location in any case.

some illustrations on the size and shape of market areas for various kinds of enterprise.[21] First, as to their size.

In the *Fifteenth Census of the United States* the sales radius also is given in part. Table 26 and Figure 70 reproduce some of the interesting results. First, the extraordinary difference in size within the same line is striking. Theoretical reasons for such variations have already been advanced in Part II: differences in population density, natural features, the characters of entrepreneurs, and so on. In judging the present data it is to be borne in mind also that the inquiry distinguished only between classes of goods, not between individual goods. Thus when firms said they supplied the whole United States the statement was by no mean true of all articles, but often of a few specialties only for which they had the exclusive selling rights.[22]

---

21. Adequate investigations on this subject are none too numerous. Nevertheless only a few selections can be mentioned here. At least the work of F. A. Fetter (*The Masquerade of Monopoly* [New York, 1931], pp. 287 ff.) on the influence of freight upon the market areas of the American steel industry may be cited, as well as A. Predöhl's excellent map in " Die örtliche Verteilung der amerikanischen Eisen- und Stahlindustrie," *Weltwirtschaftliches Archiv*, XXVII (1928), 285 Reference may be made also to R. Regul ("Die Wettbewerbslage der Steinkohle," *Vierteljahrshefte zur Konjunkturforschung, Sonderheft 34* [Berlin, 1933]), who calculated the theoretical limits for competition by British, Westphalian, and Upper Silesian coal in Germany on a basis of price at the mine and freight rates, though without considering differences in quality; to E. Scheu's map (*Deutschlands Wirtschaftsprovinzen und Wirtschaftsbezirke*, 1928, p. 53); to J. D. Black (*Introduction to Production Economics* [New York, 1926], p. 933), who published an entire scale of supply areas for Minneapolis of all sizes and in approximate form; and to H. M. Kendall's painstaking study of supply areas for markets and fairs in southern France (" Fairs and Markets in the Department of Gers, France," *Economic Geography*, XII [1936], 351–358.) His method of determining approximate limits by fares, and exact limits by personal inquiry along the the highways, is good. He describes a hierarchy of larger and smaller markets, and finds among other things that supply areas for large markets overlapped more than those for small ones. For another discussion of this subject see A. Allix (" The Geography of Fairs," *Geographic Review*, 1922, pp. 532–569). In the growing literature on areas that supply German towns there is G. Kühne's comprehensive investigation of the hinterland of Kamenz (*Die Stadt Kamenz in den Beziehungen zu ihrem Hinterland* [Dresden, 1937]), which proves, for example, that the patients of specialists are drawn from a considerably larger area than those of other physicians (Map 11). Finally, R. E. Dickinson ("Markets and Market Areas in East Anglia," *Economic Geography*, April, 1934, pp. 173–182) has written on agricultural markets in the English counties of Norfolk and Suffolk. The widening of the areas, and the dying out of superfluous centers, are interestingly shown.

22. U. S. Department of Commerce, *Fifteenth Census of the United States, Wholesale Trade in Paints and Varnishes* [Washington, 1932], p. 18. According to a questionnaire sent to 3,000 wholesale grocers, market areas increased in the following order: (1) widely known trademarked articles, (2) specialties, (3) brands of the wholesalers

For one and the same product the variation in areal size is therefore less.[23] On the other hand, this variation is often more significant than it might seem if only the number of firms is considered, and not their volume of business as well. The number of firms naturally decreases with an increase in the size of the market area, but their *importance* often increases. An example of this is the

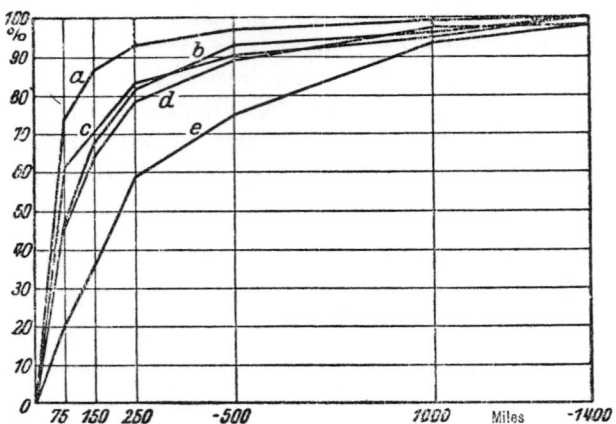

Fig. 70. Size of wholesale market areas by goods, 1929. For legend and sources see Table 26. For areas smaller than the United States, but more than 500 miles in radius, the highest value for the radius was assumed to be 1,000 miles. For wholesalers who supplied the entire United States the radius of the market area was estimated at 1,500 miles.

wholesale paint business. Firms with a sales radius of less than 75 miles have an average yearly turnover of $109,000, whereas for those that supply the world market also the average is $9,000,000.[24] An opposite example is furnished by the wholesale radio business, where the corresponding figures are $395,000 and $368,000.

Secondly, differences in the size of market areas appear among

concerned. (J. W. Millard, *U. S. Department of Commerce, Domestic Commerce Series No. 7, Atlas of Wholesale Grocery Territories* [Washington, 1927], vi.) The overlapping of areas is manifestly greatest in the third case, because the qualities are most difficult to compare.

23. It happens, also, that only commodities that will not sell are thrown on distant markets. (*U. S. Department of Commerce, Problems of Dry Goods Distribution, Distribution Cost Studies, No. 7* [Washington, 1930], p. 13.)

24. *U. S. Department of Commerce, Fifteenth Census of the United States, Wholesale Trade in Paints and Varnishes* [Washington, 1932], p. 32.

different lines of business,[25] especially in the illustration.[26] Small areas predominate for groceries, medium-sized ones for wholesale dealers in radio, paints, or hardware, and large areas for the sales offices of the manufacturers of paints or hardware. These variations are explained not only by the different importance of freight and selling costs but also by the height of the fixed costs and, on the

Table 26. SIZE OF MARKET AREAS FOR WHOLESALE TRADE IN THE UNITED STATES ACCORDING TO GOODS, 1929

Percentage of firms with at most the regular sales radii given in the table:

Sales radius in Miles	a	b	c	d	e	f
- 75	74	49	62	46	21	37
-150	87	67	71	66	36	48
-250	93	82	83	79	58	73
-500	97	93	90	89	74	84
500--*	99	96	94	97	93	94
U. S. A.	100	99	99	98	98	99
World	100	100	100	100	100	100

* The area has a maximum radius of more than 500 miles, but does not include the entire United States.

   a. Wholesale grocery businesses with $100,000–$4,000,000 yearly turnover (*U. S. Dept. of Commerce, 15th Census of U. S. Wholesale Distribution, Groceries and Food Specialties*, p. 77).
   b. Wholesale radio (*idem, Radio Sets, Parts, and Accessories*, p. 25).
   c. Independent paint wholesalers (*idem, Wholesale Trade in Paints and Varnishes,* p. 32).
   d. Independent hardware wholesalers, miscellaneous stock (*idem, The Wholesale Hardware Trade* [Washington, 1933], p. 50).
   e. Wholesale trade of hardware producers (*loc. cit.*, p. 50).
   f. Wholesale trade of paint producers (*loc. cit.* under *c*, p. 32).

---

25. E. M. Hoover ("The Measurement of Industrial Localization," *Review of Economic Statistics, XVIII* [1936]) has shown the dispersion of industrial locations in a similar manner.

26. There are simpler methods than direct investigation for determining differences in the size of market areas according to the business, but none is wholly reliable. It is not enough to know the typical number of customers since, though the number might be much larger for a baker, say, than for a dealer in automobiles, his *market area* is certainly smaller. Nor are market areas necessarily smaller, the larger the number of enterprises. In the United States there are about as many newspapers as cotton gins, but the areas of the latter are much smaller because they are restricted to the cotton belt. A relatively simple and fairly useful method is to find out through a questionnaire the distances of consumers from their usual source of supply, and then to calculate the average. For one county in the state of New York such an inquiry showed that the average distance of a farmer from a church was a little over 3 miles, from a bank about 5 miles, from a motion picture theater about 7½ miles, from a clothier nearly 14½ miles, and so on. (H. C. Hoffsommer, *Relation of Cities and Larger Villages to Changes in Rural Trade and Social Areas in Wayne County, New York. Cornell University Agricultural Experiment Station Bulletin 582* [Ithaca, 1934], p. 36.)

other side, the size of the demand. As has already been theoretically established, it is simply not true that heavy and cheap goods have the smallest market areas.[27]

Naturally this does not exclude an actual restricting effect by high freight rates if the advantages of giant enterprises are too small in proportion to them. The furniture trade provides an example of this. In the "New South," that is, Texas and the adjoining states, only 9 out of 30 furniture factories sold their products throughout the entire United States, and only one of these made a profit. The normal sales radius for [furniture] factories may be set at about 500 miles.[28] For wholesale furniture dealers it would probably be less than 200 miles. It is given as embracing 50 to 200 counties (*ibid.*, p. 25). The retail dealer's market area includes 5 to 65 counties, according to the size of the towns (*ibid.*, p. 47).

Besides market areas for different goods, a comparison of the market areas of different cities for the same goods is instructive (Table 27). Here again we find considerable differences in size, which may depend partly upon differences in market structure, but probably in part also upon a varying power of individual centers to attract qualified entrepreneurs. Even where the size is apparently about the same (both national and frontier centers often do considerable exporting) the underlying causes may be very different. Centers on the frontier export because of their geographic position, national centers because of their importance. The inland market of the one includes the entire United States and it is not surprising, therefore, that sales should extend beyond it, whereas the inland market of the other group is restricted and its market area obviously is international only because its members are near a political frontier.

Even among regional centers two groups must be distinguished. The first owe their long sales radii chiefly to natural conditions in their economic landscapes: Centers in California to the enormous length (more than 1,250 miles) and narrow width of the more densely populated coastal strip west of the Rocky Mountains. If

---

27. Weight is obviously more important for the wholesale dealer, with his lower prices and longer average distances, than for the retailer, for whom the cost of shipping by freight to the customer is less both absolutely and in relation to the price. For corresponding observations in the hardware business see W. A. Bowers, *U. S. Department of Commerce, Domestic Commerce Series No. 52, Hardware Distribution in the Gulf Southwest* (Washington, 1932), p. 32. In fact, with quality differences markets expand farther by overlapping when the freight rate is low in relation to the price.

28. W. A. Bowers, *U. S. Department of Commerce, Domestic Commerce Series No. 76, Furniture Distribution in the Gulf Southwest* (Washington, 1933), p. 3.

Simple Market Areas

Table 27. SIZE OF WHOLESALE MARKET AREAS BY CITIES, 1929
Businesses whose sales radii are in the given class sizes had the following share (per cent) in the entire turnover of their cities in the specified line of business

Sales Radii in Miles		Groceries[1]							Radio[2]					
		Up to 75	75 to 150	150 to 250	250 to 500	Over 500 But not entire U.S.A.	U.S.A.	World[5]	Up to 75	75 to 150	150 to 250	250 to 500	Over 500 But not entire U.S.A.	U.S.A.	World
Centers on boundary	Seattle.......	10	4	42	0	—		44[6]	16	47	30	7	—	—	—
	Buffalo......	60	40	—	—	—	—	—	17	34	49	—	—	—	—
National centers	New York....	47	—	1	5	34	13	1	23	2	5	3	0	65	1
	Chicago.....	28	4	1	3	23	40	—	20	19	3	18	26	12	2
Far reaching regional centers	San Francisco	26	12	13	28	23	2	—	6	7	0	34	53	—	—
	Los Angeles..	52	5	19	24	0	—	—	2	12	67	18	2	—	—
	Denver......	0	11	51	—	38	—	—	—	—	12	76	12	—	—
	Atlanta......	100	—	—	—	—	—	—	0	—	26	24	49	—	—
Compressed regional centers	Boston.......	47	17	10	—	26	—	—	36	13	51	—	—	—	—
	Pittsburg.....	69	24	3	5	—	—	—	22	54	23	—	—	—	—
		Paints[3]							Hardware[4]						
Centers on boundary	Seattle.......	3	24	54	4	1	—	14	4	5	9	2	7	9	65
	Buffalo......	9	28	4	—	—	15	44	20	4	41	35	—	—	—
National centers	New York....	18	8	8	3	6	22	36	34	4	10	7	9	18	18
	Chicago.....	13	3	7	10	33	33	—	12	5	7	16	21	11	29
Far reaching regional centers	San Francisco	25	—	—	21	21	—	33	10	1	0	22	67	—	0
	Los Angeles..	23	8	9	44	17	—	—	5	15	22	28	30	0	—
	Denver......	5	—	2	24	70	—	—	—	—	4	21	75	—	—
	Atlanta......	32	20	17	6	25	—	—	5	—	49	47	—	—	—
Compressed regional centers	Boston.......	24	2	57	7	1	10	—	14	4	31	21	26	2	1
	Pittsburg.....	25	40	7	—	—	28	—	16	45	5	—	27	7	—

1. *U. S. Department of Commerce, 15th Census of the United States, Wholesale Distribution, Groceries and Food Specialties,* p. 52.
2. *Idem, Radio Sets, Parts, and Accessories,* p. 17.
3. *Idem, Wholesale Trade in Paints and Varnishes,* p. 18.
4. *Idem, The Wholesale Hardware Trade,* p. 29.
5. Market areas that extend beyond the United States, even though they may not include all countries, even though their radii may remain less that 500 miles.
6. Much of this to Alaska and the Orient. *Loc. cit.* under n. 1.

the strip were wider the sales radius would probably shrink. The ideal location of San Francisco, almost in the middle of the strip, is clearly apparent; its sales radii considerably exceed those of Los Angeles, which is pushed into the corner, as it were. Denver has no rivals for a long distance because the market on the broad plateau of the Rocky Mountains, with their natural resources hardly yet opened up, is still more restricted than that on the half-desert of the western prairie, which forms the other half of Denver's market area. Atlanta, on the other hand, is the center for a thickly settled though partly very poor region, and has near-by competitors. It falls in the group with large market areas only because Florida, the southern tip of its market area, is of such great length. The second group is hemmed in by large adjacent centers. An extensive local demand and the demand from a vicinity that is similar in many respects predominate here.

Some data on Germany also are available. Before the war the average, not the maximum, shipping distance by rail for carload lots was, in miles: (a) *Entering*: milk, $31\frac{1}{4}$; grain and meal, $68\frac{3}{4}$; potatoes, $137\frac{1}{2}$. (b) *Distribution*: bricks, $18\frac{3}{4}$; natural stone, 75; pumice stone, $212\frac{1}{2}$; building clinker, up to $312\frac{1}{2}$; peat, $43\frac{3}{4}$; oil cake, $106\frac{1}{2}$; fertilizers, 175; peat dust, 250; newsprint, $93\frac{3}{4}$; rayon staple, $218\frac{3}{4}$; linoleum, $237\frac{1}{2}$; wine, 200; and salt-water fish, $281\frac{1}{4}$.[29] For similar goods and similar conditions (otherwise see p. 405, note 26) the average population per nonagricultural enterprise (method 1) or, conversely, the number of such enterprises or of those engaged therein per 1,000 inhabitants, the so-called occupation index [" *Besatzziffer* "] (method 2), is a clue to the *relative* extent of a market. For relative sizes in new settlements see F. Rechenberg, *Das Einmaleins der Siedlung (Richtzahlen für das Siedlungswesen)* (Berlin, 1940), pp. 29–33. The data are derived by method 2 from cities with 20,000 inhabitants and corrected by experience and comparison with the ideal.[30] For size relationships in rural districts see W. Christaller, " Die Verteilung der nichtlandwirtschaftlichen Bevölkerung im Hauptdorfbereich," *Neues Bauerntum*, 1942, pp. 139–145; and " Die Verteilung der landwirtschaftlichen Bevölkerung im Landkreis," *Neues Bauerntum,* 1942, pp. 169–176. [According to his page 169, Christaller used method 1.] For size relationships

---

29. Methods of preservation such as the deep-freezing of fish and the pasteurizing of milk have greatly extended the markets for quickly perishable goods, potentially and often also in practice.

30. The actual occupation indices (" *Besatzziffern* ") by administrative districts will be found in *Statistik des Deutschen Reichs*, 446, pp. 158–163.

within the Reich, see G. Isenberg, " Die Tragfähigkeit des deutschen Ostens an landwirtschaftlicher und gewerblicher Bevölkerung," in *Struktur und Gestaltung der zentralen Orte des deutschen Ostens* (Leipzig, 1941), pp. 21–28 (longer lists in each case). Christaller classifies nonagricultural enterprises according to the following market areas: village, environs of a main village, environs of a country town, and county. Isenberg includes all these together as providing for local requirements, in addition to which he distinguishes those that provide for district and distant requirements, inclusive of those dependent upon raw materials. His criterion for classification is whether a nonagricultural enterprise occurs regularly in every county, or at least in every province. The remainder, and a few unusually large parts of the nonagricultural enterprises first named, are classified as providing for distant requirements (method 3).

§2. Structure of Market Areas

An investigation of wholesale trade in electrical appliances (Table 28), and another of a wholesale poultry and egg house in Louisville (J. R. Bromell, *U. S. Department of Commerce, Dis-*

Table 28. DISTANCE AND SIZE OF DEMAND IN WHOLESALE TRADE, BY COUNTIES[1]

a	b	c
0- 50	5.8	0.8-16
50-100	2.7	0.4-9.7
100-150	1.6	0.1-7.1
150-200	1.6	0.0-7.1
200-250	0.4	0.0-1.1

1. Calculated from *U. S. Department of Commerce, Distribution Cost Studies, No. 9, Problems of Wholesale Electrical Goods Distribution* (1931), pp. 23 ff.
a. Average distance of territories of wholesalers, in kilometers.
b. Turnover of the wholesaler per wage earner in the territory concerned, in dollars (unweighted average).
c. The range of its variations, in dollars.

tribution Cost Studies No. 14, Wholesale Grocery Operations, Louisville Grocery Survey, Part 4 [Washington, 1932], pp. 40 f.) provide data on the structure of market areas. They show that the concentration of buyers, the total demand of each, and the number of his orders all decrease with distance. On the other hand, the average size of the single order increases. Detailed investigations in Iowa show for retail trade also a definite fall in demand with distance, which may not be continuous but is nevertheless very clear on the whole when the population of the various places is taken into account. A few examples are given in Table 29. With increasing distance only the well-to-do still come to larger towns for their purchases.[31] Thus it may be said that the richer one is the more does one buy in larger and more distant centers, whence it follows that the extent of a place's retail market areas increases with the size of the place. (See *Iowa State Planning Board, Retail Trading Areas, Series I* [Des Moines, 1936], No. 7, 7a). On the other hand, the larger is one's place of residence the less often does one purchase outside it.

Table 29. DISTANCE AND SIZE OF DEMAND IN RETAIL TRADE FOR SIMILAR PLACES IN THREE COUNTIES IN IOWA

	a	b	c	d
Montrose	8	53	100	100
Donnellson	12	11	53	94
Mediapolis	15	11	82	82
Winfield	38	3	54	75
Wayland	49	0	25	58

The inhabitants of these villages with a population of 500–1,000 made the given percentages of their purchases in the nearest town (Burlington, pop. 27,000 or Fort Madison, pop. 14,000). *Iowa State Planning Board, Retail Trading Areas, Series I* (Des Moines, 1936), No. 7, pp. 5b, 5c.

   a. Distance to nearest town, in miles.   *c.* Furniture.
   b. Kitchen utensils.   *d.* Men's clothing.

But of course this practice varies with the good to be bought. The higher the value of the purchase and the wider the choice, the more likely an article is to be obtained in a large center. Hence the strength of a rural business lies in neither specialties nor goods in whose variety the customer is interested, but in staples and cheap fashionable articles.

The investigations in Iowa, of which more will be said later, provide unique statistical material on all this. The fact that the market uniformly thins out, as it were, in respect to both size of demand and number of goods with distance from any town, and especially from a city, has an additional result. The overlapping of supply areas for cities is much less important than its extent would suggest.

W. J. Reilly believes that he can perceive regularities in the relative strength of rival towns within a disputed area, which he

---

31. For two thirds of those questioned, distance decided the place in which to buy when the state of the roads was taken into consideration, whereas less than one fifth were influenced by widely assorted stocks (*Iowa State Planning Board, Retail Trading Areas, Series I* [Des Moines, 1936], No. 6, 7a, and No. 7, 4a).

summarizes in a "law of retail gravitation" (*The Law of Retail Gravitation* [New York, 1931]). This law holds only for retail trade, only for two towns at any given time, and only in the neighborhood of the line on which both towns are equally strong; which assumes that each town is large enough to exclude the other from its local market. That is to say, the pair must not be too unequal.[32] With these limitations the law reads (*ibid.*, p. 9): " Two towns supply a smaller place in proportion to their population, and in inverse proportion to the square of the distance." [33]

In the derivation it is assumed that the "law" has the general form $\frac{U_1}{U_2} = \left(\frac{B_1}{B_2}\right)^N \left(\frac{E_2}{E_1}\right)^n$, where U_1 is the sales of town 1 in the intermediate place, E_1 the distance between both, B_1 the population of town 1; and U_2, E_2, and B_2 are the corresponding values for town 2. N and n are still undetermined. They are supposed to define what, in its general form, no one will deny: that purchases by country people in a town depend essentially upon its size and distance. Reilly states that according to his field studies $N = 1$ and n is aproximately 2. He offers figures for the latter only, which, indeed, invariably give for n an actual value between 1.5 and 2.4. In so far as the investigations in Iowa (*loc. cit.*, Nos. 6 and 7) permit

---

32. If they are too unequal, the market area of the smaller town will be encircled or entirely absorbed by that of the larger. Encirclement assumes that the cost of traveling the short distance to the small town is relatively higher than that for the longer distance to the large one. It probably is, as a rule, for certain inconveniences are the same for travel over a short or a long distance. Sliding-scale tariffs have the same effect. See Figure 71, where $BO > AC$ represents the higher prices or the more limited choice in the small town and the curves represent travel costs. Between E and F it is more advantageous to purchase in B, whereas to the right of F it is better to pass through B and go to A.

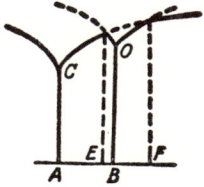

Fig. 71. Encirclement of a small town (B) by a large one (A)

33. According to W. Krzyzanowski (" Review of the Literature of the Location of Industries," *Journal of Political Economy*, 1927, pp. 278–291), Schäffle had already established a similar law, but I could not find the passage in question. In any case, that great systematizer developed many ideas on the settlement system of a country and related matters, that are stimulating even today. See, for example, his *Bau und Leben des sozialen Körpers*, III (Tübingen, 1878), 112–122.

testing of the "law," however, the range of n is very much greater. Thus I cannot regard Reilly's formula as having been verified there. Nevertheless it is a serious attempt to express quantitatively the co-operation of the most important factors.[34]

The final examples of the thinning out of markets with distance are drawn from a book by R. D. MacKenzie (*The Metropolitan Community*, 1933, pp. 76 f.) on metropolitan economic landscapes. Columns 1 and 2 of Table 30 show the proportion of retailers who bought from Chicago wholesalers in 1930, arranged in order of their distance from that city. Columns 3 and 4 give bank localities, similarly arranged, and for every group the percentage of localities in which at least one bank had business relations with the great

Table 30. DISTANCE AND SIZE OF DEMAND

Retailers Dealing with Chicago Wholesalers, 1930, by Distance		Bank Locations by Distance from Chicago		Sales of Detroit Newspaper per 100 Inhabitants in Detroit Area, as function of Distance	
Miles	Per Cent	Miles	Per Cent	Miles	Per Cent
1	3	4	5	5	6
-200	61	- 400	55	- 25	40
200-400	14	400- 800	25	25- 50	24
400-600	13	800-1200	10	50- 75	11
600-	12	1200-1600	30	75-100	8
	100	1600-	40		

Chicago banks. The higher proportion in the most distant areas results from the fact that in these groups the cities of the Mountain States and of California play the chief role, and the business relations among metropolitan banks is especially close. On the other hand, the percentage of banks having deposits with New York banks rises with distance westward from Chicago (*Comptroller of the Currency, Annual Report for 1935* [Washington, 1936], p. 10). The area from which money flows into Chicago is thus surrounded by that of New York, as theory leads us to expect, and the difference in distance from Chicago and New York is less in favor of Chicago the greater the distance west of it.[35] Columns 5 and 6 of Table 30

---

34. E. Scheu's "law" ("Der Einfluss des Raumes auf die Güterverteilung. Ein wirtschafts-geographisches Gesetz!" *Mitteilungen des Vereins der Geographen an der Universität Leipzig*, No. VII, 1927, pp. 31–37), according to which the sale of goods from a producing area decreases as the cube of the distance, is much more primitive in comparison.

35. See also a map of banks with deposits in Richmond (*Location of Reserve Districts in the United States*, Sixty-third Congress, Second Session, Senate Document 485 [Washington, 1914], p. 305).

Simple Market Areas

show how many Detroit newspapers are sold per 100 inhabitants in the Detroit area. (McKenzie, *op. cit.*, p. 83). McKenzie delimits city economic landscapes according to the center from which most metropolitan newspapers were ordered, and his book contains a map of American economic landscapes drawn by this method (p. 107).

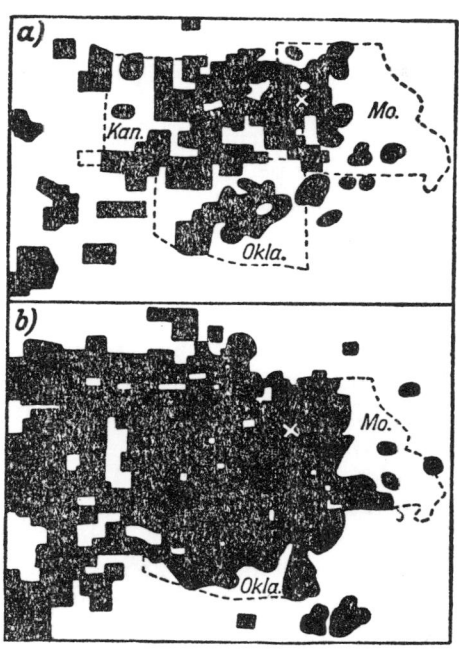

Fig. 72. Market area of a house in Kansas City (×) for (a) fine woolen clothing, (b) overalls and work clothes. (*U. S. Department of Commerce, Distribution Cost Studies No. 7, Problems of Dry Goods Distribution* [Washington 1930], pp. 16 and 21.) Counties with negligible sales are left out of consideration.

In conclusion I present the results of a study on a particularly thinly settled region in the mountainous Northwest of the United States.[36] The only fairly large town there is Bend, in eastern Oregon, with about 9,000 inhabitants. The nearest competing town lies about 125 miles distant, and as a consequence businesses in Bend have enormous market areas, of up to 7,800 square miles. But demand is slight, partly because of the sparse population and partly because of the long distances. Goods with a small possible sales radius and in particular quickly perishable foods such as bread,

---

36. E. Bates, *U. S. Department of Commerce, Domestic Commerce Series No. 51, Commercial Survey of the Pacific North West* (Washington, 1932), pp. 107 ff.

fruit, green vegetables, and ice cream are stocked hardly at all, and specialties and articles of high quality are not profitable. In theoretical terms, their supply and demand curves do not intersect. Thus there remain only a few popular articles that are produced in quantities and have long possible shipping distances. But even these cannot be carried by special establishments because sales would not be large enough, so a sort of "mixed" business prevails. As even wholesale houses are not self-supporting by themselves, they are combined with retail shops.

The lower demand in wartime is analogous to that resulting from small populations, and peddlers flourished during the Middle Ages for corresponding reasons (W. Sombart, *Der moderne Kapitalismus* II [1919], 801 f.).

§3. THE SHAPE OF MARKET AREAS

Various facts concerning the shape of market areas may be gathered from Figure 72. It shows the markets of the wholesale textile firm in Kansas City, already frequently mentioned, for woolen clothing distributed by middlemen, and for the overalls manufactured by the wholesale house itself. The gaps in markets, for which we have given theoretical reasons, are obvious. Furthermore, it is remarkable that this particular firm should be situated almost on the eastern border of the market area instead of at its center. We have met with such an eccentric placing in the theoretical part also (Fig. 46, p. 167). In the present instance this eccentric position has several reasons. First, the next competitor toward the west, Denver, is two and a half times as far from Kansas City as is St. Louis to the east. Secondly, the West is more thinly populated. In the third place, it is naturally more expensive for a place halfway between St. Louis and Kansas City to buy clothing from the East through Kansas City than through St. Louis. The border of the market area therefore lies nearer to the former. It is established by the fact that here the longer but cheap long-distance haul from New York, say, to Kansas City plus the shorter but expensive local transport from Kansas City costs as much as the shorter long-distance haul to St. Louis plus the longer local transportation from St. Louis.[37]

---

37. The effect of these three factors is still more evident in western Kansas. There the smaller market areas resemble narrow strips that stretch far toward the west along the transcontinental railroads; there are no lines running north and south. But the center that supplies these areas lies near the eastern border. See a map of the market areas for department stores in Salina or Great Bend (J. W. Thompson Co., *Retail Shipping Areas* [New York, 1927], p. 67).

Something similar is to be seen in Figure 73, though here the boundary lines are only approximately accurate. Goods for centers 3 to 5 come from the northeast in carload lots, and are distributed in small lots from these centers to their market areas,[38] which have their greatest extension toward the southwest. The coastal points 1 (Houston) and 2 (New Orleans), on the other hand, receive their

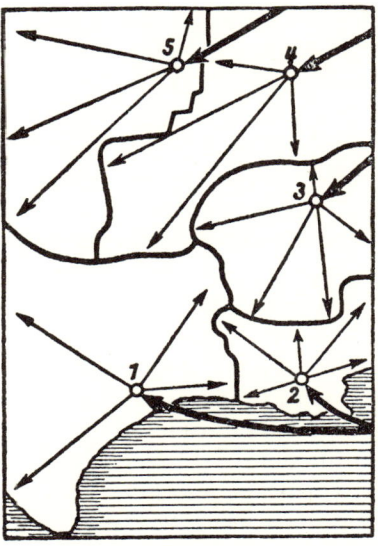

Fig. 73. Market areas of the following wholesale hardware trade centers: 1. Houston; 2. New Orleans; 3. Memphis; 4. St. Louis; 5. Kansas City. (Redrawn after W. A. Bowers, *U. S. Department of Commerce, Domestic Commerce Series No. 52, Hardware Distribution in the Gulf Southwest.* Washington, 1932.)

goods more cheaply by water, and as a consequence their market areas reach comparatively far toward the northeast. The areas established for the Federal Reserve Banks with reference to already existing banking and business conditions also fit well into this

---

38. The pattern of the movements of goods is reminiscent of a nest of rockets. First the emissions of production centers, which from wholesale centers divide anew (*in a backward direction also!*), to "burst" finally in the retail centers. Whether or not middlemen are profitable depends very much upon whether the carload freight rate is far enough below the rate per unit—unless it is purely a commercial agency. Domestic transportation does not differ in principle from international transportation, which my research group and I have begun to investigate at the *Institut für Weltwirtschaft*. In the meantime see H. Löfke, "Ursachen und Umfang des Transits," *Weltwirtschaftliches Archiv*, LV (1942).

pattern. Minneapolis, Kansas City, and St. Louis lie on the edge of their territory that is nearest to predominant Chicago.

The fact that it may be advantageous to go around the North American continent instead of across it has led to a strange splitting up of market areas.[39] Some industries that are situated on the Atlantic Coast and have rivals in Mississippi can no longer compete in the Middle West because of high railway freights, yet are enabled to do so in California, still farther west, by the lower ocean freight. For instance, the market area for New York pianos extends inland about 500 miles from the East Coast and about 1,000 miles from the Pacific Coast, where the pianos arrive by way of the Panama Canal. Between these two sections of the New York market area lies that of St. Louis, compressed within the Mississippi Valley. Were it not for the Panama Canal the entire West would be the hinterland for an industry that flourished vigorously in the upper Mississippi Valley before the Canal was constructed, just as the Mississippi Valley and New Orleans together were of greater importance and showed promise of a more brilliant future before the Civil War and the building of the Panama Canal than afterward.[40] The Civil War, the Canal, and the artificial maintenance of high freight rates on the Mississippi River [41] have hindered, if not entirely prevented, the development of this area.

The corn market furnishes another example of the influence of differences between land and ocean freights upon the shape of market areas. On both the East and West Coasts corn from Argentina is able to compete with American corn shipped from the interior. (A. Rühl, " Zur Frage der internationalen Arbeitsteilung. Eine

---

39. E. W. Zimmermann cites an impressive example of how extraordinary the difference between land and ocean freight may be. " It costs less to ship coal from Cardiff to Port Said (3,072 miles) than to send it from South Wales to London (170 miles)." (*Foreign Trade and Shipping* [New York, 1918], p. 257.) Thus the market areas for goods that are very sensitive to freight charges may extend similarly to the most distant countries if only they are accessible by ship. According to my calculation, for example, English food imports in 1937 came an average distance of 6,250 miles. From the opposite viewpoint, water routes are of vital importance to places that are far from a market. Hence the greater part of the foreign trade of the Balkan countries, even with Germany, is carried on by sea.

40. A hundred years ago New York and New Orleans exported equally large amounts of goods. The enormous supply area of the Mississippi would provide an important natural advantage for the latter, if only it were controlled. (See S. A Caldwell, *The New Orleans Trade Area, University Bulletin, Louisiana State University*, XXVIII, No. 10 [Baton Rouge, 1936].)

41. These are regulated politically, and are but slightly below railway freight rates—about 20 per cent below in 1937.

statistische Studie auf Grund der Einfuhr der Vereinigten Staaten von Amerika," *Vierteljahrshefte zur Konjunkturforschung,* Sonderheft 25 [Berlin, 1932], pp. 10, 26.)

It is also very important that the cheap water route through the Suez Canal connects Europe and eastern Asia much more closely than does the Trans-Siberian Railway. In an instance cited by E. Steinhagen [42] the railway was eleven times more expensive than the Canal. Thus Russian markets, like those of the American Middle West, are caught in the pincers.

The methodologically admirable investigations of Cornell University and of the Iowa State Planning Board are well worth attention. The books of sellers, upon which all investigations hitherto mentioned have been based, are inadequate for the delimitations of retail trade areas. The Cornell method of interrogating almost every farmer is ideal, but expensive. The results are entered on maps and boundary lines drawn in such a way that contested areas are excluded. This gives a celarer picture than that obtained when the overlapping of market areas is taken into consideration. See Figure 74 (after D. Sanderson, *Rural Social and Economic Areas in Central New York, Cornell University Agricultural Experiment Station, Ithaca, Bulletin 614,* 1934, p. 9).

In Iowa thousands of the unemployed were sent out upon the highways to ask in the homes situated along them where certain important articles were purchased. One household in every mile was questioned (*Iowa State Planning Board, Retail Trading Areas, Series I* [Des Moines, 1936], No. 6, p. 3). The rather infrequent overlaps were unfortunately disregarded in drawing the boundary lines, areas being assigned exclusively to those centers from which most was bought. The highway system in Iowa is mainly lattice-like, only the through routes being radial. An example of the former is provided by the region about Tipton (Fig. 75); of the latter, by that about Muscatine (Fig. 76). In the one case, therefore, one would necessarily expect market areas to be approximately rectangular,[43] and in the other to approach a circular shape. As the regions

---

42. *Der Einfluss der Transportkosten auf Standort und Absatzreichweite der Betriebe,* Berlin dissertation, 1937, p. 44.

43. Because the rectangular or even square shape is so prevalent in Iowa its inhabitants are jokingly called square-minded. The original state planning is still clearly recognizable today. The typical county is a square with sides 24 miles in length, the typical township another with 6-mile sides, and the typical farm still another with sides half a mile long and an area of 160 acres. Thus there would be 1 county, or 16 townships, to every 144 farms. The first settlers received lots from the Government of a fixed shape (square) and area (160 acres).

concerned are undulating or often hilly, to be sure, the assumptions for regular shapes are by no means fulfilled, but unfortunately no investigations on the level areas that are so much more typical of

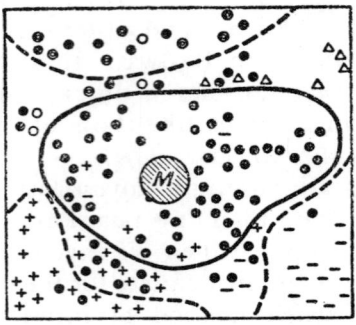

Fig. 74. Method of determining retail market areas. All farms that buy most of their groceries in Town M (Marion) are indicated by heavy black dots. The boundaries of the uncontested sales area of M are represented by a continuous line, those of neighboring competition by broken lines.

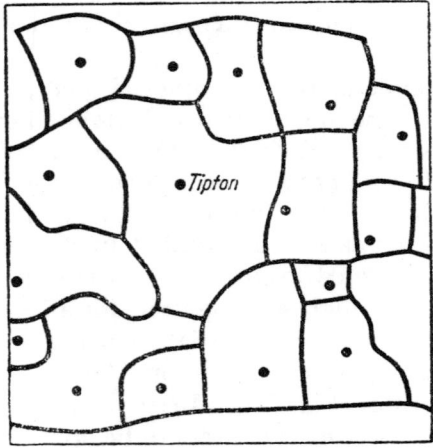

Fig. 75. Sales area for building lumber and cement, Cedar County, Iowa. (*Iowa State Planning Board, Retail Trading Areas*, Series I, No. 6, Fig. 4. Des Moines, 1936.)

Iowa were available to me. Yet even so, characteristic differences in the shape of market areas are still evident in the vicinity of Tipton and Muscatine. In the latter case, furthermore, projecting tongues of market areas are noteworthy, partially enclosing smaller places and jutting out into the market of the considerably larger Muscatine (Fig. 76). There theoretical explanation is given in Fig. 46 (p. 167) and its accompanying text. Besides differences in size among retail trade areas for various goods, Figure 76 shows also, on the one hand, the connection between the agricultural areas that supply the town with eggs, poultry, milk, and so on; and, on the other, the market areas for its retail dealers. This is easily explained. The farmer who takes his agricultural products into town for sale makes small purchases at the same time. It is different with cattle for slaughter, which go directly to Chicago as a rule, unaccompanied by the farmer; thus there is no return flow of retail buying in Chicago.

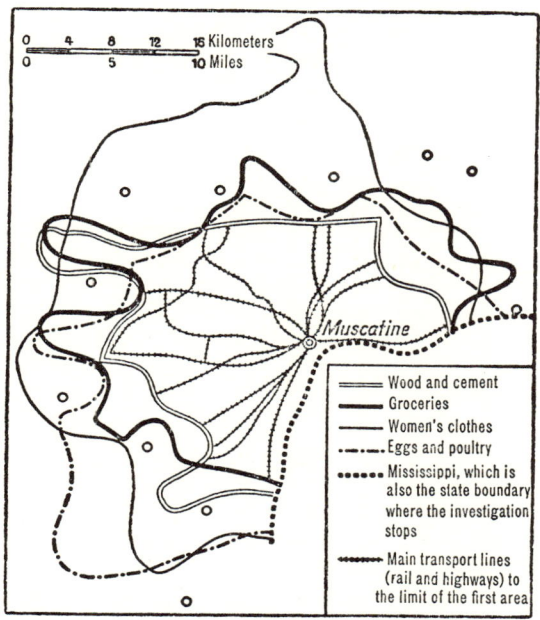

Fig. 76. Supply and market areas for Muscatine, Iowa. (*Ibid.*)

We have now passed from the market areas of producers to the supply areas of consumers. Here the literature is more abundant, probably because it is not necessary to pry into the business secrets of individual firms. Innumerable small producers are concerned, and anything worth knowing about their business connections is contained in the published statistics on trade. Hence numerous supply areas for milk, livestock, grain, and other agricultural products have been well investigated in part. As compared with what has already been discussed, they offer nothing essentially new, and so, except for presenting an admirable system of supply areas (Fig. 77), we shall limit ourselves to one last example of a more important subject. That to which we now turn is the nesting of supply and market areas that is typical of so-called world trade goods.

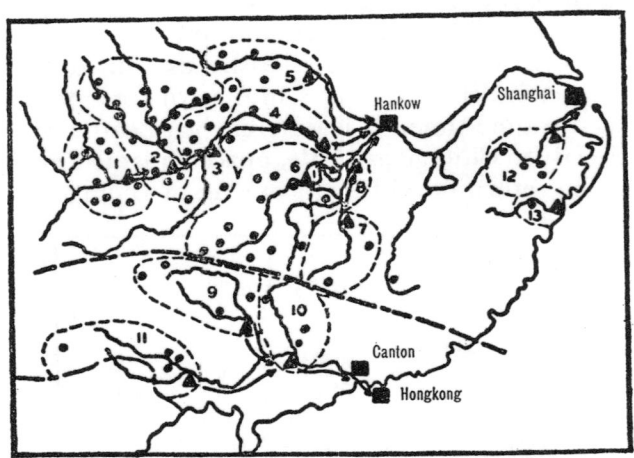

Fig. 77. Hierarchy of supply areas for tung oil. ● Larger oil mill centers (their small supply areas not indicated). ▲ Collecting stations (– – – – supply areas determined by river courses). ■ Export ports (– – – – boundary between the supply areas for Shanghai and Hong Kong). (After Deasy, *Economic Geography*, 1940, p. 265.) For English coal see K. Dietzel, ed., *Lebensraumfragen europäischer Völker* (Leipzig, 1941), p. 285.

§4. The "World Market"

The wheat markets are a good example of a complicated overlapping of regions, on the one hand, and of regions naturally important in themselves on the other. At first glance the statistics create an impression of inextricable confusion. Every exporting country seems to send wheat everywhere, and every importing country to buy everywhere. In speaking of a "world market" for wheat, should we have nothing more in mind than this universal and closely knit fabric? Figure 78 shows the farthest boundaries of their market areas for the four great exporting countries in the harvest year 1928–29, the last before the extensive transformation of markets through government interference began.[44] Only countries that an exporting country provided with less than 1 per cent of their wheat imports are considered to lie outside its market area. In a few cases, the Belgian Congo especially, the boundaries are not

---

44. Russia and India, too, occasionally throw considerable amounts of wheat on the market, but are not to be regarded as regularly exporting countries. Nor did the Balkan states export much in 1928.

certain. Furthermore, only for Brazil could it be approximately considered that sometimes not the whole country, but only parts of it, belong within any given market area.[45]

What does Figure 78 show? Though it is still confusing enough,

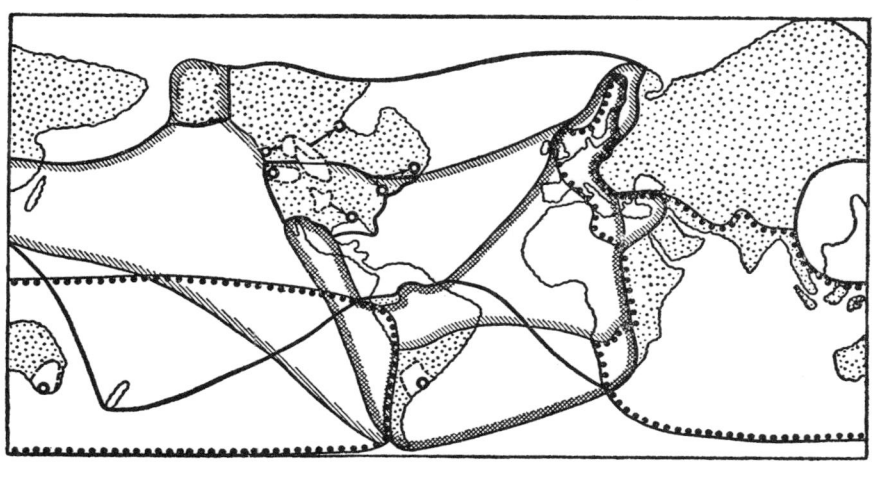

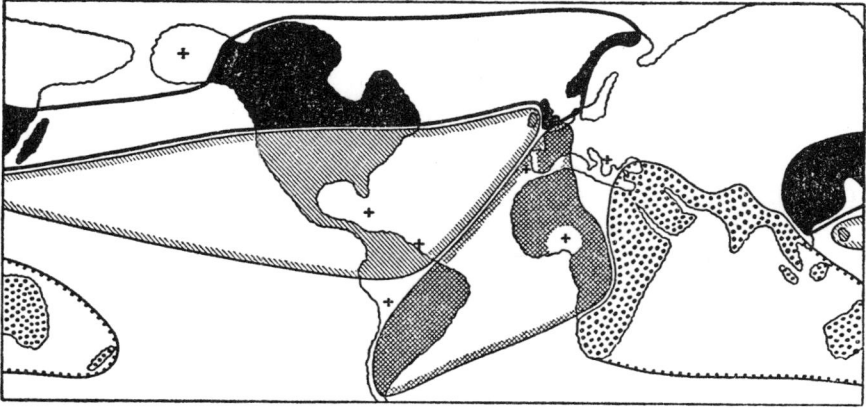

Figs. 78 and 79. The great world wheat markets

The boundaries of Canadian market areas are continuous lines; those of the American, hatched lines; and those of Argentina, crosshatched lines; while Australian market areas are dotted (after Table 31). Figure 78 shows the farthest boundaries in 1928–29. Regions importing from the principal exporting ports, which are indicated by rings, are represented by broken lines. Practically uncontested market areas are dotted. Figure 79: Dominant areas (those in which an exporting country enjoys definite superiority). Consolidated areas are outlined, exclaves designated by crosses.

---

45. South of Bahia the importation of wheat from the United States was negligible.

one can see that all sales markets are limited, and that certain regions may therefore be supplied by only one single surplus country. These uncontested areas are dotted. Figure 79 shows in addition all those regions in which an exporting country is obviously predominant. This is assumed to be the case only when it supplies more than half of the amount imported, and no single competitor provides even approximately as large an amount.

Now the picture suddenly clears. The dominating regions are grouped in a fairly rational manner about the great exporting ports, constituting closed forms with but few exceptions. The exceptions are marked in the figure by crosses. They absorb hardly 3 per cent of the world's exports of wheat, and in many cases (Alaska, the British West Indies, and others) are politically conditioned. More important quantitatively are the contested areas, in which no exporting country enjoys unquestioned predominance and to which Germany, too, belonged in the period under discussion. But most important of all is the fact that beneath the apparent confusion a definite spatial arrangement can be distinguished when the situation is reduced to its essentials.

Of course these predominant areas are not of equal importance. At that time they received more than two thirds of the Canadian, one half of the Argentine and Australian, but only one sixth of the American wheat exported. The difficulties of many American wheat growers are thus not surprising, since they are forced to such a great extent to fight for a place in the contested areas or even in the unquestioned markets of other surplus countries. Boundaries are constantly shifting, to be sure, depending on the result of the harvest, the changing structure of ocean freights, and changes in consumption and recently, above all, in trade policies. But this is more true for the boundaries of the whole area than for those of its uncontested core.

We turn now from the core regions to the contested ones, and to regional overlaps in general. How do they arise? First, through seasonal factors. Although shipments from the four supply areas continue throughout the year, they vary in amount with the season. They are largest after the harvest, that is, in the fall, from regions in the Northern and in the spring from those in the Southern Hemisphere. 'In so far as seasonal factors are at work, we do not strictly deal with overlaps at all because the shipments follow one another chronologically. A second variety of apparent overlapping is due to the breakdown of the statistics by countries. A country may get wheat from two sources, yet closer examination will often

Table 31. SOURCE OF WHEAT IMPORTS, 1928-1929[a]

Importing Country	Imports, Million Bushels	Source of Imports in Per Cent			
		Canada	Argentina	United States	Australia
Area of Canadian Predominance					
England	347	64	24	5	7
Denmark	8	52	19	29	—
Norway	6	66	16	18	—
Portugal	5	78	11	11	—
Greece	15	53	18	29	—
Jamaica	2	87	—	13	—
British West Indies	1	95	—	5	—
China	37	67	—	25	8
Japan	34	66	—	17	16
Area of Argentine Predominance					
Paraguay	1	—	100	—	—
Uruguay	0	—	100	—	—
Brazil	35	0	89	11	—
Spanish Guinea	0	15	85	—	—
French Africa	1	3	90	6	—
Spain	14	19	66	15	—
France	29	25	61	8	7
Belgium	54	31	62	6	2
Area of United States Predominance					
Ireland	5	38	—	62	—
Gibraltar	1	3	—	97	—
British West Africa	1	9	—	91	—
Cuba	6	3	0	97	—
Haiti	2	9	—	91	—
Netherlands West Indies	0	5	—	95	—
Venezuela	2	28	—	72	—
Ecuador	1	—	—	100	—
Bolivia	1	—	20	80	—
Panama	4	2	—	98	—
Nicaragua	0	—	—	100	—
Costa Rica	1	3	—	97	—
San Salvador	1	—	—	100	—
Guatemala	1	—	—	100	—
Mexico	3	13	15	72	—
Alaska	0	—	—	100	—
Philippine Islands	4	4	—	87	10
Area of Australian Predominance					
Turkey	0	10	—	—	90
Egypt	19	9	—	4	87
Sudan	0	—	—	—	100
South Africa	9	27	12	0	60
New Zealand	1	42	—	—	58
Netherlands East Indies	4	—	—	—	100
British India	26	—	—	—	100
Contested Areas					
Germany	39	43	31	20	4
Holland	63	37	43	17	3
Sweden	7	38	38	12	12
Finland	3	44	—	56	—
Italy	48	33	40	15	12
British Honduras	0	50	—	50	—
Colombia	1	45	—	55	—
Peru	4	—	49	13	38
Chile	1	—	41	16	44

a. Calculated from G. J. Carr, *U. S. Department of Commerce, Trade Promotion Series No. 130, International Marketing of Surplus Wheat* (Washington, 1932), pp. 12-24. For Germany, from *Statistisches Jahrbuch für das Deutsche Reich* (Berlin). *The figures give only an approximate idea*, since the data refer in part to the calendar and in part to the harvest year. The statistics for importing and exporting countries do not agree. Colonies are often lumped together, and the percentages for French Africa are therefore especially unreliable. Flour has been converted to its wheat equivalent.

show that, especially in large countries, the centers of the two market areas are in different sections. The example of Brazil has already been mentioned. In the third place, there is an artificial overlapping. Canadian wheat would hardly penetrate as far as South Africa and, on the other hand, Argentina would sell more there if South Africa, Canada, and Australia did not belong to the same empire.

Finally, there remain two instances of real overlapping. Different kinds and qualities of wheat are grown in different regions, and it is advantageous to mix them. The kind of mixture varies with the country and the sort of bread to be made, but also with relative prices. But the last reason for overlapping, already discussed on pages 188 ff., is certainly the most important. It is apparent from Figure 78 that all market areas include northwestern Europe, at least by a tip. This border region is no small marginal buyer, however, but the foremost wheat-importing area in the world. Its demand could not be met at all by one single surplus region without considerably raising the price. It is the center for a purchasing area that embraces all the great surplus countries, including the wheat belt of eastern Europe, which does not appear in the figure. Thus an unusual situation arises: Europe lies within the market area of all surplus countries, so that these represent in turn only portions of the European purchasing area.[46]

The world-wide supply area of the European consumer is organized into a hierarchy of smaller sources. The largest are the

---

46. The same thing is true of most world trade goods. Thus 95 per cent of the world's imports of peanuts in 1937 went to Europe; 87 per cent of the copper; 79 per cent of the hides; 78 per cent of the corn; 76 per cent of the wool; 73 per cent of the tobacco; 68 per cent of the petroleum; and 66 per cent of the cotton. On the other hand, it is not true of rubber, 31 per cent; rice, 29 per cent; and silk, 19 per cent. World trade reflects this exceptional position of Europe, and of England in particular (Fig. 80). Another such "corner market" is Berlin, where coal from England, Upper Silesia, and the Ruhr compete with one another. According to R. Regul's calculation this three-country "corner" should be about 125 miles west-southwest of Berlin. That coal from the Ruhr should nevertheless compete in the Berlin market he attributes partly to quality differences, partly to dumping, and partly to an import quota for the English coal ("Die Wettbewerbslage der Steinkohle," *Vierteljahrshefte zur Konjunkturforschung*, Sonderheft 34 [Berlin, 1933], p. 83.)

supply regions about the great export ports, enclosed by broken lines in Figure 78.[47] Difficulties in drawing the regional borders really occur only in North America. The area for hard winter wheat in Nebraska, Kansas, and Oklahoma, which is fairly well separated from the northern wheat belt, exports chiefly through Galveston and New Orleans, where the heavier wheat serves as ballast for cotton, which would be too light for shipment without it.

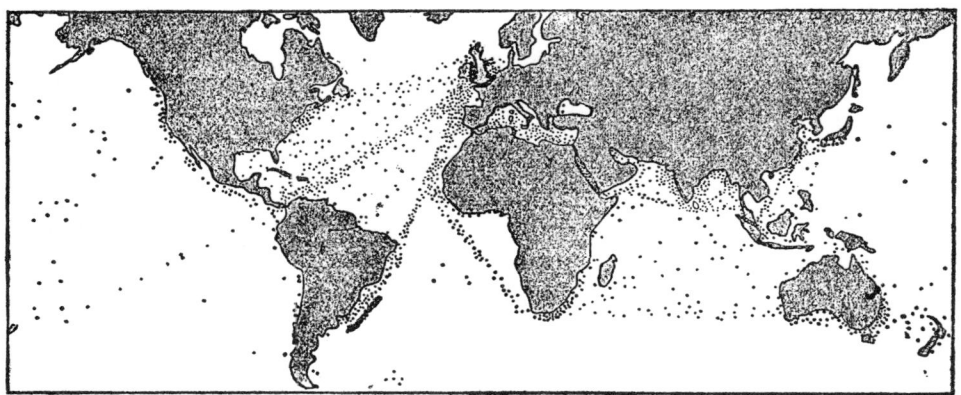

Fig. 80. England as a corner market at the center of world trade routes.

Position at sea of every British ship over 3,000 Brutto Registered Tons on March 7, 1936. (After *British Empire Shipping, 1936*, Admiralty BR 84, London 1936.) The map shows at the same time the main routes for world trade. On the other hand, the scattering on the corresponding map for November, 1937 (BR 135), is curiously wide. All small islands that might be mistaken for ships have been omitted.

Railway freight to the two ports, and the ocean freight from both of them to Europe, are the same,[48] so that on the whole, their supply and market areas are probably identical. This holds also for the two ports on the northwest coast, Seattle and Portland. But as the wheat belt here lies closer to the ports, its nearest parts divide into distinct supply areas for the two ports.

The great dividing line between the Atlantic and the Pacific ports, which in Canada runs aproximately between Alberta and Saskatchewan and continues in the United States between Idaho and Wyoming, is more important. It must not be thought of as rigid,

---

47. Not every port is shown. Most of the circles stand for a number of practically equivalent ports.
48. According to *Bureau of Railway Economics, Commodity Prices in Their Relation to Transportation Costs, Bulletin 40, Wheat* (Washington, 1930), p. 4, and to a map in *U. S. Department of Agriculture, Freight Rates on Wheat* (Washington, 1928).

however. Though railway freights change but little over the years, ocean freights change all the more.[49] Hence there are wide areas on either side of the approximate line from which grain is shipped now to the west and now to the east. Price differentials of only a fraction of a cent may decide the direction, even when the destination is the same: Liverpool. True, the westward route by way of Vancouver and then through the Panama Canal is almost twice as long as the direct eastward one, but most of the former is a cheap ocean route whereas in the second case three quarters of the total freight cost goes merely to transport the wheat over expensive railway and inland water routes to the much more distant East Coast.[50] (See the calculation of comparative costs in *Dominion Bureau of Statistics, Report on the Grain Trade of Canada, 1935* [Ottawa, 1936], p. 175.)

Hence a large part of the Canadian wheat crop, generally one fifth to one third, goes by way of Vancouver, even when it is bound for England. Fort Churchill, on Hudson Bay, is most favorably situated in respect to freight, and has a large supply area in northern Saskatchewan and Manitoba, as well as far to the south (see the *Dominion Bureau of Statistics Report* just cited, pp. 175–183). Yet only a small percentage of Canadian wheat passes through Fort Churchill. Here we encounter a new factor in the formation of regions—the season. Because of a northerly situation the harvest is late in the possible supply area of Fort Churchill, and the harbor must be closed as early as the end of October. Consequently wheat

---

49. In July, 1935, for example, the freight on wheat shipped from Vancouver to England was hardly higher than that from Montreal, whereas often it is twice as high. But because the freight from the West Coast to Europe remains higher than that from the East Coast throughout all fluctuations, the price of wheat on the West Coast must always be lower than that on the East Coast.

50. The fact that land routes are so much more expensive than ocean routes formerly caused eastern Germany to sell its surplus grain in Scandinavia while western and southern Germany were importing wheat from overseas, which could be sent by ship as far as Mannheim. (See A. Kuhner, *Die wirtschaftlichen Beziehungen zwischen Württemberg und dem Reich,* Munich dissertation, 1926, pp. 26 f.) The German tariffs could shift the central dividing zone between east German and foreign wheat; but they were not high enough to force the east German surplus and the west German deficit together. Indeed, the system of import certificates worked rather in the opposite direction. Only with the recent market organization has inland transportation increased in importance, though governmental price regulation provided for regional price differences only up to 12 per cent in the economic year 1938–39, for example. The two extremes were parts of Silesia on the one hand, and the Saar District on the other. See *Reichsgesetzblatt I* for July 1, 1938. [A discussion of the German system of import certificates may be found in Haberler, *The Theory of International Trade,* pp. 318 ff. —W. F. S.]

can be exported for a few weeks only, but during this short period Fort Churchill is numbered among the chief export harbors.

The supply areas for New York and the neighboring American ports on the one hand, and for Montreal and other Atlantic ports in Canada on the other, cannot be separated, since almost all wheat follows the same route at first through the Great Lakes, and usually not until it reaches Buffalo is the final decision made as to whether to ship it on to New York through the Erie Canal, or through the Welland Canal to Montreal. This depends mainly upon the differences in ocean freights at the moment. A great deal of American wheat is shipped through Canadian ports, and much Canadian wheat, generally one fifth to one third, through American ports. Buffalo, therefore, is a gateway, one level above the ports in the hierarchy. In contradistinction to the eastern ports, the supply area is sharply divided between Canadian and American ports on the West Coast, partly because these draw from widely separated wheat-growing districts, partly because these districts lie relatively near them, and partly, too, because cross-connections are less numerous.

As wheat shipments from a supply area stream into a port from many directions as though into a narrow gateway, so they divide again in the wide market area of the port as soon as they have passed through.[51] Both areas show in turn a definite structure. A hierarchy of smaller and larger collecting or distributing centers play the same role for their submarkets as the port for the whole.[52] This has already been discussed. Thus even in the case of the single product alone, wheat, there are many kinds of area: growing, supply, and market areas together with their subdivisions; areas for the cultivation of summer or winter wheat; supply areas for individual ports; smaller collecting stations all the way down to the local elevators or even the single farm; and correspondingly, in market areas, down to the area of the individual baker. We have been able to sketch only a few of these markets as an example, but even this short account permits recognition of the order that lies behind the apparent chaos.

c. THE ECONOMIC IMPORTANCE OF DISTANCE

§1. FOR THE DOMESTIC ECONOMY

In 1930 the cost of transportation on German railways amounted to 4.6 per cent of the value of goods at their destination; in Europe

---

51. It would have been more correct to determine the market areas for Montreal, New York, New Orleans, and so on, but the necessary time was lacking.

52. See also L. B. Zapoleon, *U. S. Department of Agriculture, Bulletin 594, Geography of Wheat Prices* (Washington, 1918), pp. 14 f.

to 5 to 7 per cent, according to Pirath; and in the United States (1928, rail) to 7.1 per cent. In Germany in the same year 4.5 per cent of the employed labor force was employed in public transportation, and in the United States 7.9 per cent. Those indirectly active therein are included in the gross receipts of the public transportation systems, which in Germany were 11.8 per cent and in the United States 13 per cent of the national income. To this there is to be added the cost of private transportation (automobiles, bicycles), or about 1.5 per cent in the United States and 9 per cent in Germany; so that the total outlay for transportation makes up in round numbers 13 per cent or 22 per cent respectively of the national income, and all costs of distance together account for 20 per cent and 30 per cent.

Obviously their wide expanse destroys a large part of the advantages that the United States (and Russia) enjoy by virtue of their natural abundance. Single examples show this vividly. In 1930 long hauls in the United States transported about $5\frac{1}{2}$ times as many ton-miles as in Germany. The enormous cost of *quickly* overcoming the vast distances in the United States is shown by the proceeds from telephone, telegraph, and radio communication: in 1931 5.8 billion reichsmarks in the United States as compared with 0.9 billion in Germany.[53]

§2. A Consequence for Foreign Trade[54]

An important conclusion must be drawn from the preceding findings on the differing size of market areas, and their "thinning out" toward the periphery. *The volume of foreign trade decreases with distance.* German statistics on foreign trade confirm this statement. For proof, the last year of flourishing and unrestricted foreign trade has been chosen and only Russia excluded, because the foreign trade monopoly there made it possible to neglect distance. Furthermore, it differs too much in size from the other countries. Even so, however, enough discrepancies in size still remain to disturb the comparison, which is upset further by the facts that distances between countries are expressed as air-line miles between their capitals and that the difference between land and ocean freights has not been

---

53. *Raumforschung und Raumordnung,* I, 366. C. Pirath, *Die Grundlagen der Verkehrswirtschaft* (Berlin, 1934), pp. 7, 8, 78, 85, 90, 99. Other figures calculated by the present author. See also G. Pavlovsky, *Zur Frage der räumlichen Ordnung der Landwirtschaft. Internationale Landwirtschaftliche Rundschau I.* XXXIII (1942), 363.

54. For the especially important costs of distance in exporting see Kapferer-Schwenzner, *Exportbetriebslehre* (Berlin, 1935), pp. 249–273.

considered. On the whole, the relation between trade and distance is clearly seen nevertheless particularly in the figure: The share of Germany in the imports and exports of European countries decreased with distance. See Table 32 and Figure 81.[55] This holds for the trend, for although the individual deviations are considerable they do not really disturb the comparison, except in two cases. The two

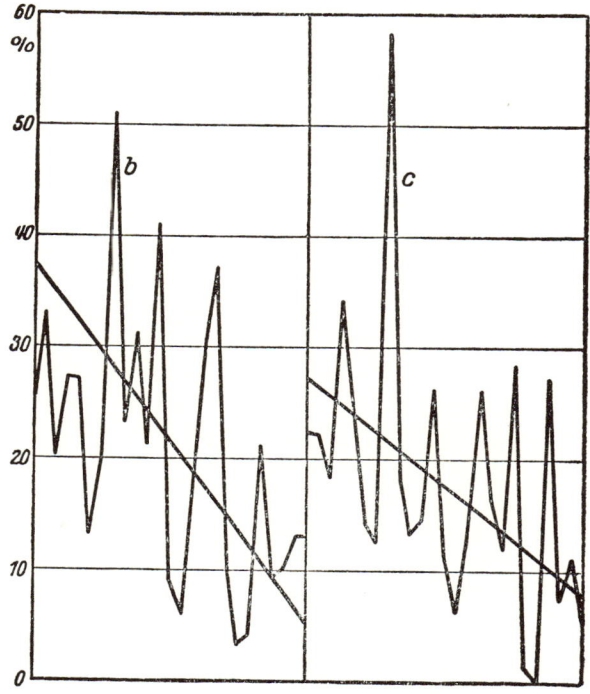

Fig. 81. Distance and foreign trade.

Germany's share in the imports (*b*) and exports (*c*) of European countries (cf. Table 32). These are arranged from left to right in the order of their distance from Germany.

exceptions are the share of Germany in Bulgarian and Greek exports. Despite the distance of these countries this share was very large, most probably because of shipments of tobacco, which made up about half of these exports to Germany. What is true of single European countries [56] is also true of Europe as a whole. In 1928

---

55. Germany's immediate neighbors bought 46 per cent of her exports in 1928, and provided 30 per cent of her imports.

56. In 1932 46 per cent of France's foreign trade went to immediately neighboring countries, and 39 per cent came from them. For Holland the figures were 55 per cent

Table 32. GERMANY'S SHARE IN THE FOREIGN TRADE OF EUROPEAN COUNTRIES, 1928

	a	b	c		a	b	c
Czechoslovakia	175	25	22	England	581	6	6
Denmark	225	33	22	Yugoslavia	638	14	12
Austria	331	20	18	Estonia	656	30	26
Poland and Danzig	381	27	34	Finland	688	37	16
Netherlands	394	27	24	Italy	750	10	12
Belgium and Luxemburg	406	13	14	Ireland	838	3	1
Hungary	438	20	12	Bulgaria	850	21	23
Lithuania	475	51	58	Albania	900	4	0
Switzerland	481	23	18	Greece	1150	9	27
Sweden	519	31	13	Spain	1181	10	7
Norway	531	21	14	Portugal	1456	13	11
Latvia	544	41	26	Iceland	1500	13	6
France	550	9	11				

a. Distance from Berlin to the capital of the country in question in air-line miles.

b. Germany's share in *imports*, as per cent of total imports of the country in question (*Statistisches Jahrbuch für das Deutsche Reich, 1931* (Berlin), pp. 90* f.).

c. Germany's share in *exports,* as per cent of total exports of the country concerned (sources as in *b*).

75 per cent of German exports went to Europe, and 51 per cent of her imports came from there *(ibid.,* p. 214). For the same reason inland European foreign trade exceeds the overseas trade. In 1928 65 per cent of the exports of European countries went to other European countries, and 55 per cent of imports were provided by these. In 1909 the corresponding figures were as high as 70 per cent and 62 per cent *(ibid.,* p. 95*). Thus it is for very goods reasons that the political interests of the great continental powers are concentrated on neighboring areas.

---

and 51 per cent. They were much lower for countries with mainly ocean frontiers, for reasons that are easily explained: Italy, 24 per cent and 18 per cent, Great Britain, 23 per cent and 19 per cent. Conversely, they were very high for Canada, which in reality is only a border zone along the United States; 61 per cent of her exports went to the United States in 1932, and 41 per cent of her imports came from there.

The number, of *Weltwirtschaftliches Archiv* in which I developed theoretically the importance of distance in international trade contains an analysis of France's trade with her colonies that conclusively supports my theory. About 75 per cent of exports from Algeria go to France, but only 20 per cent of those from Indo-China. " Distance, more than any other fact, decides in what measure colonies will contribute to the riches of the mother country." (R. Maunier, *Weltwirtschaftliches Archiv,* L [1939], 272.)

Chapter 24. Regional Systems

a. NUMBER, SPACING, AND SIZE OF TOWNS

The study of an actual regional system is an extensive and difficult undertaking. Fortunately we can refer to an admirable monograph by Walter Christaller, *Die zentralen Orte in Süddeutschland* (Jena, 1933).[1] On pages 130-132 we described regions with the same structure; that is, regions that in every size class embrace a constant number k of next smaller regions. Christaller has endeavored to explain the size and distribution of most settlements in southern Germany on the assumption that k is 3 or, in a few cases, also 7. According to our Table 8, $k = 3$ the total number of settlements per region in size-classes 0–6 is $3^0, 3^1 \cdots 3^6$, or $1, 3 \cdots 729$.[2] The number of regions in size-classes 6–0 is equally large, but the number of regional centers in the corresponding size-classes is smaller.

Table 33

Size-class of Regions	Number of Settlements per Region	Number of Regions of This Class	Size-class of Places	Number of Places of This Class
for k = 3				
0	1	729	0	486
1	3	243	1	162
2	9	81	2	54
3	27	27	3	18
4	81	9	4	6
5	243	3	5	2
6	729	1	6	1

The largest region, which includes all 729 places, has one center and the three next smaller, with 243 each, also have one center apiece, though one of these is identical with the center for the largest region. Consequently the number of towns in size classes

---

1. A rather good but much shorter presentation by O. Schlier ("Die Landschaften Deutschlands," *Allgemeines Statistisches Archiv*, XX [1930], 24–41) should be mentioned also. He shows how the influence of great cities affects the various levels of life and branches of the economy to a different degree with increasing distance.

2. Class 0 includes the original settlements without their own market area.

6–0 is equal to the difference between regions of the same and the next higher size-class: that is, to 1, 2 · · · 486 (see Table 33). The actual number agrees well with this theoretical number over wide areas, as Christaller has shown.[3] Thus in the regional system of Nuremberg (Christaller, *op. cit.*, p. 199):

Size-class of place	6	5	4	3	2	1	0
Theoretical number of places	1	2	6	18	54	162	486
Actual number of places	1	2	10	23	60	105	462

The full measure of agreement is shown only in the accompanying text, to be sure, which explains any deviations with geographical, political, and other peculiarities individually, at least for all places in the higher size-classes. The virtue of the book lies chiefly in this penetrating examination of single cases. Consequently certain methodological objections lose in importance. In regions with the same structure, at least in those whose regional networks (as with $k = 0$) cannot be "rotated," the centers of equally large market areas are themselves equally large if one assigns each center to the largest area supplied by it. Otherwise than in complete systems, every center always coincides with the same combination of smaller centers (Fig. 34, p. 128). Hence the regional centers can

---

3. Assume for the sake of argument that this predominance of regional systems, characterized by $k = 3$ and proved for Nuremberg, is universally valid. And suppose, further, that the average distance separating the smallest settlements is about 2½ miles. Since in the Germany within the 1938 borders there were 51,000 communities to 183,200 square miles, each would have on the average a region with a radius of something over 1.06 miles, which would mean a separation of 2.2 miles. Then, according to Table 8, the theoretical distance separating the various types of places would be as follows:

Size-class	Theoretical Distance, Miles	Type of Place	Example
0	2.5	Village	Many local examples
1	4.4	Village	Many local examples
2	7.5	Rural town	Many local examples
3	13.1	County town	Many local examples
4	22.5	County town	Many local examples
5	38.8	Provincial capital	Munich-Augsburg 38.8 miles
6	67.5	Provincial capital	Munich-Augsburg 38.8 miles
7	117.5	Regional capital	Munich-Nuremburg 124.4 miles
8	203.1	State capital	Munich-Zurich 223.1 miles
9	350.0	Sectional capital	Berlin-Cologne 367.5 miles
10	595.0	National capital	Berlin-Paris 675 miles

There are important actual examples for every type. But obviously they are adequate neither for a comprehensive explanation of European reality nor for verification of the theory. They illustrate only orders of magnitude in what may be an important special case.

be divided into size-classes that correspond with the size-classes of those regions and contain places with typically similar economic functions.[4]

From this Christaller rightly concluded that in such cases there must be a number of typical town sizes that should be statistically determinable as maxima of a frequency curve representing the number of towns as a function of their size.[5] He announced his classification of towns by this method in *Die zentralen Orte in Süddeutschland* (Jena, 1933), p. 65. But I cannot see that he really succeeded, except in two classes of places that he called *A* and *K* places, and that actually correspond with certain agglomerations shown on the curves on his page 326. The classification developed on pages 150–155 was not further explained. He may have arrived at it by arranging a number of places according to their functions and then finding that most places in a group fell in a definite size-class, which was thereupon regarded as typical for places with this function. But one can hardly speak of a clustering of the places about any representative central value within the size-class, save for the two exceptions mentioned. Such agglomerations, if they exist at all, would be concealed by the fact that the number of places falls rapidly with increasing size. As long as we do not know the law governing this decline I do not see how one could eliminate it in order to disclose possible hidden agglomerations.

As a classification of towns cannot be achieved statistically, only three courses remain open. To classify them by direct observation of towns with different functions, as Christaller apparently did; to derive the classification from a regularity that is independent of what is to be proved (Pareto's distribution formula, perhaps); or, finally, to obtain it by trial and error. In the last case we have one of the theoretically derived regional systems only if the actual pattern corresponds with the theoretical in more than one respect. Then, in the absence of other reasons, towns can always be so classified, of course, that their real number is equal to the theoretical number in every size-class. But only when it appears further, per-

---

4. In the *general system*, on the contrary, a place need not be larger, the greater the size of its largest area. Here the central point of the larger region is not always the central point for the larger number of regions at the same time, as is the case with regions having a similar structure.

5. He measured size not by the number of inhabitants, but in units of a specially computed "centrality," based on the number of telephones installed. For cities Schlier's method, which, using statistics of occupation, counts the "central stratum," is probably better. ("Die zentralen Orte des deutschen Reichs," *Zeitschrift der Gesellschaft für Erdkunde zu Berlin*, 1937, pp. 162 ff.)

haps, that the actual distance separating these town types from one another is the same as the theoretical distance can it be assumed that the classification was meaningful.

By such a method I shall now demonstrate the existence in Iowa of one of our theoretical regional systems. The statement to be proved is, that the structure of settlements there follows the rules that hold for regions with the same structure when k has the value 4 (see Table 8, p. 131).[6] Suppose the settlements to be collected in such size-classes (Table 34, column 11) that their theoretical and actual numbers in each class are the same (columns 2 and 3).[7] And suppose we find that their theoretical and actual distances from each other also prove to be about the same; the hypothesis would then be justified that the market areas in Iowa in all size-classes are similarly constructed and always include four areas of the next smaller size. This is actually true. The real distances deviate by only about 5 to 10 per cent [8] from the theoretical ones.

A second proof starts with Pareto's law of distribution. H. W. Singer [9] investigated the question of whether the connection discovered by Pareto between the number and size of incomes is valid also for the number and size of towns.[10] Does it correspond with the formula $\log y = A - \alpha \log x$? In this formula x is the size of a population (or of incomes), y the number of towns with more than x inhabitants (or the number of persons with incomes greater than x marks), α and A are constants for a given country in a given period of time for a given value of x and y. The formula states that the ratio of a change in y (that is, a percentage change in y) is equal,

---

6. The value $k = 4$ has nothing to do with the *shape* of a region. It holds for hexagons as well as for squares.

7. On the advice of Professor Sisam, of Colorado Springs, who grew up in Iowa, I really classified first those places with the same function according to population, counted all the places in accordance with this classification, and measured their minimum distances apart. The frequencies in the individual size-classes corresponded surprisingly well with what would be expected theoretically on the assumption that $k = 4$. Only slight changes in the classification were required to make the correspondence complete, and I have made these in order to provide a perfectly clear starting point.

8. The deviations would be still less if the the theoretical value of each size-class had been derived from the actual value of every preceding one, instead of always from the highest class.

9. " The ' Courbes des Populations.' A Parallel to Pareto's Law," *Economic Journal*, June, 1936, pp. 254–263.

10. See also R. Gibrat (*Les inégalités économiques* [Paris, 1931]) who added to Laplace's law of absolutely equal effect a similar law of proportionately equal effect. For differences between Gibrat's and Pareto's methods see *Arbeitsw. Institut. Jahrbuch*, II, (1939), pp. 203–227.

Table 34. REGIONAL SYSTEMS IN IOWA.
THEORY AND REALITY[a]

Size-class of regions	Correspondence with Theoretical System for k = 4			
	Centers			
	Number		Distance apart[b]	
	Theory[h]	Reality	Theory[h]	Reality[f]
1	2	3	4	5
1	615		5.6	
2	154	153	11.2	10.3
3	39	39	22.4	23.6
4[d]	10	9	44.8	49.6
5[d]	2-3	3	89.6	94.0
6e	0-1		179.2	

Size-class of regions	Correspondence with Pareto's Law for $\alpha = 1$				Lowest size-class[c]
	Places				
	Number		Minimum size[c]		
	Theory[h]	Reality	Theory[h]	Reality[g]	
6	7	8	9	10	11
1	819		447		180-1,000
2	205	204	1,800	1,950	1,000-4,000
3	51	51	7,200	7,500	4,000-20,000
4[d]	13	12	28,800	34,800	20,000-60,000
5[d]	3	3	115,000	94,000	60,000-200,000
6e	1		460,000		200,000-800,000

a. For sources see Table 21.
b. In miles.
c. Population.
d. Because of the small number of settlements in these size-classes, greater deviations are to be expected. If Davenport is placed in class 4 instead of in class 5, in class 4, column 10, 34,800 must be replaced by 37,600; in column 11, 20,000–60,000 must be replaced by 20,000–75,000; in class 5, column 5, 94 by 102.5; in column 8, 3 by 2; and in column 10, 94,000 by 111,000.
e. Iowa has no city of this size-class, but it lies between Minneapolis, Kansas City, Omaha, and Chicago, the first three of which fall in this class. Their average population is 490,000 and their minimum distance apart 236 miles.
f. Modal value; average value for class 5 only (because of the small number of cases). Class 1: The distances, which incidentally correspond to size 2a in Table 8, p. 131, were measured first (see p. 434, note 7) for settlements with 300–1,000 inhabitants, and the values so found were entered above in the table. A new calculation, with the inclusion of places having 180–300 inhabitants, would have taken much time, but random sampling showed that the result would not have been greatly altered.
g. Average size of places in the lowest size-class. Pareto's law, established for individual towns, thus holds also for the whole classes of towns, one more reason for regarding as representative the arrangement of classes that was chosen.
h. The values actually obtained for class 1 were the starting point for the calculation of all theoretical values.

for very small changes, to the α-fold ratio of the inverse change in x. That is, $\frac{dy}{y} = -\alpha \frac{dx}{x}$, which through integration leads to the formula given above. α is the reciprocal of the coefficient of elasticity. Singer found for a whole series of countries that the formula expresses very well the classification of towns according to size. It appears further from his tables that at present α is nearly equal to 1 in a few cases in which we are interested. This is especially true for England (0.99 in 1921), the United States (1.03 in 1920), and Germany (1.05 in 1933). But with an elasticity equal to 1, a fourfold increase, for example, in the minimum population means a quartering of the number of towns falling in this class. Conversely, if the number of towns falls to one quarter their minimum population must increase fourfold.

The classification of towns by size in a theoretical system ($k = 4$) and in Iowa corresponds with this completely. The correspondence between columns 9 and 10 [11] is either an example and a proof of the validity of Pareto's law or, conversely, if this is regarded as already proved, further corroboration of the approach of our theoretical system to reality.

G. K. Zipf (*National Unity and Disunity* [Bloomington, 1941]) gave Singer's discovery a simpler form. When the towns of a country are arranged according to size, the nth town will have $1/n$th the population of the first. If the serial number (n) of a town is multiplied by the number of its inhabitants, the product will be the same for all towns: that is, equal to the population of the metropolis. The test works for Germany to the extent that of her 104 largest towns in 1933 the product for the 25th to the 104th was without exception between 5 and 6 million (*Statistisches Jahrbuch für das deutsche Reich* [Berlin, 1937], p. 11. For the 7 largest places it was always smaller, for the 8th to the 24th frequently larger. The importance of Berlin and the capitals of the major sections of Germany (such as Munich) was decreased in favor of the centers of economic land-

---

11. To start with, 819 is given as the number of places with the minimum population 447 (819 is the sum of column 3). Columns 7 and 9 are calculated from these two numbers. The assumption that each successive number should be exactly four times, or $\frac{1}{4}$, as large as the preceding one is arbitrary, but practical. The places in Iowa should be grouped in such a way that either the minimum size (column 10) or the frequency (column 8) of the groups corresponds with the theoretical value. The assumption mentioned is chosen for convenience so that the grouping in column 3 can be employed and no new one becomes necessary. Consequently the perfect correspondence between columns 7 and 8 is due to manipulation, whereas the approximate correspondence between columns 9 and 10 gives the proof.

scapes (such as Nuremberg). Zipf's rule is identical with Pareto's if, as Singer found, $\alpha = 1$. If the serial number of the last locality in each class in Table 33 (or the equally large number of regions of this class) is multiplied by the number of settlements in such regions instead of by the population of that center, the product likewise is a constant, 729, that is the total number of settlements. Thus in regions of the same structure we get for $\alpha = 1$ the following relations:

$$\frac{\text{Size of region}}{\text{Size of landscape}} = \frac{\text{Number of places in region}}{\text{Number of all places}} =$$

$$\frac{\text{Serial number of metropolis } (= 1)}{\text{Serial number of last regional center}} = \frac{\text{Population of regional center}}{\text{Population of metropolis}}.$$

Thus also, for example,

$$\frac{\text{Population of subcenter}}{\text{Size of its region}} = \frac{\text{Population of metropolis}}{\text{Size of economic landscape}}.$$

It was no more possible to find particularly frequent town sizes in Iowa with any degree of certainty, than it was in Southern Germany. Yet one would expect such agglomerations theoretically—if not for the general system, at least for similarly constructed regions. For the present it must remain undecided whether the question is merely to discover a statistical method of making these agglomerations evident; [12] or whether differences in fertility, ability, and so on are great enough even in a state as uniform as Iowa to effect such a dispersion of town sizes that it conceals all agglomerations in this way. In this case only a classification of towns geographically and by individual size-classes, but not according to their dispersion within these classes, would correspond with the norm. Or, finally, whether size is influenced by still other factors, which underlie Pareto's law of distribution but do not enter into our theoretical pattern.

The theoretical system is fully confirmed, however, by another point. From this it follows that the distance [13] separating towns increases with their size, not only in regions with the same structure but generally, as is evident in Figure 32 (p. 127). The distance apart of all places that represent centers for one or two regions is equal. Let it be called a. The distance between centers for from three to

---

12. The few agglomerations mentioned by Christaller become clearer when the places are arranged according to "centrality" (see p. 433, note 5) instead of populations.

13. That is, the distance from the next town of equal or larger size.

five regions is a in 59 cases, $a\sqrt{3}$ in 25, and $2a$ in 1; the minimum distance between centers for from six to ten regions is a in 1 case, $a\sqrt{3}$ in 2, $3a$ in 1, $2a\sqrt{3}$ in 12, and $6a$ in 1. Thus it turns out not only that the distance separating towns increases with their size, but also that there is a typical distance for every size. This cannot be given even theoretically by one single value, however, except for regions of similar structure (Table 8), but only by a frequency curve such as we have already met with in Figures 66 and 67.[14] Such curves provide an interesting comparison between a region in which the assumptions of our theoretical deduction (similarity of natural conditions) are approximately fulfilled and a country in which they are manifestly not fulfilled. The frequency curves in Figure 66 are typical for the American Middle West, and correspond perfectly with expectation. In England, on the other hand, where the towns cluster in the five coal districts and around London, the differences are much less, practically insignificant, especially between smaller and medium-sized towns. Towns are not evenly distributed over a uniformly fertile plain, as in the American Middle West, but cluster about the few places where natural resources are to be found.

b. SPATIAL ARRANGEMENT OF TOWNS

As for the relative position of towns with different functions in respect to one another, we found theoretically (Fig. 29, p. 125) that they are grouped about the controlling metropolis in twelve sectors, of which six are thickly and six sparsely settled. The environs of Indianapolis and Toledo correspond so well with this theoretical pattern that even fine details are repeated. So, for example, the populous sectors are bounded laterally by a chain of towns; or again, in sectors with but few towns one must travel farther from the metropolis than in thickly settled areas before coming to the first town. The area without any towns which, wholly in accord with theory, surrounds many large cities,[15] would therefore have to take the form of a cogwheel, strictly speaking, rather than that of a circle.

---

14. The dispersion in Fig. 66 is theoretically unnecessary, but depends upon actual "disturbances," since we are dealing with regions of similar structure in Iowa, as we already know.

15. This fact has often been described in the literature, but never explained so far as I am aware. For Munich, Regensburg, and Würzburg, for instance, see W. Christaller, *op. cit.*, p. 256. For Berlin. O. Schlier, "Die Landschaften Deutschlands," *Allgemeines Statistisches Archiv*, XX (1930), 39. For Paris: M. P. Meuriot, *Des agglomerations urbaines dans l'Europe contemporaine* (Paris, 1897), p. 60. For Davenport, Iowa: *Iowa State Planning Board, Retail Trading Areas, Series I, No. 6* (Des

Regional Systems 439

This is actually true around Indianapolis and Toledo, where no great natural differences appear. As Figures 30 and 31 (p. 125) show, each is surrounded by a cogwheel that is deformed, to be sure, but a cogwheel nevertheless. Finally, I counted all the places within a 62-mile circumference about Indianapolis (*Standard Oil Company, 1937 Road Map, Indiana,* Rand McNally, Chicago), and found that the area containing many towns, hatched in Figure 30, included

45 per cent of the whole area,
48 per cent of the 573 places with fewer than 500 inhabitants,
53 per cent of the 38 places with 500–1,000 inhabitants,
81 per cent of the 52 places with more than 1,000 inhabitants.

Of the thirteen (there would be twelve according to theory) first-class state and federal highways that run out from Indianapolis, ten pass for the most part through the thickly settled sectors, and eight of these (again in accord with theory) along or near their borders.

c. THE FUNCTION OF TOWNS

We know from theory, and experience shows it to be always true, that is is not advantageous for those who live in the country to be associated culturally and economically with " the " town alone. They have connections with many towns, depending on the business in which they wish to engage. For certain purposes, however, such as regional planning, it might be advantageous to have also a quantitative idea of them. I have before me the results of a rather good investigation of the subject in Michigan,[16] which interests us here more for its formulation of the problem and its general results than for its details.

Moines, 1936), p. 11. For Minnesota: C. Zimmerman, "Farm Trade Centers in Minnesota 1905–1929," *University of Minnesota, Agricultural Experiment Station, Bulletin 269*, p. 11. The cause is that *all* nonagricultural enterprises are represented in a central town, so that agglomerations of such enterprises with long sales radii cannot maintain themselves in the neighborhood (see Fig. 28, p. 125). Retail revenues also are smaller in places that lie in the shadow of a large city. Thus according to R. D. McKenzie (*The Metropolitan Community,* 1933, pp. 323 ff.) retail sales in dollars per capita in 1930 were

In Los Angeles and Chicago respectively	738	638
In towns 0–20 miles distant	529	406
In towns 20–40 miles distant	709	637
In towns 40–80 miles distant	857	619

16. C. R. Hoffer, "A Study of Town-Country Relationship," *Michigan State College of Agriculture, Agricultural Experiment Station, Special Bulletin 181,* East Lansing, 1928.

More than 1,000 farmers, a sufficiently large number when it is recalled that in the United States most farmers live on separate farms rather than in villages, were asked: (1) the location of their banks, and where they bought: (2) clothing, (3) furniture, (4) groceries, and (5) hardware. It appeared that not even half of their business was transacted in the same town (chiefly by farmers living near a large one), while on the other hand only a negligible fraction of those questioned patronized a different town for each separate purpose. Most of them were satisfied to transact all five types of business in two or three places. They did not change about indiscriminately from one to the other, however, but had their regular places for banking as well as for the purchase of clothing, fruit, hardware, and so on, but these places themselves did not coincide. On the average the distance of their sources of supply increased in the following order: hardware, groceries, furniture, men's clothing, women's clothing. The order for services was: bank, physician, motion picture theater, tailor, hospital. A third order was: church, amusements, post office, newspaper.

d. TOWN PLANS

In many respects towns are miniature copies of economic landscapes. They, too, are composed of market areas for merchants and workmen and of supply areas for offices and various enterprises, but also for parks, transport points, and so forth. The advantages of an agglomeration of locations at the center [17] determine also the plan of a town and the most suitable course for the main traffic routes. Similarly, and especially in the case of retail trade, smaller agglomerations of locations are found in the suburbs,[18] which correspond

---

17. It is better to have buildings high and set close together in the heart of a town, but with broad sidewalks; and lower and farther apart toward the outskirts. At the center cluster the buildings most frequented by both inhabitants and outsiders for widely different purposes: markets, post office, town hall, and others. Only constantly visited public buildings deserve this situation in the community. Today there is a tendency to have the centers of towns and even villages too scattered and disconnected; this pleases the eye, but is a nuisance for those who have business to transact. The building of a town is no merely aesthetic or hygienic problem; innumerable economic proportions must be correct, and the entire layout must be convenient for the public. See F. Rechenberg, *Das Einmaleins der Siedlung*. (*Richtzahlen für das Siedlungswesen*) (Berlin, 1940); W. Christaller, "Raumtheorie und Raumordnung," *Archiv für Wirtschaftsplanung*, I (1941), 122–126, 131–133; Uebler, on Fallersleben, *Raumforschung und Raumordnung*, 1940, pp. 121–126.

18. An investigation of Baltimore will serve as an example. (J. K. Rolph, *The Location Structure of Retail Trade, Domestic Commerce Series 80*, Washington, 1933). The Abercrombie-Forshaw plan for the rebuilding of London provides for the individ-

to the provincial towns of an economic landscape. No wonder, therefore, that cities should be like reduced economic landscapes, the more so because their main lines of communication are essentially determined from without by their position in the landscape, and because in the ideal case all nonindustrial enterprises of their economic landscapes are represented within them.[19] In one respect modern towns are even ahead of landscapes: They are more a product of planning than of unsupervised growth. The most promising layout need not develop painfully and incompletely [20] through the free play of forces, but can be consciously made a foundation for the whole structure from the first.

Has this come to pass? Examining modern [21] town plans and the literature on town planning, one is struck by a strong inclination to abandon the lattice arrangement. Many large German cities have, like Berlin, a radiating street system, though the pattern is seldom so clear and perfect as in cities founded in modern times—Karlsruhe, for example. The medieval town center, which generally had a rounded form for the sake of better defense, and the modern through traffic routes that radiate from it, combine to produce this result. Such an arrangement is less often seen in smaller towns. First, distances are too short to make the time saved by radiating streets of any importance. Secondly, small towns frequently lie on but *one* through highway or at most on but one right-angled intersection, as is evident from the pattern of the theoretical economic landscape (Fig. 32, p. 127). Thus they can enjoy the advantages of the right-

---

uality of parts of the metropolis and of neighborhoods with from 6,000 to 10,000 inhabitants by developing such cultural and economic subcenters, as well as by directing through traffic around them. *The Times* (London), July 10, 1943.

19. Here origin remains an open question—whether the metropolis is an original or a copy, the seed or the fruit of its landscape; whether its purpose and, even more, its view of the world, originates here or merely rises into consciousness; or whether town and country mutually condition one another.

20. Yet here, too, there are examples of good spatial arrangement with a free choice of location. See Doxiades on Athens, *Monatshefte für Baukunst und Städtebau*, 1942, No. 2.

21. The concept of an ideal town blossomed first with the Renaissance. Octagons and squares predominate in sketches of that period, and a twelve-sided shape seems to have been proposed first by Francesco de Marchi (after 1540). But only once was one of these theories put into practice. Palmanova, founded by the Venetians in 1593, has a hexagonal plaza in the center with radiating streets. (G. Münter, *Die Geschichte d. Idealstadt v. 1400–1700*, Danzig dissertation, 1928, p. 16.) For a concise description of the plan and network of streets for all German cities see E. Keyser, ed., *Deutsches Städtebuch* (Stuttgart, 1939, and following years).

angled pattern without its disadvantages becoming of any real consequence.[22]

The advantages are the simplicity of the system, easy orientation toward street crossings, and adaptability to the right-angled shape of houses. In order to avoid the corresponding disadvantages of the star-shaped arrangement, the individual angles of the star must be conspicuously different; at the center there must be a large island around which traffic rotates, and this limits greatly the number of street intersections; the single sectors must not be built over as far as their points, for on the one hand this obstructs the view of traffic emerging from neighboring streets, and on the other makes too noticeable those departures from the right-angled ground plan that are not entirely avoidable with close building.[23] But when these requirements are fulfilled, a radiating network of streets facilitates metropolitan traffic considerably. For this reason diagonal streets at least have been cut through subsequently in many cities that were laid out on the chessboard plan. Then eight streets instead of four radiate from a crossing, which is no doubt the reason why several newly established cities have been laid out octagonally from the first, like Littoria, in the former Pontine Marshes, and most districts of the Australian capital, Canberra. Yet this remains a compromise after all between the square and the radial pattern.

22. Fig. 82 shows how a settlement would have to be laid out if every nonagricultural enterprise were to be represented but *once*, and the settlement were situated at a simple crossroads. Trade and nonagricultural businesses are concentrated at the center, and the condition under which all houses on the outskirts of the settlement

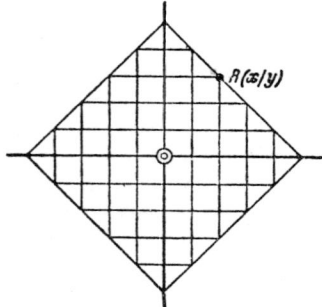

Fig. 82. Shape and street network of a small town

shall be equidistant from the center is $x + y =$ constant. From this it follows that the shape of the settlement is that of a square standing on one corner. This is reminiscent of Washington, D. C., and its environs, but in the case of such a large city the assumptions according to which this is the best shape are no longer fulfilled.

23. In the case of overland highways this corresponds to the difficulty of plowing in the sharp corners.

In the first place, a few diagonal streets are not enough for a large city, and secondly they do not permit the most suitable shape for the subdivisions—the hexagon.[24] For cities on a plain, a hexagonal center where six main streets cross [25] and from which twelve streets radiate has a good theoretical basis. This pattern is seen in Washington, for example, with the Capitol as a center, though in combination with the chessboard pattern. The White House constitutes a secondary center. The hexagon is still more clearly evident in Canberra around the site of the city administration and, unless I am mistaken, around that of the Government offices as well.

But just as the isolated market area is circular, not hexagonal, so also the environs of a town (which is thus always isolated), in contradistinction to its center, have a circular form; or rather, the outermost houses, situated on through traffic routes, lie on a circle. The periphery itself, on the contrary, is star-shaped. This is plainly evident when one considers the course of the isochrons for the trip from the suburbs into the heart of a town. The nearer one lives to one of the main traffic lines (street cars and so on) the less important becomes the distance from the center. Hence the isochrons have approximately the shape of a diamond,[26] and their long axis is the street railway. Superimposition of six such diamonds gives a twelve-pointed star. This corresponds throughout with the experience that towns extend farthest outward along a through traffic

---

24. H. J. Triggs (*Town Planning* [London, 1909], p. 112) called it "the most successful form that has yet been devised," and Cauchon (*Journal of Town Planning Institute of Canada*, February, 1926, p. 12) praised it for saving 10 per cent in street length.

25. Whereas through traffic is directed tangentially around it to the outskirts, the railroad is best run underground, or tangentially to the center of the city, where the passenger station, restricted to the minimum requirements, is situated. Freight stations should be distributed on the radially emerging tracks, along or on the other side of which factories may be located. Switch yards, freight depots, and other extensive installations should be in the outer districts. There, in contradistinction to the heart of the city, cross traffic is less than radial traffic, so that this layout cuts across the fewest roads. For a careful consideration of the question see R. Wentzel, "Eisenbahn und Stadt," *Grossdeutscher Verkehr*, 1942, pp. 180–186, particularly his Example 1; see also Niemeyer, *Raumforschung und Raumordnung*, 1941, pp. 531 ff.

26. For their exact shape see H. von Stackelberg, "Das Brechungsgesetz des Verkehrs," *Jahrbücher für Nationalökonomie und Statistik*, Vol. 148, p. 687. The feeder streets are at right angles to the sides of the diamond-shaped figure, and thus enter the main line at an oblique angle. The obliquity of the diamond depends in turn upon the ratio of speed on the main street and on the feeder streets. See also B. Wehner, *Grenzen des Stadtraumes vom Standpunkt des innerstädtischen Verkehrs* (Würzburg, 1934); and F. Ratzel, *Die geographische Lage der grossen Städte. Kleine Schriften*, Vol. 2, p. 441.

route (See, for example, Chemnitz, *Raumforschung und Raumordnung*, 1941, p. 65).[27]

Even on a level tract of land, town planning does not imply a dull uniformity. As villages are displaced eccentrically to a country town, and this to the metropolis (Fig. 46, p. 167), so suburban centers also are diverted toward the more influential city. Even in individual houses the most important room and its window may be situated with respect to a view (of interesting traffic). In small places such imperceptible deviations from symmetry, associated perhaps with a slight rotation or moving forward of selected buildings, may not only create a compact and dynamic street pattern but also greatly facilitate the orientation of traffic, as K. Bozenhardt has so well shown (*Das Gesicht des schwäbischen Hauses im Strassenbild* [Stuttgart, 1941]). Careful designing in detail often results in very effective refinements like this.[28]

---

27. In England this is made more difficult by the Ribbon Development Act of 1935.

28. Of course such deviations must be justified by adaptation to nature or to some practical purpose, or by an assured artistic result. There must be no perfunctory or affected enlivening, as in so many modern settlements. This is one of the reasons why so few modern village or town plans are satisfying. The problem of our large cities in particular can seldom be solved today by the principles, and still less often by the methods, of yesterday's architects.

Chapter 25. Frontier Regions

A classical example of the economic problems of the so-called "small border traffic" ("*kleiner Grenzverkehr*") is provided by the hinterland of Geneva. The city lies about at the tip of a tongue of Switzerland that projects far into French territory. The political boundary separates it almost completely from its immediate natural supply and market areas. This creates exactly the same difficulties for the Swiss businessmen of Geneva as for the French farmers in its environs. Thus the hinterland of Geneva, hatched in Figure 83,

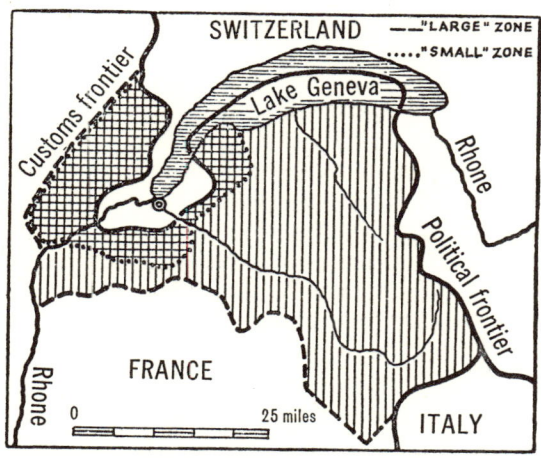

Fig. 83. The French hinterland of Geneva. The "large" zone, broken line, after C. B. Fawcett, *Frontiers* (Oxford, 1918), p. 23; the "small" zone, dotted line, from *Neue Zürcher Zeitung* (October 19, 1930).

was excluded from the French customs area, partly by State Treaty when Geneva became Swiss again after the Napoleonic Wars, and partly by a voluntary decision of France when Savoy became French in 1860. Matters remained so until 1914 and 1923 respectively. In 1932 the Hague Tribunal decided that the former state of affairs be restored, at least in respect to the "small" zone imposed upon France in 1815–16. On the other hand, Switzerland whose customs and political frontiers had coincided since 1849, was to facilitate the importation of products from this zone. During the first four years after the new establishment of the zone, Geneva exports to it increased tenfold.

In a country as small as Switzerland the so-called small border traffic plays a really important role. The economic situation of its frontier cantons has become especially bad since the last depression.

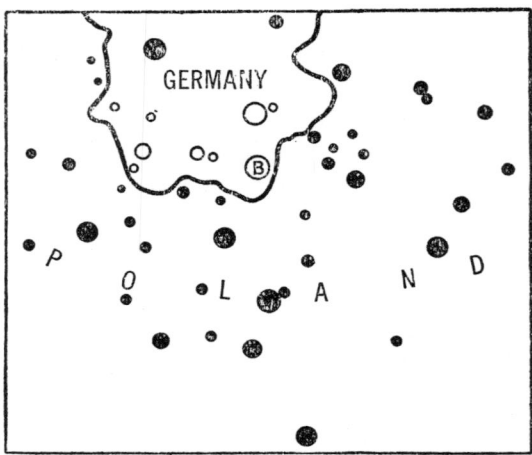

Fig. 84. Influence of the drawing of the boundary upon the market area of Bischofswerder (B), in East Prussia.

The places indicated by black dots belonged in 1913 to the uncontested supply area for its shops and artisans. The importance of B was so reduced by the boundary of the Corridor that it lost even two places that had remained German to competing Freystadt. (After W. Volz and H. Schwalm, *Die deutsche Ostgrenze. Unterlagen zur Erfassung der Grenzzerreisungsschäden* [Leipzig, 1929], Map 1a.)

The Canton of St. Gallen, and the upper Rhine Valley in particular, now suffers severely under the compression that resulted from extension of the German exchange regulations to Austria. The Canton of Ticino also is in a highly unfavorable frontier situation, compressed as it is between Italy and the rest of Switzerland; by the former through tariff walls, by the latter through especially high railway rates (additional mountain charge).[1] On the German side the revenue of groceries in Constance, which were some distance from the frontier, rose by 50 per cent in 1933–1937, but that of businesses nearer the frontier by only 12 per cent.[2]

As for conditions on the Canadian-American border, one fact

1. See *Frankfurter Zeitung*, March 26, 1939, "Dauerkrise in den Grenzkantonen."
2. Hartung, in *Raumforschung und Raumordnung*, 1939, p. 317.

is clearly shown in Figure 85: International trade is restricted to a few gateways. On the 687-mile stretch of frontier between the two Canadian wheat provinces and the United States only eight railways cross the line, though nearly two dozen branches approach it closely! Yet the terrain is perfectly flat, or but slightly undulating, along almost the entire border. Even to the West, toward the Rocky Mountains, where the hills become higher, many rivers flow in a north-south direction and thus offer natural traffic routes, but for 312 miles not one single railway crosses the line! This supports the general belief, which must be relied upon here in the absence of statistics, that the small border traffic is insignificant on this border,

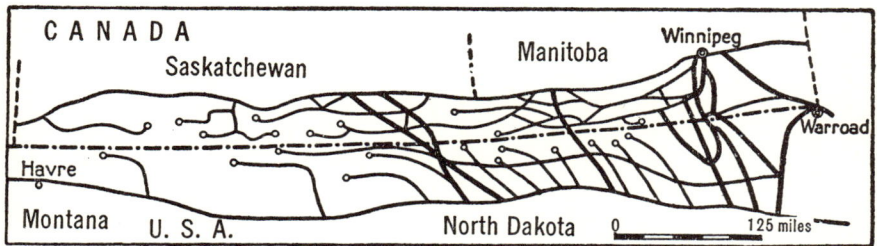

Fig. 85. The network of railways on the American-Canadian border

and lawful trade in particular. The only exceptions are the few gateways and these, of course, are the center for market areas of a special kind, which often reach exclusively into the neighboring country. Here large quantities of articles are sold that can easily be smuggled, or that make it worth while to spend two days as a "tourist" in the neighboring country, after which purchases up to a value of $100 monthly can be brought in free of duty. But regular purchases of goods with a short sales radius are uncommon.

One who enters the frontier city of Detroit by way of the wide pasture lands of Ontario will hardly believe that after the tariff had been increased during the Great Depression practically not a single drop of Canadian milk was sent there, whereas previously it had been shipped as far as New York. This restriction of retail trade in particular and of the importation of agricultural products along a frontier, may lead to the establishment of twin cities where one city would have sufficed. Each one then attracts completely the trade that otherwise would have crossed the boundary in spite of the tariff. So instead of one market area, intersected by an international line, there arise two that extend only as far as the border. Twin cities are typical of the northern boundary of the United

States, but it must be assumed in almost all cases that the split would have occurred anyhow in smaller degree, since a river always hampers connection with the opposite shore, even a bridge making no change in the situation.

Before the Federal Reserve Banks were located, the regions controlled by the various bank sites under consideration were determined. The findings for El Paso are of interest, because it lies directly on the Mexican border. Exactly the same regional form (Fig. 86) was found as we have deduced theoretically for ordinary goods (see Fig. 60, p. 341). It will be proved that distance affects capital transactions and trade in physical goods in exactly the same way.

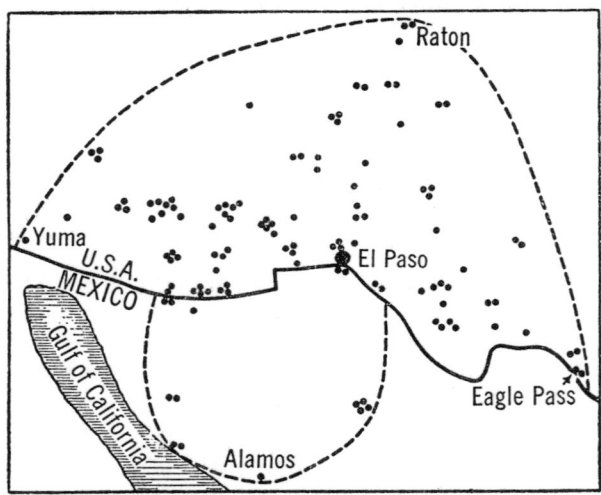

Fig. 86. The financial sphere of influence of El Paso. Each dot indicates a bank keeping an account at a bank in El Paso. (From *Location of Reserve Districts in the United States*, 63rd Congress, Second Session, Senate Document 485 [Washington, 1914], p. 149.)

When an international boundary is drawn through an already existing group of market areas the damage caused by their separation is manifested in an especially painful way. A comparatively recent example is provided by the South Baden–Switzerland–Alsace economic area.[3] The outlying parts of this three-country corner were tightly woven together without regard to national boundaries by shuttling workers and entrepreneurs, by interlacing capital, by branch enterprises, and in particular by a vigorous finishing trade.

---

3. See in particular, L. Dedi, *Die oberbadische Textilindustrie unter dem besonderen Einfluss ihrer Grenzlage*, Göttingen dissertation, 1935.

into a homogeneous production area, especially for textiles, that had already been outlined by nature. The central point, particularly in a financial sense, was Basel, as in general the Swiss had been the chief leaders in developing the region.[4] South of Freiburg there is hardly a great enterprise that was not either founded or continued by the Swiss.[5] Until World War I, the national frontier influenced the choice of a location in many instances, as we have already seen, but made no change in the homogeneity of the region, thanks to the encouragement of border trade and the finshing business. Only with the tightening of frontiers by the war economy, unfriendly Franco-German relations after the War, and now by exchange control was the region cut up into its political divisions. Individual enterprises thereupon lost wholly or in part their sources of raw materials, labor, and capital, or their market area for finished products. The Wiese Valley, for example, opens toward Basel, in whose natural hinterland it lies, and toward Alsace, whereas it is closed off against Germany. After loss of the neighboring Alsatian market, its textile enterprises had to seek new customers in much more distant parts of Germany.[6]

Only then was its unfavorable situation with respect to the German market fully felt. Yarns from the upper Wiese Valley reach even the relatively near-by weaving mills of Württemberg only by way of long detours through Basel and then on through Karlsruhe, or through Singen. This means high freight costs and delayed deliveries. Consequently, competitors in Augsburg enjoy a considerable freight advantage. Upper Baden, on the other hand, had to change from near-by foreign to much more distant German sources of supply. Thus in 1926 the cotton industry of Upper Baden received or shipped 90 per cent of its wares over a distance of more

---

4. Consequently the cheapness of Swiss capital, a result among other things of century-long neutrality and frugal Calvinism, can have meant for Basel only a negligible locational advantage in comparison with the German frontier area (W. Mangold to the contrary notwithstanding, *Standortsanalyse der Basler Exportindustrie seit 1870*, Basel dissertation [Basel, 1935], p. 97). On the other hand besides the abundance of capital a whole series of reasons speaks for the three-country-corner; for example, despite a certain eccentricity of location in some respects, at least with free trade, it is rather favorably situated at a great traffic intersection, it maintains contact with three nations, and so on (see W. Jaeger, *Der Standortsaufbau der Basler Industrie*, Basel dissertation [Cologne, 1937]).

5. According to E. Waldschütz (*Die schweizerischen Industrieunternehmungen im deutschen Grenzgebiet*, Frankfurt dissertation, 1928, p. 39 f.) more than half the enterprises in the frontier zone were still Swiss in 1922; 80 per cent, indeed, in the food industry and 100 per cent in the tobacco industry.

6. For an example see *Raumforschung und Raumordnung*, 1939, p. 317, Fig. 2.

than 156 miles (L. Dedi, *op. cit.*, p. 105). Insufficient regional flexibility in the wage rate, exactly as in the depressed areas of England, made it impossible to relieve the regional distress by lowering regional prices.

The damage caused by disruption of markets by borders is even more evident in the German East,[7] because the border was drawn in later and in an entirely arbitrary manner. It cut up thousands of agricultural and industrial enterprises. which happens much less commonly with old boundaries. Furthermore, the lengthening of the road brought about by the boundary was more annoying than usual, partly because the border was new and hence there.were no suitable connecting roads running along it for those who wished to avoid it, and partly because those who had to cross it were allowed to do so only at a few points. German farmers in the Marienwerder district whose cattle grazed a few yards across from their farms on Polish soil beyond the dikes had to walk up to 7.5 miles a day to milk their cows, since they were allowed to set foot on the dike only at special " economic " crossings designated by the authorities (*ibid.*, p. 27). These crossings were often as much as 12.5 miles apart. Many lanes and highways ended blindly at the boundary (*ibid.*, p. 21). Of 34 railway lines cut by the Corridor, 19 were closed to all through traffic (*ibid.*, p. 16). This was especially bad because formerly the main stream of traffic had flowed in a west-east direction,[8] so that the later north-south barricade of the Corridor lay directly across its path. Together with customs duties and the Polish railway rate policy these effects of the boundary on traffic led to an extensive change-over of supply and market areas. A regional deformation like this is disadvantageous to start with. Still, the loss of an area by one town ought to be the gain by at least one other, but for special reasons the losses here were chiefly German, the gains chiefly Polish. For many more towns close to the boundary remained German than became Polish, a situation that resulted in particularly large regional losses. Thus Bischofswerder, like Geneva surrounded

---

7. My presentation is based on the detailed investigation by W. Volz and H. Schwalm (*Die deutsche Ostgrenze. Unterlagen zur Erfassung der Grenzzerreissungsschäden* [Leipzig, 1929]) and information from W. Vleugels, former Director of the Institut für Ostpreussische Wirtschaft, in Königsberg.

8. Traffic between East Prussia and Upper Silesia was very heavy. The eastern provinces traded chiefly among themselves because they were unfavorably situated with respect to the rest of the Reich, and cut off from neighboring countries by tariffs. At present [1944] Upper Silesia's principal trade is northward, to regions that were formerly Polish and to the seaports (Teubert, in *Raumforschung und Raumordnung,* 1941, pp. 286–287).

almost entirely by the boundary, lost nine tenths of its market area (see map, Fig. 84), and its population fell in consequence from 2,314 in 1913 to 1,792 in 1933. Before World War I the market areas of the industries of the Grenzmark stretched toward the east, because toward the west they encountered the vigorous competition of Berlin and other great cities. The new boundary therefore cut them off from the largest part of their market area, and many enterprises had to be closed down. Extensive agricultural areas, too, lost their natural sales center. Thus instead of near-by Danzig, Eastern Pomerania supplied Stettin, three times as far distant, and a large fraction of East Prussia surpluses became valueless if they could not be processed to something lighter (for example, the converting of potatoes into starch, fodder and so on). On the Polish side, the new boundary severely affected the coal mines of eastern Upper Silesia. As the German market was almost closed to them and the Polish market alone was inadequate, this coal made its way to Scandinavia, thanks to a subsidized railway tariff especially after the strike of English miners.[9]

Under normal conditions an effort is made to soften the economic effects of a political boundary, at least for those who live directly on the border and are therefore most nearly concerned, by encouraging so-called small border trade. Thus residents of a frontier zone some six to nine miles in width, say, are generally allowed to bring in free of duty certain articles for prescribed purposes and in limited amount, especially such as have a short sales radius.[10,11]

---

9. See R. Regul, "Die Wettbewerbslage der Steinkohle," *Vierteljahrshefte zur Konjunkturforschung, Sonderheft 34* (Berlin, 1933); G. Wende, *Die Auswirkungen der Grenzziehung auf die oberschlesische Montanindustrie* (Stuttgart, 1932).

10. From this it is clear that, contrary to the usual statement, so-called "local," or "domestic trade" goods are by no means exempt from the effects of customs frontiers, though within a limited area to be sure.

11. On this subject see R. Riedl, *Die Meistbegünstigung in den europäischen Handelsverträgen* (Vienna, 1928), pp. 94–106; also Boggs-Bowman, *International Boundaries*, 1940, pp. 107, note 18, 124 (Geneva zone); and Baumgartner, *Grenzsetzungskunde*, 1941 (geopolitical).

C. Trade

Chapter 26. Price Levels in Space

We are inclined not to take regional price differences seriously. The cases in which a monopolist fixes a uniform selling price are too numerous. Even in our theoretical analysis we found that it pays the seller to absorb one half the freight costs. And how low the rates have become in comparison with earlier ones! The same transport costs are frequently in effect over wide zones. But on the other hand, it must be said, first, that when the freight is absorbed, not prices but profits differ interregionally. Second, only a part of regional price differences is caused by freight. But let the facts speak for themselves. They show that regional price differences are regular and wide.

a. PRICES OF FACTORS OF PRODUCTION

In the theoretical section only the demand side was really analyzed, because we should have discovered nothing essentially new on the cost side. Like the purchase and sale of products, the acquisition and utilization of factors of production are influenced by space. As the price of agricultural products rises with proximity to a demand center, so also do the value of land of the same quality and the wages of labor. And as nonagricultural commodities decrease in price as we approach their place of production, so interest on capital also falls with proximity to great financial centers, or wages in areas of surplus labor.

§1. SPATIAL VARIATIONS IN LAND PRICES

Regional price differences are greatest in the case of land, and the most expensive square yard even in a German economic landscape may easily cost a thousand times as much as the cheapest. But at the same time these variations are most irregular, because qualitative differences are hard to exclude and because there is no central market for land. However, there is a tendency for prices to be highest at the center of every settlement, especially if it is a city, and to fall for comparable sites toward the outskirts (Fig. 87).[1] This *local price gradient* is continued as a *field gradient* that surrounds every community. With increasing distance from a place even equally good arable land should necessarily become progressively cheaper, since each additional mile eats up an absolutely equal

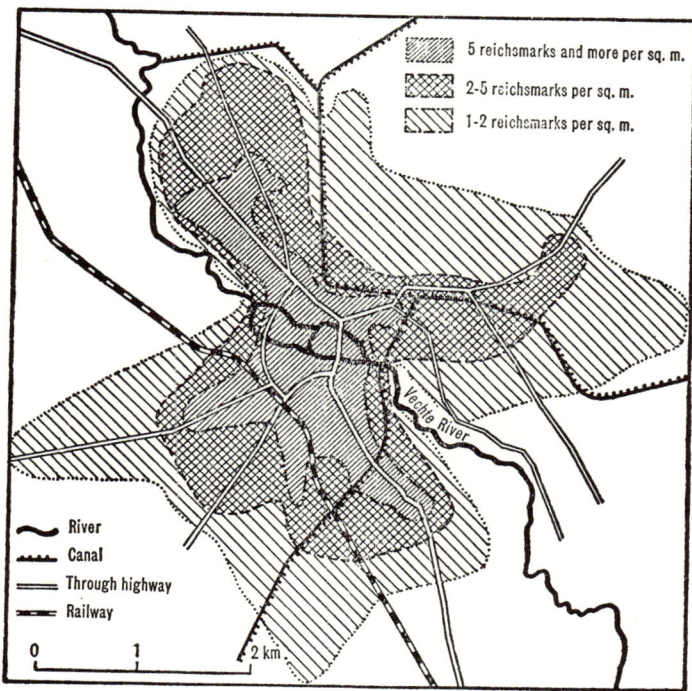

Fig. 87. Price of land in Nordhorn, 1926-29. (From R. Klöpper *Niedersächsische Industriekleinstädte* [Oldenburg, 1941], p. 111.)

put percentually increasing part of the rent (see H. v. Thünen, *Der isolirte Staat in Beziehung auf Landwirtschaft und Nationalökonomie* [Waentig edition, Jena, 1921], p. 103). The price summits for every town and, in regions with the same structure for the next lower places belonging thereto, lie on *regional price gradients*, of which the steepest is the *economic landscape gradient*. A cross section therefore shows the following patern: Prices of land are highest in

---

1. According to a map prepared by Wiesener (*Reichsstelle für Raumordnung*) the price, carefully ascertained, that could be had for every lot in Stuttgart likewise showed great regularity. For the price of land in various distance zones see also A. Spiethoff, *Boden und Wohnung* (Jena, 1934), pp. 132-135, 149-154.

the metropolis, and fall around it in the shape of a cone. Above subcenters and villages smaller apexes rise, but with increasing distance from the central point of an economic landscape the decline becomes progressively more irregular (Fig. 88). (See also *U. S. Department of Agriculture, Value of Farm Land and Buildings per*

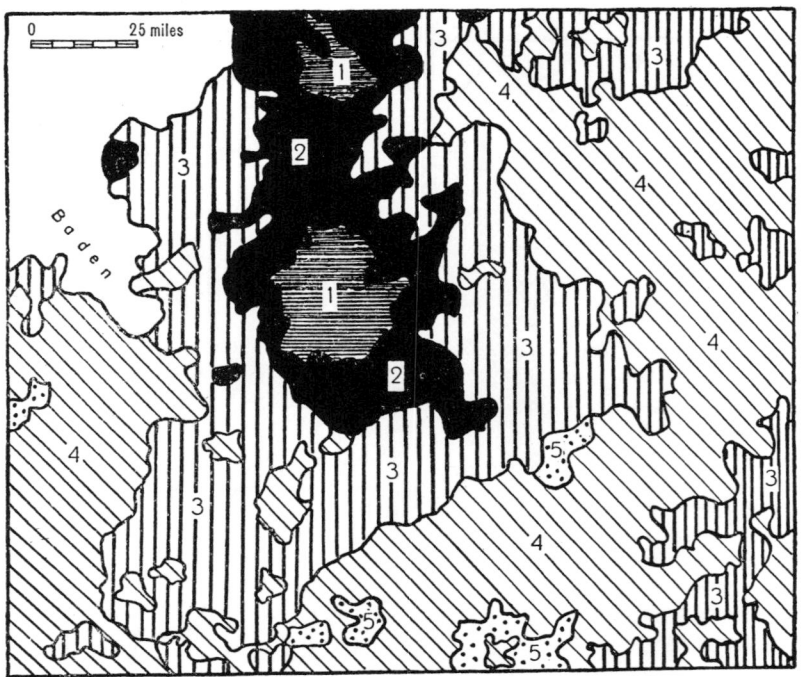

Fig. 88. Value of agricultural units around Stuttgart and Heilbronn (1) in 1935. (After P. Hesse and others, *Landvolk und Landwirtschaft in den Gemeinden von Württemberg-Hohenzollern (Kartenwerk)* [Stuttgart, 1939], Map 9.)

	Reichsmarks per hectare	1	2457 and more	4	568–1134
		2	1920–2456	5	–567 and less
		3	1135–1919		

Acre, Based on 1930 Census, map.) In *national gradients* land values are highest where the soil is especially fertile (lowlands, Iowa) or especially scarce because of a dense population (the Rhine Valley, central Germany [average prices per agricultural unit], the northeastern United States (see p. 374, note 16).[2]

2. Land in Chile about 1897 was almost dearer by 300 pesos with every additional inhabitant per square kilometer (1/3 of a square mile) approximately (K. Kärger,

§2. WAGES IN SPACE

The spatial patterns for wages and prices are similar in principle. As factory prices differ irregularly between production sites, so also do wages. But as local prices rise with distance from the same production site for industrial goods, or from a great agricultural surplus area, or the price to the producer of agricultural goods falls with distance from the same site of consumption, so it is also with wages. According to whether working or living places are more numerous, we can distinguish demand and supply areas for labor exactly as we speak of market and supply areas for goods. An example of the first case would be a great community of miners who work in the various mines of the neighborhood. The second is more common: a town into which workers come daily from the country. In the first case, the *efficiency wage at the place of residence must be the same for all workers* under otherwise similar working conditions, except for certain compensations for greater or less loss of time on the way to work. On the other hand, wages at the place of employment are higher by traveling expenses and compensation for time the farther away this is from the home. In the second case the worker receives a lower wage the farther away he lives, and only the *efficiency wage at the factory site is the same for all.* Thus the structure of market areas for labor is exactly the same as that for goods and capital.[3]

Landwirtschaft und Kolonisation im spanischen Amerika [Leipzig, 1901], II, 105–107). In the German *Länder* and provinces, the value of an agricultural unit for every additional inhabitant per square kilometer approximately averaged something like 1,100 marks higher in 1928 if areas with more than 200 inhabitants per square kilometer are disregarded (correlation coefficient 0.67 as compared with 0.88 for Chile exclusive of Valparaiso).

3. The size of commuting areas for workers varies considerably, and radii of some 45 miles are not uncommon. Their structure resembles that of commodity markets: The number of commuters decreases with distance. The same thing is true of regional form. Figure 90 shows the supply area for Stuttgart (given in greater detail in C. Pirath, *Verkehr und Landesplanung* [Stuttgart, 1938], Figs. 9–11). Again we see the indentations that appear in all cases when weaker centers adjoin a vigorous one (see Fig. 76, p. 419). Where centers that are about equally strong lie next to one another the regional form is much more rounded. The commutation area about Heidenheim furnishes an excellent example of this. See G. Jahn, *Heidenheim und seine Industrie, ihr Einfluss auf Landschaft und Bevölkerung* (Öhringen, 1937), Map 2. Not only are there overlaps of supply and market areas around a metropolis as in the world market (see our Figure 52 and M. Eckardt [or Landesplanungsgem., Sachsen]: *Die Hauptströme der Pendelwanderung in der sächsischen Industrie* Pt. II [1940], p. 47, Fig. I); many centers receive and supply at the same time. On balance, the nearer places about Dresden get more commuters from it and the farther ones send more into it *(ibid.,*

As with land prices, there are other gradients besides those for the market. The *town-country gradient* deserves special attention. It is calculated from the various regional gradients without regard to geographic location, and is to this extent an abstract average of the various regional gradients. For instance, according to *Wirtschaft und Statistik*, 1942, p. 426, the actual hourly wage for unskilled casual workers in Germany in September, 1941, in a simple average of 20 nonagricultural pursuits was higher than the corresponding wage in place-class 1 in places with:

		by
1.	Less than 10,000 inhabitants	0%
2.	10,000–25,000 inhabitants	2. %
3.	25,000–50,000 inhabitants	5.4%
4.	50,000–100,000 inhabitants	5.8%
5.	100,000–200,000 inhabitants	8.5%
6.	200,000–500,000 inhabitants	13.9%
7.	500,000–1,000,000 inhabitants	14.2%
8.	Over 1,000,000 inhabitants	30.9%

On the *national gradient* there is a depression for Bavaria between a high point in northwestern and another in southeastern Germany. Perpendicular to this saddle-shaped gradient there is joined toward the northeast, in the direction of Bohemia, Silesia, Warthegau, and East Prussia, a flattening that finally bends somewhat upward and is known as the " west-east gradient " (Fig. 89). I leave open the question to what degree this corresponds to an efficiency or living-cost gradient, since I have discussed it elsewhere in full detail.[4] For the European *continental gradient* see page 476, note 40.

In the United States pronounced differences in wages and, with a sufficiently large group, slight differences in character lead to extensive one-sided migrations. Figure 91 gives the pattern of agricultural wages there. It is based on state averages, which are entered on the map in the middle of the states concerned. The problem of drawing in approximately the lines for equal wages corresponds exactly with the cartographic problem of finding the

---

pp. 49 ff.). In Bavaria places with up to 5,000 inhabitants have more outgoing commuters on the whole, larger places more incoming. See *Bayerisches Statistisches Landesamt, Die Pendelwanderung in Bayern. Beiträge zur Statistik Bayerns*, Vol. CXXXIII (Munich, 1943), p. 7*. This contains also some very good maps of Munich and other towns.

4. For example, in *Zur Beurteilung des west-östlichen Preisgefälles* (unpublished memorandum).

Price Levels in Space 457

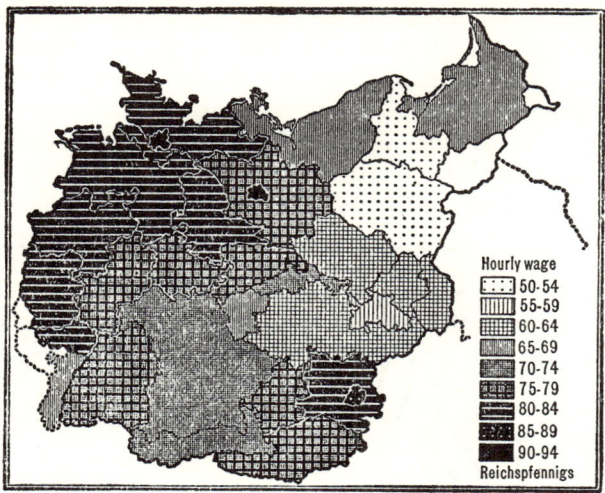

Fig. 89. Gradation of wages in the German Empire. Hourly wage of nonagricultural unskilled casual workers, September, 1941. (From *Wirtschaft und Statistik* [1942], p. 283.)

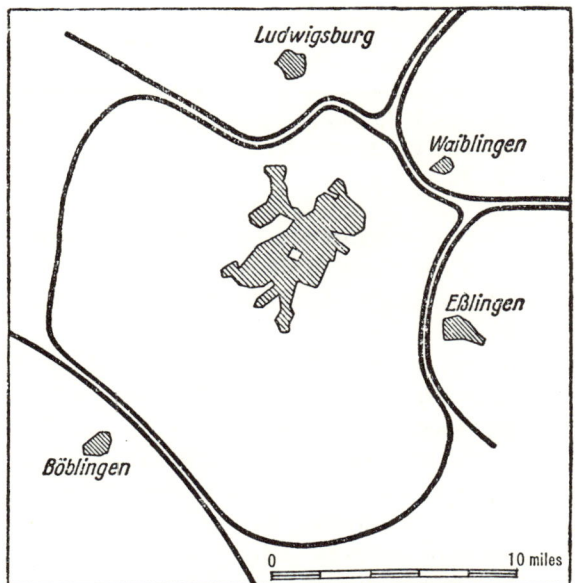

Fig. 90. The Stuttgart commuting area

(from which more than half of all the commuters travel into Stuttgart). (From H. W. Mayer, *München und Stuttgart als Industriestandorte* [Stuttgart, 1937], pp. 27, 155.)

probable course of contour lines when the height of a number of points is given. In both cases the lines have only the value of an interpolation, but approach nearer to the truth the larger the number of points given.

Moreover, the pattern will be more reliable the more easily it can be logically explained. In Figure 91 wages are lowest in the heart of the old South, with its great excess population that is rela-

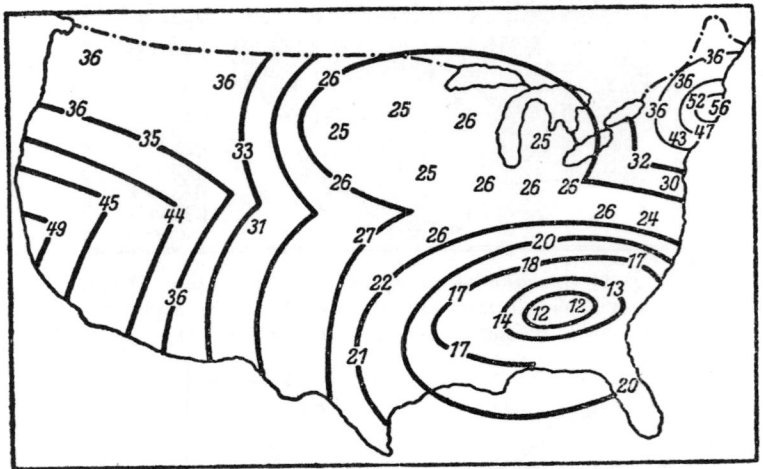

Fig. 91. Monthly wage, without board, of agricultural workers in 1933, in dollars. (Figures from Ch. Roos, *NRA Economic Planning* [Bloomington, Indiana, 1937], p. 161.

tively little inclined to migrate.[5] From this low point they rise in all directions, to reach their peak in flourishing California and highly industrial New England, where they are almost five times as high as in the South.

The two following figures, 92 and 93, do not show wages as such, but the prices of certain services, which, however, are largely dependent upon the wage level. Once again, therefore, we find a low point in the old South, and probably for the same reason, also in Kansas: for in this farming area only agricultural wages are relatively high. The region around Philadelphia may be so cheap for shoe repairs because it is a source of leather.[6] I have no explanation for the low

---

5. Of course these money wage differences are not entirely relevant, since in part they reflects only the smaller productivity of the Southern worker; nor do they affect him to the full extent, because of lower living costs.

6. The price difference between Philadelphia ($1.10) and Seattle ($1.73) is real; that is, it holds despite the use of sole leather of the same quality and heels of the same brands.

Price Levels in Space

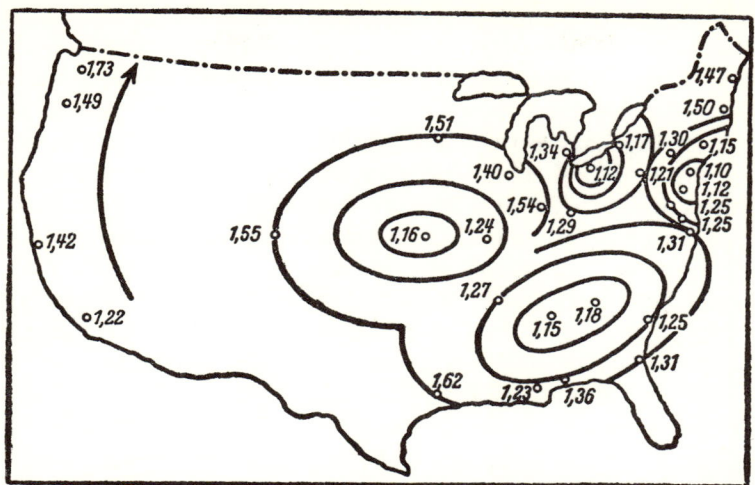

Fig. 92. Price in dollars for resoling and heeling a pair of shoes in 1936. (For source see Table 38, column h.)

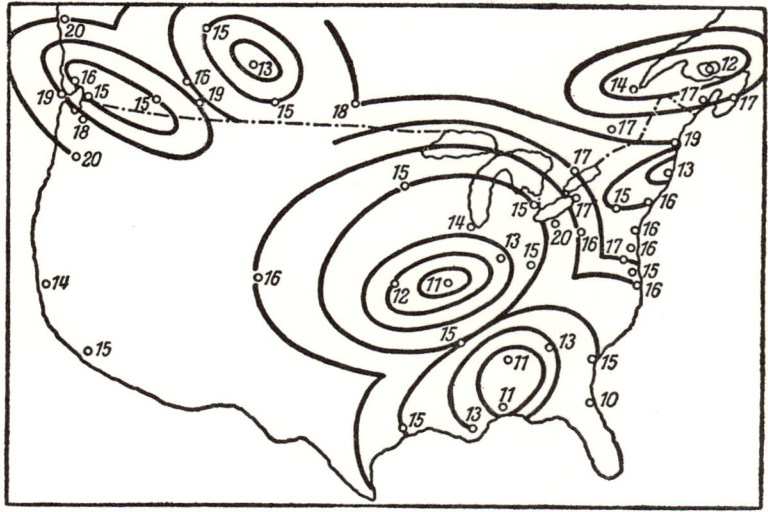

Fig. 93. Price in cents for laundering a man's shirt in 1936. (For source see Table 38, column i.)

area around Cleveland; on the other hand I suspect that the price increases northward along the Californa coast are due at least in part to quality differences caused by climate. Laundry prices, finally, are connected partly with the general wage level (the South, Kansas, Saskatchewan) and partly with the proportion of Chinese, who have most of the laundry business. On the East Coast they are especially numerous in Massachusetts, hence the low around Boston; and on the West Coast, in San Francisco and Vancouver, both cheap places. Among the three price rings about Vancouver those places on the innermost ring have on the average 6.4 per cent of Asiatics and an average price of 15.4 cents; those on the next one have 5.04 per cent of Asiatics and a price of 18.7 cents; and those on the outermost ring 3.9 per cent of Asiatics, with a laundry price of 20 cents.

For Canada as a whole all statistics substantiate the fact that wages rise from east to west, even though there are some fluctuations. No doubt these can be easily explained by the different degree to which the country has been opened up. The main stream of migrants comes from the East and gradually loses itself in the great expanse, so that only a few eventually reach the man-thirsty West.

Regional wage differences of 50 per cent are no rarity in North America.[7] Yet a few years ago the Department of Labor declared that there was no economic basis for this variation, and Roosevelt's economic planning agencies hastened to abolish or at least decrease the differences.[8]

The result of this equalization of wages was that industry, in places or regions that formerly had been profitable locations chiefly because of low wages began to languish and even to move away: from small towns[9] and from the South.[10] Uniform wage scales necessarily depopulate regions that are unfavorably situated, and it was only because of the brief duration of NRA and the laxity with which its decrees were often carried out that the migration

---

7. Many additional examples are to be found in *U. S. Bureau of Labor Statistics, Wages and Hours of Labor, Bulletin No. 616* (Washington, 1936).

8. From an intimate knowledge of events C. Roos wrote: "With crusading zeal the NRA eliminated or very drastically reduced sectional wage differences." "Without adequate appraisal of facts it faithfully followed the dogmatic advice of the Department of Labor that pre-code differences should not have existed, and proceeded so zealously to eliminate them that few, if any, of its policies upset business inter-relations and balances to a greater degree." *NRA Economic Planning* (Bloomington, Ind., 1937), p. 154.

9. Wages are lower in small towns because living is cheaper and also, perhaps, because labor is less productive since the more skillful tend to wander off to the large cities. To these may be added a number of other reasons, such as the less active competition for labor, its lack of an inclination to migrate, the fact that wage labor is merely a supplementary pursuit, and so on.

10. The lower wages in the South are explained in part by the preponderance of small towns. Yet Roos is of the opinion, which is probably too extreme, that the smallest part of the difference between wages in the North and South, in so far as it is a real difference, is a result of geographic factors.

did not assume greater proportions. Yet even so the effects were apparent. Employment in the cotton-spinning mills [11] of New England and the wood industry of the West increased much more than in the South (*N.R.A. Hours, Wages, and Employment under the Codes* [Washington, 1935], p. 58).

§3. Interest in Space

Seldom noticed and still less often explained, yet of special importance to our interpretation of the spatial organization of the economy, are geographic differences in interest. They must therefore be discussed in some detail.

α. *The Facts*

1. SPATIAL DIFFERENCES IN THE DISCOUNT RATE

To the European living in a comparatively small country the discount rate seems to be fixed politically, or at least by the position of a politically defined economy. He is but little acquainted with the idea that there may be differences in the discount rate even within a country, or in any case that they would be sensible. Even in the United States, where the reasons for inequalities are perfectly obvious, politicians and even the Federal Reserve Banks have periodically closed their eyes to them. Thus in 1926 the same discount rate of 4 per cent prevailed throughout the entire country, whereas in March, 1934, it varied between $1\frac{1}{2}$ and 3 per cent according to locality. From New York ($1\frac{1}{2}$ per cent), the ruling financial center, it rose toward the North (Boston, 2 per cent), toward the West (Cleveland, 2 per cent; Chicago, $2\frac{1}{2}$ per cent; Minneapolis, 3 per cent), toward the South (Philadelphia, $2\frac{1}{2}$ per cent; Richmond and Atlanta, 3 per cent), and toward the Southwest (St. Louis, $2\frac{1}{2}$ per cent; Dallas, 3 per cent). The difference was

---

11. Between the middle of 1932 and the middle of 1933 77.8 per cent of all spinning time fell to the share of the South, whereas in 1933–34 its share had fallen to 73.7 per cent. Conversely, the share of the North rose from 20.2 per cent to 24.1 per cent. See J. J. Lane, *Migration of Selected Industries as Influenced by Area Wage Differentials in the Codes of Fair Competition.* (b) *Cotton Textile Industry* (NRA, Division of Review, Work Materials No. 45) (Washington, 1936), p. 37. Roos (*op. cit.*, p. 368) wrote in similar vein. Chiefly as a result of government action the hourly wage of male textile workers rose in the North from July to August, 1933, by 45 per cent, and in the South by 67 per cent; for the women by as much as 56 per cent and 100 per cent. See A. F. Hinrichs, "Wage Rates and Weekly Earnings in the Cotton-Textile Industry, 1933–34," *Monthly Labor Review*, March, 1935, p. 6.

greatest toward the end of May, 1931, when the rate of the Federal Reserve Bank in New York was 1½ per cent and that in Minneapolis 3½ per cent.

2. SPATIAL DIFFERENCES IN INTEREST ON BANK CREDITS

(aa) *Differences among Landscapes.* Until 1933 the *Federal Reserve Bulletin* published the interest rates on prime commercial loans, largely as estimated by representative banking houses, for each of the 34 most important banking centers in the United States.

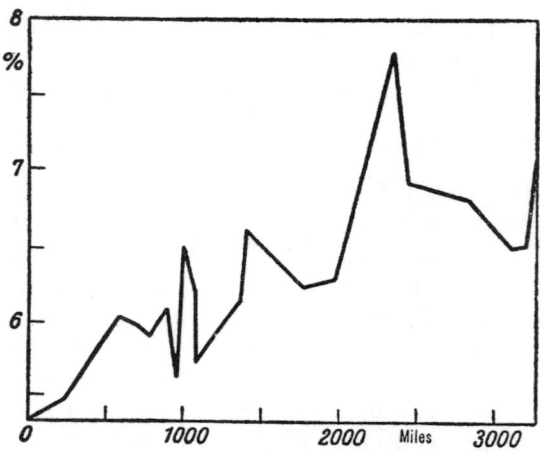

Fig. 94. Increase in the rate of interest with distance from New York, 1919–25.

The last figures, for the middle of December, 1933, varied between 1½ and 8 per cent. The rates were lowest in New York (1½ to 3 per cent) and highest, as usual, in El Paso, Texas (7 to 8 per cent). That these differences in no way reflected merely differences in risk is proved by the interest rates on loans that obviously are equally safe. Early in June, 1923, a time selected at random, the interest on bank loans covered by Liberty Bonds was 4½ to 5½ per cent in New York and 8 to 10 per cent in El Paso. (*Federal Reserve Bulletin*, July, 1923 [Washington], p. 857). These examples show the size of the difference, and their spatial pattern demonstrates once again the characteristic rise from the North Atlantic coast toward the South and West. Thus the interest rate on bank loans for the average of 1922 to 1926 was 6.32 per cent in the Northeast (around New York), 5.45 per cent in the Middle West (around Chicago), 5.99 per cent in the South, and 6.49 per cent in the Far West. Going somewhat more into detail, we discover a phenomenon that we shall encounter again in connection with the prices of a few goods: Interest does not increase uninterruptedly toward the West, but reaches its highest point in the Mountain States, with an average of 6.84 per cent, and, within the mountain region, again in the far south (El Paso, 7.63 per cent) and the north (Helena, 7.73 per cent), decreasing toward the Pacific coast (6.05 per cent).[12] This final decline and the tendency of the interest rate to rise with distance from New York, are shown with special clarity in Figure 94. Twenty financial centers are entered on the abscissa according to their distance from New York by rail, and on the ordinates are arranged the average interest rates on six principal varieties of bank loans in 1919-1925.[13]

(bb) *Differences within Economic Landscapes.* The great banking centers are all subordinated in turn to New York, the leading financial center. To this extent the United States constitutes one single economic landscape. Yet the regions surrounding the large subcenters have a still better right to this name, because their economic activities as a whole are oriented even more completely toward their centers.

Within these economic landscapes, too, interest rises with distance from the dominant banking center, but no data have been published so far that would allow proof of this thesis. It could be proved only indirectly, by comparing the interest rates (published up to 1928) for places of various size. Here the ordinarily justifiable assumption is that a smaller place is, on the average, farther away from the main center than a larger one, because it deals with the center only through the larger place. On a basis of bills and the like rediscounted by the Federal Reserve Banks, it was found that the member banks had demanded the following rates of interest from their borrowers in June, 1928: in towns with a population of over 100,000, 5.3 per cent; of 15,000 to 100,000, 6.2 per cent; of under 15,000, 7.0 per cent. (*Annual Report of the Federal Reserve Board for 1928* [Washington], p. 102.) Differences were still greater in a recent special investigation that compared total interest received with total outstanding bank loans of all sorts. In the first six months of 1936 and for central reserve city banks the ratio was: New York,

---

12. Calculated after F. C. Mills (*The Behavior of Prices* [New York, 1927], p. 184), who gives the rates for 34 cities. As most statistics on regional differences in interest have not been published in recent years, it is often necessary to go back to old data.

13. From W. W. Riefler, *Money Rates and Money Markets in the United States* (New York and London, 1930), p. 97.

2.36 per cent; Chicago, 3.22 per cent; and in reserve city banks, 4.28 per cent; for county banks, 5.62 per cent. (*Federal Reserve Bulletin* [Washington, 1937], p. 296.) [14]

Naturally an exact pattern of the interest rate within one and the same economic landscape is especially convincing, and I am fortunate in being able to furnish such an example. The Federal Deposit Insurance Corporation asked each of the insured banks for the ratio in 1936 of total interest received to total average loans, which represents the average interest on bank loans. At first sight it might appear disturbing that all kinds of loans were included, but for our purpose this is actually an advantage since, besides the figures for the same type of loan, we wish to know also the interest on loans of the form actually obtainable at the time.[15] I have arranged the banks in Texas according to their distance by rail or automobile from the chief financial centers: Dallas (location of a Federal Reserve Bank), and Houston, San Antonio, and El Paso (with branches of the Federal Reserve Bank), and collected them in groups of about the same distance. The average interest was calculated for each group as a simple arithmetical mean, without regard to the varying size of the banks. In every case interest increased at first with distance, and then fell off as a competing center was approached. The increase extended over the widest areas (about 155–220 miles) in the case of the three branch offices,[16] among which we select Houston, the largest city in Texas, because with it the rise is steeper than in San Antonio and based upon many more observations than that for El Paso (Fig. 95). When short distances are measured the increase is found to occur beyond the immediate environs (50 miles circumference) and irregularly, mainly because the influence of smaller subcenters makes itself felt intermittently. But when the banks are grouped by longer distances, as in the lower part of Table 35, these secondary fluctuations disappear. Random disturbances as well as secondary fluctuations are most completely

---

14. The rate was highest in the Dallas, Texas, area, where 10 per cent on agricultural loans was the rule. (*Federal Reserve Bulletin* [Washington, 1937], p. 298.)

15. The rate of interest is often the same anyway on all types of loans to the same customers because the long-term total profit on the business connection in question, not the single transaction, decides what it shall be (Riefler, *op. cit.*, p. 87). On the other hand, a regional interest differential may arise because, although interest on the same type of loan is the same everywhere, more distant customers are excluded from the cheaper varities.

16. But for Dallas over only some 63 miles. Interest rose from 8.4 per cent at a distance of 0 to 10 miles to 14 per cent at 50 to 60 miles. This may have been because large parts of the Dallas area lie near the St. Louis and Kansas City areas, which on the whole are cheaper.

Price Levels in Space

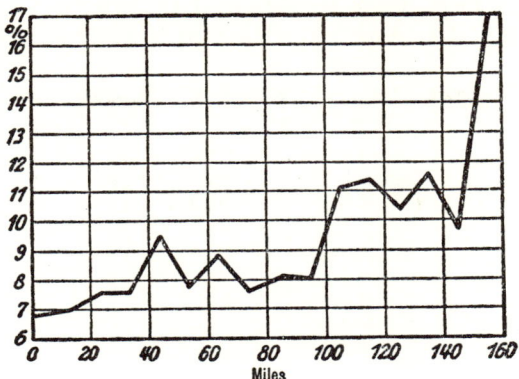

Fig. 95. Increase in the rate of interest with distance from Houston, Texas, 1936. (For source see Table 35.)

eliminated, however, and the clearest result is achieved, when the figures for all four centers are combined. Every one of the 218 banks under consideration is then assigned to its nearest center (Table 35).

Table 35. INCREASE IN INTEREST RATE ON BANK LOANS WITH DISTANCE IN TEXAS, 1936[a]

Distance in miles	Interest in Per Cent according to Distance from	
	Houston	Nearest of the four locations
0-10	6.9	8.2
10-20	7.0	8.7
20-30	7.6	9.1
30-40	7.6	9.6
40-50	9.6	10.2
0-40	7.3	9.0
40-80	8.6	10.1
80-120	9.3	10.5
120-160	11.0	10.7
160-200	11.3	11.0

a. Arranged according to distance from the original data of the Federal Deposit Insurance Corporation. I am deeply indebted to Dr. Donald Thompson, who made this valuable material available to me.

On a basis of the same survey the average interest on long-term bank deposits was calculated also, and I have arranged it according to distance, but here the data are less complete and less reliable.

In several cases the interest was found to be above 2.5 per cent, the maximum legal rate. I was unable to determine the causes for these fluctuations, and therefore offer the result with reservations.

Table 36. INCREASE IN INTEREST RATE ON BANK DEPOSITS WITH DISTANCE IN TEXAS, 1936

Distance from Dallas or Houston in Miles	Interest on Time Deposits in Per Cent
0-20	1.60
20-60	2.19
60-100	2.24
100-140	2.34
140-180	2.70
180-200	2.74

3. SPATIAL DIFFERENCES IN BOND INTEREST

The rate of interest on long-term debts also probably tends to rise with distance from New York, but of course the proof of this is not so simple; partly because the differences are smaller, since naturally the security market is open only to known and fairly riskless borrowers, and partly because manifold differences in the conditions of issuing and repaying, and the frequent difference of apparent (local branch enterprises) and real (national mother enterprises) debtors make comparison difficult. Hence conclusions have to be drawn from only a small number of similar cases.

First, the rating [17] of public bonds falls with the distance of these corporations from New York. Only one state west of the Mississippi River, Iowa, received the highest rating without reservation in 1937. All the other states in this class (New York, Delaware, Virginia, Massachusetts, and Vermont) are near New York. Most of those in the second class are not, though in the main they lie east of the Mississippi. The majority of those in the third class are west of it. We must leave open the question to what degree this classification expresses actual financial reliability, and to what degree it reflects the caution that grows with distance from the situation to be appraised. But even if reliability west of the Mississippi really is less, this might be because, among other reasons, the higher rate of interest prevailing there, which itself is influenced in turn by distance from New York, makes financial obligations more difficult to fulfill. Hence according to circumstances distance would have an influence upon presumptive or actual reliability.

17. According to *Moody's Manual of Investments, Governments and Municipals* (New York, 1937). First-class paper is designated by Aaa, next in rank by Aa, A, Baa, Ba, and so on.

The yield also rises with distance. Moody (*op. cit.*, p. a6) gives a list of " representative " public loans, with information as to their average yield in 1936. Bonds of the State of New York yielded 2.48 per cent, of North Carolina 3.46 per cent, of Louisiana 3.89 per cent, of North Dakota 3.90 per cent, of Arkansas 5.35 per cent, and of Alberta, Canada, 6.15 per cent (this is the complete list). The distance from New York increases (except that Arkansas is a little nearer than Louisiana), and the yield rises, and Moody's rating falls in this order. But interest rises with distance also, independently of the ratings. In the same place, Moody gives the loans of a few cities, all east of the Mississippi and all in class A; thus they should be more or less equivalent and should be felt to be so. Nevertheless, the yield also increases with distance: New York, 3.30 per cent; Philadelphia, 3.33 per cent; Toronto, 3.84 per cent; Birmingham, Alabama, 3.89 per cent.

Finally, the coupon rate, too, increases with distance from New York. Of the fourteen states that floated bonds in 1928, most of which matured in 1945 and were used principally for highways, only New York could issue them at $3\frac{1}{2}$ per cent and its neighbor, Vermont, at $3\frac{3}{4}$ per cent. With the single exception of California, which had to pay from 4 to $4\frac{1}{2}$ per cent, only loans for states east of the Mississippi had a coupon rate of 4 per cent. The states that had to offer at least $4\frac{1}{2}$ per cent all lie west of the Mississippi River except Mississippi itself, which borders on the east bank and is, of all the states on this side of the river, farthest from New York. Montana, in the far Northwest, had to pay as high as 5 per cent for its loan even though, like three states east of the Mississippi that had to offer but 4 per cent, it had an A rating (data taken from Moody).

One final example of different interest rates on equivalent paper is provided by the bonds of electric power companies (Central Hudson Gas and Electric Company, New York; Edison Electric Illuminating Company of Boston; Consolidated Gas Electric Light and Power Company of Baltimore; Cleveland Electric Illuminating Company; San Diego Consolidated Gas and Electric Company). All were issued during a period of four months, March–July, 1935; all fall due in 1965 (payment before maturity only at a higher rate); and all were rated by Moody as first class (Aaa). The issues of companies in New York and near-by Boston and Baltimore have a coupon rate of $3\frac{1}{2}$ per cent; those in more distant Cleveland of $3\frac{3}{4}$ per cent; and those in San Diego, on the California coast, of 4 per cent. The difference becomes still greater when the issuing price is taken into account. In Boston this was 103.8, but in New York only

100, so that the effective interest was higher than in Boston (now and then interest rates in Boston are still lower than those in New York). Baltimore was sold privately, without any statement as to the price, while Cleveland and San Diego were issued in 102.5 and 101 respectively. Thus the interest differential between Boston and San Diego, without regard to the repayment loss, was 0.6 per cent. Assuming that neither loan is repaid until 1965 (premature redemption is permissible under exactly the same conditions), the difference in interest, when the repayment loss is considered, rises to 0.7 per cent. (Moody, *op. cit.*, pp. 647, 2050, 2275, 2464, 2559).

β. The Explanation [18]

1. THE MARKET RATE OF INTEREST

We have maintained from the first that the wide regional differences in interest depend upon differences in distance from the great financial centers of the Northeast, above all from New York. But now this must be explained in detail. This we shall endeavor to do, not in general terms but by using the example of the East-West interest differential,[19] in order to facilitate the presentation. Why is interest higher in the West? Why are the supply of and the demand for capital balanced there only at a higher price?

In ordinary language, there are two reasons. First, the formation of capital in this still partially developed area lags behind the great demand for it. Second, connection with the capital markets of the East, where the situation is reversed, is not perfect. This must now be shown more exactly and in detail.[20]

1. Other things being equal, the demand is greater in the West at the same rate of interest because there are more undeveloped possibilities there, and more credit is demanded to bridge over agricultural losses.

---

18. Although this explanation agrees in principle with that given for all prices it seems to me suitable, considering the importance of interest and the strong doubt that what holds for other prices holds for it also, to repeat the explanation in greater detail and in a form more nearly adapted to the special case of interest.

19. The reader will soon notice that most arguments can be applied also to differences in interest between large and small towns, or between western and eastern Germany.

20. Several of the following arguments have been taken from the extensive work of S. E. Harris (*Twenty Years of Federal Reserve Policy* [Cambridge, Mass., 1933]) and an admirable study by W. W. Riefler (*Money Rates and Money Markets in the United States* [New York and London, 1930]) Others are based on my own investigations and personal inquiries.

2. Other things being equal, the total supply is smaller in the West at the same rate of interest. (aa) The supply of *local* capital is smaller, mainly for three reasons: Less capital is formed, a smaller part of this is in liquid form, and the costs of lending are higher. *First*: Less capital is formed in the West because agriculture predominates there, and its profits are lower than those of the great industries in the East. Furthermore, there is less forced capital formation through credit creation, because with the more uniform economy of the West less of the money lent is spent locally to return to the banks as a basis for further credits. *Second*: A smaller amount of local capital is free for further loans in the West.[21] In the first place, the banks have to keep larger cash reserves on hand, because of the less liquid state of their borrowers and the greater average distance of their Reserve Bank. Furthermore, part of their capital finds its way to New York for clearing purposes, as a last reserve [22] to spread out the risk and as a temporary excess reserve. It may find its way in part to New York, indirectly, through regional centers where some of it is absorbed. Only a portion returns as payment for obligations of Western debtors. The larger a money market the more additional money it attracts. *Third*, and finally: The costs of banking are higher in the West. This is certainly true for management and general expenses, in part directly because of the greater distance from New York (appreciably larger outlays for travel, postage, telegrams, telephone, insurance on valuable shipments, and so on) [23] and in part because of the sparser population, which makes the individual bank smaller [24] and its district larger.

21. In the middle of 1935, for example, the total loans (including bills of exchange) by banks in the East amounted to 41 per cent of the deposits, in the Middle West and Mountain States to only 29 per cent. (*Comptroller of the Currency, Annual Report for 1935* [Washington, 1936], pp. 102 ff.)

22. The *legal* reserve ratio is, of course, highest in New York and Chicago: 13 per cent for demand deposits. In the other Reserve cities it is 10 per cent, and lowest, 7 per cent, for country banks. The gradation of actual cash reserves, on the contrary, is reversed; in 1930 cash on hand was 0.8 per ecnt, 1.25 per cent, and 2.25 per cent of the deposits, respectively. (*Annual Report of the Federal Reserve Board for 1932* [Washington, 1933], p. 269.) When we consider the fact that the smaller and more distant banks maintain additional balances also with larger banks and banks in the financial centers as a reserve, it turns out that they actually have a higher reserve ratio than New York banks.

23. Expenses of this sort for all Federal Reserve Banks, for example, averaged two-thirds of their net profits in 1936, whereas for that in New York alone they amounted to less than one third. (*Federal Reserve Bulletin*, February, 1937 [Washington], pp. 116 f.)

24. In 1935 the loans per bank averaged $3.8 million in the East, in the Middle West and the Mountain States $200,000. (*Comptroller of the Currency, Annual Report for 1935*, p. 103.)

The size of the districts results in large outlays for the overcoming of distance, while the small size of the banks is responsible for a high proportion of general expenses in their total cost.[25] The necessity for larger cash reserves and the limitation on the creation of credit, furthermore, are equivalent to a lower utilization of the available capital. The individual agricultural loan is generally smaller than the industrial, so that the fixed costs associated with it become more important. On the other hand, it must remain an open question whether or not the lower land rents are more than counterbalanced by higher bank salaries here and there. In addition to the higher cost of running a bank there is the increased risk, caused partly by greater insecurity on the frontier, partly by the greater one-sidedness of the economy, which is chiefly agricultural,[26] and finally, also, by the longer average distance from the money center and from customers. This last makes contact with a market and the supervision of borrowers more difficult. According to Riefler (*op. cit.*, p. 108), losses of member banks from 1919 to 1925 amounted in the East to 0.61 per cent of their loans, and in the West to 0.75 per cent. As a third important factor in costs, the higher rediscount in the West may be mentioned.

(*bb*) The supply of *eastern* capital is smaller. Despite the great interest differential, eastern capital does not flow freely enough toward the West to equalize the difference. The various causes have a common denominator: the higher cost of loans toward the West to both debtor and creditor. Again there appear the direct costs of greater distance, which may also take the form of a greater loss of time. Thus a country bank in the middle of Mississippi can obtain an emergency loan from a larger bank in Memphis in three days,

---

25. According to the Comptroller of the Currency (*ibid.*, p. 678) general expenses for national banks of various size in the first half of 1935, expressed as percentages of the deposits, were as follows:

	Deposits per Bank in Dollars		
	Up to 100,000	750,000 to 1 million	Over 50 million
Salaries	1.64	0.65	0.40
Other expenses	1.15	0.41	0.25
Unpaid loans	0.80	0.44	0.27
Net receipts in per cent	1.35	0.66	0.49
Absolute in dollars	1040	5700	1,110,000

26. This one-sidedness leads to an expansion of bank areas, in order that they may include at least a certain amount of economic diversity. Risks could be spread even better if great regional branch banks could be developed whose districts would be still larger, but in the United States this is forbidden by law.

whereas it would take a week if it borrowed directly from New York, unless it went to the expense of telephoning or telegraphing. Many banks therefore prefer Memphis, even though interest is somewhat higher there. Other banks and industrial enterprises in the West are denied direct access to the New York market in any case, because they are too small or not well enough known.[27] They can all deal with New York only through middlemen (Riefler, *op. cit.*, p. 2). Hence before the abundant eastern capital reaches the small western borrower, numerous commissions to middlemen have made it more expensive. In addition there must once more be mentioned above all the risk to both parties, debtor and creditor, which is increased by great distances. Even to the debtor, since he can rely on the fact that even formally short-term loans by a local bank will not be inexorably recalled when money is short, because the bank is interested in him from a long-term standpoint (Riefler, *op. cit.*, p. 87); but with eastern surpluses lent out temporarily in the West, the possibility of sudden recall must always be reckoned with. For the eastern

27. Various classes of western borrowers may therefore be distinguished (Riefler, *op. cit.*, p. 75 and elsewhere), for whom the rate of interest is variously high. It is lowest for the first class, large enterprises that can choose between the New York open market for first-class bills and the great New York banks. It is highest for small enterprises, whose credit is good only at one local bank. Thus a certain class of customers and banks always deal with one another. The larger both are, the more distance loses in importance. J. P. Morgan is as well acquainted with General Motors, although it is a thousand miles away, as is the village bank with the baker around the corner. Hence any distance can be small for certain classes of firms (and for certain kinds of transactions).

From this standpoint one can adopt a definite attitude toward the German discussion of the early 'thirties on *regional banks*: In so far as objections to the large banks were sound, they amounted to saying that these did not limit their customers to the great enterprises that would have been appropriate to them. They should have been reproached less for fostering small and medium-sized credit too little than for attracting so many small and medium-sized deposits in defiance of all economic principles, merely because they knew that the State would guarantee them. It could be objected further that in exaggerating their function of bringing about an interregional equalization they paid too little attention to regional differences in risks. Their regional credit policy was too regular, their personal policy too irregular. From this a special purpose for regional banks, as middlemen between medium-sized deposits and medium-sized credits on an agricultural basis followed. In order to equalize the risks the only problem was to locate them in such a way that the borrowers should be engaged in different pursuits; or, if it was desired to root out the evil entirely, to bring about a more balanced development of individual economic lanscapes. Regional banks have the advantage over the large banks that during the depression medium-sized credits proved to be more liquid than large ones. (See *Untersuchungsausschuss für das Bankwesen 1933* [Berlin, 1933], II, 172. Also my letter: "Für die Bank von Württemberg," *Stuttgarter Neues Tagblatt*, May 3, 1932.)

creditor there is, in addition to the more or less objective great risk which also exists for the western creditor as we have seen, the additional risk of distance.[28] He does not know men and conditions from his own long experience and cannot keep in touch with further developments, which in pioneer regions particularly may be stormy and uncertain. Information and credit bureaus may compensate partly for this lack of personal knowledge, but they cannot make up for it entirely.

In addition there is a political risk when capital is transferred to a region under the control of a different public authority, whose future course is hard to foresee and still harder to influence. In such cases one must be prepared for anything, from confiscation by the state down to special local taxes. Foreign capital is the first to suffer from national emergencies or social reforms. This is true not only of international capital movements, for which it would be superfluous to cite examples.[29] The situation is no different even within the same country. The hostility of the American West and South toward " exploitation by eastern capital " breaks out now and again. I recall the activities directed against the banks by the social reformer Earhart, in Alberta, and against the oil companies by the Louisiana dictator, Huey Long, later assassinated. The price of this hostile reaction, of course, is still higher interest since capital shies away from such states, districts, or cities.

Two groups of phenomena underlie this association of distance with risk, which can be observed again and again: in surplus regions, the efforts of those with capital to invest it in their own businesses or in the place, the economic landscape, or at least the state to which they belong; in deficit regions outside the great financial centers, the complaint of capable small entrepreneurs that the large banks will lend them no money. I shall mention only a few examples: The attitude of those with capital before the war, who held that in general their money was most safely invested in their own countries;[30] and Ford, whose factory is situated in the city

---

28. No matter whether he lends directly to the western borrower or through western banks. The solvency of the latter depends in the last analysis upon the solvency of their customers. Even western branches of eastern banks would not make up for the risk, even if they were allowed, because their supervision would be made more difficult in turn by distance.

29. That they put up with it so frequently since 1914 is partly a cause and partly a result of the decline of the European powers.

30. According to *Untersuchungsausschuss für das Bankwesen 1933, Untersuchung des Bankwesens 1933* [Berlin, 1933], II, 443–447, about three quarters of savings-bank deposits and demand deposits in Württemberg around 1931–1933 went to savings banks

of his birth because he could find no one in Buffalo to finance him. Like Ford, many other great entrepreneurs had to be financed locally at first; outsiders had to be shown that things could be done.[31] Even in the southward migration of English industry the fact that the capitalists live in the South of England and prefer to finance industries there, where they can maintain contact without long journeys, is said to play a role.[32]

In the American West, furthermore, Federal Reserve policy has done little so far to decrease the risk and cost of an East-West flow of capital. It might be thought that the Federal Reserve Banks in the West are large and secure enough to attract abundant capital from the East at lower interest by rediscounting with the eastern Reserve Banks, and then to get it into circulation by rediscounting bills presented by their own member banks. But this is prevented because the Federal Reserve Board certainly does not wish a greater effectiveness of the discount rate. Member banks are not supposed to rediscount with the Reserve Banks merely to profit by the difference between the market discount and the Reserve Bank discount (Riefler, *op. cit.*, p. 29). But even if this were permitted on a large scale it would only moderate the drop in interest, as is easily seen, not equalize it.

The multiplicity of factors that force interest up in the West must be described in detail, to meet the objection that an explanation by distance alone is too simple. It is now easy to see that in the final analysis almost all [33] the factors cited depend upon distance. All conditions in the West, its stage of development, its industries, its population density, are in every respect fundamentally determined by its distance from the Northeast. The important migration (not that of the Spanish and French) came originally from there,

---

and credit unions, which lent them out again locally for the most part, or at least in the same *land*; in the Reich as a whole, exclusive of Berlin, this proportion was approximately one half, in Berlin one twentieth (on the other hand, almost two thirds of all deposits went to the large banks).

31. See also F. S. Hall, "The Localization of Industries," *U. S. Department of Commerce, Twelfth Census of Manufactures, 1900*, Pt. I, pp. 211 ff.; M. Keir, "Economic Factors in the Location of Manufacturing Industries," *Annals of the American Academy of Political and Social Sciences*, 1921, p. 89; and others.

32. *PEP (Political and Economic Planning) Report on the Location of Industry* (London, 1939), p. 9.

33. Among independent factors the fixing of legal maximum rates of interest might be mentioned. These in turn, however, adapt themselves to the independent interest differential. As a rule they are higher in the South, and especially in the West, than in the East (6 per cent in New York, for example, and 12 per cent in New Mexico). In general they are very high, but can be circumvented by additional credit terms.

and as a consequence the West is a step behind the East in its development. At the same time the soil over wide areas is younger and more fertile, and therefore better suited to agriculture. Similarly the continental climate, with all its risks to agriculture and its influence upon the density of population, depends upon long distance from the sea. But even when these chance historical and geological factors are disregarded, the number of inhabitants, industrialization (especially in the form of large-scale industries), and diversification of the economy are greater at the center than at the edge even in a theoretical system. To these indirect effects of distance upon interests are to be added all the direct effects, which need not be repeated. Whoever is still in doubt need only imagine New York shifted from its eccentric position to the middle of the continent in order to be convinced how greatly this would lower the rate of interest in the West.

2. DISCOUNT RATE OF THE FEDERAL RESERVE BANKS

Spatial differences in the discount rate are much smaller in the United States than the differences in market interest. This is possible only because the discount rate is not in close touch with the market rate, as it is in Germany. The causes are institutional and political. Purely economically, the readiness of individual Reserve Banks to rediscount is determined by their available capital (and thus finally by their gold reserve, which sometimes can be increased by rediscounting through other Reserve Banks), whereas the demand of member banks to rediscount could be thought of as determined by profits (difference between the discount rate of the Reserve Banks and that of member banks), by necessity (exhaustion of their own means), and by competition (difference between the discount rate of Reserve Banks and that of outside banks). Discount rates originating in this way may differ regionally by at least as much as the discount rate of a Reserve Bank in the cheapest financial center differs from the considerably higher rate [34] of interest on loans between ordinary banks. For example, if the discount rate in New York is 2 per cent and member banks there will not lend to other banks at less than 3 per cent, the Reserve Bank in Atlanta can immediately fix its discount rate at 3 per cent without having to fear that its member banks will turn to New York.[35] Indeed, it can

---

34. It is only slightly below the rate that other customers pay. See Riefler, *op. cit.*, p. 92.

35. For the lower rates in the impersonal open market compete only for the most important banks with the Reserve Bank discount. If a bank can obtain means still more

go even beyond 3 per cent, because not all its member banks can borrow in New York at the lowest rate, or borrow at all, and because in any case borrowing is associated with higher costs.

But the Reserve Banks have not used their gold reserves to the limit, and therefore have never been interested in an effective discount rate that would facilitate international transfers. Nor was the Reserve discount very effective as a business cycle policy, partly because of the objective market conditions and partly because of the Reserve Banks themselves. Because of the abundance of American capital, the creation of credit does not play such an important role as it does in Germany, and there is a smaller need for notes since payment by check is widespread, so that the point at which banks have to rediscount if they wish to extend their credit still further, is reached later. Thus the Reserve Banks do not exert very strict control over their member banks through the discount rate, and try to make up for this by changing reserve requirements [36] and by open market operations.[37]

Furthermore, this abundance of capital leads member banks to reduce their securities holdings at a favorable price during an upswing, when money is tight, rather than to call immediately on the Reserve Banks for help. These arguments, however, apply entirely to the rich Northeast only, whereas it is impossible to escape the impression that the Reserve Banks in the capital-hungry West and South often do not promote the creation of credit to a degree that would be actually possible. Only too often they are restrained by regulations and principles that appear to have grown out of conditions in the Northeast, and hence are not suited to the West and South. The prohibition of rediscounting from motives of profit seems to me especially open to criticism. For the Reserve Banks do not want member banks to rediscount bills that they have extended at a high rate of interest, with their Reserve Banks at

---

cheaply in the open market, it will not deal with its Reserve Bank even though this has the same low discount rate as the New York Reserve Bank.

36. Within certain legal limits the Federal Reserve Board can change the reserve requirements.

37. I doubt their efficacy. When the Reserve Banks want to sell Government securities, for example, to reduce the liquidity of the banks, the question is, especially when the banks themselves are supposed to be the buyers, whether they are disposed to make an investment that bears such relatively low interest (except with a substantial fall in the price of securities), or whether they would not prefer to make industrial loans bearing a high rate of interest. If the latter is possible they will buy no Government obligations; if not, no tricks with Government securities are required to make them refrain, no matter how welcome this investment of capital might otherwise be to the banks for lack of a better.

their lower rate, merely to profit by the difference in interest (Riefler, *op. cit.*, p. 29).[38] The Reserve Banks themselves thereby restrict still further the already limited effectiveness of their discount rate.[39] On the other hand, this slight effectiveness of discount rates allows a discount policy that would not be tenable with more effective rates. Low and equal discount rates are not only considered politically desirable, but are welcomed by the Federal Reserve Board also because they are supposed to strengthen the position of the Reserve Banks. That is to say, it is expected that with low and equal discount rates member banks will deal more often with their own Reserve Banks instead of with outside private banks. This, of course, is inconsistent with the other principle just mentioned: that the Reserve Banks are to help out only in an emergency, and then only temporarily. In so far as this happened—and in areas with but little capital there actually was much rediscounting from time to time (in 1928–29, for example)—it had the further result, of course, that the Reserve Banks which were thus used had to rediscount with the Reserve Banks in regions where capital was abundant. Thus they strengthened their position vis-à-vis their member banks at the price of greater dependence upon other Reserve Banks, and the end result was always that they finally raised their discount rate, partly because they did not want this dependence to continue and partly because the means of even the rich Reserve Banks are limited.

Thus actual circumstances together with self-elimination of the Reserve Banks make it possible (and, indeed, because of a certain striving for power the banks even consider it desirable) for interregional differences in the discount rate, though often considerable, to be smaller than interregional differences in the market rate of interest. The contradictory effects of these two activities, which seem to produce the same result, appear only when the Reserve Banks really wish to exert their power, at least within the restricted limits that are actually possible. For to the extent to which discount rates become effective, they must naturally also increase regional differences to the extent that we have deduced above.

b. PRODUCT PRICES[40]

It is not always easy to tell a priori whether local differences in the prices of any particular good will be large or small. At first

---

38. Hence rates in the open market may often be higher than the discount rate of the Reserve Banks.

39. The moment at which member banks rediscount after exhaustion of their own means is affected less than the degree to which they do so.

40. Useful data are so rare, so difficult to collect, and take so long to explain that

one is tempted to suppose that the differences are greater for raw materials than for finished products, because their unit of weight is cheaper and the freight therefore higher in proportion to the producer's price. Then the following, say, are mentioned as examples of the first group: ore, coal,[41] iron; wood, paper; bricks, cement; [41] oil and salt,[41] as well as potatoes, hay, animals, and fruit. Typical of the second group would be jewelry, watches, tobacco products, drugs, clothing, and so on. But in the first place, the freight rate also is generally lower for the former group; and second, in many if not most cases, the shipping distance is shorter. For instance, it is shorter for paper than for books, for iron than for machinery, and for potatoes than for potato spirits. Third, interest and insurance during transit are lower; fourth, competition is keener because qualities can be compared more easily than in the end product; and finally, in the case of raw materials, prices are usually f. o. b. prices plus freight, whereas with finished products the retail prices include selling costs, which vary greatly in different localities. Thus at first glance it is not at all certain which group will show the greater regional price differences. At any rate, the labor of examining individual cases cannot be saved by a few general reflections.

§1. Agricultural Products

α. Wheat

The geography of grain prices in the United States was investigated at an early date by T. H. Engelbrecht,[42] whose pioneer work

---

market, regional, and national price gradients can frequently be shown only in fragmentary form and not sharply separated one from the other. According to A. Jacobs (" Die räumliche Ordnung der Preise in Europa," *Wirtschaftsring*, 1941, pp. 205–207), the European continental gradient for groups or averages of single prices at the opening of 1940 was as follows: Food was most expensive in Germany; for industrial materials she was between the more expensive southeast and the less expensive northwest. The same was true of real wages, which in Germany were twice as high and in Denmark more than three times as high as in Bulgaria.

41. In 1931–1933 the freight on cement in the United States, for instance, amounted on the average to 1/3, on lime to 1/2, and on coal to 1/1 of the f. o. b. price. (T. K. Urdahl and L. J. O'Neill, " Operation of the Basing Point Provisions in the Lime Industry Code," *NRA, Division of Review, Work Materials*, No. 65, 1936, pp. 59, 71. F. E. Berquist, " Economic Survey of the Bituminous Coal Industry under Free Competition and Code Regulation," *ibid.*, No. 69, I, 34.) According to some sources, August 13, 1940, salt prices in Mexico varied between 95 and 230 pesos per ton. On the whole, regional price differences are said to be great there during the rainy season because of loose economic relationships and difficulties in transportation.

42. *Die geographische Verteilung der Getreidepreise in den Vereinigten Staaten, 1862–1900* (Berlin, 1903).

for the latter half of the nineteenth century is still well worth reading.[43] He introduced the concept of isotims, lines connecting places with equal prices. More recent price maps for wheat are based on an admirable investigation by L. B. Zapoleon.[44] It includes tables of producers' prices by counties, that is, relatively small areas, for the years immediately preceding World War I. Corresponding statistics for recent years are in the files of the Department of Agri-

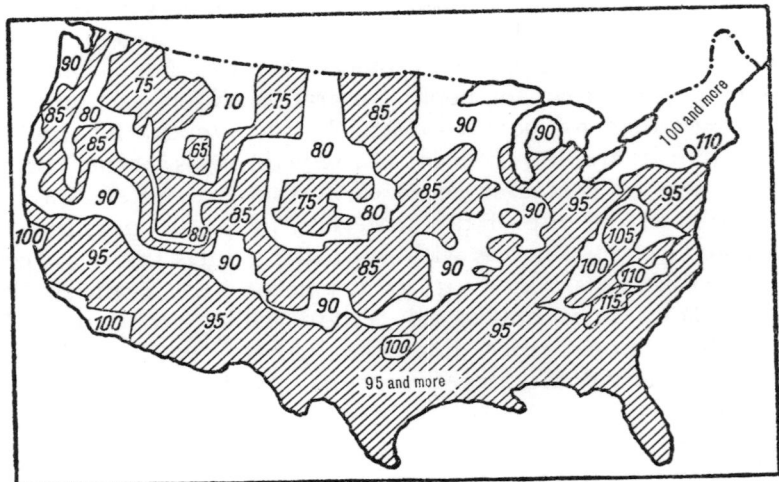

Fig. 96. Spatial pattern of wheat prices in the United States (producer prices in cents per bushel, 1910–14). (From F. A. Fetter, *The Masquerade of Monopoly*, p. 295, after L. B. Zapoleon, *Geography of Wheat Prices*, U. S. Department of Agriculture Bulletin No. 594 [Washington, 1918], Map 3.)

culture, but have not been released for publication. Zapoleon's maps give prices only for the wheat-raising areas proper. These do not constitute a compact whole, however, which makes a review of their connections difficult, but by interpolation, F. A. Fetter (*The Masquerade of Monopoly* [New York, 1931], p. 295) has prepared a new map that affords a good general view of the whole field and gives price zones for the entire United States (Fig. 96).[45] The lowest

43. In this period, for example, occurred the great cheapening of transportation, which diminished local price differences.

44. *Geography of Wheat Prices, U. S. Department of Agriculture*, Bulletin 594 (Washington, 1918); Map 3 in particular.

45. It is based on producer's prices regardless of quality differences, but as the interpolation includes also regions where no wheat is grown, it may perhaps come nearest to a map of wholesale prices. Zones are given, not lines of equal price, partly for the statistical reason that prices are rounded off one way or the other to the nearest five cents, but partly also for the actual reason that freight costs are often the same over entire zones.

price prevails in the surplus region that is farthest from the market,[46] namely eastern Idaho. Here, therefore, is the great divide between the supply areas for the Pacific and Atlantic exporting ports. Along the main transport routes to these ports and to the inland markets, prices rise about in proportion to freight costs (Zapoleon, *op. cit.*, p. 16). Here price differences are smallest and most stable. Smallest because of well-organized interlocal trade, and most stable because even in the years of poor harvests, the great surplus regions continue as a rule to supply wheat, so that the flow of traffic hardly changes its direction. In smaller and more remote wheat areas, which sometimes have a surplus and sometimes a deficit, local price differences on the contrary are greater and more variable.

Zapoleon's map includes also, though only in rough form to be sure, the smaller price cones about the main collecting stations in the wheat area. However, only the two great price funnels around distant Idaho and the great surplus region of Nebraska appear clearly. About the ports on the northwest coast fragments of price cones, at best, can still be recognized. Thus the map does not show with perfect clarity to what degree price cones (which in my judgment must predominate), and to what degree price funnels, actually determine the pattern. This is partly because of the rounding-off; partly too, no doubt, because of Fetter's interpolation, which seems to start from the conception of price funnels as the regulating principle; partly because freight rates are not given; and finally, in part, because the eastern ports are so far from the relatively small surplus region.

But however this question is decided the significance of, and a certain regularity in, regional price differences are clearly apparent on the map. This does not exclude the fact, however, that agreement with the rule is never complete in all details. Thus there is a striking example of three places in Kansas with the same freight rate for wheat to Kansas City, the collecting station; yet only once in the entire harvest year 1929–30 did the storehouses in these three places buy wheat of the same quality, on the same day, and at the same price![47]

β. Potatoes

The price of potatoes just about doubles as it rises from the North, the surplus region, toward the South. A comparison of Figures 97 and 98 will show how the importance of Idaho and

---

46. Not in North Dakota, the region of *largest* surplus.

47. Bureau of Railway Economics, *Commodity Prices in Their Relation to Transportation Costs, Bulletin No. 40, Wheat* (Washington, 1930), pp. 2 f.

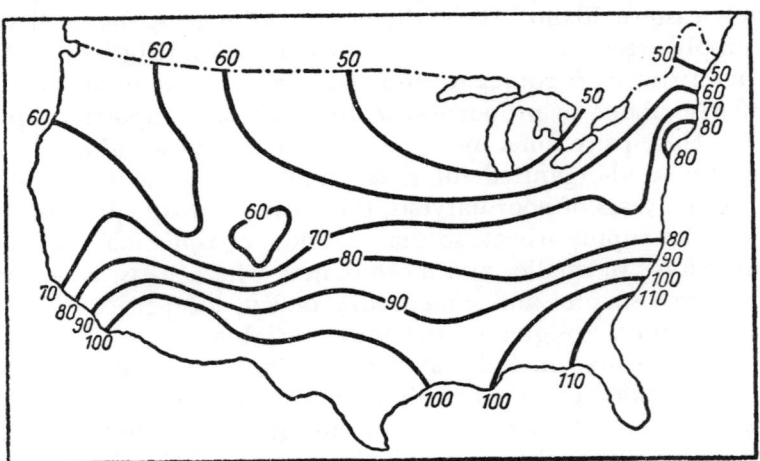

Fig. 97. Producer prices for potatoes in cents per bushel on December 1, average for 1906–15. (From H. Working, *Factors Determining the Price of Potatoes in St. Paul and Minneapolis,* Minneapolis, 1922.)

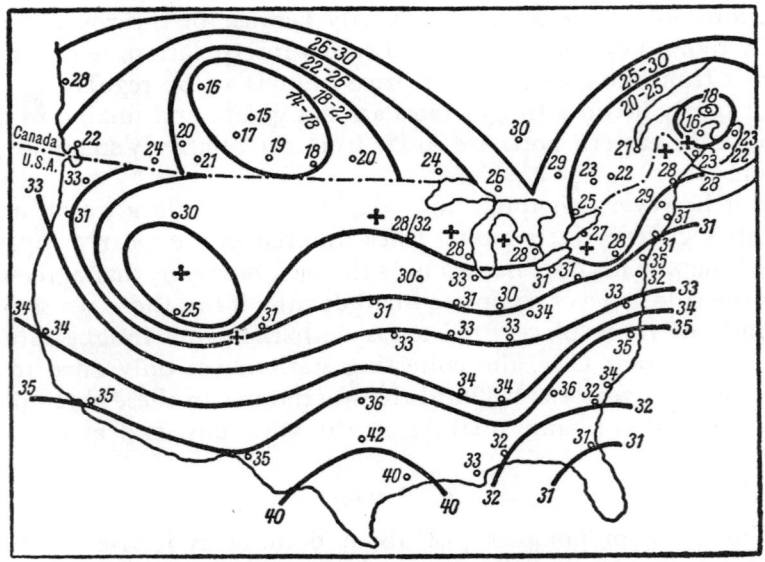

Fig. 98. Retail prices of potatoes, 1936, in cents per 10 pounds. + = surplus regions. (Sources for the figures: Canada, Dominion Bureau of Statistics; United States, Bureau of Labor Statistics.)

Colorado has increased since World War I. The low price around Florida is a result of large imports from Cuba and Bermuda. That around the Canadian province of Saskatchewan requires special examination, because its potato production, though considerable, is nevertheless low in proportion to the population. For the rest, the isotims, which had to be derived from comparatively few price data with due consideration of transport conditions, naturally represent but a rough interpolation.[48] Even at the best they constitute only a sound, yet for that very reason a useful and important, presumption.

γ. Oranges

Over two thirds of the American production is furnished by California, where the largest groves are gathered closely about Los Angeles, and a bare third by Florida. About both these centers there are definite rings of rising prices.

Table 37. ORANGE PRICES AND DISTANCE
Retail Price per Dozen, 1936

Cents[a]		Distance from Los Angeles in miles (rail)
16.0	Los Angeles	—
25.7	San Francisco	470
26.8	Salt Lake City	780
27.6	El Paso	820
21.2	Portland (Oregon)	1220
31.9	Denver	1370
33.5	Omaha	1930
35.0	Minneapolis	2280
36.9	Chicago	2430

a. From the Bureau of Labor Statistics, Retail Price Division.

Table 37 shows how greatly distance from a producer affects the price of oranges. As both great producing areas supply the principal markets in the Northeast at about the same time,[49] but Florida is

---

48. The smaller price cones simply disappear in the interpolation, yet they are often highly significant. Thus in the Minneapolis supply area differences in producers' prices up to 66 per cent, according to distance, have been shown to persist over long periods. (L. F. Garey, *Local Prices of Farm Crops in Minnesota,* University of Minnesota, Agricultural Experiment Station, Bulletin 303, 1934, p. 29.)

49. This lies partly in a contested area that in 1936 stretched approximately along the lower and middle Mississippi River, the Ohio River, and the northeast coast. Southeast of this area Florida controlled the market, while northwest of it California was in possession of more than two thirds. (*U. S. Department of Agriculture. Carlot Unloads of Certain Fruits and Vegetables in 66 Cities and Imports in 4 Cities for Canada 1936* [Washington, 1937]). Chicago and New York are similar " corner markets " for oranges, as northwest Europe is for wheat.

nearer to it, prices must be higher there than in California. For example, it is hardly half as far from Chicago to Jacksonville (Florida) as to Los Angeles. It could therefore be supposed, and statistics confirm the presumption, that the price in Jacksonville (27.3 cents a dozen) would be somewhat above the mean for Chicago and Los Angeles prices.

δ. *Milk*

As the shipping distance for milk is usually short, local price differences may be especially large and irregular. Thus the producers' prices paid by Canadian dairies in 1936 fluctuated between 12.8 cents a gallon on the East Coast (Charlottetown) and 45.3 cents on the West Coast (Vancouver).[50]

ε. *"Heavy" and "Light" Goods*

It would be wrong to dismiss the wide regional price differences in the preceding examples on the score that they concern exceptionally heavy goods. Salt, too, is a heavy product in the sense of our argument: that shipping over a given distance raises the price disproportionately. Yet in so far as data are available,[51] the retail price in Canada on the border of any area is never more than one third above the price at the production site, and generally much less than that, merely because salt is produced in almost every Canadian province and the actual shipping distance is therefore relatively short. Coffee, on the other hand, is a " light " commodity; that is to say, the freight rate is less important. Yet in the interior in 1936 a pound cost half as much again as in a Southern importing port (New Orleans, 21.4 cents; Denver, 31.8 cents).[52] The insignificance of the freight rate in proportion to value was obviously balanced by the long haul. This comparison shows that not only the " weight " of a commodity, but the extent of its market area as well, determines the importance of its regional price differences.

---

50. See *Dominion Bureau of Statistics, Prices and Price Indexes 1913–33* (Ottawa, 1934), pp. 54 f.; also J. M. Cassels' isotims for milk and butter fat (*A Study of Fluid Milk Prices* [Cambridge, Mass., 1937], pp. 161, 165).

51. Source: *Dominion Bureau of Statistics, Internal Trade Department.*

52. Differences in quality may not have been eliminated with complete success, but in the general region of Denver prices were equally high (Salt Lake City, 31 cents; Sioux Falls, S. D., 31.4 cents).

§2. Nonagricultural Products

a. Homogeneous Goods

1. NEWSPAPERS

The New York Times, the leading American newspaper, formerly sold for 2 cents in New York itself; for 3 cents in the environs of the city; for 5 cents in Boston, 220 miles distant; for 6 cents in Montreal (440 miles); and for 7 cents in Ottawa (550 miles). The price of the Sunday edition varied between 10 and 15 cents. Considering its weight, about 3/4 pound on weekdays and about $2\frac{1}{2}$ pounds on Sundays, the explanation lies largely in the fact that freight costs rise with distance whereas sales decrease, so that a greater proportion of the fixed selling costs falls upon the single copy.

2. AUTOMOBILES

The price of a Chevrolet that sold for about $600 in Flint, Michigan, its production site, rose in accordance with the freight rates prevailing on January 10, 1935, by $16 in Chicago (270 miles); by $37 in New York (670 miles); by $78 in New Orleans (1,160 miles); by $91 in Miami, Florida (1,460 miles); by $115 in El Paso, Texas (1,650 miles); and was highest in San Francisco (2,540 miles) and California as a whole, where the price increased by $130—that is, by more than 20 per cent.[53,54]

3. CLOTHING

Summer suits bearing the Palm Beach label sold for $16.75 at retail everywhere in the United States in 1936. But it would be absurd to conclude from such cases, which are well known to be numerous, that distance is apparently of no consequence for sales. With a prescribed uniform price the costs of distance deter the manufacturer or retailer, of course, not the consumer. Instead of the price level, it is the profit level that varies from place to place.[55]

---

53. Information kindly supplied by Mr. S. du Brul, of the General Motors Corporation.

54. The buyer does not always pay all the freight, of course, for a dealer often takes a used car at more than its market value as part payment.

55. Sometimes, however, the price level only seems to be the same. Thus in the western branch of a large Canadian department store I found that towels, which came from the East, were something like an inch smaller instead of more expensive. In another case the conditions under which a mail-order house would deliver in the West were less favorable, and the assortment included more expensive qualities.

In the present instance Palm Beach suits were not to be had at all in remote San Francisco, according to reports of the Bureau of Labor Statistics.

4. EUROPEAN RETAIL PRICES

A study that is particularly valuable because of the method employed is that undertaken by the French Institut Scientifique de Recherches Économiques et Sociales. Retail prices in European countries were to be compared, special emphasis being laid on obtaining prices for actually comparable qualities.[56] For this purpose the same investigator with the same sample case visited leading department stores in the various capitals and obtained the prices for 200 goods and services. It was found that prices in France, Holland, England, and Sweden averaged about the same, or at most, somewhat lower in the two latter countries; whereas in Switzerland, an important health resort, they were very much higher and in Belgium much lower. This price inquiry preceded the French and Swiss devaluations. Belgium, England, and Sweden owed their low prices to early devaluation, and Holland to its policy of free trade.[57]

β. Similar Goods

The range of trade-marked articles obtainable anywhere in the United States and recognizable as such is not so wide as it is striking. However, almost all the available material on retail prices relates not to identical but to similar qualities. Even this has not always been so. Until 1935 the Bureau of Labor Statistics, in Washington, determined prices in single localities, not for comparable articles but for those that were then most widely purchased.[58]

The standardization of production goes especially far in the United States, and the Bureau of Labor Statistics has commendably endeavored for years to obtain interlocally comparable prices by exact instruction, central training, and supervision of its outside investigators. (The Canadian Bureau abandoned such an investigation as hopeless because of its limited means.) Yet, although I worked for months to choose from this material particularly such articles as might be most readily assumed to be of somewhat comparable quality, the results show the extraordinary difficulty of the

---

56. Nevertheless, qualities for some finished goods could be only roughly compared.

57. Charles Rist, *Écarts de prix, France-Étranger* (Institut Scientifique de Recherches Économiques et Sociales, Paris, 1936), pp. 20–22; supplementary information by Dr. Herberts, Paris.

58. Hence F. C. Mills' calculations of average local differences in retail prices based on these findings (*The Behavior of Prices* [New York, 1927]) are also useless.

task. Even an orderly over-all pattern of local prices could not be established in every case, nor could this spatial order always be logically explained; that is, it did not always correspond with what would be expected from a knowledge of the production site,[59] freight rates, and local conditions. But of course it must never be forgotten that this knowledge itself is incomplete, and above all that one must be prepared from the first to find that retail prices, even for exactly the same product, differ locally to a greater degree and more irregularly than the prices paid by retailers.[60] For retail margins vary considerably from town to town, and even between neighborhoods,[61] different businesses, and single businesses in the same place [61] because of variations in ground rent, wages, interest, taxes, advertising costs, conditions of competition, ease of supervision, size of store, and so on.[62] Hence irregular price patterns are not always illogical simply because they are irregular. Especially when production also

---

59. Where this was not already known it was obtained from business directories (Thomas, *Register of American Manufacturers*, 1932–33 edition; *Canadian Trade Index*, 1936) and *American Census of Manufacturers* or the statistics on production of the Dominion Bureau of Statistics.

60. Thus, in all stores investigated, a certain package of aspirin cost 12 cents in Jacksonville, whereas in Mobile an identical package cost 15 cents. For another brand the prices were 10 and 15 cents respectively; the difference, that is, was much greater than would be caused by the insignificant difference in freight, since both places are almost equally distant from the production center, New York. Similarly, the great difference between the price for spectacles in New Orleans ($9.00) and Los Angeles ($15.50) is apparently genuine; it is not explained by the freight situation, however, but rather by the wage level. In the same way, even without dumping, exported goods may be cheaper at retail in the country to which they are shipped than in the country of origin.

61. For example, in November, 1932, the prices of 19 important foods were 10 per cent higher in the west end of Berlin than on the north side. (C. Boehm, " Zur Frage der Preisstreuung," *Vierteljahrshefte zur Konjunkturforschung*, Vol. XI, No. 4A [1937], p. 460.) Fruit and vegetable prices were higher in the outskirts than at the center of the city, because it cost more to transport goods from the great central market to the shops; because the population density was down and sales were accordingly fewer; and because competition was farther away. Extraordinary price differences prevailed in the case of goods that spoiled easily or had but a small sale. Thus in average stores on November 18, 1930, onions of medium grade cost from 5 to 13 pfennigs a pound, and spinach of the same quality from 5 to 25 pfennigs. As perishable goods cannot be withdrawn from an overstocked market, their prices differ by more than the costs of distance. Hence, though competition is perfect within the same wholesale market, it is limited between markets. (Well demonstrated by H. Liebe in *Preisbildung bei Obst und Gemüse* [Berlin, 1931], pp. 12, 17–19.)

62. These differences are eliminated in dining cars. The increased price at each succeeding meal between San Francisco and New York (in 1935 from $.70–$1.10 in the West to $1.30–$2.00 in the East) no doubt depended upon differences in the cost of supplies.

is regionally scattered, a regular pattern is seldom to be expected when comparisons are drawn between a few central places, because the smaller price funnels around a single factory simply drop through the wide meshes of the including network. This is true of mattresses, for instance (Table 38, column *l*), where, in addition, quality differences cannot be wholly eliminated.

Nevertheless there remain a fair number of price patterns that are regular and logical at the same time, and thereby furnish proof of the correctness and reliability of the manner in which they have been collected. In such cases rings of increasing prices surround the site of surplus production (soap, for example), or those places where an important factor of production is especially cheap: labor (laundries), land (motion pictures), a raw material (shoemakers). When occasionally a price is nevertheless wholly out of line, further investigation, wherever possible, has generally shown a difference in the quality of the product or in business methods, or perhaps special local conditions such as a price war, for example. In this way we obtain at the same time a clue as to where the statistical inquiry should be critically tested.

1. SOAP

The most important production centers for soap of the variety investigated here are Cincinnati, in the United States, and Toronto, in Canada. Prices rise appreciably with distance from these centers (Fig. 99 and Table 38). As the unit of weight is cheap and the shipping distance for the brand concerned is long, freight plays an important role in the explanation of price differences. For soap shipped from Cincinnati to Boston in cartons it amounts to 75 cents a hundred pounds, or about 4 cents for 10 cakes, which corresponds exactly with the difference in the retail price. Toward the South the isotims lie closer together, because freight rates there are higher than in the Northeast. Toward the West conditions are not entirely clear. In California there seems to be a local product, made in Los Angeles, since prices rise toward the North.[63] In Buffalo and Detroit imports from Canada may play a part. In Kansas and New Orleans, and perhaps throughout the South as a whole, there are differences in quality. As for Philadelphia, it could not be determined whether

---

63. On the Pacific Coast, along which only a narrow but very long strip is populated, the influence of distance can be followed with special ease. For example, a surplus of overalls is made at the northern end of this strip, and prices accordingly rise toward the south: Seattle, $1.30; Portland, Ore., $1.42; San Francisco, $1.47; Los Angeles, $1.55 (from data of the Bureau of Labor Statistics for 1936).

Table 38. LOCAL DIFFERENCES IN NONAGRICULTURAL RETAIL PRICES IN THE UNITED STATES AND CANADA, 1936

	a	b	c	d	e	f	g	h	i	k	l
Boston, Massachusetts.........	59	1.56	94	91	1.21	45		1.50	13	45	21.2
Portland, Maine...............	60	1.60	97	93	1.17	25	11.8	1.47	19	39	23.7
Buffalo, New York............	56	1.63	100	85	1.32	25	13.2	1.17	17	42	
New York City, New York.....	59	1.41	72	89	1.13	39	10.5	1.15	16	41	21.0
Philadelphia, Pennsylvania.....	56	1.38	80	66	1.13	30	12.6	1.10	16	42	19.8
Pittsburg, Pennsylvania........	58	1.56	89	74	1.16	32	13.8	1.21	16	46	20.7
Scranton, Pennsylvania........	57	1.56	69	68	1.23	40	9.5	1.30	15	41	20.9
Chicago, Illinois...............	58	1.34	67	73	1.15	36	11.0	1.40	14	56	19.8
Cincinnati, Ohio..............	55	1.75	69	89	1.13	33	10.8	1.29	15	44	19.0
Cleveland, Ohio...............	60	1.51	67	102	1.18	29	12.3	1.12	20	50	22.0
Detroit, Michigan.............	56	1.48	68	98	1.17	40	11.3	1.34	15	36	18.3
Indianapolis, Indiana..........	58	1.62	73	86	1.11	36	10.8	1.54	13	45	23.6
Kansas City, Kansas...........	73	1.99	89	83	1.15	24	13.1	1.16	12	29	19.7
Minneapolis, Minnesota.......	61	1.88	72	99	1.17	25	12.3	1.51	15	33	22.7
Saint Louis, Missouri..........	60	1.74	73	92	1.12	38	11.5	1.24	11	44	21.0
Baltimore, Maryland..........	57	1.53	65	88	1.28	39		1.12	16	39	20.7
Washington, D. C.............	58	1.68	68	96	1.18	35	12.2	1.25	17	37	26.8
Norfolk, Virginia..............	62	1.81	72	96	1.23	28	14.8	1.31	16	46	20.4
Richmond, Virginia...........	61	1.96	84	86	1.31	36	12.2	1.25	15	43	22.4
Atlanta, Georgia..............	68	1.65	68	74	1.20	20	13.7	1.18	13	34	27.9
Savannah, Georgia............	67	1.70	78	92	1.19	22	13.1	1.25	15	39	26.3
Jacksonville, Florida..........	63	1.51	72		1,05	28	12.9	1.31	10	32	27.8
Birmingham, Alabama........	68	1.66	70	69	1.10	24	12.3	1.15	11	46	24.2
Mobile, Alabama..............	64	1.86	67	60	1.14	24	12.4	1.36	11	28	22.6
New Orleans, Louisiana.......	47	1.96	71	76	1.17	32	9.0	1.23	13	33	24.1
Memphis, Tennessee..........	64	1.74	69	82	1.24	30	12.6	1.27	15	35	23.0
Houston, Texas...............	70	1.86	71	91	1.19	31	12.3	1.62	15	46	25.1
Denver, Colorado..............	66	1.73	74	101	1.25	31	11.6	1.55	16	32	22.5
Los Angeles, California........	54	1.68	71	86	1.16	39	15.1	1.22	15	40	19.1
San Francisco, California......	59	1.57	81	102	1.05	30	14.5	1.42	14	50	28.3
Portland, Oregon..............	59	1.83	67	94	1.05	33	13.3	1.49	20	44	22.7
Seattle, Washington...........	62	1.83	80	111	1.07	35	13.6	1.73	18	50	24.0
Montreal, Quebec.............	46	1.87	87	.	1.59	.	.	.	17	32	.
Toronto, Ontario..............	46	2.00	79	.	1.49	.	.	.	17	39	.
Winnipeg, Manitoba..........	55	2.00	117	.	1.59	.	.	.	18	.	.
Regina, Saskatchewan.........	47	2.00	.	.	1.68	.	.	.	15	35	.
Saskatoon, Saskatchewan......	51	2.00	150	.	1.49	.	.	.	15	.	.
Calgary, Alberta...............	44	2.18	97	.	1.43	.	.	.	16	35	.
Edmonton, Alberta............	50	2.00	100	.	1.52	.	.	.	15	35	.
Vancouver, Brit.-Columbia.....	47	2.25	79	.	1.44	.	.	.	16	36	.

a. Kitchen soap (U. S. A.) or laundry soap (Canada). Price for 10 cakes of 6 (U. S. A.) or 8 (Canada) ounces each in cents (less sales tax in U. S. A.). Other Canadian cities: Halifax, 51; St. John, 50; Quebec, 47; Kingston, Ont., 49; Port Arthur, 50; Nanaimo, B. C., 51; Prince Rupert, B. C., 52.

b. Men's cotton shirts with attached collars, medium quality (more detailed description added). In dollars less sales tax. The chief centers of production are New York, New Jersey, and Pennsylvania.

c. Cotton work shirts with collars (according to more detailed statement) in cents (less sales tax in U. S. A.). The Canadian surplus area is Quebec. In the United States production is divided especially among the original cotton belt, the Middle

West around Chicago, and Pennsylvania as well as Maryland. Other Canadian cities: Halifax, 96; Quebec, 87; Ottawa, 87.

d. Cotton union suits for men, summer weight, size 6. Price in July, 1936, in cents, inclusive of sales tax. The production center is the Pennsylvania area.

e. Bed sheets, 81 × 99 inches (according to more detailed statements). Price in dollars (less sales tax in U.S.A.). The states along the East Coast are the chief production area.

f. Motion pictures. Admission price for adults, weekdays, dress circle, in cents.

g. Glasses. Examination of eyes, frame, lenses. Price for the more popular of two varieties described in more detail, in dollars (less sales tax).

h. Resoling and heeling men's shoes. Sewed, best quality leather, well-known brand of heels, in dollars (less sales tax).

i. Laundering a man's shirt with collar. Price in cents. Other Canadian cities: Halifax, 17; St. John, 17; Charlottetown, 12; Quebec, 14; Lethbridge, Alba., 19; Nelson, B. C., 15; New Westminster, B. C., 15; Victoria, 19; Prince Rupert, B. C., 20.

k. Haircut. Adults, cents. Other Canadian cities: Halifax, 32; St. John, 28; Ottawa, 25; London, Ont., 35; Medicine Hat, Alba., 35; Nelson, B. C., 50; Trail, B. C., 50; Prince Rupert, B. C., 50; Victoria, 35.

l. Mattresses, according to more detailed statements. Price in dollars (less sales tax).

Sources: *United States.* Calculated by the author from original data of the Bureau of Labor Statistics, Retail Price Division (original data obtained by field surveys). *Canada.* Compiled by the author from original data of the Dominion Bureau of Statistics, Internal Trade Branch (original data through correspondence with the large department stores). Prices for work shirts come from a special inquiry of November 1, 1936, in which importance was attached in the United States to *comparable* qualities, whereas in Canada prices of the *most popular* qualities were entered.

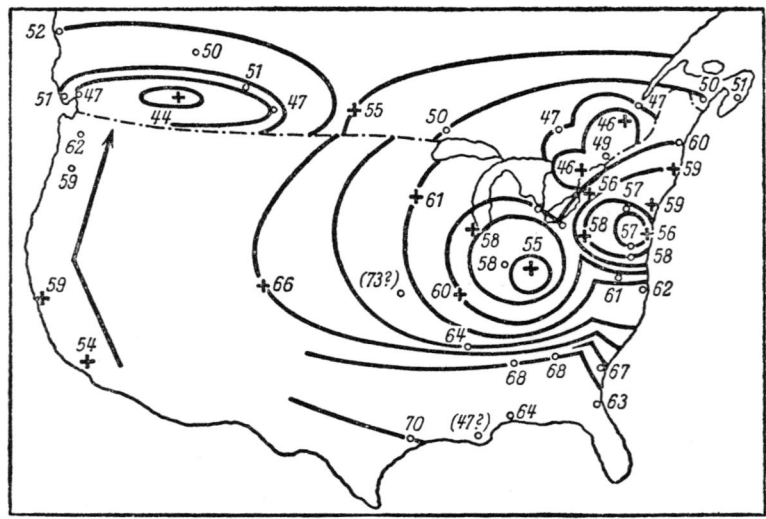

Fig. 99. Isotimes for soap, United States and Canada, 1936. + = important production centers. (Sources: see Table 38, column a and last footnote.)

the figures refer to another brand produced there, or whether the competition of this likewise important soap center lowered the price for the Cincinnati product also.

2. TEXTILES

In the case of textiles, which are expensive per unit of weight, distance would necessarily play a smaller role if freight rates were not considerably higher than they are for soap, say, if prompt delivery of seasonal and fashionable goods especially were not preferred, and if shipping distances were not often very long. Thus, in 1929 80 per cent of all men's shirts were made in the comparatively small area about New York City and Philadelphia. Prices increased definitely around this center, at least in the industrial belt, with the single exception of Chicago: Zone I (about $1.40): Philadelphia, New York; Zone II (about $1.55): Boston, Scranton, Pittsburgh, Cleveland, Detroit, Baltimore; Zone III (about $1.65): Portland, Maine, Buffalo, Indianapolis, Washington, D. C.; Zone IV (about $1.85): Cincinnati, Minneapolis, Richmond, Va., Norfolk. In Canada prices rose westward from Quebec, the chief center of production (Table 38, column *b*). For union suits, too, there are definite isotims about Philadelphia, the center of production, and about Chicago and Mobile. In the case last named I rather suspect that a lighter quality must be involved. In Canada pajamas are made almost exclusively around Montreal and in eastern Ontario. Quebec is the only surplus area, with an average price of $1.50.[64] The average price in the Atlantic provinces east of Quebec was $1.64; in the more westerly provinces, in order of their distance, it was: Ontario, $1.60; Manitoba, $1.67; Saskatchewan, $1.64; Alberta, $1.72; and British Columbia, $2.01. Prices rose similarly toward the north within the individual provinces.

For a few varieties of Canadian textiles such as bed sheets and work shirts one gets the impression from the inquiry of November 1, 1936, that prices do not rise steadily from the production centers in the East toward the West, but fall again from about the eastern edge of the Rocky Mountains to the Pacific Coast.[65] This observa-

---

64. For men's cotton pajamas. The prices refer to pajamas that were deliberately chosen because of their comparable quality (according to the Canadian special inquiry of November 1, 1936).

65. The same is true of cement, of which British Columbia imports a rather large amount by rail. (*Economic Council of British Columbia, The Trade of British Columbia with Other Canadian Provinces and with Foreign countries, 1935* [Victoria, 1937], p. 97.) In 1933 a 350-pound barrel of Portland cement cost at wholesale in the following cities, arranged in order from east to west: Montreal, $1.70; Toronto, $2.10; Winnipeg, $2.68; Regina, $3.35; Vancouver, $2.60. (*Dominion Bureau of Statistics, Prices and Price Indexes, 1913–33* [Ottawa, 1934], p. 74.) The wholesale price of gasoline increased similarly in 1933 from 16.8 cents a gallon in Montreal to 23.8 cents

tion, if accurate, could easily be explained. For example, it costs $4.54 to ship a hundredweight of bed sheets from Montreal, the chief production center, to Calgary, 2,240 miles distant and just east of the Rockies. But if it is shipped farther on to Vancouver (2,880 miles), the freight for the entire stretch from Montreal to Vancouver falls to only $3.27 because of the competing water route.[66] As a second factor there may be added more the risk than the volume of cheap imports from China, just as on the Atlantic Coast of the United States certain products are especially cheap because of European competition.[67]

c. COST OF LIVING[68]

§1. GENERAL PRINCIPLES

For practical reasons, indices of living costs are generally calculated by determining from time to time the total cost of a constant aggregate of goods and services (the method of Lowe or Laspeyres). If this collection were representative—that is, if it consisted of the typical total requirements of every individual member of a group according to economic landscape, category, occupation, income, and size of family for similar persons—the method might be considered meaningful. But there still remains the difficulty that an aggregate of needs can be typical only of the period for which it was estab-

---

in Regina, and fell again toward the west to 20.2 cents in Vancouver (*ibid.*, p. 72). With eggs the situation was exactly reversed, because Saskatchewan is the most important surplus region. The average price of a dozen eggs of the highest grade was 18.2 cents in Saskatoon in 1933. From there the price rose toward the east and west to 24.5 cents in Vancouver and 28 cents in Montreal (*ibid.*, p. 57).

66. Western railway freights dropped similarly in the United States until 1916. (A. Predöhl, " Die örtliche Verteilung der amerikanischen Eisen- und Stahlindustrie," *Weltwirtschaftliches Archiv*, XXVII [1829], 279.)

67. For instance, in so far as freight plays a role, northern Europe can compete easily in New York with Pittsburgh in the case of pig iron, since the railway freight from Pittsburgh amounts to about twice the ocean freight from Europe. (L. B. Zapoleon, " International and Domestic Commodities and the Theory of Prices," *Quarterly Journal of Economics*, XLV (1931), 442.) Furthermore, an iron industry has developed in the seaports of the East Coast that uses foreign ores exclusively from the shores of the Atlantic Ocean. (A. Rühl, " Zur Frage der internationalen Arbeitsteilung. Eine statistische Studie auf Grund der Einfuhr der Vereinigten Staaten von Amerika," *Vierteljahrshefte zur Konjunkturforschung*, Sonderheft 25 [Berlin, 1932], pp. 10, 26). The East Coast belongs in part to the market area of northwest Europe for Portland cement also (*ibid.*, p. 28).

68. For the sake of argument it will be assumed at first that there are such things as " utilities," and that in principle they can be measured. The reader will recall from Part III that I share neither view.

lished, which, however, for technical reasons generally lies far in the past. This is not a disadvantage if only the price *level* moves; that is, if every price changes in the same direction. If, for example, all prices rise by 10 per cent, the total needs also will rise by 10 per cent. Those who cannot afford to spend more will therefore get fewer goods, though it cannot be said how many fewer because their decreased purchasing power affects different goods differently. The aggregate of needs will be reduced unequally. It also will provide a smaller total utility, whose decrease, however, must be less than 10 per cent, according to Gossen's law—as, conversely, a deflation of 10 per cent increases the utilities of those with fixed incomes by less than 10 per cent.

It is different when the index has gone up because the price *system* has been dislocated, some prices having risen whereas others have fallen. More of the cheaper and fewer of the dearer goods will now be bought. The typical aggregate changes, but without anyone being able to say that either it or the utilities it provides have increased or decreased. Cases can be imagined in which a " *drop* in real wages," calculated in the usual way, may actually mean an increase in utilities. On the other hand, a *rise* in real wages, similarly calculated, is actual in every case, for if one still wished to do so one could buy the same things with less money than before.

Hence the Laspeyres index may be relied upon to show a rise in the standard of living, but not a fall. Conversely, the Paasche index, based on the typical aggregate of goods and services for the given rather than the base year, is dependable in case of a fall, not a rise, in real wages. From this G. v. Haberler concluded in his thoroughgoing analysis (*Der Sinn der Indexzahlen* [Tübingen, 1927]) that a combination of these two indices, as in Irving Fischer's " ideal formula," would necessarily decrease the error. But of course only the degree of uncertainty, not the fact of uncertainty, would be altered. Even the ideal formula definitely shows a change in living costs (in direction, not extent) only when the result agrees with that of each of the two component formulas.[68] To publish only the result of the ideal formula without the results of the two component formulas is worse than simply to calculate the index from one of them alone. This would give an accurate result in some cases at least, whereas the ideal formula by itself alone is always uncertain.

69. The third case, in which the Laspeyres index of living costs falls whereas the Paasche index rises, is certainly impossible. The fourth, in which the Laspeyres index rises whereas the Paasche index falls, remains possible, uncertain, but especially important.

The procedure is the same when living costs are to be compared in space instead of in time. For instance, if it is desired to compare a German with an American economic landscape—Württemberg, say, with New England—it must first be established what the aggregate needs typical of Swabians at home would cost in New England (Laspeyres' formula). Even this is not easy, because many typical Swabian goods are simply not to be had in the United States. Hence one must compute, when possible, how much they would cost if they were to be imported from the homeland. If the cost of living index falls despite this, it is well.[70] But if it rises, as it usually will, one must calculate next the cost in Württemberg and New England of the aggregate needs, not of a New Englander, but of a typical Swabian living in New England and enjoying the same nominal income (Paasche's formula). If this index also rises it is certain beyond any doubt that living costs for a Swabian in the United States are higher than at home.[70] But if both indices change in a different direction, as they generally will—that is, if the aggregate needs of a Swabian living abroad are more expensive at home, and those of a Swabian living in the homeland more expensive abroad—this question must remain *objectively* unanswered.

The individual Swabian, on the other hand, may know very clearly where he requires more money in order to live equally well. This tempts even the statistician to measure at least *subjectively* what cannot be compared objectively. (*a*) He can either determine what aggregate needs most Swabians in the United States regard as equal to those customary at home. (*b*) Or he can decide for himself which aggregates are held to be equivalent. Here he may start with requirements at home, and substitute only what is not to be had in the United States. (*c*) Or he may assemble an entirely new aggregate of goods that is adapted to American conditions.

§2. Statistics

α) *Subjective Comparisons:* The Reich Statistical Bureau (Director Jacobs) compared the living costs for German officials abroad by methods *a* or *b*, and the International Labor Office established for 14 European cities by methods *b* or *c* the costs of living that correspond to those of a worker in Detroit.[71] As it was soon found that many articles bought by the Detroit worker were not obtainable

---

70. Except when the same aggregate provides a different utility in the United States.

71. *Internationales Arbeitsamt, Beitrag zur Frage der internationalen Gegenüberstellung der Lebenshaltungskosten* (Geneva, 1933). (The so-called Ford Inquiry.)

in Europe, an aggregate of local needs equivalent in the opinion of the investigators, was substituted. Interlocal differences in costs as great as 80 per cent were found, those in Detroit being that much higher than those in Barcelona (*ibid.*, p. 33).

β) *Objective Comparisons:* So far as I am aware no interlocal comparison of living costs has been carried out according to the correct principles developed above. On the other hand, the WPA endeavored to discover the cost of the same aggregate of needs in all parts of the United States. Yet despite the rather uniform conditions in America the attempt succeeded only with important limitations. The need for fuel, ice, and transport facilities was determined locally, and in addition there remained significant qualitative differences, no matter how great the effort to avoid them. Washington was found to be the most expensive city, its living costs being 25 per cent above those in Mobile, on the Gulf Coast, which was the cheapest. The range in the price of food was only 17 per cent;[72] for housing, where local conditions and difficulties in comparison play an important role, it was 125 per cent. These figures are interesting, even though they do not measure differences in the cost of living as they were intended to do, but represent simply an interlocal price comparison—a comparison not of different prices for one product, which often vary considerably, but of the much more nearly equal costs of a group of products. The error sets in only where a special significance is attributed to this group of commodities; that is, by regarding it as representative of the American standard of living. Regional differences are not so small, even in the United States, that this has meaning for interlocal comparisons.[73]

---

72. This is strikingly small, contrasted with the fact that for Germany the Institut für Konjunkturforschung found, by a procedure that methodologically was not entirely satisfactory, however, the price level for the most important foods in Saxony to be one third above that in East Prussia. ("Materialien zur Frage der regionalen Preisunterschiede und ihrer Bedeutung für die Lebenshaltung," *Vierteljahrshefte zur Konjunkturforschung,* Vol. X, Heft 3B (1935), pp. 185–189.) Nevertheless it was true of Germany also that in the case of the main expenditure category (food) the price differences, and in the case of wide price differences (rent, heat) the expenditures, were not so great (see, for example, *Arbeitswissenschaftliches Institut, Jahrbuch,* 1937, p. 86).

73. How differently regional variations may be viewed according to income level is illustrated by a little incident. I asked the American Consul in Vancouver (Canada) whether it or the neighboring American city of Seattle seemed more expensive. He found Seattle cheaper, an opinion that was contradicted by his secretary. He was thinking of such things as automobiles and gasoline, which cost more in Vancouver by a good third, as well as of many other nonagricultural products, whereas she naturally had in mind her principal expenses, food and housing.

Occasionally such a method is justified by asserting that with sufficiently small chronological or geographical intervals the aggregate of needs is hardly changed, and that a useful series of indices can therefore be obtained by the chain method. But with small intervals either price differences also are small, and hence exactly as much affected by slight errors in the aggregate of needs; or price differences are wide, in which case changes in this aggregate cannot be small, except with deflation or inflation.

The Arbeitswissenschaftliche Institut (*Jahrbuch,* II (1938), 26 ff.) ascertained for 9,000 places the prices of goods of a quality usually found in each (!), added the unweighted figures (!) [74] separately for food, light, and heat, weighted only these three groups among themselves with constant (!) weights, and took the result to be interlocally comparable indices of living costs. Wrongly, since according to this method living costs may be greater not only where prices are high, but also where people live extravagantly because they buy a better quality of product. At best, only the indices for housing are usable.

In 1938 the International Labor Office compared the retail prices for 19 articles of food in the capitals or principal cities of 25 countries and assembled them in eighteen groups, for each of which the same aggregate of goods was taken as a basis; for example, Group III, Germany, Holland, Belgium, and, earlier, Czechoslovakia (see *Jahrbuch,* 1941, pp. 152–153, 162–164). A good feature of the investigation is that both the Paasche and the Laspeyres indices were calculated for each pair of countries, since according to what has been said above it would be a pity to publish only the geometrical mean. In addition, the comparison was supposed to hold for incommensurable types of people, instead of for the same type in both countries. As for the restriction to international foods, see the end of footnote 74 (above).

Finally, there remains to be mentioned the most serious argu-

---

74. The weights would have to be very different. For example, in 1927–28 families of equal size and with equal incomes consumed: in Brandenburg, 7,820 calories daily; in Nordmark, 9,323; in southwest Germany, 11 pounds of fish yearly; in Pomerania, a little over 114 pounds; in Bavaria, 583 pounds of bread yearly, in Pomerania, 911 pounds, and also 618 and 1,976 pounds of potatoes respectively. (" Unterschiede im Nahrungsmittelverbrauch der deutschen Wirtschaftsgebiete," *Institut für Konjunkturforschung, Wochenbericht,* 1937, pp. 162–166.) In 1937 the Schleswig-Holstein household smoked 87 cigars, 350 cigarettes, and $5\frac{1}{4}$ pounds of tobacco; the Berlin household, 141, 1,421, and $1\frac{1}{2}$ respectively. (*Arbeitswissenschaftliches Institut, Jahrbuch,* II (1939), p. 45.) To limit oneself to the part of consumption that is common to all places objectively or by subjective substitution is to eliminate precisely the most variable peak requirement (in reply to Keynes, *Treatise on Money,* 1930, I, 105 ff.).

ment against all objective comparisons of living standards: the aggregate of needs varies not only with changes in relative prices, but also independently with changes in time and place.[75] No objectice index can take account of these variations. Every index is either subjective or an unrealistic static construction that becomes less reliable the further one departs from its foundations. Such a construction is better employed as an index of living standards than of real wages, and better as a price index than as an index of living standards.[76] But is loss of the measure so unfortunate when the object to be measured itself evaporates? When the concept of utility is revealed as but a vague word after all?

75. People drink more in the South, even though drinking is not cheaper there. In the country one raises one's own vegetables at small expense, so that the market price becomes irrelevant (Rompe). As far as drinking is concerned, life is more expensive in the South than in the North, even with equal prices, and in the North cheaper in the country than in the city (see p.492, note 70.).

76. Even though the index of real wages, too, is meaningless, scientifically speaking, nevertheless in countries that are changing over from a free to a planned economy and thus experiencing labor troubles, it fulfills a social function similar to that of the entrails of sacrificial animals in antiquity: it guides decisions on war and peace.

Chapter 27. Price Changes in Space

a. SPATIAL DIFFERENCES IN THE MOVEMENT OF COMMODITY PRICES

At the time of their great traditional football game, which is regarded by high and low as an event of extraordinary importance and every year attracts from the surrounding country many times the population of the little place, I found myself in a small American university town. Prices rose temporarily with the transitory increase in demand, the cost of a night's stay, of refreshments, of having one's shoes shined, and so on, suddenly doubling. Although we observe this sort of thing again and again it has not yet received the attention necessary. Incorrectly, under the influence of the prevailing theory of foreign trade and because of a lack of regional statistics, a national average of price movements passes as an adequate description of what happens. In a few cases and for a few purposes this may be justified. But, as the following examples will show, the differences between economic landscapes within a country and similarities in the price movements of economically related parts of different countries are generally too impressive to be disregarded. The proof of such differences and similarities constitutes the concluding part of our entire system.

§1. DIFFERENCES DUE TO REGIONAL BUSINESS CYCLES

Schäffle wrote of the business crisis of 1857: " With devastating force the avalanche [at the end of August] raced unchecked from the banks of the Ohio . . . toward the East . . . to descend after a mightly leap across the ocean [at the end of October] upon England and to overrun the Continent of Europe [Hamburg in the middle of November] as far as the plains about the Baltic Sea."[1] Business indices in Iowa, available for even small districts, show clearly how the great depression gradually advanced between the end of 1929 and the beginning of 1931 from the eastern to the western border of the state (see Fig. 100). The progress of business cycles was surprisingly slow, a little over half a mile daily on the average. At the

---

1. *Gesammelte Aufsätze,* II, 23–24, 42.

Price Changes in Space

Fig. 100. Westward movement of the depression in Iowa, 1929–31. The figure gives indices of business activity for ten counties in the state, whose position, like that of Chicago, the nearest focus of disturbance, appears on the map. (Assembled by the author from *Iowa State Planning Board, Second Report,* 1935, pp. 194 f.) The depression period is indicated by heavy lines. In correspondence with the west-east course of the main traffic routes, the depression spread most rapidly in this direction. The economic center of the region, in District 5, was relatively soon affected by these influences from without, as would be theoretically expected.

end of 1937 consciousness, or even signs, of the business recession were hardly noticeable in distant parts of the United States; Texas, for instance, whereas it still continued its full course in the East, near the center of political unrest. Similarly, the last upswing in South Wales progressed but slowly from the coastal towns up the long valleys of the depressed area (*Economist,* October 30, 1937, pp. 199 f.). In short, business cycles differ geographically in their timing and amplitude, and these differences are reflected in price movements also. Thus during the last great depression prices of the most important foodstuffs fell from 1927–28 to 1932 by 30 per cent in Essen, at the heart of the most severely affected Ruhr district, but in Stuttgart, the center of the least affected economic landscape, by only 21 per cent. Conversely, the following upswing affected the area of heavy industry more strongly, and from 1932 to 1935 drove prices upward by 4.6 per cent as compared with only 0.7 per cent in Stuttgart.[2]

A comparison of American cities in different economic landscapes with one another, and with neighboring Canadian cities of similar character, is especially interesting (Table 39). First, a nationwide movement of prices appears in the effects of currency devaluation. As this was not forced by the foreign exchange situation, it resulted in a national tendency toward higher prices. Table 40, calculated from Table 39, compares the price level before and after devaluation, which in Canada occurred at the end of 1931, and in the United States at the beginning of 1933. After the Canadian devaluation prices fell less in Canada than in the United States, and after the American devaluation they rose more in the United States than in Canada. The few exceptions are limited to rent, which lags because at first it is purely locally determined,[3] and influenced only indirectly by a change in foreign demand. As the Canadian devaluation took place before, and the American devaluation at the turning point, American prices fell on the whole more than Canadian prices.

The same regional differences appear on both sides of the international boundary. Take rents, for example. As a consequence of the disturbance in world trade they fell at the beginning of the World War I in the seaports, Seattle and Vancouver, whereas they rose in automobile and other industrial cities. See Table 39 in connection with the following remarks. After the war, prices reached

---

2. " Materialien zur Frage der regionalen Preisunterschiede und ihrer Bedeutung für die Lebenshaltung," *Vierteljahrshefte zur Konjunkturforschung,* XX, Heft 3B (1935), pp. 188 f.

3. The smaller the market areas for a product, the more slowly do price movements advance.

Price Changes in Space

Table 39. COMPARISON OF PRICE MOVEMENTS ON
THE AMERICAN-CANADIAN BORDER

	Food							Rents						
	Industrial cities			Seaports		Automobile cities		Industrial cities			Seaports		Automobile cities	
	Buffalo	Hamilton	Toronto	Seattle	Vancouver	Detroit	Windsor	Buffalo	Hamilton	Toronto	Seattle	Vancouver	Detroit	Windsor
1915	102	102	102	98	.	104	101	101	100	94	98	84	102	100
1916	126	117	125	108	.	124	116	105	102	102	95	79	117	104
1917	161	150	162	137	.	156	151	109	112	122	99	91	133	109
1918	188	167	180	173	.	182	170	121	119	132	144	126	139	117
1919	193	172	188	181	.	195	181	128	130	147	161	158	153	128
1920	208	204	216	195	200	211	216	147	151	166	176	188	188	144
1921	152	159	163	139	151	149	161	161	165	178	172	201	196	156
1922	152	136	139	142	131	149	136	165	172	188	164	200	189	154
1923	156	138	144	143	129	144	132	171	176	191	163	190	202	160
1924	154	135	140	145	129	151	130	176	176	190	164	191	205	166
1925	172	148	147	158	141	171	136	179	171	181	164	192	198	169
1926	176	152	157	152	141	172	147	178	165	174	161	193	195	169
1927	171	147	153	151	140	170	142	175	165	171	158	192	187	169
1928	165	141	147	145	135	159	137	173	164	171	155	190	179	162
	163	153	152	146	141	159	144	169	164	171	154	190	178	162
1929	167	144	147	150	142	166	142	167	165	173	152	189	177	163
	169	157	161	152	151	164	149	166	165	173	152	189	178	163
1930	162	145	153	150	144	157	138	165	171	176	150	189	173	161
	144	130	141	126	124	138	126	162	171	176	148	189	160	161
1931	126	110	116	118	105	121	101	156	171	177	144	178	145	158
	112	106	113	112	98	111	95	150	173	177	137	178	131	158
1932	110	91	96	102	89	98	81	140	173	162	125	152	118	126
	103	99	101	96	90	91	84	129	159	156	115	152	101	105
1933	104	94	98	100	91	96	84	120	144	145	108	130	89	105
	109	100	105	100	95	105	89	115	144	145	103	126	84	92
1934	117	101	108	103	97	115	90	113	144	150	100	120	86	98
	116	102	108	110	97	112	93	112	147	156	99	120	93	98
1935	126	103	109	117	96	123	95	112	147	156	99	120	96	98
	129	101	107	115	99	126	93	112	147	163	100	124	100	105
	125	108	113	113	103	124	99	113	159	163	101	124	109	113
1936	129	111	118	119	104	127	101	113	159	163	101	124	111	113
	125	106	113	116	99	124	94	114	159	163	102	124	114	113
	137	108	114	121	106	133	99	117	167	163	103	130	116	113
	130	113	117	120	109	133	105	117	167	163	105	130	117	113
	130	113	116	121	109	128	103	118	170	172	107	146	125	117
1937	134	112	120	130	114	134	104	119	170	172	108	146	127	117
	139	115	120	127	114	139	103	126	173	179	109	152	131	117

Basis: U. S. A., December, 1914 = 100. Canada, 1914–15 = 100.

Sources: U. S. A., *Bureau of Labor Statistics, Changes in Costs of Living,* Washington. Canada, Department of Labour. The Canadian figures, published here for the first time, were kindly placed at my disposal by Mr. C. W. Bolton, the director.

The figures for 1928–1933 apply to June and December; for 1934 to June and November; for 1935 to March, July, and October; for 1936 to January, April, July, September, and December; for 1937 to March and June.

Table 40

	National Price Increase after Devaluation of the Currency in			
	Canada		U. S. A.	
	Price level, December, 1932 (June, 1931 = 100)		Price level, June, 1934 (December, 1932 = 100)	
	Food	Rent	Food	Rent
Buffalo, U. S. A.........	82	83	114	87
	∧	∧	∨	∧
Hamilton, Canada.......	90	93	102	91
Toronto, Canada........	87	90	106	96
Seattle, U. S. A..........	75	80	108	87
	∧	∧	∨	∨
Vancouver, Canada......	84	86	108	79
Detroit, U. S. A..........	81	70	127	85
	∧	∨	∨	∧
Windsor, Canada........	86	67	107	94

their peaks in the seaports between the end of 1920 and the middle of 1921, and in the automobile and other industrial cities from the middle of 1923 to the end of 1925. The great depression reached its trough in the automobile cities toward the end of 1933, but in the two seaports mentioned, not until the beginning of 1935.

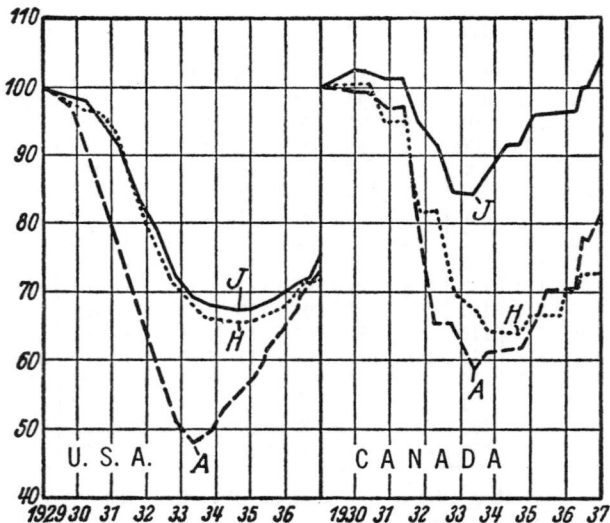

Fig. 101. Comparison of house rents in the United States and Canada, 1929–37. J: Buffalo or Toronto. H: Seattle or Vancouver. A: Detroit or Windsor. (Based on Table 39.)

Rents dropped in both countries, most in the automobile cities, which are especially sensitive to business conditions, and later increased most there; they fell less in the seaports, and least in the other industrial cities (Fig. 101). The similarities in the developments in neighboring cities of different countries, and the differences between distant cities in the same country, are striking. Besides their geographical proximity, the parallelism of the developments is certainly due also to the fact that we are dealing with cities of similar economic character. But it must not be overlooked here that this very character itself is decisively formed by their similar geographic situation.

§2. Differential Price Movements Caused by Regional Changes in Structure

We have already discussed the fantastic price increases that accompany a gold rush in regions where the presence of deposits is suspected. Its opposite can be observed today in chronically depressed areas, though as a consequence of stupid adherence to the customary national wage scale unemployment often takes the place of a fall in prices.[4] If the pressure on prices here is caused by the removal of locations away *from* the depressed area, in another case it depends conversely upon the removal of locations *to* the area concerned: when the area develops from an importing to an exporting region. Thus wheat prices in Idaho during the 1880's, when it still imported wheat, were above the average for the United States; but before World War I, when Idaho had already become a surplus region far from its market, they were below this average.[5]

An excellent example of regional shifts in price levels is furnished by the price changes in the southern and northern parts of the United States that accompany alterations in the tariff policy. The prices of nonagricultural goods and of cotton are taken as representative of the North and the South respectively. The proportion of tariff receipts to dutiable imports is an adequate yardstick of tariff policy. During the protectionism that prevailed until 1830 this proportion rose. Then, under the attacks of the South, the tariff was lowered, with a negligible interruption in the 1840's, until the lowest rates since 1816 were reached, just before the Civil

---

4. For Great Britain see J. Uhlig, "Die Notstandsgebiete Grossbritanniens," *Wirtschaftskurve*, 1938, p. 75.

5. See Zapoleon's diagram, *Geography of Wheat Prices, U. S. Department of Agriculture Bulletin*, No. 594 (Washington, 1918), p. 25.

War.[6] Curve *b* (Fig. 102) sinks accordingly from 1830 to 1861. From the latter date onward, duties began to rise again, with a few unimportant reversals after 1872 and 1894, until the opening of the century. The greatest increases took place during the Civil

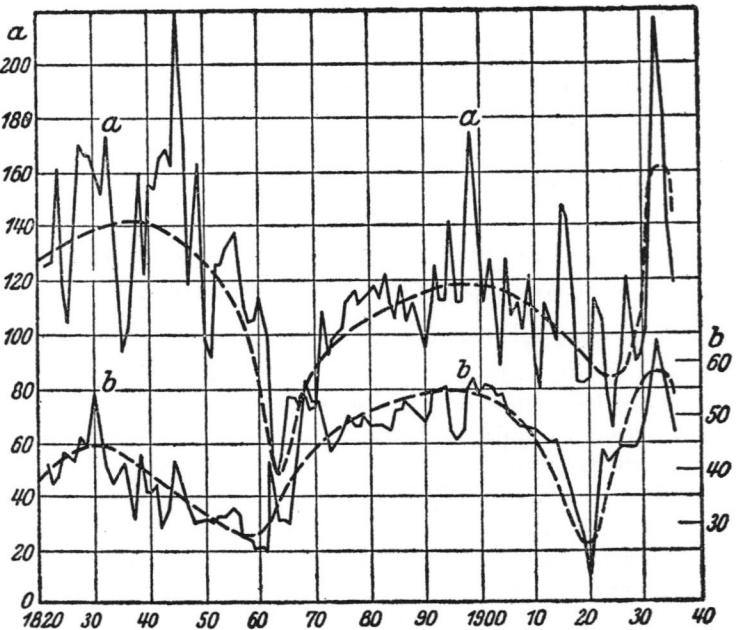

Fig. 102. The ratio of price levels in the North and South in the United States and its dependence upon tariff policy, 1820–1935. *a*) Level of American industrial prices (L. Myers and M. R. Cooper, *Cotton Statistics and Related Data* [Washington, Department of Agriculture, 1932], pp. 3–5) relative to the price of middling upland cotton in New York (pp. 7–9. The 1861 ratio is set at 100. *b*) Customs receipts as percentages of dutiable imports. (*Statistical Abstract of the United States*, 1891, pp. 15 ff.; 1936, p. 436).

War years, partly because tariff revenues had decreased in consequence of the preceding depression, and partly because Government expenditures had increased enormously. This period, too, is well characterized by curve *b*. The fall between 1900 and 1920 was caused, in addition to the relaxing of the protective tariff—particularly in 1913, by special conditions associated with World War I and by the fact that after the tariff increases of 1897 many rates were

---

6. The energy of the protectionists was weakened because most of the infant industry tariffs had fulfilled their purpose in the meantime. (See F. W. Taussig, *The Tariff History of the United States* [New York, 1922].)

prohibitive and thus for lack of imports are no longer expressed in the curve. After World War I duties were raised again in a new wave of protectionism, especially in 1922 and 1930. Little as the smaller fluctuations in curve b need depend upon changes in the tariff, the curve obviously reflects well the main developmental tendencies of the tariff policy.

Comparison of curves a and b shows on the whole a remarkably close parallel movement, particularly for the larger tendencies. After a short lag, the price ratio changed in favor of the South, which depended on exports, when the tariffs that protected the North were lowered, and grew worse when they were raised. The Civil War marks one of the most pronounced turning points. In the period preceding its outbreak a closer and closer approach to free trade raised prices in the South as compared with the North. The free-trade southern states fought on this point also for real economic interests, and from this side, too, their defeat meant at first a real economic disadvantage. In time, of course, these wounds began to heal at the expense of the victor. The cheaper conditions in the South, due in part though not entirely to the protectionist tariff policy, attracted northern industry. What irony of fate! The northerners were intent only on protecting their industry from foreign competitors,[7] and when they succeeded in this after a bitter struggle and at the expense of the South, the South lured away a large part of their laboriously protected industry!

The industry of New England was intent only on erecting a high tariff wall, without realizing that behind such a wall violent changes in location would necessarily take place—to its disadvantage. Regions threatened by imports are not merely protected by a tariff; they are also made more expensive, and therefore less favorable locations than those parts of the country that depend on exports and have to make up for their lessened chances of exporting, brought about through the tariff, by lowering prices. Thus before the Civil War the cotton industry of the South was insignificant absolutely, and declining in addition. After the war and up to the turn of the century, that is until the protective tariff reached its then highest point, cotton spinning and weaving mills moved from the North to the cheaper South at a constantly increasing rate.[8] From 1850 to

7. However, the Northeast is protected against the rest of the United States by freight rates that favor it, particularly as against the South. But this artificial protection by freight rates was less than the tariff protection.

8. In 1859 the average wage of the industrial worker in the South was only 12 per cent under the wages in the North, but in 1869 it was 45 per cent below these. (C. Heer,

1860 the share of the states south of Virginia in the total production of cotton goods had further decreased by 53 per cent; in the decade 1860–1870 it rose by 15 per cent, in the decade 1870–1880 by 36 per cent, in 1880–1890 by 70 per cent, and in 1890–1900 by nearly 100 per cent. In the following period, up to 1920, the price level in the South rose in comparison with the North, as we have already seen; and wages especially increased more in the South than in the North; the rate of growth of the southern cotton industry fell correspondingly to 35 per cent between 1900 and 1910 and to 34 per cent from 1910 to 1920. After World War I there were fresh orgies of tariff protection (1922 and 1930), the South became cheaper, and the rate of growth jumped back again to 41 per cent between 1920 and 1930.

This interpretation is strengthened by the development of wages and cost of living. If the 1901 level is set at 100, the wages of cotton workers in 1920–21 [9] at 335, were higher than those of industrial workers, at 315.[10] From 1922 onward they dropped below these until, in 1932–33, the levels were 106 and 245 respectively. Thereafter they rose again more sharply (up to 1934–35 by 18 per cent as compared with 13 per cent). At the end of 1920 living costs in five cities of the Northeast whose records go back furthest (Boston, Portland, Buffalo, New York, Philadelphia) were 95 per cent above the level of December, 1914, and in five southern cities (Jacksonville, Norfolk, Sanvannah, Mobile, Houston) 98 per cent. Conversely, in the period of rising tariffs (1920–1932) living costs in the Northeast fell by only 30 per cent, and in the South by 37 per cent. From the middle of 1933 to the end of 1936 duties fell again, and living costs in the South went up by 11.7 per cent and in the Northeast by only 9.1 per cent.[11]

Incomes and Wages in the South [Chapel Hill, 1930], p. 25.) The difference is less for strictly comparable labor, to be sure, and particularly is it less for skilled labor than for unskilled.

9. L. Myers and M. R. Cooper, *Cotton Statistics and Related Data* (U. S. Department of Agriculture, Washington, 1932), p. 95.

10. *U. S. Statistical Abstract*, 1936, p. 312.

11. Calculated from *U. S. Bureau of Labor Statistics, Changes in Costs of Living* (Washington). After what has been said it is not surprising that regionalism, which arises everywhere, even in England and especially in France, should be so strong in the American South, with its vivid memories, its great poverty, and its wide possibilities. Hardly anywhere else does one encounter a more lively interest in regional investigation. Among the many scholars we can mention only H. W. Odum (*Southern Regions of the United States* [Chapel Hill, 1936]) and R. B. Vance (*Human Geography of the South* [Chapel Hill, 1935]). P. Molyneaux (*What Economic Nationalism Means to the South*, World Affairs Pamphlet, No. 4 [Boston, 1934]) has worked out the effects of

b. SPATIAL DIFFERENCES IN THE MOVEMENT OF INTEREST

On October 30, 1929, the average rate for bank credits (customers' rate) in New York was 6.08 per cent; in eight other cities of the Northeast, 6.25 per cent; and in twenty-seven western or southern cities, 6.29 per cent. From November, 1927, up to the date mentioned it rose by 1.73, 1.43, and 0.73 per cent, and then fell until the end of September, 1931, by 2.15, 1.77, and 0.97 per cent. These figures are typical. The cyclical fluctuations are regularly greatest in New York, the chief financial center, and least in regions that are poor in capital. The result, as can be seen above, is that geographic differences in interest are least at the end of a boom and greatest during the downswing.[12] The following table corroborates this. The yearly averages of interest rates for bank credits

| 1: | 5.88 | 5.19 | 5.15 | 4.69 | 4.67 | 4.60 | 4.53 | 4.49 | 4.47 | 4.22 | 4.02 | 3.33 | 2.70 |
| 2: | 0.26 | 0.75 | 0.55 | 1.03 | 0.94 | 1.11 | 1.07 | 1.13 | 1.11 | 1.17 | 1.54 | 1.84 | 1.99 |

in New York from 1923 to 1935 are arranged in row 1 according to magnitude. Row 2 shows by how much these rates were absolutely below those of twenty-seven financial centers in the South and West.[13]

The explanation is simple: the more member banks have to rely on their Reserve Banks, and the more the Reserve Banks have to rely on the Federal Reserve Bank of New York, the more uniform will be the rates; the tighter the reserve position of banks throughout the rest of the country becomes, the more reserves and surplus liquid funds must they withdraw from New York. In times of plentiful money New York absorbs these excess liquid funds from

---

the tariff policy rather well in popular form. But I do not wish to give the impression of attributing all the poverty of the South to this. The most potent single cause of its condition, of which the tariff policy is only a part, appears to me rather to be its defeat in the Civil War, which destroyed both its abundance and its self-confidence.

12. Similarly, with constant freight rates, fluctuations in commodity prices are greatest percentagewise at the center of production, and decrease toward the edge of the market area. (Where competition prevails or the demand is very elastic producers' prices, contrary to the ruling opinion, are especially flexible precisely *because* of high fixed costs, since if necessary they can fall as low as the relatively insignificant variable costs.) In Tsarist Russia the wages of agricultural laborers seasonally fluctuated most in regions of inward migratons—thus again in central markets. (G. Pavlovsky, " Zur Frage der räumlichen Ordnung der Landwirtschaft," *Internationale Landwirtschaftliche Rundschau*, Vol. I, No. 33 [1942], p. 357.)

13. *Annual Report of the Federal Reserve Board* (Washington, various years).

everywhere (which depresses its interest rate to an especially low level), but helps out everywhere when money is scarce (hence the more than average increase of its interest rate). The higher the interest rate structure as a whole, the less important the costs of distance become. This explains also the observation that the small country banks change their interest rate on local loans less frequently.

The same thing is true of the discount rate of the Reserve Banks. In July, 1928, for example, when the most frequent rate was 5 per cent, the regional spread amounted to but 0.5 per cent. By May, 1931, the most frequent rate had fallen to 3 per cent, and at the same time the regional spread had gradually risen to 2 per cent. Nevertheless, and especially after what we have said about the slight connection between American discount rates and market rates, it is pertinent to ask whether they really play the same role as the discount rates of European central banks, say, in facilitating transfers.

To anticipate: Despite the similarity in technical function between the Federal Reserve Banks and the European central banks, disturbances in the balances of payments between Federal Reserve districts in the United States are more easily overcome than corresponding disturbances between the countries of Europe. The causes lie partly in the political unity of the United States, and partly in its special history. Its enormous gold holdings, which it owes to its position as creditor nation, to its protective tariff, and to its policy of gold sterilization (and thus, among other things, to the desire to minimize the effect of international payments on American prices) permits internal payment also to be made without any great shifts in relative price levels. The gold reserves of the Reserve Banks far exceed the legal minimum, so that transfer of gold between them is generally possible without reaction on the circulation of notes or on the credit structure. Furthermore, the legal gold reserve in itself is already high, which, as we have seen, mitigates price movements at first at the expense of gold movements, even with full utilization of the gold reserve. But even if the point is reached where a Reserve Bank has lost so much gold to foreign countries or to other parts of the United States [14] that a European Central Bank would be *forced*

---

14. Generally no gold is actually shipped; deposits in the Interdistrict Settlement Fund are merely transferred. International gold shipments, too, could be made unnecessary in the same way and, finally, expensive hoards of monetary gold could be abolished and replaced by credits in an international clearing house, such as London was before World War I. (A. Lösch, " Verrechnung und Goldwährung—ein Vergleich," *Die Bank,* August 21, 1940.) The gold points would thereupon coincide and there would be practically no further scope for fluctuations in the rate of exchange, just as today the price for payments between any given place in the United States is the same.

to raise the discount rate under similar circumstances, the Federal Reserve Bank can still avoid this. For it can easily force credit movements in its favor, partly by disposing of government securities (that is, so to speak, "foreign assets") in the districts of other Reserve Banks, and partly by rediscounting bills of exchange with other Reserve Banks and thus, as it were, forcing credits in its favor.[15] Only when even this does not suffice must it fall back upon a change in the discount rate as a last resort. On the whole, however, discount policy in the United States is intended more to influence business conditions than to facilitate transfer, but without, even in this respect, playing the same role as in Europe. It is less the construction of the currency than actual conditions that create these differences.

One road is closed to the Reserve Banks, however, when they have to make interregional payments, and it is important to note this. They cannot pay with their own notes beyond the bounds of their own districts. If this were allowed, an ambitious Reserve Bank could buy gold with its notes from other Reserve Banks, issue new notes on the basis of it, repeat the maneuver, and finally acquire all the monetary gold in the country and supplant the notes of all the other Reserve Banks by its own; in short, set itself up as the dominant bank of issue. It is therefore one of the most important legal requirements,[16] that Reserve Banks are obliged to return all notes received from other banks to the bank of issue. As it appears to be of a purely technical nature this regulation has received but slight attention in the literature, yet it is the foundation for the independence of the individual Reserve Banks, and the reason why Reserve districts constitute transfer communities between which, as between countries, net balances can be paid with gold alone. Only because of special circumstances are these transfer communities less frequently forced into a rapid completion of transfers through district-wide price movements.

---

15. In 1920–21 the Reserve Banks in agricultural regions borrowed more heavily than usual from those in industrial areas.

16. Section 16 of the Federal Reserve Act of December 23, 1913.

Epilogue.[1] On Space

If everything occurred at the same time there would be no *development*. If everything existed in the same place there could be no *particularity*. Only space makes possible the particular, which then unfolds in time. Only because we are not equally near to everything; only because everything does not rush in upon us at once; only because our world is restricted, for every individual, for his people, and for mankind as a whole, can we, in our finiteness, endure at all. The extent of this horizon differs, of course, from man to man. But in economic affairs, as in all other affairs, our ken is limited for acting intelligently and for finding our way through the complexities of life. And even within this little world, we are familiar with not more than its innermost circle. Depth must be bought with narrowness. Space creates and protects us in this limitation. Particularity is the price of our existence.

To let this space-conditioned particularity grow without letting the whole run wild—that is political art. For me one of the happiest results of my study is to be able to show for the spatial organization of the economy that the free initiative of normal men produces results that in general are wholly desirable, politically as well as economically, provided only that man can build on rational conditions. Because the powerful forces of spontaneity, if rightly guided, are an ally to national economic policy, this is saved the superhuman task of planning everything down to the very last detail. The mighty elements of spatial discipline tend toward preserving geographical and cultural roots in spite of freedom.

For our science, finally, the question how the economy fits into space not only opens a new field but leads in the final analysis to a new formulation of the entire theory of economics. Even static theory enters upon a late flowering. For, as is not the case with distance in time, the static picture itself changes with distance in space. Life consists not only of development in time but of spatial diversity as well. Space stimulates the creative forces. And I see in my mind's eye an economic science that, more like architecture than like the history of architecture, creates rather than describes!

---

1. He who wishes to recapitulate a system can do no more, after all, than set down once again the thoughts upon which it is based.

Subject Index

T.: Table   n.: footnote

Aarhus, 269n.
Abercrombie-Forshaw plan, 440n.
"administrative principle," 132n.
Agglomerations, 6, 10ff., 15, 149n., 164, 343n.; areal, 10, 90; chance, 77; dissimilar enterprises, 75-77, and economic stability, 76; of pure consumers, 78, 90; and freight rates, 172, 175; production cost, 261; punctiform, 10; effect of price discrimination on, 164ff.; restricted, 79ff.; of similar enterprises, 68-72
Agricultural substructure, 374; unevenness of, 380f.
Alaska, 356n., 407n., 422, 423T.
Albania, 430T.
Albany, N. Y., 354
Alberta, 385, 425
Algeria, 430n.
Alsace, 383, 449
Antwerp, gateway, 251
Appalachians, 35n.
Arbeitswissenschaftliches Institut, 494
Argentina, corn exports, 416; wheat exports, 421, 422, 423T., 424
Arkansas, 374n.
Athens, 441n.
Atlanta, 407, 408, 461
Australia, wheat exports, 422, 423T.
Austria, 430T.
Autarky, 323f.
Autobahnen, 183n.

Bahia, Brazil, 421n.
Balance of payments, 97n., 98n., 233, 298; migration and, 307
Balkan countries, 416n., 420n.; *see also* names of individual countries
Baltimore, 81, 440n.
Bank clearing, 126
Bank for International Settlements, 281n.

Barcelona, 493
Basel, 449
Basing point system, 31, 157f., 164, 165
Bavaria, 456, 456n.
Belgian Congo, 420
Belgium, 258, 430T., 484, 494
Belts, 12, 372; formation of, 15, 85ff., 179, 182, 380; of industrial population, 258; wheat belt, 386, 425
Bend, Oregon, 413
Berlin, Germany, 129n., 216n., 370n., 402, 424n., 430, 436, 438n., 441, 473n.
Bermuda, 481
Besatzziffern. See Occupational indices
Birkenfeld, 381, 382
Bischofswerder, 446, 450
Black Forest, 383
Black soil areas, 258; Texas b. s. a., 392
Bohemia, 258, 456
Bolivia, 423T.
Border wasteland, 205
Boston, 81, 386, 407, 460, 461, 504
Boundaries, 13, 384; German-Polish, 450f.; Canadian-American, 384f., 446f.; German-Swiss, 382f.; overlap, 13, 168; payments across, 275f., 282n.; political and economic, 103, 192, 196, 199f., 292, 384, 445; prices at, 251; between market areas, 117, 166, 252; Swiss-French, 445f.; twin cities at, 447; width of, 207f.
Boundary region, 136f., 181, 448; demand in, 143n., 181, 387, 424; competition in, 153n.
Bradford, England, 218n.
Branch enterprises, 383, 384f.
Brandenburg, province of, 370n.
Brazil, 421, 423T., 424
Breslau, 216n.
British East Africa, 171n.
British Honduras, 423T.

British India, 423T.
British West Africa, 423T.
British West Indies, 422, 423T.
Budapest, 187n.
Buffalo, N. Y., 407, 427, 473, 499T., 500T., 504
Bulgaria, 429, 430T., 477n.
Burlington, Iowa, 410
Business cycles, 76, 120n., 293f., 298, 318, 322f.; and wars, 209; transfer through economic capitals, 275; and formation of large economic areas, 339; spatial transmission of, 496f.

California, 334n., 406, 412, 416, 458, 481
Canada, 355n.; wheat market, 421T., 423T.; price and wage differences, 460ff.; Dominion Bureau of Statistics, xiv, 480; Dominion Tariff Board, xiv
Canberra, 442, 443
Cannstadt, 354
Capital movements (exports, imports, flow), 209, 265, 278, 284, 289f., 301, 305, 321, 470; formation in Eastern and Western United States, 469f., 472
Cardiff, 416n.
Carpathians, 258
Cedar County, Iowa, 418T.
Cement, 367n.
"Centrality," 433n., 437n.
Central sites, 126, 134, 216n., 342, 350, 354, 354n.
"Central stratum," 433n.
Chemnitz, 444
Chicago, 11, 82, 166n., 354, 371n., 378, 379, 385, 390, 407, 412, 416, 419, 435T.n., 439n., 461, 481n., 497
Chile, 423T., 454n.
China, 423T., 490
Cincinnati, 371n., 486
Clearing, 339, 469
Cleveland, 459, 461
Coal, 11, 379, 380, 380n., 386n., 403n., 424n., 477; attraction of, 83, 90, 258, 367n., 374, 438; freight on, 170; Illinois, 11; location of individual mine, 35n.
Coefficient of localization, 369T.
Colombia, 423T.
Colonial policy, 193n.

Colonies, 424n.; value of, 335f.; saving of foreign exchange, 335n.
Colonization, 330
Colorado, 481
Combination problem, 305-314; compared with transfer problem, 312; impediments to new combinations, 327f.
Communication, lines of, 22, 32n.
"Communication principle," 131n.
Comparative cost, 229ff., 250f., 259n.; applicable to choice of occupation, 229f., 232-236; applied to many countries or persons, 230-232; and emigration of factors, 310
Comptroller of the Currency, 469n., 470n.
Copper, 424n.
Cornell University, 417
Corn market, 416f., 424n.
Costa Rica, 423T.
Cost of banking, 469f.
Cost of living, regional differences: US, 295, 490ff., 493, 504; international, 492f., 494; Germany, 493n., 494, 494n.
Cotton, gins, 11, 366; goods industry, 378, 449, 503f.; imports of Europe, 424n.
Cowles Commission, xiv
Credit creation, 276f., 469, 475
Cross hauling, 157, 165
Cuba, 423T., 481
Currencies, effect of different construction on transfer, 276f.; with different gold cover, 279f.; paper, 280f.
Customs unions, 340f.; possible American-Canadian, 385f.
Czechoslovakia, 430T., 494

Dakotas, 374n.
Dallas, 461, 464
Danzig, 451
Davenport, Iowa, 435T.n., 438n.
Denmark, 423T., 430T., 477n.
Denver, 407, 408, 414
Depressed areas, 200, 250, 326, 380, 449, 501
Depression, 283n., 318, 332, 333n., 400n., 500n.; westward movement of, 496ff.
Detroit, 371n., 385, 388, 412T., 447, 492, 493, 499T., 500T.
Discount rate, 277, 278, 286, 290, 293, 299, 300, 318, 319, 320n., 461, 474f., 506, 507
Distance, importance underestimated,

396f., 401n.; of bank locations from Chicago, 412
District, 12, 182, 372
Division of labor, 223f., 264, 265
Donets area, 258
Dresden, 455
Duluth, 257n.
Dumping, 157f., 163n., 234

East Prussia, 373T., 456, 493n.
Economic landscape, 127, 130, 325, 375, 436, 496, 498; empty corners, 136, 204, 205, 448; metropolitan, 412f.; affecting price waves, 275, 496; in reality, 216f.; relation toward each other, 135f.; square, 134; and states, 196-210
Economic provinces, 13, 216
Economic regions, overlapping of, 168f., 173, 191, 205n., 401, 410, 420f., 424; in reality, 215-220, 431f.; size of, 109; with equal structure, 431, 434f.; theory of, 8, 101ff.
Ecuador, 423T.
Efficiency wage, 231T.n., 309, 455
Egypt, 423T.
Elasticity: and distance, 146, 149; of industrial and agricultural demand, 141n.; geographic differences in, 141f.; local vs. regional, 143f.; and size of region, 146n., 180n.; monopolists and, 322; and tariffs, 300; of volume of traffic with respect to freight rate, 171
Electrification, 379
El Paso, 448, 462, 463
Employment, fluctuations in level of, 265; full employment policy, 322f.; through control of foreign trade, 323
England, 337, 339n., 424n., 430T., 444, 473, 484, 504; corner market, 425; devaluation of 1931, 321; distribution of towns, 389f., 394, 436, 438; market areas, 403n.; sources of wheat imports of, 423T.
Entrepreneur, location of, 244-245, 248; ability, 191f., 403, 406; profits and location, 330
Erie Canal, 427
Estonia, 430T.
Exchange, control, 320, 321, 339, 449
Exchange depreciation, 293f.; American depreciation, 294

Exchange rates, 97n., 231T., 233; fluctuating, 281, 284n., 299n., 318, 506n.
Exchange stabilization fund, 284n., 318
Expenditures, importance of local, 269, 308n., 369n., 370n., 469
Export industries, 252f.; premiums, 301n.
Extra-economic factors, 27n., 32n., 33, 34, 35, 302f.

Factors of production: international migration of, 251, 305f., 316, difficult, 309f., prevention of, 328f., substitute for movement of goods, 307, and shift of demand, 307; movements of factors and goods compared, 310, 329; redistribution of factors, 305-314
Federal Deposit Insurance Corporation, 464, 465n.
Federal Reserve Banks, 277n., 281n., 415f., 448, 461, 469, 473, 474f., 505f.; compared to European central banks, 506f.; interest differentials, 461f.; of Kansas City, 416, of St. Louis, xiv, 416, of Minneapolis, xiv, 416, 462.
Finland, 423T., 430T.
Florida, 408, 481, 482
Ford Inquiry, 492n.
Foreign trade, 327; proportion of Europe's overseas trade, 338; as function of distance, 428ff.
Fort Churchill, Canada, 426, 427
France, 258, 283n., 403n., 429n., 430T., 484, 504; devaluation of 1936, 321; location of sugar refineries, 367n.; source of wheat imports, 423T.
Free entry, 8, 260
Free trade, 328, 339, 341n. and *passim*; see also Comparative cost, Tariffs, Customs unions
Freight cost, for different goods, 334, 396n.; lowest, 260; and agglomeration, 72ff., 83n.; affecting price spreads, 267
Freight rates, 170-178, graduated, 171-173; level of, 174f.; as protective device, 210, 503n.; ocean, 425f.; discriminatory in US, 258, 486, 503n.; on Mississippi River, 416
French Africa, 423T., 424n.
Freystadt, 446

Galveston, 425

Gary, Ind., 379
Gateways, 187, 187n., 188n., 189n., 191, 251, 447
Geneva, border zone of, 445f.
Georg-Weierbach, 381
Germany, 258, 259, 373, 379, 386n., 396, 397, 400, 416, 422, 426n., 427, 428, 430T.n., 477n., 494; number of medieval towns, 393; distribution of cities, 431f., 436; supply of wheat, 423T.
Gibraltar, 423T.
Gold flows, 277f., 279, 280, 282f., 318f.
Gold standard, 318f.; *see also* Transfer problem
Gold sterilization, 285n., 290, 316, 319, 506
Gossen's law, 491
Great Lakes, 258, 378, 427
Greece, 423T., 429, 430T.
Ground rent, 247f., 259n.
Guatemala, 423T.
Guelph, Ontario, 387

Häusern, Maschinengenossenschaft, 400, 402n.
Haiti, 423T.
Hamilton, Ontario, 499T., 500T.
Heidenheim, 455n.
Heilbronn, 454
Helena, Mont., 463
Hennigsdorf, 379
Hides, 424n.
Hohenstauffen, 342n.
Holland. *See* Netherlands
Hong Kong, 420n.
Houston, Texas, 415, 465, 504
Hungary, 393n., 430T.
Huygen's principle, 275n.

Iceland, 430T.
Idaho, 425, 479, 501
"Ideal index," 491
Illinois, 371n.; distribution of towns, 392
Import premiums, 301n.; certificates (German), 426n.
India, 420n.
Indiana, 366, 371n.; distribution of towns, 392
Indianapolis, 125, 371n., 438, 439
Indifference curves, 225
Indo-China, 430n.

Industrial areas, 275n.; of US, 257, 375n.; of Europe, 257; English, 258
Industrialization and foreign trade, 337f.
Industrial location theory, 16ff.
Institut Scientifique de Recherches Economiques et Sociales, 484
Insurance companies, 402; different from other businesses, 402n.
Interest, and capital movements, 305f.; interlocal equalization of, 306
Interest differentials, 461ff.; of commercial banks, 463f.; of corporation bonds, 467; of Federal Reserve Banks, 461f., 474f., 505f.; within Texas, 464f.; of state and municipal bonds in US, 466f.; reasons for, 468f.; movement in space, 505f.
Intervention, into combination of factors, 324f.; compulsory, 334f.; into transfer process, 316f.
Inheritance, division of land through, 65n.
Institut für Weltwirtschaft, xiv
International trade: and interpersonal trade compared, 231-232; classical theory criticized, 312f.; classical theory and location theory, 103f., 104n.
Iowa, 257, 365, 366, 389, 409f., 417, 418; business cycles in, 496f.; distribution of towns, 389ff., 434ff.; land values 454; market areas, 417f.
Iowa State Planning Board, 417
Ireland, 423T., 430T.
Isochrons, 443
Isodapanes, 19, 20, 25, 28
Isostants = lines of minimum transport cost, 28n.
Isotims, 25n., 28n., 481, 482n., 486, 489
Isovectures, 19, 20
Italy, 258n., 423T., 430T.

Jacksonville, 504
Jamaica, 423T.
Japan, 423T.
Joint production in agriculture, 60
Jones Report on Nova Scotia's Economic Welfare, 386n.

Kamenz, 403n.
Kansas, 414n., 425, 458, 479
Kansas City, 399, 413, 414, 415T., 435T.n., 479
Karlsruhe, 441, 449

Subject Index

Kentucky, 371n.

Land grabbing, 348
Large economic areas (Grossraum), 339f.
Laspeyre's index, 490, 491, 494
Latin America. See names of individual countries
Latvia, 430T.
"Law of retail gravitation," 411
Leeds, 218n.
Leipzig, 82
Lithuania, 430T.
Littoria, 442
Liverpool, 426
Location policy, 315ff., 346f.
Locations (actual): automobile, 371n.; banks, 365f., 377; close to consumer, 365f., 370; even distribution, 371; of fairs, 366, 367, 403n.; of farms, 374ff.; regular distribution, 365f.; irregular distribution, 376f.; of production, 365ff.; of shoes, 377n.; soap, 371n.
Locations (theory), agricultural, 36ff.; agriculture and joint production, 60ff.; agricultural and industrial compared, 63f., 256; interdependence of all locations, 8, 28, 92ff., 255, 259, 261n., 263, 343; influence of nature, 33n., 256f.; lack of coincidence of best location for producers and consumers, 98f.; at center of gravity, 121f.; of ports, 188; stickiness of location system, 81, 217n., 352n.; effects of political boundaries on, 203f.; shift of location to adjoining state, 206; historic forces, 256, 259, 330, 352n.; changes in pattern, 305f., 325; in reality, 329; ecentric location, 414; military considerations, 344
Location triangle, 18
London, England, 129n., 259, 416n., 440n.
London, Ontario, 387
Lorraine, 21, 379
Los Angeles, 407, 408, 439n.
Louisville, Ky., 409
Luxemburg, 430T.

Madison, Iowa, 410
Maggi, 384
Manitoba, 386
Marginal product of land, 306; of labor, 226, 238n.

Marginal workers, 239
Marienwerder, 450
Marion, Iowa, 418T.
Market areas, 9, 105ff., 395f.; consolidation of, 401; circular, 417; corner, 204, 481; with equal structure, 128, 130f.; in Germany, 401, 408f.; networks of, 109ff.; possible vs. actual, 120; possible sizes and locations, 116f.; restriction of, 211ff.; square, 133f., 355n., 417; shape of, 110, 182, 248; for tung oil, 420T.; in US, 395f., 417ff.; for wheat, 386, 420ff.; wholesale, 404ff.; retail, 396f., 419; system of, 124ff.
Massachusetts, 378, 460
Maximization of number of competitors, 8, 259
Maximum shipping distance, 108
Mecklenburg, state of, 393n.
Memphis, Tenn., 415T.
Mexico, 423T., 477n.
Michigan, 371n., 439
Middle West. See names of individual states
Minneapolis–St. Paul, 218n., 385, 403n., 435T.n.
Minnesota, 439n.
Mississippi, 374, 416
Missouri, 369, 375; distribution of towns, 392
Mittelgebirge, 258
Mobile, Ala., 504
Mobility of labor and goods compared, 243n.
Montreal, 257, 386, 426n., 427
Mortgage credit, 402n.
Motorization, effects of, 183n.
Mountain States, 412
Multiplier, 308, 308n.
Munich, 129n., 216n., 436, 438n.
Muscatine, Iowa, 417, 418, 419T.

Nationalization, 332n.
Nebraska, 425, 479
Netherlands, 423T., 429n., 430T., 484, 494
New England, 369, 458, 503
New Orleans, 294, 415, 416, 416n., 425, 427n.
New York, 354, 407, 412, 414, 416, 416n., 427, 447, 461, 462, 481n., 504, 505; gateway, 251; harbor, 81, 82, 330

New Zealand, 423T.
Niagara Falls, Ontario, 387
Nicaragua, 423T.
Nordhorn, 453
Norfolk, 504
North Carolina, 375
North Dakota, 479n.
Norway, 423T., 430T.
Nova Scotia, 386
NRA, 460, 460n.
Nuremberg, 432, 436

Occupations, choice of, 236-240; location of, 240ff.; women's, 237n.
Occupation indices (*Besatzziffern*), 408
Ohio, 371n., 378; distribution of towns, 392
Oklahoma, 425
Omaha, 435T.n.
Ontario, 385, 447
Open market operations, 475n., 507
Oranges, price of as function of distance, 481f.
Orient, 407n.
Orientation, 17, 33n., 34, 377; cost orientation, 17, 23, 261; minimum transport cost, 18, 35, 261; mechanical model, 18, 20, 21; one-sided, 17, 30, 35; by profits, 27ff.; by gross receipts, 26ff.; technical, 23; and specially favored locations, 32f.; and raw materials, 35n.

Paasche's index, 491, 494
Palmanova, 441n.
Panama, 423T.
Panama Canal, 186, 416, 426
Paraguay, 423T.
Pareto distribution applied to towns, 433, 434f.
Paris, central location of, 82, 129n.; internal customs duties, 210
Pennsylvania, 378
PEP (Political and Economic Planning), Report on Location of Industry, 16, 369T., 473n.
Peru, 423T.
Petroleum, 424n.
Philadelphia, 458, 458n., 461, 504
Philippine Islands, 423T.
Pianos, 416
Pittsburgh, 11, 164n., 166n., 407, 490

Poland, 258, 430T.
Polish Corridor, 450f.
Population, interlocal distribution of, 99, 143n., 146, 181, 246n., 256f., 342; distribution between occupations, 226ff.; difficulty of marginal approach to, 226; according to principle of comparative cost, 229f.; and market networks, 109f., 260, 403; and possible market areas, 115f.; advantages and disadvantages of scattered settlement, 115n.; optimum size, 350; of agriculture in US, 375; effect of increase in, 176n.; irregular distribution, 179; density of, 180n., 257n., 258n., 311, 382, 403, 474, 485n. and *passim*.
Population cycles and business cycles, viii, 209; effects of a declining population, viii
Portland, Maine, 504
Portland, Oregon, 425
Port Said, 416n.
Ports, 217, 344, 367, 424; location of, 188; simplify price pattern, 189f., 427
Portugal, 423T., 430T.
Potato market, 479f.
Prague, 129n.
Prices (actual): US domestic goods, 294; US regional differences 295, 426, 449, 452ff.; retail price differences, 387, 484f.; regional shifts in, 501f.; of products, 476ff.; in cost of living, 490ff.; spatial movement in time, 486f.; after US and Canadian devaluations, 498, 500T., at US–Canadian Border, 499
Prices (theoretical discussion of): spatial price differences, 24n. 126f., 139ff., 168n., 176n., 180n., 188, 189n., 251, 265, 272, 333; of land, 253f.; lowest delivered price, 261; price gradients, 263ff., 273n., 333n., 453ff., 462ff., 477n.; price fluctuations, 265f., 282; price waves, 267ff.; neutralization of price waves, 274, 279, 286; interspatial price movements, 270f.; with credit creation, 277; changes of prices in the large and in the small, 296
Price maps, 329, 478, 480, 488
Price policy, geographical, 139f.; and competition, 160-164; uniform f. o. b price,

Subject Index

159f.; uniform c. i. f. price, 140; price discrimination, 147-159
Product differentiation, 168f., 189n.; compared to definition of location, 245n.
Production cost, lowest 261; and distance, 399
Profits, spatial differences, 195n., 211; monopolistic, 259, 260
Quebec, 385, 386

"*Raumforscher*," 349n.
Reaction. *See* Transfer problem
Refraction, law of 184f.; limitation of, 186
Regensburg, 438n.
Regional banks, 471n.
Regionalism, 504n.
Regional planning, 249, 346ff.
Regions, of demand, 9, 455; of supply, 9, 12, 188, 190, 217, 403n., 455; production as per cent of demand, 367-371; objections to method used, 371-374
Reparations, 266
Reserve ratio, 279f., 283, 469n., 475, 505
Reserve requirements, 475
Retail sales, Windsor and Ontario compared, 387; areas in Iowa, 409-410; Los Angeles and Chicago, 439n.
Rhine, 258n., 259, 454
Rhode Island, 374, 375
Ribbon Development Act, 444n.
Richmond, 412n., 461
Risks, 212, 402n., 469ff.; and distance, 399, 470, 472; and regional banks, 470n.
Rocky Mountains, 35n.
Romania, 258
Rothenburg, 333n.
Rubber, 424n.
Ruhr, 21, 218, 258, 333n., 373T., 379n., 424n., 498
Russia, 401, 420n., 428, 505n.

Saar district, 426n.
St. Louis, 414, 415, 461
San Francisco, 407, 408, 460
San Salvador, 423T.
Sarnia, Ontario, 387
Saskatchewan, 386, 425, 426, 459, 481
Savannah, 504
Saxony, 258, 493n.
Scrap, 379

Seattle, 407, 425, 458n., 493n., 498, 499T., 500T.
Selling costs, 212; as function of distance, 397f.
Shanghai, 420T.
Siemens-Martin process, 379
Silesia, 426n., 456
Situation (as distinct from orientation), 33
Soil quality, differences in, 178-182, 257
South Africa, 338n., 423T., 424
South America, 228n.; *see also* names of individual countries
South Wales, 416n., 498
Spain, 423T., 430T.
Spanish Guinea, 423T.
Spatial planning, 333
Springfield, Ill., 354
Stages of economic development, 223n.
Sterling area, 339n.
Stettin, 216n., 451
Stratford, Ontario, 387
Stuttgart, 216n., 354, 382, 453n., 454, 457, 498
Substitution equilibrium, 20f., 24n., 29n.
Suchard, 384
Sudan, 423T.
Suez Canal, 417
Sweden, 423T., 430T., 484
Switzerland, 382f., 386n., 430T., 445f., 484

Tariffs, 200n., 201, 206, 208n., 210, 213, 300f., 322, 411n., 501; American, 202, 300, 386; Canadian, 384, 386; infant industry, 328n.; effect on market area, 341; and regional price shifts, 501ff.
Tariffs, graduated, 19n., 22
Taxes, 345n., 383, 472
Technical progress, 259n.; tax on, 345n.
Terms of trade, 285, 286, 341n.; of Northern and Southern prices within the US, 502T., 503f.
Texas, 406, 496; distribution of towns, 392, 393
Thomas process, 379
Thünen rings, ix, 13, 14, 51, 62n., 380; boundary between, 44ff.; conditions for emergence, 40ff.; milk-cream-butter example, 46ff.; applied to production systems, 50, 61; inversion of, 52ff.; effect of uneven soil quality on, 59, 62, 85, 86

Time costs, 212, 257n.
Tipton, Iowa, 417, 418
Tobacco, 424n., 429
Toledo, Ohio, 125, 438, 439
Toronto, 384, 486, 499T., 500T.
Towns: formation of, 15, 68ff., 179; size of, 178, 389f.; as function of distance, 390f.; attraction of the more gifted into, 246n., 406; function of, 126, 178, 275, 439f.; distribution of, 127, 136, 178, 180, 389ff., 431ff.; size of demand compared to country, 143; plans, 440f.; Canadian, 344n., 386
" Trade follows the flag," 336
Transfer aid, 287, 290f.; cost of transfer, 291f.
Transfer community, 293, 298, 507
Transfer problem, vii, 265-304, 316f., 506f.; real transfer, 274, 279, 282; preliminary transfer, 276-278, 279, 282, 287f., 299; final transfer, 278-279, 288n., 299; reaction with transfer, 279, 285; with different currency systems, 276f., 283f.; difficulties of, 281n.; speed of, 282-283, 285; and terms of trade, 285
Transport cost in practice, 396, 427f.
Transport density, 127, 129
Transport lines, effect of, 184-187, 354
Transport points, 187ff., 217; nodal points, 187
Transport surface, 19, 182
Transshipment points, 188
Trans-Siberian Railway, 417
Troy, N. Y., 11
Turkey, 423T.

Ukraine, 258
Unemployed, 239
United States, 283n., 364; agricultural substructure, 374f.; distribution of production, 356ff.; distribution of towns, 436; population distribution, 256, 374, 375, 428; land values, 374n.; market areas, 395ff.; wage differentials 456ff.; wheat exports, 421ff., 423T.; *see also* names of individual states and towns
United States: Bureau of the Census, 366n., 367, 371n., 372, 396n., 399f., 403; Bureau of Labor Statistics, xiv, 295n.; Bureau of Mines, xiv; Department of Agriculture, 295n., 374n., 376n., 454; National Resources Committee, 306n., 395; Works Progress Administration, 210n., 493
Upper Silesia, 258, 424n., 450n.
Uruguay, 331n., 423T.
Utility, 224f., 246, 260, 309, 315n., 326n., 490n., 491, 492n., 495; interlocal equalization of, 241, 242f., 306n.

Vancouver, 426, 460, 493n., 498, 499T., 500T.
Venezuela, 423T.
Vienna, 129n., 216n.; a gateway, 187
Villiger, 384

Wage differentials, 25, 43n., 99n., 170n., 240-244, 243n., 306, 309f., 326n., 334, 380, 383, 384, 449, 455ff., 501, 503n., 504
Wages, efficiency wages correspond to international prices, 234, 309; hourly wages correspond to exchange rate, 233; time vs. piece wages, 237n., 239, 309; real wages, 305
Warthegau, 456
Washington, D. C., 257, 354, 442n., 443, 493
Weber, Alfred (theory), assumes inelastic demand, 17, 27, 104n., 108n.
Weights, 21, 22, 33n., 406, 482
Welland Canal, 427
Westphalia, 393n.
Wheat market, 189, 190, 420ff.
Wheat prices, 477f., 501
Wiese Valley, 449
Windsor, Ontario, 385, 387, 388, 499T., 500T.
Wisconsin, 354n.
Württemberg, 331n., 334, 348n., 354, 357n., 373T., 449, 472n.; stability of economy, 194-196
Würzburg, 438n.
Wybert, 383, 384
Wyoming, 425

Yugoslavia, 430T.

Zollverein, 340n., 383

Name Index

T.: Table   n.: footnote

Aereboe, F., 89
Allix, A., 366n., 367, 403n.

Backe, H., 51n., 288n., 380n., 402n.
Baker, O. E., 376n.
Barfod, B., 269n., 308n., 309n.
Barlow, Report, 25n., 348n., 380n.
Barton, Minister (Ottawa), xiv
Baumgartner, 451n.
Beaver, 218n.
Beckerath, H. v., 208n.
Bell, J., xiv
Berquist, F. E., 477n.
Black, J. D., 229n., 403n.
Blum, 180n., 187n.
Boehm, C., 485n.
Böhm, F., 332n.
Boggs-Bowman, 451n.
Bohnert, 348n.
Bolton, C. W., 499T.n.
Bortkiewicz, L. v., 25n.
Bosch, R., 195n.
Bowers, W. A., 406n., 415T.
Bozenhardt, K., 444
Brinkmann, C., 104n.
Brinkmann, T., 60n., 85n., 89
Bromell, J. R., 409
Brüning, K., 346n., 383n.
Buchman, 21, 377n., 379n.
Bücher, K., 104n., 393
Bülow, F., 349n.
Burger, H. O., 196n.
Burns, A. R., 164n.

Caldwell, S. A., 416n.
Carr, G. J., 424n.
Cassels, J. M., 482n.
Cauchon, 443n.
Chamberlin, E. H., xiv, 64n., 66, 69, 72, 74, 108n., 109n., 112n., 120n., 205n., 340n.

Christaller, W., xiv, 104n., 114n., 115n., 126, 131n., 132n., 218, 350n., 393n., 408, 409, 431ff., 440n.; criticism of system, 433
Cooper, M. R., 502T.n., 503n.
Cournot, 70, 272n.
Culemann, C., 132n., 133n.

Dannenbauer, 342n.
Dean, W. H., 29n.
Deasy, 420T.
Decken, H. v. d., 380n.
Dedi, L., 448n., 450
Dennison, S. R., 28n., 250n.
Dickinson, R. E., 403n.
Dietzel, K., 420n.
Dorner, Z. G., 332n.
Doxiades, 441n.
DuBrul, S., 483n.
Duddy, E. A., 177n.

Earhart, 472
Eckardt, M., 402n., 455n.
Economist, The (London), 498
Edwards, A., xiv
Eggers, 21n.
Eikstedt, E. v., 213n., 246n.
Ellis, H. S., 322n.
Engelbrecht, T. H., 51, 364n., 376n., 477
Engländer, O., 8, 45n., 46
Erlenmaier, A., 183n.
Eucken, W., xiv, 123n., 198n., 332n.
Evans, xiv
Everett, H., 380n.

Fawcett, C. B., 445
Fetter, F. A., 403n., 478, 479
Feucht, O., 353n.
Fezer, H., 396n.
Fischer, W., 346n.
Fisher, Irving, 491

Florence, P. S., 369T.
Ford, Henry, 472, 473
Friederici, G., 355n.
Friedrich, C. J., 18n.
Frisch, R., 120n.
Furlan, V., 211n.

Garey, L. F., 481n.
Garver, xiv
Geer, Sten de, 35n.
Gibrat, R., 434n.
Gillman, 90
Gini, C., 336n.
Goodrich, C., 216n.
Gras, N. B., 104n., 386n.

Haase, A., 85
Haberler, G. v., xiv, 158n., 229n., 233n., 309, 328, 335n., 344n., 364, 380n., 426n., 491
Haenelt, D., 356n.
Häpke, R., 130n.
Häring, J., 331n.
Hall, F. S., 379n., 473n.
Hansen, Alvin, viii
Harris, S. E., 294n., 468n.
Hartsough, M. L., 218n.
Hartung, 446n.
Hasenclever, C., 380n.
Haufe, H., 114n., 258n.
Haushofer, K., 218n., 339n.
Heberle, 174n.
Heer, C., 503n.
Hegel, 93, 358n.
Heiser, 346n.
Hellpach, W., 192n., 246n.
Herberts, J. H., 252n., 484
Herrenberg, 400
Hesse, P., 195n., 454
Hinrichs, A. F., 461n.
Hoffer, C. R., 439n.
Hoffsommer, H. C., 405n.
Holmes, W. G., 365
Hoover, E. M., xiv, 47n., 107n., 141n., 147n., 212n., 377n., 405n.
Horn, Charles L., xiv
Hotelling, H., xiv, 6, 72ff., 162

Innis, H. A., 355n.
International Labor Office, 492, 494
International Magazine Company, 396n.
Isard, W., ix

Isenberg, G., xvii, 195n., 218n., 269n., 346n., 353n., 369n., 373, 409
Iversen, C., 223n.

Jackson, Colonel, xiv
Jacobs, A., 477n.
Jaeger, W., 449n.
Jahn, G., 455n.
Jefferson, M., 392, 393n., 394

Känzig, W., 118n.
Kärger, K., 454n.
Kann, F., 346n., 348n.
Kapferer-Schwenzner, 428n.
Kautz, E. A., 81n.
Keir, M., 172n., 473n.
Kendall, H. M., 403n.
Keynes, J. M., viii, 251n., 308n., 315n., 339n., 363n., 494n.
Keyser, E., 81n., 441n.
Klöpper, R., 453
Koch, H., 88n.
Köster, xvii
Krzyzanowski, W., 411n.
Kühne, G., 403n.
Kulmer, A., 426n.

Lagger, L. de, 393n.
Lane, J. J., 461n.
Lardner, D., 174n.
Launhardt, W., 7, 9, 18, 104n., 107n., 114n., 162, 166n., 174n., 175n., 186
Lehmann-Lenoir, F., 31
Lenschow, 171n., 336n., 355n.
Leontief, W. W., ix, xiv, 100n.
Liebe, H., 485n.
List, Friedrich, 17n., 51n., 76, 198n.
Lively, C. E., 183n.
Löfke, H., 415n.
Lösch, A., 46n., 118n., 147n., 165n., 182n., 183n., 201n., 203n., 209n., 251n., 320n., 324n., 335n., 338n., 339n., 340n., 350n., 357n., 506n.
Lowe, 490
Lubin, J., 380n.
Lutz, F. A., 285n.

McCarty, H. H., 366n., 389
McGregor, xiv
McGuire, C. E., xiv
Machlup, F., 260n.

Name Index

McKenzie, R. D., 104n., 213n., 412, 413, 439n.
MacPherson, L. G., 378n.
Mädge, W., 331n.
Malthus, Th. R., 262
Mangold, W., 449n.
Marchi, Francesco de, 441n.
Marquardt, H., 62n., 63n.
Marshall, A., 364n.
Marshall, H., 207n., 384n.
Maunier, R., 430n.
Mayer, H. W., 457
Mecklenburg, G., 159n.
Meinhold, H., 350n.
Mellerowicz, 369n.
Metzdorf, M., 334n.
Meuriot, M. P., 438n.
Meyer, F. W., 281n., 285n., 290n., 298n., 320n., 322n., 323n.
Meyer, K., 351n.
Meynen, 355n.
Michels, R., 194
Miksch, L., 332n.
Millard, J. W., 396n., 397, 401n., 404n.
Mills, F. C., 463n., 484n.
Mitze, W., 236n., 246n.
Möller, H., 120n., 159n.
Molyneux, P., 504n.
Moody's Manual, 466n., 467, 468
Morgan, J. P., 471n.
Moulton, E. S., 217n., 366n.
Müller, K. V., 246n.
Müller-Miny, H., 381n.
Müller-Wille, 381, 382
Münter, G., 441n.
Münzinger, A., 65n., 400, 402
Muhs, H., xvii, 346n.
Myers, L., 502T.n., 503n.

Neue Zürcher Zeitung, 445
Neupert, 393n.
New York Times, 483
Niemeyer, 443n.

Odum, H. W., 504n.
Ohlin, B., ix, x, 24n., 103, 104n., 223n., 252n., 307n., 309n.
Olin, F. W., xiv
O'Neill, L. J. 157n., 477n.

Palander, T., ix, 18, 19, 22n., 28n., 73, 120n., 162, 166n., 173n., 183n., 184n., 185n., 188, 207n., 261, 377
Paullin, 365n.
Pavlovsky, G., 36, 51n., 338n., 428n., 505n.
Peeters, M., 378n.
Peter, H., 100n.
Petersen, A., 46n.
Pfannschmidt, M., 349n., 377n.
Pfeifer, G., 334n., 355n.
Philip, K., 243n.
Pirath, C., 37, 174n., 183n., 428, 455n.
Powell, xiv
Predöhl, A., 20n., 24n., 28n., 33n., 92n., 166n., 201n., 257n., 378n., 403n., 490n.
Preiser, E., 196
Priebe, H., 65n., 195n.
Puttkammer, W., xvii, 346n.

Rath, 402n.
Ratzel, F., 82n., 192n., 197, 198n., 201n., 443n.
Rechenberg, F., 370n., 408, 440n.
Regul, R., 403n., 424n., 451n.
Reilly, W. J., 410, 411, 412
Riedl, R., 451n.
Riefler, W., xiv, 463n., 464n., 468n., 470, 471, 473, 474n., 476
Rist, Charles, 484n.
Ritschl, H., 28n., 104n., 177n.
Robinson, A., 28n., 250n.
Robinson, J., 66, 109n., 150n., 152n.
Rockefeller Foundation, xiv
Röhm, H., 67n.
Röpke, W., 177n.
Rolph, J. K., 440n.
Rompe, 495n.
Roos, Charles, xiv, 458T.n., 460n., 461n.
Roosevelt, F. D., 460
Rostovtzeff, M., 201n.
Rühl, A., 45n., 416, 490n.

Sanderson, D., 417
Schäffle, 411n., 496
Scheu, E., 403n., 412n.
Schiller, Friedrich, 4
Schiller, K., 357n.
Schiller, O., 216n.
Schilling, A., 166n.
Schlie, A., 340n.
Schlier, O., 177n., 183n., 218n., 258n., 369n., 431n., 433n., 438n.

Schmidt, H., 113
Schmidt-Friedländer, R., 402n.
Schmitz, J., 173n.
Schmölders, G., 332n., 349n.
Schmoller, G. v., 104n.
Schneefuss, 187n.
Schneider, E., 62n., 92n., 107n., 108n., 120n., 162, 299n.
Scholte, W., 338n.
Schultze, J. H., 90n.
Schulz-Kiesow, P., 170n., 177n., 183n.
Schumacher, H., 21, 379n.
Schumann, H. J. v., 380n.
Schumpeter, J. A., ix, xiv, 64n., 237n.
Schuster, E., 69, 72
Schwalm, H., 446, 450n.
Schwenkel, 352n.
Scott report, 348n.
Seidler, G., 158n.
Seyfried, E., 382
Siebrecht, 402n.
Singer, H. W., 150n., 434f.
Sisam, C. H., 112n., 434n.
Smith, A., 46n.
Smith, G. H., 354n.
Sölch, J., 198n., 202n.
Sombart, W., 6, 76, 78, 170n., 194n., 337n., 414
Spengler, J. J., xiv, 335
Spiethoff, Arthur, ix, xiv, 343n., 358n., 453n.
Stackelberg, H. v., 120n., 184n., 443n.
Stamp, 218n.
Steinbeis, F. v., 195n., 331n., 334, 357n.
Steinhagen, E., 417
Stewart, xiv
Stewart, Mrs. S., xiv
Stigler, G. J., 195n.
Stockmann, G., 195n.
Sulzbach, W., 198n., 210n., 281n., 336n.
Swabia, vii, xv, 195n., 196, 492

Taussig, F. W., xiv, 502n.
Terborgh, G., viii
Teubert, xvii, 450n.
Thaer, A. v., 51n.
Thompson, Donald, 465n.
Thompson, J. W., 395n.
Thompson, T. E., 371n.

Thünen, J. H. v., ix, 5, 7, 8, 9, 13, 36, 45, 46n., 50, 51, 85, 104n., 130, 133n., 376n., 380n., 381n., 402, 453
Tintner, G., 107n.
Triffin, R., 254n.
Triggs, H. J., 443n.
Turner, F. J., 355n.

Uebler, 440n.
Uhlig, J., 380n., 501n.
Umlauf, J., 21n., 218n., 351n., 352n.
Urdahl, T. K., 157n., 477n.
Uthwatt report, 348n.

Vance, R. B., 504n.
Veit, O., 338n.
Viner, J., 108n.
Vleugels, W., 450n.
Volz, W., 446, 450n.

Wagemann, H., 381n.
Waldschütz, E., 383, 449n.
Walras, ix, x, 92, 163n., 226
Weber, Alfred, ix, 5, 9, 18, 19, 20, 24, 25, 27, 28, 29, 92n., 164n., 179n., 186, 261, 330, 338n.
Weh, Max, 382, 383
Wehner, B., 443n.
Weigmann, H., 349n.
Wende, G., 451n.
Wentzel, R., 443n.
Whittlesey, Ch. R., xiv, 297n.
Wiedenfeld, K., 194n., 339n.
Wiesener, Diplomatvolkswirt, xvii, 453n.
Wilbrandt, R., 242
Wilcox, S. W., 182n.
Willeke, E., 194
Williamson, W. F., 396
Winkler, E., 130n.
Working, H., 480
Wright, 365n.

Young, xiv

Zapoleon, L. B., 242n., 427n., 478, 479, 490n., 501n.
Zeuthen, 120n.
Zimmerman, C., 169n., 439n.
Zimmermann, E. W., 178n., 223, 416n.
Zipf, G. K., 436f.

DATE DUE